KU-411-012

SOME
FANTASTIC
PLACE

CHRIS DIFFORD

SOME FANTASTIC PLACE

MY LIFE IN AND OUT OF SQUEEZE

WEIDENFELD & NICOLSON

First published in Great Britain in 2017 by Weidenfeld & Nicolson
an imprint of The Orion Publishing Group Ltd
Carmelite House, 50 Victoria Embankment
London EC4Y 0DZ

An Hachette UK Company

1 3 5 7 9 10 8 6 4 2

A CIP catalogue record for this book is
available from the British Library.

ISBN 978 1 474 60567 0

Typeset by Input Data Services Ltd, Somerset

Printed a[...]RO 4YY

For Louise, my beautiful children,
and in loving memory of Maxine and my parents.
Dedicated to my brother Lew and Glenn Tilbrook

KING GEORGE STREET

My first home was 98 King George Street in Greenwich, south London. Six prefabs, three pubs, a school, a church and a yard where the electricity board kept cables. Two long rows of terraced houses faced each other at one end of the street; at the other, big houses with big doors and even bigger windows. There was a phone box next to one of the pubs and when it rang everyone came out to see who it was for. It was a tiny road – at one end of which was Greenwich Park. It was heaven being there. Its beauty shone on me from the trees at sunset and from the bushes in the rain. I was there in all weathers. It was 1964, I was ten years old and this is when my memory really begins.

In the early 1960s, our family was working class. We had a green bath and matching basin, a tin bath for outside and a shed. We had a cardinal-red doorstep and a budgie called Joey. Dad had a bicycle but never a driving licence. Sunday roasts were traditional and wonderful; there was lots of it and crumble for afters. The radio played in the corner as we sat and ate our greens. A black-and-white telly occasionally spluttered into life; lines would move up and down the screen until the valves warmed up, and then they stopped. Life was good and I was happy killing ants with hot water and playing games in the garden with my mates, all two of them. Coconut – whose real name was Jimmy Thatcher – lived just down the street. We went to the same school and shared many adventures. He was called Coconut because he had three crowns on the top of his head. My other mate Gary Meades lived what seemed like miles away, by the river. He was tubby and had a ruddy face like me; we shared a love of collecting stamps and model aeroplanes. Each weekend we'd make things and paint them, mostly badly, while listening to the radio. Even today when I hear 'You Really Got Me' by The Kinks, I'm transported back to small tins of paint and a tube of glue.

Our prefab was the perfect home to grow up in: no stairs to climb and a huge garden to hang out in which went up a slight embankment at the back. My mum, who loved me and took me everywhere, was bright-faced and slightly round, like me today. A staunch Protestant from Coleraine in Northern Ireland, she enjoyed dancing and shouting at my dad when he occasionally came home from work drunk. She was a great cake-maker and I used to sit beneath the table and watch her and her friends bake. Icing sugar would fall like snow, currants would occasionally drop on the floor and I would pick them up, chewing the life out of them. It was a bit like being in a Tom and Jerry cartoon – all I could see were their legs and their knees. I was told not to speak unless spoken to. I was given jelly, cake, white bread with lemon curd spread thickly on top. It was all about food and legs, handbags and toys.

Mum and Dad had met in World War II during his time in Belfast. He was waiting for a ship to take him to Africa, Mum was serving up food in the mess, and I guess they saw each other over the steaming Irish stew and fell in love. I can imagine them walking along the docks holding hands, watching the stars and trying to stop each other from crying at how wonderful life was. Her ship did come in but it took my dad away from her, off to war, to fight the Germans. They had just enough time to fall deeply in love – and other stuff. Nine months later, while he was away, a telegram arrived to inform Dad of my brother Lew's birth. It was 1943. Three years later, he came home to see his young boy. There on the dockside was Mum with Lew, waving flags and crying, and down the gangplank walked Sidney Lewis Difford, beaten by the years of war but overcome to be on dry land. His son ran right past him – they were meeting for the first time. The drums must have been banging, the pipes piping and the ship's horn blowing. Belfast in 1946; he wasn't home yet, but peace had broken out and the war was a shadow that would follow my father around for the rest of his life, although he said nothing, ever.

Coming home from war would mean moving mother and child over to England from Coleraine. They went to Charlton, south London, where my dad's parents lived. Reluctantly, Mum moved into the spare room and brokered a deal – she would get to go home every year for a few weeks in the summer. She'd been up-rooted and forced to move in with my grandparents, who I knew very little about. I only met my grandmother once or twice; she had a beard and lived in one room in a big house close to the Charlton Athletic football ground. Beside her sat a bell, which she would ring if she needed tea or a newspaper. She lived to the ripe old age of ninety-two and had a colostomy bag for the last thirty years of her life. My uncle Bert lived with her and tended to her

every need. My other three grandparents all died of cancer before
I was born.

As soon as my mum moved into the house in Charlton, she
contacted the council about getting a place of her own. A prefab
came up a few miles away in Greenwich and they moved in. It
must have been a palace to them, a reward for being together
and surviving the war. Les was born in Woking four years after
Lew; and I came along in 1954 – an afterthought. They were so
much older than I was and they left home before I moved into
adolescence.

Dad was tall and handsome; I could imagine him at Monte
Cassino, in Italy, charging around with a gun, though this was
probably far from the truth. But what was the truth? As much
as I asked him about the war, he would never tell me what it was
like. He did say that seeing your friends get blown to pieces wasn't
a story that needed telling. He was the breadwinner, working as
a wages clerk down at the gasworks. Mum managed his income
well and we seldom went without – there was always food on the
table and socks in your shoes. Dad worked the same job all his life
and never missed a day; he was dedicated to the coin. He knew
where every penny went, and unlike me, he was extremely careful
with money.

Being with Dad was a very different experience to being with
Mum. We would cycle to the allotment on a Saturday down by the
Blackwall Tunnel, me strapped to the wooden crossbar on his bike.
We would take trips up the Thames on the riverboats. We went
to his office. The gasworks was a huge place built on marshland
called Tunnel Point. It's now better known as the O2. Dad sorted
out the wages and all the men on the site had genuine respect for

him. In his office I would play with rubber bands and paper clips; there were also yellow Bic pens with 'Gas Board' written on them – well worth nicking at the time. As a young lad I loved being there, surrounded by men, stationery and large dumper trucks. Next to the office was a huge furnace where the coke would be smelted to make gas. It was roasting hot, and massive trains would carry the coal away to a siding by the dock for shipment. I was in awe.

The office was robbed a few times at gunpoint and Dad was caught in the crossfire. I'm not sure about the whole story, but I imagined cars pulling up, men with sawn-off shotguns and hands in the air from inside the office windows. The only security they seemed to have was a floppy plastic disc on a small record player in a cupboard which was hooked up to a phone line and, with the tap of a button, the arm would drop and it would play to someone at the other end over at the Greenwich Police Station. A delicate female voice would calmly say, 'There has been a break-in at the Gas Works, emergency, emergency.' How do I know this? The disc ended up on my record player at home.

The Gas Board held Christmas parties and we would all go for dinner on folding tables and receive little presents from the managers on the stage. It was all very jolly and great for the morale of the workers; bringing everyone together to say thanks was a wonderful idea.

Harry Lynham was a close friend of my dad's. He fell in the furnace one afternoon and burnt his face and hands as he scrambled to climb out of the scorching coal. His leather gloves and his patched eye always scared me, but I could see that he and Dad had a very close bond. They would even hang out at weekends together; a few beers in the Tolly House on Royal Hill. A friend of

Harry's would deliver a wooden crate of beer to our house each Saturday morning; he was tubby with Charles Hawtrey glasses and he always wore a brown cardigan, and his van was full of similar wooden crates.

The allotment was next to Dad's office: he was the manager of this vast marsh on which men would come and turn the soil and grow vegetables. He would weed and sow while I would run around in the dirt with my toys. There was a disused van at the allotment and I would sit in it and pretend to drive – I'd travel as far as I liked, sitting on the leather seats with springs and mud everywhere. People would drop by and buy things from my dad: lime, string, seeds and cane. Across the allotment on a green field, men in whites played cricket at the Gas Board cricket ground.

When Dad wasn't working, at the allotment or in the garden digging up weeds and sorting out the shed, he was a home bod. Feet up by the telly, reading a newspaper, pouring out a beer; this was the man I saw from way down on the rug where I'd be playing with my Dinky toys. And it was from these toys that the roots of inspiration were formed. I created my own world where I could speak as much as I liked, but in happy silence. I had a few buses and cars, a lorry and a tractor; inside my head I had a world of things going on, a whole planet of people and places that only I had the bearings of.

King George Street was a great place to grow up. Milk was delivered by a horse and cart at first, then later by a three-wheeled electric death trap that would slide all over the place in the snow. Bread came from the bread van, rag-and-bone men took your disused bits away, and the fish lady pushed her barrow once a week up to the corner, where she would sing and sell her fresh cod.

Cars were few on the street, but they were mostly black and very impressive.

I would play with my toy cars and buses all day long, and often drove them from one end of the street to the other along the kerb, lying in the gutter with my chin on the pavement.

Life was all bees in jars and Fairy Liquid bottles filled with water on hot days. Rhubarb crumble and yellow custard, green gooseberries and upside-down cake with tinned pineapple. Harry Secombe and Doris Day, Harry Worth and Tony Hancock. Voices in the living room other than our own. *This is Your Life* and *Sunday Night at the Palladium* on the telly; *Watch with Mother*, *Blue Peter* and *The Woodentops*. Mum singing along with Jim Reeves and The Bachelors. There was always music playing – not all of it brilliant. My older brothers Lew and Les were generally out or in their bedrooms; Mum was always in the kitchen. Lew suffered from asthma. His wheezing did not go down well with Les, who shared a room with him. Les was born with a hole in his heart and this made him treasure each day as it came, in a more rebellious way than Lew. The two of them never really saw to eye to eye. I was always on the floor: the pattern of the rug made for a network of roads all leading to the same place, a traffic jam of Christmas and birthday toys all in a row.

Home was warm and black and white while we lived in King George Street. My elder brothers were at school, Dad was at work; it was just Mum and me. I loved being with her. She was gentle and tender, her whispering Irish accent gliding like harp music up and down my spine. As most mothers do, she kept each family member's plates spinning with selfless love. I had my brothers and my dad in the evenings, but during the day it was women who surrounded me. Mum and her church ladies would sit in the front room and talk all day long, or bake cakes in the kitchen. There was always cooking, and Mum's meals were a treat – worth waiting for. To me, cooking seemed like a play with three acts. Preparing – me peeling the spuds and podding the peas. Cooking – me stirring the gravy and watching the meat. Eating – all of us sitting quietly around our tiny kitchen table, which I must have laid in order to gain brownie points. The encore was the washing-up, which Dad always did. Our house was a home full of memorable smells and food fresh from the allotment or the local shops on Royal Hill.

I don't remember too much tension. My many therapists over the years have tried to locate deep-buried memories of conflict and familial unhappiness, but to no avail. Life was normal; we lived simply. Sometime before I was ten, I was joined by my imaginary friends. Only an addict would have more than one. Together we were soldiers, pilots, seamen and spies; in the garden, in the bath and under the table during cake-making manoeuvres. We went everywhere together and were inseparable. My mum cottoned on to how close we'd become and laughed about it with her friends. She even had my imaginary mates babysit me; she'd encourage me to hang out with them in my bedroom when she wanted some time to herself.

I have no idea where they came from. They joined me one day while I was playing in the garden and came back the next day for more; they stayed with me until I was about sixteen years old. We formed a band – but not Squeeze. We were good mates. I never took them to school, but we walked together as far as the gates outside the playground and they waited for me there. We were the Men from UNCLE, invisible and invincible. I can't describe them, but they would have been good-looking and a little burly one moment, and slim and slender the next. They could have been sulky like me. I remember the one called Paul; he wore the same jumpers as I did and the same grey flannel short trousers. Sandals in the summer with socks, Wayfinder shoes in the winter. Together we grew up in summer gardens and in the park. We would talk to each other and romp around. On the way to school, the three of us would pretend to be on a train. We would chug along the park wall, down to the school gates and there the train would stop for me to get off and go to school. They'd be there at the end of the day to pick me up, though I would wait for the bigger boys to fade away before I launched into the full train-like sound. Sometimes steam, sometimes electric – both were as sexy as each other.

August provided holiday time for us all. Heavy-looking cases, two of them black-and-white check, were packed and left in the hall; we were off to Coleraine. We would lock the front door and walk down the side of Greenwich Park to the 177 stop, where we would catch the bus to Euston. Dad would be in a suit. Upstairs was the only place to sit on a bus, my brothers and I pressed up against the front windows looking out over the south-east London landscape of working-class lives. Across Tower Bridge and into the unknown of north London. Euston was a huge cathedral of steam and noise, the smell to be consumed like a stew. My dad would grumble as he hauled the cases onto the train, and then there we all were at the table, heading north. Porridge for breakfast, black faces from looking out of the window at the steam engine up ahead pulling us nervously along the tracks. My imaginary mates would occupy the bench seat with me, and if people came into our compartment my mum would simply say the seats were taken. The wonderful journey would go on for days in my head. For a little boy, it was magical. Steam trains and ships; what was not to like?

When we arrived at Heysham, the train would wobble onto the ferry and we would spend the night crossing the rough sea to Belfast. Our cabin was small and musty, and in it I half-slept and half-imagined being in the navy. With all of us in one cabin, it was our prefab at sea. Bleary-eyed, the five of us would be led back to the train for the last part of the journey up the country to my mother's home town. Aunt Sarah and Uncle Robert were always there to meet us at Coleraine station. She was every bit my mother's sister and he was quiet and gentle. A pipe-smoker. He talked with a whistle, very softly and with a huge grin always at the ready. He was a skilled carpenter and drove a Mini; it was immaculate and I loved to sit on his knee and hold the steering wheel as we went up the back road to the garage behind the house. We would decant ourselves into their small terraced house on James Street. How we did that I'll never know. It was smaller than the prefab; we must have all been in one room. I loved the journey and the holidays we had there – fourteen in total. My Aunt Ginny had a shop just up the street: she sold potatoes, sweets and just about everything in between. This was my Willy Wonka's, and my fingers were often caught in the many jars behind the counter. Out the back in her living room there was the sweetest smell of peat burning on the fire and her pet pig lay snoring and farting in front of it.

Trips on old local buses to the south for cheap fags and gifts, walks along the Antrim coastline to the Giant's Causeway, powerful cliffs, castles and streams. Portrush for Morelli's ice cream, toy shops and naval vessels, all moored up with nowhere to go. Tea shops, fish and chips, playgrounds and funfairs. That was all we needed each day – and the local club at night for a knees-up while the kids sat outside trying to be good. Crisps and orange Fanta. I'm sure there were rows and we used to fight; like any other family we must have had our moments. The great thing is that I don't remember it being anything other than wonderful.

This was mid-Sixties Northern Ireland, though, and beyond our idyllic little world, there was tension in the air. Not that I knew much about it, of course. I was dimly aware of there being a gulf between the Protestant community in Coleraine, of which my family were a part, and the Catholic area. The streets I knew over there were warm and friendly places, where people left their front doors open for each other, while the Catholic parts of town seemed dark and unwelcoming, places to keep well away from.

My mum never made a big thing of the religious divide, even when the Troubles really kicked off in the late Sixties. But she did tell me I must never marry a Catholic – or a black girl. Yes, we used to go and watch the Orangemen march through Londonderry on the Glorious Twelfth, and my mum would sing 'The Sash My Father Wore' as loudly as any of them, and I remember going to Belfast with her and seeing barbed-wire fences and British army vehicles on the streets, but I never identified with the Loyalist cause.

Once at my cousin Trevor's house in Belfast I was shaken in my bed by a large explosion a few streets away. It was very frightening for a young lad like me, but somehow I felt safe in the arms of my family back in the calm of James Street in Coleraine. When we sat together on the rocks at the Giant's Causeway, my mum would stick her nose out to the sea and the sun, and she would pray. She felt her prayers would wrap us all in safety. She sat there for hours on end while I jumped from stone to stone, fishing for reflections in rock pools. I never interrupted her prayers. I was told to speak when spoken to. It has served me well over the years. She, however, was in constant conversation with the Lord and his shepherds.

Ireland was our second home. The Antrim coast was our faraway nest: the cold rocks and the salty breeze, the rain and the long, hard walks up and down the cliffs around the Giant's Causeway. Shopping for handkerchiefs and tablecloths, tea towels and postcards. Pac-a-macs protected us from the constant summer rain and the wind and the spray from the sea.

Once my mum took me to the Lammas Fair, a gypsy gathering in the County Antrim hills. She led me into a caravan to see an old lady who looked at my hand, held my fingers back and in a deep Irish accent told me, apparently, that I would marry several times and have many children, have a long life, play an instrument and find happiness in music.

I was sidetracked by her hairy face and was far too young to know what was being said. Mum told me about it one night at home before she died; we discussed the reading of hands as though we'd just opened a bag of crisps. If it were true, the old gypsy woman was right.

Music was a big part of my mum's life. At home, she'd play love songs – Jim Reeves and Frank Ifield – and she loved to sing and dance to Irish music. On holiday in Ireland, we would go to a pub called The Salmon Leap and listen to folk music; I'd sit there with my crisps and lemonade and watch as she swayed and sang along with her friends and family. Her Irish roots were planted firmly in a fertile soil of religion and music. It's a good foundation for life.

Dad told me that Mum breastfed me for two years after I was born, and during that time she was drinking Guinness. He said I slept for days – so much so that they took me to see a doctor. He saw nothing wrong with me, but thought my doziness might be linked to the velveteen black stuff. I slept on and the doziness continues; I was in at the deep end at a very early age.

My mum's connection with the local church meant she did lots of good things, like taking in a young girl whose mother had cancer. She moved into the prefab for a few months. My imaginary friends were not impressed. My mother doted on her and for those few months my nose fell out of joint. Dad meanwhile was treasurer of the church and also did good things. They were do-gooders, you could say, but in a nice way.

My mum and dad were on the waiting list for a new house for many years. We were getting very crowded and there was damp everywhere – which didn't help my brother Lew's chronic asthma. In 1965, we moved from 98 King George Street to 98 Combe Avenue, a house on a council estate at the edge of Blackheath, built from grey breeze blocks and glass. The fronts of the houses had no windows; it was the new way, a Swedish design, they said.

Inside it was open-plan: a chimney breast coiling up to the roof from the large bricked fireplace, the tiny kitchen covered off with a sliding glass hatch, three bedrooms and a bathroom, and a green bathroom suite, again. Once more, a house with a flat roof. Change was unnerving at first, but soon I got into the swing of living in a modern house on Blackheath. Outside, there were garages with floors that sloped down under the ground and washing areas to hang clothes out to dry; there were open spaces paved over to play on and across the road the very green heath. On the corner of the estate there was a tower block so ugly that nobody wanted to live there.

My brothers had left school and gone on to work by the time we moved in – Lew was an articled clerk on his way to being an accountant and Les worked in a tailor's shop in Lewisham where he nicked suits at the weekend for parties and returned them on Monday morning. Smart lad. They were both in relationships and girls often came round to the house. Scooters were polished every weekend, music was played on the newly bought record player. A stereogram hogged the whole of the front room; it was fun to listen to and I would lie beneath it with my head on the floor, absolutely entranced. One minute I was bathed in the gentle sounds of The Searchers, and the next the more down-to-earth rhythms of The Rolling Stones or Bo Diddley. Music cradled my little imagination and transported me into a safe place, one that would become my home for life, it seems. Even my mother's records grabbed my attention; Ray Conniff and The Bachelors rolled me up in a passive state of comfort.

I was in some ways an only child, with a mother who let me get away with most things, including staying up late listening to music with her by my side. The smell of Persil wafting from the kitchen and a blast of Jim Reeves: what was not to love? Les came back to live at home every now and again; Lew drifted in and out. He provided the balance in our house when I was young. He was the yin to Les's yang. He always loved me with real and genuine warmth, and introduced me to The Beatles and The Searchers

– music Les would have thought too soft. Lew's asthma meant he would cough all night, keeping us all awake. It was so unfair; Les would just hit him and tell him to shut up. Mum was so worried about his health, she got him to start swimming – an activity that opened him up and helped him breathe without pain. Even though he's now got a replacement hip, he still swims seventy lengths once a week at the golden age of seventy-three. He puts me to shame health-wise. I feel more at home in the shallow end and have never been sporty at all.

The house was a more grown-up version of the prefab. Mum was so proud of it and dusted every day. New curtains and new carpets, a smaller cardinal-red door and a coal bunker. We were living the council-estate dream. Still I hung out mainly with my imaginary friends. They gave me the chance to be sociable in another world, one in which I felt safe, loved and happy. Today I still long for this place. Yes, I have friends, but they sometimes pass like the breeze. Maybe that's my fault though. There's been so much water under the imaginary bridge, so many changes – family, recovery, touring the world . . . It's very different from those short-trousered days when I could storm houses and fly low across open battlefields, and I'm sad to say I think I preferred it the way it was. Back then, my imagination was endless, my hope eternal, and I thank my imaginary friends for being there for me. It's been a gradual uphill climb ever since, but then life seems to be like that. King George Street was the cradle of my youth.

COMBE AVENUE

Walking to school through Greenwich Park was a daily treat. I loved its changing look through the year: the snow of winter, the colours of spring, the heat of summer and the orange-greys of autumn. On its avenues of tarmac I began to stretch my imagination, surrounded by nature and big open skies. Mum walked me in most days, as by now she'd found a job and was working in the canteen at the local police station. This was where, most nights after school, I had my tea. Sitting with the Old Bill on benches looking out over the rooftops of Greenwich right next door to the town hall. The men flirted with Mum and she with them. It was good-natured and all I cared about was the pie and chips, a sneaky teacake and a possible ride home in a police car.

South London was safe in those days for a young lad and I remember that I could ride my bike for miles along the towpath by the river or across the heath and even down to Lewisham. The towpath was my route into the future and my imagination came with me everywhere. I'd pedal past moored barges, bored-looking cranes and tired and silent lorries. This was my manor and I was lord of all I encountered on my green Chopper. I was following in my father's footsteps – feet that had walked across Europe during the war, had walked the steps to the church where he married my mother. They were big shoes to fill.

Mum changed with the new move and the new job; poor old Dad could never stand up to her and would run around like a slave for her. 'Do this, Sid . . . bring me that, Sid' – her constant commands would wear him down. And me too. He would dust, hoover and cook while she sat by the fireplace with her whiskey; he would finish work and come home with the shopping while she sat in the garden in the sun. She had changed from the quiet one to the mother with a bee in her bonnet.

Mum was a jealous person and next door to us lived Mrs Jones, who Dad always got on well with over the garden fence. She was attractive and looked a little like Joan Sims. Her husband was a fireman – Mum liked him – and his whistle would sing across the lawn over the picket fence and into my mum's lap. Nothing ever happened, but it was flirtatious. My mother's jealousy sadly made her burn many of the love letters my dad sent her in the war; she struck the match one day when she thought my dad was seeing someone at his Gas Works club. He wasn't seeing anyone as far as I know.

Dad did everything for Mum to keep the peace; even – I believe – turning a blind eye when she became a bit too friendly with a policeman she worked with. There were so many unsaids in our house at that time. I remember silence being a big part of our family life from an early age: on the train going on holiday, on the beach with our jam sandwiches. One summer, en route to Ireland, Dad got off the train at Crewe to get some tea and KitKats, and never got back on. I still don't know why. Mum said nothing; she just sat there looking at her reflection in the glass as the train pulled out of the station. I cried and looked out of the window too. No KitKats! Just the reflection of my mother's eyes straining not to cry in front of me. Two weeks later, we were home again and nothing was said. Dad had come back.

Therapy has explained none of this. Dad loved Mum, of this I'm sure, and in all the pictures I have of our family, I only see the two of them smiling and laughing together. This makes me happy; glad to know that love was there even during what must have been long periods of domestic emptiness. Even now it makes me smile when I remember one night on holiday in Coleraine, Dad staggering home with Mum and stumbling up the stairs. I could hear him singing and laughing, and though he was obviously trying to have his way with her, she was having none of it. 'Go in the bathroom and sort yourself out, Sid,' I heard her say.

By the time I was due to sit my 11-plus in 1966, it was panic stations. Short trousers were becoming a thing of the past and being a mummy's boy was not a cool look around our estate. Gary Meades, who was always allowed to wear long trousers, was my new best mate. Together we had fun being silly on school trips and in the upper forms of primary education. He was chubby like me and we shared a boring hobby: plane-spotting. We also spotted ships and sometimes lorries on the A2 from the roundabout on Blackheath. We were nerds in floppy hats. Once on a school journey to the Channel Islands me and some friends took a boy's pants down and polished his nuts with black shoe polish. I quite literally fell through the bedroom window in tears laughing. The teachers didn't think it was so funny. We'd been to Guernsey to talk about how they grew tomatoes and why the Germans had invaded this small, boring island. A day trip took us all on a ferry to Herm, an island close by, and someone said that Eric Clapton had sailed his yacht up to the beach one afternoon. 'Get Back' by The Beatles was number 1 and two hundred 555s were bought and stowed away in my hand luggage. I smoked myself sick, but it looked good.

Dad had always hoped I'd be a grammar-school boy, like he had been, but because he worked so much he could never keep his eye on the ball when it came to me and homework, and I managed always to skip it or disguise the fact that I had any. I failed my 11-plus at James Wolf Primary School and I didn't end up going where my dad wanted me to go. We stood in Greenwich Park by the bandstand and he read me the riot act as he thumbed through my exam results. Mum in his shadow weighed in with her wistful Irish wisdom and we all marched back to the house with me twenty yards behind, head hanging low as if I was on my way to the gallows. I was a let-down. Mum always wanted me to remain four years old, cute and a little bit in love with her. The schooling wasn't a huge issue for her, but she had to take Dad's side and stand close by when he shouted at me.

I spent the six weeks of the long summer holidays nervously building up to the new place – Greenwich Secondary School for Boys. But for the first time ever we went on holiday to somewhere other than Coleraine; we went to the Isle of Wight. Dad, who was sick of going to Northern Ireland, had got his way, so we sat on the beach drinking tea and eating gritty hand-made sandwiches, walked the cliffs and came down in the morning at the B&B to a sunlit room filled with people like us. It was so great to be somewhere new and I think even Mum enjoyed the change, a new home and a new holiday destination all in the space of a few years. We went back a few more times to the Isle of Wight, and I remember seeing the *Queen Elizabeth* sail by each time we were there. It looked so graceful and so much of another world: way above our station.

Lew was now too old for family holidays and Les was trusted to stay at home and house-sit. We came home after one break and opened the door to find the furniture all out of place and the fish in the tank gasping for food. Behind the sofa was a pair of girl's knickers; in the kitchen empty bottles of beer and wine. Mum hit the roof and Dad was hunched over, resigned to something he knew all along – that the boy couldn't be trusted.

The new school beckoned. A 53 bus from the edge of the heath took about six minutes to get down the hill into the dark and dangerous world of Deptford. I had to walk past Carrington House on the corner of Deptford Broadway, a doss house outside which I'd trip over women with walking canes and men with matted grey hair and long, flowing Dickensian coats. The smell was urinal and high in octane – one dropped dog end and the whole lot would have gone up. At first I was petrified. The rest of the walk was along Friendly Street to the black gates of the lower school, passing the corner shop that sold single fags to school kids. I'd heard about the tradition of tie-label cutting and bog-dipping, and I was nervous my head would be stuck in some shitty white toilet bowl.

I said goodbye to my mum at the black gates. I wanted to hug her and cry, just like I had on my first day at junior school, but the new young man inside me dragged me off into the playground – into the lions' den. When I had a chance, I took my own tie label out and threw it away; it did the trick and in some ways made me feel part of the flock. The early years in the lower school were spent dodging games and looking out of the window at the trains heading up the track to London. I had some friendships to build; I also had some old mates, like Coconut, who was big enough to offer me some security. It was time to toughen up a little, too, as without it I'd get eaten alive by the bigger boys. But there was too much Mum in me and not enough Dad.

My classmates and I grabbed each other's balls on the stairs going to and from class, we rubbed bogeys on the banisters so teachers would put their hands in them and we tripped weaker boys up in the main hall at assembly. Hardly tough nuts. I had the nickname Mo; it was seen as an insult, but I had no idea why. I was hopeless at games, so in the eyes of my peers, my masculinity was immediately in question. At best, I played in goal; in cricket I batted like a little girl and in running I walked. In the brutally cold showers our teachers would force us into after every game of football, I found looking at other boys uncomfortable; they never looked at me.

The balance had shifted at home, and Mum working at the police station wasn't going down well with Dad. This was the end of the 1960s and working mothers were still a rarity – especially around our way. Dad was miffed about it, though he was the first to admit we could do with the extra money coming into the house. His problem, I think, wasn't this first flowering of women's liberation, but the fact that she spent her days surrounded by burly, cocky policemen. She seemed happy, though, and was always being chauffeured to and from the station in police cars, which I thought was impressive.

Dad sat at one end of the sofa and Mum the other, then she moved to the chair next to the fire. They pointed themselves towards the TV and watched the heaps of inspiring programmes that came into our front room back in those days. Wednesday plays, *Morecambe and Wise*, *Tomorrow's World*. The cigarettes seemed more and more important and the new spinning silver ashtray on a pole in the centre of the room was always full. Drinks were poured but each night felt increasingly empty of conversation. Dad worked as hard as he ever did and treated himself to a moped. It was scary to see him ride it, as he'd never driven anything more dangerous than a bicycle. The tubby man with the brown cardigan and Charles Hawtrey glasses seemed to follow our move, and again every Saturday he would pull up in his small van and Dad would smile and pass him some cash.

Dad was frustrated with my schoolwork and the fact that I was academically useless, unlike my older brother Lew, who was as bright as a button and had got a good job and a new home in Overton, Hampshire, with the love of his life, Christine. Lew was the generous older brother who would bring me toys and look after me with a warm arm around my young shoulders. He always called me Henry, my middle name, the only person who does so, and his affection for me made him seem like a third parent. By council house standards he was doing pretty well for himself. Unlike me, who struggled with maths, English and all the things Dad wanted me to excel in. They said I was backward at school – whatever that meant. Dyslexia by another name. Homework was boring and I sat there long-faced as Dad stood at my shoulder waiting for me to turn into some kind of Billy Whizz, which I never did. I turned into Billy Liar instead.

My stammer and my lack of self-confidence slowed me down. I sat at the back of the class next to kids who chewed crayons and threw paper and rolled nose-pickings into a matchbox. I went to elocution lessons in Deptford to try and correct my speech impediment.

I was often gasping for words with my friends at school and this always made me feel one step behind the rest. I felt frightened. I'd never conform to Dad's way of thinking and in the end I think he saw that my way was the only way I'd make myself happy. I was nice but dim, and I was never going to be an accountant like my big brother.

School dragged on. I can't remember too much about the lower school, but once I transferred to the upper school, things changed. The 53 bus took me from the same stop on the heath down to the bottom of the hill again, but not as far as the doss house on the Broadway. The upper school was a tall imposing building and it felt dangerous, bigger boys and bigger balls to grab. In the playground there were two long buildings, one for metalwork and one for woodwork. The top floor was where the art room sat – the first class that made me feel engaged in this education I'd previously assumed I simply had to get through. It takes a good teacher to show you that learning can be fun, and we had a few. Good friends can always help, too. Eric Stuckey was my new best mate; he was so funny and so focused on his work. A magnificent goalkeeper, he would scoop the ball in his arms, choose a player on the pitch and lob the ball right to their feet. I played left back so I could be close to him for some chilly laughs on bleak open fields deep in the south London suburbs.

Eric lived right next to the Millwall football ground, and we spent our evenings either in his bedroom or in mine on Combe Avenue. Going anywhere near Millwall filled me with fear. It was such a dark, grey environment, and I always felt scared walking the streets around there. I quickly learnt to keep my head down and not invite trouble. You had to look confident, like you knew exactly what was around you, and to walk purposefully. Danny Baker was a huge Millwall fan; he was in a lower year than me, so full of life and charisma, a good football player and all-round happy chap. And like me, he had a keen interest in music. Danny never seemed to be one of those football fans that would round you up with a few punches and a boot to the ribs.

We shared many of the same experiences in that school; you can read them in his book after you have read mine. The smell of school still lives with me today: the sweetness of timber being shaved in the woodwork room; the harshness of metal being drilled on a lathe. The smell of custard creams being cooked at Peek Frean's factory a few miles away in Bermondsey and, in contrast on another wind, the sickening smell of dog biscuits being made down on Blackwall Lane. Stewed greens at lunchtime, tar soap in the changing rooms, the dry crusty odour of socks in football boots. The smell of boys in grey flannel trousers, and pencils – ah! The sweetness of pencils.

The leap from childhood into teenage utopia seemed to happen overnight. Suddenly I was in a place where girls seemed oddly interesting, where Airfix kits were to be left in boxes and what you had in your trousers was worth occasionally investigating, especially when wiry hair started to take root. I started to notice the shape of things to come – particularly in the form of Greenwich Girls' School, across the road. At the bus stop I became friends with a girl who caught my bus each day; she was taller than me and very serious-looking. A few times I walked her home even though it was nowhere near where I needed to be.

Finally I plucked up the courage to ask her to hop off school with me. To my delight she accepted. My daily routine was this: I'd arrive at the school gates and tumble into class for the register; then, in the first break, I'd sneak back out of the gate and onto the bus. I had a key to the house and was trusted by my parents. She agreed to join me and we met on the bus going back up the hill to my estate. I turned the key and in we went to the cold, empty house. Suddenly I lost my nerve, and after a cup of tea and some awkward chat, we headed up to listen to records in my bedroom. Her hairy legs and her serious face made me feel like crying, and just at that moment I heard the pop-pop-pop of my dad's moped coming down the road. White-faced, I told her to get under the bed, where the floor was littered with electric toy trains and top-shelf magazines nicked from the corner shop. Dad came in and hunted around downstairs; he'd left something behind. He must have known I was home, as the teacups and the sugar bowl were out on the serving hatch. The door slammed and pop-pop-pop, off he went back to work. By this time, any passion I had was gone.

My attention span was minimal. When being taught history, I drifted; when being shown how to make a wooden stool for my parents' kitchen, I lost interest and the stool was forever lopsided. Maths was for the bright kids in the front row of the class, not for me. Geography, though, was something I enjoyed. Mr Cosgrove, our teacher, was seven feet tall and his hushed Irish accent and total love of rivers and valleys won me over. I was gripped by his voice and embraced his descriptions of limestone and clay. We once went on a field trip to Box Hill in Surrey, where he stood in a river in his corduroys to show us how the river was deeper on one side than the other. His enthusiasm drew me in.

I also enjoyed English, especially when, from time to time, it was taught by a stand-in teacher. He was young and tuned in to my dreamy, curvy handwriting, which would dribble words in rhyme onto the backs and fronts of my school books. I knew about daydreaming and I knew about poetry, and to pass the time at school I married the two together. I was fascinated by the rhyming images of Spike Milligan, his humour and the rhythm of the words. Poetry was something I had read, but not understood, at my brother's house in Hampshire when he first got married. I flicked through a book of verse by Tennyson. The pattern of the words and the meanings hung like fluffy clouds above the empty pallet of my receptive young mind. Nobody in my house seemed the least bit interested in words; there were no books except the Bible and a few unread encyclopaedias. We were not a well-read family. I'd been unsure about writing but this teacher inspired me.

In an early long poem, I wrote about a land that could only be discovered from within the lamp post outside my prefab. The cold metal door would open to reveal a mystical place full of friendly children my age who would talk in rhythm and offer you sweets. Day was night and night was day. I went there in my imagination and inbetween the words I had created. Xiom was a far-off land of peace and sunshine, full of little people who lived in cream-cake houses and drove around in sherbet-dab cars and buses. Rivers were lemonade and the clouds were candyfloss; almost everything in the lamp post was edible. I could lose myself in the poems I wrote; along with my imaginary mates I was in a safe place far away from the rigid structure of school.

One afternoon my teacher carted a record player into the classroom and out of his bag he pulled a Bob Dylan album. We studied the lyrics and talked about them. This was new. He unveiled the link between words and music. I must have subconsciously swallowed this idea and the seed was planted gently in the fertile ground of my youth. Most of the other teachers were too old to teach and way out of touch with the music of the day, and sneered at his forward thinking.

One day the careers teacher sat me down in his office surrounded by Join the Army pamphlets and guides to local colleges. He asked me what I might like to do when I left school – something I really hadn't given any thought to. He was a bit of a know-it-all, and whenever I suggested something, he knew better. When I said I wanted to be a pilot in the air force, he laughed and said I'd have to work jolly hard for that to happen. He said I needed to go away and give it some more thought. That same week, I read an exciting interview with Pete Townshend of The Who in *Melody Maker*. He had all the drugs in the world, fast cars, drink and private planes, money and a busy touring schedule. It sounded great. The next time I saw the careers master, I sat down in his room with a large grin and told him I wanted to be in The Who. Again he laughed. Prodding me, he asked me what I'd really like to do. I sat and thought. A pig farmer?

Art wasn't my finest hour. I could paint, but not with anything other than an abstract brush. I was good at matchstick sheep. Our art teacher was good-looking and a bit of an enigma. She had long hair and all the boys and male teachers followed her with their eyes. She drove an open-top car and swaggered up and down the stairs to the art room. She took me to another place. She was young and used music to inspire us in class, which meant we could bring in LPs. My collection at this time was thin, but Eric and I were starting to take an interest in NME and Melody Maker. We were watching and reading everything to do with music; it was our hobby. The 53 bus took us up west to HMV to see and hear the albums there. I would listen to Frank Zappa and The Allman Brothers Band, King Crimson and The Who. Those trips were the foundations of my musical journey; the anticipation of hearing new music was so special. Albums were listened to and collected with pride and devotion. It was a boy thing, except she wasn't a boy – she was our teacher, and being asked back to her place was a bit weird. At her flat we listened to albums and sat on the floor a lot. It was all Chicken Shack and wholemeal bread, candles and sideways looks that seemed full of meaning. When she came close to me, I was aware of something stirring in my underpants. But I knew that was a line that could not be crossed, and anyway I was terrified.

Albums were key to all forms of communication; they were the talking points that could turn a friend into a closer friend. Eric had a cool collection including records by Canned Heat and Jethro Tull. He did a fine impression of a man playing a flute, in his socks with a ruler in his hands. I wasn't a big fan of that, but he turned me on to Chicago and a band called Heaven, who reportedly had the most complicated album sleeve in circulation. It opened up into a large cross the size of my bedroom. The music wasn't great. Sleeves were the thing, and with King Crimson we had album sleeves that were so artistic it was hard to believe there could be anything better. The music inside seemed great, too. With a Pink Floyd album under your arm, you could walk through school and say all you needed to say about how you felt about life and who you were.

Eric and I started going to see bands play live – Genesis, Canned Heat, Crimson, and lesser-knowns such as Camus and Gong. The norm was to sit on the floor and nod to the music, coming away with what we felt was an innate understanding of time changes and non-emotional lyrics about mythical creatures and dreams. Lunchtime concerts at the Lyceum were good tickets, but we had to hop off from school to see them. No big deal as our art teacher would cover for us. Van der Graaf Generator, Patto, Atomic Rooster; all great sets, over which the smell of patchouli and fags would hang sweetly in the afternoon air.

We were distracted from our musical adventures briefly when we bumped into two girls in the park. Eric was confident and soon moved into a short relationship with his; me, I stumbled forward like Frank Spencer. Diane Twigg was tall and very lovely; we were both fourteen going on fifteen. She lived in Lee Green, where I made a few visits, soaping up her parents with my good behaviour. I think I even washed her dad's car. Once I was in the family I was allowed upstairs to her room to listen to her records. She put a Leonard Cohen album on the turntable. She gazed into the light of the window; I gazed at my monkey boots. I was not vibing with her on this one. Her dad took us to see Cat Stephens at the Coliseum in September 1971. Cat was magical and gentle, like Diane. The concert was an eye-opener: I had never seen such a soft concert before but I think I loved it. A few weeks later, Diane dumped me. I went and bought the Leonard Cohen album she had played me; suddenly I understood the darkness she was looking at, and now it belonged to me.

I may have been a sort of hippy at school, but such dreamy affections would never have cut it back on the estate. A skinhead gang was forming as the houses were being put up around us, and the Combe Avenue Killers – a name I once painted onto one of the shed walls nearby – were starting to come together around Les Grimsley and Trevor Chambers, kids a couple of years older than me. Les walked with a limp and his lips were never very far from a cigarette. He could explode at any minute, he seemed to have such a short fuse. Trevor was more cunning in looks and by nature. There were two sides to the gang – those who leant towards creative mischief such as removing people's gates and reattaching them to their neighbours' gateposts, and the out-and-out thugs who were into nicking cars and breaking into houses. At first, they petrified me (I'd always veered towards the nerds in floppy hats), but ours was a small estate and social options were limited, so I was soon hanging around with them once school was over. It was boredom relief. We would often gather on the heath on a piece of rough ground we called Cowboy Land. Snogging in the bushes and lazing about being hard was the nature of the beast.

One night a man arrived on our estate delivering the football pools; he had a small black car and was very friendly. He asked me and a mate if we wanted to help, and told us we could earn a few bob too. I went around posting the forms through the doors of our estate and others close by. One night he took me to an estate on the other side of the water, in east London; it was scary and exciting. He asked me if I liked model aeroplanes, which I did, and the next time he picked me up he had a box with a model Lancaster bomber in it. My face lit up as he rolled another cigarette.

He then drove the car into a dark spot off the heath and touched my leg, smiling and in search of reward. I slammed the door and scarpered. The following day I gathered my mates together and we went to his house. We broke into his car and rolled it down the side of the incline that would become the new A2 bypass down to the Blackwall Tunnel. To top it off, we smashed his front window. Nothing was said. I'd dodged a very hairy bullet.

I did have some softer friends on the estate. John Barnes lived just behind us, and his parents often took me with them for Sunday lunch in a folk club down in Kent. We sat outside submerged in the tenderness of folk tales played on fiddles and banjos. I do recall a woman singing songs one afternoon and being smitten by the storytelling value of her words. John and I got on well and I found his home a place to retreat to when things got hot under the collar around the washing lines. Other softies included Andy Driscoll, who played the drums in his bedroom, much to the annoyance of his neighbours and his parents alike. He lived opposite two boys who were into The Who and The Small Faces. We would bounce off their parents' sofas with tennis rackets singing along loudly to 'Lazy Sunday Afternoon' and 'Happy Jack'. The estate was a mixture of emotions: one minute I felt safe in a woolly jumper, the next on edge in a pair of turned-up jeans and a Fred Perry shirt.

The skinhead scene may have become synonymous with racism, but in our corner of south London that couldn't have been further from the truth. A lot of people in the area were uncomfortable with seeing more black and brown faces on the streets in the late Sixties – I remember my dad once telling me he'd got off the bus and walked all the way back home from Lewisham because three 'darkies' had got on and sat behind him – but ours was a very white estate so it just wasn't that much of an issue for us. Plus our gang had huge respect for Jamaican music, so the black kids we'd go clubbing with were good friends. There was a definite sense of segregation at school. The Jamaican and Ghanaian boys gravitated towards each other in the playground, and the white kids hung around in separate groups. But there was never very much tension. I was once in a fight with a boy called Dingle Fullerton, who stabbed me with a fountain pen on the ground outside the woodwork room; there was a stand-off around us, but it was soon broken up by the seven-foot geography teacher.

I loved the music I heard at the Tamla Motown parties I went to with my skinhead mates every Saturday night, followed by the Savoy Club in Catford on a Sunday. My record collection was full of reggae and ska; my wardrobe consisted of tonic suits and polished shoes, white shirts and white socks. Brut and spray-on deodorant was a mixture I won't ever forget the smell of. My skinhead days intertwined with my early days in the upper school and my dual life split me into two camps. Combe Avenue, and the estate I lived on, provided the lads and the little masculinity I managed to harvest; school nurtured the more feminine musical-poet teenager who was focused on doing as little as possible but enjoying the ride. Being a skinhead made me walk tall and connected me to dancing and girls.

My skinhead girlfriend was Sharon, she was as skinny as a rake; we dressed the same and danced the same, but somehow I always knew she was looking over my shoulder at better-looking boys. I say girlfriend, but nothing ever happened; it was a long walk home for a kiss. Nothing else. One night we won a dancing competition judged by a slick black DJ in a reggae club. I was buzzing. Outside I was talking to a very pretty girl in a Prince of Wales check suit. From behind me leapt Sharon, who stabbed me in the hand with her silver comb. We fell to the ground and had to be pulled apart. It was over, and she moved on to a taller skinhead with a chiselled face, sculpted no doubt by large amounts of uppers.

Speed was the first drug I ever took; it pinned my face to the back of my head and made my teeth grind like millstones. We danced all night and we danced all the next night too; me and Trevor at his mum's flat on the estate. He was a thug and started aggro without any fear. Together we often picked fights with hippies on the street – easy targets. But then he beat up a boy on the heath whose dad was head of CID at the local police station. Not so bright. He was arrested. A big black girl and her sister joined the clan; she was a nutcase from Lewisham and punched people for no real reason at all. She terrified me. One night she tried to force me to take my pants down on the heath. I ran away and hid under the washing lines. Another girl, Chrissy Mayers, was connected with friends in local record shops in Deptford so we always had the newest releases from Jamaica on the decks. My life was livening up.

I was once caught in a house with Trevor and some other boys when the police raided the place for drugs after a tip-off from a neighbour. Handcuffs were exchanged for held-out arms, but not me: I was taken to one side. The policeman I knew from my mother's canteen gave me a stern talking-to in the back seat of the police car just up the road and then let me go. Mum was none the wiser. A few years later, I walked into our front room at Combe Avenue to find the same policeman in my mother's arms. He was sitting on her lap; I could see her stocking tops. I think they were both on the brandy. I ran upstairs to my room to sit with my tropical fish and my record player. I wasn't sure what to think or feel, so I played *Beggars Banquet* by The Rolling Stones. A few days later, I found him waiting for me outside the house in his car. He got out as I walked past, and gave me The Beatles' *White Album* as a gift. I took it from him and went to my room trying hard to pull a long face. I don't think I said thank you. The record still sounds amazing despite its connections to Greenwich CID. He wasn't *The Sweeney*, more *Z-Cars*. A nice man with a soft Irish accent. I left a big scratch on his car with my front-door key. Revenge was not sweet. Playing 'Revolution 9' loudly every time he came round to the house was.

On Saturday, 26 April 1969, Leicester City played my team Manchester City at Wembley Stadium. Colin Bell was my hero. Dad got two tickets and took me to see the game. The journey through London on the bus and the tube swallowed me up. I was fifteen, but I still held tightly to Dad's hand. The experience of being around so many people, mostly men, made me scared and anxious; I was not so much excited as petrified. We stood in the stands as the crowd as one swayed from side to side, men in hats, boys in scarves; it seemed powerful. Dad stood by my side while I tried hard to see the game on tiptoes. The winning goal was scored by Neil Young – the other Neil Young – and the place erupted, except for my dad, who stood silent and motionless. I was beside him trying hard not to explode; I was the firework that fizzled out under my father's giant shadow.

Manchester City won the cup and we returned home on the tube and bus. It was a damp squib of a day, but the journey and the vibrations of so many people in one place stayed with me for a very long time. It was tribal if nothing else; it's just my dad wasn't into crowds and expressions of manhood. Back home in my bedroom I looked at the poster of Colin Bell on my wall, next to the one of The Who's *Maximum R&B*, and beamed with pride as I took it down. It was replaced by a poster of a girl scratching her arse while holding a tennis racket. On my copy of The Small Faces' *Autumn Stone*, I can still see the words 'Man City' written in biro on the front of the sleeve. Mixed-up days indeed. I didn't go to another football match until I was in my thirties.

Our rival skinhead gang lived in Charlton – just above the Valley football ground on the Charlton Road estates. They were into causing trouble at Charlton Athletic games, a new kind of fun for many young working-class boys in the late Sixties and early Seventies; and something my dad, a lifelong Charlton fan, could never understand. We couldn't be bothered with that, but we were always up for a fight with the Charlton mob. Equidistant between us was The Standard pub, which was the crossing line. You had to go mob-handed if you went anywhere near it, as once you passed it, you were in enemy territory. The fight would normally be led by one or two people – the gang leaders – who would start rucking while everyone else stood around and occasionally stuck the boot in. Then, when it got too much, we would all run off in different directions. There was another gang over in Kidbrooke, which included the comedian Jim Davidson and his brother, that we had an easier relationship with. I remember teaming up with them to oust some Hell's Angels from their local pub, The Dover Patrol. But when we got there, the Angels came out of the door and we all legged it.

These sorts of events were seemingly all in fun, if a little nasty in reality. All local gangs would taunt each other but it never seemed to reach me on a deeper level. It was all part of being a lad. Les Grimsley and Trevor were more cut out for villainy than me. They had anger issues and liked to get involved in any kind of scrap. One evening they pulled me into something I knew was going to be uncomfortable. They needed money to buy drugs, mostly speed, or wiz as we called it. It was such a misty night, they suggested we just grab someone on Blackheath and rob them. We hung around the bus stop for a while, waiting for someone to get off, but no one did, so we went down Langton Way, a narrow, dark lane, where we saw an old woman walking a dog.

It all happened quickly. It was a misty night and I was choking with fear. As things started to escalate, I knew I was doing something that wasn't really me. It shook me up and made me think about the peer pressure that I seemed always to be under. I was impressionable and drawn into the danger of teenage stupidity. We were like a pack of wolves as we ran towards the woman from behind. She was knocked to the ground, the dog was kicked into a hedge and the bag was wrenched from her shoulder. And for what? All that was inside was a pack of Polo mints, a couple of quid and some keys.

I felt terrible all the time we were doing it. Really upset. We'd tipped the scale too far and I realised I'd had enough – that my journey onward wasn't going to be with the gang. Les was the sort of person who had no fear and little emotion; he was clearly destined for prison. Many years later, he died outside his home, frozen in the snow, high on drugs. Trevor went to prison and later died from an overdose. The day after the mugging, I had to take the victim's handbag and lob it in the Quaggy River at Deptford Bridge. I was petrified and tearful; I knew I wasn't cut out for the danger and the violence of council-estate life. Deep down, I was still under the table watching my mother bake cakes: a sheep in wolf's clothing.

I loved my estate and all of the people who lived there; we had a good laugh and grew up with equal amounts of danger and fantasy. Our parents worked hard for the rent and with some ducking and diving we all managed to scrape by. People kept themselves to themselves but I always felt that the arm of friendship was always close at hand. I loved it despite being dragged into some sticky situations.

My hair started to grow longer, and heavier music appeared on my turntable. I was moving from the dance floor to the bedroom floor, from Marvin Gaye to The Nice in one short year. Prince Buster made way for Pink Floyd. My parents were confused and the poems I began to write were a constant amusement for Les and Trevor and the rest of the gang. One minute I was coming home high on speed from a Tamla Motown party, tanked up on a Party 7; the next I was slow as a snail glued to the sounds of Black Sabbath or Cream. The role change was very swift, but I think it probably saved my life. We went our separate ways; the gang got more and more dangerous and I grew more reserved and introverted. I was seventeen and all over the place inside, until the day I heard some loud music coming from the end of the block.

THE THREE TUNS

Some boys followed football teams and the muddy world of the leagues. But I wasn't into that; I followed the charts. I tracked record companies and their acts with passion. I read music papers as if my life depended on it. My hair grew down my back and my world focus zoomed in on music and groups. Some boys thought I was a girl. I was sliding down some scary helter-skelter on a rug made of surreal lyrics. The best thing about adventure is not to question it, and I didn't know what to ask it even if I could.

Bob Blatchford lived a few doors down on my block in Combe Avenue; he was heavily into music and making model planes, which we often flew on the heath. His fingernails were mashed to shreds from catching his fingers on the rotating propellers. He had a small moustache and slicked black hair. He smelt of 3-In-One oil, and wouldn't have been out of place taking tickets on the dodgems at the fair. Bob was older than me by a few years and came from a lovely family. His father was a trade union leader on the docks, and looked angry all the time. Bob adopted me and introduced me to an alternative lifestyle. He had some loud records by MC5 and The Stooges. He would pump up the volume and his big black speakers would rattle the windows. I held on for dear life. I borrowed his guitar and took a chord book out of the local library, along with a Donovan album called *A Gift from a Flower to a Garden*, which never went back. I'd started writing songs in my bedroom and, heavily influenced by Bowie and Donovan, was making my first attempts at putting words to music. Bob heard me strumming these and recorded them for me on a tape recorder and some microphones he owned.

I have to thank Bob for inviting me into this world. He listened to me, and took interest in my growing passion. Times were moving on and poetry was my thing, now in full motion. Across the street were the remnants of the Combe Avenue skinhead fraternity; they had whittled down from about twenty to just three or four of them sitting on the wall, gobbing and trying to look hard. But I'd hung up my Doc Marten boots and was now mincing around in plimsolls. We would nod but seldom exchange words; the whole mood of the estate had changed and I was moving on with my life. Two other boys from the estate toyed with music, one with a drum kit and one with a guitar, though it was only a passing fad. But I was not letting my focus shift like the others and spent more and more time with Bob.

Bob took me to Cambridge one afternoon in his father's Austin Metro, and there we hung out with his mates in a student flat where there was a party. I may have rubbed shoulders with my heroes; there were meant to be members of Pink Floyd hanging about but I'd never have known, as I was indulging in the room spin of my first joint. Meeting David Gilmour would have certainly made my year. The odd thing is, maybe I did. The party was slow; we sat on the floor and listened to music, but there was no Smokey Robinson or Prince Buster in sight. Skinhead parties were all about dancing and holding onto the girls, the music steaming up the rooms. Now it was time to sit down and take it all in. There was a lot of dope smoking going on, something I was new to, but joining in seemed the best thing to do, and it didn't take long for me to become very passionate about rolling joints. I rolled them as if my life depended upon it; they were neat, round and tipped to perfection. I had a friend called Keith who lived across the road from the estate. Together we smoked our way through Pakistan and back, his eyes squinting narrowly together. His brother was a dealer; we got all the good stuff, and sometimes the good stuff made me sick. Other times it would make me giggle all night long. It was delightful.

One of the first concerts I went to with Bob was Pink Floyd at Crystal Palace; they were supported by The Faces, Mountain, the brilliant Sutherland Brothers and Quiver. On the top of the 75 bus from Blackheath, sitting right at the front, I found myself surrounded by hippies.

One with a sweet bag offered me a mushroom – it was a magic one and I obliged. By the time we made it to Penge, I was flying. The bus had become a spaceship and I was the pilot. I giggled all the way to the front row, where I sat down just in time to see the show. The Floyd were amazing; they inflated a massive octopus from beneath the lake in front of the stage. This was it, I was in heaven, and it tasted like mushrooms. The whole experience was enhanced by quadrophonic sound and a dark-blue overcast London sky. My early experiences of going to gigs were mostly like this, stoned and happy, studying every aspect of what the musicians were doing, staying up late and being in a haze of quietly spoken friendships. Nice one.

I would walk across Blackheath with my imaginary friends, and we would often form a band and make up songs, some of them long and progressive like ELP or King Crimson. We were forward-thinking with our bass and drum solos. I would sing and play guitar like Jerry Garcia, then switch to being like Frank Zappa. I would make up lyrics and if, when I got home, any of them were worth keeping, I would jot them down in a notepad. I still do this today, but without the bass and drum solos. When people walked by, I would quieten down and hum softly until they had passed, then crank it up again. If the concert wasn't over by the time I got home, I would walk around the block a few times.

Walking and being in the imaginary band helped me to find words and melodies. My days would be full of drum crashes and guitar strums, keyboard swells and crowd noises, and even introductions from the DJ. It was a full-time job being in an imaginary band. We never got on *Top of the Pops* or *The Old Grey Whistle Test* but we had a good go at being famous in my head and in my bedroom, where we imitated every record that hit my turntable. Once I saw Soft Machine, though, my walks with the band changed shape. I suddenly found myself in the world of slow jazz pieces complemented by sporadic vocal lines; often this would go on all afternoon if the weather was right. I realised, though, that any band I played in could never be as intelligent as Robert Wyatt or Mike Ratledge. And I'd never have the sheer musical talent of Keith Emerson of The Nice, who I also saw play around the same time at the Festival Hall – he was another hero of mine. This was a huge realisation for me, and one I'm probably still coming to terms with. I wasn't to know, but a real band would soon follow and my imaginary band mates would take a back seat while I learnt to bluff my way around the local music scene.

Tony Bachelor was a close, quietly spoken friend from school; he rolled the best joints in the class, apart from me, that is. We enjoyed the same kind of music and it was with Tony that I played my first few songs. I had a bass guitar – a Bill Wyman Vox from a second-hand store in Lewisham – and he had a drum kit, and we played in his bedroom in New Cross. His mother was usually downstairs glued to the TV; she was housebound with agoraphobia. She liked knowing where Tony was, so she put up with the noise. We were rough, but it was fun. And the more stoned we got, the better it sounded. We jammed for hours on Velvet Underground songs; it was perfect. Eric Stuckey faded into the background as he needed to study for his exams. I was intent on learning the bass and playing music for the rest of my life – I'd decided exams weren't going to get me anywhere. Tony was like me; we couldn't care less about grades. Cheese on toast round at his and a few hours of 'In-A-Gadda-Da-Vida' was all we needed to get by.

I formed my first band in 1972. It was called Porky's Falling Spikes and was a mixture of jamming, dope-smoking one-chord wonders and good intentions; at one point we had two drummers and I played bass. We played a few shows I managed to sort out in a local pub. The band was made up of some school friends; they weren't as good as my imaginary band, but for a while they helped me live in the real world. As I remember, I wore a boiler suit when we played; I thought it would make me look like Pete Townshend. I had the look – just not the style or the talent. I had learnt how to play bass by pressing it up against the wardrobe to amplify the sound, and slowly plodded along with some Velvet Underground songs on my record player. I took the root notes and made the most of it. We supported Nick Lowe's band Brinsley Schwarz. Nick was a real gent, and kept me in jokes and roll-ups all night long.

Our second gig was headlined by The Flamin' Groovies and Dux Deluxe, a fair old night. The pub was called The Harrow Inn at Abbey Wood, and I made the stupid mistake of wearing silver make-up and getting it all over the neck of my bass guitar. I slid up and down the frets sounding dull and wrong. But I looked good. Tony's mother had put me in touch with a charity who were trying to raise awareness of agoraphobia, so I made a few calls to managers and agents and put the show together. I was boldly going in a direction I had no clue about, but it worked. We raised £250 and even made the *Daily Mirror*.

We did have Nigel, who had joined the band and wrote most of the songs; he was a grumpy sod, and everything had to be his way or he would sulk. It seems that every band has this dynamic from time to time. The syndrome. Nigel wrote some good songs and so did I; we swapped ideas and met in the middle. I was just a pothead with some decent poems on lined paper. He played a Telecaster and was a real musician. I never liked him. Our covers would include 'White Light, White Heat' by the Velvet Underground: it sometimes went on for days. Plonking around on a bass guitar was very satisfying, but I knew that one day I would progress to something a little more musical. Eventually the band broke up. I'm not sure why. I think it was due to apathy, not enough skins, a lack of cheese on toast – or any fans.

Then there was the hippy band. A fiddle and a mandolin, a twelve-string guitar and a cello, some drums and me on piano.

The bluff was total. I had a piano in my bedroom at home and over time it became a place where I would try and practise being like Keith Emerson. I got as far as stabbing knives into the keys, but beyond that I was hopeless. I couldn't play the piano, but I could score drugs, load the truck while on acid and add lyrics to some otherwise average folk songs. Barry Bartlett was our leader, a tall, thin, angelic chap with a love of all things Neil Young and Stephen Stills, and a beautiful girlfriend who came everywhere with us. Barry was a fine player, the first person I'd met who carried a capo. I'd just left school, so we went to a small village in Wales called Boncath to get our heads together; the rest is a blur. I do remember an owl being nailed to the front door of our rented farmhouse. I was tripping and it freaked me out. That evening we sat around a fire and listened to *Dark Star* by The Grateful Dead, then jammed all night and went for a walk. We played some music as we drifted over the hills.

Our driver John Reed was a lovely chap with a long beard that he loved to stroke. He smiled all day long and scored the drugs for most of Blackheath and Greenwich. Acid was his drug of choice and sometimes I'm sure he drove while tripping. It was hairy stuff. I recall being on stage in a local hall in the middle of Wales. We were in the heat of a set, intense then laid-back, with long fiddle solos followed by delicate guitar, followed by silent piano parts. I was bluffing, remember. During one solo, a tin of blue pills fell to the floor and opened up; the pills all rolled out and fell down the gaps in the wooden stage. The music stopped as I got on my hands and knees to save them from the void. After the show I went beneath the stage to find the ones that had got away. The addict had landed. We stayed up all night on the back of the pills

I'd prised from the floor. It was my first summer of madness; it was wonderful.

When we got back from Wales, the band split up – just when I thought I would be on *Top of the Pops*. I wasn't ready. We weren't ready. Life was on hold. When I returned home from my adventure, I walked into my bedroom to see my upright piano had been removed by my parents, back to the church hall where it had come from in the first place. They could see the disappointment in my gaze as I lay on the sofa dreaming of buying a Hammond organ.

I'd left school, and unlike the kids who were sent out into the world just a few years later, there were plenty of jobs available for us. The problem was that they were all crap. At school we were taught how to make things out of metal and wood, and how to kick a ball around. Nothing practical. There was no one attempting to guide us down a suitable career path. None of this mattered to me. My only intention was to play music. But my mum and dad were determined I should have a proper job, so to keep them quiet, I worked at a succession of rubbish places in between signing on for the dole. I did a week in a cardboard factory, flattening boxes. Another job involved editing soft-porn films onto reels of Super 8. It was an eye-opener, hot work and very tedious. It was all very tame, with naked men and women bouncing balls over nets; it was topping and tailing, making tea and watching the clock. Mum and Dad were sleeping in separate rooms at this time, apparently because of his snoring – he had massive problems with his sinuses. In Dad's bedroom, which was the larger of the two, hung his neatly kept work suits. One afternoon I had a feel around his suit pockets, and to my surprise I found he kept small wads of cash in them: each suit had different amounts. I fell into a bad habit of removing a few large notes from time to time, small numbers so he would not notice. I wonder if he did. Sometimes I would find myself at the bar in the pub with £100 of my dad's hard-earned cash making its way to the till. It was not a nice thing to do, but it helped tide me over between jobs.

For a while I worked as an office clerk for a local solicitor's office run by a tall, scary-looking lady called Miss Griffiths and a thin, tired-looking man with glasses called Mr James. They seemed to never speak to one another: I was working for my parents, it seemed. There was a staff of about twenty spread over two offices – one in Tranquil Vale in Blackheath, the other in Charlton. My job was to fetch files from here and there, and take them up to London to the law courts. On the train from Blackheath to Charing Cross, I would write poems that I had started to fall in love with in my notebook and dream of better days ahead. I enjoyed the work as it took me to a wonderful part of town where history loomed down on me everywhere I walked.

They liked me there and my £15 a week was soon raised to £18, plus travel and notebooks by the score. My parents were happy. I looked smart and I had a job; I was on the road to great things as far as they were concerned. One day I might even be a lawyer. After ten months of being a good boy and arriving on time I was given the keys to the office. I was such a nice lad. One of my jobs was to close up at night and tidy the desks. But after a year in a suit and tie, I decided that life was too precious to waste on studying law at night school, and going up and down to London on the train in clean underpants. My social life seemed a better alternative to the working one, so one Thursday night I emptied the safe of the entire wages tray – all neatly collected and counted in brown envelopes. I was loaded and it felt fantastic. It simply didn't occur to me that I wouldn't get away with it. All I had to do was cover my tracks, come up with some story and it would all go away. It didn't bother me at all.

That night I went to the pub, The Three Tuns in Blackheath, and scored some speed. I bought some albums and still had enough left over for the deposit on a rented flat of my own. I was off sick for three weeks, spending my way around London, then my dad got a letter asking where I was. I was busted. No more carrying briefs for barristers in chambers; no more arse-licking Miss Griffiths in the office; no more job. My dad promised to pay them back the money so long as the police weren't called in.

I was a chancer and I was stupid and naive to even try to rob people of their wages, but at the time I was dipping in and out of reality, in and out of drugs and in and out of the pub. I was not thinking logically. Dad was losing the plot with me; Mum was drinking too much and generally losing the plot, but not the same one as Dad. It was time to move out. School was done, skinheads were done, but the bug for music was just getting under my skin. I was in the very small world of experimentation and song. I was writing three lyrics a day, I was in another place. Mum and Dad got the raw end of the deal. I remember standing in the kitchen at Combe Avenue with my dad, and him saying, 'If you join a rock and roll band, son, you'll end up an alcoholic, a drug addict and skint.' And, as it turned out, he was absolutely right. I was tripping, though, and in no mood to listen. I was more amazed by the fact that I was able to put my hand right through his chest and watch it come out the other side.

'What are you doing?' he asked.

'That was amazing,' I said.

'Have you been drinking that cider again?'

They asked me to move out the next day.

I had started spending all my time in The Three Tuns, a pub Bob had introduced me to. It was a bohemian kind of place with jelly babies stuck to the walls, where hippies and builders mixed with local villains and estate agents. The landlord had a moustache and was very shady; it seemed like everyone had a moustache in those days. He smelt of roll-ups and, with his very tight jeans, wouldn't have been out of place in a porno film or alongside Bob on the dodgems. He was strict but smoked dope like we all did and turned a blind eye to most things. It was there that I met Jim Giles, who ran a sheet music shop in Soho. Across the road from Jim's shop was Dean Street Records, where I spent many an hour thumbing through the collection of musical and theatrical cast records. I bought Judy Garland albums and musicals as wide-ranging as *Easter Parade* and *West Side Story*; I was in love with the diversity and the brilliant songwriting. My dream was then, as it is today, to write the lyrics for a musical.

Jim took over where Bob left off. He introduced me to many great things and took me under his wing. We became like brothers, and he was the conduit for my transformation from schoolboy to unwashed dropout. I went to stay with him and his girlfriend Christine on Shooters Hill Road. It was 1972 and life was good considering I had little money and no real focus. Christine seemed to like having me around, and when Jim was at work, we hung out together in Blackheath or in the park. Jim had thrown out a met-aphorical rope and I hung onto it, as I knew it was taking me out of my home life and into a new and magical place, away from the drabness of the estate and the lads. He loved my songs, and one day he took me to see where David Bowie lived. We stood outside in the darkness for an hour; I'm not sure why. Bowie wasn't there, no lights were on. I imagined he was in some smart Soho club mincing around drinking cocktails in a serious mime pose.

Blackheath was becoming the well where I would fish for reflections and replenish myself with love and hope. I was in a place where I could now blossom. I picked up a girl from the pub called Diane. She was blonde and from Sweden, and she was a nanny for a local well-heeled family. I bored her with music and dope. We lay in my room at Jim and Chris's flat with its black walls and tried to keep ourselves from falling off my tiny bed. I played her Todd Rundgren's *Something Anything* album and tried to have my way, but she was cold and left me hanging. The album's total length gave me enough time to gently wrap my arm around her and try to nestle in for the kill, but I was very Woody Allen yet again and slipped from the bed on to the record player. We saw each other a few times but it never really worked out as it was planned in my mind. And then there was Tina, a girl I met on an acid trip at a friend's party. We gelled well, but a month later I came down and so did she. We had fun and explored the possibilities of a long-term relationship while rolling joints and snogging, and I introduced her to my mum, who hated her. She was both Catholic and black. Up in my bedroom I could feel my mother seething in the living room below. Love felt like something far away. I had no idea what it really looked like; all I really loved was music and the idea of playing in a band.

To pay my way, I got another job, this time at the Ready Mix concrete plant in Catford. This had a Wednesday-afternoon film

club, and it was my job to shut the curtains, bring out the pro-
jector and load it up, then stand at the back as the film clicked
through the shutters and the drivers watched with sandwiches in
hand. I saw some smutty films at that place. Nuns in trouble on a
bridge over a stream; one was drowning. Oh no! Mouth-to-mouth
resuscitation was needed, and the habits were off. Film over, back
outside to sweep the gravel. It was filthy work.

I ended up working down by the docks with my brother Les in
a huge warehouse stacked high with forty-five-gallon drums of
oil. My job was to count the contents of the trucks as they left the
yard. Drivers would give me money and I would turn a blind eye. I
was young and the cash was burning a nice big hole in my pocket.
Mum and Dad weren't happy. I'd gone from wearing a nice suit
and tie to jeans and a T-shirt, smelling of beer and cigarettes. But
to me, Les seemed like a safe pair of hands; elder brother, what
could go wrong? We went to the Rose of Denmark pub on the
Woolwich Road at lunchtime to watch strippers dance to Slade
songs. Sometimes I'd spend whole afternoons at the back of the
pub, sipping lager and just watching naked girls dance in and out
of time to the hits – even 'Clair' by Gilbert O'Sullivan got a past-
ing. It was never Legs & Co; never anything more than a clumsy
ballet in front of sixty men in overalls dripping beer onto the floor
through a fog of cigarette smoke coloured by the cheap flashing
lights on the makeshift stage.

I was a man – well, a boy who was pretending to be a man
by smoking untipped fags and walking home with a stagger on
a Friday night. Naked women, money in the pocket, drink and
drugs, record shops on a Saturday, pubs and nicking things. I loved
the warehouse world and forklifts. I loved the smell of oil drums

and the lorry drivers with their wives waiting at home and their dinner in the oven. I loved the sun coming up over the warehouse in the morning and the moon when it rested on the roof of the pub when it closed. Life was sweet. *Minder* and *Top of the Pops* on the telly; 'Maggie May' on the jukebox. Working with Les made me feel protected. With him and his dodgy mates I started to feel and smell the first signs of adulthood. Long hair was not an issue at the warehouse gates as it had been in the cosy confines of the solicitor's office in Blackheath. But then the company went bust and we all lost our jobs, the warehouse was closed and the strippers went home. I was back in a void.

Jim and I went on a trip to Devon together in his old London taxi. We went down there to drink cider and find ourselves, but in fact we found ourselves calling the AA every day as the taxi wasn't built for long journeys. In Plymouth we made our camp as we waited for the spare parts to arrive from London by train. We went to see Arthur Brown play, dropped acid and turned into versions of ourselves that resembled elves in a Disney cartoon. Jim was a dealer and drugs were never very far away; people called for him at night, they met him on street corners in Soho and we often had the leftovers. Devon was slow; we crawled back and slept in the car park at Stonehenge, having stopped off at a festival along the way, possibly Glastonbury. It was magical, cold and damp. The sun came up and we struggled homewards up the A303. I moved back in with my parents as I'd run out of money and food.

It was only a few years after that that Jim died. It was very sudden and very sad; he caned the old drugs and died from a brain tumour. I once slept in his shop in Soho. He sold sheet music, and I tripped to the faces of all the greats there staring at me; I was on a wild one. Soho was a dark place and Jim was well known around the local pubs. He passed the social baton on to Will Palin, who worked for David Bowie's Mainman company.

I met Will in The Three Tuns one night, when we started talking after he recognised me from the hippy folk band. All the girls fancied him. He was tall and impressive, suave and blond, and so gentle in everything he said and did. Will looked out for me, and when Bowie played a show in Lewisham, I went to watch the Thin White Duke sound-checking. Angie was there making tea backstage and Mick Ronson was amazing to watch. Will and I went to a builders' yard and came back with some wood and paint; we made the lightning strike on the circle that hung above Woody's drum kit. This was Ziggy and he played guitar. It was a very inspiring night. The band were so thin, they were from Mars, though we all knew they were really from Hull. I thought they were taking speed, so that night I went to the pub and scored some for myself. My teeth almost came out as I tried to sleep that night. Grinding my upper jaw with my lower. I'm sure I woke my mum up at one point as I lay there watching the bloody sun come up, again.

Bowie was a big figure for me. I always imagined he must have had many imaginary friends too. Through his lyrics he told me it was OK to be spaced out and in another world. He gave me the right to be feminine and lovely, to wear big hats and walk with a wiggle. His songs lured me into a place of hope. I saw him play once at Eltham College. I loved the way he walked into the crowd with his blue twelve-string guitar and handed it around. We were all sitting down – that's what you did in those days. That or idiot-dancing, when hippies used to leap about in the air as though they'd got electric shocks going through their testicles.

They should bring that back; it was so funny to watch. In my diary at the time I recalled walking home to Blackheath with a bottle of wine and my friend Andy; I was planning to write more songs and wanted nothing else but to be like David Bowie. He must have ignited so many dreams for so many young people at that time, and I was one of them.

After living with Jim and Christine, I moved into a flat with Graham and Suzy, another fine close couple from The Three Tuns. Graham was a chippy and was always working; at home I lay stoned in front of his hi-fi, zoning out on Stevie Wonder and *Tubular Bells*. I was transfixed by the album's cadences and its magical production, but I'm sure being stoned helped. When I hear it today, it sounds shit. We had a three-bar electric fire which we toasted white bread on when we couldn't be bothered to get up and walk to the kitchen. We put our electric train sets together and sent joints around the room on wagons. They lit up as they went through a tunnel made of a cornflakes box. We were too stoned to do most things and just giggled our lives away, it was hilarious. I was falling around on other people's floors, paying little rent and learning how to listen to music from a different angle. Horizontally. The flat was too small for us being stoned all the time, and they needed some head space of their own so it was time to move back in with my parents again for some home cooking, a washing machine and the start of something very special: the rest of my life.

LLOYDS PLACE

Blackheath was where I first met Glenn Tilbrook, back in April 1973. I put an advert in a shop window for a guitarist to join a band. I had no band. It said I had a pending record deal and a tour lined up. I had neither deal nor tour. The advert cost me 50p – I took the money from my mum's purse. That 50p got me to where I am today, which is some journey. I was looking for a friend. I was a lonely young man, fresh from being a skinhead and now, with long hair, slipping into flared jeans and leaning gently toward the hippy. From beating people up in Dr Marten boots to loving people in bare feet. A change of clothes, a change of music and now a change of friends.

Maxine, Glenn's girlfriend, talked him into calling the number on the ad. At home my mum had a phone table by the front door, and when the phone rang she would take her time perching on the velvet chair next to it before lifting the large green plastic receiver. It was like she was pretending to be royal. 'Christopher,' she called. 'It's for you.' I raced downstairs and spoke for the first time to Maxine – Glenn was too shy – the only person to call in two weeks of the ad being in the window. I was thrilled.

We met a few weeks later at The Three Tuns. Through the

frosted window I could see two young hippies standing around outside, one in pink trousers with no shoes, the other in an angel-like white dress and sandals. They both had long hair and looked like brother and sister. I recognised the boy as being that annoying hippy who played mandolin by the zebra crossing in the middle of Blackheath Village. At other times he would sit in the flower beds playing guitar and looking like he floated rather than walked. I also remembered seeing them together at the Osmosis Club in Kidbrooke, idiot-dancing to 'All Right Now' by Free on the dance floor; he looked like a deer caught in the headlights as he leapt around the hall. I didn't know what to do. But as fate would have it I strolled outside and introduced myself.

When Glenn and I first met that day outside The Three Tuns in 1973, I was wearing a psychedelic coat made of paisley tinsel, which I'd found in the local Oxfam shop. At least that's how Glenn remembers it. I seem to recall I was wearing a donkey jacket of the highest order. Either version will do – they're both sides of the same coin. Glenn and Maxine were dressed in silks and cotton, cheesecloth and beads. Shoeless Glenn looked like Jesus without a beard; Maxine like an angel – beautiful and glowing with life. Glenn I knew from the long hair falling over his pretty face, and Maxine because she was always by his side, looking so calm and beautiful. They were like Mary and Joseph. I may have been the donkey.

I got the sense he was more nervous than I was as we stood there outside the pub. We talked for about ten minutes, then they said I should come to Maxine's house, a short walk away, to hear Glenn play and hang out for the afternoon. I was still very nervous and unsure. One side of Tonto's Expanding Head Band later and we were joined at the hip. The house was on four floors; it was the first posh home I had ever been to. It was like a palace to me – I'd been living on a council estate made of breeze blocks. In Maxine's bedroom, Glenn played along with Jimi Hendrix, and I sat and watched as he effortlessly ran up and down the guitar fretboard. She made jasmine tea, which I'd never heard of. I was in love with them both from that moment and I went home that night lost in the idea of being part of this new world. They were the opposite of anyone I'd ever met before.

Glenn was locally famous for being kicked out of school for refusing to cut his hair, and had been in the local paper. Oddly, it was the same school Boy George attended. A rebel at an early age. He seemed similar to me in some ways. I think we were both a bit lost – musical, but with deep distant dreams of stardom at whatever level. Glenn had a small band of friends at the time who all seemed soft-natured and very gentle. I had not had people around me like this ever; it was quite a wake-up call. I felt like a leaf that had fallen from a tree onto a bed of flowers.

Shortly after we first met, I called and invited them both over to my house in Combe Avenue. We sat on my single bed and I played some of my songs. They seemed impressed, and before long we were seeing each other from time to time as we built up our friendship. Within a few weeks they were inviting friends around to hear my songs too. I would sit cross-legged on my single bed as I treated people to 'Welcome to Mars', an earnest song about space travel that was inspired by the lyrics of Peter Hamill from Van der Graaf Generator; or 'To Catch a Girl's Eyes', taken from the paws of Neil Sedaka, a mixture of light and shade, minor and major keys. My small audience filled my bedroom. I was an indifferent guitarist but managed to make my way through the chords I had written for what were mostly naive lyrics. Glenn played me some of his songs too; it was as if we were courting each other. My parents, who were sitting downstairs watching *Some Mothers Do 'Ave 'Em*, had no idea a partnership had just been born. Neither did I.

Glenn and I got on well. I'd never been a great communicator and I wasn't really sure what 'well' was, but I think we achieved it. He was often shy like me yet had the ability to suddenly entertain the whole room with songs plucked out of thin air. He was a big fan of 'Summer Holiday' by Cliff Richard; like Cliff he could smile and play at the drop of a hat. Glenn's own lyrics weren't as deep or as floral as mine, though my chords were more basic than his textures and arrangements. He began to teach me some new chords and slowly I found myself more at home on the fretboard, though never as fluent as him. He could tune a guitar, something I couldn't do. His singing style was way more versatile than mine; his high-pitched and mine drone-like. I would sing like Lou Reed while he was more like Paul McCartney. It was a good mixture. Those first few months of our friendship were a lovely time of tea-drinking and strumming. We were sifting around at the bottom of the riverbed, searching for flecks of gold. They weren't far away.

Glenn had a narrow face with a distinctive nose, and long hair that fell to both sides of his cheekbones, and he spoke softly – almost with a lisp. He wore stuff from Oxfam that was perfect for his angelic features. He and Maxine would sometimes swap clothes. I'd not seen this before and thought it sweet. I found him an incredibly soft character and I never felt threatened by him. I'd grown up on an estate full of hard nuts, so Glenn was a revelation. He was from a working-class family who lived close to me in

Blackheath. His parents had split up and he lived with his mother but spent most of his time with Maxine at her house. His mother, Margaret, was lovely and welcoming; his stepfather less so. I once stayed at their flat and borrowed his stick shaver; he hit the roof. I was not welcomed back very often. Glenn's dad Peter lived all over the place; he was a welder and travelled around Europe where the work and money was.

Our first mentor and manager was Ron Reid, an Australian photographer who was a friend of Maxine's family. He lived in Notting Hill with his boyfriend Johnny, had long wavy hair and was considerably older than us. The first time I went to Ron and Johnny's basement flat in Notting Hill Gate with Glenn and Max, I got nicely stoned and sat around playing songs. After a full-on night of dope-smoking, I fell into a very deep sleep. In the morning, Ron, who was a vegetarian like Glenn and Max, prepared a healthy breakfast of muesli, something I wasn't used to; I was a cornflakes boy. Johnny raved about this cauldron of white goo and rolled a joint to accompany the delight. As I took my first mouthful, Ron gleefully told me that he and Johnny had both ejaculated into it. They giggled like Cheech and Chong. I felt the gluey lumps in my throat and didn't know what to say. I swallowed. Soon I was a vegetarian myself; it seemed to make life easier, as by this time we were all living together and Maxine and Glenn were both streets ahead of me in the health stakes. I missed the bacon, if I'm honest.

Ron was a softie: he managed to find us gigs, which was helpful. He would drive us around in a converted transit van with a double bed in the back, which he called his 'fuck truck'; it was in here – while driving along the A4 – that Glenn and I wrote our first song together. I gave Glenn a lyric, he sat on the mattress and strummed, and the next thing I knew we had a song. It was simple and brilliant. I decided to put down the chord sheets and just concentrate on the words from that point. The song was called 'Hotel Woman'. I had no idea what that was, and had no experience of prostitutes, but my imagination had a good go at it. The song was rocking and bluesy; Glenn sang like a bird and so our partnership was formed. My groaning theatrical voice took a back seat, and my Bowie-like cadences slipped slowly into the sunset. Ron got us our first ever gig, at The Butts – a small bar up at the Elephant and Castle – and followed this up with a slot at Trentishoe, a hippy festival on the cliffs in north Devon. He managed to squeeze us onto the bill between the Pink Fairies and Hare Krishna – obvious bedfellows. On stage, Glenn and I were about forty feet apart and totally unable to hear each other. We ploughed on, though, and went down awkwardly. Ron looked out for us and found us some more shows. These were more festival gigs, and we were shitting ourselves in front of bigger crowds as we tiptoed through our acoustic set (we stayed a duo as we couldn't fit a band into the fuck truck). We ate wholefoods, smoked joints, painted our faces, laughed and danced, shat in fields and tripped out to midnight fires and Hawkwind.

Within a few months Glenn and I gathered some other people around us and formed a band. Norman – another long, thin person with a big nose – on bass, and John, who had curly hair, round glasses and a huge smile, on drums. We worked hard, and though the band was fragile in its commitment, it sounded OK.

Windsor Free Festival was very special and was our first real gig. I played without a guitar in bare feet in front of a few hundred unenthusiastic stoned hippies who were surrounded by police officers. It was an illegal festival in Windsor Park which ran for a few years and was always watched closely by 'the pigs'. We played before Ducks Deluxe Camel and Ace, who had Paul Carrack as their frontman. I felt like one of the new generation of layabouts, creatives on dope ready for the revolution that would never happen. We were giving power to the people in our three-minute pop songs.

In the first year of meeting Glenn we had chalked up no less than 137 songs – 'Take Me I'm Yours' was one of them. We were so happy writing and we seemed to impress each other with each new tune. Golden days. We wrote some obscure songs – 'Clipper Ship' was about a sailor on a clipper ship, can you believe? – we wrote songs about distant lands and fanciful tunes about strange places beyond the mind; songs about being sixteen and being in love. We sang together and Glenn would teach me the chords. I found some of them tricky – something that hasn't changed – but I persisted. We sang into the night, candles flickering, joints burning, friends sleeping and record decks revolving. If the sun came up while we were still singing, it was normal. Hundreds of songs were born in that period. We were like sponges absorbing all the music we could, from Sparks to Elvis and back with a bit of Jake Thackray and Pete Atkin in there for good measure.

I was constantly surprised by how different we were as people. He was outgoing and I wasn't. He would jump on the table at parties to lead singalongs on his guitar, while I sat in the shadows at the back pretending to be Leonard Cohen (I'd get girls, but they were the intense, gloomy ones in delicately printed skirts). Our friends loved the fact that we were so different, but even then we often found it hard to communicate directly. Maybe we were just shy of each other.

Maxine and Glenn's friends soon became my friends, and my old mates faded into the background. That's a lot of people. I had to let them go to make the next move of my life, though I didn't really know I was doing it at the time. My skinhead mates were gone, my folk music friends had gone; I was in the world of experimentation and song. It was like being in a fairy tale. Maxine was Glenn's angel and sometimes I felt jealous. I was embraced by her beauty – most people were. I remember once seeing her in a towel. She'd just taken a bath. She was standing with me in her father's study, and as we talked, I felt something I'd never felt before. I had never been around a woman who was so natural and at one with her body; I was used to fat skinhead girls who were welded into tight skirts.

Maxine's mother Anthea was wonderful too – the first person ever to call me 'darling', while holding a gin and tonic and smoking a fag. She was so full of love and life, even when she was pissed, which she was most days, and she seemed constantly to be playing a part in a Richard Burton film; everything was done with such grand, dramatic gestures. She let me stay at the house, and I came and went as I pleased. Often I would sit by her bed and talk her down from a heavy hangover or listen to her jealous ranting over the love of her life, Maxine's father Felix. He was a lush with the women and would call me 'dear boy', which he did with a great sweep of his voice – condescending, but with grace. I loved his study on the top floor of the house; it was full of books and dust and newspapers. This was an inspiration to me. Sometimes I would sit in that study and pretend to be educated, like Maxine's elder brother Kent. I was never sure how he felt about us invading his house while he was at university, but I do remember him being very stern with me when he caught me and others smoking some of his cigars by the fireplace.

My moods were up and down at the time. Glenn and Maxine's relationship was inspiring but at the same time made me think that I could never have anything so warm and tender myself. One night the gin from the sideboard laid me low with loneliness and depression. I locked myself in my room and started to cry. I had the wardrobe against the door and I was ready to take some of Anthea's pills. Everyone else was downstairs watching the TV. When I realised that nobody could hear me, I removed the wardrobe and stood outside the room. Then I sat on the stairs. Eventually I made my way to within earshot of the TV room. Max came to rescue me. I was a sorry case, looking for attention in such a dramatic way. Maybe it was the gin talking; maybe it was a cry for help, or the start of something deeper. I cheered up once I was sitting and watching the telly with everyone else, and Glenn started to play the guitar along to The Monkees. He never put the guitar down and would accompany bread being toasted. It was something different for me.

During our first summer together, Maxine took me to her family's country home in Benenden, Kent. The house had been built around the time of Shakespeare. It had wooden beams that twisted across the ceilings, bedrooms with floors that sloped to one side, huge open fires and acres of garden with a lake. It was my first smell of country life. One night we had a bonfire and sat around with loads of our friends; her parents were asleep but they didn't seem to mind. When the fire ebbed down to a glow, we decided to lob on some old deckchairs we'd found leaning up against the house – fine Victorian ones, as it turned out. The next day we were raked over the coals by Felix. I walked to the local pub to get out of the way. I'm good at that; walking away is a dance I can do standing on my head. Her dad wasn't impressed, though Kent found the situation very amusing.

Maxine gave me the space to write by letting me stay at her house. She gave me the love that no other woman had before, not even my mother. She introduced me to femininity, to beauty, to jasmine tea and sunflowers, pretty music and Marmite. She showered love on all of her friends. She and Glenn were so generous with their love and with their passion for all things rock and roll.

The band's first name was Cum, but it didn't stick so we changed it to Squeeze. Maxine's mother picked the name out of a hat for us, after the terrible album The Velvet Underground released when Lou Reed left the band. Unfortunately, we'd sprayed 'Cum' all around Blackheath with a stencil. Maxine kindly invited me to move in to her brother's room while he was away at Cambridge. I soon got into the swing of writing words and leaving them on the stairs for Glenn. I'd then listen to him plonking on a piano upstairs or strumming on a guitar. He'd spend hours up there with Max by his side, weaving melody around my words in the most beautiful way. It was fun and gloriously uncomplicated. Glenn and Maxine introduced me to Jools Holland, who would come around to the house on his motorbike and play the piano. I had never heard of boogie-woogie music before and was mesmerised by his left hand, his ability to plough through so many notes and make it all sound so great. His tasselled leather jacket always seemed strange in the context of our hippy-trippy world, but he wore it well and his motorbike looked brilliant.

The girls loved Jools and I loved him too. The two of us quickly became close friends. Jools added such great things to our songs. I was attracted to his masculine side – it reminded me of the skinhead in me – and soon I was hanging out with him more than I was with Glenn. Jools felt dangerous to me. He was much more of a lad. Like Glenn, Jools could hold court with his wonderful musicianship and knowledge of rock and roll. I was blessed to be around the two of them.

In the summer of 1974, Bob from the estate asked me to help him down at Charlton Athletic Football Club. I walked down the hill to where The Who were headlining with Little Feat in support. That night, 120,000 people filled The Valley – a record that has never been broken. Backstage, I loaded charged batteries into walkie-talkies for the road crew. I sat and watched Little Feat play, then I watched Keith Moon slide around on flight cases while playing the drums. I was only feet behind him. It was amazing to watch. I sang 'Magic Bus' all the way home with my imaginary band, the percussion part going on for days. I could smell the fame, I wanted it, and I could sense that, if I was stupid enough, it might just happen. I didn't want to load batteries, I wanted to be on stage. I had a feeling that one day Glenn and I could be in a band like The Who, just like I had wanted at school, and with Jools in the team I knew it was going to be something very special and possible. All we had to do was believe in ourselves and fall in with some luck.

Jools was, and still is, blessed with luck. I loved to ride on his motorcycle, and without crash helmets it was even more fun. We raced down to Benenden along the A21 one weekend, the sound of his Velocette throaty and majestic. We were pigs in shit . . . until we got arrested for driving without an MOT or licence, for being underage and for not stopping when asked to by a policewoman on the Sidcup Bypass. As luck would have it, Jools's dad, Derek, came to bail us out of the nick in Eltham. When the police took us home, they saw all the things we'd stolen on our journeys in Jools's garage – road signs, cones, bits of old bikes. Nothing was said. Derek covered for us. He was so supportive of the band and, like Glenn's dad, gave us the space to do what we needed to do. My dad less so.

By now, Jools had officially joined the band on keyboards, with Paul Gunn on drums. Paul was a really nice person but he wasn't a strong drummer; his timekeeping was always up for discussion. Norman was on bass again, but he soon left, to be replaced by Harry Kakoulli, who came equipped with a new bass, leather trousers and a tasty wife called Mary. Harry looked the part and he made us all laugh. He was a lazy bass player, paradoxically full of energy. He looked as though he could have been in The New York Dolls, who I loved and had seen play once at The Rainbow Rooms above Biba in London. His mop of dark hair and Mediterranean good looks attracted the attention of our local female fans. He was quiet but not shy and loved to be funny for the sake of it. He was also a keen dresser, more so than the rest of the band. I really liked Harry: he was simple to hang out with and never went over the top drinking in the pub. Unlike me.

Together we got a set together in a rehearsal room in Greenwich. We played in pubs for beer money and slowly managed to attract a local crowd. Glenn led the band from the start and always knew instinctively how the songs should sound. He draped us in his ideas and moods, and we coiled around his playing, his fantastic voice and ability to lead. He was a born leader – something I've fought against from the start, for no real reason. After all, I could never do it myself. The rehearsal rooms were dark and mysterious, down there under the street; sometimes you would cross paths with Jeff Beck or musicians of a more mature persuasion. David Bowie and Lou Reed had rehearsed there too; it was a cool place to make some noise.

Glenn and Jools were close in a musical way; they could reach each other as they flew through the songs, even if it was just the two of them in a pub. They loved the same kind of music and would jam for hours, playing twelve-bar blues. I tried to dig in, but I was never very good and could only support them by buying drinks. We also rehearsed at Max's house, and sometimes over at Jools's. He had a huge piano his parents had treated him to. Once or twice I slept there beneath its ceiling of notes, wood and strings. His mother, June, would look after us all and make us feel welcome; later in our lives, she became our fan club manager.

Those were the days. Our first studio experience was in Polydor Studios just off Oxford Street, recording one of my songs, 'Black Jack'. I have no idea where those recordings are and I can't remember much at all about the session. In May 1974 we played at the Northover pub in Catford; later in the year we played at Camden Girls' School, supporting the band Deaf School. My diary of the time says we all played well but Paul was not very good with the endings.

As Squeeze, our first real show was at Greenwich Town Hall in April 1975. My friend Will Palin helped us by letting us rehearse at his house in Devon, and by supplying a huge PA from Mainman, Bowie's own PA company. The cavernous hall could not stand the sheer weight of sound, and the few people who were there went home deafened by our excited set of twenty three-minute pop songs. We then played at Catford Girls' School and my new girl-friend Nicky thought I might like to wear make-up like her idol Marc Bolan. I went on stage looking like Lou Reed. It was a great show and I think the girls loved it.

Nicky looked very much like Marc herself, with shoulder-length curly hair. She once took me up to Bond Street to wait outside his offices. We were there for hours, and I got very bored. She was in a gaggle of girls all waiting to see him. Eventually his green Rolls-Royce turned up and out he got. He walked over towards the door, pinned Nicky to the wall and seemed to put his tongue in her mouth in a huge passionate kiss. I was shocked, but it seemed that Nicky was over the moon. I was forever walking home alone in those days, second best, it seemed, to men of a more fabulous nature. I did briefly manage to pull myself from under Nicky's spell by going out with her posh best friend from Golders Green. One night I sneaked into her house for a sleepover. In the middle of the night she screamed out so everyone could hear – every-one being her parents – 'There is semen all over my leg!' She was being overdramatic, but the next morning her father sat me down in the front room and asked me what plans I had in life. I said I was in a band. I never heard from her again. I did write a song for her, with the lame lyrics, 'Nicky D, Nicky D you're the one for me'. It was early days.

Ron felt we needed a more dedicated manager, so he introduced us to Mark Cooper, a suave, impressive, suited man with ideas and money, and a smart office in Pimlico. He'd formed a company with John Leyton, who was famous for singing 'Johnny Remember Me' in the early Sixties and being in films with Frank Sinatra, but who was running a food stall at Waterloo station by the time we met him. We had a promising early meeting with Mark and John, in which we discussed some lyrics of mine going into a book to accompany Ron's photos of the festival scene, but the whole thing was doomed to failure. John dropped us off at Waterloo after the meeting, and as I stepped out from his brand-new Ford, a bus shot past and took off the door – and very nearly my leg. The one thing Mark and John did for us was to buy Glenn and me some leather trousers. That tells you everything about how wrong their vision for us was. They quickly faded into the background. The book, *Tomorrow's People*, did get released; today it's hard to find and very rare but worth the search just to see Glenn and me with painted faces at a festival somewhere, not to mention my lyrics, so juvenile and harmless, printed on the page.

Our first serious manager, Lawrence Impey, was introduced to us by Peter Perrett from fellow south London band The Only Ones. Glenn had played guitar with them at one point and our bassist Harry was Peter's brother-in-law. I felt threatened by Peter and always thought that Glenn would jump ship and end up in The Only Ones; that gave me a few sleepless nights to deal with along the way. By that point we had only really played a handful of local gigs in pubs and we didn't have two shillings to rub together. There was nothing any of us wanted to do more than be in a band.

Lawrence was a young, skinny, curly-haired, well-spoken, well-educated chap, who couldn't have been more different from us. He drove a flash new car and had wealthy parents who lived in a big house in Bournemouth. He introduced me to some Bob Dylan songs I had never heard, and they inspired me to push harder with my stories. He also turned me on to Carmen McRae; her voice charmed the long nights at his house. His father was a very successful lawyer in Nigeria and in the garden of the house they had a servant who lived alone. Thompson was always on hand to supply sandwiches and drinks. One night Lawrence hired a small truck and I went with him to collect two dozen three-wheel disability bikes, which he then shipped to Nigeria – I had no idea why. We got home in the early hours and Thompson rustled up some breakfast for us. We got on well. Soon Lawrence was carting us to and from local gigs in hired vans, and running up a big tab. He was out of his depth, though, and we all knew he needed help. Then one day he revealed he'd been to school with Stewart Copeland, who was the drummer in Curved Air. Copeland's brother Miles was a proper manager. It was all falling into place.

Miles Copeland became our manager in 1975. He bore a striking resemblance to John Denver, wore a tweed jacket and grey trousers, and had a convincing optimistic chant about life that at the time I found appealing. He walked into our rehearsal room beneath the A2 on Blackheath Hill with his brother Ian (who would later become our touring agent in the US), we played him a few songs and his eyes lit up. It was our moment. The Copeland family were a dynasty of some note. Dad was head of the CIA in the Middle East. What could go wrong? Within a few months a contract had arrived from Miles, a thick wad of paper.

None of us could understand it, so we showed it to our parents, who also had no idea what it all meant. We signed it anyway, and wrestled £15 a week out of Miles, as agreed. Miles was convinced we would be as big as The Beatles, which made us all feel really good about ourselves, and he quickly found us some gigs so we could sharpen up our act. We supported bands he had floating around on his prog rock and blues label BTM. It wasn't really our cup of tea, but it was work. We were soon playing up and down the country with Curved Air and The Climax Blues Band, Renaissance and Caravan. It kept us off the streets and firmly in the back of a noisy Transit van. Miles would always put us on right at the beginning of these shows, in front of audiences that couldn't have given a toss. They didn't want to see us. Plus the headlining bands wouldn't move any of their equipment to fit us in. Caravan would set up with Hammond organs and mellotrons, leaving us two feet at the front of the stage to play on. I loved the album *In the Land of Grey and Pink* so I stood and nodded along secretly with the crowd. At least they let us sound-check.

I thought Darryl Way, the violinist in Curved Air, was a complete dick; on the shows we did with them, he told us he needed all the time before the gig to get his sound right, and we'd just have to make do setting up as the doors opened. I remember watching him perform these endless, boring violin solos, with his long hair flowing behind him like an Afghan hound in a gale, and thinking, 'What a tosser.' He was everything you didn't want to be.

The touring began in earnest at the Marquee Club in London. At the opposite end of the scale we played at RAF Brawdy in Wales. It was exciting to jump in the van and head off all over the country, playing to people who mostly didn't want to see us.

Throughout 1976 the band also built up a sizeable south London following, securing a residency at the Bricklayer's Arms in Greenwich, run by Harry Rodgers, who paid us in lager. Here we cut our teeth covering songs and slipping in many of our own along the way.

Travelling in vans all the time was boring. We played cards to see who would go in the front, and the losers would sit glumly in the back as we weaved our way out of London towards various motorways. One afternoon on the A40, I was in the back of the van with Jools and our friend Mark Smith. Bored, we wrote messages on pieces of paper and stuck them up at the window. One of them said: *I can see your tits, now show us your cunt.* Behind us in the traffic, though we couldn't see her or her motorcycle outrider, was the lady mayor of Acton. The van was pulled over – much to the confusion of those in the front – and the next day we had to appear in court, where we were fined. We missed the gig and Miles made us send flowers to Annie Haslam from Renaissance, the band we were meant to be supporting.

We wrote new songs and recorded them at Pathway Studios in Islington; sixteen songs over two weekends in a tiny space. The recording was funded by Miles and it was an incredible experience; the first time we had heard our songs up close. The studio was a place that Glenn seemed at home in; he always paid more attention to the detail than Jools or I did. The engineer was called Barry, and he did a fine job of easing us into this new world of recording as a band. The light would go on and we would play the songs we had rehearsed back in south London. Overdubs were few, but Glenn seemed to know better than the rest of us just what the songs needed. I really liked recording but always thought it took too long to get the right takes, though maybe that was the band and its inability to glow in the dark of a small room covered in orange and brown pegboard.

Shortly afterwards, we recorded with legendary producer Muff Winwood – famous for producing The Bay City Rollers – at Basing Street Studios. Although Muff seemed to be on the phone most of the time, he did come out of the control room to express his doubts about our drummer; it was becoming increasingly apparent that Paul's days with the band were numbered. Being in the studio was a new experience for us, and it felt as though we'd suddenly stepped into the real world of being in a recording band.

When Glenn broke up with Maxine, I was devastated for both of them. Their long and beautiful love affair had come to an end. Glenn and I moved out of Lindsey House, Lloyds Place to share a flat in Bennett Park just down the hill in Blackheath Village. It was our first step into the real world, and we confronted it head-on by writing songs and recording demos all day long. Glenn was providing more and more amazing music to my lyrics; his arrangements were melodic and beautiful. Together we had carved out a new way of writing and it had begun to hit a new peak. We ploughed on, hoping we would get a record deal full of cash to hold us up while we wrote some more. After Maxine, Glenn started seeing Nicky. He went out with her for a few years; she then started seeing Jools (or was it vice versa?). Our band was a right old chicken run in those days; we stood in each other's shadows but nobody seemed to mind very much, which was just as well.

The flat was in the basement and our landlord was insane. He told us that he worked for the secret service and that he knew all the nuclear codes for a war. We kept him away by building a wall of cardboard on the stairs. I would work in the room beneath the stairs and Glenn in the living room. It was tidy most of the time. Ron came to shoot our photos there once and invited all the girls from the girls' school across the road. They were younger than us and it looked and felt wrong. We sipped whisky and giggled a lot. One night the cardboard wall came crashing down and in fell the landlord, swearing and sweating. He accused us of being Russian spies and tipped us into the street. Next thing we knew, fire engines were racing towards our flat; he thought it was on fire. Joss sticks were calmly burning in a jam jar. We moved on. He was sectioned and never seen again.

We went to Island Records and Richard Williams, the label's A&R man, turned us down, again pointing towards our drummer. Glenn and I were no longer writing about clipper ships. We'd set sail on a new course – writing about love, and imaginary people and places. We even wrote a short musical called *Trixie*, influenced by reading Damon Runyon and indulging in Sparks, a band we both loved. The song cycle was ambitious and ahead of its time for a young band like us. My lyrics were dreamy and colourful, and I'm proud of them to this day. But in the Island audition, nerves got the better of us and we stuttered through the arrangements. Paul was all over the place and possibly more nervous than the rest of us. Richard looked on from his chair in the corner of the studio, and Glenn and I were convinced this was it. Luckily it wasn't. I have always been so pleased that Richard passed on us; the cake was still in the oven and nowhere near rising at the time. Richard crossed the hall into the next studio to carry on working with Bob Marley.

We put an ad in *Melody Maker* and auditioned drummers in a rehearsal room beneath the main pool at Greenwich baths. Paul had his P45 and had left the building. It was loud in there but upstairs you could get a bag of chips and a white slice for 50p. The space was handy for when we played the Bricklayer's Arms next door. Gilson Lavis, a former session drummer, turned up in his mother's Mini with all his drums stacked inside. As I helped him unload, I could hear the clink and rattle of empty whisky bottles as they rolled around the floor. Gilson's drums took up most of the space in our rehearsal room. He played with six toms on racks; it was ridiculous but it sounded amazing. He got the job. All the others we'd heard that week were so tippy-tappy compared to this powerhouse. Our songs sounded brilliant with him playing on them. We were complete. We were Squeeze. Gilson was a big fella with a lovely chunky cardigan with a zip; it opened up to reveal a hairy chest and a cigarette lighter on a cord. He was vocal about arrangements and came from the world of session playing – he'd just been on tour with Chuck Berry and Johnny Cash, no less. He had also auditioned for Wings. We naturally were impressed by his CV.

Gilson lived in Bedford so it was a trek for him to get to us in south London, but he always turned up when needed. He liked a drink, it's fair to say, and with him in the band I felt we had grown up both musically and at the bar.

Since we'd met in 1973, we had grown into young men. I was twenty-two years old. It was now 1976 – pre-punk, the tail-end of hippy and all things self-indulgent. Glenn played the guitar like no one I'd ever seen before – he was amazing around the frets, and with him and Jools in the band, we had a fantastic line-up. Gilson brought up the rear with his inventiveness and flair, and Harry plodded along behind with me. We had tons of songs and we rehearsed all the time before trying out numbers in the Brick. We were on fire most nights and we packed the place out. We played for the booze and for the fun of it all. Covers went down well, as well as our own songs. We played 'Junior's Farm' and 'Get Back', and some obscure Merrill Moore songs that Jools brought to the table. Jools sang some and I sang some, but Glenn sang the most. He had the best voice by a mile. When he sang 'Riot in Cell Block Number Nine' everyone's jaw would drop open. Gilson was so loud; his drums took up all the room and he was not a light player, but he could be tender when he wanted to be. I was out-of-tune, pissed and having a great time of it all.

Miles got us a meeting with RCA. They sent us to Rockfield Studios in Wales, where we recorded with the BBC Welsh Symphony Orchestra, no less. The songs were sweet but not sweet enough for the label bosses. Here we recorded 'Take Me I'm Yours' for the first time. We also nailed 'Cat on the Wall' and 'Night Ride'. This was the first time we had been away from south London as a band together to record, and it was the first time we witnessed how much experienced drummers could drink. I was impressed and found it hard to keep up.

That summer Glenn's dad Peter booked us some shows in Holland. Some nights we played three sets, mainly for beer. After two sets one night, I was so drunk I had to sit the third out on a beer crate. It was good fun and being in Amsterdam meant real bonding sessions for the band. A museum with Jools by day, a seedy bar by night. We drove around in a Luton van, playing cards as usual for the front seats; if you sat in the back, your view of Holland was through a small hole only fit for one eye at a time. Fame trickled in slowly in those days. When we went on stage one night in a place called De Brak, a huge potted tree was put in the middle of the dance floor. It turned out to be a marijuana tree. A handful of giddy people arrived to hear us play our rapid and excitable set. By the end of the evening we were all doing the hokey cokey around the tree, giggling and falling over each other, having a really good time. Thanks to Peter, we learnt how to have fun and play music with people with broken English.

Those dates in Holland further illustrated Gilson's thirst for a good time. He was often angry but I was never sure why. He tried to get off with our roadie's girlfriend; he tried to pick a fight with a hotel manager in Amsterdam; he threw a bike into the canal. But then, who didn't? We all liked a drink in those days, but Gilson had a completely different threshold to the rest of us.

One night at the Milky Way club we all succumbed to some space cake, and after about an hour we were off with the fairies. When the police came in to ask us to move our van, three of us took the back of it and the other three the front, trying hard to push it. It had broken down and we were in no fit state to move it, or play a set. We did make it on stage, though, and I remember well the feeling of not knowing what a guitar was for, or why it was around my neck. Jools's keyboard sounded like shards of ice dropping from the sky, Gilson had rubber sticks, Glenn was Hendrix, in my head. Harry was cool and posing as usual at the front. My jaw remained sealed for days after so much laughing and giggling like a child.

Our roadie on that tour was Les Grimsley, skinhead from Combe Avenue. I thought it would do him good to get him out of harm's way. He drove the van, and in one small town took the awning off an ice cream shop.

He got stopped by the customs officers at Dover and was asked to unscrew all of the speaker cabinets, at which point he handed the screwdriver back to the officer and said, 'If you want to see what's inside, go ahead.' They were having none of his lip. Les took the speakers apart and two hours later we moved on. He was a handful, as he had been on the estate. There was no getting him out of harm's way.

Our only other ventures into Europe included a brief trip to Denmark where we visited the Heineken factory in Copenhagen and came out much the worse for wear, having sampled a few gallons of Elephant Beer. The other time was a trip to Sweden where we were invited to a party by one of the girls from Abba. Phil Collins was there as he had produced her album. I got very silly, I was also hallucinating on some heavy dope I had been smoking, which made me feel slightly paranoid. I was in a hotel room with a man dressed as a woman. I made a hasty exit when I figured it out. Back down in the bar Phil kept us all entertained with his Genesis stories. I felt like the lamb that almost laid down in Gothenburg that night. Europe was never a big marketplace for Squeeze. I think my lyrics were lost in translation along the way, which is not surprising.

Suddenly, in 1977, punk happened. Fashions changed and we watched, slightly bemused, from south London. Touring was our staple diet; we seemed to always be on the road trying to impress people with our outrageous energy and short songs. Miles had several punk bands on his books, so we mixed with them a lot in those early years, but I never really liked the music. I was always looking for the lyric and I felt there was no depth to it; it was just kids trying to get a record deal. The music sounded like it was falling down stairs. I moved to a flat on the Crossfields estate in Deptford, and it wasn't until Dot, my flatmate, played me the first

Clash album that I heard a punk record I loved. It had a depth and energy to it that was totally lacking from stuff like The Sex Pistols. They annoyed me in the same way that Les Grimsley had done when I was a skinhead. The aggression was too much for me to handle. I was leaning more toward the pub rock troubadours and their gentle venom which I knew was only skin deep. Downstairs lived a band called Dire Straits – how they survived the headwind of punk aggression I will never know; maybe it was the constant rehearsing in the flat. To me it sounded like they were knitting; it was polite and drifting. But then what did I know? They seemed like nice lads. Glenn and I were never natural punks, but we tried our best. Jools, though, couldn't be persuaded at all. Miles wanted us to ride the bandwagon, so we untucked our shirts and I bought a few safety pins that I wore like brooches on my shirt. I didn't mind dyeing my hair either. It was blond for a while, then orange, then blue.

Punk meant that record companies would now make the effort to come and see us play, and so Miles had an idea. We'd record an EP, which would send a signal out to record labels that we were serious. He and his brother Ian were promoting a tour with John Cale, who happened to be in London biting the heads off chickens, and was invited down to hear our songs in a rehearsal room in Chelsea. I was beside myself. My hero from the Velvets was coming to hear us play! I sharpened up my act; I found some cool dark glasses and a leather jacket and tried hard to look out of it all the time. Cale walked in and sat down, and asked us to play for him. We raced through twelve new songs; he fell asleep. We prodded him but he wouldn't wake up, so we moved the PA closer to his head and ploughed on. Still no life. Then Jools grabbed a marker pen and wrote 'I am a cunt' on his forehead. We woke him up and sent him in a cab back to his hotel. The next day, he came back to the room. The writing was still clearly visible on his head, though it was a little faded, but nothing was said. He then got us to play again before stopping us mid-song and telling us our songs were all crap and we should rewrite everything.

We chose three of our current crop for the EP and quickly recorded them with John Cale at Surrey Sound, an out-of-the way studio in Leatherhead, Surrey. 'Cat on the Wall' was a fun song to play; it had shades of The Who about it, and was noisy with grains of attitude. 'Night Ride' was in the same boat. 'Backtrack' was also lively and mildly aggressive. All three songs promoted the use of Gilson's drums. Toms were the order of the day – he played an Octaplus drum kit at the time – served up on a bed of brittle guitar in a gravy of lumpy bass sprinkled with some flakes of fine keyboards from Jools. Glenn and I were the salt and pepper.

John Peel played the resulting *Packet of Three* EP on Radio 1. It was pretty amazing to hear our record for the first time in full mono on a small transistor radio in the kitchen while the cheese was melting on the toast. We were on the radio, everything was new and exciting, every day was a huge adventure on a journey I instinctively knew I had to make. *Packet of Three* sold 25,000 copies on our own Deptford Fun City label. We were courted by other record companies and most of our London shows were all about impressing A&R men: Sony, Arista, Warner. We eventually ended up at A&M Records on the King's Road. Miles walked us in and dropped us off as though it was our first day at school, and I loved being there. The staff were welcoming; the whole building was alive with music and people who loved music. It was a breath of fresh air. A&M were really great at developing their acts; they gave us time, there was no rush to get things right, which was just as well. We were stablemates with some odd people, but it was 1977 and that was all about to change. Supertramp were giving way to The Sex Pistols. Punk and new wave were marching towards us up the King's Road.

WILLESDEN HIGH ROAD

Recording our first album was like a daily trip to the moon. John Cale had booked us into a studio in north London that took us an hour or more to get to, and when we did get there, there was nothing to do. Willesden was an oasis of kebab shops. We spent our days setting up and trying things out. John hated everything we'd written up to that point; he just wanted us to be vulgar and rough, so all our lovely pop songs were put away for another day and we charged into the unknown, with guitars being dragged across chord changes that were out there (though, somehow, Glenn managed to shine through it all). Jools's talents were mostly buried in functional keyboard parts, and lyrically, I had to delve into the weird and wonderful demands of Cale: 'Sex Master', 'Strong in Reason', songs that made me feel at odds with myself. It was frightening.

After the awe of meeting John Cale had worn off, I really couldn't understand why we were working with him, because he was unremittingly difficult. He was angry and late. We'd always be waiting for him. Then when he did show up at the studio at midday, one o'clock or whatever, after we'd been there a couple of hours, he would poke us with insults or come in with a whip

and start cracking it against the floor, things like that. On our first
session, he made us swap instruments then turned all the lights
off in the studio, telling us he wasn't going to let us out until we'd
perfected 'Amazing Grace'. There were times when I couldn't see
the direction we were being driven in and that would piss me off.
But I think when somebody's that out of it, they don't really know
what's going on. He would throw a hand grenade in every now
and again just to liven things up, and I think that was a good thing
looking back, but at the time I was terrified.

   We did manage to rock out, though, with 'First Thing Wrong',
'Get Smart' and 'Out of Control'. We were confused and on a mission, but in our own naturally gentle way. 'Strong in Reason' is a
favourite of mine from that album, and 'The Call' was inventive
and really showed Gilson off at his finest. Cale pulled in the girl
who worked in the downstairs canteen to scream over a few takes;
she had no idea how mad he was and neither did we. During one
session that never saw the light of day, we recorded a smutty song
about phone abuse called 'Deep Cuts', and she embraced the part
fully, swearing and giving the mystery caller grief. It was light
relief from the eccentricity of Cale. He hated the name Squeeze
and wanted us to change it to Gay Guys; that never happened, but
that's how strange life was in the studio with John. In retrospect
he was a genius. His engineer was John Wood, who kept a steady
hand on the tiller, with his lovely jumpers and beard. He came
with a polished CV that included Nico and Fairport Convention,
not to mention Nick Drake.

   Our first album was a mixture of the wilfully weird and pop
promises. It was a muddle of two worlds pulling apart; our youth
in one direction and our hopes of being serious songwriters in the

other. Miles seemed as confused as we were, but the record company embraced the result, warts and all. My favourite song from that album is, of course, the single 'Take Me I'm Yours', which Cale had nothing to do with as he was ill that day. Rather than waste time in the studio, Glenn persuaded us to lay down a backing track with electronic keyboards and drum machines. To do this we had to hire in the equipment and two men in white coats to work it for us. Jools, Gilson and I were concerned at the time, as we felt the song was becoming more about machines than a band, but in hindsight it was a real coming-together of the two.

A&M loved the sound of it and they released it as a single and suddenly we were on *Top of the Pops*. It was fabulous and a dream had come true. I was recognised at the baker's shop, my mum and dad liked me again, I was on the telly with my mates and we got to number 19 in the charts. As soon as we heard we were going to be on *Top of the Pops*, we were forced by the Musicians' Union and A&M to go back into the studio to re-record the track – a farcical situation brought about by union pedantry. The Musicians' Union chap turned up and was immediately taken out for a lunchtime drink by our A&R man, returning to the studio several pints later. By this time, we'd re-recorded the song – albeit a very splintered version – and swapped the tapes, so that the original version was used. This happened every time. The Musicians' Union representative was none the wiser. Or was he? To be an A&R chap in those days you had to really like a drink.

Top of the Pops wasn't at all as I'd expected. It was like being back at school, complete with a headmasterly producer and DJ Peter Powell, who played the role of head boy. I remember heading downstairs to the dressing rooms and walking along a corridor seeing the names of all these famous acts – Thin Lizzy, Tubeway Army, Gerry Rafferty, etc. Jools and I headed immediately to the door marked 'Legs & Co.' to introduce ourselves and try to convince them we were the band that were going places, but when I opened the door we were met with the sight of Bucks Fizz's David Van Day swanning around in a polo-neck jumper and way-too-tight trousers, chatting to the girls. Every time I go to Brighton and pass his hot-dog stand by the Churchill Centre, I look back at that moment and wonder which of us had the better journey.

I bumped into Gary Numan in the corridor and the first thing that struck me was how bad his make-up was – I wondered why he'd bothered with it. I was never a big fan of his, especially when his record kept 'Up the Junction' off the number 1 slot. We also met Thin Lizzy, who we got on well with. My 'in' with Phil Lynott was being able to tell him we'd recently stayed at his mum's Manchester B&B while we were touring, and that I'd had to sleep in the bath due to Gilson's snoring. Downstairs in the bar, the scene was like something from *O Lucky Man!*, with Manchester United footballers, CID officers, the local mayor and some scantily clad women surrounding Phil's mum, who held court all night long. I remember being served beans on toast at four in the morning. It was bliss.

I'd expected *Top of the Pops* to feel inclusive and open, a community of artists coming together in mutual support, but it actually felt like the opposite. Everybody seemed surprisingly guarded and distant during the recording, but things opened up a little once we all headed up to the BBC rooftop bar. Here, the record company plied us with drinks – making sure they also got a few in for the producer – and we hung out with the other acts, while casting glances at various newsreaders and the Two Ronnies. I think we were at a crossover point, where the poppier bands from the Seventies became arseholes because they couldn't quite cope with the youth who were coming up, so they didn't really know how to react. We'd be in a little circle with the record company, who'd be buying us drinks, and we'd just be avoiding everyone else on the other side. DJs at that point had an ego because they were on TV a lot, which was far above their station, so in other words if you weren't nice to them they wouldn't play you on Radio 1. And I found that a trap really – because I didn't want to get to know them but I did want to be on Radio 1. Being on telly lifted the step. I was walking into the pub just waiting for people to recognise me. The feeling of being on TV was a feeling of having arrived, but where? My parents loved it and rushed all the neighbours into the house to watch the programme with them. Being on the radio was now commonplace. John Peel gave us a few sessions live in the BBC Maida Vale studios. Fags were lit and smoked on one side of the mouth as I waltzed along the high street in my blue jacket with a black velvet collar, tripping up on thin air. My dreams of being in a band and taking off were taxiing to the runway. We were now vaguely famous. Storm Thorgerson filmed the band on Deptford High Street (though I've never actually seen the footage) and we were photographed by Jill Furmanovsky, who was Miles's squeeze at the time. It was wonderful. We were being filmed and photographed locally, which made me feel important. We had arrived, albeit on Deptford Broadway in south London.

The record company put up massive posters publicising the album – one could be found in Deptford at the end of the high street. Three pink musclemen pulling shapes. Our faces were never going to sell the album and our reputation in front of the camera let us down. On an early photoshoot, we hired outfits from a costume shop. I was dressed as a vicar, Jools was an egg and Glenn a giant bird. On the back cover of the album we were in our swimming trunks, some eye make-up here and there and a few socks down the pants. On TV we managed to confuse people by swapping instruments. Jools sucked on a large cigar, Harry had no top on; we were desperate to avoid being branded teenage pin-ups. We were rebels without any real cause. Any attempt to mould the band would have been useless as Miles, I'm sure, would testify. One day in his London office just off Oxford Street he gave Glenn and me £500 each to buy some smart clothes to wear on TV. Glenn bought a kaftan and some brothel creepers; I invested in a cardigan (yellow with red triangles) and some brothel creepers too. We swapped a creeper, so we each had one blue and one red. We looked hopeless and not at all like The Beatles as Miles had wished for.

It was all about our songs – and on this first album I'm still not sure how we survived the hand of John Cale, with his constant colds, his brandy-swilling rants and late arrivals in the studio. The *Squeeze* album came out in March 1978. In the racks at the same time you could find *Jesus of Cool* by Nick Lowe, *This Year's Model* by Elvis Costello and *The Rutles* album. Life seemed as it should be. We were making records and we were on *Top of the Pops*. We were flying. It felt like there was a movement afoot: every pub was filled with great new music and the bands from the past seemed to fade away or adapt a newly tailored rough edge. Although I felt like we were part of this movement, I never really hung out with our contemporaries; there was no time. We were busy with promo and radio sessions, loading up the van and getting to the next gig. There was a crest of a new wave but we seemed to surf in the shallow waters of south London and did not venture too much into the swinging circuit of central London or Camden, where everyone else seemed to be gathering. I really loved the feeling of being in a band, rattling our way around every venue that would take us. We played to our strengths, loud and fast. Our first real live break came in the shape of a support slot with the very lively Eddie and the Hot Rods; we played a thirty-minute set each night and blew people away. I still look back on that tour as being the opening of a window. The view was of the future and us being the headliner. But first, America.

Miles had great connections in the States. His brother Ian became our agent over there and a tour was booked. Our first date was in New Jersey at The Lighthouse in Bethlehem on 23rd May 1978. We literally played to one man and a dog. We were forced to play a second set by the owner. The dog left. We went everywhere in a small blue Chevy van with Gilson in the back like a bear with a sore head. Jools was the joker. Glenn played banjo all day long while Harry hung out of the window in the breeze, trying to look cool in shades and no shirt. When you see dogs in cars, they always like to hang out of the window – Harry was a bit like that. Miles took charge of the truck with the gear in it and John Lay, our tour manager, drove us from place to place. In each town Miles would head to the local radio station and demand they play our EP. He worked really hard knocking on doors. Radio over in the US was mostly about 'Baker Street' and soft rock. It was terrible.

We were flying Freddie Laker, we were touring in America, the sunglasses were on and the cameras were out. Real musclemen were joining us on stage; and at the Whisky a Go Go in LA, I shocked A&M boss Herb Alpert by playing in a T-shirt that Miles had made for me that stated, 'I can see your tits, now show us . . .' Yes, that old chestnut. You'd have thought I'd have learnt from that incident on the A40. His wife was not impressed. The whole of A&M were there to see us play at the Whisky that night; we were brilliant, but it had been a long tour and we were fading around the edges. We were going slowly stir-crazy in our Chevy van. The three-month tour eventually drove us all mad.

Touring in those days was compact; we stayed mostly in motels on the edge of town. Glenn, I think, shared with Harry on most tours and Jools shared with Gilson as the rest of us were, I think, too scared. I shared with John Lay. John was a dead ringer for John Cleese with his narrow moustache, and I loved his no-nonsense style at hotel check-in. One day as he was sorting out our rooms we noticed the name of the concierge – Beau Bumgardener. We fell about with laughter and spent the next couple of days thinking up excuses to call him to our room. Silly, but then touring was an extension of school for most of us – and laughter was the raft that kept us afloat through our boredom.

Smoking dope also helped, but American weed was strong and one toke would make my teeth grip together. My eyes would change dimensions; I would stare at nothing for hours and laugh at the daftest things. English marijuana was lemonade compared to this pungent smokestack of dreams. We did enjoy a party as a blob, which was how Jools always referred to our collective self. Once we finished a show, we'd invade the hotel bar or a neighbourhood dive for our entertainment. Best of all was if they had a piano. We'd pretend Jools was blind and raise money for drinks

Dad with his mates tucking into some grub, post-Second World War.

Mum in her WRAC uniform.

Brothers in arms but not in fashion.

A jolly old Christmas time at Combe Avenue.

Mum on a mobile phone, me heading for the moon and Dad squinting.

My first bike
on King George
Street.

A toy bus, an ice cream, a holiday
…and I'm still wanting more.

Sunday lunch, always a treat,
served up by Mum.

Happy days waiting for Glenn to arrive, prior to my early demos.

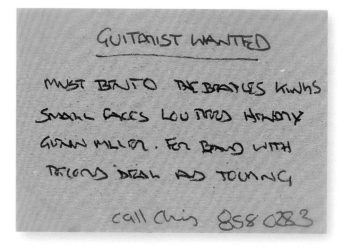

The ad from the sweetshop window:
50p well worth spending.

Windsor Free Festival, with a
man in his underpants.

Maxine in Blackheath Village.

Squeeze down
the foot tunnel in
Greenwich, me with
a whisky bottle.

Jools and Gilson in
a Deptford pub.

Me and
Glenn looking
innocent in
paradise.
(Jill Furmanovsky)

That fateful day when I signed my life away for £15 a week.

as he boogied his way through some Meade 'Lux' Lewis or Merrill Moore. One night in New Orleans we watched in awe as James Booker played Jools into a cocked hat; it was a very dark night in every sense of the word.

The band at this time were joined at the hip, and went from party to party and from bar to bar tripping the light fantastic. We all liked a drink, but it affected us in different ways. With Gilson, alcohol seemed to propel him into another universe. He would swing from being mild as a baby one moment to unpredictable the next. One night we were at a party at someone's house in New Orleans, and rather than leaving by the front door, he decided to throw himself through the French windows, ending up on a balcony below. It was possibly a cocktail of vodka and local marijuana. Sometimes he would turn blue and we'd have to call for medical help. The rest of us were no choirboys either, we also liked a party. I was always really worried about Gilson. Jools was the only one who'd share a room with him, which probably laid the foundations for their lifelong friendship.

I loved Gilson as our drummer and was in awe of his inventiveness and courage, but I was constantly terrified he would do damage to himself or deck me. He did try once. We were both sitting in the front seat of the Chevy van, driving into Cleveland, and I asked him to turn the radio down. He ignored me and the rest of the band, who were pleading with him to sort out the volume, and out of nowhere he let me have it with both barrels. I wanted to cry. An hour later, I was sitting in my hotel room wondering if I could get the phone number for Keith Moon, who seemed like a pussycat compared to Gilson, when he started knocking on the door. I ignored his requests to come in. After several more attempts, he kicked the door off its hinges, walked into the room and hugged me, telling me he was sorry. He was a lovable old bear who sometimes wouldn't be caged.

The tension of that tour and being trapped in that small blue van often made us all boil over; we were mad, bad and dangerous to know, as Jools used to say. Sometimes the heat and the hangovers would get to me. Harry's constant posing often drove us all nuts. There was one occasion when I pushed him off stage mid-gig because he was posing so much, but it was all in good fun. We all signed the plaster on his leg and so did our many newfound fans. Thank God the Sony Walkman had been invented. It kept me happy while soaking up those long journeys. Any detailed memory of this time has been eradicated, but I bet it was a lot of fun along the way.

We became a 'new wave' band when we went to America, along with Blondie, Elvis Costello, The Stranglers and other great bands that had both the attitude and the musicality that punk lacked. We were much more comfortable with that tag. We played endless sets at CBGB in New York, which had become the epicentre of the new wave scene over there. Though the gigs went well and the place was rammed, CBGB wasn't a place I loved. It was in the Bowery and there were always rumours of people wandering around outside with guns. I wanted to get in and out of there as quickly as possible. But we'd play our part, hanging out there or in a bar called Grass Roots around the corner where I would smoke local grass, drink warm beer and play pinball with The Ramones or Television for a couple of hours. We never became mates, though. That's the thing about musicians: when they're together, they don't really talk to each other. We might have crossed the floor of the bar to have a beer with Debbie Harry and Chris Stein, but we never got to the stage where we were sending each other postcards. If you're in a band, you've got to have a sense of coolness about you. And if you're cool and Tom Verlaine's cool, then you risk things freezing up. We might have been in the same class, but we were all too cool for school.

America was so much fun, even in the heat of a small Chevy van. What was not to like for a bunch of young men from south London: enthusiastic audiences, watery beer, long drives and dodgy motels. We were loud and very much enjoying the accolades of respect we would gather along the way. It was all of our dreams come true and I had never been happier.

We were riding the new-wave wave and getting credibility on the back of it too. But Squeeze were always a pop band in my eyes. Of course, I'd never have admitted that back in the late Seventies. Pop then meant Cliff Richard and Gilbert O'Sullivan, and the musical landscape had changed completely from the one I'd grown up with. But whenever I listen to great pop music from the Seventies, I get a warm glow. It takes me back to a safe place, when there was food on the table, sun in the sky and everything was really happy. Christopher Rainbow, Todd Rundgren, Carole King – all voices that dissolved me like sugar in a warm cup of tea.

Back in London, The Bell in Greenwich – a small pub on the edge of a dodgy council estate, outside which Squeeze had performed a short set on Jubilee Day in 1977 – became my second home. It was an afters pub, which meant it closed at 11 p.m., doors bolted, but with us all inside. Most of the drinks were on the house. My tipple would have been tequila sunrise after lock-in and pints of lager up until then. The Bell was run by some shady people and often I had no idea what was going on, what was being bought and sold or agreed to. We were local celebs, though, and just for us to be seen perched on a stool at the end of the bar was enough for them.

A mile away, there was a pub called The Deptford Arms, where we also played a short rooftop set on a hot summer's afternoon. The punters in there enjoyed our company too. The pub was heaving with villains; the gangs from south London would gather there to mastermind bank robberies and break-ins – or at least that's how it felt to me – though our local-hero status kept us shielded from anything untoward. I smoked differently when I was in the villains' company; I could see myself pulling on a tip as if it were stuck to my soul, looking at its ash as it roared into life. I walked with swagger and bravado. I knew I was safe.

Pubs were where I lived. In Blackheath it was The Crown, where toffs, estate agents and villains alike would stand at the long wooden bar. Here I would sit with notorious local criminal and dealer Johnny Edgecombe – he who supplied the gun in the Christine Keeler affair – or talk nonsense all day long with Alan from the City. In The Bell, I hung out with the locals. One of the regulars invited me to go and see Frank Sinatra at the Albert Hall with him, an offer I couldn't refuse. He picked me up from the pub in his Bentley and drove me across town with classical music blaring out of the windows. It was a memorable evening, and on the way home he turned down the Mahler long enough to give me some advice. 'Any girl that wants to marry you,' he said, 'get them to sign a contract. Offer them nothing and you won't be robbed if you end up getting divorced.' At the time it seemed ridiculous, but when I did end up getting divorced some years later I naturally thought of my dodgy friend from The Bell and wondered what had become of him. I'd simply got out of the car when he dropped me back home and never saw him again.

It was also in The Bell that I met Derry, a sweet girl who lived in a block of flats nearby. She loved the band, so I invited her along to *Top of the Pops* on one of the nights we were appearing on the show. But when she asked me to drop her off in Soho on our way home, I discovered she was working the streets for some Maltese pimps. I went back to her flat in Greenwich to ask her mum if she thought this was a safe thing for her to do, and it turned out her mum and sister were on the game too. It was a colourful time.

Punk was still going strong in London and going to clubs was a mission. I once went to the Vortex to see Generation X, who were supported by The Lurkers, Art Attacks and Steel Pulse. Walking down the steps into the club I felt out of place and intimidated. I had been before to see The Cortinas and Chelsea, who we shared an office with at the time, but it was still a big walk. The punk movement felt aggressive and reminded me of my skinhead days a few dark years before. Young drunk wannabes fell about all over the place looking for someone to bump into, shove or spit at. The best I could do was try and blend in, so I went to Boots and bought some safety pins. I attached them to my shirt and swaggered in with my leather jacket hanging open. Billy Idol made a good job of winding everybody up; the place shook to the foundations. I liked his attitude but not the songs, or his pumped-up ego, which he chucked around like a bad smell. The room overheated and soon the crowd was swaying this way and that until I had been levitated without lifting a leg or moving a muscle. It was like being down the Valley at a Charlton game before the nice seats were cemented into place. I left for a Chinese meal, deaf and a little drunk. It was a bear pit of a place, and as much as I longed to be part of the scene, I think I preferred the cosy pub on my street corner.

Maxine came back into my life around this time when she started seeing Squeeze's tour manager John Lay. She had become a young woman, yet those angelic features remained. It was so good to see her again and to have her back in our circle of friends. It could be a zoo, and from time to time chaotic, but it was a secure place nonetheless. Glenn and I were both in new relationships. He had fallen for Jo Davidson, a local girl who lived in a big house on Blackheath, and who'd been to a much better school than us. She made him happy and content, and became a fixture of the Squeeze social scene. She even sang backing vocals on 'Cool for Cats' when we recorded it a little later.

I was now with Mary – Harry's ex-wife – and we went everywhere together, holding hands. She was calm and supportive, enjoyed the same kind of music as me and made me feel special. And as everyone would fancy her whenever we went to a pub together, she made me feel incredibly proud too. Even though she'd been married to Harry, it didn't create any divisions in the band, either in the rehearsal room or on stage. It all happened very suddenly, the hop from bass player to guitarist; we seemed to fall for each other very quickly. They hadn't had a very happy relationship, and before I knew where I was, I was staying at their flat – with Harry in the spare room and me in the matrimonial bed. Harry didn't seem to blink an eye about it; I remember him bringing us tea and toast in bed one day. It was almost as if he knew it was going to happen. It was all very confusing. I think this was my first taste of love and never wanting to leave each other's side, which can be suffocating, but for us it seemed natural. I discovered what a relationship was and I hated to be apart from her. I always kept a diary and it's beautiful to read it now, to see how much I was besotted with Mary. She would write in my diary too. Everyone did. Jools would draw pictures in it from time to time. Both Jools and I were avid diarists. They say if you keep a diary it might one day keep you. Well, we shall see. Reading it now, I see and feel this time of my life as very special. Being in a young band was fun, that development stage can often be overlooked, but for me it was one dream followed by another in rapid succession. I had nothing to complain about.

OLD CHURCH STREET

In late 1978, we started work on our second album. At first we tried recording with one of Pink Floyd's producers, Brian Humphries, at their studios in north London. We managed to almost get to the end of the album, but the record company rightly thought it was too dull. The songs sounded flat, and so were many of the performances. Brian once told me not to touch the recording desk, and hit my hand with his ruler. I was not impressed. So we changed horses in midstream and hooked up with John Wood. We were writing and recording up near the King's Road with John, who'd engineered our debut album. It was another daily cab ride across town, but this time there was loads to do around the studio. Chelsea provided a completely different atmosphere from that of Willesden. After all, Old Church Street was slightly posher than Willesden High Street. All the fashionable shops were within walking distance, I think we made it as far as the café at the top of Old Church Street. John had built the studio with his bare hands and it was his musical version of my dad's shed – complete with soldering iron and wires with boxes everywhere. Here he'd recorded Nick Drake, among others. It was a very productive place to work, with a nice pub across the street with brilliant cheese on toast. Writing was fast and we were released from any constraints – no John Cale telling us what to do, twisting our creative nipples. We were on a roll; a new trajectory that would gather pace over the next four years.

Cool for Cats was recorded in a few months. Glenn put a lot of time into the arrangements and played most of the keyboard parts too, as Jools wasn't always on hand to contribute – he was in the pub with me. It's an inspired album in many ways and I'm very proud of it. I think of it as our first record because it feels like that to me; it's certainly the first of our albums that sounded how we wanted it. Lyrically, I was scooping up things I heard in the pub, and writing in a dialect – cockney from the south bank of the Thames – that's now almost vanished, 'It's Not Cricket' being a prime example. The songs came quickly; the inspirational tap was on full flow. The music I was hearing on the London pub circuit – Ian Dury, Elvis Costello, Nick Lowe, etc. – was making me raise my game. I knew my lyrics had to be of a high standard to compete.

'Goodbye Girl', the first single from the record, was written on the previous US tour, and when I hear it now, it reminds me so much of Boston – a place I loved to visit. It's the percussion that makes the track, and Glenn and Gilson's genius was to work up a rhythm by hitting bits of metal, empty vodka bottles and the odd tambourine. At first I was uncomfortable about this, and we even recorded two versions of the song – a traditional rock 'n' roll number as well as the more offbeat Kraftwerk-style one. In hindsight, I think it's brilliant. Both versions are. Throughout our career, Glenn has often taken our songs in a direction that at first I'm not sure about. I naturally err towards simplicity. Now I'm older, though, I've realised that much of his talent has been hidden from me by a low-level mist of jealousy. Thankfully that's no longer there.

I wish I had been more engaged with him at this time. I could not convey my ideas in the way that he could, and that often wrong-footed me. It was like a musical stammer but I had no time to learn how to speak my mind clearly. If we had any disagreements during the recording or during a rehearsal, I would simply sulk. I don't remember any full-blown arguments with Glenn at that time. Other disagreements were too subtle and often left hanging like underpants on a washing-line. Sulking was not very grown up of me, but then I had no tools to deal with such a close friendship. For the most part my friendships had all been passing or on one level.

It seems to me that most major songwriting teams follow similar patterns. When you meet, you share the same views and ambitions. You set sail with the band in your rowing boat until someone drops an oar and you spin in different directions. Lennon and McCartney; Townshend and Daltrey; Page and Plant; the Gallagher brothers. We have all followed a similar journey. Luckily our relationship is not as fractious as the Oasis boys'. It's really OK not to agree about everything you do. It's healthy to go and pull in different directions. The tension was often the weight that ended up keeping our friendship balanced, and in those days I needed all the balance I could find. The scales of our friendship were mainly tilted in favour of mutual respect.

The lyric for 'Up the Junction' was inspired by the BBC *Play for Today* episodes I used to watch as a teenager. Those kitchen-sink dramas, written by such greats as Alan Ayckbourn, Dennis Potter and Mike Leigh, appealed to me because I could zone out and go into another world. My imagination could be rested for the time they took to weave their story. Like all of my best lyrics, I wrote the song in one sitting, and Glenn wrote the music on our day off in a motel room outside New Orleans while we did our washing. Miles, our manager, said it would never be a single because it didn't have a chorus, but thankfully we and the record company were more open-minded.

The videos for 'Cool for Cats' and 'Up the Junction' were shot by Derek Burbidge at John Lennon's old house in Surrey, Tittenhurst Park. Both were completed in one day, two versions of 'Cats', and one of 'Up the Junction' shot in the kitchen on our way out the door. Jools and I were keen to get to the pub to chat up the girls from the shoot, but they were off home to their respective pin-up boyfriends. Videos were the new bolt-on to the record, a way to show the song around the world. Our slapstick approach went down well with the BBC and the videos were shown many times on different shows. It was fun making them in those days.

'Slap and Tickle' is one of my favourite songs from the album. It gave Glenn and me another opportunity to do our trademark octave-apart vocal, and the story I put into the lyric was incredibly satisfying for me to write. The song's metre is heavily influenced by Ian Dury.

I'd never heard anyone recite a lyric before he did, and it gave me an opportunity to experiment with an entirely different kind of rhyming couplet. Contentiously, Glenn recorded a rhythmic mini-Moog part, which I was unhappy with at the time. And when we went out on tour to support the album, the mini-Moog came with us. I'd cringe when Glenn started playing it. It was never in tune, and the part would have been much better on a guitar. For a while it became the bane of my life, though nowadays it's very much part of the Squeeze family. I've grown to like its sharp edges.

The original melody of 'Cool for Cats' was much more laid-back and the lyric wasn't anywhere near as good. But Glenn felt the song had legs and asked me to have another crack at the words. So I took the backing track back to my flat on Crooms Hill and listened to it over and over, trying in vain to come up with something that would work. Nothing happened until I took a break for some Welsh rarebit and a cup of Earl Grey, with a bit of Benny Hill on the telly. Watching him perform his comic songs, I was struck by the metre of the verses, the quick-fire lyrics and the vivid images, and decided to try something along the same lines. The words then came quickly, each verse a vignette about the various TV shows that followed – Wagon Train, The Sweeney, Minder and a bit of Grease. At the studio the following day, I read the lyric to Glenn and John Wood, and a consensus quickly developed that I should be the one to sing it. I did it in one take. We employed the services of our girlfriends to sing the backing vocals and the job was done.

When the album came out, Sounds magazine said the lyrics were sexist, but I was just observing things around me. This was the late Seventies and I didn't really know what sexism was. I was sharing a flat at one point with a girl who worked for the feminist magazine Spare Rib and she agreed with Sounds. She said I should take a long, hard look at myself and my attitude to women. But I didn't know what she meant. I grew up in a family where my dad gave my mum spending money each week and I didn't know any different. I've always been very feminine-minded and I saw my lovers and female friends as my equals, so it hurt me to think that a woman would think I was sexist. Misogyny to me was what we'd witness every time Squeeze were on *Top of the Pops*. There the DJs acted with grand superiority, and shamelessly exploited the girls who came to watch the show being filmed while they were on set. It seemed that if you wanted to sleep with the drummer from Slade, you would first have to get filtered through one of the DJs on the studio floor. At the time it all felt very friendly and nothing seemed out of the ordinary. Jools and I held our fingers in our nostrils live on TV behind the Hairy Cornflake as he introduced the next band; the producer of *Top of the Pops* told Jools that he would never work in TV again. Jools seems to have done OK.

Now that we'd made a bit of a name for ourselves, touring was much more fun. We played a series of bigger gigs with Dr Feelgood in 1978, then 'Cool for Cats' was released as a single and went to number 2 in the charts. We were beside ourselves. A few months later, 'Up the Junction' came out and also stormed up to number 2. They were giddy times and my feet barely touched the ground, but when they did, I was usually in the pub. Two massive singles and a huge tour with The Tubes got our fire well and truly lit. Success was dribbling into our lives and it felt comfortable to be in the public eye. We were on TV all the time: *Top of the Pops*, *The Kenny Everett Show*, even *Jim'll Fix It*. The only thing I remember about that experience was that it was fixed. A fourteen-year-old girl had written a letter saying she was a huge Squeeze fan and wanted to sing a song with us. So we went on the show and performed whichever hit it was at the time, and she chirped away in the background somewhere then went and sat on Jimmy Savile's knee. We all knew that it was fixed by our record company, but it got us on the telly so we went along with it. And that was that. We turned up late to record *Tiswas* in Birmingham after a long night in the hotel bar, even though the hotel was right next to the studio. We found it hard to show up on time. Chris Tarrant was livid. He seemed furious with us, throwing all of his toys out of the pram. Not a nice look.

Despite selling out the Hammersmith Apollo five nights in a row with The Tubes, my memories of playing in London at this time are all of pubs and small clubs. From Deptford to Camden and back again. It was a wonderful feeling playing in our home city, and taking the stage there, I felt connected to a greater musical movement. It always made me walk a little taller. We were supported by some great bands – The Specials, REM, The Jam, Dire Straits, U2 and XTC – who'd go on to have huge success. We generally got on well with them and there was never any bitterness between us and other bands, apart from with The Jam. They supported us at The Marquee and Paul Weller's dad, who was their manager, was really forceful about them getting the maximum amount of time. They brought their own microphones and all sorts of things, and I think we probably sneered at them a bit and took the piss. But when I watched them I remember thinking, 'Fucking hell, this band are amazing. The songs are brilliant, Weller's a great guitar player, it's just so exciting.' They'd certainly earned my respect, but the next time we found ourselves on the same bill, Weller's dad came up to me and pinned me against the wall. 'Where are our fucking microphones?' he shouted in my face. 'Last time we played with you, some of our microphones went missing. You were the only person who knew they were there.' He was going to lay me out. I had no idea where they were.

We went back to the States in 1979, to support The Tubes in large halls all across the country. Nobody wanted to see us. One night the curtain went up and bottles were thrown. The audience were expecting to see hard rock act April Wine, who were second on the bill. We lasted four songs and retreated to the cold dressing rooms backstage. It was a learning curve.

On one flight to New York I sat next to a woman who was interested in the fact that I had a Nikon camera. She asked me what pictures I took; I said pictures of the band. She was much older than me, possibly mid-forties. We talked about photography and she asked if I would like to meet a famous photographer if I had a day off in the city. We met one day outside the Chelsea Hotel where we were staying and she took me to see a fragile old lady called Lisette Model. We walked her around the block very slowly and talked. Lisette had been a mentor for Diane Arbus, who I adored, so it was a very inspirational visit. I went to see her on later tours too; she was gentle and I'm sure had no idea who I was. She had just had a book released called *Aperture*, which she signed for me. It was a chance meeting that inspired me to keep taking pictures. A hobby that slowly passed, I'm afraid.

Quentin Crisp stayed at the same hotel as us. I often saw him flamboyantly strolling around the lobby. I went to see him read from his many books, all of which I bought and all of which he signed for me. He was a strange-looking figure whose glance could buckle my feelings and make me wonder if I could ever be that glamorous and intriguing. New York was full of such interesting people.

I met Cindy in New York at the bar in CBGB. She was small, thin and funny, like the character Anybodys in *West Side Story*; the tomboy. She showed me around the darker side of Manhattan and introduced me to her friends and to Bob Gruen, the photographer she worked for. The New York scene was great fun. If there was a seedy party to be had, then Squeeze would be there. We'd seek out the underbelly of whatever was going on, and enjoy whatever we found. One night, Jools, Glenn and I went to what was basically an orgy in a warehouse, although as observers it was way too far out for me. There were people screwing each other and doing heroin to eardrum-shaking music while we watched bemused. I ended the night sleeping on a park bench. It was all very appealing to an Englishman who until very recently had never gone further than the Isle of Wight.

New York was the place to be and we were playing all manner of shows; we even played at Lou Reed's birthday party, attended by Divine and Andy Warhol. There were not many people there at all so we raced through our set. Underneath the disco lights of the club I could make out a gaggle of people by the bar, half interested in our performance. New York was as magical as I thought it might be, the glamour of having no money but getting by on the pure energy provided by the people you met late at night in clubs and bars was enough. I would walk everywhere just to involve myself in the electricity of the city; I felt plugged in all of the time, even when nursing a hangover.

I came home from that tour with a New York Monopoly set and some T-shirts and found myself homeless outside The Crown in Blackheath. Mary had booted me out of her parents' home where I had been staying with her between tours. She'd had enough of me being away all the time and she may have had a whiff that the band had been having a very nice time while on tour. I was stupid, but being in a band had its fascinating moments, and being away from home was dangerous.

The following summer we played the Reading Festival, headlining the Sunday night supported by Deacon Blue and the Hothouse Flowers. We were ready to go on stage but Jools was nowhere to be seen, so we went on anyway without him. We were furious. As I looked back at Gilson, I could see Jools turning up behind the stage in his Buick with Mary beside him; he casually got on stage and we raced through the set. At the end, we took a bow. When I looked around, Jools had gone, driving out past security. It was a stylish moment, like a scene in the movie *Grease*. The festival was so different from the way they are today. We had been canned on stage by a sea of very drunk people. Meatloaf had been canned the night before. I hated the atmosphere – it was nothing like the gentle stages of the free festivals from my not-so-distant youth.

Mary was now living with Jools, and I was soon to be married, all in the space of one small year. Cindy and I moved quickly to cement our relationship. It all happened so quickly. When two magnets meet and it's hard for them to be separated, that's what it felt like for me with Cindy at that time, like it had been with Mary before. Marriage was a large part of my family's life; both my brothers had had traditional weddings and now I was following suit. St Alfred's Church in Greenwich was where we tied the knot, and the sun shone as we walked to the altar to take our vows. I was locally famous, so people from the newspapers wanted to come to take pictures; we had a vintage American Buick car to drive away in. I was fresh from the pub across the road and a little light-headed, as was my mother. It was a giddy day all round. Drunk at the reception in my flat, my mother told me I should have married Mary, and then, giggling, promptly fell down the stairs and had to be taken to hospital with a broken ankle.

We spent our honeymoon upstate in New York with Cindy's parents. Her dad was a gentle soul who ran the local drug store and her mother was a talkative smiling bubble. We walked in the mountains and lakes together and really enjoyed our time away from the electrifying hub of New York. I had found another home in the Catskills and it felt very different. I was the first in the band to be married. At the time it seemed like part of my journey, but later I found out how much it had upset Glenn – it put a wedge between us and I'm not sure why that happened. Yet he was such a good best man. It was here where we began to drift a little. All good friendships have to oscillate from time to time and eventually recalibrate.

Our journey as a band was about to gradually change, although in a good way. I was married and had all the trimmings of fresh new relationships as Cindy and I amalgamated our friends, and the band were young and exciting with records in the charts. Somehow, during this very busy time, we had to write the next album, which A&M were gasping for. I wrote it in a month – either in Cindy's flat, or in Grass Roots or around the corner at CBGB. In the little time we had between tours, Glenn and I managed to put together another set of demos. Glenn's demos are legendary, second only to Pete Townsend's in quality and delivery. I would hand him twenty or so lyrics, and a few weeks later he'd send me a C60 cassette containing all these fantastic, fully formed songs. I miss those days – waiting to hear what might be. The songs we wrote together shone in demo form, so when the band got hold of them they could only shine further. I was driven by the demos; they inspired me to write more and more to impress Glenn. He always managed to surprise me, though, and often I would have to pinch myself with the joy our songs would bring me.

But then there were the curveballs. The songs with odd changes in them, the ones that would make my toes curl, songs that were just not my cup of tea. But how could I tell him without upsetting him? So I didn't. Sulking is passive bullying and not very nice, but it was my default setting and I never knew any better. Touring was a perfect place to frame a bad mood. If I found I didn't like what was going on, I would isolate myself and keep quiet about my feelings, then dance like a nutcase across the stage. The isolation promoted secret drinking in my hotel room, and all of this together started to silt up the emotional waters. I'd not been taught the art of emotional communication by my parents, so I invented my own, which was primal at best. I was mostly in a good place, but that place tended to be in the pub with my friends. If I could find no friends to take I would take my imaginary ones.

Home life was contained within a steady beat of parties, trips to the pub and driving around in my first car, a white Morris Minor convertible. I was proud as Punch of it. I loved living on Crooms Hill in Greenwich with Cindy. Glenn was in the basement, and Cindy and I were on the top floor. It was such a madhouse, full of music and the odd porno film (thanks to our eccentric landlady, who would rent out the middle flat to makers of 'adult' movies), and it became the new hub for our songwriting. Across the road was The Rose and Crown, up the hill the heath, all around us our friends, who would drop by from time to time. It was a stone's throw also from King George Street where I had been born. I felt warm and happy in that house, and sometimes the worse for wear. But that was all part of enjoying our new-found success.

There were other local bands, such as Stone Cold Sober and The Red Lights, but we were way out in front – we were the dogs. Minicabs home from the pub were a regular event; the new thing was Indian and Chinese takeaway food. I had some money in the bank thanks to PRS, which is money collected from TV and radio play; I was in the record shops every week snapping up all the new releases. Music had become the daily bread I broke with everyone in my world, and my childhood dreams were being achieved.

Because Mum suffered from agoraphobia later in her life, she seldom came to see Squeeze. She was coaxed out once, though, to the Albany Empire in Deptford, and danced with Dad in the balcony – and of course she cried to see her son so very happy. Coming home one day, I gave her my gold disc of 'Cool for Cats'. She was so proud of me, and all the neighbours were invited in to witness the trophy being hung above the TV. (It hung there until Dad died; and now it hangs in my house.) I was on telly. The flags were out on Combe Avenue where once I had been a skinhead beating kids up with my mates; smoking dope with Bob Blatchford and listening to The Stooges and MC5; playing strip poker in the shed with girls and losing happily. I had come home under a cloak of fame. A Rolls-Royce once picked me up from the house to take me to *Top of the Pops* and all the neighbours came out to see me; the only other time fancy motors turned up on our estate was for funerals and weddings. Some years later the bill for the car arrived with my royalty statement, proving that nothing is for free.

Touring was as mad as ever and we all got on extremely well, basking in our own success on various stages and at the corner of many late-night bars. Jools and I almost got arrested again on the way back from a crazy New Year's gig in Glasglow. We stopped the van for a breakfast at a Happy Eater. Jools and I tried to order fish fingers. The lady behind the counter said that they were on the kids' menu. We offered her £20. She told us that was bribery and called for the manager. We then offered him £100 for two plates of fish fingers. He called the police, who turfed us outside while the band looked on unamused in the van. After our unsuccessful bid to buy fish finger for £100, we signed autographs for the two policemen and hopped back in the van happy days indeed.

CROOMS HILL

Argybargy was part two of the *Cool for Cats* album, recorded in much the same way. John Wood was still at the mixing desk at his Sound Technics studio in Chelsea, and he proved to be a steady hand on the tiller yet again. Both albums are classic young Squeeze. Glenn was focused in the studio, playing some amazing solos and holding the songs together. Jools had a song on each album, which I co-wrote with him, and this allowed him and the band a chance to show off their musical roots. Glenn and Jools were the band historians when it came to rock 'n' roll. They knew every song on every jukebox and together they ignited many a quiet bar. I watched from the side and wished I had the talent to amuse in such a wonderful way. Writing with Jools was slightly different to the way I wrote with Glenn – I would hand him some lyrics handwritten on A4 paper and he would present a song in the rehearsal room rather than demo it.

John Bentley had joined the band on bass. He turned up late for the auditions – we'd already chosen someone to replace Harry, who we'd had to let go – but John insisted we set back up and let him have a play. He got the gig and we were off on another twist in our tale. John was fun to have around and got on well with Gilson. Recording proved very simple with our new rhythm section – Gilson was always so inventive. John was from Hull and enjoyed a wicked sense of humour; he had the gift of the gab and fitted in so well with our band. He played with great confidence and was creative. He looked like Dudley Moore on a good day and dressed well, though mainly in the same clothes. He liked small joints and the ladies, who loved him too. He was a handsome chap who played without having to look at the frets.

The record company seemed happy enough with the two hits to come from the LP, 'Another Nail in My Heart' and 'If I Didn't Love You', though I've never felt attached to the former. Like a lot of lyrics on that album, it was written quickly and has its roots in the constant flow of verses and choruses I was forced to produce rather than in me unearthing any deep emotional thoughts. Glenn had this idea of having a guitar solo rather than a second verse, and he worked long and hard at getting all the notes in the right order. It was the correct decision. 'If I Didn't Love You' is my favourite track on the album. The line 'singles remind me of kisses, albums remind me of plans' comes from the days when I used to take girls up to my room at Combe Avenue and put on records with long running times, to give myself enough time to get my arm around them. 'I Think I'm Go Go' was the first song I'd written about travel – it mentions a New York radio station and references my time in the city. 'Vicky Verky' was a continuation of 'Slap and Tickle'; in some ways, it had the same sort of characters, a similar metre and a beautiful melody by Glenn. 'Pulling Mussels (from the Shell)' was inspired by going on holiday as a teenager with my next-door neighbour, whose dad had an Austin A40. We drove down to a caravan park near Margate and saw The Small

Faces play in the local social club while we were there. Lyrically, I tried to imagine how Ray Davies would write a song about this most English type of holiday, and the words came quickly and easily.

I still love the *Cool for Cats* and *Argybargy* albums, but I hate both record sleeves. With *Argybargy*, we were left to take the group photo ourselves with a foot switch; we all took turns pressing it. On the one hand, it does represent the band as we were at that time – a bit lively, a bit mad. But on the other, it was very rough around the edges. I suppose we were too. We were seeing less and less of Miles. His younger brother Stewart – once the drummer in Curved Air – had formed a band back in London called The Police, and Miles was grooming them for success in much the same way as he had the young Squeeze. They recorded at Surrey Sound, they signed to A&M, they recorded hits and toured America following the same route we'd taken. There was a theme. I'd even been present when the band had been auditioning for a singer. Sting turned up and I told everyone he couldn't sing for toffee. I was wrong, obviously. Greater involvement with another band didn't stop Miles sending us off on tour to Australia, though.

My daughter Natalie was born just before we went; I got the news that Cindy had gone into labour while we were doing a Christmas gig with Madness and The Specials in Birmingham. Miles had kindly installed a phone at the side of the stage for me and it rang just as the audience applause was dying down. I leapt into a waiting car and the driver raced me down the M1 to London. By the time we got to Kilburn, I was gasping for a beer, so we did a pub crawl down the Edgware Road, making it to the hospital in Lewisham, a little the worse for wear, just an hour before Natalie was born. Later that night, Gilson turned up at the hospital with a McDonald's and a bottle of whisky to help me celebrate fatherhood. I was so happy to be a dad. Even through all the alcohol and hamburgers I'd consumed, I could see how beautiful Natalie was, and over the next few days I puffed up with pride whenever her name was mentioned.

One minute I was telling everyone how amazing my life had become and the next I was being handed my plane tickets. Cindy being pregnant had been a wonderful time; the expectation of birth and the slow realisation that I was going to become a father were something else, taking me away from the band and the journey I was on. That whole year was emotionally draining and in some ways I needed the tour to steady the internal ship. That was the nature of my life at the time: tour, album, tour, album.

Australia was one of the first straws to start bending the camel's back of my marriage. At first, Cindy coped really well with me being away, because she knew that was what I did. It was like she'd married someone in the merchant navy. She had a great group of friends around her in south London, including Jo Davidson, who stayed by her side, but it must have been hard because her parents were in New York and I was away on the other side of the world, separated from my new family by travel, the band and the pub. We were on such a roll at this time that it was difficult to focus on both my lives at the same time. There was the success I needed to chase, but equally there was a wife and child I needed to be there for. Australia was a long way away from Crooms Hill, where Cindy and I had made our nest with Natalie. Once in Sydney I hit the Pernod to numb the feelings. I had no idea what day it was, or for most of time where I was. It was summer down there and it was hot – too bloody hot for me – and I slowed to a drunken crawl. We were treated well, the crowds were great and we met some good people to party with. On a rare day off, we went out on a speedboat, and I tipped some cans and sat in the sun. Back at the hotel that night, the pain started to cripple me. I was red like a crab. I resorted to covering myself in calamine lotion and wearing my pyjamas everywhere I went, including when I was up on stage. I could hardly stand. Gilson could hardly stand either, but still managed to surf on top of a car in the hotel car park.

Melody Maker came to review our quest, and asked us what we thought of Australia. Tactfully, we said it was shit. We never went back and the hits over there dried up. One of the most memorable shows was in a small coal-mining town called Wyella. It was an hour's flight in a small plane. After the show, I made the mistake of getting stoned, and then got into the plane with the pilot who had been waiting for us. Once up in the warm night air, Gilson asked how long he had been flying; he told us he had just got the all-clear after a recent heart attack. At this point he could not get through on the radio to the control tower at Adelaide. He said the only thing we could do was quickly land so that he could call from a phone box, but the lights on the runway were on a timer. We'd only just made it down to the ground when they went off. I was so scared that I was ready to die while holding on for dear life to Jools's arm.

I was never home, and home began to crack. We were being worked hard by our agent, our manager and the record company, but what else was there to do? This was my journey and no destination had been programmed into the sat nav. We all wanted success at whatever cost, even an emotional one. Touring the album in America was hard work but so much fun. We were young and full of beans, all sorts of beans. We had a tour manager called Mike Hedges who always called us before a show with his catch-phrase 'last pisses and shits, five minutes'. He was a barrow boy from south London and gifted with the gab. He once walked us on stage in New Jersey and in the corridor was a smartly dressed elderly gentleman. Mike pushed him out of the way. While we were ploughing through the set, Mike head butted the guy, who just turned out to be the Italian owner's dad. We came off stage and Mike hid in a guitar trunk. We were all in towels when three big chaps burst in wanting to kill him. I was shaking with fear and chucked a can of beer at one of them, which bounced off his chest. We legged it out the back door into Miles's hire car and into the city. Our gear was impounded and we lost the fee. Mike was wheeled out into the back of a van inside the case. It was a close call, a brush with the local Mafia. Touring was exciting and nerve-racking and it was our way of life.

Back in the UK one night we had an unplanned meeting in a hotel bar that set us off in another direction entirely. Elvis Costello was performing in a town near where we were playing in Malvern when we bumped into him and his keyboardist Steve Nieve – who we knew from days of yore, gigging around the pubs of south London. We lined them up, talked shop all night and tried our best to solve the world's problems. It was good fun. Being in total awe of Elvis, I was all ears and hung on his every word. To me he was the lyricist of the time – the king of retort and pun. Jake Riviera, Elvis's manager, told us we were brilliant, but latched on to how tired we all were and asked us why we weren't doing more as a band. Jake was a colourful person who stood up on imaginary hind legs when making his point. He was like a corgi, snapping and barking orders and ideas. I was impressed. He shone a light on our journey that would turn us upside-down. He was inspired and full of great ideas; he cared about music and knew how best to rule the world.

This new world, as it turned out, wouldn't include Miles or Jools. We parted from Miles and went over to west London to Jake's offices, where lawyers were employed to look over our previous contracts and sort out a severance. Miles was furious and kept calling to say it would be a massive mistake, one that the record company would not entertain. He was welcome to clutch at straws as we marched on regardless. Unlike Miles, Jake had an impressive record collection which spoke volumes to me about his passion. If they had been cars, Miles would have been a Reliant Robin and Jake a Corvette: Jake had tons more class and style.

Meanwhile, back in south London, Jools called us all in for breakfast at a café in Blackheath, where he broke the sad news that he was going to leave the band. He would stay with Miles and record on his own. My throat became dry and I felt like bursting into tears. It was like losing a finger. We sat around in the café patting each other on the shoulders, but Glenn seemed completely let down and left as upset as I was.

Jools was swiftly out of the door and on to the next thing. He had plans that he may have been weaving for many months before. In my heart I wished him well, although I was devastated. I felt I'd lost a really close friend. I didn't see him for a long while after that. Jools and I were both lads and wanted to be in a gang. Gangs had been a huge part of my life pre-Squeeze, and when the band first got together I was looking to form a musical gang

– inspired by The Small Faces and The Who. Jools had the gang mentality so I'd hang out with him, sleep round at his house, write the odd song with him, get arrested with him. On tour, we'd be the first people to call each other in the morning and would go for breakfast or just hang out. Miles had seen something in Jools that went beyond playing keyboards in a pop band. He'd already become our spokesman on stage after Miles had come to one of the gigs and said, 'No one's talking on stage. Jools, why don't you do the introductions because Glenn and Chris don't want to do them?' So Jools would get the microphone, introduce everybody in the band and just start talking and be the entertainer. He was a natural, like the ringmaster in a circus tent, and he was always very funny. Miles saw potential in that, and when TV came along, he took him to *The Tube*.

Back at camp, Jake Riviera had an idea. Ex-Ace and Roxy Music keyboard player and vocalist Paul Carrack was free, and Jake thought he'd be a wonderful addition to the band. Paul was managed by Jake, so it all fitted together nicely. My tears soon dried and we went into Nick Lowe's basement studio in Shepherd's Bush to rehearse with Paul. Suddenly it was 'Jools who?' Paul, or PC as we all called him, was confident and always in good voice, an ardent football fan and a dear friend, who I shared a room with on some US tours that followed. He was a family man, and the warmth of his company glowed brightly. I loved being around Paul, as he was dry with his humour and always up for a good night. He was an inspiration to be around.

Elvis, Jake, Nick and Paul became part of my new gang. We were all in our mid- or early twenties – hanging out, recording, writing and being in bands. We went to the same parties together, we toured together and hung like bats off each other's ceilings talking nonsense for days together. It was fun all day, and at night things got even better. Jake would call the shots, and you could see how Stiff Records must have been in its heyday, full of wild, exciting moments. I was always over at Jake and Toni's house in Chiswick for dinner, or with Elvis and his wife Mary at theirs. Nick would meet me in the pub, so long as it was local, while Paul was more of a home bod. It was great.

Nick was married to Carlene Carter, daughter of Johnny Cash; she was so much fun, and very generous. We had some great nights together and Cindy fitted right into the American-girl, let's-all-have-a-good-time vibrations. These loud nights scared me sometimes, as I couldn't keep up. Cindy and Steve Nieve's wife got on really well, and to be around them was to be within spitting distance of madness and dizzy drunken conversations that went on all night long. None of which I could understand. Steve and I became close friends, I loved his playing and we had both become fathers at roughly the same time. We even tried writing together but couldn't get past the manual on the complicated Fairlight computer we had borrowed. We were also exceedingly happy on good red wine and other nonsense.

One night, Elvis surprised me by asking if I could write some lyrics for a song he had called 'Boy With a Problem'. I was stunned. I went home and kept playing the demo on my cassette machine, trying urgently to come up with some words that would knock him out. Elvis liked the lyric I delivered, and though he made a few changes, the version he recorded was mostly mine. This was a milestone in my life for which I'll forever be grateful. Elvis has always been such a generous friend. He gave me a guitar when he knew I was on my last hundred quid, he invites me to his shows, and we email from time to time in a novel exchange of 'How's it going then?' He is a pedigree, albeit long-distance chum.

Cool for Cats and *Argybargy* were ships in the night, gone and behind us, though the hits from those albums will follow us for the rest of our lives. It was an intense time, and it had to be; you only get one shot at the target, at least that's how it seemed at the time. Elvis had 'I Can't Stand Up for Falling Down' in the charts, Madness had 'Baggy Trousers' and The Nolans had 'I'm in the Mood for Dancing'. The Police were number 1 every week with quirky videos of them hopping about on recording studio desks. They could afford to. Everyone was gearing up for the future. We were content, however, to keep it simple. We just wanted to record great songs and enjoy our life of constant touring around America and Europe. We were up all night and all day; we were burning every candle at every end and having loads of fun with our new mates.

Nick Lowe was great to work with and we never messed around. We would bang it down, as he used to say, then head to the pub to celebrate. Jake's idea was for us to record a four-sided album: Nick Lowe would produce one side, Dave Edmunds another, Elvis Costello and Paul McCartney the other two. Sadly, it never got off the ground. More cab rides across town – this time to Acton, where we spent six weeks writing and recording the album in Eden Studios. We started at 11 a.m. and finished at 10 p.m. most days, with salads and light meals supplied to keep us trim and healthy. I enjoyed the regime Elvis dished out. Cider but no lager, as I recall. At home, life was as you might expect for a young father, full of baby things and early-morning calls. Hangovers and kids didn't mix. But for the most part, I was on alert; I knew this record had to be good and we had to be at the very top of our game.

We cracked on at a furious pace with one take after another, each song tenderly looked at and devoured by Elvis and Roger Bechirian, who engineered the sessions. Glenn got on well with Elvis and I was still in awe of his work, so every time I handed him a lyric it was like giving it to a cute teacher I fancied at school. I was inspired like never before; I was up all night picking through every pun and each story. I really enjoyed the challenge of writing the album and both Glenn and I came up with the goods. We were very much focused on this new-found grown-up way of working. Elvis provided the umbrella of credibility beyond that of our own.

During the recording we got the sad news that John Lennon had been shot. We downed tools and stood stunned in the pub at the end of the road. Friends were invited over to the studio where a mass expression of appreciation and disbelief took place, it was so devastating. The next day we picked up sticks and rolled on with the recording. That was a very powerful day for us all.

We'd had 'Tempted' up our sleeve for a while. We'd already recorded it, with Glenn singing, for Dave Edmunds. Unfortunately, it sounded like ELO and not like Squeeze at all. Elvis thought Paul should sing it, so we went into the studio and nailed the track in one take. Glenn looked shell-shocked, but was man enough to admit that Paul really could sing the song better than he could at that time. Elvis arranged the song and played the guitar riff, and provided backing vocals with Glenn, while I sat around eating salad and jotting down lyrics, content that history for Squeeze was being made. The whole process of the album was never to be repeated. It's by far the most complete album we ever made, from the genius 'F Hole' to the sublime 'Labelled with Love'. Elvis's bass player, Bruce Thomas, came up with the title *East Side Story* – and it fitted Squeeze like a glove. The sleeve was arranged by Barney Bubbles, who was out there with the fairies but in a beautiful and inspiring way. Chalkie Davis was taking our pictures. What more could we ask for? We were surrounded by genius.

Jake had another great idea, he was full of them. Two bands on one bus going around America together, taking over the world; a magical mystery tour across several states with nine band members, Jake, a tour manager, a driver, an accountant and a security man. Elvis Costello and the Attractions supported by Squeeze. The tickets flew out the door and we tore up every town we went to. For the first week it was like a holiday; there was loads to drink and marching powder, the hotels were top notch and we wanted for nothing. Backstage, our world was exclusive and good-humoured; there were many jokers in the pack. Steve Nieve and Elvis's drummer Pete Thomas were like Pinky and Perky, up all night on invisible strings playing jokes on everyone. Elvis and Glenn were more serious and looked mostly in opposite directions. The bass player was Bruce Thomas – otherwise known as the Rhino – who was always in a bad mood. His Fender bass would often take flight across a crowded stage, hurtling mostly towards Elvis. Gilson was under lock and key, John Bentley was having lots of fun and was very Dudley Moore-like. And me? I was knocking about the bus in search of the next beer, a bottle opener or some headphones to avoid the madness with my Walkman. Jake sat at the front of the bus reading a restaurant guide. This was thick with places to stop for a meal, none of them any good, but we gave the book quite a thrashing. We drove off route one day for some Welsh rabbit – this turned out to be a plate of melted Kraft cheese with ears cut from a slice of white bread. We were not amused. Another stop-off was to Buddy's Ribs, a rib joint at the end of a runway at the airport where Buddy Holly took off for the last time, or so the guide led us to believe.

Jake was great at organising events for us; it was exciting and hard to keep up with, but we all did our best. Touring on a bus filled with mischief was something I hadn't bargained for. It taught me so much about the dawn, the bars and dark corridors in hotels, and about how touring really should be: full speed ahead until you pass out. And then some. During one journey from New Orleans, we were stopped by the Ku Klux Klan, who got on the bus with guns to look for donations. We were in our bunks and stayed there until they got off. The tour rolled on and our shows got better and better, apart from the fact that we were mostly chasing hangovers.

A&M were on tenterhooks. They didn't think they liked Jake or the way he managed the band, and I saw a telegram (yes, they were still being sent in 1981) from the label's co-owner Gerry Moss saying: 'Avoid Jake Riviera; he is rude and is mismanaging the chances of this album being a hit.' What did he know? In San Francisco that year, Mr Moss was waiting for us when we came off stage. Jake asked him what the B-sides were called on the singles we currently had out, then grabbed him by the nose and dragged him along the hall away from the dressing-room door. Brilliant. After the same show, Jake took me aside and asked me what was so fascinating about my shoes. I was lost for words. 'All you do on stage is stare at your shoes,' he shouted. 'Look at the fucking audience. Pick a girl, smile at her and the connection with the crowd will be made.' It was a great tip.

We had another number 2 single in the UK with 'Labelled with Love'. We were back on telly again and I personally felt reignited. We had a new manager, a new keyboard player and some great plans for the next album, for the next year and beyond. Videos were starting to take shape as MTV was creeping around the corner, and more and more record companies were investing huge sums of money to get bands seen by a wider audience. True to form, however, we had Barney Bubbles push some mops around a flickering screen for our single 'Is That Love'. Jake told us not to chase the MTV rainbow; we were never going to be Duran Duran anyway.

I had made it, whatever making it was. I seldom had the time to go and see my mum and dad – and when I did, I just went to the pub. Life was good. I was famous for fourteen and a half minutes and I wanted to make the most of it. Hanging out with local villains, being large at parties. I was on the dial, and drink and drugs took centre stage, though in a secret and private way, behind closed doors. My nose became over-familiar with the toilet seats in public loos; pub car parks and lay-bys in country lanes were new places to swig beer and sleep. Anywhere but my own home with my wife and daughter, or my mum and dad's house. By the end of 1981, we had been on tour for months, and in a short break in August Paul Carrack left the band. Like Jools before him, he had other fish to fry: a record with Nick Lowe and Carlene Carter, solo albums and a path into his own future. It was very sad the way he left so abruptly, but I understood why.

He went on to form a band with Nick and I became one of their biggest fans. Meanwhile Jake turned up with a massive contract for us to sign – we didn't, and he resigned, spitting feathers. Our original contract with him had been verbal, but we'd just had a hit album and he understandably wanted to get the financial side of things nailed down. He wanted us to use his lawyer to go through the contract, though, which was a big problem for us, as we were only just becoming aware of what we'd signed away to Miles. The lawyer he kept pushing on us was called David Gentle, who'd been a fixture at all the festivals we'd played at when we were younger, and it just didn't smell right to me. Jake put us under pressure and didn't want us to take the contract anywhere else; he kept saying that we could do it all in-house and save money, but because we'd had our fingers burnt with Miles, we were being really careful. It was never easy and sadly we went our separate ways. Jake had inspired us to look at our deal with Miles in the first place. He was right to point out what a rum deal we had signed up to. I'm grateful that he helped point this out to us. He never took a penny from the band in all the time he looked after us.

Glenn and I decided to take Miles Copeland to court with the help of my brother Lew, who was passionate about helping us find some justice and recompense. Our original contract with Miles signed away the rights to all of our songs, masters and copyright, never to be returned. His company owned 50 per cent of my words and Glenn's melodies for life. We had been completely taken in by everything Miles had told us. Everything in his contract was cross-collateralised, which is totally illegal now, so if we didn't make any money from the touring but did from the publishing, one would pay for the other. Miles knew we'd sign it because we were young, we didn't know any lawyers and he was promising us fifteen quid a week each, which seemed a great deal to us at the time. That was fundamentally wrong and you couldn't do it today – you'd get banged up for grooming a young band in such a way. He had really taken advantage of our naivety. Just as we were about to go to court, we had a call from Miles asking if he could come over and see us. He wanted to avoid the hearing at all costs. He came to Glenn's flat in Greenwich, and we sat and asked him questions that were neatly aimed at getting him to reveal the truth about how much we'd really made and how much we were owed. Behind a curtain, on the window ledge, was a microphone; in the next room was a reel-to-reel tape recorder to slowly gobble up each word. Miles's father, the ex-CIA head, would have been proud of us. We did resolve the case, but were none the wiser or wealthier. My brother Lew and our very talented young lawyer James Harman worked so hard on that case, and in the end we were all relieved just to close the door on a chapter that was fairly painful and somewhat costly.

Paul Lilly was our manager for a brief period while all of this was going on; he was our sound engineer and had convinced us he could do the job better than Miles, which he could. My mum could have done a better job. He got us to invest our money in a PA company; it was an odd thing to do, but it helped us with our tax situation at the time. Paul was gentle and kind. He opened an office in Greenwich Market and employed Jayne Homer to be his secretary, poached from the offices of our record company A&M. She is still with us today. He took on management of Chris Rea and left us behind when Chris hit the European jackpot, a number 1 record across the board. Managers were beginning to really annoy me. There seemed little loyalty. Either that or we were becoming harder to handle.

We were high, then low; a band collectively experiencing bipolar mood swings. Somehow we pulled things together to write another album. *Sweets from a Stranger* was a dark album to record; that's my view. We started it with legendary producer Gus Dudgeon, widely credited for making Elton John a worldwide star, but we replaced him with Phil McDonald, formerly The Beatles' engineer. We tumbled into Ramport Studios in Battersea, owned by The Who. Phil dined out on the stories over expensive dinners late at night. He was calm to work with but never really lit any fires. Don Snow was now on the revolving keyboard stool, and we rolled up our sleeves. Don was impressive and could play most instruments; he was a very funny man who could imitate anyone, but he had another side to him that I could never read, and neither could he. He was up and down with his moods just like I was; together we oscillated like valves in an old radio. Gilson was becoming darker and harder to read too. He constantly turned up in a foul mood and seemed disconnected from the band. And by this time he and Glenn had built up huge resentment towards each other because Glenn would try to tell Gilson what to play, and Gilson would kick against it. It was miserable.

The best song on the album was 'When the Hangover Strikes', on which Glenn surpassed himself melodically. It's a crooner's song with fantastic chords, worthy of Sinatra. I was very proud of my lyrics too. The record company glazed over, but put out a few singles. 'Black Coffee in Bed' was too long but did get some plays on the radio after a brutal edit. Record companies back then were in the habit of playing with your art without you knowing about it. We first heard the new version of the song when a promo cassette arrived through the post. It was hilarious and very, very wrong. We were livid. Elvis and Paul Young dropped in to sing on 'Black Coffee in Bed', and that was the highlight of the recording for me. Paul Young was topping the charts at the time and was in fine voice, and with Elvis there too we sounded like The Drifters. It was a friendly afternoon filled with back-slapping banter, but I felt like I had fallen from the lyrical challenges of the previous album and had delivered some lazy writing. I was not on my game and had gone backwards into a safe but untidy mind. It seems like a dark album to me for so many reasons, not least because I was still mourning both the loss of Paul Carrack and our management situation with Jake. I felt lyrically homeless.

Our new manager, David Enthoven, who'd previously managed King Crimson, T. Rex and Roxy Music, had his work cut out for him. He was introduced to us by someone at A&M, and our first meeting was at the Greenwich Theatre, right across the road from where I lived. David had been schooled at Harrow and could not have been more different from us, but his warmth and ambition shone through his wicked smile and straight talking. After the album he came on the road with us and soon became a very good friend. He was so much fun and mucked in wherever he could. Like us, he enjoyed a drink and a game of cards; we toured well together. He was gentle with everyone and enjoyed the slapstick camaraderie of touring life. I was once invited to his country house, where he lived with his wife, heiress to the Wills cigarette dynasty. On a winter's walk, all wrapped up, David would eat raw beef from a bag like he was eating sweets. We were both mostly drinking fine wines and blowing things up our noses while sitting by roasting fires eating very little and talking bollocks.

David talked us into a 'greatest hits' album and we added a new track called 'Annie Get Your Gun', which was recorded by Alan Tarney, who was famous for the songs he'd written for Cliff Richard. Alan put Squeeze into a computer and recorded the song without us; we came in to sing on top of the track. Gilson added some drums and moaned all day long about how technology was stealing his job. 'Annie' made the radio and to this day is still always in the set. Lyrically I have no idea what it's about. It was a strange marriage – Alan and Squeeze – yet somehow I think it really worked.

Touring went on and on, and on a train en route to Paris from Hamburg, Glenn and I decided the band sounded tired and agreed it was time to close up shop – a rare coming-together at this point in our relationship. It was like a black-and-white movie. I was looking out the window and so was Glenn; we just came to the same conclusion right at the same time.

We were both knackered, Gilson seemed beyond reach and our keyboard seat could not take another swivel. As a band we no longer seemed like a unit. It felt as though we were winging it. The break-up was a mixture of exhaustion and sadness because the constant touring had taken its toll on Gilson more than the rest of us. I felt helpless around his drinking and, although I didn't know it, mine too. Little did I know that I was to follow in his footsteps – in a gentler and more devious fashion perhaps.

I didn't really know what I might be saying goodbye to. It had been such a magical ride, from the first time I met Glenn in 1973 to that day on the train in Hamburg. I had no clear idea of where we might go from here, but as ever, I had no fear about the future. Stages had grown from the corners of pubs to Madison Square Garden; we had come a long way.

Glenn and I kept it all under our hats until the last show of the year, at the Jamaica World Music Festival. We told the band just before we boarded the flight out there. Perfect timing. Gilson and John were furious, and though Don took it in his stride, he was angry too. Sitting behind us on the flight was Rick James and his band, and mid-way through the flight Rick got up and walked into the cockpit, which was only partitioned off by a curtain. As he stood up he lit up a huge joint, and as he disappeared in to see the captain I felt the blood rush round my body ridiculously quickly. I could almost feel the pilot getting stoned on the fumes and flying the plane into a mountain. I watched as Rick walked back into the front of the plane where we were all sitting, a massive grin on his face. I looked out of the window hoping for the best.

I once saw a film of us playing at that festival, and I could see in me a person who was stoned out of his head, playing the wrong chords to the wrong songs, dancing about like there was a nest of spiders in my pants. My head was all over the place and I could not wait to get home. And right after we came off stage, I headed for the airport and boarded a plane home.

It had been a great festival: The Beach Boys, Yellow Man, The Grateful Dead, The Clash and Aretha Franklin; racing crabs on the beach with Joe Strummer; smoking joints in a rowing boat at the back of the stage; falling asleep to Jerry Garcia sweetly playing 'Dark Star'; dancing to Peter Tosh. Not a bad way to say farewell. Jamaica was the oddest place to be at that time; we were completely distant with each other and gone from the band feeling in so many ways. The hotel we stayed in was on the beach: to get a phone call to England you often had to wait several hours, the connections were that bad, so it felt very isolating to be there. Cut off from the reality of home and living in this tender world of impending separation and doom, I had no idea what was going to happen next. After the tour, Gilson became a cab driver, John went to live in Cornwall, and Glenn and I went into partial obscurity for a rest. David stepped to one side, taking my brother Lew with him as his accountant, which I was very happy about. I went home and trod water for weeks on end, contemplating my future. By the end of 1982, I felt as though I was suddenly in a forest. There were shadows and fallen trees, and I had only sunlight from gaps between branches to guide me along the way. David Enthoven was there too; I could see him ahead of me. He had come along to pick up what was left of Squeeze – and what was left was a singles album and Jamaica. He did his best with what he had; we parted ways; it was all amicable.

TOYS HILL

Cindy and I were living in the country when she became pregnant again. I was over the moon. My son Riley was born at Pembury Hospital in Kent, and as I held him for the first time, sitting alongside Cindy's mum, who'd flown over from New York for the birth, I felt so proud. I was a father again, and this time to a boy. He came out of the sunroof because of some complications, which meant that I had first cuddles. Afterwards I headed straight to the pub to wet the baby's head, then drove home with one eye shut and the other peering out for oncoming traffic.

We were happy out in the sticks with our little family, albeit in an isolated way, though Cindy enjoyed it less than me. I'd become firm friends with the photographer Chalkie Davis and together we would enjoy the country life and go for long walks to Toys Hill where there was a nice pub and Winston Churchill's old house, Chartwell, which was close to my home. I loved Churchill and his colourful paintings, his wall-building and chair designs, but I drew the line at his cigars. Fine wine and champagne were on my radar – I was at Berry Bros & Rudd most weekends stocking up on red wine and sometimes sherry. It was a fine way of keeping out of harm's way and from working on any new songs. I was

Burlington Bertie. 'Tempted' and Jake Riviera seemed years ago. I
wrote by night and slept by day; I snorted and drank my way from
one month to next. I was not of this world and it terrified me, but
it never stopped me. Squeeze was behind me now and it was time
to smell the roses, but my nose was constantly too blocked up.

I was not missing the treadmill of recording and touring, the
headaches of management changes and keyboard players coming
and going like wasps. I was enjoying my time in the Weald of Kent.
Home was a place people liked to come and spend weekends, parties were many, but I felt increasingly lonely in my own skin. I was
unsure as to why. It just might have been the drugs catching up
with me. At one of our wild weekends Pete Thomas and his wife
Judy came to stay. They slept in the loft with the electric radiator
on full. Six months later I went up to get something from a case;
the heat was overbearing and the flies were swarming about in
wonder. Our electric bill literally went through the roof. All good
fun.

Glenn and I worked on *Labelled with Love*, a musical that ran for
three sold-out months at The Albany in Deptford. We had been
approached by writer John Turner with a script; it seemed like
a great idea. It came completely out of the blue and woke the
sleeping giants in us both. The experience of having our songs
sung by other people and watching them weave a story from one
to the next was inspiring. The show had a weak plot but it was a
happy one, unlike most of my songs. And being there backstage
each day was incredible. I was Andrew Lloyd Webber on Deptford High Street. The shows kept me from the darkness that was
falling slowly about me. The reviews were really positive and the
cast, including Alison Limerick and Danny John Jules, were beside

themselves. A review from one paper said, 'Tim Rice, who knows a thing or two about musicals, was in the audience the night I went, checking out the competition. He will not be the only writer looking over his shoulder at a theatrical career blossoming in this unlikely corner of London's dockland'. I wish it had travelled up to the West End; maybe it was too scruffy for the larger theatres. Most of the songs came from the *East Side Story* album so there was a thread there, one I had not seen. Now it makes sense to me, there is a narrative within the songs on that album and on stage it seems to work.

One night at an after-show party, Glenn walked down the stairs to dance with Pam the wardrobe lady. I had not seen Glenn want to dance since the early Seventies. I watched from above and knew I wouldn't see him again for some time. She was attractive and danced like she was in a Sixties hippy movie. They looked en-twined in boogie wonderland. It was awkward for me as I was not in her good books. At one of the rehearsals she'd laid into me for supposedly being sexist when I'd asked her if she'd mind sewing a button back onto my jacket for me. 'What the fuck are you asking me to do that for?' she yelled at me, in front of everyone. 'That's not a woman's job. You should be able to do it yourself, you're a grown man!' It was a fair point – even though it was delivered in such a horrible way. With wonky buttons on my tweed jacket I did try to like her but she always seemed to pour her words over me like they were hot tar; all it needed was for me to add the feathers, and I was good at that.

Pam and Glenn became inseparable; they were a really, really tight couple. I could not get a cigarette paper between them. And part of me wanted to applaud that but there was something suspicious about it for me. I just didn't trust Pam because she wasn't the sort of person I could warm to – she seemed cold and wouldn't engage me in conversation unless it was something to do with her or Glenn. So I felt excluded. It was a wedge between us, particularly when I discovered he'd started taking heavier drugs. I was scared for Glenn. One day I picked him up in my car and he said, 'I'm getting married to Pam. Will you be my best man?' I felt as though I was picking up a red-hot poker. What could I say? This was somebody I dearly loved – despite our differences – and I didn't feel I could say no, even though I knew I wouldn't do a good job or be able to come up with a convincing speech. I'm ashamed to say that at the wedding I simply couldn't think of anything to say, so I gathered the courage to get up on a table in the back garden of Glenn's house, said a few words and left as quickly as I could. Not very nice of me or supportive but I was trying to understand the situation from a very lonely place. They drifted from my radar for several months and even went to India, coming home with, of course, a sitar. I was drifting too, but I never got as far as inside my head which was a bit like India at the time.

Another manager came and went – a very mature Shep Gordon, complete with a different Hawaiian shirt for every day of the year. He had hoped to sign Squeeze but settled for Difford and Tilbrook as we both thought we should change our identity and respect the past. Glenn was very careful to make sure that we didn't use the name Squeeze without the primary members being present in the line-up. Shep was good friends with Gerry Moss – the 'M' in A&M – and for a while he and the dangling carrot of his impeccable connections re-energised us. His Muttley laugh was infectious and his humour uplifting, and I really liked his company even if he did spend most of his time out in LA or Hawaii.

With Shep guiding us, we recorded the *Difford & Tilbrook* album with ex-Bowie producer Tony Visconti. It was like being in a school play – I felt shy and out of place all the time. The songs had little power and never tickled my scales in the way Squeeze did. We were strange fish. Glenn grew his hair into a long, flowing mane and I grew an appetite for cocaine. The two of us had drifted apart and didn't speak a word to each other during the entire recording of the album – we very rarely even threw each other a glance. Glenn would wander in and out, and I developed an uncanny knack of disappearing just before he turned up. Tony Visconti thought he was signing up to record the new Lennon and McCartney, but that was not to be and it was frustrating for everyone.

Musically Glenn did a masterful job of arranging those songs, because they were complicated. 'Love's Crashing Waves' was about as commercial as we got on the whole album. And that pissed everybody off, particularly Shep, who wanted us to be as big as Squeeze. Despite this, off the back of this period Glenn and I signed a healthy publishing deal with Steve Lewis and a young Richard Branson at Virgin. I remember meeting Richard; he appeared nervous, and eye contact was not something he seemed to do. I chased his face around the room but he kept hiding from me. Maybe it was the amount of money he was about to give us. The album in retrospect has some genius moments: 'Hope Fell Down' and 'On My Mind Tonight' are musically so sublime. Lyrically I think I might have been coasting but I'm proud of what I coasted with. The album is a rare treat for our fans, it's always so hard to find online or in record shops. Debbie Bishop, who starred in our musical at The Albany, sang some lovely parts on the record, a great contrast to Glenn's voice, and mine.

With money in the bank it was time for Cindy and me to move back to London, and we moved from Toys Hill and bought a nice big house on Lee Terrace, on the edge of Blackheath Village. My parents were well impressed with me: I was in a posh house on four floors with hundreds of windows to clean. The country had been a field too far for Cindy, and she'd felt isolated when I was away working or up in London taking meetings. The move back was good for her. I also treated myself to a jaw-droppingly cool black Jaguar MK11, hand-built by a company in Coventry called Vicarage Cars. It was my pride and joy. Sadly the taxman came and the car had to be sold to pay the bill, but just for a few months I was that rock star with a rock-star car in his garage. Glenn and Pam bought a massive house in Blackheath not far from ours. They had two huge black poodles and lived a surreal, almost prog-rock lifestyle.

At that time, I was doing everything I could to look after myself and not be controlled by Pam. Imagine my disbelief when I turned up for a video shoot one day to discover she'd made all the clothes. She thought we'd look good in eighteenth-century frock coats. It was curtains for me. I went to see my designer friend Scott Crolla, and he and I went to Heal's, where we bought some fabric and he made me a suit. It really was curtains – nice flowers on a bright-blue background. Splendid. It must have hurt Glenn's feelings that I wasn't signing up to what his wife was going out of her way to do, but I didn't have the ability to communicate my feelings at the time. I just went into lockdown. I was still smarting from Pam's request that I send her all my new lyrics so she could edit them before passing them on to Glenn. I felt suffocated by her needs. It was not her fault, it was a time and place that invited bad behaviour and misunderstanding. I often wonder which direction our career might have taken had Pam not come along.

The record company got us on *French and Saunders* with the song 'Wagon Train'. It was a comedy show and uncomfortably I think we fitted right in with this rather weak song. It opened up a few doors and we were asked to write theme tunes for two TV shows, *Father's Day*, which we got Paul Young to sing and *Girls on Top*. We were sort of in demand.

Looking back, 1982, 1983 and 1984 were odd years that were muffled by introspective soul-searching. We were serious writers with serious faces, but we were losing our connection as people. In New York, while touring, we went to hang out with The Sugarhill Gang at their studio in New Jersey; this was one of Shep's ideas to get us involved with the upcoming East Coast hip-hop scene. Doug Wimbish and Skip McDonald played bass and drums like I'd never heard, and being in the studio with them was a powerful experience and such a great twist to our journey. We cut a few songs and made good friends with Eric 'ET' Thorngren, the studio engineer. We could have made an album there and turned a corner that might have taken us into a different league. But that never happened, instead we went on tour with a bunch of white, middle-class session musicians and painted ourselves into a very white-sounding corner. Imagine if we had made a record at Sugar Hill; it would have been so cool for us and I always feel robbed that it never happened. The good news was that ET helped finish off our album when Tony's mixes were very sadly rejected by the record company. He flew over to London and patched it up in the best way possible. ET and I hung out together and became close friends. He loved my Morris Traveller and called it a Tudor car because of its woodwork.

I had a soft spot for Shep, but Glenn and he didn't always see eye to eye. Pam got in the way. I'm sure she meant well, but her over-protection and fussing about the running of the band's affairs led Shep to cup his hands and say goodbye. Shep never commissioned our work. I have always respected him for that and for many other personal reasons too. Managers came and went in our lives, and he was one of the good guys.

LEE TERRACE

After the darkness of the *Difford & Tilbrook* album and the tender high of the musical *Labelled with Love*, I was lounging about in an empty field of inspiration. Early in 1984, Jools called Glenn and invited us both to play a charity event with him and Gilson in the Northover pub in Catford, where it had all begun ten years earlier. We agreed to this one-off and without any rehearsals played a blinding show in front of a packed pub – and Miles who was there with Jools. The magic on stage was so amazing, like old times; the electricity of our songs oscillating between these great musicians was food for thought.

We all called each other the next day to see if we could get back together. Jools, despite his new-found astronomical fame from *The Tube*, was onside, but only if Miles could come back as our manager. Miles got in touch and said, 'Look, I can make you a great deal with the record company if you're serious about going back out on the road. I can get you a merchandise deal and an uplift on your deal at A&M.' For me, it was the devil we knew. It was difficult to be around Miles at first but his John Denver smile soon had us all back in his rocky mountain ways. The Police had sold millions of albums so his star was at its highest, and he could use this to open more doors for us. It sounded good to me.

Squeeze were back. The dynamic, however, was odd. Gilson had sobered up and at first I couldn't get on with his new way of life, despite being full of admiration for him. Jools was always on the telly; his profile was enormous, thanks to being on Channel 4 each week. For some reason things didn't click with John, so we asked Keith Wilkinson, who'd played on the *Difford & Tilbrook* album, to join the band. He was a tender and precise bass player, and a kind person to tour with, but Miles thought his baldness was an issue and tried to get him to wear a hat. Not so kind. Miles chewed strips of paper that he constantly pulled from notebooks, and somehow the flame was relit.

Glenn sent me the first set of demos in the post. There were some real gems in there, 'No Place Like Home' being one of them. The tape contained re-workings of some songs we'd recorded before, but the newer stuff sounded inviting. It was a progression from the lonely Difford and Tilbrook days, but at the time I thought only by a few degrees. For my part I think lyrically I was not firing on all cylinders and I'm sure that didn't help Glenn find new inspiration to work with. However, the songs were good enough to open the door into our first album in a few all-at-sea years. I was writing about the tragedy of exhausted home life and the old chestnut alcohol and its effects. The domestic masterpiece on the record was 'King George Street' with more lyrics and chords than you could shake a stick at, it was brilliant. It's not one that gets many call-outs from the audience which is just as well, it's a fistful of chords. We met up with record producer Laurie Latham, who'd recorded *New Boots and Panties!!* with Ian Dury and the Blockheads and who was keen to work with us on a new album. He'd scored tax-exile status, though, which meant we had to work outside of the UK – so we went to Brussels. Dog shit on the pavements, nouvelle cuisine on the plates and cocaine in my pocket; it was an inspired choice. Prince's 'Paisley Park' was on constant play on my Walkman; life seemed oddly optimistic. Brussels was a beautiful city to walk around (if you could avoid the dog shit), but there was no real nightlife – just the studio. The best place to eat was the Indian Pont De Indes, I think I went there most nights for a curry, a table for one in the corner.

We recorded there for about a month, with Jools flying in and out of Newcastle, where he was shooting *The Tube*. He was the big young TV face of the time and we had to share him, which was fine. At least for me. But the recording dragged on. Laurie was slow at making things happen – he pored over the sounds endlessly. Laurie and I got on really well, and we once hired a Mercedes to nip down to Switzerland to see Paul Young (who he had produced) play. With some bat food in my pocket and plenty of red wine, we raced across Germany, stayed one night and raced back the next day. It was so mad but fun. I loved to drive, and to drive fast, but I excelled on that occasion with the added weight of a nasty Swiss hangover.

Miles was asked by Bob Geldof to contribute bands to Live Aid, the biggest stage ever, and he chose to put Adam and the Ants up for one of the opening slots. We were dumbfounded that we hadn't been asked, and when we watched the event on TV, that was all we could concentrate on. Sometimes Glenn was hard to reach but I must have been impossible. We were at different places together. I was isolating and deeply out of touch with my marriage back at home, where I never seemed to spend any time, and things were rapidly falling apart. Despite all that, Cosi Fan Tutti Frutti is a good album with some very fine moments, 'I'll Never Go Drinking Again' being one of them, written after some nasty hangovers. It's the most dated of our records, though; it sounds very much of its time. With hindsight, it was a stepping stone to the album that followed. Maybe we'd gone into the studio too soon.

We toured when the album came out and poor old Jools had to constantly fly in and out on Concorde; his head was all over the place. Pam also came on tour with us and immediately annoyed Robin, the bus driver, by turning up with hundreds of hat boxes she insisted he find space for. I remember her falling out of her bunk one morning, and hearing the 'oof' as she hit the floor. A curtain opened on the bunk across from me. It was Jools. We looked at each other, closed our curtains and went back to sleep. Gilson put a copy of the Alcoholics Anonymous Big Book in my bunk one morning. I was interested, but not enough to start reading it or stop drinking, though I was secretly inspired. Gilson was clean and serene and wonderful to be on the road with. How times had changed.

My house on Lee Terrace at the edge of Blackheath Village became a real party house. On one occasion the actor Keith Allen arrived completely naked with his girlfriend to play endless board games and drink wine by the caseload with me and Cindy. It was a nutty night, and I remember wearing an all-in-one velvet romper suit that was modelled on one Churchill once owned – I had two, one in blue and one in green. It was high times and money wasn't an issue, so getting Scott Crolla to make my clothes seemed as normal as ordering Jaguars from eager salesmen. I wasn't having much luck with Jaguars, though. One blew up on the M6, but as Jools was with me, the AA were only too happy to tow us all the way to the stage door for our next gig. It was replaced by a new model, which also broke down. I wasn't far behind.

At the end of 1985, I went to see my mum one Sunday and she had a brown mole on the side of her head. She said it was nothing to worry about, but she had tears in her eyes. I spoke with my brothers, who were also concerned. Mum was reluctant to go to the doctor. We managed to get her to see one eventually, when the mole had got much larger, and he sent her to Guy's Hospital for a check-up. The results came back: she had cancer. We felt the stunned silence of the word as it entered the family vocabulary. It was like a shark that chases you around in shallow water until you're forced to give in to it. Mum cried, and as her hair started falling out from the chemotherapy, she cried some more – a lot more as she saw her beauty fade away, melting like ice on a spring morning.

Cancer mixed with agoraphobia, brandy, sleeping tablets and anti-depressants made her life too difficult to handle. She was taking a tray of pills each day, and she did little but sit by the fire and pray, sip from her glass or sleep. It was shocking to watch, but I dulled the pain by drinking and managed the grief with regular visits to the local pub with Jools's dad, who had become a close friend. On the last Mother's Day of her life, I visited her with my very good friend Barny after being in the pub for most of the day. 'Oh God, it's Mother's Day!' I remember saying as we came over the heath. I went into the off-licence and bought her some cherry brandy – God knows why. I knew she wouldn't like it. By the time we got to the corner of the street, the bottle was three-quarters empty. She laughed and we finished off the rest around the chair that had become her throne and soapbox.

With a few whiskies she was lucid and funny with it. She did drift in and out of herself, but she managed as best she could with the inevitability of cancer. She took to her bed from time to time and visits to see her revealed a scared and retreating mother figure; this woman who had once held me in her arms, baked cakes and prayed for me with such emotional strength. In December, when she went into Greenwich Hospital for another check-up, my dad, my brothers and I gathered to have words with the doctor. Through the glass we could see Mum sitting upright in bed. He told us she had about two months to live. He then left us to talk to her about it and decide what we should do. Nothing. There was nothing we could do. She was leaving us and we were unequipped to deal with it. I flew to New York for a TV show that night, but when I tried to board the plane, I was so drunk I cried and fell over. The pilot came to talk to me, and in the end he upgraded me to first class. I sat next to a nun and fell asleep on her shoulder. Ever since then, flying has been a major issue for me.

That Christmas was Mum's last. I went into the intensive-care room feeling numb and hungover. We were a long way from the cold stones of the Giant's Causeway and prayers in the sea breezes. She was praying, though, and I remember her saying prayers for me, for my kids, for everyone except herself. I left and sat in a waiting room, and a few hours later my brother and father appeared to tell me she'd gone. It was a cold moment. The clock stops when a parent dies and you wonder where on earth time has gone and why you've been robbed of their love. Suspended in shock, we fell to our emotional knees.

No more jelly cubes, no cake, no mother's love. Just the wonderful memories. She died on New Year's Eve and we buried her on her birthday – 10 January 1986. It was a big funeral with lots of policemen there, loads of people from the church, and friends from far and wide – even Mum's sister from Ireland, who could hardly walk due to multiple sclerosis. It was cold and I was trapped inside my head and my heart, but my brothers and my father held me and loved me. It was so grim saying goodbye, yet that's what we do until it's our turn to be lowered into the ground.

The wake was at my house – a home she loved so much yet seldom came to. With tears in my eyes, I raised many glasses of vintage brandy from Berry Bros & Rudd. I was the pop star with too much money; she'd have been proud of me tipping them back. Dad soaked up the compliments and looked totally lost for the first time in his life; the war was over and the cancer had won. He looked defeated, like we all did. He tore into some old jokes and sang a little on his way out of the door, back to the house in which he had lived with the girl of his dreams for all those years. He loved to be alone, but this was different.

My connection with Mum is a sum of many parts – a bit of this, that and the other. A bit of the Irish, too. When I pick my nose, I think of her. When I laugh, I laugh like her. When I worry, I worry like her. She'll be part of me forever. I miss my mum. It would be so great to go around and see her; to smell her roses and introduce her to my beautiful wife Louise, the love of my life, and all the children. But it's so long ago, I can hardly even access the feelings of her death. I was numb then as I am now. Not because I didn't love her, but because time has iced over each image of her – just like the icing on one of her cakes.

A few months after the funeral, Dad's next-door neighbour Mrs Jones started to invite him in for his tea; her husband had also passed away recently. The two of them became very close and my mother would have been turning in her grave with jealousy, but she had no reason to, Mrs Jones was just being a good neighbour and Dad was happy to accept her company. I'm sure it never went any further than tea and a read of the paper over a few glasses of sweet white wine.

After a month or two it was time to get back in the studio, this time to record *Babylon and On*, which we started working on in late 1986. It took months to record and cost us a fortune. Glenn and I wrote together in the same room for the first time and 'Hourglass' was the result. Oddly I think that was Pam's idea. We had a lot of fun writing it, but it didn't feel very natural. It was like being on a first date, slightly awkward at first, but then we were in with the tongues. My favourite song on the album is 'Tough Love' because it tells the story of someone with a drinking problem who's in a volatile relationship at home. It was a reflection on the reality I found myself in. Glenn and I sang it together in our trademark octave-apart vocal, like we had all those years ago on 'Take Me I'm Yours'. It's a sound like no other.

There was yin with our yang. ET Thorngren, who Glenn and I had met in New York at Sugarhill, made the album sound fresh and original by keeping things as simple as possible. We got on really well together, though I never knew how he managed to drink so much alcohol and smoke so much pot while still mixing the songs with such clarity. He was a dead ringer for Jack Nicholson, and when he burst into a sweat sometimes he would have the ability to scare you with his goofy smile. He was full of love and so brilliant at his work.

It was a time of excess. I spent my way out of the emotional darkness by prising open some strange and wonderful personality malfunctions. It was pretty good fun. We had run up bills of about £100,000, but it didn't sound like it. We filmed three huge-budget videos for the album, and even managed to win an award for the 'Hourglass' one. That video, a two-day shoot in a studio on the Thames, directed by Ade Edmondson from *The Young Ones*, with a large helping hand from Jools, was amazing. We dressed as babies, we dressed as lords and had a bizarrely built set realised mostly by Jools. The cost was enormous, one we would never repeat again. It was great fun playing around on set and being lads for the first time in many years; everyone seemed at home and at ease with being back in the band. I thought it would last forever. A follow-up video for *Trust Me to Open My Mouth* was shot on the Old Kent Road in a warehouse. A huge mouth had been erected, and we played inside. The song lacked the chart success of 'Hourglass' but it provided another great big moment of happiness as we danced around giant tonsils.

MTV was the thing to be on and we were on it all the time, along with Sting and Dire Straits, Duran Duran and the other all-male bands that wore make-up. On the screen we had none of the seriousness of some of our contemporaries – thankfully. Our childish take on life served us well and kept us apart from the pouting pencil-thin bands that filled the MTV screens across the world with their well-tailored collars sticking up.

My memories of the video shoot for 'Footprints' are less happy. We'd gone up a mountain in Salt Lake City, and it was snowing and bitterly cold. As we walked to the location, an angry Glenn and I had a huge falling out. Glenn was furious and the atmosphere during the shoot was incredibly uncomfortable. I couldn't wait for it to finish. Apparently, I had been complicit in some gossip about his relationship with Pam, but it was never clear what was said to whom and when. That evening, when Pam arrived at the hotel, they had a huge row and the hotel room was wrecked. We had a gig later that night and Glenn refused to talk to anybody in the band – he even insisted on having his own dressing room. At the end of the set he wouldn't come off stage and stayed there angrily playing the guitar Hendrix-style. I'm sure if he'd had some lighter fluid he would have set light to his guitar. I was deeply sorry I'd fractured our friendship, but I couldn't find a way of apologising as it was impossible to get close to him. Neither of us was in a great space at the time. We could have both done with some therapy.

'Hourglass' was a hit in America and it charted in the UK too, and we were soon back out on tour. In the States, we sold out Madison Square Garden twice and did huge arena shows with all the trimmings. We flew out to the US on Concorde with a *Mail on Sunday* journalist, David Thomas, to show him and the UK how big we were in America. We had a New York radio station invite fans out to JFK airport to meet us – with the carrot of them getting a mini CD and a one-off single available only on that day. We landed giddy with free champagne and BA gifts, and as the doors opened we steeled ourselves for the forthcoming Beatles moment on the tarmac. But when we looked outside, there were only about twenty people milling around in the cold. How we laughed. We were rushed off in a limo to the hotel for a stiff lie-down.

Touring then was in plush hotels; we had fake names on check-in, nice food – we'd discovered sushi – smart tour buses with big screens, good-looking fans with long legs, and comfortable seats on aeroplanes. America was all about limos and trucks, and backstage knees-ups. The stages were bigger than we were used to, so we asked our crew to help us fill the blank spaces. Our tour manager also worked for U2, which was how we ended up with a set that had steps on each side of the stage, leading to a walkway that crossed over Gilson's drum kit like a bridge. It worked fine for Bono to race up and down these during U2's long instrumentals, but for Glenn and me it was ridiculous. I ran up the stairs for the first time during 'Pulling Mussels (from the Shell)' and by the time I got to the top, I was already due back at the microphone to sing the chorus. I was out of breath, hungover and lacking in any stadium-rock nous. Glenn tried it once and also got stuck during a solo.

Though it was wonderful playing those huge venues, I felt a bit embarrassed most of the time. On big stages, road crews have often made the mistake of setting Squeeze up wide apart, but we're not that kind of band. We need to be close together – like The Beatles at Shea Stadium. Touring was getting out of control again and I began to feel the strain. I was the distant one, still finding it hard to communicate my feelings in a manageable way. Our tour manager made us come to his hotel room in LA; he sat us down and asked us both to speak our minds. He was metaphorically bashing our heads together, but nothing much was being said, and within the hour I was back up on the roof in the pool with a cold beer. It was painful, yet on stage I'm not sure anyone would notice the brick wall that I had erected between us. I never crossed over to his side of the stage. Roger Waters had nothing on me when it came to building walls. I feel so sorry that we never got to share those touring moments from a healthy place. We missed each other from my inability to come out of a self-imposed sanctuary.

Being in New York at this time was a cocktail of very late nights and heavy heads in the morning. The Limelight club was my den of iniquity and often I found myself behind a red velvet rope at the end of the club with other celebs of the time: Daryl Hall, John Oates and other bods with big hair. One night the guitarist from Def Leppard joined me for a beverage. He had his arm in plaster, so I asked him if he had played a minor chord. He didn't see the funny side of my off-the-cuff quip and left me to my laughter. Other nights I danced like Woody Allen on the dance floor chatting up New York ladies, none of whom took the slightest bit of notice of my over-engaged swinging of the hips. Their loss. New York was limos and record company visits, club nights and bigger stages like Meadowlands, a massive venue for Squeeze. I was swanning about with an American Express card, a nice suit and a record on MTV.

Back in London after the tour I was asked to help organise Sport Aid on Blackheath, a fun run inspired by Bob Geldof. It was nice to be asked but I was welded to my stool in the pub most nights and was not a natural runner. I did some small preparations, I got some nice trainers, and headed out onto the heath. On the big day Jools fired the starting gun and off I went with about 10,000 runners behind me. The route took us through Greenwich Park to the *Cutty Sark*, where Simon Le Bon's catamaran *Drum* would meet us at the jetty. I was told there would be a big photo of us all on the deck. Bob, Simon, Paul Young, Sting and others. However, *Drum* pulled away before I could get my foot off the jetty. My foot starred on the front page of the *Daily Mirror* the next day just out of shot. The best bit of the run was getting a lift on a friend's motorcycle down through the park.

Squeeze supported U2 at Croke Park in Dublin. It was one of the most exciting shows I've ever played at – like being back at the Charlton Athletic football ground in 1973, watching The Who. Thousands of people were there, and so many of them sang along to our songs, especially 'Labelled with Love', which is a pub sing-along favourite over in Ireland. U2 blew us away, though. They knew how to fill large stages; we never looked comfortable in such a setting.

I was big on cocaine and hung out with all the right people on tour; the tour managers who carried and the dealers who came to our hotel rooms. One of these, called Gig, was tall and had a runny nose; he would treat me to lines of cocaine longer than most coffee-table tops. I would shake and feel good for about an hour, then fade fast only to be propped up by vodka and red wine. It went around in a circle day after day. We also had a tour manager called James Sliman who blow-dried his hair. I thought it was weird at the time. I loved James: he knew everyone and where to go and be seen. His voice was deep like a native New Yorker from a Damon Runyon story.

We were back on tour, back in the charts and back in debt with the record company. The result was the follow-up album *Frank*, which came out in 1989. It had to be made on a tighter budget than we were used to, so we went into a studio on the Old Kent Road called The Chocolate Factory. It was funky and inexpensive; it had ants crawling from the faders on the mixing desk. ET was dumbfounded by this and complained all the time. Glenn argued that by saving money we would benefit in the long run – and with the cash we saved, he started to build his own studio in Black-heath, which was a smart move. No more expensive sessions in

New York or London, and videos with silly budgets. It was time to tighten the old belt. Except that I had no belt to tighten. I was broke. My marriage to Cindy was over. I was away, she was a single mother at home alone; we didn't talk, we argued. We'd moved from the big house on Lee Terrace to the White House in Kidbrooke. A new house, but the same old feelings and resentments. Whenever I came home, there'd be conflict because Cindy would be lonely and I'd be high from being on tour. We'd paper over the cracks with parties, where in my view we'd become competitive with our drinking, but generally I wanted to recuperate.

Cindy and I were very close when we met, but by the end we went off in different directions. Natalie and Riley were such great kids and I loved playing with them and being there when I could; they lit up my life and I was so proud to be a father. But I found it difficult to get my head around fatherhood when I was always about to be whisked away on tour. Home was very much a place to put down your bags, fill the bath with children, pack and then leave again. It was a warm place and I think the kids had fun growing up in the houses we tried hard to keep happy for them. I remember leaving and seeing them at a window on the first-floor landing that looked out onto the road. I sat in my car and cried as they waved with such bright rosy faces. They had no idea what was going to happen, and neither did I.

Divorce from Cindy made me a shard of my former self. In court the judge deemed that because the singles album had sold so well, my income would always be roughly the same. He never saw the sales of *Difford & Tilbrook*, a very different picture. On the steps of the court by St Paul's I broke down, in my head singing 'Feed the Birds', in reality on my way to the bankruptcy courts next door. A tax officer present at my hearing asked for my autograph. I was twisted in knots. Divorce can be brutal. It wasn't anyone's fault. It's very difficult to be the partner of a musician – it's like being married to a submariner. There's very little time to have a relationship in a meaningful way and when I did come up to surface I was lost inside my own head.

After the split from Cindy, I went seamlessly from one relationship to the next. Heidi was a wardrobe mistress on the *Babylon and On* tour, and when I'd first met her I hadn't fancied her at all. I thought she was hard work and not at all friendly; in any case, I thought she was seeing one of the crew. But one night in Philadelphia, reeling from the final death knell of my marriage, I got so drunk that I ended up in a swimming pool with two beautiful women and a large bottle of Vodka. Heidi pulled me out, took me upstairs, brushed my teeth and put me to bed. One minute I was Jon Bon Jovi, the next I was Eric Sykes. Heidi was twenty-one and lived in Chiswick with her mum. Her father she never saw; he lived in Essex. I met him twice. He was a keen drinker and cigar smoker, and he gripped my hand so hard when shaking it that my ring cut into my finger. I never liked him very much. Her mother was fun; she balanced out our disagreements and floated between us sweetly. I really liked her. Our early courting days were spent mostly on two tour buses, she on the crew bus and me on the band bus. We got to see each other at the shows at least. Back in the UK we never had time to court in the old-fashioned sense, we just moved right in together to my flat in Wapping above the River Thames. We had amazing views of Tower Bridge to one side and to the other a building site that would become Canary Wharf.

Frank was a fun album to record, and the songs were more

earthy and more like the Squeeze of 1979. ET Thorngren saw to that. Glenn pushed me to sing more, so I bagged myself two songs – 'Love Circles' and 'Slaughtered, Gutted and Heartbroken'. It had long been an issue for me to sing on the tracks. Glenn was the best person for the job, the storyteller; yet he'd always been a great advocate for my singing. It gave him a breathing space on stage, but I had little confidence and always felt in his shadow. The way he writes is so structured melodically and it's difficult to sing. The tunes are written for him and mostly him alone. The high point of the recording for me was how Jools played the piano; he really became part of the band again, even though he was still on TV duties from time to time, and I felt like we were making music together as one. One of my fondest memories of the album was the sleeve. Our art director Rob O'Connor wanted to put a drawing of Frank Bough on the front cover, but the art depart-ment at the record company could not see why. There was a lot of scratching of heads. We ended up with a tortoise on the cover. We loved it and thought Rob was a genius, which he is. The record company sighed deeply into their gin and tonics. I love the album. It's so honest and was refreshing after a few years of much knob-twiddling production.

Glenn and I get on well during promotional tours, which can be gruelling. We seemed to bond in interviews while talking up our songs and our band. Some of the tours around the Frank album meant flying every day to different cities in America. A morning radio, an afternoon of press and more radio on drive-time. Glenn supported my tiredness and my fear of flying in a very patient way. To get through the flying I would drink vodka for breakfast just to get on the plane. The promotion for the Frank album was the most exhausting I have known. Glenn is a master at being positive and often leads the conversation. People tend to ask Glenn questions before they come to me. It must be my face. He handles the property of conversation better than me, although we share in the spoils of self-congratulation like pros. Playing songs in this situation drives me nuts sometimes, early morning radio being the worst. Poor Glenn has to sing for his breakfast, and I strum away in support. I'm not that good before midday at the best of times. Never the lark, more of an owl.

Frank was followed by a live album – *A Round and a Bout* – in 1990. It was recorded in Newcastle, which was now Jools's second home. But it wasn't long before Jools left the band again for more TV, and his big band albums and tours that followed. Glenn was livid with him for leaving the band again. I didn't see it coming, but was respectful of his needs to plough his own fields. After all, his musical landscape was yielding a very nice crop of its own. He wanted to concentrate on his solo career again and didn't need to be in Glenn's shadow or mine, and I totally understood how he felt. Naturally, I was sad to see him leave. His parting shot was an inspired piano solo on 'Peyton Place', a one-take, breathless piece of playing. It's pure genius.

Heidi fell pregnant very quickly and I was beaming with pride, yet nervous about becoming a father again. I planned to tell Natalie and Riley over a Chinese meal. I was sweating and trying to time the whole thing right. I did not want to upset them or make them feel awkward around a new branch on the family tree. I stumbled my words out just as the main meals arrived at the table. Nat was beaming with smiles and Riley wanted to know if he could eat the ornamental carrot.

Even more work fell into the band's laps; a summer of shows at universities came into the calendar, easy shows to do and fun. We were playing a show at an Oxford college ball, supporting the band Imagination and off to one side was a pit for mud wrestling. A typical night out for Oxford wallahs. Don Snow was back in the band on keyboards, but he had changed his name; this time he was called Jonn Savannah. It was an interesting show: a May ball, everyone swanning around in ball gowns, the men in dickie bows. At the sound check, Jonn stayed behind while the band went to catering, the most important part of any show. Glenn had kindly asked him to take a guitar solo in a new song on stage that night. At the point at which this happened, all the lights swivelled around to illuminate Jonn in mid solo, face grimacing, with the notes being eagerly ripped from the fretboard. My jaw dropped. I took my hat off to him for missing a great bit of catering to have the lighting guy work on his new routine.

My phone went as I was hanging around backstage after the show. Déjà vu. Heidi was in labour and on her way to hospital. I jumped in the car with a six-pack and a bottle of wine, and hurtled down the motorway to her bedside at the Ashford hospital. By the time I got there, things had calmed down and she asked me to go home and come back the next day. I headed back the following morning a little the worse for wear, and at 2.30 in the afternoon was rewarded with the wonderful sight of my new daughter Grace. I was beside myself. She was angelic and made me so proud. In the corner of the room was my shortwave radio. I could hear the gentle sounds of Wayne Shorter playing the song 'Misty For Me', a heavenly backdrop for the birth of my daughter.

Home now was a farmhouse in Sussex, one I could ill afford.

I was living beyond my means. Within a year it was back on the market and this time I was seeking rented accommodation. I found the perfect place, Old House Farm, near Rye; it was huge and cheap to rent. A rare bit of luck, you might say. Six bedrooms, outbuildings and 650 acres of land. It needed work, and Heidi did not shy away from that. It was £600 a month. Imagine. Natalie and Riley came at weekends to enjoy the countryside, the fields I'd put myself out to graze in to get away from my past and the sadness of a broken marriage.

Our neighbours in Sussex were Paul and Linda McCartney, and ever since we'd moved in I'd been concocting plans to pop over to borrow a cup of sugar. Then one morning Linda invited us over for brunch. We took Grace with us, and Paul was very gentle with her – even dancing with her at one point. He played us a new song, 'Real Love', that he and the remaining Beatles had recorded with Jeff Lynne over an old John Lennon demo, and it sounded amazing. Then we sat down to a meal of vegetarian sausages at their small kitchen table. I really liked Linda. She even suggested that Paul and I should sit down together and write some songs, but Paul was more guarded about the idea and the moment passed. We stayed friends all the time we lived near Rye, and got together many times until Linda passed away, which was heartbreaking.

Despite my money problems and the fact that my drinking and drug-taking was spiralling out of control, being in Sussex felt good to me. It was my home; it was where I felt at ease. But *Frank* had confused the record company – there was no 'Hourglass' to send to radio, no hits or videos for TV, and it sounded slightly flat. So we were dropped. We'd been back together for five years, we'd had another good crack of the whip, made some money on the road, broken MTV, broken a record company and were about to break another.

Miles got us a deal with Warner in LA, who at the time seemed excited to have signed us. A lot of record-industry people in the US have a soft spot for Squeeze, as we're the absolute antithesis of American music. They see us as being a bit like The Kinks – a picture-postcard version of Englishness. Lenny Waronker, the label's president, called us personally to ask us to come to the States to record. And producer Tony Berg, who'd worked with Public Image Ltd, flew over to London to hear the new songs we'd written. I liked him immediately. He looked like Cliff Richard from the side, he played guitar incredibly well and was an all-round nice chap. At Warner's request, the band flew to LA to record at Tony's house. I didn't want to go. There was too much to leave behind, and I was enjoying, if that's the right word, my drinking.

When the band decamped to LA, I didn't deal with it well. We moved into a rented house in Hollywood, and after the first night, I moved out. I wanted to be alone. The idea of being in a house with the band terrified me at that point. I couldn't contemplate the idea of partying with other people; I wanted to do that on my own. I was at the end of my drinking and drug-taking days, and there was no let-up. I'd start on Indian lager (much stronger than the American brands) in the afternoon, then move on to vodka and tequila, and finish early in the morning. There was no moderation with cocaine either. Whenever it ran out, I could get more. I never did more than a gram a day, but that combined with the drinking made things mental.

I moved into a small apartment and the rest of the band stayed put. Glenn was very upset about this, but because of my state of mind I'd no idea how he or anyone else was feeling. I didn't really know how I was feeling either. He saw the album as a new beginning, but because of our lack of communication, nothing was ever said. I wanted to be at home, but I also wanted to record the album. I was no good to anybody. My apartment became a den and the curtains were drawn most of the time. It was my bat cave. Back in the UK Rob Dickens, the head of Warner, very helpfully wrote to his American counterpart warning him they had made a massive mistake signing Squeeze: we were washed up, he said. I met him in a lift one afternoon. He stood by his word which I guess shows how much he cared about our music. We ploughed on regardless.

In a break in the busy recording diary, I flew home. Maxine and I had drifted in and out of each other's lives over the years, but each time I saw her my heart was lifted. In 1990, that same heart broke when I heard she had cancer. She was so young. It was so wrong. I went to see her in hospital, and there she lay with this horrible disease that had taken her face and turned its palette into one of smears and dark colours. We were all so shocked. She came out of hospital some weeks later and went to a retreat in Spain, where she did some focusing work on the cancer, determined not to be beaten by it. She was strong and that has always inspired me.

She got better, and then she got worse. I called her and she invited me to Benenden for afternoon tea in the garden. Her face looked bruised but her spirit was glowing. She had her back to the setting sun, and all I could feel was the love I'd first witnessed when we met outside The Three Tuns all those years ago. She drew breath and gave me a gentle lecture about my life. I sat there with my scone and my Earl Grey tea while she told me I should consider some sobriety. She had become worried about my drinking. She told me to spread my wings and try to write songs outside of my partnership with Glenn, which I'd never really thought about. We talked about my relationship with Heidi and how it might have become volatile. In reality we were as bad as each other. I'd fucked up so many things and hidden behind the bottle. Maxine picked it out like a pearl from an oyster. There was no way I could avoid the inevitable. That afternoon my life was turned on its head, and I had plenty to think about on my way back home.

Meanwhile there was a record to make. The recording at Tony Berg's house and at Real World in Bath was sporadic but brilliant. We had no keyboard player at this point, so we trimmed down to a four-piece and we sounded tight. Steve Nieve did come in to play some sublime keyboards on the album, and I hoped he might join the band, but he was on Costello duties. The result, *Play*, is one of my favourite Squeeze records, with more than a few songs I found utterly mesmerising when I first heard them. I was writing dark, confessional songs, and when I heard Glenn singing them, the hairs would stand up on the back of my neck. 'Letting Go' is one of the best songs Glenn and I have ever written; its chord changes are beautiful and clever. I always feel a deep sadness when I hear the song, it's so attached to a very personal emotion with me. 'The Truth' says everything about how I was feeling then, and it hurts to hear it. And 'Walk a Straight Line' is inspired. Its opening line – 'I need some help' – was me reaching out through a fog of people I knew well but had pushed away to the point where they'd become strangers.

These were dark days indeed. I'd always felt that Glenn and Tony were more than a match for each other, both headstrong

and constantly creative. The yin and yang of the recording sometimes felt strained, but I was in the shed at the end of the garden
tuned into my Sony shortwave radio, listening to the war in Iraq
unfold on the other side of the planet. I was drinking and dis-
tancing myself from Glenn and everyone during the recording of
the album, and not being very useful. I was fried then refried. I
had no real idea what I wanted apart from to go home. I binged
on cars and gadgets, and became insolvent again. I couldn't pay
my tax bill and things were starting to be repossessed back in the
UK. One night in LA I went over to see Nick Lowe for some light
relief; he was in town with his new band Little Village. I loved
his company so much. We drank at his hotel bar and laughed for
hours, then I attempted to drive back to my place. I could hardly
see and drove the wrong way down the freeway before getting lost
in a dodgy Latino district. I was then chased by some Mexicans in
a car and somehow lost them along a dark road in an industrial
estate. I went to bed, woke up and thanked God I was alive. It was
a close call.

Most of the *Play* album is pure art; it's as deep as you want to
go. It was never pop, never what Warner wanted. The album came
out in June 1991, and by August we'd been dropped by the record
company. We were not the Squeeze they had signed, and it all
went sideways. Despite Miles re-signing us to A&M just a couple of
weeks later, we were on a downward spiral. The record company
were hungry for a classic Squeeze album, but the best we could
offer them was another greatest-hits package. It sold thousands
and kept the bank account out of the red for a few more years.

We did a US tour in support of Fleetwood Mac. It was a disaster
– no one wanted to see us, and we played to almost empty venues.

The Mac were in another world; they kept cancelling shows all over the place, pleading illness, though we all felt it was more to do with cocaine psychosis. Our equipment was in their truck, so we had to just hang around until they felt like playing again. Nice venues and catering, but that was it. As ever when I was away from home, hotel rooms had become safe houses for my dull head and insatiable thirst.

Glenn and Gilson were never on the same sheet of paper; they often fell out over drum patterns and tempo – the usual pulling and pushing between writer and drummer. The two of them rubbed each other up the wrong way, particularly in the second phase of the band. On Glenn's demos, he'd use a drum machine to lay down a very precise rhythm track. He'd play them to the band and Gilson would grumpily say, 'Well you might as well get a fucking drum machine then, if that's what you want. You obviously don't want a human being.' When Gilson did get into technology and started to try to bring it into the band, he fumbled and wasn't very clever with it – it just wasn't his forte. And that used to frustrate Glenn. So he would take over, and that would create more tension. When we played live, I think Gilson would do things on the drums just to wind Glenn up, because he knew he couldn't do anything about it. I'd listen, knowing exactly what he was up to. He'd play a double-bass drum part when there wasn't meant to be one, or he'd put a flam in where there was no flam. You could see him looking daggers at Glenn's back as he was singing. Invisible sparks would fly around the dressing room; it was not a very nice atmosphere. Gilson, however, was the genius behind so many of our songs. His inventive patterns live proudly to this day. I felt for them both, but had no way of expressing my views.

Gilson was lured away to play with Jools's Rhythm & Blues Orchestra, which was a smooth move for him to make. I was sad to see him leave the band, as he'd inspired me to think about things in a different way. He'd sobered up and was a different person from the one that used to scare the shit out of me each night on stage. He was tender and in repair emotionally from the demons in his life. It touched a nerve with me and I'll always thank him for that huge inspiration. I loved Gilson like I had Jools, so when he left the band the sadness rippled deep into the well, the dark well that was almost dry.

REHAB

The first time I remember experiencing high anxiety was when the band were in New York in 1987. We were signing albums in a record store. I'd been up for a few nights on the cocaine and was feeling more than a little worse for wear. My mum had died the year before and I was dealing with my grief via a constant intake of fine wines and white powder. I felt overcome by the number of fans in the room, but I did my best to stay focused until the line of people had trickled down to one or two. Then I legged it to the hotel. I raced up to my room, ordered room service and lay on my bed. The red wine arrived with two chilled beers; it was late afternoon. This was the first time I felt scared because of a hangover.

Since my mum's death, flying had become an issue for me. I had broken down at the gate on a BA flight from London to JFK to do some promotion before another tour and was led gently to one side by the airline staff. The pilot in his crisp white short-sleeved shirt came to see me, reassuring me that the flight would be safe and not too bumpy. He even supplied me with the weather maps. I drank my way across the ocean and back home again.

In 1990 I was flown to Cupertino, California to work on some musical ideas with Apple Computers, a sort of brain-storming event. Sadly my brain was not behaving itself. Each day a group of us would sit around talking about the future, and if Apple could help music expand via the internet. It did, and sadly I missed the boat due to a hefty hangover. I really enjoyed my time there and wished I'd stayed around the table with the other people I met, who later went on to be part of Facebook, Twitter and Apple Music. One morning, while staying at a hotel in San Jose, I got up to watch David Frost interview Elton John about his drinking and new-found sobriety. I sat on the bed in my bathrobe in tears as I saw myself reflected in his every word. I knew I had to change, but I just didn't have the courage to. Back home, I met up with my good friend Barnaby; he'd been into rehab and was a new man. To see him like this was an inspiration, but sadly I still didn't want to stop. He had been in Farm Place, a rehab down in Surrey. I visited him there but thought it was full of Mars-bar chomping alcoholics, which they were. Barnaby and I used to be in each other's pockets when I lived on Crooms Hill. We smoked and drank and stumbled together. I've still got a broken scaphoid bone in my wrist from a drunken fight we had in my flat one night. All harmless fun. The landlady had a cellar full of sherry and we managed to clear a few cases out one weekend and for some reason stuffed the empty bottles up the chimney breast. When I moved out some months later they were all discovered. We went to any lengths to quench our thirst in those days. In the bad old good old days when we were naughty boys we used to visit Will Palin in Devon and be all *Withnail and I* on the moors and in the villages of the north Devon coast. Barny and I enjoyed our dizzy friendship.

A few months later I went down to PROMIS, a rehab centre in Kent. I drove by in my car then drove home again. I went back a week later for an interview, and the counsellor tried to check me in there and then. But I drove home again in denial, hiding behind the fact that Squeeze were about to go on tour. Another few months passed, and this time I went to see a Dr Robert Lefever in London. He recognised my anxiety and the state I was in, and how it needed to be cared for. He said I could benefit from a few weeks in treatment. I sat in my car and wept. Soon afterwards, I had lunch with our former manager David Enthoven, who had sobered up after years on drink and drugs. I sat there with him, talking rubbish and gradually making myself feel worse, until he put his hand on my shoulder and said, 'Come back, Diffy, when you sort yourself out, and we can talk again.' David held his lantern up for me to see the light, but I refused the offer, even though I could feel the penny dropping at an alarming rate.

Squeeze were sliding into a never-ending date sheet of venues that were getting smaller all the time, the songs weren't as engaging as they once were, and lyrically I was drilling down into the deep underbelly of my self-centredness. Being away from home and in a place that made me nervous and scared did me no favours. The drugs gave me panic attacks, I couldn't ride in lifts, and my flying phobia took off. I was thin then fat; up then down. I was drunk then drunker. Nothing had changed in five or six years and I'd pushed Glenn away, possibly the closest person to me. I knew Glenn wasn't happy and I often felt rejected and I felt the rejection had worked both ways. We were like two clouds that came together to create thunder. We'd managed to use our songwriting as a bridge between our often complicated personalities, but there was precious little other communication. At least, that's how it seems to me.

In 1992, a tour came up that began at a Fourth of July fireworks event in Chicago. I scanned the dates with fear. I was in no fit state to go on the road but I knew I had to. I couldn't let everyone down. At home, things were tense. Grace was growing fast and Heidi had banished me to the spare room as my drinking had become too secretive. I must have been a heavy weight to have around the house with my intensive mood swings. A usual evening for me would be to put Grace to bed, sit and watch TV with Heidi till 11 p.m. or so, then wait for her to go upstairs. Once she did, I'd get out a bottle of red wine and start tipping that back, then go to my desk with some cocaine under the pretence of writing. Heidi's father had been an alcoholic, so she knew exactly what she was living with, and once I'd been sent to sleep at the other end of the house, the loneliness and fear collided and I was scared. I felt so depressed but had no idea what to do with it, or what it was. It came and held me with its black sheet, cradled in the breath of stale wine and fags. Her cold shoulder defiantly gave me food for thought, which of course now I'm very grateful for.

I packed my suitcase, said goodbye to Heidi and my beautiful daughter Grace, who looked so sweet in her little crib, and left Sussex for London. En route I'd planned to see Riley and Natalie at their mum's house in Greenwich. I had to stop the car on the A21 to be sick at the side of the road. It was as if I had a Norman helmet on my head, it was so painful. I knocked on their door in Greenwich and waited. The door opened and there was Cindy. I walked in and cried in her arms. I was overwhelmed with sadness; I was leaving home again and abandoning my children for the shelter of a few more beers and some American fans.

In my pocket was the number of another good friend, Chris

Briggs. I called him and he called Barnaby. This was how it worked; the sober army were out to get me. In Barnaby's car, going around the roundabout on Blackheath, he called Squeeze's manager John Lay and told him I wouldn't be going to the States with the band, who were at Heathrow, waiting for me. Then he called PROMIS. Two days later and I was in a very different group, with tears rolling down my face – sweet and salty tears of hope and regret. Over the years my drinking had got slowly worse and my inability to communicate was choking all my relationships, including with Heidi. It was growing on me like a beard, and by the time I fell into PROMIS, it was way down to my knees. I could not feel the emptiness because that was all I knew; I could not feel the loneliness because that was exactly how I wanted to be. The darkness was like treacle, I could not move for its attraction and sweet taste; I wanted nothing more than more of the same each day. Chasing the hangover around the room was never much fun, but once I caught up with it I was back on target in the frame for another bullseye of red wine, cocaine and beer.

Every drunk's story is different. There are a few obvious similarities, but each of us builds slowly to our fall. Mine started when I was eighteen years old, and without a day off for good behaviour it slowly ploughed on until I was thirty-eight and on the ropes. My first drink was harmless enough: a few pints at The Sun in the Sands in Blackheath with my brother Les. The taste and the way it made me feel lifted me from my teenage angst and propelled me into being a young man. Within a few years I had to drink, I thought, to get to sleep, and along with the smoke and the crafty drugs I was building into a nice long progressive overture of darkness. On tour I drank at first with everyone else as part of the crowd, the payoff to a good gig, which we always had. Then it took on more of a central role. My whole day would be geared around the brew; it was pivotal that nothing got in its way. Hangover followed sound check followed show followed drink, and then back in my room the secret bottles of booze, wine and sometimes vodka. The cocaine drifted like snow on the mountains of insecurity that it conjured up on a daily basis, again some of it secretive. It changed my mood, made me even more devious than normal, and destructive.

It was fun at the time, or so I thought. Staying up late on my own was dangerous. I found myself falling into bad habits and making perfectly easy relationships very complicated, especially with people I loved, like Glenn and Cindy, and in the end Heidi too. I stacked up dark clouds above my head that were fed by hours of dedicated drug-taking and wine-glugging. I was not that nice and I'm so sorry that for so long I caused people such deep hurt. Having been there and done that it was now time to understand who I was, and why I had let myself down in such a way. It was not so much the amount of drink and drugs I took, it was more the way they made me feel and how I reacted to them, given that I have always been prone to the darker feelings of the soul. My imagination can lock me in, it can drug me and fold me over. It was time to put my cards on the table, the few I had left. I had become stuffed with sadness, but at last I was being unpacked.

I wasn't allowed a phone call for a week. I couldn't see Heidi for a week. I just stewed. Squeeze toured on until the end of August, and every now and then I would get reports of what was happening: the usual madness, but this time augmented by the addition of Steve Nieve and Pete Thomas, who were devils with good intentions. This is from a local paper that reviewed a show: 'Guitarist-vocalist Glenn Tilbrook popped out onstage first for a solo rendition of "Pulling Mussels (from the Shell)" and then was joined by regular bassist Keith Wilkinson, keyboardist Steve Nieve and drummer Pete Thomas. Notably missing was guitarist and lyricist Chris Difford – the Lennon to Tilbrook's McCartney. Who, in Tilbrook's words, "ate a piece of bad fish".' Not only had I eaten some bad fish, but I was breaking bread with a bunch of people who would change my life for ever – a day at a time. I was sharing a room – with a Japanese diplomat addicted to sleeping tablets and the drummer from a world-famous 1970s rock band – and sharing my feelings. Feelings I'd no idea I had. I was surrounded by like-minded people, and for the first time, I felt loved and understood as an addict. I was safe.

The only communication you could have was from a phone box under the stairs; it would only accept calls in. The first call I got was from David Enthoven; he simply said, 'Got ya!' and laughed loudly down the phone. I fell into his laughter. I'd done the right thing – I knew I had. I'd been feeling guilty about missing the tour, but it soon passed. My career could be put on hold while I sorted myself out, and luckily the band were hugely sympathetic. They wrote to me almost every day from the tour. I was so grateful. They were having fun without me, but I knew I was in the right place. Miles was slipping into the background again, but I was fond of John Lay and happy for him to take a larger role. John handled the whole thing with dignity and understanding.

Rehab was a strict regime. Up at 6.30 a.m. for prayers and readings, breakfast and group therapy. There was a break, then another group before lunch. Afternoons were spent in small groups, then in workshops or psychodramas, which I felt nervous about at first, but which ended up making me inquisitive about myself. Family day was on Sunday. Heidi would come with Grace, or my dad would arrive with my brothers. It was awkward (my dad thought I was in a nuthouse and kept making jokes about straitjackets) and I was pleased when they left so I could get back into the pain and anger groups.

The head counsellor was called Beechy. He was a softly spoken man from Belfast, and was so clever with his workshops. He got people to gently let their feelings be realised, and he cunningly used music and visualisation to open us up. 'I Can't Make You Love Me' by Bonnie Raitt did it for me – it cracked me in two. I was in pieces the day he played it to me while asking how I felt about my family. Psychodrama work is extremely skilled; some people are opened up but can't be put back together again. It scars them. There's a rhythm to it. You go around the room and find someone who's feeling emotional and ready to open up. It's like a Mike Leigh play; there's no script, but you know that in the last twenty minutes you've got to bring the person back and give them affirmation. Often sessions would end with someone lying on the floor with everyone laying hands on them to leave them stronger.

As well as the psychodramas, we had groups that dealt with our various other personal issues. One of the things I had to deal with as an addict was my secrecy. My secret life was incredible, a dizzy out-of-kilter balance of reality intertwined with a furtive imagination. I was ducking and diving between the two. It was put to me that I should let go of my secret life in favour of a more honest relationship with myself. I revealed to the group one afternoon that I had been keeping in contact with a girl I had once met in Boston. We communicated by way of letter-writing and the odd meeting here, there and on various tours. I really liked her; she was calm and wrote to me with such love in dark moments. It was time to let her go. When I next flew to LA, we arranged to meet for lunch. I had made up my mind to say goodbye to her. She beat me to it; she revealed she was getting married. It was over, and we were both free. We have never been back in contact and she remains very firmly in the fairy tale of my past.

One secret down, many more to go. The addict loves a secret, but they can be the death of good friendships and often marriages. It was a tough lesson to learn so early on in sobriety. A secret world provides many things; it fuels the imagination and has me walking a tightrope above the gasping, frustrated people below me. It takes me back to my childhood, where it all began, where the imagination first leapt into action. There is nowhere to hide when you are in rehab and all of your emotions and behaviours are being observed by eagle-eyed counsellors. One morning every-one seems in good spirits in the group, smiles are exchanged and a general hum of friendships vibrates from chair to chair. Then in walk two of the counsellors, who put two chairs in the middle of the room and ask us one by one to take a seat. We take it in turns to sit back to back. For five minutes you have to sit and listen while the person behind you tells you exactly what they think of you, followed by a brief affirmation. And then it's your turn. It's so hard to say what you feel about someone, but they can't respond: they have to sit in silence as you speak your mind. It seemed like the whole group hated each other; it was just like being in a band but without the honesty. By the end of the day everyone seemed closer and on a more even level of emotional captivity. I tried to

imagine this happening on a tour bus in the middle of a tour. It
would be murder, but then touring is not recovery. I was up to my
ears in treatment, recovery, psychodramas and meetings. Then
there was a phone call from the box under the stairs. It was John
Lay, calling from the States to tell me that Maxine had passed
away. I walked into the front room of the house and cried like a
baby. My roommate, Simon, gave me a cup of tea, and to this day
I can still taste it on my lips. The next day we did a workshop on
'the passing of Maxine'. One of the counsellors, Philip Bacon, put
a red velvet cushion in the middle of the room, telling us that it
was Maxine and this was my chance to say goodbye and to tell
her how I felt about her. At the end, a jug of water was passed
around and everyone's glass was filled. They all lifted the glasses
up to their heads, said a prayer and put the water back in the jug. I
then poured a full glass containing everyone's affirmations, which
I drank down. It was so moving; so perfect. My counsellor let me
go to the funeral at the church in Benenden, and there were all
her friends and family. It was a service full of love, as befitted her.
Jools played the piano. Sadly Glenn was still on tour in America
– the tour I was meant to be on – and couldn't be there. The fact
that I wasn't with him and the band made me feel awkward and
guilty, but in Maxine's passing I found the strength to know I'd
done the right thing.

At the wake, her mother hobbled about on her crutches and
took hugs from everyone, which she embraced with a whisky kiss
and a sob of great control and gesture. She'd lost her husband
Felix just before Maxine died and was now grieving the loss of
her two most beloved people. 'Darling,' she said. 'Give me a kiss.
She always loved you so very much.' Anthea never gave up the

fags, the afternoon nap or the whisky. I went to visit her several times after Maxine died. She always managed to greet me with a big hairy kiss and a 'Darling, how nice to see you!' Behind her baggy red eyes was the love of youth and days gone by. Radio 3 was always on in the background. She gave me some pictures and press cuttings she'd kept of the early Squeeze days. I was so grateful. Her head tilted to one side as we sat and talked about Maxine and how wonderful life had been; about Felix and Benenden. She died shortly afterwards. It was so sad. The family were moving on, and their world was passed down to their son Kent, who looks after it all now with such great care. After a walk to Maxine's grave, I got in the car and was driven back to PROMIS, where I dedicated my sobriety to her – and still do. Because without her in my life, there'd have been no songs about people who live in Clapham. Of course I placed the ad in the shop window, which was how we found each other, but she made the connection – no one else did. And nobody else held it in their hands like she did. That ad in the sweet shop window cost me 50p, and from that I have my whole life, my children and my future. A 50p I had stolen from my mother's purse. It stuns me when I think about the path I might have taken had we not come together. So I thank Maxine, as the keeper of the keys that unlocked my small and complicated world.

Beechy had me in his office one day and told me I might need a sponsor. The phone in his hand was given to me, and on the other end was Elton John. I couldn't believe it. Just the evening before I'd been listening to him on the radio, and 'Someone Saved My Life Tonight' and 'Don't Let the Sun Go Down on Me' had reduced me to tears in the back of the minibus that took us to meetings in

Dover and Canterbury. It was he who'd first pulled the trigger on my addiction back in that hotel in San Jose. Elton said he would look after me and that I was to call him every day without fail or he'd rip my head off. I was beside myself. We were in daily contact for the whole of that first year.

Immediately after coming out of PROMIS, I was on a pink cloud. I went to AA meetings three times a week. Rehab is like a bandage – you can put it over the wound, but you still have to heal the wound afterwards. The hard work comes later. Luckily, I lived near a fantastic meeting at St Mary's Church in Rye. It was such a great, strong group of men and women, and we all supported each other. Sometime later, in 1993, Elton played at Earl's Court for two nights to raise money for his AIDS foundation. I went along to meet him for the first time. We'd talked daily on the phone since he first called me at PROMIS, but we'd never come face to face before – though I had seen him play back in 1974. I arrived backstage two hours before the show. A square of Portakabins served as dressing rooms and Astroturf had been laid down in front of them. A few tables were set up on the fake grass and generally the atmosphere was homely – or as homely as backstage at a gig can ever be. Elton was dressed in blue shorts. He was no taller than me, and for the first thirty seconds of our meeting, I tried to stop myself from gawping at him like some star-struck fan. We got along very well. We talked in a backstage kind of way – very short paragraphs about how things were, what was going on.

Elton and his friends tried to make me feel at home, but I felt very out of place most of the time. There were all these very wealthy people milling about, and here was I, insolvent and wearing a worn-out suit as best as I could. The backstage zoo consisted of some very exotic creatures, from Joan Collins to Stephen Fry. Paul Young was there too – it was good to see him again. His youthful face had dropped since the last time I'd seen him, six years ago; the grey hair had found a home on his head, as it had, no doubt, on mine. Elton's close friend John was a lovely chap who ushered me around and never let me stand alone in a crowd. His brother James was just as polite. They came from Chapel Hill in North Carolina, where Squeeze had played in the past, so we talked about their love for the band, about Chapel Hill and about Joan Collins.

It was a long night; the show was two and a half hours. It was a re-education in the talents of Elton. His piano-playing was much better than I remembered it to be, and his voice was powerful. 'Don't Let the Sun Go Down on Me' sent a shiver through the 16,000 people in the crowd and the chill bolted down my spine, bringing a welling of tears to my eyes. It is such a fantastic song. In my car on the way home, Radio 1 broadcast the concert. I turned it up loud and cruised back to Rye on a high of satisfaction. After that, I went to Elton's house, we went to meetings together, I went to his shows. He inspired me so much to keep coming back, because it does happen if you work it. Being sober isn't easy when the world around you mostly drinks, but in time it becomes a way of life. Elton had meetings each Sunday at his home in Windsor. It was a large, warm and friendly house with a well-stocked garden and grounds; indoors, rose candles burned in every room and flowers lit up every corner. The meetings were strong and afterwards there was Sunday lunch.

One night Elton called me and asked if I could send him some words – he told me what the brief was and gave me his fax number. I went to my office and looked out of the window toward the sky. I was in my happy place; the place where words are gifted to me. I sent the lyric over to him, and the next day he called and invited me to his home. He placed the fax on a piano and the song, 'Duets for One', was written in about three minutes flat. I stood behind him wondering if this was really happening to me. It was. We drove over to a studio he had close by, where a band that included Chris Rea was waiting, and the song was played through and recorded in about half an hour. I was in heaven. The song can be found on Elton's *Duets* album; it's the only one he sings on his own. I felt blessed.

The one-day-at-a-time mantra suits me – I like taking it slow, seeing what each day can reveal. I open my arms and life walks in. When I feel weak, I return to the meetings and to the places where I got well. I'm never far from either. Today I like to work with sober or like-minded people, and I find drinking as a culture ugly and unfriendly. If I'm in a room with someone who has been drinking, I have to make my excuses. But it seems that the music industry has changed over the past fifteen years, and more and more people shy away from the drinking culture, the drug abuse and the darker corners of stardom.

Younger people naturally have a need to push their boundaries, and alcohol can help break down the walls of communication. And for a time, it worked for me. So I understand the good-time person who hasn't got the same issues as I have – he can dance and drink, he can be in a happy place. It's just not my happy place. As a drinker, I never had a day off; it was a constant dedication and commitment. I was always thinking about the next drink or planning the next secretive meeting with someone who could feed my addiction. I really enjoyed my time in the headlights. I regret not a single day. Though the happiness has been tinged with darkness, it's got me to where I am today.

The order of sobriety is a simple one: it's keeping it in the day, making sure you come back and sticking with the winners – those who are sober and in a good place. And I feel so grateful to have discovered this way of life, for without it I would be a very different person. One drink was never enough for me, and the energy I put into being a drinker was enormous – more than I'd put into anything else in my life. Everything took second place: the band, being a father, being me. Slowly I listened to the advice I was being given and in time the order fell into place. I was one of the lucky ones. To be in rehab is a very privileged place to be; most people have to find the light from AA meetings alone, which must be a struggle. I can't describe the feelings I'd found; they were open and full of life and colour. One-day-at-a-time is a mantra that most people now have heard of, but you don't hear it so clearly when you are blinded and deafened by the drinking that rules your life and emotions. Drinking can be fun and most normal people have healthy drinking habits. Sadly I can't be one of those. Nonington was a wonderful place to get sober, and in the Kent countryside I felt the cushion of love soften my fall, providing me with the simple steps that would guide me for the rest of my life.

ROYAL PARADE MEWS

The first thing that struck me about being sober was that I could read my watch – when I was drinking, my hand would shake so much I had to guess the time. I was enjoying life again, and when the band came back from the 1992 tour, Glenn called me at PROMIS to see how I was doing. He sounded happy for me. We had a meeting in London, so I picked him up in my car en route from Rye and he quizzed me all the way into town. He was inquisitive in an understanding way. I was hopeful the heavy penny might drop for him, but then I wanted to convert everyone to this new way of life – over the years I've learnt that it works through attraction rather than promotion. Glenn was supportive of my recovery and was very kind. He kept his drinking to himself and the parties he loved out of my earshot, which was very respectful.

By the end of the year we were in the studio – the one that Glenn had built on Royal Parade Mews in Blackheath. It was small, compact and homespun; it was Glenn in every way. At first I was uncomfortable there, but soon I was feeling relaxed and at home myself. It was situated above an alleyway in which rats would run between the bins at the back doors of the local restaurants. There was a long mixing desk and boxes of leads everywhere. This was

Glenn's shed. Glenn would be busy with gaffer tape and T-shirts, as he and Pete Thomas tried to deaden the sound in the room in which the drums were set up. From the outside, looking in through the window, the studio must have looked like a shop on Carnaby Street. Old tour T-shirts hung in rows, like a museum to the years of Squeeze that lay behind us. I could look at them and see my life stretched out in cotton. It was touches like these that made this very much Glenn's studio – a nest of tidy bits and bobs, hundreds of LPs and old copies of *NME* and *Melody Maker*.

He was happy in his new home and I was more than happy in mine. I was going to AA meetings and aftercare, and generally managing myself well. But once in the studio, I was sprung back into a place of mismanagement, a place of shared misunderstandings. When you get six-year-old boys together in a playground, you often find a leader, a scapegoat, a bully, a joker and a pleaser. Add thirty-five years and you find those same boys at a recording session in Blackheath. As well as Glenn and me, there was Keith Wilkinson on bass and Paul Carrack back on keyboards which was a nice surprise. Pete Thomas, who'd played drums for Elvis Costello when we toured with The Attractions, was now in the band – he was the only drummer I've ever worked with to call me before an album and ask to see the lyrics. We had the greatest line-up and Pete was a brilliant addition to the band; a very safe pair of hands.

The album was co-produced by Pete Smith, a cockney sparrow who'd worked with Sting on his *Dream of the Blue Turtles* album. He was fun to be around – as was his drumming namesake – so the atmosphere was generally buoyant, but he was also forthright and incredibly driven; his ear was well tuned and he took no prisoners, particularly when he thought he was right about something. Sadly Glenn was exactly the same, and the two of them often clashed. The songs were hard to arrange, as we all had strong opinions about how they should sound, and we spent hours working out feel and pace, often chasing our tails. It was Glenn's studio, so he stayed back and fiddled after we'd all gone home.

My drive back to Rye took more than an hour, so I was in the car for upwards of two hours each day with just my friend the radio for company. I was really enjoying writing again, and ideas seemed to flow when I was behind the wheel. I wrote 'Loving You Tonight' on the A268 on my way home one evening, and 'Cold Shoulder' was also written in the car. It was raining so hard that I pulled over and went into a church to scribble down the lyrics I had in my head. My notebooks were brimming with words, colours and ideas. Sobriety offered so much creativity and hope.

Sunlight streamed through the windows of the studio where five went mad about recording, and mad about getting it right. The heat was turned up as we pulled arrangements around like a pack of wolves over a skinny carcass. We tugged verse and chorus to and fro. Long faces melted into smiles, though happiness could quickly turn into furrowed brows. Strangely, though, there seemed to be little tension. That could be because we all had the same goal in mind. Success. A hit. *Top of the Pops*, the glory of which was fading at this point but still worth a punt. Big stages that stretched around the world, and food and water for our families.

'Third Rail' became the first single and we all had fun recording a video for it on the Tenterden steam railway down in Kent. The song shivers in the shadows of 'Is That Love' but still packs a punch. The big song on the record, though, was 'Some Fantastic

Place', inspired by Maxine's death. The first few lines were written at my desk in PROMIS, the rest on my kids' school desk in the playroom at my house in Rye. I cried when Glenn first played me the song; it was beautiful. Cunningly, he'd lifted the guitar solo from a tune we'd written together when we lived in Max's house in 1973. Another gift. The song has to be one of my proudest moments. It was as if Maxine had come into my soul to write the words. It was a truly spiritual experience. Delicately we sculpted our way around this song, as it meant so very much to us. We both loved Maxine and we wanted to do 'Some Fantastic Place' justice. Glenn and I often come from very different corners of the spectrum, but for this song we met in the middle and came up with something that would evoke the love that she – our closest friend – gave to us.

At home the weekends would fly by. Being there with the kids around meant that time never had a chance to stand still – Monday would come even though Friday wasn't quite finished with. Riley and I played a lot of football. He loved to come to the house. He would play with Grace, and with Sybil, our bull mastiff, as though he lived there all the time – and I wished he did. Natalie also loved to come and see Grace, and she loved the house and all the freedom she had to roam there. I was never happier than when all three of them were in the garden running around with each other.

Miles Copeland was somehow still lurking around the perimeter fence of Squeeze trying to manage the band. He'd signed Keith our bass player to a publishing deal and then persuaded us to have one of his songs on our record, a song that did nothing for me. Glenn was more understanding than me and helped him work through its recording. I was still really happy with the album. Bob Clearmountain, who'd worked on Bruce Springsteen's *Born in the USA*, flew over from LA to mix it all at Real World Studios near Bath, where we'd recorded *Play* a few years earlier. It was such an idyllic location, nestled down in a lovely little village called Box. The food was amazing, the river ran beneath the studio floor and there were ducks on the pond. You could see them from the mixing desk. It cost a fortune, but it was worth it.

Glenn had co-produced with Pete Smith, and all of his hard work was rewarded in the sound and arrangements of the record. I will never forget the thrill I got listening to the album on the A21, driving back home after the last day of mixing. My car has always been the best place to listen to music, it's my stereo on wheels and I bathed in the album's glory on that sunny drive. Glenn has always been closer to the songs and the production than I have, that's not my skill. It takes a tidy mind to listen and balance the nuances of each song. I don't think I've ever wanted to produce records, but Glenn has always been there at the sharp end of the ship, painting with his musical palette of many colours.

That summer Glenn and I were invited to play at part of the Phonogram Records convention by our loving A&M MD Howard Burman. The *Devon Belle* river boat cast off and headed upstream for a night of handshakes and cold salmon along the River Dart in Devon. The firmest handshake belonged to the head of Our Price Records; my hand was squashed like a melted KitKat in his grip. I was warned that it might be hell, but that it would be a good thing for us to do. Out on the upper deck tales of the riverbank were exchanged, and we slowly mingled with the mainly male population of executives. Only a handful of women were spotted on board. Then after the buffet and chat it was time for us to play.

'A&M without Squeeze would be like A&M without its trumpet,' Howard proudly announced. Howard was a nice enough chap but really never filled me with any confidence as an MD. Unplugged and in front of the heads of this, that and the other, we blew our very own trumpet: our songs. We played six numbers to a warm, respectful crowd who encouraged us back for an encore, not that it takes much to do that. We had just arrived back alongside the dock as we strummed the final chords of 'Tempted'. What a relief. It was a miracle that I got through the set – I had zero confidence. Being back in the promotional saddle reminded me of how much I hated it, playing largely to people who are too busy thinking about themselves and what's in it for them. If it were a board game I would always try and miss this square out.

Maurice Oberstein, the head of Sony, made the evening for me by reflecting on the days when he once came to see Squeeze play circa 1977, and remembering smugly that he didn't sign us then as he knew that we would never make it. The skin on Howard's face visibly dropped into his beer. I was newly sober and to me this really felt like hell, record company hell. Squeeze was, and still is, a business like the corner shop, and we needed to bear that in mind as we weaved our way from album to album, and from tour to tour. So evenings like this could only do us good, as even in our matured years we still needed to convince the people upstairs in the record company that we are worth our salt. Back on dry land I ran for my car.

The following night we were on stage at The Inn On The Park in St Helier, Jersey, to a sell-out audience who were crammed up against the stage. 'Smashy' the DJ, with all the nauseating presence of a chihuahua, introduced us, and on we bounced into the lions' den to play our first date of the Some Fantastic Tour. It was loud and fun; our set consisted of seven new songs and a random selection of old chestnuts. The first encore was packed full of them, glowing and pulsating for the eager sweating crowd. Paul Carrack sang and played with great soul and confidence, it was so great to have him back in the band. Behind me on drums, Pete Thomas kept the whole thing pegged to the floor, the finest of song drummers. Keith Wilkinson and Glenn smiled a lot, grooving on the club atmosphere, it was good to be playing again. Technical problems can often throw all best intentions out of the window, and I had a few that night. There we were playing what our fans like best, the ones they know. However, the new songs found comfortable ground within the set and went down equally well. We had attracted some people with their baseball caps on the wrong way, they gave us the old swinging arm treatment, even on the slow songs like 'Cold Shoulder', a valiant show of appreciation, but then this was the Channel Islands.

All the greats had played there before us. Gerry and the Pacemakers, Stan Boardman and Lindisfarne, to mention a few. Was the scampi-in-the-basket circuit just around the corner, I wondered. Back at the hotel I got on my knees and prayed. On the way home I took the catamaran across the Channel, plain sailing all except for the piped music, 'Tubular Bells'. It created a soundtrack for my tiny but imaginative mind; I found myself in a movie along with people of all shapes and sizes who lived in little worlds all apart from one another.

When the time came to disembark and collect luggage, they all came together to fight for their places next to the six-foot stretch of carousel. Four hundred people all in one or another stage of being animal and all I dislike about crowds. I waded in elbows out and retrieved my bags as they passed by. The hairs on my face grew by the minute until I was safely in my car, another place of refuge. I turned on the radio and there we were, our new single 'Some Fantastic Place' in all four speakers, sounding wonderful. We were back.

Touring and promoting the album felt like a new lease of life with me being sober; I started to really enjoy the ebb and flow of our show from a new angle, a new head space. Playing live was always fun, the circus life we led was very comfortable. We were fed and watered at each show after the sound check, our washing was taken care of, all we had to do was prance about, try to look good and keep time. It's a doddle being in a band when things are going well.

On stage one night in Bristol the band were on top form, with my funny legs bending back and forth across the stage; Glenn sang like he was in heaven and we hit the audience between the eyes. In the second encore after 'How Long' I introduced the ace up our sleeve. 'We have had many keyboard players in our time, Jools Holland, Don Snow, Paul Carrack . . . Please welcome Elton John!' The crowd looked at me as if I were joking and near silence fell on the hall, followed rapidly by a huge roar as Elton sat at the piano and started playing the opening riff to 'I Heard it Through the Grapevine'. I too was in heaven. We then launched into 'I Saw Her Standing There' and the place went nuts. When I looked around the stage the ecstasy on people's faces was so pleasing to see, not a grumpy jowl in sight. After the show it was hard to contain my excitement, hugs all round in the dreary dressing room. Elton really enjoyed it too, praising Glenn up and down the hall and shaking Paul's hand with true admiration. Outside in his car I heard tracks from his new album, which practically blew me away – with sixteen speakers blasting out it was hard to remain in my soft leather seat. I felt like a little boy who had just climbed into a car for the very first time with my legs dangling down. What I heard was very special, my emotions were tickled to the roots. Elton sings with such great power and confidence; he was on full throttle with this new album. I felt very privileged.

The next day in the local paper we were front-page news, with a huge picture of his nibs at the piano. The new album *Some Fantastic Place* was soon sold out in the Our Price down the road from the Colston Hall. Bristol was suddenly our kind of town. The same day Elton had been out to his local record shop to buy up all stocks of the album to give to his friends, so we might get a chart position yet. Touring was special again for me, I really loved it: the atmosphere seemed new and exciting. The sobriety I had been working on definitely helped open the valves of appreciation, and with a good sponsor and regular meetings I was doing well. I lost weight and looked trim in a nice stage suit. All I had to do was keep the emotional ball in the air.

We then took the album to Japan for the first time on a short but very successful tour. Sadly, Paul Carrack couldn't come with us so we took Andy Metcalf instead, a man who liked to party and play well for his supper. Japan was so interesting, and the first thing I wanted to do was find an AA meeting. My old roommate from PROMIS met me in Tokyo and took me to an English-speaking meeting, it was hard to concentrate as the savage jetlag was hounding me to sleep. I flew with my friend Chris Topham who was captain of my Virgin flight. I first met Chris in Norfolk, Virginia many years before when he flew as an RAF pilot on an F16 with his mate stumbling Lou. They were top gun in every sense of the word. Chris is such a big music fan and these days he still flies for Virgin but he also finds time to run a vinyl record label.

On the flight to Tokyo I sat up the front with him as we flew across Russia for hours on end. The turbulence scared me but he had his feet up reading the newspaper. I found it all reassuring but terrifying at the same time. These days being in the cockpit is of course impossible.

The tour around Japan lasted about ten days, it was an eye opener and very calming as we visited the temples and sushi bars of each city we visited. The audiences were passionate and loved to involve themselves in our songs, it was orderly and brilliant. The flight home, without Chris to cuddle up to, was not so brilliant. The turbulence still vibrates in my consciousness today. I loved the gadget shops in Reppongi but wrestled with the constant promotion schedule that was timed to the minute, each day all day. I managed to find some lovely gifts for Grace in a department store one afternoon when the building started to shake: it was an earthquake. I'm not sure how big it was, but it was enough for me to stand and shiver while shoes in racks moved about and comedy music was piped through the intercom to calm the nervous shoppers. We were well looked after in Japan, it was a great experience, I just wish it wasn't so far away or I would visit more often.

It was a busy year for us promoting the album and we gave it everything we could but there were things to deal with in our own lives; it was tricky to balance home and work. *Some Fantastic Place* was a huge hit for us. Elton bought twenty copies for his various homes and cars, and we had rave reviews in Q magazine and *Mojo*; musically we were back in the saddle. Paul Carrack then left for more solo work, and Pete Thomas went back to Elvis's commitments on tour and in the studio. I was sad to see them both leave. The next year Glenn got divorced from Pam – there were some tiny hats in the air around Blackheath in celebration – and the following year married a lovely woman called Jane, who was a schoolteacher. Their wedding was down at Huntsham Court in Devon. Huntsham was a place that had become a drinking hole for me over the years, a dark Gothic hotel set in the red Devon soil. The sun shone for them on that lovely day, which was nice to see, and the air was thick with old faces. Glenn settled into a new life in a different tempo from the one before, and seemed happier for it. He then became a father for the first time, a wonderful thing for any young man. We both seemed to be in a good place.

In 1994, I went on my first writers' retreat, as a guest of Miles Copeland at Chateau Marouatte in France, a grand purchase he had made mainly from Police royalties. I drove down in my Saab, of which I had a total of fifteen over time, and was very nervous. But once inside the castle walls I was relieved to find friendly faces. Twenty writers from all over the world gathered in one place to write songs; it seemed magical.

Miles made each group work with one of his writers – of course he did. I had a nice room in the main tower with a sloping floor and a grand four-poster bed. I wrote with Alannah Myles on the first day. She insisted on lighting frankincense and the room filled with a mystical fog, so much so that I couldn't see her across the table. A crap song ensued.

Cher was joining us the following day, and when she arrived, Miles showed her the rooms around the castle. She chose mine to move into, so I moved out, but not without first taking with me the peg of wood that kept the bed steady on the sloping floor. Cher ruled the roost and chose who she wanted to work with. I got on really well with Patty Smyth, a lovely person with a great voice, who spoke the same new language as me, both of us being sober. She was dating John McEnroe and they were going to get married. I kept in touch and later that year I met up with her in New York.

Driving back through France after the retreat I thought, 'I could do that – I could run my own workshop.' So I called my publisher EMI and organised a week down at Huntsham Court in Devon. It was filled with talent – Suggs, Kirsty MacColl, Lamont Dozier, Graham Gouldman, Cathy Dennis and Gary Clark to mention just a few. Some great songs came out of that week. I have been running songwriters' retreats for twenty-five years now, sometimes twice a year. We moved location from Devon to Kent, to Italy and back to Devon and then Wales, mostly in old houses, or hotels. I love the writers' weeks. I've never made a bean from them, but it's a worthwhile thing to do. Recently I have been running them in Glastonbury, a stone's throw from the festival site, at Pennard House, an eccentric and wonderfully run place. The Buddy Holly Foundation now fund the event, and it has established itself as one of the leading writing camps in the UK. Peter Bradley helps me put the show on the road, along with the ever-so-whispering Bob Harris and his lovely wife Trudie. We had forty-two writers caress our retreat with some amazing songs in 2017. I felt so moved and proud to have reached the milestone of the 25th year. Pennard House is a very special location and the event seems to grow and grow with each year, like the roses in its beautiful garden. I'm so proud of all the songs that have been written at the retreats down the years. It's more about the friendships made than the songs. The songs are merely stepping-stones, hopefully to lasting relationships between the writers who attend.

One of the most interesting writers' weeks I have worked on was on Cunard's *Queen Mary 2*. I have crossed to New York four times teaching people to write songs. I take with me close friends and fellow writers and together we instil confidence in would-be writers of all ages, but mainly the over-sixties. On the first ever morning at sea I was greeted by 150 punters all keen to learn how to write a song. Thank God I had with me Squeeze drummer Simon Hanson and writers Chris Sheehan and Matt Deighton, among others.

Over the course of the five-day journey to New York we gradually mould songs from blank faces and perform them in the theatre on the last night. It's so much fun. On one crossing we had Roger Daltrey on board. He insisted on having my cabin as it was the largest, which I had no problem with; after all, he is one of my idols. We played a secret show for the crew below decks, which resulted in chaos. Some great songs come from those crossings and it can be very moving. Coming into Manhattan on the deck of the *Queen Mary* is something else, well worth the crossing in whatever the weather. Mostly fog.

GALSWORTHY LODGE

My memories of Miles Copeland are of a man whose first record was 'Wake Up Little Susie' by The Everly Brothers. I can remember him playing it to me in his house in St John's Wood when we first met. We listened to the song together and I watched him being taken to a different place by the harmonies, then he turned and wrote down the expenses for the meal we'd just eaten on a piece of paper. That kind of summed him up. Miles was sacked for the last time just after the touring had finished for *Some Fantastic Place*. He had pushed us too far with his handling of certain issues. He and John Lay went around the same time.

The Police came closest to the success he had imagined for us, but when they broke up, Miles then sold their family silver, and his share of their publishing deals went roughly the same way as ours. I'm still in touch with Sting, who I admire for the way he sees his past as being as important to him as the present. He just acknowledges how Miles played a vital role in his success, but times move on. I'd like our songs back please, but that's just not going to happen. The masters are owned by Universal for the rest of my life. The publishing is with BMG and they won't even talk about readjusting our share more evenly. It's sad really, my kids will never own my songs or benefit from all the hard work, they can never be handed down. All because we signed away our future for £15 a week to a man who doesn't even get a mention on our Wikipedia page.

I think Glenn despises Miles for what he did, but I can't harbour resentments in that way; it's done, we move on. Yes, he groomed us expertly. He was a devious manager, unlike Shep, unlike Jake and certainly unlike David. Miles now manages a troop of belly dancers. I think that says everything we need to know about karma.

So with Miles out of the picture it was time to think again. Step this way, new manager Paul Toogood. Paul took the role on for a year and made a hash of the VAT payments, so he went too. He would drink tea with me and beer with Glenn. It's a shame it never worked out.

We ploughed on with another album, another new band. Keith Wilkinson was still on bass, but we now had Kevin Wilkinson (no relation) on drums, with the keyboards open to session. Kevin's drinking was even slyer than mine used to be – he knocked them back in secret but always delivered a great show. Pete Smith was still on board as a producer. It was a small miracle. *Ridiculous* felt like an extension of the previous album, though the songs were harder to come by. Again we spent days pulling teeth over the arrangements. The album was rich with layers of sound, but the hits had to be torn from our hands. 'Electric Trains' was a powerful song we were proud of, while 'This Summer' was a dead ringer for 'Sunday Street' on our *Play* album. Danny Baker championed the song on London Radio but that was the extent of the album's radio appearances. Another Keith Wilkinson song and the album was complete – a complete extension of where we'd already been.

Were we repeating ourselves? Who cared? A&M cared enough to keep fussing with the mixes and treating us like possible new wave pop stars, which we were not. Some of the songs were mixed in Sweden – the obvious place to mix a Difford and Tilbrook song – and Glenn and I weren't even consulted. It cost us a fortune. A poor show all round. Things were in decline; the music industry was hanging on to anything it could find to keep its apparent greed alive. Britpop was one such animal, and we were soon to be hailed as its ambassadors. Oasis were huge, Blur were at the fun end of the stick but we seemed to be hanging around like confetti left on the church floor after a wedding. We even tried to write in that Britpop style; we were clearly clutching at straws.

Touring was amazing fun, though. It was all starting to feel very grown-up – especially with the likes of Kevin Wilkinson and former Sly and the Family Stone member Andy Newmark on the revolving drum stool. We had already done a tour of full acoustic shows during this period with Aimee Mann and Paul Carrack, which threw up some lovely moments in faraway places. Aimee was so much fun to work with; she carried an air of intelligence about her that was mixed with deep and clever humour. We recorded with her in London at Konk Studios, owned by The Kinks. I sang on a couple of songs, as did Glenn; one song he sang on I think was about him, which was very odd. Aimee was easy to love as a friend and we got on really well.

For the first time in my life on that tour I felt as though I could play the guitar properly. For many years I'd had a default setting, which was 'bluff'. I managed to get through the songs with just enough accuracy to not upset Glenn – though he often held me up to the light for not paying enough attention. Glenn's always been a very good teacher, but I'm not a very good student. And perhaps I couldn't hear what he was trying to say because it was him saying it. He has always been so patient with me. Over the years my playing had been at best muddy. Gilson used to call me pork-chop fingers and in the studio most of my guitar parts would be replaced as Glenn always felt he could play them better. I'm not even sure if I feature on any of our albums up to *Some Fantastic Place*. There are some background parts on *Frank*, but most of what you hear on there is Glenn.

Early in 1995 Elton called me and asked if I would like to come over to listen to his new album called *Made in England*. I drove over the next morning very excited to hear the new record. En route I was bursting for a wee, however there were no services at that time on the M25 in Surrey. I thought I would hold it until I got to his house. As soon as I arrived I was whisked into his Bentley and sat in the front seat. All 200 speakers blasted the new songs at me at high volume and I was suitably impressed. Gradually though my bladder was warning me of imminent danger. I did not have the heart to ask to step out of the car for a toilet break, so I held on. The album rolled on and I found myself distracted in a big way. As the last track skipped by, a song called 'Blessed' which was five minutes long, I felt trouble brewing. At the end of the song he looked at me as if to say, what do you think then? All I could say was could I use the loo – naturally he had no idea that I was in so much pain, almost fainting from the strain of holding in my requirements. Doors slammed and I left out. I was red-faced and totally embarrassed. Relief and a cup of tea followed in the kitchen moments later and, to top it all off, there was Elton wearing Marigolds washing up a few cups. Thank God these days we have the Cobham services on the M25.

A few months later and Squeeze were dropped by our label; A&M passed on us. This was final. Glenn suddenly separated from Jane, which was very sad. He soon found happiness again when he met Suzanne Hunt at one of our rehearsals. She was one of our road crew. Suzanne was a lovely person, easy to talk to, easy to like, and she did a great job on the road for us; she worked hard. I remember well when Glenn met her. We were in New Orleans, and I saw them come into the hotel very early one morning looking happy and embracing. They were like soulmates on two different tour buses that became one. After a few tours Suzanne became the band's manager, which was a natural promotion and as a team they worked well. So much seemed to happen at once. They formed a record label together and had ambitions to take Squeeze and go it alone without the safety net and all the trimmings of a major label. I, on the other hand, wanted to hold on to the umbilical cord that was attached to the major labels and felt we might lose everything.

I was confused and slightly worn out by all the sudden changes. I was also missing the valuable AA meetings which had become the backbone of my sobriety.

At the beginning of 1995 my third daughter Cissy had been born (in a birthing pool in Hastings) and I now wanted more than anything to be at home with my family. I was so happy with that part of my life. Cissy was my pride and joy; she would come everywhere with me, walking the dogs in the woods or into Rye for shopping. Grace was always by our side too; she was a good sister and they seemed to get on well together. Nat and Riley enjoyed the extended family and gave both the girls plenty of cuddles and time to play.

There was an empty barn in my garden at Old House and I decided to build a recording studio, which would be for everyone to use – a chapel of music in the most idyllic spot. Despite Heidi not wanting it there, she eventually became studio manager and helped run it, which she did really well. At the same time, for my sins, I was producing a record for Eddy Grundy from *The Archers* as a favour to my brother Lew who was an avid fan. One afternoon the owner of the studio marched in and said that everything was for sale, as her husband Alvin Lee had deserted her for a younger model. I said I would have the desk, but first I called Alvin who seemed not to care at all. It was meant to be. It was great having such a fine creative space across the lawn with its newly plumbed-in Helios mixing desk from 1971, and lots of old classic equipment besides. It took a few months to build but it was worth it. The studio became a great place for me to co-write, which I did, having been inspired to do so by Maxine. At first it seemed like infidelity and I kept it from Glenn. I was shy; I felt awkward sleeping outside of our marriage. Once I became more comfortable with the idea, though, I was off like a balloon that had been let go.

The recording of the next Squeeze album, *Domino*, was much harder work than the previous two. I sat in Glenn's studio for weeks while he tried to separate oil from water. It must have been so hard for him to read the empty words I had presented to him for the album, I could hardly believe it myself. I think I was well and truly drifting at this point, the passion was waning and the last gasps of a band were being shuffled about on the studio floor. I wanted to be at home, and I wanted to spread my wings above my own nest. Some of the backing tracks from the album were put down at my studio in Sussex and I enjoyed having everyone down to the house. I think it gave us all clear heads after the small confines of Glenn's studio up in London. Once the record was done it came out as *Domino*, as was the plan. There was no money to promote the record and no vision for its release other than touring with yet another new band, which comprised Ash Soan on drums, Hilaire Penda replaced Keith on bass, and on keyboards Jools's little brother Christopher Holland. In retrospect, I'd given up the ghost inside. Ash was a great drummer to work with, but Hilaire – though brilliant – was a complicated jazz player trying to bend his way around simple pop songs.

I didn't enjoy the experience very much, though there are two songs on that record I really love – 'To Be a Dad' is a fine piece of work and 'Without You Here' is a beautiful song that I wrote for Glenn, mindful of the fact that Jane was taking his two sons to live with her in Australia. It was unkind and he was in a great deal of pain.

The rest of the songs were tossed off like pancakes on a less-than-emotional grill. The band had become just Glenn and me, really, and it didn't feel like the full shilling. I had drifted from the dream of being in a band to being almost an employee of a band that was going around in circles. Glenn had these wonderful ideas about change and how the record industry was the enemy. I was holding on to the castle walls as people were being tossed out into the moat. He was right in a way, but it was all going too quickly for me. I was scared to lose what I could not keep. People I knew in the industry were being put out to graze; perhaps he was right.

Glenn always says at that point I left the building, but it was up to him to turn the lights off. We were both heaving the elephant in the room further and further up the hill. I had clearly left the band in my head but just not told anyone about my feelings, mainly because I had lost control of them. If only we had talked things through and been more responsive with each other. Or maybe it was just me. I was prepared to accept that. Glenn had been playing solo shows, and had already put out a solo album that I'd not heard – and at that point I wasn't in a rush to hear it either. I was envious of his new career path but sadly I had no way of communicating how I felt to him. He was in another space and time from me. During the same period, Squeeze had gone through three drummers, two producers, three managers, two bass players, a dozen tour buses and crew. At our peak we had written 'Some Fantastic Place' and at our lowest ebb we'd written a song called 'Bonkers'. Which summed it all up. Being at home with Heidi, Grace and Cissy was now more attractive to me than work, and with the building of my studio I knew I could bring work home with me. The wheels had come off the bus.

The early Nineties were years of lost hope and feelings of unmanageability. I was skating on thin ice all the time and not thinking things through very well. Not even my brother Lew could fathom out the darkness I had found myself in. When music became my life, Lew had supported me – as Les did too. He always came to see Squeeze play and was full of encouragement. I wrote my first poems when I went to stay at his house in Hampshire, where he lived with his wife Christine and their two children Sarah and Simon. I sat by the River Test and scribbled words in my A4 pad; words that became covered in dust before being reborn as song lyrics.

When Squeeze were being managed by David Enthoven, Lew became our accountant. He very cleverly tipped money into a pension for me; he sorted out my tax and helped me invest. He remained my accountant – and Glenn's – until the 1990s. Lew knows more about Squeeze than I do, I think; his constant mining for royalties and who is owed what seems to be a dedication no other accountant could match. He has always been fair and hugely generous with his time. I love my brother. It was hard for him to say no to me though. From my perspective, he was the ideal person to be controlling the chequebook. Cars were the bane of his life and he had to be incredibly patient with me. I almost bought a Bristol one afternoon, but he intervened. He called the garage to tell them I was on day release from prison and wasn't to be trusted. He missed the Maserati, though; it ended up on my driveway at the farm in Rye. Heidi wanted to kill me for buying it as we had no money to pay for food, or the taxman, but Lew cleared up the mess and the car was returned. I managed to sneak another car in the following week.

In the morning, ta-dah, the curtains opened to reveal the gleaming new Maserati. A car I could not even get down our lane or get the kids in! It did not go down well and the addiction went on until I went completely skint. I had no money, but I had a nice car. Heidi was not impressed with my behaviour. I was spending to feel better; it had got out of control. From cars to simple things like DAT players or shortwave radios, which I had many of. Sometimes I would hide things in the boot of the car, and when Heidi went to bed I would sneak them in, hide the boxes they came in, and make them look like I had had them for ages. I flew on Concorde and stayed in all the best hotels; I was out of touch with reality. Heidi and I were at rock bottom and I was lost in a secret world with Squeeze, where my confidence had been kicked into the long grass. My addictive behaviour had begun to creep back in the form of shopping, poor relationships and not standing up for myself. I was reduced to a weak and empty complicated shell – one I couldn't break out of. Again the anxiety grew. I saw yet another tour schedule I couldn't face. Home was a house with many cracks forming in its foundations.

I had stopped going to AA meetings altogether – this was my downfall. That's the lesson we learn in AA and one I always manage to brush aside: the further you drift from it, the more you start falling apart. It's meant to be a bridge to normal living. Some people think they've already reached this, but it's not possible for addicts to do that. After years of sobriety, people assume you're all right, but you need to regularly reconnect to the goodness. I had found the old black dog again, sleeping just underneath my bed. Depression was not visible from the outside, but I felt it from within and in my relationship with Heidi. Things began to drift. I was conning counsellors into thinking I was doing OK in a fifty-five-minute session of hoodwinking, and then leaving with a bombshell. Squeeze were off on tour again, this time on the back of an album I had lost faith in and with a band that was not really Squeeze, although it was full of great people. Steve Maidment, who helped run the studio with me, came to see me off at a hotel close to Heathrow airport. I broke down in tears and kicked the room to pieces as I looked out at the runway in front of me. Steve helped me calm down but could not get me onto the plane. I could not take the pain of separation and the onslaught of what I knew would be a long and possibly difficult tour. I did not get on the plane: I watched it take off and then drove by myself to the gates of The Priory, where I collapsed in a heap on the steps. I was done.

Once at The Priory, my counsellor told me I needed to get back on the programme and work hard on myself. They poured me into their Galsworthy Lodge treatment centre which was on the same grounds as the Priory Hospital. I also needed to find another accountant – my counsellor felt Lew might have been complicit in my actions and I needed someone in charge of my finances who I couldn't manipulate, but I didn't completely agree with him. However, Lew was replaced, but by this time he'd gone to work for Elvis Costello, whose affairs he ran successfully for many years. It was good for our relationship and he was brilliant with Elvis.

In all honesty, Lew had nothing to do with my bad behaviour. I was the guilty party, the one who shopped and stole and lied and cheated his way around. Addiction is a very patient disease; the darkness is right there on my shoulder, waiting for me to creep into a weak and empty place. I was soon on antidepressants. I stayed on them for many years. My time in The Priory was in effect to get me through the depression I had been suffering, and suffering in silence. I was not sharing my concerns or speaking my mind to Glenn or to Heidi about the way I thought things could be; I was just going with the flow. Sometimes the easiest option, but not always the best. I was not speaking my mind; I was not man enough for that. I was on the ropes with myself, and with Glenn I was losing the focus on my creativity. It was so sad. I was all over the place and needed to find my feet again. I had let everybody down, again. Depression came to me in many different disguises. I didn't want to look out and check for the reality around me because I felt safe in its darkness. I felt I had let my children down who were young and at home wondering why, and where I had gone. Riley and Natalie seemed understanding, maybe because they were a little older. They supported me with equal amounts of love when Heidi and I were at each other's throats. It was often tough for them being in the middle and I felt for them. Riley followed in my footsteps a few years later with his own trip into treatment. We ended up supporting each other. Maybe it is a family disease after all.

To go back into rehab meant I had reached a new rock bottom and to prove how mad I was I had dark windows put in on my new car; it was taken away for tinting while I was in The Priory, picked up from the car park and replaced the very next day. I think that sums it all up pretty well, as did my peer group at the time, who raked me over the coals in a Wednesday-afternoon anger group. I was in group therapy all day long, and going in the minibus to meetings in Chelsea and Richmond; four weeks of step work in which I wrote down how bad I felt and where I'd been, then shared it with the group. As at PROMIS, there were good people to hold my hand and there were complicated relationships to unravel – the ones with my brothers, Heidi and Glenn all needed a good seeing-to. One afternoon Pete T came in to visit me. He came in twice more to help me understand what being in a band can do to you; how the relationships born out of youth and a shared vision can, over time, give way to anger, resentment and fear. It was so kind of him to spend those hours with me and I felt very lucky to sit with him – he had been a lifetime idol, and now he was a personal mentor. It was his job I had been after all those years ago when at school, and here he was in front of me: larger than life but softer than I could ever imagine.

The group at Galsworthy did some empty chair work one afternoon. Chairs seem to play a big part in any rehab routine. In this exercise, you place someone you need to speak to in the chair, but they of course are not present. Heidi would not come to therapy so she was in the hot seat. It took some doing to verbalise how I felt. It was painful and, egged on by counsellors and the group, I screamed and shouted, something I never do – I normally prefer the quite life. It was an incredible experience. I repeated the process a few years later at Cottonwood, a workshop in a hotel in London. I went into a long weekend with a fantastic counsellor, Rockelle Lerner: her workshop on letting go of fear really helped me out of a tight emotional spot. The empty chair work she is so skilled in had me reaching deep inside. She broke me down and then built me back up again and it really worked for me. It was similar to the feelings I had during psychodramas back in PROMIS. It hurt but I knew it would do me good.

My time at the Galsworthy was just a sticking plaster over a deep wound. Rehab and weekend retreats can only be this. The real work is achieved in the everyday world. A high wire above the emotional streets below walking between the mother, the sea and the father, the forest, it's a bloody nightmare some days. With the help of anti-depressants, I kept a level head and the word Cipralex became as visible in my bathroom as Colgate.

Glenn came to see me one fine afternoon. It was brave of him, especially as we hadn't seen each other for a long time while he was on tour. There were four of us in the room – two counsellors and Glenn and myself, sitting opposite each other – and though it was a sunny day, I remember Glenn being very frosty. Eventually my counsellor opened up the discussion, which was cordial. Then he got up and left. I wonder whether he came in to get an apology from me. All I really wanted was to be back on stage with him singing from the same hymn sheet, which would come, but not for a long time.

Take two of Squeeze had been everything I never thought it might be, and yet I came out of it with more than I went in with. The most important thing for me was that I had four wonderful children and a lovely house in the Garden of Eden. I was sober and full of hope. I'd said all I had to say lyrically and I was on the point of repetitive overload. Tours were a thing of the past. I found that home and being still gave me what I needed. I wanted very little, but AA meetings had taught me it was important for me to feel included. And in the studio with Glenn, I felt like a piece of the furniture. Squeeze seemed to be over. Naturally Glenn was really upset and hurt. Other than that brief meeting at The Priory, we didn't speak again for the next eight years, at least not with any feeling. We did meet once at Home House in London to discuss a musical I wanted us to write together. Suzanne told me that Glenn didn't have the time to be involved but gave me the freedom to develop the idea. Eventually he came to see a workshop held at Andrew Lloyd Webber's office in London. It didn't really work out as planned and was shelved before it had a chance to be properly developed. A musical is something we both very much want to be part of, but it has to be right. Maybe one day our songs will be heard on the theatrical stage again; it's where some of them belong. After all, there has been so much drama in our lives, it seems only natural that we should find a home somewhere on Shaftesbury Avenue.

OLYMPIA

In 1997 when I first went to meet Bryan Ferry, I was nervous and shaking with fear – which was just how he liked me, as it turned out. I was introduced to him by Squeeze's ex-manager and mentor, David Enthoven, and at first I was employed to help him write songs. 'Lyric doctor' was my full title. His offices were pristine and ran with a quiet hum, everything in its place. There were cupboards full of notepads and Berocca; drawers full of files and files full of photographs. Tour posters leant against the walls. Books were piled neatly on tables – tables that were covered in white blotting paper. Jars full of pencils; cups and saucers, tea-pots and silverware in the kitchen, to one side. Beyond the office, there was his bedroom, bathroom and drawing room, with its grand piano covered in books. Downstairs there was the studio with its antique Trident recording desk; guitars and keyboards – all vintage.

Most of the time Bryan marched around the office finding things for people to do, including me. His style was that of an old school-master, and I liked that about him. His tea was always poured to perfection. And why not? I'd adored his music as a twenty-year-old, obsessing over Roxy Music records. I even took his first solo album, *These Foolish Things*, to a hairdresser in Kensington one day and said I wanted my hair like his, lagoon blue!

It was intelligent pop music and the whole sound of it was so well-crafted and unique. The glam side of me desperately wanted to be part of it all. Every nuance of Bryan's recordings over the years had been thoroughly thought through and I'd been totally in awe of his lyrics and vocal style – which I found so touching. The journey that Bryan took us all on was incredible. It's a style I've tried to emulate many times without success.

In his recording studio was Phil, who ran the mixing desk and chewed pencils. He had the patience of a saint, as did we all. Robin Trower, his guitarist and co-producer, bit his tongue most of the time and clapped loudly in time to the things he liked, like a dad trying to be hip. Alice was nineteen, French and beautiful – she made the tea and filed the photographs. She stayed in a hotel as she hadn't yet got a place to live. Mr F had discovered her in Spain, babysitting a friend's children. She talked on the tracks we recorded in a young, polite and sexy way. Alice was being watched at all times and she knew it. She was no fool. Auntie – Miss Mann – sat by the phone and ordered olives. She was an all-round wonderful woman who'd known Bryan and Roxy all her life; she was part of him in every sense. Without her, the day would crumble. Nigel Puxley, otherwise known as The Doctor, hunched over his Mac, his hair hanging down over his eyes to cover his age and historical drug habit. I wasn't sure what his role was at first, but gradually I understood that he and Bryan went back to the very beginning, and like Auntie he knew where all the bodies were buried.

One of my first days with Bryan involved going to the Dorchester

Hotel, where Sasha, a Russian pop promoter, was waiting with his Orthodox priest. Yes, really. First things first, he asked me to join him for an early-evening Chinese meal. We sat together and ate our food, which he chose, getting to know each other while holding chopsticks. Our first date went well. I was in a black suit with a white-spotted black tie; he was also in a black suit with a white-spotted black tie – we were a strange couple. I drove a Jaguar XK at the time and he loved sitting beside me as we raced around town in the darkness. After the meal, we drove over to Park Lane. The eighth-richest man in Russia, with gold teeth and a whole floor of rooms, was waiting for us. At the hotel door we met his bodyguard, who spoke into his arm and took us into the lift. My car was parked for me. On the fourth floor, the door opened and we were met by another dark-suited man with an earpiece. We were seated in a suite down the hall and told to wait. In came Sasha with another bodyguard and his interpreter, and we shook hands and sat down. Sasha was a big man with a mysterious beaming smile. We watched a DVD of Bryan playing live; he looked awkward. A tray of cold vodka appeared and, being teetotal, I refused. The guard said it would be bad form for me to refuse. I said that if I drank the vodka it might be bad form all round. I took a glass and feigned sipping. Mr F tipped his back with a face like a child taking his medicine. We talked about future shows in Moscow, then in marched two chefs with a chariot of Chinese food. Apparently we were to eat with the Tsar. This was not on my memo. Gingerly tossing rice and giant prawns around our plates, we both tried to look surprised and hungry – which of course we weren't. After a few long hours, we managed to leave with firm handshakes all round. Back in the Jaguar, Mr F said nothing. I dropped him off at his place and he still said nothing. I then drove on to my new lodgings at The Gore Hotel in Kensington, where I stayed during the week.

We had many slow days in the studio working through lyrics – pulling teeth springs to mind. But soon I could add something new to my CV: chauffeur. I drove Bryan around town all the time; to Sotheby's and Christie's, where he'd dive out to look at the paintings. I would sit in the car by the kerbside with the radio on. All I needed was the chauffeur's hat. I mentioned this in passing to Bryan, and he went to Jermyn Street and bought me one. The gesture would have been funny if it weren't so loaded. After this, we drove up to Alastair Little's restaurant in Notting Hill for lunch. For a chauffeur, I was extremely spoilt. The food was beautiful.

Most afternoons were like this. Bryan always liked to have a dinner date. If it wasn't me, it was Lord Somerset. Two or three times a week we'd go out for lunch – usually to Cibo, an Italian in Kensington. We always had the same seat. To regularly have dinner with someone I'd grown up dreaming of getting to know was wonderful. My feet didn't touch the ground. I felt like a little boy in the company of his favourite teacher. The icing on the cake was a trip into the West End for dinner at the Groucho Club with Mrs F, David Enthoven, Brian Eno and Michael Stipe of REM. Eno had toothache and made good with a salad and some painkillers. He balanced the conversation very carefully and seemed charming. Moving to Russia was his main topic; he was going there for six weeks to get away from it all. He could have saved himself a trip and come to my hotel – it was full of Russians.

Mr F sat at the head of the table, Mrs F at the other end, smoking delightfully and looking debonair. They were like bookends that glared at each other through cigarette smoke, words drifting like clouds from one end of the table to the other, nothing much being said. I'd have been so happy to be in Bryan's shoes, let alone in his jacket. I'd never met a fifty-one-year-old who looked so cool. Michael Stipe sat like a leprechaun hunched over his small plate of food. I looked at him and saw no signs of the 80 million dollars he was meant to be worth. His head kept folding into his body as his eyes fixed like headlights into the distance. Jet lag. We talked about the past and how REM had once opened for Squeeze; it was some years ago and I was in a very different place now. I was a huge fan of the band and loved the way they stuck together as a team. Squeeze were never normally team players, and the grass always did look greener on the other side. We exchanged admiration for each other's work, and the butter was passed. The apple crumble was cooked to perfection and was the envy of all present, which made me feel very fat as I delicately spooned in each mouthful. Stipe had the yoghurt.

Life in the camp was often farcical. If Bryan fell ill with a cold, everything came to a standstill while we all figured out what was for the best – though nothing ever was. He would sing a couple of high notes, which would then snap, and we'd be diving into the vitamin cupboard, putting ginger in hot water and generally hopping about. My job one morning was to listen to what had been going on musically over the previous few weeks and make notes on what I thought. Then Bryan came in, read the notes and walked away without comment. I listened again to all the songs on the CD and made more notes; this time he agreed with me but wanted another opinion. The Doctor came down from his busy desk upstairs and shuffled about on his heels. He looked earnestly at the boom box and shrugged, then I tried to write down what his thoughts were. Mr F walked back in and asked me if I'd brought my video camera, but I hadn't, so he tried to send John, the other driver, down to my house in Rye to collect it – a round trip of nearly 200 miles.

I was also asked to watch a rare French film and note down each time the woman screamed. Halfway through, I thought to myself, 'Didn't I used to be in Squeeze?' One day at The Gore, I looked into the mirror and saw this fat face there. I was a pink balloon in tartan underwear. The great white chin of pride ducked down onto my shirt, and everywhere I looked, impressions were confirmed. I had put on weight that year, eating up my teenage dreams at delicate lunches and dinner tables for two.

One day Alice, who worked in the office as studio gofer, asked me if she could come to the studio in Barnes where we had been working. I asked Bryan and he said of course. As I walked in with her, a very famous guitarist turned up to work in another studio just at the same time. He saw her and set about finding out more. He came to me and asked me to pass on a message to her: perhaps she'd like to meet him for dinner one night? She thought this was very funny, but I saw more than humour in her smile. Her red lipstick painted a very different picture. That night, he made a pass at her and the next morning invited her to hear his new album.

When Bryan got wind of it, I was banished from the studio. I was left so confused. I slithered about in the garden at Old House Farm and waited for something to happen. The phone didn't ring, so I picked it up and made some calls to the office, but Bryan wouldn't speak to me. So I faxed him. The next morning, he called me and we made it up – sort of – then it was back into the Jag and up to London, where the frost was thick on the ground. We shook hands and the week ended with a cordial smile.

Life returned to normal for a few months. I enjoyed my car and my hotel room. I loved my life with Mr F. Dave Stewart was producing his new album – I found Dave so interesting to work with; he was a buzzing bee who was always here, there and everywhere pollinating his wares. He filmed everything, he stored all he saw, he was mad as a hatter. What to make of it all? I could not. I dared not. Mr F took me to the Royal Albert Hall one night to see a band I'd never heard of called Blackstreet. The place was buzzing with atmosphere, and the bodies in the crowd swayed and shook as the music lifted everyone to another place – not bad for a Tuesday. The band were great, the drummer was an amazing player. It was nice to wake up in the morning not knowing about something as great as this then going to bed exhausted, having been fully educated. We were two middle-aged white men in tweeds trying to look cool. We stuck out like sore thumbs. But he always managed to carry off the look wherever he happened to be.

Back at the studio, the mood was altogether different. I picked Mr F up from his house in Kensington and he was in a very happy mood, with a teenage smile. Funny things happened, though. The lyrics to the new album were on my PowerBook, but they didn't match those on the Mac shared by The Doctor upstairs. We were both summoned to the table and commas were moved and hyphens created; spellings were changed. The Doctor was barked at – the whole thing got very heated indeed. 'Let's see now, does martini have a capital M or a baby m in this case?' Such things were very important in Bryan's world. It was all about spacing, timing, interpretation of the master vocal and what Bryan wanted. His attention to detail in everything we did was inspiring and exhausting all at the same time. I loved to try and keep up with him, but of course I never could.

Meanwhile in the studio, a tribe of people worked on bringing new beats to old songs. The studio would always employ at least one programmer to try new things out. Long, boring hours in front of a screen with the latest plug-ins. It was like Grand Central Station and all trains were running late. But we all knew that when they eventually left the platform, Mr F would be in the signal box sending them in different directions, having first checked that The Doctor and I agreed with Robin Trower. Then Robin would agree with Bryan and, in turn, he with us.

Auntie would then arrive to agree as well. We all agreed that Bryan was, of course, right after all. I sharpened pencils until they were all the same height in the jar. I made tea with just the right amount of milk. I kept quiet when I was not spoken to. It was a dream job helping Bryan to find lyrics from his notepads and transform them into verses and choruses for new songs for an album that didn't come out for another four years. But I was tired of that room and I was tired of that coffee, those sandwiches and the crisp white shirts. My chin rested on my collar and my tummy created a schoolteacher's paunch in my ever-blue jumper – I was tired of that too. I was tired, but not really of my job or Bryan – just of me. Suddenly I was let go, my term had come to an end, so I packed my school bag and I raced back to the country to the family and the studio that had just been built. I was missing my girls, the dogs and simple walks in the woods at weekends. One

did pay for the other, but it was hard work. There was no room for
a lyric doctor at Avonmore Place any more.

Three years later, I walked back into his office. Nothing had
changed. Although my life did have its own changes, as I was now
living back in London in a flat in Wapping overlooking the Thames.
I was a single man again. Bryan grilled me to within an inch of my
life. Did I really want to be his personal manager? David Enthoven
had once again put me forward and I drank the poison from
the vial. Bryan's recent divorce from Mrs F had turned his world
upside down and he wanted to work.

My role was to find him shows, and the corporate gigs came
thick and fast once I put the word about. This was all new ground
for me and I had to learn on the hoof, which made my heart race
with every call I had to make. It was testing but rewarding. The
first of these was at the Natural History Museum, just a mile or so
from the office, at which Bryan was supported by James Brown. He
was paid a fortune, but still demanded a hotel room close by, even
though he could have walked back to his own bed in less than ten
minutes. He delivered a short but stylish set of hits, then went
home and left the hotel room empty. My sub-role that evening
was to get his son to video the female dancers, who were sexy and
outrageously good. He would use this footage to teach his dancers
how to move. Dancing underneath the dinosaurs of the museum
was a sight I will never forget: I was as transfixed as he was.

At around the same time, I was asked to help arrange a photo
shoot for an advertising campaign featuring Bryan that would
run in glossy magazines all over the world. The photographer
was Lord Lichfield. The plan was to meet in Hyde Park and the
shoot would take place in the orange glow of fallen leaves in the

autumn morning light. Again, Bryan insisted on a hotel room, at the Four Seasons on Park Lane – though this time he did actually stay there, with me in the next room. On the shoot, I stood by and watched, throwing in words of encouragement every now and again as Lichfield snapped away. I was trying to be in the right place at the right time with the right comments, but it was hopeless. Bryan hated the cold and the park, and although I could tell he admired Lichfield he found it hard to work for him, and things seemed to become frosty. And when, a few weeks later, the pictures arrived, he was not keen on them. He asked Lichfield to airbrush out a gap between his legs as he felt it made him look as though he was wearing an ill-fitting suit. This didn't go down well and I was caught in the middle. It was almost pistols at dawn. But things moved on quickly; other pressing matters arose. We'd run out of Fortnum & Mason Earl Grey. Bryan was recording again, but the output wasn't enough to excite EMI so I was summoned to an office to discuss another hits collection to fill the gap. The sleeve design for this took longer than the making of most albums, and each picture suggested was pored over for days, leaving grown men weeping over cold coffee. I was inspired by Bryan's keen eye and attention to detail but it was something I was not very good at. We eventually released the album and went on tour to promote it. It was a very strange time. In Australia, Bryan's guitarist Mick Green had a heart attack on stage – he was saved by two doctors who were at the show. Bryan didn't seem to notice it happen behind him and carried on singing.

Since my last stretch at Avonmore Place, poor Mr Puxley had passed away, and Bryan had replaced him with a Glaswegian fan who knew more about Bryan than Bryan did. It seemed ridiculous to me that you'd not only employ a fan to work in your office, but you'd also fly him down from Scotland on a Monday, put him up in a hotel all week, then fly him home again on a Friday night. There was a strangeness about the man that meant I didn't trust him, and his snooping around the building bothered me. When he took some time off sick, the studio engineer and I noticed that some boxes had been moved and that tapes were missing from the collection. Later in the day, I saw that some posters from old Roxy shows were also missing.

I was summoned to Bryan's room and ordered to fly to Glasgow to watch the man's every move – stalk him if needs be. I'd gone from chauffeur to spy in a few short years. I couldn't track the man down: he wasn't at home and his phone had been cut off. Months later, we found him in a hospital, suffering from serious depression and being constantly watched by the nurses. We never recovered the tapes or posters. Bryan was understandably shocked by the betrayal and it felt as if everyone in the office suddenly became guilty by default. I think it took him a while before he trusted any of us fully again.

During this second stint, I had a call from a wealthy fan who wanted a private show from Roxy Music – and was prepared to pay whatever it took. Bryan asked me to call around and I managed to persuade all the old band members that this was a good idea. I even got them in the same room at the same time to discuss things – a huge feat in itself – but it felt like the first day of primary school. Everyone was ridiculously shy and there was lots of standing around, much twiddling of thumbs. Phil Manzanera was the one who knew how to open Bryan up the most. They got on well and there was a glimmer of hope. There'd be no rehearsals, it

Glenn in midair outside The Bell in Greenwich on Jubilee day.
(*Jill Furmanovsky*)

The centerfold from Squeeze's Madison Square Garden tour programme.

Me with a fag down The Albany, before it burnt down.

Squeeze with JB, backstage at the Marquee Club in London.

Oh no it's the Nineties – and I'm in a nice suit!

The three amigos looking happy and ready for business.

Brighton Pier, a little worse for wear after a long night.

Looking into the future.

Playing live in the early days, when we could both get off the ground without needing surgery!
(*Jill Furmanovsky*)

An *NME* front cover taken at Crooms Hill in thinner days.
(Jill Furmanovsky)

Chewing the cud with Glenn in his studio during the recording of *Cradle*.

Mrs Difford and me, on the most important of all stages.

was agreed, and Bryan would take the largest portion of the fee.

The show was magical. There were only about a hundred people there, which was a shame – a lot of very rich people, it seems, have plenty of money but not many friends. And afterwards, Phil asked Bryan and me to his studio to hear the bones of some new songs, which Bryan very reluctantly agreed to. We stood and listened, and I was absolutely thrilled at what I heard. Bryan didn't seem too impressed, but the next day he was back in Phil's studio pushing some of his own ideas around, some of them involving lyrics I'd turned up in old notepads I'd found in a cupboard. The fire was lit, but it soon went out.

The tension of being on call all the time slowly got to me. There were no gaps in the week. I managed to see my kids from time to time, but with Bryan in my life too it was becoming too much. He couldn't make up his mind about another show I was organising for him – even though things like private jets were being thrown into the deal – and it all came to a head. I drove back to Wapping and called in sick for a few days, then spent hours each day asking myself whether I needed this in my life. When I returned to work, I was let go. Bryan wrote me a letter, which remains unopened to this day.

I felt a massive sense of regret. Though I was relieved to be free of Avonmore Place, I felt as though I'd failed. There was no new album, no reunion with Roxy, no more dinners at Cibo. And for all Bryan's faults, I missed him. He was a man with whom I was besotted as a teenager, and whose records I'd constantly played and studied. He was mysterious and generous, he was angry and he was gifted. The week I left, we were in the studio and he sat at the piano and sang Traffic's 'No Face, No Name, No Number' while

I stood behind him and felt the tears come to my eyes. His voice, though fragile, reduced me to rubble.

It was a tough job and each week I bailed water out of the sinking boat with nothing more than a china cup. But a very expensive china cup, as you can imagine. David Enthoven always told me that I should stand up to Bryan and shout back at him if he barked at me. Man up, he would say. It was good advice. But I was just a boy, a fan in very expensive sheep's clothing.

THE STRAND

In 1999 I was invited to the Ivor Novello Awards in London. It's without doubt the best music-award ceremony you can go to; it's well-run and each year I know more and more people there. I have two Ivor Novello awards on my desk and I'm very proud of them both. On this occasion, I was a guest of my then-publishers EMI. The manager John Reid was there too, and on his table was Marti Pellow, lead singer with Wet Wet Wet. In the papers recently there'd been pictures of Marti being wheeled away from a hotel looking gaunt and wasted during his much-publicised heroin addiction. But tonight he looked fresh-faced, suited and booted.

We had met once before when I wrote some lyrics for Marti's band. I remember going to a studio in Berkshire where they seemed to be living at the time and working with Graham Clarke, who was their main writer. Sometimes they used the studio to do their laundry; so decadent. At the height of their fame they'd fly in curries from Glasgow to studios in Norway on private planes. Marti was sitting in a dark room eating chicken on the bone. He asked me how I managed to keep myself sober; I could only just see him as the light was so bad. He was on drugs then without doubt. He was like Marlon Brando, sitting in the darkness whispering in his Glaswegian accent. I was scared for him and felt his pain.

At the Ivor Novello Awards, though, he was very much sober – but nervously so. I gave him my number in case he wanted to chat about recovery or go to a meeting with me; that's what AA people do. He called a few weeks later and I arranged for him to come to Old House Farm. He arrived in his car and we sat on the lawn. It was a hot summer's day and we talked about writing songs, about recovery and about him leaving his band. After a few cups of tea and some cake, we looked around my studio and he met the girls, Grace and Cissy. Later on we had a takeaway curry from Rye and he moved in.

Marti stayed at my house for almost two years. Slippers and pipe, Ferrari and a sense of humour; he was a funny and delicate soul. He asked me to hook him up with songwriters I trusted, so each week became filled with people coming and going to the studio in my garden. He had swapped one addiction for another. We were up all night and all day chasing songs with bemused writers down from London. It was good fun. Marti was self-obsessed, though. Not necessarily a disadvantage for a frontman in a successful band, but fucking trying for those surrounding him when the hits dried up. We all had to live with his mood swings and eternal disappointment that he was no longer number 1 in the charts.

I was in Rye town centre one chilly day when I heard a Wet Wet Wet song playing at top volume. That's weird, I thought, immediately thinking of Marti at home. He didn't see me, but I saw him several more times as he drove round and round the town's one-way system with the Wets' greatest hits blasting out. He found a parking space and fell out onto the cobbled street, where I was buying bread.

After a few months, Marti asked me if I fancied managing him. I accepted, as I was already organising his diary with his PA Rowan, who was lovely but lived way up in Scotland. I walked into Universal to discuss a possible solo album but they wanted me to work with someone more skilled as a manager, and that person was Clive Banks.

Clive and I met, and I agreed he was much more suited to the job than I was – his track record was impressive, and he had an enviable reputation in the music industry. His wife looked after Madonna's press at the time. Clive was a creative and loving person who I really liked hanging out with; it seemed to work and we formed a company to look after the boy. Marti and I had a friendship and some good people to work with; we had 110 songs, but still we had no album. I'd write the words, plucking them out of thin air as Marti sang, and another musician would provide the vamps and chords. A three-way split. We had everyone down to try and co-write, Andy Caine, Gary Clark, Gary Kemp and Graham Lyle. Graham Gouldman, the postman, the baker, the farmer and anyone else who would be passing by, it was exhausting. Then we had a programmer who would stay up late and make the songs sound great. This was mostly the job of Paul Inder, a tender man with eyes the size of computer screens, who was the son of Lemmy from Motörhead. He was fast and he was patient too, but he did have very smelly feet. He lived in a converted ambulance in the garden, which Heidi found intolerable. They fell out constantly. Especially one night when the handbrake on his ambulance stopped working and it ended up in a field; it had to be pulled out by the local farmer. Heidi was not impressed. She sent him packing and it took me a few days of negotiating with her to allow him back. He was priceless in many ways.

One night when I was in bed, I opened my eyes to see Marti bending over me, whispering for me to come and hear a new song. It was 3 a.m. I got dressed and crossed the garden to the studio. I could smell something; it was too much aftershave mixed with something else. He was slurring and bullying me to stay awake and write more words for him. He wasn't well and the next day he drove himself to The Priory, where he stayed for the obligatory twenty-eight days. I visited him each week. My driveway, I later discovered, was strewn with empty vodka bottles hidden in bushes and ditches.

When Marti returned to Old House Farm, he threw himself into work. He was on a mission and we all had to ride with whatever it was – often I would try and creep away, but he was on full burn most of the time, writing as much as he could. It tired me out. I'd pick out lyrics, order food and cars, plan tours and book musicians, then write more lyrics. He was a funny sod and really good company. He got on with my kids and became like an uncle to them, buying them sweets and picking them up from school. And I enjoyed going to Glasgow with him, meeting his folks, who were much like mine.

Marti paid rent and mucked in – sometimes. He was generous and kind. The first solo album gathered mixed reviews, but he wanted to push on; the next one was being written and in his head the one after that too. He had his sights on being the next Robbie Williams, and talked to us constantly about getting film work or appearing on stage. He wanted nothing less than James Bond as his first role. Clive and I knew, what with his strong Glaswegian accent, that this would be hard work and at the very least he'd need some help. But in Marti's mind he was a superstar.

One day he went to the local shops to buy the latest issue of Q magazine, and returned fuming. 'Call yourself a manager?' he shouted at me. I was sitting out in the garden with my kids. 'There's not a single fucking mention of me or the new album in here.' I explained, as patiently as I could, that he wasn't the big news he'd been a few years ago and that there was never going to be the same level of interest in his work as there had been when he was with the Wets. He wanted badly to be a great solo success but Marti, unlike Robbie Williams, didn't have the likes of the very talented Guy Chambers to help mould his songs into hits. He had me. This infuriated him and we ended up nose to nose, with him yelling and swearing into my face as Grace and Cissy looked on from the trampoline. To say sorry, he bought a curry from the Indian in Rye for everyone that night – and picked it up in his Ferrari. He would often shoot from the hip, but he would make it up soon after. He felt embarrassed by such outbursts; he was really a softie and full of love. I understood his concerns and tried hard to shelter him.

Clive and I managed to get him an audition for Billy Flynn in the West End show Chicago, and I drove him up to London. I pushed him into a small room with two young men from the theatre; one in red braces, the other in a running suit.

I stood outside on tenterhooks and listened to him singing. When he came out, we walked through Covent Garden together with him cursing about being stuck in a room for an hour. He got the role. Marti had to work hard to speak and sing in an American accent, and his teacher was consistent and patient – much more patient than I was. He was practising at the Pineapple Dance Studios in Covent Garden, so I'd wander next door to watch girls warming up in leotards. As a manager, I was on the lookout for talent. That was my excuse anyway. It was the highlight of my day. I went to see *Chicago* with Marti, in a checked shirt and dark suit. I was welcomed as the guy who supported the star, who showed up on time and got the coffees from Starbucks. Clive very kindly pointed out to the producer that I'd done my own show only the other night and that it had been fantastic, but they couldn't have cared less. Marti had his picture taken and hung out with the cast members, who surrounded him like mist around a mountain. They swam behind him in the room, smiling and trying to under-stand what he was saying.

Rehearsals were a success. Sitting in the stalls watching Marti go through his paces, I imagined how great it would be to write a musical and have it staged like this. Choreography and story are so important; there is so much to learn, but where do you start? Maybe having that passion is enough. Being backstage at the Adelphi Theatre on the Strand watching Marti was a lot of fun; and the cast laughed and joked and generally made the new boy feel very welcome. The Royal Room – in which the Queen hung out whenever she came to the theatre – became my office, and between its red-and-gold walls and its framed posters for West End hits of the past, I started to breathe again. Marti's life was now cushioned by daily rehearsals; I was needed less and less. Marti nailed it – he was brilliant at being Billy Flynn – and I felt very proud.

One evening, on my way home from the theatre, I walked into the NCP car park and saw a young man beneath a makeshift shelter in a dark corner of the exit ramp. He was sitting cross-legged on a sheet of card fixing heroin by himself. I passed him slowly, and though I was in a pinstripe suit and carrying a briefcase, I felt closer to him than I did my own shadow. I said the serenity prayer and left him there to enjoy his evening, to sail the night fantastic. In my Jaguar, I calmly pulled out into Drury Lane and set off towards the calm of the country with Radio 3 playing and a nice empty road in front of me. Worlds apart, maybe. The following week, I receive a call from young Marti: he has jammed his Ferrari in the pinch points of the ticket barrier in the same NCP and he can't move the car. I'm asked to come and help, which I refuse to do. Some things are just out of a manager's remit.

I watched the show about twenty times. I really loved it. Marti did us all proud, but he was soon on to the next task: Broadway. Clive and I delivered his request, but sadly, when he arrived in New York, there was an actors' strike and he ended up sitting in his hotel room for a few weeks. He was fuming – which he was an expert at doing – but there was nothing I could do but wait for the strike to end. So he came back to the West End, then toured *Chicago* around the UK.

Meanwhile, he recorded two more solo albums in Memphis with producer Willie Mitchell. We took Phil Brown to engineer, who we totally trusted; he had worked on Marti's previous solo albums and on my solo album a few years before. A steady pair of hands. The recordings were incredible; I had never heard Marti sing like that, with so much soul and tenderness. We also recorded a fantastic album of country songs with John Wood; not sure what happened to them. We were never lazy and I was on full spin all the time.

One day I took Marti to see Deke Arlon, an old-school manager with a big desk with inkwells and a house in Spain, who had looked after Ray Davies. I left him there with his new carer. It was like dropping him off at boarding school.

When Marti lost his mother, I went to Glasgow to hold his hand at the funeral. It was a bright day, but cold. I stood to one side as his family took centre stage; the other members of Wet Wet Wet turned up to pay their respects. I was the only Englishman there and I felt it. After leaving the graveside, we moved down the hill to a small hotel where some sandwiches had been laid on. I walked in and the band's keyboard player came up to me and said, 'You've stolen our singer.' His look scared me. The atmosphere was sudden and cut from glass; I was on the edge of another band's empty stage.

Sadly Marti and I have not kept in touch. He called me a few times for directions to various theatres, and then nothing. Our backgrounds were similar; his parents had the same three-bar fire as mine, the same furniture, the same sons who'd gone off to do what they wanted and followed a dream. We had different needs, but we'd both had to grow up in a world of minibars, fast cars and Top 10 records. And, in Marti's case, tons of cash too. Working with him was great fun. I enjoyed the tours and the fun we had up and down the country. I was his manager-cum-chauffeur-cum-writer-cum-takeaway-orderer-cum-backstage-guide-and-confidant. Hotels were always of a high standard and his car became my home.

Who would have thought it just four years before, when he was on heroin and every bit the fallen pop idol? He was lucky to be in such a great place. And I was lucky to have been there with him, for better or for worse. He is one of the hardest-working singers I know, on both stages: the theatrical and with his band the Wets.

HELIOCENTRIC

Francis Dunnery came to my house in Rye to change my life forever. We had first met at a writers' retreat at Huntsham Court in
Devon, which had become something of a bolthole for me during
the last few years of my marriage to Cindy. I'd go there to write
and relax, drink, eat and walk in the beautiful countryside. Francis had been in a band called It Bites; he was a larger-than-life
human being and a great guitarist – he was from that prog-rock
school of musicians that had really learned to play their instruments properly. We wrote together on that trip. One evening he
knocked on my door yelling, 'I need a meeting, let me in!' I knew
what he meant, and we went to his room and sat around a copy of
the *Big Book* – the AA bible. We soon got to know each other well.
His presence was immense and it was almost as if he could read
my mind. It was he who led me to the microphone to make my
first solo album. I was terrified as I stepped up to the plate.

I'm not sure how it all fell into place, but one day I was at home
doing nothing much and the next minute he turned up and set me
writing and recording. It was an intense session that ran for about
a month, with people coming and going – notably Dorie Jackson
on vocals, who magically managed to lift my voice on invisible

strings, tuning it and keeping it warm. Dorie was a very gentle person who was so lovely to work with. Ash Soan, who'd played on Squeeze's *Domino* album and was someone I loved being with also, came in to play the drums. He was so creative. We had Matt Pegg on bass, who I knew little about, and the rest was down to Francis. He played guitar, he played the upright piano we based most of the songs around and he cradled everything in his way.

We listened to his words and fell to his views, rightly or wrongly. I loved working from home. My studio – called Heliocentric after its unique Helios desk that I'd got from the famous Basing Street Studios in London – was in the garden and I could look out of the window and see my girls, Grace and Cissy, riding horses. Heidi kept house, and fed and watered us all through the recording. The sound we evoked was that of childhood, and the deeper we went, the harder it was to keep from crying. Phil Brown, who'd engineered Jimi Hendrix, The Small Faces and Robert Plant, brought his tender touch to the album.

The studio – my studio – was a nest of chords, words and feelings, and felt unlike any place I'd ever worked in before. Francis had to wrestle vocal performances from me – and with some patience, too. He knew it would be difficult. I tried so hard to sing in tune for him, and spent hours working on each line to get it right. I was not a natural singer. I never have been. He was well versed in astrology and drew on my curiosity from time to time; he even read my chart one afternoon. He was spot on. We sat, he talked and he described my life back to me. He could feel my present self and where my journey had taken me. It was very emotional when he revealed my life, shallow and painful as it had been. Before this reading the closest I got to astrology was reading my chart in the

Sunday papers for fun. This was the real deal and very deep, just like Francis.

During the recording we talked all the time and had a good laugh. It was open and fun, like no other album I'd ever made before. 'Parents', a song about my mum and dad, was emotional and so haunting to record – its lines prised every feeling I had about them out of me. I was in therapy, but on a couch of guitar, bass and drums. Francis wanted me to get deep down into family – about what it was like for me growing up.

We used a school piano as that link to childhood. He'd studied psychology and believed that by dredging down, you reveal treasures that have been deeply buried. In doing so, he opened me up to being a better writer in many ways.

'One Day', a wonderful, dark song, had me flying into the unknown, exploring the anxiety of fear. Francis knew exactly where that came from and how to lance its boil. He really knew how to reflect me. He made me look at my feminine side with 'Cowboys Are My Weakness', and even managed to rake me over the hot coals of Glenn with a song called 'No Show Jones'. 'Get it off your chest,' he said, so I wrote the song about me not turning up for the tour when I went into The Priory, and tried to address the differences between Glenn and me. I don't think Glenn paid much attention to 'No Show Jones'. He had also written a song about me, on one of his solo albums. We were both hissing like snakes in the undergrowth of our separate lives. Silly really.

I was so proud of the studio as a creative place to work and enjoy. Thanks to my brother Lew and his close management of the situation, we were able to balance the books. Elvis Costello part-funded the build, yet he never came to record there, which

I always found odd, but very generous of him. Other than during the sessions for that album, the only other time I recorded at my home studio was with the jazz musician Guy Barker. We wrote an album together. I was the Chet Baker of Rye. This is a record I'd love to revive at some point, as I really enjoyed singing in the jazz style. Guy was imaginative and fun to record with, but his band were way above me in terms of musicality. I was merely mucking out to their intelligent brass lines. They were way too smart for me.

Bands came down all the time to record on my treasured Helios desk, the studio's homely atmosphere being one of its selling points. Heidi grabbed hold of the situation and began to manage it on a daily basis, supplying lunches and dinners for our musical guests. Bryan Ferry came to record there once; The Pet Shop Boys came and ate scones while programming tracks. Paul Weller spent a month there and named his album after the studio. Supergrass recorded there and named a song after Grace, which thrilled her to bits. We had musicians from all over the world: India and America, Canada and west London. Trilok Gurtu came with his drums for some recording and we wrote together. It was a very uplifting event, even though I felt out of my depth. Once we had Wayne Shorter fly in for a session with the incredible Portuguese singer Dulce Pontes. He stayed at the Oast House B&B up the road from the studio. Bob, who ran the B&B, found it all too much dealing with such people; all he knew how to do was full English with fag ash as a topping. But the comings and goings of such famous people never fazed him. Paul McCartney would slip into his bar for a pint every now and again; it was that simple.

On my own album with Francis, we couldn't get the vocals right at my studio in Rye. Francis rightly thought I was too distracted by the house, Heidi and the kids, so he took me back down to Huntsham Court. It was torture as he lashed me line by line, stretched me on my metre, tied me to the depth of each word. He beat me up so I'd deliver the goods. Driving back from Devon, he revealed his plan to release the album, *I Didn't Get Where I Am*, on his own record label in early 2001. Without a major label there was no money for promotion or PR, it was not going to come out of thin air. It reminded me of when *Domino* was released a few years earlier; yes there was ownership but there was no clear benefit from its value if there was no money to let people know it was out there and in the shops. It was clearly just my take on things, and possibly one a dinosaur would own in these modern times of indie home-spun records that nobody would hear. The right people heard it in the end and I'm very proud of each and every song, and I thank Francis for his determination to get it right and make it sound wonderful.

My album was a success as far as I was concerned. Good friends were constantly in touch to tell me how much they liked it: Elton bought ten copies, which was lovely of him and very supportive; Elvis Costello wrote a glowing review. *I Didn't Get Where I Am* was never going to rock the charts, but that was a thing of the past for me. Like skateboards.

BRUNSWICK SQUARE

The day my dad passed away in May 2001, the sun was shining on the hospital and on the cemetery in which my mum lay waiting just a few streets away. Ha Ha Lane, Charlton – a funny name for a street with a graveyard. I'll never forget the day. Dad waited for me to come into the room before he drew his last breath; he wanted all three of his sons by his side. There he lay, head propped up on green pillows. I'd been downstairs on my mobile talking to Heidi, who was at home with our daughters in Sussex. The nurse called for me and I came up from the car park. Dad looked at us all, and then he went. In the yellow room where he lay, we stood and cried and held each other. The family tree had lost its major branch.

Hours later, I sat outside in my car with the sun beating down on me, looking out at the Technicolor world my dad was no longer part of. At eighty-three years, he had had a long and good life. The next day, in the car park outside the hospital canteen, I bumped into my very first girlfriend, Sharon. She was still thin and tall; her features still much the same as when we first kissed on West-combe Hill in 1970, and when we used to go dancing in Catford all those years ago. It was a complete shock to see her there. She hugged me and I cried. I cried most of that week following Dad's death. It was odd to find someone that removed from my life yet somehow connected. All the wonderful weaves of this great tapestry seemed to come together.

Later that day, I went walking in the woods near my home, and reflected on my life with my dad. The dogs I'd been walking looked tired and lay down in the fallen leaves. And in that moment, I could taste the rhubarb he always stewed for me to have on my Weetabix before bed. I could smell the chicken boiled in a bag on Saturday nights. I could taste the sweets – milk bottles, blackjacks and the fruit salads I liked the most – bought for me when we went down to the allotment, where he was among his friends. This was our hideaway from the rest of the family. Dad did what he did all afternoon and I played with my cars in the heaps of earth and bits of mud and stone. The smell of his shed was a cross between wood, lime, old cans, nails, creosote, brushes, oil, damp and heat, earth and clay. Smells that are with me today. They pin my memories to the past almost as much as records do.

The gasworks on Tunnel Avenue had been my dad's life outside the home, a grown-up world of big trains and big lorries. Right up to his death he would go back there and enjoy the company of other retirees he knew; the last of the summer wine. They all came to say goodbye at his funeral. It was moving and very funny. The gasworks folk were our second family, who would come and go through our lives. It was nice to know my dad was being looked after when he left the house in the morning.

From the hospital in Charlton, they took Dad's empty body to a funeral home on Blackwall Lane, across the road from Greenwich Hospital, where my mum had died a few years earlier and where

I had been born. Across the road from where I saw my first racy film at the Granada Picture House and from the gasworks where he spent most of his life. Lew picked out a suit for him to wear; around his neck was the old Gas Board tie. I didn't want to see him there made up like he was leaving for work. He was on his final journey and this time he wasn't coming back; and though he looked great, I remember his hands were like fallen autumn leaves in texture, lined and faded with life.

Outside, in the busy traffic, I sat in my car and thought about all the times we'd ridden past this corner of Greenwich on his green bike. Then I drove up to Combe Avenue, where time stood still. The fish still swam in the tank above where he used to sit, the kitchen was cold and still smelt of leaking gas. I looked around and decided not to take anything but memories from the house in which I learnt to listen to music, where I learnt to kiss, where I enjoyed colour TV for the first time and where I learnt to play the guitar and write my first songs.

The wake was held in a hotel on Blackheath; Lew organised everything. Sandwiches and cake; beer, and sherry for the ladies. Pictures of Dad hung on the walls, and books of remembrance were laid out neatly on the tables. He was loved so much – I was proud to be his son. Everyone said nice things about my old man. Elvis Costello came in support, as did Glenn. We hadn't seen each other for some time, but this was not the moment to mend bridges. I felt his love and was grateful to him for joining me on this moving and very sad day. My dad was respected by all of my friends. Jools would often say he'd seen him at the shops and that he'd made him laugh. Funny old sod that he was. Mrs Jones from next door was there to say her goodbyes, with a fag on the go and a large glass of sweet white wine in her hand. She was so generous to my dad; it was so nice to see her again.

I sat outside the hotel and looked out across the Heath towards our old home at Combe Avenue. A perfect, simple vision. There I was: schoolboy, skinhead and hippy. There I found love, football and drugs. There I found music. The Who live at Leeds, David Bowie, Frank Zappa, King Crimson, Prince Buster, The Small Faces and the rest. I thanked my dad for giving me my home and my roots. I thanked him for giving me my first pushbike, which in turn gave me my first taste of freedom.

I write about my dad in my songs. 'Sidney Street' on my *Cashmere If You Can* album is about his journey to war. I was always asking him about the war, but he never wanted to talk about that part of his life. Unlike a lot of men of his generation, he never glorified those days and I admire that. War isn't pretty, unlike rock 'n' roll. I can talk about that all day long. I'm that bloke in Squeeze; the one who sang 'Cool for Cats'; the one who wears his inside on his sleeve, etc. My dad's formative years were much more meaningful. What an easy life I've had in comparison to his. Out of bed into my socks and jeans, on to the stage, wreak havoc with some songs and walk away happy with some cash – no dead bodies.

Dad was never sure about the music I was playing, but he grew to love it, and it eventually made him proud. The support he gave me at first was non-existent, but then my piano-playing did only consist of three notes and some very basic thumping, mostly inspired by The Velvet Underground. From there, I moved on to a bass guitar, then a guitar with four strings, and then a band. From pub gigs in south London to touring shows in America. After my mum died, I flew my dad to New York – him, Lew and Les out in a limo all night long. Squeeze were playing Madison Square Garden. A second sell-out show. It was his first journey on a plane, his first trip outside the UK since the war. He loved the city, but he couldn't understand why all the lights were left on at the World Trade Center at night. It was money being wasted, he moaned. A constant refrain.

After Dad died, his three boys went in different directions. Perhaps I could have seen that one coming. Les and Lew fell out over money, and I was piggy in the middle, but refused to be drawn into the fray. I prefer to think back to the hospital room in which we stood and hugged each other, and held on to our past, trying never to let it go. But that's what we've had to do. Each day flicks past, one after the other, and here you are one minute and gone the next. The man in the doorway no more; the funny man with the jumper and the slippers. Tall and handsome, hair to one side like Bobby Charlton, a cross between Eric Morecambe and Gregory Peck. Priceless humour, dry and pointed sometimes. Lovable from a glance. A hard worker and a keen gardener. A drinker in moderation, a smoker in the evening also in moderation. A soldier with medals. Ruddy-faced and hunched over, distant and tired, shaky and fragile.

Sidney Lewis Difford spent the last years of his life watching football and snooker on the TV, and reruns of *The Two Ronnies*. He enjoyed his own space more than most. I often felt uneasy when I went to see him, but now I understand the comfort provided by being alone – that space created, carved in precious time. If there is another world, I will see Dad there and we can sit together and not say very much; we were so good at that after all. But we will know, just by being father and son, that what we're saying is all we need to say. We never did play football together, or board games, we never built train sets or climbed mountains, but we did love each other. He rooted me in a garden where I flowered into the person I am today, complicated but calm, a chip off the old block maybe. How could I look back and say anything other than thank you, for giving me the best years of my life.

After my dad passed away, I went back home, but my time at Old House Farm was coming to an end. My relationship with Heidi had run out of steam; it was flat and both of us were to blame. Therapy was not going to glue us back together; she thought there would be nothing to gain from it. She had been told that I would always be an addict and therefore always be the way I was. It's here where I think she threw in the towel. Telling the children was the worst thing. We sat them down and told them I was moving out, as Mummy and Daddy weren't getting on. We still liked each other, but we couldn't be together any more. They went to their rooms to smash things up and slam doors. I walked through the fields and cried as I felt the curtains coming down on my family. Heidi and I had put so much work into our thirteen years together, but now we were just too tired and were hopeless around each other. We weren't talking and it seemed that every corner we turned, we had issues there. I do think that underneath it all there was love, but our communication had emptied and the relationship just slipped away.

I moved into a cottage in the garden, which worked for a while, but I realised it was totally over when I got back from a gig at Glastonbury. I booked a van and packed up all my stuff the next day. Leaving was quick and very sad. I remember so well seeing the house in my rear-view mirror as I drove away. The girls were standing waving in the garden, and I felt my heart breaking in two. I cried all the way to London and felt very depressed about the way things had ended up.

I left Rye with my writing desk, which was hand-built in the style of a pile of neat books, a design I stole from the original *Queen Mary*'s Art Deco library. I also took many of my books and clothes; a few pictures and gold discs followed along later. It still felt like I had lost everything in a separation that, like the divorce, seemed brutal and cruel. It was agreed that sometime in the future I could take more of what was mine including my original writing desk which was bought with my first PRS cheque. Sadly its roll-top beauty remains at Heidi's house and not at mine. I moved to Wapping: a view of the Thames in a very nice flat above the cobbled streets. I knew Wapping well and managed slowly to rebuild my life. The kids liked coming to visit me, we had great times walking up and down the river. It felt like another stepping stone. The studio carried on and Keane recorded their two big albums there. Heidi seemed happier and life moved on for us all.

After my years in London working with Bryan Ferry, I then moved to Brighton. I found the sky and the sea intriguing; I loved being able to walk everywhere and soak up the youthfulness of the city. On a sunny day it's the best place in the world. It was such a creative place to be and it was important for me to be close to Grace and Cissy, who were now at school just up the road at Brighton College.

I lived in Brighton for six years, and did some teaching at the local college of music, which was really enjoyable. In that time I moved flats six times, so I got to know the area very well. I also met some lovely people along the way. It was different from London and more like a village, but by the sea. I needed to find a home but that wasn't possible. I was packing and unpacking, chasing mixed emotions and a relationship up and down the flats and mews of Brighton and Kemptown. It's a long story best left to another time. Thankfully I had the safe ears of Martin Freeman, a local councillor who I trusted. Emotionally I was not always a happy bunny in my relationship there, and at the end of the six years I snapped. I ended up back in rehab for a few weeks, this time for relationship issues. It was very painful, but not made any easier by the neglect, in my view, of the counsellors who allowed mobile phones in the rooms. People were constantly on them and losing their focus, including me. My friend Gordon helped me more than rehab could with his pearls of wisdom and love, as did my manager Matt. I vowed never to return to those helpless feelings again, but it would take some doing. I was grateful that my girls Grace and Cissy were at school just up the street. It was always so good to see them, but it must have been hard for them to see me often in such a fragile space.

While living in Brighton, I decided I needed to get off my arse and learn more about myself, so I signed up for a diploma of counselling at the CCPE in London. Each Thursday and on some weekends I would join a group and work through the various basic challenges of being a counsellor. By the end of the year I was working in triads learning my skills, but my head was side-tracked by work and I could not always concentrate, and so many books and essays tested my patience. I was not very focused, but I was enjoying the group therapy, which was at times intense. Tears were often shed over sandwiches at break time with the other members of the group, most of whom went on to work in social services or have clients of their own. Which is what I would have liked.

I took some of my skills into treatment centres, where I would lead a group with music and therapy. I found this really rewarding. Some people fell asleep – which was fine; I would have too – but others joined in with the songs and the story I had to share with them. At one centre in Bournemouth we collected enough songs for an album, which we printed up for friends and family. I also had time to take the workshop into Wandsworth Prison, where I had a captive audience. They loved to muck in with the songwriting.

My next solo album – *The Last Temptation of Chris* – was recorded in Brighton, in my small flat in Brunswick Square, and at a studio not far away in Eastbourne. Singer-songwriter and close friend Boo Hewerdine and I wrote most of the songs, and Boo co-produced the record with me. It was a very different experience from working with Francis, but Boo still had to work hard to tease out the vocals from me. John Wood, who'd worked on the early Squeeze albums, came to share engineering duties with him. But sadly, he wasn't keen on the computer technology Boo was using, and I felt him slip into a mist. I'd pulled John from retirement to record the album, and it wasn't long before he went back to Scotland to concentrate on running his B&B.

I enjoyed the writing process with Boo. He was easy to work with and we had loads of fun. When I wrote for him I felt inspired in a different way than I did with other people. I was very pleased with 'Reverso', a song about vasectomy changes. I'd had my knackers bricked so I knew a bit about the subject. After Cissy was born,

Heidi had decided she didn't want any more children, so I did the manly thing and agreed to have the snip. I remember lying on the bed just before the anaesthetic kicked in and a beautiful Australian nurse came in and whispered kind words then said, 'Did I see you on *Top of the Pops* a couple of years ago?' If I think very deeply about it, it does feel like being put out in a field on your own to graze. Heidi made me feel hollowed out like an old tree, and with not much left inside I buckled with loneliness and dreamt of someone to hold.

'On My Own I'm Never Bored' summed up my time in Brighton; its lyrics reveal what I saw from my front-room window. 'Battersea Boys' was a story told to me by a man called Jim who was in a hospice close to where I lived. I wrote his story into a song and gifted it to him. He sadly passed away, but his brother, who the song is about, turned up at one of my solo shows. It was surreal, and wonderful to meet him. It was a very special moment.

Eastbourne was an odd place to record, but the results were really great. It's a fantastic second album and I'm very proud of it. Boo and I had forged a relationship that I knew would last a long time, as it has. It felt odd to tour on my own – though this was helped by the fact that I was never actually on my own. Dorie Jackson and Francis came with me on my first tours supporting Elvis Costello and Chris Rea, and Boo was by my side the rest of the time. Dorie helped me to tune myself when I first stepped back out on the road, her voice being so correct and powerful. These days I tour with Melvin Duffy on guitar and Arcelia, a vocal group from Kent, who are magnificent and need no rehearsing.

At first, walking on stage without Glenn and the backdrop of Squeeze frightened me. I'd quiver in the dressing room, waiting for the call to stage, worrying about what to say to the crowd. But soon I was in conversation with an audience who mostly hadn't come to see me, the support act. Francis helped me warm up, and made me think about what to say. He also helped me rearrange Squeeze songs to sound like they were mine, which they were – despite me assuming for years they were Glenn's. Francis was a hard taskmaster, making me grumpy before I went on, but it worked. Supporting Elvis was the perfect introduction to being a solo artist, and – good friend that he is – he looked after me from the top of the bill. The Chris Rea tour was more difficult – his audience seemed uninterested, even when he was on stage – but Boo made the experience fun with his dry sense of humour and his harmonies. Dorie was a good person to have on the road, too; she was fun and often balanced out the workload, selling merchandise and so on. I was a very happy boy.

Touring became a new place for me to be; driving around with an acoustic guitar in the boot of the car was easy work. We played all over the UK, but sadly we couldn't sell out the venues. It was a bit embarrassing and I had to pay the band's wages whatever happened – mainly by selling CDs after each show, which also helped to pay for the endless curries in the dressing room. To change the mood, I made some home movies and bought a big screen to show them at my shows. It was a pain getting it in the car, but the audience seemed to love my editing skills; it gave them something to watch instead of a fat bloke and another bloke with a beard. Matt Deighton joined us on guitar at some of the shows, and as I got to know him more, I wanted to write with him. The chemistry between us was calm. We wrote his album *Part of Your Life* – one of my favourite records – together at my house in Rye and, just as Francis had done with me, I listened to his story and reflected what I'd heard back at him as lyrics. I was the rhyming psychotherapist. Matt at the time seemed confused and depressed, but I'm pleased to say that's behind him now. He was a diamond to work with; he had a fantastic imagination and a pure gift for melody and darkness.

Cashmere If You Can, my third solo record, was an album of deep darkness. I was in the wrong place at the right time in my head to record it, but one thing led to another and soon I was in the thick of it all without ever thinking it through. I worked on the record with Leo Abrahams, a fine guitarist and producer, and – at great expense – a band of top players he'd put together. I felt a little out of my depth. Leo co-wrote some of the songs with me, but I don't think I did them justice – I let him down by metaphorically nodding off on the job. The ones I'd written with Boo in earlier sessions fared slightly better. 'Goldfish', with guest vocalist Kathryn Williams, and 'Wrecked' are the two tracks that stand out to me now. On reflection, we did well to come out with an album at all. Leo had the patience of a saint. *Cashmere If You Can* was expensive, and my manager, Matt Thomas, and I coughed up a heavy price to put it out on the internet. An app was built; it was all going off-piste. And I finally realised there was no money for me in making records any more. But even though solo touring and recording is largely vanity-driven, it's so enjoyable and fulfilling for me to play alone on stage to a house of happy faces that I continue.

During the recording of *Cashmere*, I was playing a solo show in Blackheath. The usual appreciative crowd appeared at the venue as I sat in the dressing room warming up with my customary take-away curry and tea. There was a knock on the door and in walked

Bob from Combe Avenue, who I had not seen for so many years. In his hand was a Tesco bag. After we'd said hello, he handed me the bag with its contents of quarter-inch tapes on reel-to-reel of me as a seventeen-year-old singing and playing my songs. I had completely forgotten about them. I was so moved to have them in my hands. In the studio we found a tape recorder and I heard this young voice singing songs in Bob's bedroom. It was the voice of a passionate young person slightly influenced by Bowie and Reed, the songs deep and dark, the playing gentle, simple and oddly in tune. I was blown away as I was transported back to the young me, at the beginning of the journey that was always going to lead me to this moment.

Being a solo artist is like wearing different hats; sometimes it makes me look like Elvis and at other times it makes me look like a pantomime horse. It's a role I've found difficult to cultivate, but I'm finding that the more I do it, the more I like it. Being on stage is good fun. I talk more and try to engage the outside world with what's going on inside. My history with Squeeze carries weight, and people want to know all about this part of me.

It's an honour to share my journey, which I do in between solo strummings and gentle versions of classic Squeeze hits.

I continue to enjoy a writing partnership with Boo Hewerdine as he delivers something very different to Glenn. We have an unreleased album in the wings. When we come to release it, I think people will like what they hear. The new songs are funny and charming, very me-and-him in some ways. I also love to write with Paul Carrack; I send him words, he sends me melodies and somehow it all fits. Hearing his voice wrapped around my lyrics often finds me crying in the car; the soul is enormous. I also enjoy working with Jools, who comes from another place musically, though it doesn't happen as often as it used to.

We do tour together from time to time and it's a wonderful experience to sing with his Orchestra and play alongside Gilson, who I love and admire for being a wonderfully poetic drummer and good friend. Who would have thought that back in 1973? As I cast my eye over each of my solo albums, I can see a different me to the one in Squeeze. Working with other people engages another part of my soul and I like it that way. It's the writing that I enjoy – it opens me up and hopefully reveals something new every time I put finger to keyboard. It's what I do. If I were a plumber I would be fixing sinks; if I were a pilot I would be flying planes. But I find it's writing that connects me to my higher power. I feel plugged in, sparked up and nourished if I manage to hook something great. It's a hobby more than anything. And today, my solo career simmers in the background feeding my new-found hunger to be heard as an individual, not just that bloke who sang 'Cool For Cats' in Squeeze, lovely though he is.

ANCHOR AND HOPE LANE

Les was the troublesome brother; the tall, skinny one who drank and smoked and swore at my dad and never came home when he was meant to. My mum would be up all night with worry. My parents struggled with him when he was a teenager; he once knocked my dad out on the stairs after a drunken night, and he pushed my mum to her limits as he borrowed more and more money from her. Money she never really had. He fought with my other brother Lew over most things, too. Lew was the academic one and this was to be a lifelong bone of contention for Les, who thought our parents loved Lew more because he was brighter than him – or indeed me. You had to love Les, though; he was such a warm person. He played football really well and enjoyed riding his scooter with girls on the back down around Combe Avenue. If ever I were in trouble at school or on the estate I would go to Les for help. He looked after me, and when I started out in a band, he would always come to the shows and support me. His musical tastes were Bo Diddley and The Rolling Stones, Eric Burdon and – in the end – Squeeze. He tipped my scales musically when I was younger; all that R&B he played in the house drove Mum nuts, but it showed me that nice wasn't always right or good.

The first time I vomited from drinking too much was when I went to visit him up at the Sun in the Sands pub in Blackheath when I was about eighteen. It was lunchtime. He was at the bar on his stool with all his mates around him, and they all gave me their time and support even though they thought I was a dippy hippy. I had a pint and a pie then I had another pint. I was trying to be the man Les was – the bloke who played darts, followed the football and drove home drunk. An hour later, I was outside the pub being sick against the wall; inside my brother and his mates just ploughed on as if nothing had happened. Les got me work, too. I helped him scree walls with plaster in a new housing estate down by the river, then we'd go and get plastered ourselves in the pub. I worked down the docks with him, and at Ready Mix concrete in Catford. He looked out for me and showed me the basics of ducking and diving. Les was my 'fence' once when I was working at Biba in London. I was in the stockroom and found myself moving some gold lighters around. The next day I came to work with an empty guitar case, filled it with the lighters, struggled home on the train with it and took it to Les. He sold them around the pub and gave me a cut of the profit. I managed to keep my job, everyone was at it. My prize steal was a folder covered with a fine leopard-skin print. I still have it, still with nothing in it.

When Squeeze went on tour in 1986, we took Les with us as a minder. He was a big chap and looked tough, and he brought along his mate Terry Kibble from the pub. Terry had been in the army and had served in the Falklands War, and was very scary. Having the two of them on a tour bus was delightful: cards and beer, women and song. Terry managed to get us out of bed some mornings for a bit of training, running around the hotels so we could keep fit. Running on a hangover is not a good idea, and I bailed out very quickly. Those two and our manager David Enthoven were a team, big drinkers all and very funny with it. A good mixture of private school and secondary modern.

Les had a good heart – even if it did have a hole in it. He managed to maintain many friends and was always there when I needed him. But I could see he needed help – his drinking had become an issue and his wife wasn't happy with his anger and temperament. He watched me like a hawk as I got sober in 1991, and one afternoon he came to my house in Rye and asked for help. He moved in for a few days while I sobered him up, then I arranged for him to go into PROMIS, where I had been. They kindly took him in even though we couldn't afford the fees. He got sober and remained sober. It was great for his health and for his family; he has two lovely daughters, Kim and Claire, by his first marriage, and a son, Josh, by his second.

Without Les in my life, I'd have had nobody to call when I felt lost and in need of family support. He gave it in a way that was non-judgemental, and with so much love and understanding. He hadn't got a pot to piss in, but it never mattered to him as he lived a day at a time. He always knew the hole in his heart might kill him, so he was carefree and never worried about tomorrow. When he got sober, it all fell into place for him. He enjoyed the community of AA meetings and gained many new and dependable friends. It was a joy to see.

Then in 2007 he died in hospital from *Clostridium difficile*. He was Squeeze's biggest fan. He used to drive me to the airport and held my hand, and collected me again when I returned from wherever I'd been. He gave me all the love I needed to get on that plane and beat the anxiety that had lit its fire in my soul. He was a lovely man and a wonderful brother, and I miss him every day. He lived the champagne lifestyle on lemonade money; he really did live a day at a time. Some days I'm in the car and I think, 'I know, I'll call Les,' and then I remember he's not here. It's like losing an arm but still feeling it.

By 2007, Glenn and I hadn't seen each other – or even spoken very much – in eight or nine years, since I'd recoiled into rehab. But after we buried Les in Benenden, a few plots away from where Maxine lay, I flew to New York to honour his passing and to be with him in the sky as he left for the heavens above. When I woke up the next day in my room at the Soho Grand, the phone rang, and it was Glenn congratulating me on flying after such a long time. He knew what I was going through; his own brother had died as Squeeze were just beginning to take off, when he and I were living in the house on Crooms Hill. His brother was a haemophiliac and sadly died through complications. When I see footage of us playing outside The Bell in Greenwich on Jubilee Day, I can see him in the crowd, but I don't ever remember there being any more than a passing hello – but when he passed away, Glenn was knocked for six. I remember seeing him crying and distraught, but we just didn't share our feelings in those days in a way we might do today.

My good friend and US touring agent Steve Martin boldly found me some solo dates to play while in America. On our date sheet were Nashville, Birmingham in Alabama, Chicago, Minneapolis and New York. I flew out Dorie Jackson to keep me in tune and Melvin Duffy to add sparkle. Glenn had already toured in the US a number of times but this was my first adventure, and sadly it was not well populated. We played well and travelled well, and in doing so I suppose I showed a new-found commitment to touring and, more importantly, flying. It was a start. Glenn takes to the road much better than I do, he is a dab hand at the old soft shoe on stage with his masterful fretboard work and his voice which never grows old. Mine however at that time was in need of some work, and on that tour I felt the scaffolding rising into place.

While I was in New York, I went to see Nicky Perry, my girlfriend from all those golden years ago. She had a tea shop called Tea and Sympathy, and that was what I needed. We talked for hours about Squeeze and our journey; she was hoping we might get the band back together. I was still grieving the loss of Les.

A month after touring in America, Glenn and I met for a nice lunch in Blackheath. My then manager, Peter Conway, and Suzanne, Glenn's manager, were there too. Glenn looked much the same as ever. He sat uncomfortably opposite me and we may have mirrored each other. It was good to see him again and I was excited about the possibility of being back together. Suzanne and Peter played hosts to our delicate conversations and our tiptoeing closer and closer to each other. Trust was hard to find, for both of us, I guess. It was potentially a big moment in our lives. I was struck by how serious Glenn was about us working together again, and how he carried himself; there was little room for light or laughter in that meeting.

He was considering re-recording our hits so we had some ownership of our masters, and we talked about touring with the band again. At first I wanted a fresh sweep of the broom, but Glenn would benefit from his band, The Fluffers, who already knew the songs from playing them at his shows, which made sense, although a brand-new band would have been exciting. The Fluffers were made up of former Death in Vegas drummer Simon Hanson, Stephen Large on keyboards and Stephen's wife Lucy Shaw on bass. It was a job lot. John Bentley's name came up and it was decided he'd be better on bass and would give the new-look Squeeze wider appeal. I hadn't seen John in hundreds of years, but when we did meet again he was just the same: small in stature, but large in love and musicianship. The most perfect person for the job. The band was formed and we quickly made hay in Glenn's studio down by the river on a trading estate in Charlton, on Anchor and Hope Lane.

This studio was a larger version of the one he had in Blackheath, ample amounts of chaos gathered together around the creativity of love. And a collection of Hoovers, a Steptoe and Son front room of stuff. Word got out and we were soon back on the road – first in the States and then in the UK for one of our legendary Christmas tours.

2008 was a very busy year. My album *The Last Temptation of Chris* came out on Stiff records no less, to great reviews, but sadly it was dwarfed by the touring of Squeeze. Glenn and I were giddy with awards: we got a lifetime achievement award at the Ivors, which I cherished, and the same at the Nordoff Robbins. At the Ivors we were given our award by Mark Ronson, whose mother I had just had tea with in New York. He was very humble and I was beaming with pride. Glenn and I hugged on stage in front of the music business' great and good. It was a fabulous day. This was my second Ivor, the first being for the lyrics for a film I had worked on called *Still Crazy* featuring Bill Nighy and Jimmy Nail, another proud moment.

Lily Allen gave us the Nordoff Robbins award a few months later.

It was all making sense to me, we had re-engaged with ourselves and our history and the respect around us fired our ambitions to get things right this time and make it last. We were back on the map and people wanted to reward us for our dedication and ambition down the years. However, the old behaviour quickly set in. Peter Conway was my voice and he very softly expressed my words and feelings to Suzanne, who'd then speak with Glenn. He in turn would bat the verbal ball back the other way. We communicated through emails and managers. It was exhausting for us all, and heavy work for Peter. Squeeze went on tour to America and it was agreed that Peter would oversee the first half and Suzanne the second, which seemed fair enough to me. Then one day Peter called me from LAX airport to tell me he was quitting the tour. He wasn't happy and found the whole Squeeze banquet hard to stomach. I had to let him go. He was such a nice man, but I had to agree with him that it was sadly just not working. I started to feel the claustrophobia of the past creeping back in. But playing live again on the bigger stages made me feel happy.

Glenn had this mad but wonderful idea to re-record all of our hits on the *Spot the Difference* album, and it was pure genius on his part. Simon Hanson was Glenn's anchorman; he worked hard at playing exactly what Glenn wanted him to play. He was replicating the brilliant drum parts laid down by Gilson over the years, a tough job that he did well. Glenn played all the rest of the instruments, even sometimes on the original guitars and keyboards. The end result was an almost perfect replica of the originals. Thanks to the co-production of Andy Jones, the record was well received by our fans, who wondered why we would ever cover our own songs. It took some explaining.

My new manager Matt Thomas tried hard to find a small label to help promote it and cover some of the recording costs. He felt this would give it the best chance of being heard and for the songs to be used in films and on television commercials. The album was a great idea, masterfully achieved. We would finally own the rights to our songs. Sadly nothing happened with the recordings, it was expensive too and the tour profits seemed to soak away into the black hole of recording the album. Hopefully in the future they will turn a coin.

In 2010 our Christmas tour took old fans by the horns. By this time Matt, who I'd met at a therapy workshop in London a year before, had his feet under the virtual management desk; he handled the strange and delicate set-up carefully and diplomatically. He was a master of balancing emotions. Matt was my voice and he very softly expressed my words and feelings to Suzanne, who'd then share them with Glenn. What we really needed to do was talk to each other a little more. Matt did instigate various meetings and for the most part they were fruitful. It seemed like we were sparring with one another when we didn't need to. Maybe there was an issue of trust, I'm not sure.

In rehearsals for the tour, Glenn told me we were going to learn a dance routine to perform on stage. I handled it badly and walked out. I was not in the mood for dancing.

Steve Nieve was in the band for this tour, and the two of us remained at the back of the stage each night while Glenn and Simon led the routine from the front. It was Chuckle Brothers time; we looked like five minicab drivers. It was uncomfortable for me and I hated it. My head wasn't in the right place. I was distracted by a relationship that was turning me inside out. I had

lost all grip on reality. I was tending the emotions of my adolescent self, who in turn was chasing the same in the other person. I
dipped in and out of depression once again, only to be held by my
good friend Gordon. He had been security for Sting, Robert Plant
and others. He was a kind and very serious person who lived off
Portman Square, where I spent a lot of my time at a club called
Home House. Matt Thomas was wonderful on that tour, as was
Gordon, who drove me from show to show and kept the dressing
room jolly and me partly sane. I wore dark glasses on stage to hide
my puffy eyes and the emptiness beyond. I was feeling deeply
depressed and in no-man's-land emotionally.

Squeeze ploughed on with more tours across the States, which
were fun. My cloud lifted. We made money, we lost money. And
the last UK tour we set out on was amazing – we sold out all the
shows and made CDs of the performance available to fans in our
Pop Up Shop, as soon as it finished. One of Glenn's inspired ideas.
It was hard work selling them at the merchandise stand. It kind
of breaks the magic, or any slight magic a band might have. Up
close our fans are lovely people, but after two hours on stage I'm
knackered and want a warm bed to lie down in. But it was worth
the effort. It was a Christmas tour to be proud of. Our royalties
were once large cheques that came in the post twice a year; these
days it's embarrassing. Thank God for PRS. This keeps the pie
in the oven, as Squeeze manage to get good historic radio play
across the country. We are something of a national treasure, a
heritage act, which makes me feel as though we should be behind
a twisted red rope in a museum.

Matt was a brilliant manager and close friend; he held my hand
during some fragile relationships that came my way. He was in

the room with me, so to speak; he was bright and focused on my chaotic, complicated world. I felt for him. I could take my darkest fears to Matt and share them with him, and that's what a good manager should be, a person who listens and loves and enjoys your music too. In 2012, the band went into the studio and recorded some new songs – our first new material in fifteen years. The BBC made a documentary about us, which was revealing and wonderfully put together. Our story was out there. With all the tension and lack of communication between Glenn and me laid bare, it was sad to watch, but overall I was proud of our journey, warts and all. Controversially, Glenn grew a beard for the filming, and everyone whispered how awful it looked, but we were in the spotlight once again and the old fans who had remained dormant came out to see us play because they had seen us on the telly.

Beard or not, Glenn was on a mission, and I wanted to be there by his side. In the grand scheme of life, the beard meant nothing to me. But the new songs did. And I initially felt excluded during the writing and recording of them. I had sent more than twenty-five lyrics to Glenn since we'd been back together, which he had largely ignored, and I was beginning to wonder how bad they must have been. Inside, I knew that my stories of heartfelt sadness inspired by the recent break-up were not filling him with fire. Looking back at them I can see why.

One survived from the wad of tears in my notepad, a song called 'Tommy', a lyric inspired by a real-life incident, when my then girlfriend, now wife went into a post office and saw a timid black man and his son being attacked by a drunken racist idiot. I'd heard nothing from Glenn in the six weeks since I'd sent the song to him, and then one night the demo arrived via email. I was blown off my chair; it was incredible. He'd recorded it with beautiful strings laced over his lovely melody and my tragic words. The song took on another beautiful life of its own as 'Sonny' on our most recent album, *Cradle to the Grave*. His musical genius had returned and I could see and feel the future about to change around me.

'Cradle to the Grave' was a typically great Squeeze song too; its chord structure turned its wheel precisely over the verses and we rolled along. It came about when, one afternoon in Glenn's studio, he asked me to write something that would capture life's journey, from the cradle to the grave. I found the idea appealing and went home and worked on a lyric.

The new songs went into the set; then, before I could catch my breath, they were mixed and out on an EP. I argued to slow things down, but Glenn was driven as he always was by another imminent tour. Suzanne had an idea for a 'Cradle to the Grave' video and soon we were in The Pelton Arms, a Greenwich pub in which Glenn loved to play, making a cheap but fun promo with our children playing us as younger Squeeze members. My son Riley looks so much like me on the screen it's scary, and the older cast were locals and friends of Glenn's. 'Tommy' also had a short video made for it, and we used both as backdrops on the Christmas tour. Our tours were beginning to look properly produced, and to good effect. We could not afford just to swagger on stage and play our songs; these days people wanted more, and with videos and lights we managed to shape a really good show around our songs. I felt part of this new creativity as gradually we shared our ideas. We added some of our solo songs to the live shows; we played 'Still' and 'Black Sheep' from Glenn's albums, and 'Cowboys Are My Weakness' and 'On My Own I'm Never Bored' from mine. It was lovely to play all of these songs together, and the band made them sound like Squeeze songs. My two were rearranged by Glenn, which gave them a slight left turn that the audience seemed to like.

More recently I discovered what Glenn thought of my solo albums. He liked *I Didn't Get Where I Am* but seemed ambivalent about the other two. His solo records mostly passed me by, though the most recent, *Happy Endings*, is really great. Lyrically it's very strong, and I can see now why he pays more attention to the lyrical side of things in Squeeze these days. He really digs in and magnifies his thoughts in an open and honest way with me. Sometimes it's frustrating, but often inspiring. His album melds family with a happy spirit, which is Glenn. He likes a night in the pub, friends around the house, good food and song, and it's all there in this honest and open recording. I have never been to his house – I don't even know where he lives!

Summer festivals were great for the band to play. WOMAD, where we played a proper set, was amazing in the July heat; we played full tilt and went down a storm. Latitude was exciting, as were some of the smaller festivals. We had come a long way from the playing on the wooden pallets of 1973. At V Festival in Essex we had a short and sweet set to play, and the best thing for me was meeting the brilliant comedian Peter Kay backstage after we played. We got on like a small house on fire. He was a huge fan of ours and I was a big admirer of his. Peter knows where all the B-sides are buried. He told me about the time, years ago, when he'd been waiting to get his record signed by the band outside the Manchester Apollo. Apparently he'd offered me an extra-strong mint, which I turned down; then I signed his album and knobbed off in my car. Now look where he is, and who's laughing now!

At the Coachella festival in 2012, I got to feel what it was like to play a US festival. This one was neat and tidy and it ran like clock-work. No beer cans in the grass, and no feeling of claustrophobia because of the crowds. Radiohead inspired and lit up the hot night sky with a mystical coming together of collective minds, a band all singing from the same hymn sheet. As a band I thought we were not as cohesive as I imagined Radiohead to be, but we could be just as serious with our music.

At this point I was feeling like I was drifting again. I was over-thinking everything and everyone. The short festival sets didn't appeal to me, and there was an internal yearning for new songs. I was seeing things through those old rose-tinted glasses you find in the dressing room after a good show. I found it harder and harder to put pen to paper.

When Glenn and I first met in our teens, we shared a place in our minds where we could have ambition, with shared ideals. Compromise was always going to be painful; after all we are two very different people bound in a powerful creative partnership, both struggling to be heard and respected. Both of our lives have changed so much since the early days – and for the better. When we first started writing together, the sun seemed to shine every day. I would write pages of words and Glenn would beaver away at the piano or guitar, coming up with the most amazing melo-dies. He was patient and gentle as I got my head around his often complicated chord structures, and as a result, I'd try my hardest to learn from him. We spent that summer of 1973 up to our ears in music, as his record collection and mine came together in the giant listening booth that was Maxine's house. Our journey

slowly gathered pace, and between then and now we have written hundreds of songs, played hundreds of shows and recorded
thirteen-plus albums. I have been in awe of Glenn's musicianship
all this time – even when we weren't talking to each other. And
I've always wondered what it would be like to be him, up on stage
sweating like a goose but being able to pluck any song out of thin
air and deliver it perfectly. It's a gift he has. Being in Squeeze in
this third act of our lives has had its moments, but walking out to
face an audience with Simon on drums, John on bass and Stephen
on keyboards made me feel confident and very happy. Having the
band back together was a learning curve. Our songs drilled deeply
into the history book of my life.

We are lucky: younger people are coming to our shows, as fans
bring their children – and even grandchildren – to see us play,
and I love that so much. As I get older, I understand that we have
a contract with those who buy tickets to see us. The songs they
want to hear must be in our set and we must play them no matter
what.

It's a tall order to keep all of the people happy all of the time,
but we have a good crack at it.

CAVAN

There I was minding my own business when I was asked by a friend to record a young band from Cavan in Ireland. It was September 2012 and I was fresh back from a fantastic Squeeze tour of the US. The only spare time I had was before our biannual knock about Britain that December, so I went up to London to see this band – The Strypes. I met them and the drummer's dad Niall Walsh in a coffee shop and it was obvious to me they were going places. They were all fifteen and sixteen years old, smartly dressed and very friendly. Their broad Irish features made them look like jockeys ready for the rock 'n' roll hurdles ahead.

I booked a studio, Yellow Fish, close to where I lived in East Sussex, on the advice of Boo Hewerdine, who was keen to co-produce the sessions with me. Boo was the perfect person to have on board; he's a really good producer and has a keen ear when it comes to building songs. The band came down and set up shop, and within the day we had twelve great songs – mostly covers, but full of excitement, youth and passion. It reminded me of early Squeeze recordings. The circle had been joined in my head in a unique way. I was observing myself back at the starting gate. We were all stunned by what was taking place. Ross, the singer, was bunking off school to be in the studio; he was very shy and had to wear dark glasses when he sang to summon up enough confidence. Josh, the guitarist, blew me away; his playing and his writing were way beyond his years, and he was such a nice guy too. Pete was just sixteen but his bass-playing was so informed, inventive and right on the button. Evan was amazing on the drums, especially for someone so young – he kept great time while knowing so much about the music he and the band were covering. He was the historian, just as Glenn and Jools had been in Squeeze, and he was the most opinionated, but in a very inspiring way. He had the future all planned out, though this as I know can be fateful.

Niall, Evan's dad, was doing all the running around for the band, playing the role of dad on the one hand and manager on the other, and he'd mentioned to me a few times how he felt a little out of his depth. There were actually two other managers in tow, who had organised a few shows for the band and had paid for the studio and my small fee. But I felt the band needed more experienced management. To me, it was obvious they were going to be something special, and I knew I wouldn't be on their journey for long. They needed a record company and a producer who could hone their future for them. I couldn't do that.

So they went off and we kept in touch. Niall called for help here and there as contracts appeared and the two managers took more of a role. It gathered speed very quickly. The penny really dropped when I went to see them at the 229 club on London's Great Portland Street. I was so excited that night – watching them live was an exhilarating experience. Niall came up to me afterwards and asked my advice. The contract they'd been offered was too heavy

and far too restrictive for a fresh-faced outfit at the very beginning of their career. My own experience of rum deals lit up a few
red lights on the internal dashboard.

I was rehearsing with Squeeze that December when I got a call
out of the blue from Elton. He said he'd heard about The Strypes
and that I'd been working with them, and he asked me if they'd be
interested in meeting with him and possibly signing to his company, Rocket Music Management. I called Niall, and before I knew
what was going on, Elton had called him at home in Cavan. Niall
was blown away. Cavan is a small town, about an hour's drive
from Dublin, and not much happens there. Then suddenly Elton
John calls and puts Lily Allen on the phone to say how much she
loves the band too. They had a simple choice to make. They came
to London to meet the team at Elton's office, and the next thing I
knew they'd signed a contract and Elton was back on the phone
asking me if I'd consider working with them again as a mentor.
I was thrilled. Within a month, I was there in the Rocket offices,
finding my feet at the beginning of an entirely new journey. It was
magical to see the excitement in the band's faces.

The Squeeze Christmas tour came to an end and I pondered the
changes to my life. I was back in co-manager suits and ties in west
London, just two roads away from Bryan Ferry's office. In fact, Mr
F and I had an Audi-off in the street one day, when I parked mine
next to his – the same one I'd ordered for him a couple of years
before. All his windows were darkened glass, but he had them half
rolled down. I could see him in his dark glasses, peering out at me.

The Strypes' two previous managers sued the band, they settled
the case, and in my view the move to Rocket was the right one. Not
that it was any of my business. Record companies offered up all

the toys they could muster – iPads, CDs, box sets, bags and other swag – to court the boys, and every day was like Christmas. It was exhausting, but it was amazing to watch and be on the edge of it all. After a bidding war, Rocket signed them to Mercury Records. It was the right home. Plans were hatched for the first album and Elton was keen for the band to record with his old friend Chris Thomas, who'd produced part of The Beatles' White Album and had worked with some amazing artists – The Pretenders, The Sex Pistols, Pink Floyd and Pulp among them. I had lunch with Chris and Julian Wright, The Strypes' manager at Rocket, to discuss this, but Chris wasn't keen. He had retired and was resentful of the industry he'd left behind. Elton pushed him, though, and eventually he gave in. Before recording the band set up in a house near to where I lived in Sussex called Tilton House, and there the boys rehearsed some of the new songs. One afternoon I invited Jeff Beck over to surprise them, and to his credit he jammed along with them for an hour, faces beaming with the genius in the room, a complete legend and a very magical afternoon for us all. He wanted them to play The Yardbirds in a film he was making, but sadly nothing came of it.

We booked Yellow Fish studios as the band had liked their time there with Boo and me, but as Chris would only work short weeks, the band had to fly in and out from Dublin all the time. The momentum was stuttering. They were cool with it all, though, and in between sessions we booked London shows to keep the pulses racing. My diary had become very full all of a sudden and I wasn't at home very often. But important seeds were being sown. I desperately wanted the band to have the success that had eluded me at their age. I'd watch them from the side of stages, feeling the rush and excitement I'd had back in the days when Squeeze would play pubs and tiny clubs, before our lives changed forever.

Elton had the boys over for Sunday lunch one afternoon; I picked them up from Heathrow and we drove up to his house at Windsor. The gates opened and in we went to be greeted by His Nibs, his hubby David Furnish and creative consultant Tony King. Julian Wright and the lovely Charlie Dunnett, who'd first spotted the band, were there too. Sunday lunch was to die for, though the band seemed timid – I think they were a little intimidated by the surroundings and the banter. As I drove them back to the airport, I asked them what they'd thought of the day. Ross said the roast potatoes were the best he'd ever had. That was it. We were off and running.

The shows that followed were amazing, and Elton even turned up to a few – once arriving in a helicopter on his way back from Thailand to see them in Brighton. The crowd packed into a small pub was amazed to see him there as large as life. The set got tighter and tighter, and I managed to pull together a great team of people to work with them. It was going well as far as I could tell; everyone seemed happy and taken care of, which is all you can ask for on the long and winding road to fame.

Chris Thomas worked hard to get his head around the limita-tions of Yellow Fish, and he did well to record the band in the way he wanted. Chris was such a nice man to be around, although sometimes difficult to read. He'd tell the boys stories about The Beatles and the session would stop while all ears leaned towards his words. I enjoyed the recording, too; the songs developed well, with lots of venom and youthful verve. I even enjoyed the sandwiches that Niall and I had to go into nearby Lewes for every day. The band stayed at Mount Harry – a wonderful old pile on the other side of the town. Its owner, Chelsea Renton, was so welcoming. She looked after them and provided them with fry-ups and chips all night long. She was happy to entertain and support them away from the studio heat. She created a home away from home for them.

Short days and short weeks meant it took three months to record the album, and it was during the final stages that the band really started to take shape as young people. They were growing like triffids. Either that, or I was shrinking. Looking back, I remember that period of my life so well: being in a band and witnessing the dynamic starting to change. It's subtle and it takes time for it all to sink in. But then sometimes you're pissed off with the guy who stands in front of you on stage. I remember not being able to express my feelings, cringing when other members of the band had the courage to banter with the audience whilst I stayed silent, angry at myself. A riff you think is yours is now someone else's. An idea you think is great is tossed aside for someone else's better idea, and it hurts but you won't concede and you sulk. It's your band, then it's not; you divide and rule with subgroups; you're not the lead singer, but you want to be. You think you look cool, but you know someone else in the band thinks you look like a wanker. I've been there and I've survived.

In a short space of time, The Strypes had the album mixed in LA, were offered a tour with The Arctic Monkeys and had a sleeve shoot with the photographer Jill Furmanovsky. Jill took pictures of Squeeze early on; it was like going back in time for us both. One thing just led to another and there were always a million balls in the air. The album mixes proved to be the last straw for Chris Thomas; even though he didn't want to do them himself, I think he felt hurt when others took his place, and he left the building. He refused to have his name anywhere near the record – which was a shame as his production was so incredible.

As the album promotion rolled on, it was clear the band had lots to say; almost all of them wanted to talk, but in the end they had to learn how to share the spotlight. Interview slots were dealt around. It worked well. The Strypes are so knowledgeable about themselves and music, the old iPad being their history book. They are always digging deep into the YouTube vaults to find new old things to listen to, and there's not much you can teach them. Not that I ever attempt to try. Japan licked the band up like fresh cream; they were adored and were waited on hand and foot during two sell-out tours in 2013. Europe started to come to the party, and though gigs in the UK were selling out too, the audiences were mostly men of a certain age.

The band thrive on the mosh pit and I can see them raise their game when people toss themselves about like lemmings. Bodies fly around; it's as if a school of salmon has suddenly reached a row of rocks – they leap into the air and land on each other with tails wagging. Watching the band reminds me of being on tour in the early 1980s, and sometimes it's as though I'm seeing myself in an earlier life – with my mouth wide open, breathing in the heavy fumes of excitement from the crowd as they hear my songs for the first time, watching girls looking longingly at the lead singer. The energy you provide in that situation is massive and it comes from deep inside; it's a need to impress and be the leaders of the pack, wolves on heat, sweating under lights, running around on small stages, using the monitors as springboards for height. It's so great, but now I'm in my sixties all I can do is watch like a parent, hoping they don't break a leg or faint from the heat.

At the end of the show, I hand out the water and hug the band one by one as they come off stage. In the dressing room, Niall really justifies his role as the fifth member of The Strypes; he translates how they feel and deals with any niggles or cross words. He also doesn't mind picking up their pants. I've heard a few healthy rows in their dressing room, but nothing nasty. It's all very understandable and typical of a young band. Again, it takes me right back to the early days of Squeeze: a small, hot room with sweaty clothes thrown on chairs, boots on the floor and a rider of crisps, Skittles and soft drinks – though in my case it was always crates of brown ale or lager. Now I'm the one who makes it all possible – I'm not the Wizard of Oz, pulling levers behind a velvet curtain though; they are.

When Squeeze were first signed, we knew that if we didn't make it with our first record, we could hold on for a few more. The music industry just isn't like that today, but at Mercury Records with Mike Smith in charge, it's as close as you can get to that situation. Mike is a generous person, and gives his acts plenty of guidance and ideas about co-writers and producers – essential in an industry that has changed beyond recognition from the one I first entered in the late 1970s. Music is now listened to in a totally different way. The internet has created so much freedom for artists and it has taken away the power of the major labels. Squeeze sold 30,000 singles a day at our peak. If you sold 30,000 records now, you'd be at number 1 all year round. The Strypes sold 129,000 copies of their debut album – mostly in Japan and the UK, with Ireland a close third – but they make a much better living on the road than we ever did, thanks to record company support. Mike is aware of all of these parameters. His job, along with the effervescent Ted Cockle who runs the label, is to sell records and advance the band's talents, and all sides have to listen to one another for this to work. It doesn't always happen, though. How could it, when we all know what's right?

Elton gives so much to the boys; he calls to see how they are doing, he comes to see them play and he always invites them to the Rocket Christmas party – which, for all the glitz, is a work do just like the ones back in those black-and-white days when I used to go with my dad to the parties at the Greenwich gasworks. Elton feeds everyone well, then makes a speech about each and every artist he has on the books. He thanks the assembled staff, he makes jokes and I'm deeply touched by his care and attention. David stands by his side and is just as impressive with his encouragement to one and all.

The boys were not naturals at all this swanning and schmoozing, though; Josh seemed the only one who would mingle and make small talk. The rest of them looked slightly out of place – like they wanted to go home now, please. I know that feeling well. I however enjoy the mince pies with Ed Sheeran and Elton, and discuss the comings and goings of people way more famous than me or The Strypes. We are all a little out of our depth. But the band is held in high esteem by the great and the good. There's Jeff Beck, who jammed with them when they were staying at Mount Harry; Jimmy Page, who was at the side of the stage at Earl's Court; Wilko Johnson, who joined them on stage at Canvey Island; Paul Weller, who gives them studio time. Their music and attitude seems to

touch performers from a certain time and place; it moves creak-
ing limbs. It's always been my dream, though, to turn younger
people on to live music and the excitement it brings. And though
it's mostly mods at their shows, the front row is expanding slowly
with younger wannabes. In Derby, I saw a front row that was completely young and female. How the band raised their game that
night! It was magical to see.

The Strypes went back into the studio at the end of 2014. Album
number two was recorded in the Dean Street Studios where Glenn
and I had made the *Difford & Tilbrook* album in 1984. It was great
to be back in Soho, but this time I took more of a back seat, and
watched and listened as the band got stuck into twenty new songs.
Josh was now nineteen and had discovered girls and vodka, and
he'd also got heavily into hip-hop music. I don't think the rest of
the band were impressed. I sensed Evan and Josh – the band's two
leading factions – pulling in different directions. Josh was spreading his wings, hanging out in London and jamming with a new
set of friends in Chiswick, while Evan was steadfastly devoted to
the bluesy garage sound that had become the band's trademark.
One day, when things took a mellow route with loops and backing
tracks, Evan got so upset that he kicked a sofa and stormed out of
the studio into the busy Soho night.

I knew exactly how he felt and it was hard for me not to take
sides. Change is so hard, so difficult to embrace when you're clear
in your mind how your world should be. You genuinely feel your
band will be wrecked by one strange turn of events. All I ever
wanted in Squeeze was the simplicity of bass, drums, keyboards
and guitars, and when change came into the room it rattled me.
The irony is that it's been Glenn and all the change he's brought

in over the years that has kept Squeeze going. Staying in the past would only have hindered our progress.

With The Strypes, Josh was only trying to open up the way for the new. Being radio-friendly does require compromise, and there are decisions to be made about credibility versus success. For me, it's obvious. Success pays your pension. But try telling an eighteen-year-old that they should be thinking that way, and all you'll get is blank looks. When you're that age, you're on the front line – nose against the mud as you climb out of the trenches with your drumsticks and guitars. You're on a crusade to change the world with your music and your know-all attitude.

Being involved with The Strypes has connected me with a younger part of myself and that's an amazing feeling. So what is my role? I'm a mate and sideboard for them to put their drinks on; I'm personal management, and a mirror for them to wash their faces in; I'm observer and hod-carrier while they tuck into bowls of chips and takeaway food in the dressing room. Whatever my role, it's doing me the world of good. Because of them, music excites me again. They are now on album number three called *Spitting Image*, and Pete the bass player along with Evan the drummer have knocked up some fine songs with some very inspired lyrics. Josh has had to raise his game, which is no bad thing as the band have grouped together more closely thanks in part to the wonderful production of Ethan Johns. Ross is singing better than ever and with miles more confidence, and Evan is still the best young drummer I have heard. Josh is a big talent and a very special player. Paul Weller was only too eager to pluck him away for a few days to play on his new album.

The band recorded the new album at the legendary Rockfield

studios in Monmouth, where Squeeze had recorded in 1976. I went to visit them while they were recording and nothing much had changed over all of that time. In a cupboard were the very tapes on which we had recorded. I had no idea we had recorded so much. Golden days – ones I find hard to recall. Like The Strypes I'm curious about the past and find it hard to live in the present, but that's where we all are, for now at least.

NUMBER 18

Ziggy Stardust, Obscured by Clouds, Talking Book, Eat a Peach, Honky Château, Exile on Main Street, Something Anything, Transformer and *Clear Spot*; all these albums appeared in 1972. I was on a musical journey that has brought me to where I am today. During that fruitful and inspirational year, I was mostly stoned and living on the dole. I had nothing to complain about. I celebrated my seventeenth birthday, and the same year, Louise Fielder was born.

In 2011, Squeeze were asked to play on a Radio 4 comedy show. It was something I really didn't think we should be doing, but my manager Matt Thomas thought I was wrong, so we did it. I turned up at comedian Arthur Smith's house and sat on my amp in a crowded kitchen filled with radio people and invited guests. That day I was feeling very positive as I'd just come from seeing Maureen, my therapist. She was straight with me; she made it abundantly clear that I should know what I wanted from a relationship and have all the boxes ticked. At that moment, I had no boxes to tick. All my relationships had chosen me. I was feeling delicate and extremely lost. As Squeeze played another version of 'Pulling Mussels (from the Shell)', I looked out across the busy room and saw the most attractive smile I had ever seen. For a moment I was lost. 'I could spend the rest of my life with that woman,' I thought to myself, and inside I was pulling loads of impressive shapes, like James Brown.

On the way out we said a brief hello, and I walked to my car and dragged out my departure from my parking space as long as I could, in the hope that she might leave at the same time. She was standing at the door with Peter Curran, one of my favourite radio voices and lovely all-round chap; they looked like they were in fits of laughter together. Later that night we searched for each other on social media and words were exchanged. We had bitten the bait on the hook and the discovery began. I sat in my flat watching the screen for words, a mint tea to one side, tantalised and smitten with her humour and wit. She seemed exciting to me.

A week later, we had dinner at Home House, a club in London's Portman Square that I've been a member of for many years. We sat at a table by the fireplace and glanced at the menu; Louise looked nervous and incredibly beautiful. We talked things over, forking small pieces of our meal, then I drove her home. Home – that was a place I'd not yet found in that period of my life. I was living in Bentinck Mews in Marylebone; very expensive and smart, but it wasn't really home. It was a place of cold nights and long afternoons on the sofa thinking about the mess I had got myself into. The boxes needed ticking. And packing, again. I drove Louise home in my Audi, which might as well have been my home in those days, as I was driving around so much, and when we got to her house, where her family were sleeping – three kids and a husband she was in the process of separating from – I carefully leant over the gearstick and armrest to kiss her goodnight. She turned, and our lips met just below the rear-view mirror. That short kiss lit a fuse inside of me and the fireworks went off all at once.

I drove back to my mews house and started emailing her again; each day we were engulfed in chapters of humour and openness. We were finding out about ourselves. A few days later she dropped the kids off at school and came over to see me. I was waiting on the corner of the street; we hugged and went inside my bachelor pad. The discovery continued for some hours. In the few, very fast months that followed, the boxes were ticked one by one; we were in each other's lives as though we had been there forever. Maureen was gently prodding me to take care and slow down, but how could I? I had fallen in love with a wonderful person, there was clearly no doubt about that.

Some months later, after Louise's husband had moved out, he was on holiday with their children at their house in France when he was taken ill and very suddenly died. It was all so unimaginable and sad. He was a talented TV producer with many friends. Louise and her children were shattered. I stepped away; it was not my place to do anything other than support Louise from a distance, who proceeded to manage the passing of her husband with such courage and love for her young children, who had been there at the very end. It was heartbreaking. I retreated to Marylebone for my daily AA meetings and coffee with Gordon. He was so close to me at this point and like Maureen gave great advice. Louise wanted me nearby, so far from being in the shadows and giving her the space to grieve, I was there alongside her to give her love and comfort.

A few months later David Enthoven very kindly invited us all to see Take That at Wembley Stadium. The children were excited, and so was I. Robbie was the highlight of the show and came on stage via a long rope high above the rest of the band, bursting into 'Let Me Entertain You' right on cue. It was a night on which I could really see how wonderful Louise was with her children, and how close a unit they were. I felt privileged to be part of the outing. I think it was tough for everyone, but David made it as smooth as only he could.

Louise is warm-hearted, a loving and patient mother, a very trustworthy friend and a person who supports me in ways I'd not thought possible. I'm so lucky to have met her and to have her at my side. I have found her humour to be a constant flame that keeps all of our friends warm. She listens without prejudice and gives without expecting to receive. The fact that she has so many good friends tells me everything I need to know – she loves all of them and is loved by them in return.

My time in Marylebone had come to an end; I was running out of money again and needed to move somewhere more realistic. I had just read a book by the clergyman and writer Peter Owen Jones and it inspired me to go and see him read from the book at The Old Market theatre in Hove. We met after the reading and I asked him if I could come and visit him at his house in Firle, a small village near Lewes in East Sussex. When I went to see him, he sat in his small office and let me talk about my life and how low I was feeling before I met Louise. I cried and he listened with love. He said that what I needed was home and community. Then he led me down the street to a house and said, 'You should live here.' Number 18, The Street. It was a biblical moment. I met the person who was living there, Chelsea, and Peter told her I might rent her spare room. It almost happened, but fate took that moment away from me. A few months later, though, not only the spare room but the entire house was available to rent. I was in heaven. Louise thought I was mad to move to a small village; at that time, she was not a country person. But I was.

Firle is the most beautiful place on earth. In time, Louise and her children, Linus, Pebbles and Mitzi, moved in too. She sold the London house and committed to a life in the countryside with me. A year later, I walked her up to the beacon on the Sussex Downs just above Firle and asked her to marry me. She said yes. Her face lit up as we walked and hugged the sky around us. We had the most romantic wedding, with curry, music and all our friends, on a cold and very wet day in April 2013. It was perfect – even with the horizontal rain. Peter married us in St Peter's Church in Firle; the circle was being joined together. I had found home for the first time in years. Gordon Hough was my best man, and what a great best man he continues to be. Gordon is a wonderful friend who has saved my life many times; he is funny, he is love. His stories are incredible. Lou's father gave her away.

Glenn and Suzanne were there too, and Glenn was in tears when we walked down the aisle. I was in tears as well, and we hugged as we left the church. It was a very significant cuddle; it felt deep. People from all corners of our lives were in the congregation; family on both sides. From school there was Danny Baker and his wife Wendy; from the big stage, Peter Kay, who had been so kind to me during my darker times, and his wife Susan. Lou's dad made a very funny speech and my brother Lew gave us his well-rehearsed look back at my life. He was very funny too and had everyone in stitches. Gordon's speech was poetic and honest;

he gave me a cheese sandwich in a bag as a closing gesture – it was what he often gave me in the car after a show when he was driving me around the country. He made a perfect chauffeur, when I let him drive, which was not very often. The Strypes flew over from Ireland to play for us. Niall and his wife Anne came over too. Tony King and Julian Wright represented Elton. Outside the riding school, where our reception was held, the rain lashed down and the wind gusted in from the beacon and the Downs above. We were all cosy inside, though, with our massive heaters and bellies full of curry. After the reception we drove to Lucknam Park in Wiltshire for a brief honeymoon and a very long sleep.

Apart from me, Lew is the only Difford left from our branch of the family tree – a tree that goes back through the foggy 1960s and down the ages to Somerset and France, where the Diffords struggled up from originally. In September 1993, Squeeze had been playing at Bristol's Colston Hall. After the show, as I hung out with the band and our friends in the cavernous space downstairs from the depressing dressing rooms, Lew came in and introduced me to a woman – a Difford by birth – who'd spent the past few years researching the family tree. The first traces of the name now synonymous with a songwriting partnership that stretches back some forty years appeared, aptly enough, in and around Glaston-bury – home now, of course, to the legendary music festival. Many of my forefathers were buried there and documents dating back to the 1700s show we weren't a wealthy lot. The odd sheep was passed down from generation to generation, but that was about it. When the railways came, my great-grandparents took work on the track, following it all the way from the West Country to

London, where they settled in Charlton, which is where Lew, Les and I came in.

The woman had our genealogy all mapped out on a long white roll of paper. I could clearly see where Les ended and his family preceded him. I could see Lew there with a million grandchildren and I could see family members I've either never met or who appeared once or twice when I was a young boy. There I was too, with my twig growing from the tree: four children, and now the new Mrs Difford and her brood. And as our wedding climaxed, I could feel the family tree growing.

My children were all there and embraced our marriage – they have always supported me with open hearts. Natalie and Riley, Grace and Cissy are the cornerstones of my life. When Natalie was born, I walked with her strapped to my chest through the woods on Toys Hill, near where we lived in Edenbridge. She was loved and educated in London and at Sussex University. Now in her mid-thirties, she lives in New York, where she has been since 2006. She loves the New York city life, and she loves to travel. Her work in film is finding her awards and mentions in Oscar-winning films. I'm very proud of that. Recently she has produced two great films, *Gimme The Loot* and *Tramps*. When I was her age, I was on tour – no surprise there. It was 1987 and I was in New York with Squeeze at Madison Square Garden.

Riley was the second best man at my wedding – he read the serenity prayer for me, which was lovely. Riley is sober like his dad. I loved taking him on long drives when he was a child; he would sit in the passenger seat as we raced around London and the Kentish countryside.

He is one of the nicest people in my life; a wonderful, big-hearted son, dreamy and full of dizzy ideas like me. He also lives in New York, married to the lovely Natasha, who is related to Florence Nightingale, which will come in handy for young Riley.

Grace is a talented photographer and is working all of God's hours to make a name for herself and to afford to live in East London which is so expensive. She enjoyed horse-riding, shooting and swimming as a child. Her journey from Brighton College to St Martin's in London was colourful, as is her way. She is fun to work with and she has been on many Squeeze tours as a production assistant. She always seems to be happy and is fiercely independent, which is a good thing. She is a sweetheart and loves a curry just like her dad. She has been to India several times, and I'm green with envy.

Cissy came along in the early days of my sobriety, and to me is a sobriety gift of love. She is like me in many ways, and I remember long walks with her as a child, taking the dogs up through the woods and back in all weathers. She excelled at Brighton College and she went to London to study English literature. Not an easy transition for someone as tender as she is. With her English degree under her arm from Goldsmiths college I'm sure she will light up many an empty page with her imagination and words. Cissy works hard, also loving living in East London not far from Grace.

Linus, Mitzi and Pebbles, Louise's children, are very special young people. Bravely they have accepted me into their mother's life and into theirs. They are all growing rapidly and bringing with them the focus of early-teenage life; the house is a cauldron of social demands and domestic issues, some of which I have not had to deal with for many years so that I am retraining myself to control my expectations. Family is a beautiful thing and Louise is so good at being mother and wife, controlling all our needs one at a time with grace and good temper. It can't be easy. Binding the new family with the old has been a steady and gradual journey. At the wedding, all seven of the children – mine and Louise's – danced and joined in with the happiness of the evening.

Francis Dunnery once told me I was the *puer aeturnus*. I had no idea what he meant, but it is Latin for 'eternal boy'. It is a Jungian concept and applies to men like me in their fifties and sixties who have retained the emotional characteristics of an adolescent. Some of us had fathers who were partially or totally absent, others had dads who were weak and passive and left the upbringing to the mother. All of us have an inappropriately strong tie to our mums, for better or worse. And if the young boy doesn't learn to differentiate himself from his mother, he struggles with his sense of masculinity – it has to be won by taking a stand, overcoming inertia, deciding and acting more, reading and knowing more, gaining muscle and competence in the world of men. Or by joining a rock band and touring the world. We *puer aeturni* are known for our wandering, our many relationships and Don Juanisms. This has to do with seeking the perfect mother in a woman, looking for someone who can give us everything – always to be disappointed.

We long to be fathered, and throughout my life I've always latched on to strong male characters, be it Glenn, Jools, Francis, David or friends in recovery. We are impulsive and impatient, we have a low frustration tolerance and our main pursuit in life is ecstasy, often at the expense of everything else. We are drawn to drinking, gambling, pornography and drugs to get that rush. And I'm here to tell you I tried them all, it was wonderful and I was momentarily happy without knowing what true happiness really was. In many cases, we are charming and attractive – like me, obviously – but we also have a concealed sadistic streak that you would hardly guess was there until it strikes. Many women I've known will attest to that.

It's a tough thing to own up to, and to grow up. Charm might make a great first impression, but intimacy, commitment and involvement are needed in relationships. Louise is helping me find a balance. She has endless patience; she is fine-tuning me like a Patek Philippe watch. Time, however, is not on my side. On the positive side, the *puer aeturni*'s willingness to begin anew, take risks and be spontaneous can work in our favour. Being creative and childlike is helpful, and if we can harness this energy consciously, it can transport us to a good place. One like mine, where a dreamer and a chancer with the most incredible luck in friends and in love can turn things around.

All those years ago, when my palm was read in a small, colourful caravan at the Lammas Fair, I never thought the reading would come true. But I've had a big family and a life in music – though the prediction of the long life remains to be seen. Maureen, my therapist, asked me to open my hands each morning and let whatever was out there into my life. I did just that, and Louise walked in. I'm not afraid of what might happen in the future now. I'm grateful for everything I have. I have nothing to complain about, no real regrets. Life, I've realised, is about belonging and having dreams you'd still like to realise. I do. I'm just not sure what they are yet.

WORTHY FARM

Glenn and I are a very odd couple, but that's what makes us special. So in 2014, after we'd rehearsed being together in the guise of Squeeze, we began rehearsals for our next tour – one involving just the two of us, which would begin with us getting out of bed Eric-and-Ernie style and end in rapturous applause and a few giggles. The 'At Odds Couple Tour', a title my wife Louise came up with, was one I'd been looking forward to for a long time, and unlike previous acoustic jaunts, I found myself feeling more at home on stage with Glenn and with myself. The nakedness of acoustic music brings honesty and fear in equal amounts to the table, but after just a couple of gigs I felt my confidence return to the point where I actually enjoyed being under the bright lights. Alongside all the old favourites – 'Tempted', 'Up the Junction', 'Black Coffee in Bed' – we each played a solo section, which made our combined musical journey join up. The show was glued together with a Q&A led by Miles, Glenn's driver. He was the man in a golden cape running down the aisles with a roving microphone. He wore it well and it seemed to work.

I have known Glenn for forty-four years, and though we're not always close, we know each other well. We have travelled so far together and risked many things musically and sometimes emotionally. In this third period of Squeeze we find ourselves getting closer than before, but it took time to find our feet with each other. It was a slow but fruitful build.

At first the tour was hard work – I felt the old feeling creeping back in, the weak confidence within me and the yearning to slow down. I called David for advice and we went for lunch. He was so understanding and told me how I might handle the new world I had entered into.

I let go of all of my fear around my relationship with Glenn and the way I played on stage and freed up the emotions that had been locked inside. And by the end of the tour I was wanting more and more of the same. We went to America for five weeks, which was very tough on us both, but it brought us closer than we had ever been. Hugging each other in the dressing room and both missing home and, more importantly, missing our families. Walking on stage was hard, but I adopted the mantra 'Tits and teeth, darling, tits and teeth.' Tonight, Matthew, I will be Chris Difford of Squeeze. It was another of David's simple tips. Speaking of Matthew, sadly myself and Matt Thomas went our separate ways. It seemed to make sense for Rocket to look after me as I had managed to get to know them all so well and I trusted the process of change. As a company they are locked into the music industry in a way that perhaps Suzanne and Matt would not have been. I was sad to lose Matt, but it was very amicable and we still work with each other closely together on charity work. He runs Music Support, a haven for people in the industry who seek help with their addictions and depression. Matt has done a fantastic job bringing this out into the open, and I help where I can.

After all the duo touring, we turned our minds to the new album. In the second week of January 2015, I got a call from Glenn to wish me a happy New Year and ask whether I'd like mackerel soup for lunch in the studio. Suzanne sat us down to talk about plans. There were many. Most pressing was the new album to accompany my old school friend Danny Baker and Jeff Pope's new TV sitcom *Cradle to the Grave*, based on Danny's memoirs. The show was so funny and I felt so lucky to have been given this massive opportunity. Our task was to produce one song for each episode of the show – eight in all – plus the title track, which was already in the can. But though the TV people were over the moon with the songs, things had changed a lot from the early scripts, and they found it hard to place them in the show, which was really disappointing, though we did manage to get a few on screen. I watched each episode as it came off the machine in the editing suite and was blown away by them. They were funny and brilliantly scripted, and Peter Kay was totally believable as Danny's dad Spud. It's a hilarious show from start to finish and I was so proud to hear our songs coming out of the TV. It was hats-in-the-air time all round.

Glenn and I were drafted in by Jeff Pope to play cameos. I was the grumpy drummer, which suited me well, and Glenn the pub organist. We spent the day together in Manchester, mostly in the good company of Peter Kay in his trailer. I love this man; he is so gentle and funny, a real one of a kind who has helped me through many a tough moment with a shoulder to lean on. Laughter filled the day, and with Danny there too it was a belly buster of a visit.

The album was a coming-together of minds; we really worked hard to be in each other's company, and it paid off. It's as good as

East Side Story, filled with precious moments and well-produced songs. 'Open' was about my wedding to Louise, and 'Nirvana' was a story that Glenn and I worked on together from my idea about a couple reaching old age and the kids having left home. It was a struggle to wrestle some of the songs from within, but it made the recording interesting. Glenn would challenge me from time to time on what I was writing – I was finding it hard to focus on the metre of some of the songs, mainly because they fell over older melodies. It was not writer's block as such; more writer's drift.

I was blown to the side of the road by the weight of our new relationship. He would pore over each line almost word by word like a member of the musical forensic branch. The dynamic had changed; we were writing songs as one. I think that his time apart from me, having to write his own lyrics, had made him a more detailed and mature writer. The balance of our separate views on life would change the words sometimes for the better, and my share of the partnership began to alter. At times we almost wrote in the same room, but we settled for the next room with the door open. It seemed to work. Glenn's words would be more factual than mine and mine perhaps more emotional and dreamy, a good combination for this album.

Laurie Latham co-produced the *Cradle* album with Glenn, and we used Jools's studio to mix. John Bentley was replaced by Lucy Shaw on bass. John did at least play on half of the album. I was sad to see him go, but I agreed with Glenn that we needed the change and to his credit he said if we ever needed him back he would be at the end of a phone. A true gentleman. My voice, alongside Glenn's, is the sound of Squeeze. For the first time in years we were joined at the vocal hip, and I believe that was one of the secrets of the success of the record. However, I had no leads on this album; it has been seventeen years since I sang a song on a Squeeze record, and that was 'Bonkers'.

We got great reviews for the new album and were back on form. 'Happy Days' was a radio hit and we were being playlisted for the first time in years on Radio 2: a great feeling. The *Cradle* album sold 50,000 copies and was well received in the press and by our loyal fans. Since our first album all those years ago, times have moved on. Spotify is now the parental record company to one and all: it pays pocket money to artists like us, and I have no idea how much that might be. Although I did hear that 6,000 streams of one song equates to £1.90.

We shot two cheap but effective videos and got on to *Later* with Jools. I only wish he had joined us for a number, and people tweeted to say the same thing. It was a big moment; we were back on the telly and we missed a trick. After the show we were invited around to Jools's castle for dinner with him and his charming wife Christabel. I remembered that when I first met Jools he would write, like everyone else, in my diary, and once he drew a Rolls-Royce outside a castle next to a princess, his dreams in a doodle. They all came true.

We shared stories around the table with Danny Baker and Jeff Pope, and then he took us to see his train set, which covered the whole of the top floor. It was magnificent. There was even an underground train network and scale models of the Thames down at Greenwich where we all grew up. His house was rebuilt with his loving passion for architecture; the detail is stunning. He has done well for himself and very much deserves it. I have always kept in touch with Jools, singing as a special guest on tour in his fabulous orchestra. Their arrangements of Squeeze songs go down well with his dedicated fans.

As a hobby while all of this was going on I had been working with Boo Hewerdine on some songs we had collected over a five-year period. I got to sing which was nice, it boosted my confidence in that neighbourhood. The album was the polar opposite of *Cradle*, but sadly it didn't come out as it clashed with Squeeze activities, which naturally take precedence. It was maybe over-ambitious to record twenty-three songs and try to strap them loosely around a thin storyline, but the songs really worked and will be released at some point. They are very much worth a listen. Doing other things in the background gives my life balance and I think I need that. It's good to prod around and write, it keeps the songwriting muscle in shape. Those songs will see the light of day, but first I have to find a window in which to release them. That may be tricky, but it will be worth it. There are some great songs floating around in my bottom drawer.

I'm growing more and more confident in my solo shows as well. I love the one-on-one contact I have with my audience, and these days I seem to know most of them. One of my favourite solo shows during a break from recording *Cradle* was when I was playing at the Arts Centre in a town called Oswaldtwistle, not far from the home of Peter Kay. I invited him along to introduce me. The small crowd of maybe 150 in total, were stunned to see young Peter come out on stage and walk up to the microphone. I stood in the wings. Twenty minutes later he finally introduced me as Glenn Tilbrook from Squeeze. When I walked on to the stage, he said 'Oh no, we've got the wrong one, the one who can't sing, ask for your money back!' I fell about laughing and indeed it was hard to sing a note without belly laughing all night long. 'Look, he doesn't know the chords either,' he went on to say – sadly he was not wrong. It was a memorable night for us all. The next day it was back to work, back to the studio for a check on reality.

The tour that followed the *Cradle* album felt very grown up; the production was key and many of the songs were supported by fantastic videos made by a friend of mine called Sam. We invested in a tailor to make sure the band looked good, and we made sure we took care of ourselves on the road. As touring goes I think I was as comfortable on and off stage as I had ever been before. It was a revelation not to be stressing about what other people might think. I started to put myself first, something I often find difficult. When men get to a certain age they start to wear their trousers up high just below their tits and not care. I think I was reaching this point in life. If I got things wrong, it was OK. I learnt from it and moved on. If I got things right I proudly owned my feelings and savoured the moments. What was not to like, the reviews told us that the new songs were just as good if not better than the old ones.

Touring in the past ten years has gradually grown; we have taken more care of our presentation and it looks and sounds great, and our audiences are growing in numbers. We of course travel differently and separately, Glenn in his bus which is his home from home, and me in the Audi sometimes with Gordon driving me, although I do prefer a comfy hotel. Suzanne has managed things well, a hard balancing act, the two of us with our very special needs. It can't be easy, and now with Rocket on board with their expertise I think we have a balance that protects us both. Julian Wright is expert at diplomacy and driving a good deal through the record companies' door. Rachael Payley has also been active in the delicate task of management. I feel safe in their hands, they are well respected and have good hearts.

America is still a very strong playing field for us and recently the long tours over there have certainly paid off. Old faces pop out of the woodwork and now too their children are at our shows, loving the old and the new songs. Our tours now include nannies for children, drivers for both Glenn and me and a complicated accounting system that nobody seems to understand, but we all get paid eventually – sometimes it takes as long as five months to get paid! It makes me feel like a jobbing plumber. For the first time in many years I can honestly say that I enjoy touring again; it's a great place to get to know oneself and learn how to cohabit with friends. The world is a smaller place these days so it's possible we could spread our wings, if I can get my head around the flying a little more.

At the beginning of 2016, after touring the UK, Squeeze were invited onto *The Andrew Marr Show* to play 'From the Cradle to the Grave'. One of the other studio guests that day was the Prime Minister, David Cameron, who before we went on told Marr that his government was planning to knock down council estates and build more houses in their place. This is a particular bugbear of Glenn's; he has always leant to the left politically, and feels really strongly about young working-class people being priced out of the areas they were brought up in. However, it was still a complete surprise to me when, as we were playing the song, he decided to change the words of the final verse. 'I grew up in council housing,' he sang to Cameron. 'Part of what made Britain great/There are some here who are hell bent/On the destruction of the welfare state.'

Predictably enough, the media went mad about the story – especially as Cameron, who obviously wasn't listening, sat there clapping politely at the end. Squeeze were back in the news again and suddenly I found I was a hero on Twitter, because people know I'm the lyricist in the band and assumed I was the one sticking it to the PM. I said to Glenn, 'I want to go on social media and remove myself from this because you should be the one taking the credit.' But he disagreed with me. So I was high-fiving people on the streets of London for days after the show as I was mistaken for the mastermind behind the lyrical changes. People always get the two of us mixed up; they stop me in the street thinking I'm Glenn, and I was once booked for a private show and introduced as him. I stood at the microphone and held my hand up. I got paid, sang, and went home happy. It was a stroke of genius when Glenn changed the lyrics that Sunday morning. David Cameron came over to us at the end of the show and said, 'You know I think that song is going to be a hit!' Wanker.

Later in the summer of 2016, we played at Glastonbury on the Pyramid Stage – a cathedral of happiness and a dream come true. It has housed all the greatest artists in its time and it was a complete honour to be there for the fifty minutes of our set. The band smiled and played so well, Simon so gracious, Lucy adding femininity to our songs, Stephen as dapper and professional as ever, and Melvin Duffy the sunshine in our sky. His smiles keep me warm and distract me from over-thinking. Louise and my daughter Cissy came to support me. She was covered in mud most of the time, as we all were; that's Glastonbury in the summer.

Glenn looked happy too, like I had never seen him before in his nice shirt and suit. He played so well; he is one of the great guitarists, and his singing is sublime and never ages. Our songs in his hands are incredibly safe.

Being on stage has changed very much over the years. I once felt intimidated and scared, shy even. I would clatter about in a haze following the shapes of the chords, trying desperately to get them right. The energy of the younger me and the younger crowds was so addictive, everyone bouncing about like wasps in a can. There was nothing better than chucking myself from one side of the stage to the other, high on the adrenaline of the moment. The younger me dished up the crowd with rough hands; stage talking was not polite and often aggressive. There was a swagger that we all adopted as we walked on stage, similar to how you see football players whaling on to a pitch, shoulders up and down, head high, in for the kill. But I often looked scared and felt empty. Repetition of a song can often render it soulless, and remembering words has always been a mission for me, but somehow it slowly sinks in. I bluffed my way through the creeping success from the smaller pub stages to the larger arenas.

I have learnt to hold my own and not be looked down upon by others in the band. I feel like I have grown into the mature(ish) person I am today. The same rush and the same swagger applies, but there is no fear. I feel at home on any stage, in a small club or a large concert hall. In my solo skin I play house concerts, and that is very different, being in a living room with twelve people listening to me singing my songs. When I see myself on YouTube now, I see a very happy chappy, dashing about high on excitement, content with his lot, triggering off the other members of the band like a piston in a racing-car engine. And all this without the old Cipralex.

I do enjoy it, though. The pinnacle of 2016 was to play at the legendary Glastonbury festival on the Pyramid Stage, a peak experience that took me to another place, a place somewhat spiritual and free. It's not like walking on air, it's like being air itself.

As we leapt through our set, and the years, my eyes soaked up the growing crowds, who seemed to be miles away from the stage. Yet the connection to the front row and beyond was easy to embrace. It was our time to link arms with our songs and the people who have made them what they are on our journey. I saw many smiling faces and people singing, I saw flags and hats, I saw clouds and sunshine. Time raced by and it seemed as soon as we were on stage, it was all over and we were walking back into the wings. We hugged each other and hovered in our place, the place where we had triumphed. There were tears in eyes and lumps in throats, and with hugs all round we reluctantly shuffled back to the dressing room.

Like at every show, the audience is key: they are your reflection. They reflect your happiness and love, and sometimes all the mistakes you make too. When I sewed all of my dreams together as a teenager, they made a magic carpet for me to ride on. Being on stage at Glastonbury was like being on that magic carpet.

When I got home from the festival I watched us on the telly, and I was right: it was really great. I watched other bands too. Coldplay can grip a huge audience in the palm of their hands with such control; I find all that very moving. I loved the way they paid tribute to Viola Beach who had died in a car accident while on tour a few months earlier. Young lads on an exciting journey, but sewn together by their sudden and very sad destiny. The inspiration I had experienced at the festival made me want to look ahead and think about the next album, the next Glastonbury. I sat up at my desk and prayed. After all these years suddenly a spike of clarity mixed with fear had centred me in such a wonderful place. It's as though our songs and our journey had found their place back in people's hearts and minds, and I was feeling so excited about the future and what that might mean. They say a cat has nine lives, but I feel like I've had more.

ST PETER'S CHURCH

The very next day after I had driven home from Glastonbury with Louise, I received a text from David Enthoven: *Just saw you on BBC4. Big hug and looking sharp, Sir Christopher. David E.* It was uplifting to read his text, the very fact he took the time to contact me with his love really made my weekend complete. A few weeks passed by and we had turned the corner into August when I received a text from my old friend Chris Briggs, it came out of the blue. David was in hospital and was very ill. I was in shock. Lucy from his office called me to confirm the worst. I quickly sent him a text, and a day before he died he replied, sending me his love in return. I could not comprehend the magnitude of his passing; he was such a big figure in my recovery and in my life. Barny, who I had not seen for a few years, called me, and we met for lunch and shared David stories, of which there were many.

Barny and David were big on men's groups and discovering the male within, which meant poetry and tears in a cold open field. I once went on one of these weekends, New Age Warriors it was called. I was shitting myself – I had turned up to a disused airbase, where I was told to go to the man with the lantern in the opposite corner of the field. He then told me to cross back over the paddock the same way, ending eventually in a line outside a Nissen hut. We were told not to talk. One by one we filed into the darkness of the hut. When it was my turn, I looked around to see David. 'Go on, Diffy,' he said. At the door was Barny. I broke down and was led away. I drove home wondering what I had missed.

David ran a men's group of his own after that, and once I left The Priory I went there every week for a good kick up the backside. The group was facilitated by a very gentle but firm therapist called John McKeown from Liverpool. Ten men in a circle sharing deep feelings and being there for each other, risking and being supportive. As they were when my father had died, and when things at home at Old House Farm were less than perfect emotionally.

At David's funeral in the King's Road, the church was full to the rafters with friends and people from the music industry in which he had successfully spent his life. Behind myself and Louise was the quiet figure of Bryan Ferry, sat on his own off to one side. I went over to say hello and to ask if he was OK or needed anything; he passed me a casual nod. Brian Eno and Robert Fripp paid careful respects with quiet words, Phil Manzanera shook my hand and we exchanged stories about David and his passing. The church was also full of counsellors, most of whom I had seen over the years. Maureen was there, as was Gerrard from The Priory and Martin Freeman from Brighton, who I loved seeing. It's fair to say, I felt safe.

A eulogy was read by David's business partner, Tim Clark, who managed it without succumbing to tears as only a fellow Harrovian could have. David would have been so proud. He told the story of David's life in the music industry, from Marc Bolan through to Robbie, with Roxy Music along the way. He was bold and full of heartfelt anecdotes. Robbie Williams sweetly performed 'Moon River' with Guy Chambers playing beside him and Lucy Pullin, who worked with David, sang a beautiful rendition of 'Angels' that made us all swallow very deeply, letting the tears fall upon our cheeks. Such a wonderful send-off. When Craig Armstrong sat down to play one of my favourite pieces called 'Hymn 3' on the piano, I lost it. This piano piece is always with me when I fly, it's in my ears, it escorts me through the clouds into the air. His piano music is my meditation for my fear of flying. In my pew with Louise beside me my heart floated up inside my chest, I felt safe within as I said goodbye to my dearest friend, and as my eyes reached up to the sky through the stained-glass windows I cried.

I sat and looked out of the window above the altar as the sunshine poured in from above, and thought about my own mortality, my own life in its present form. I knew that in David I'd had a true friend who held up the lantern for me, showing me the way at each difficult twist and turn. Who would replace him now? Nobody could. But I would learn from his courage and from the way he gave so much and submerged himself in gratitude for the things he had in his life. I must do this too. I went to his home-group NA meeting that week, and everyone in that tiny room wept and shared the love of David. A brick in the serenity wall had been taken from us, and all I could do was gain strength from his passing. I was heartbroken. His coffin was driven away with four Hells Angels outriders, they roared up the King's Road stopping the traffic as they went. The low rumble of the bikes made us all feel connected with David's wicked humour. He would have loved it.

A month later, Squeeze embarked on a sell-out tour of America. It was another five-week marathon, bookended by that enormous fear of flying I still suffer from, although it is getting slightly better. This was the last drop of *Cradle* promotion; after this we could focus on the future, a dangerous thing in itself. On stage each night I decided to take a piece of David with me in my soul. I imagined him being there with me. 'Smile, Diffy, be in the moment and enjoy yourself, tits and teeth, tits and teeth,' he would say. 'Have a fry-up, Diffy, if you feel low'; 'A Twix will sort you out'; or 'Call the missus and tell her you love her.' All sound advice. The tour was tough from one end to the other. But one thing that struck me was the friendship that grew between Glenn and myself; we gave each other space and we performed each night and enjoyed ourselves, mistakes and all. Mine not his. The band were playing so well together, like never before, and the future simply seemed ours to make. We fell into the last week of the tour exhausted, and there we were again, me and him in the dressing room embracing in a hug.

We had driven for three solid days and after forty-four complicated years together, I never expected a hug to mean so much. Just like on our first US tour, we travelled across the country, from the west coast with its warm and beautiful people to the east and the chill winds with even more beautiful people. We had come a long way from the Chevy van of 1979, the miles still seemed as gruelling even though there were many more comforts than there used to be.

Another year in the saddle drew to a close and all of my children gathered round the Christmas tree at home. I could feel the passing of time and the many Christmases before us all. This one felt really special. The girls, Cissy and Grace then flew to India which they seem to love, maybe one day I'll get there too. Louise keeps family well, and without her in my life I'm sure I would be driven back into that dark place. She has my back and is a real team player. In the past being a team player was alien to me, thankfully I'm still learning how important the commitment of relations is. Not just with Louise but with everyone.

Christmas passed and in early 2017, Louise and I saw a house come up for sale in Firle. They are mostly owned by the Firle Estate and rarely come on the market. Not one in seven years in fact. We pored over the email and photographs and the next day went to see the house. And then a call from Peter Owen Jones: 'It's Peter, there's a house for sale and I think it could be your new home, come and see it.' Another biblical message from our vicar. We told him we were on our way. Peter is like all three of the main characters in *The Wizard of Oz*: he is made of straw, he is the tin man and the lion, but most of all he is the wizard himself.

Within two days we had the house under offer. At last a place to call home, a home that I will own with Louise. The first home I have owned for thirty-six years. It was time. Having always lived out of a suitcase, renting seemed like the best option for me in life until I met Louise, who very much believes in roots and own-ership. I stood in the garden as we looked around the cottage. The house was next door to the church where I had been married, and in the village where I found my family and my feet again.

The bell struck from the Saxon spire of St Peter's church and suddenly I felt reconnected with my stumbling journey through life, from south London to the breathtaking Sussex Downs. When I heard the sound of the bell as it started striking the hour, time

stood still for me while Louise and the vendors, two lovely ladies
of the village, walked around the garden. I seemed to enter a zone
of deep thought. I was off with the balloons. For that second I felt
connected with the turning of another page, part of the long walk
home. As I looked down the garden to see Louise so excited about
the house and the plans being made there, I felt that perhaps this
was the time to let go of my old values and embrace the home
we are lucky enough to be able to afford at this time of my life. If
only we could have gone to the pub to celebrate with some fruity
wine, laid back in the afternoon and blissfully rolled over into a
long nap. I could dream on. Eleven chimes passed and there I was,
walking back to the car, the house was ours. Now all I have to do
is work around the clock to pay off the mortgage – I've not had
one of them in about twenty-nine years. We got home from the
viewing and the phone rang: it was Glenn.

When I see Glenn's name pop up on my mobile phone I find
myself in conversation with someone who I have now known all
of my life. The only person I have known longer is my brother Lew
which is a very deep thought in itself. I think we are closer now
than we were all those years ago. How great is that? Relationships
have come and gone, cars and guitars have come and gone, rehabs
and tours have come and gone, yet Glenn still sits in the middle of
my life like the musical maypole.

It was time to write the next album. I sat down at my desk looking out to the South Downs before me and started to write the
lyrics. Another adventure was about to begin. Some predictable
moments perhaps, followed by odd exchanges of unpredictabil-
ity. That's the nature of our relationship. Writing takes me to my
happy place. I feel at home dissolving myself in the many issues

of the day, and in my imagination. January and February are always inspiring months to write. I love the darker nights and the cosiness of home, and when the house quietens down I can really sink into my word bath. I eventfully sent Glenn my new lyrics and waited for his response, which sometimes can take weeks. When he had read them, he said that they were the best I had written in a long time.

When the songs finally arrived back from Glenn in the form of his infamous demos, I pulled them down from my Dropbox – how I miss the C60 cassette – and listened hard, ears leaning towards the speakers in my car, the only place where I still love to listen to music. I was really happy to hear what he had written. It's often a magical feeling to hear his voice singing my words and to hear the songs glide in such an unusual way, from the serious chord jungle in one song and then suddenly back into the chic for another. The record at this stage seemed to be taking on a very different shape from the last, it seemed very exciting. The pressure of *Cradle* had lifted and I felt this time we could relax into a new, unscripted direction.

By March I was back up at Glenn's studio to gather round chord sheets with the band, just like on the album before and the many more before that, a daily drive of around three hours. There is a price to pay to live in the arms of nature, but I think it's worth it. We all sounded magnificent when we started to play, and why not? With the masterful Simon Hanson on drums, a better person would be hard to find for the job. A sweet man with a bright outlook on life, even when it sends him into a spin. Stephen Large on the keyboards, the ever-so-popular one who is on tour with so many other acts but finds time to put our band first, which speaks volumes. New on bass for this album was Yolanda Childs, who is smart and soulful and very adaptable with her playing. She knows a song and she feels where it needs to be, and couples up well with Simon. Laurie Latham set us up at the beginning of the session, but couldn't finish the album with us as he sadly had to record with Jools. Andy Jones, a friend of Glenn's, stepped in to focus things in the studio as Glenn had become swamped with ideas and inspiration. Andy was that gentle person who knew how to juggle the ever-changing studio emotions, and I really liked working with him. I was not helping very much, as my production skills are seldom useful, or always heard.

With twelve songs under our belts it felt like we were off to the races. Some of the new numbers sounded baffling in their arrangement but over time they sunk into this thick skin of mine. I had the feeling that we were making another great record; a couple of the songs stood out as early favourites: 'Patchouli' and 'Innocence in Paradise'. Glenn worked really hard producing the album, putting in maximum hours to place the songs in production. Fourteen albums down the road and his strive for perfection I still find inspiring. I may not have always recognised this, but playing back the new album I can feel the love we still have as songwriters, and for each other. We stand out from the crowd as gifted songwriters. Nobody sounds like us. It's been some journey and I hope it goes on for many years to come. He reminds me of a brother, someone who will look out for you and give you their shoulder to lean on, and at the same time manage to bring out the complicated emotions that only time can dissolve.

During the recording we took time out to head back to Glastonbury, this time for a duo show on the acoustic stage. Only a year and a chapter since the last visit to Somerset when we held our own on the Pyramid Stage. We went down on site a few days early this time so that we could write and record in Glenn's RV. Sadly the heat got to us both and that never happened. This year was incredible, I managed to play three times in the space of one day, with Jools on the Pyramid Stage, with the inspirational Gilson on drums, and with Glenn on the acoustic stage, plus a BBC TV slot singing *Up The Junction* backed by a Kazoo Orchestra. It seemed strange with so many other past members of Squeeze being around on the weekend. Paul Carrack played a fine set and sung three of my songs in a row on the Friday. I was welling up with pride as he sailed through his version of *Tempted* and *Bet Your Life*. Having Glenn on stage with Jools on the Saturday would have been a special TV moment but it was not to be. Jools thought it was a great idea but best saved for the future. Our acoustic set went down well, and we raced through our hits like men with trains to catch. I think we were both looking forward to some new songs joining the canon of our acoustic repertoire. Grace and Cissy joined me and Louise and it made for a calm and very special family weekend. They got to party and I got to blag meal tickets backstage and wristbands.

I got to hang out with Johnny Depp, a name I find embarrassing to drop. We had met before at a previous show in LA but this time we spoke for over an hour. He was softly spoken and leant into my every word, which felt surreal. He dressed in the way that he does, like a pirate. We tried to get on the side of the stage to see Radiohead but it was full on the gantry where guests stand to watch. Beside us on the stairs also stood David Beckham. There I was between two massive celebrities, neither of whom could get the right wristbands. I tried to help by talking to a passing tour manager. Johnny then said to me, it's OK I think I'll give this one a miss. When the Foo Fighters played we were there again trying to get side of stage. The same thing; no special wristbands. Along comes Liam Gallagher with his 30-strong entourage and they walk right by us up the stairs on to the gantry. It was like a pub arriving, them all drinking and smoking like the lads they are. His brother Noel we met earlier the day before, a true gentleman, who when I introduced him to Louise said I was punching above my weight. He may be right about that. Soon after that comment Mrs Difford was having her picture taken with Brad Pitt, and she looked very happy with herself. He said he was a huge Squeeze fan and shook my hand. And me just a simple bloke from King George Street with no such celebrity to match his. The real celebrities are the backroom staff at festivals, the dressing room managers, the drivers in their Land Rovers, and the kind people who give out the wristbands. I ended up with an armful. I have never been completely comfortable with the celeb palaver, much preferring to ride shotgun with the crew, or keeping it simple with my close friends along the way.

Before we left the magical staircase that leads up to the Pyramid Stage, Lou and I watched Barry Gibb. He sang *Staying Alive* and the whole festival burst into song and dance. For me nothing could top this, but it did. The next band up were Chic. They had me crying with deep emotion. If only Squeeze could get a crowd reaction like that. Maybe we do, I sometimes just don't recognise it. I'm not sure what it is when I see bigger bands take to the stage. I get very churned up, not envious but full of joy. It's what I was seeking all those years ago when I first saw The Who on stage down at the Charlton Football ground and when I began to write songs with Glenn. I guess I get all the emotional stuff from my mother, who would cry watching the weather forecast.

When I look back at my relationship with Glenn I feel blessed that we have survived so long. I think we still have the same differences we always had, but today they seem more transparent. Keeping a good relationship tidy is bloody hard work sometimes, but it's worth it if you work at it. It's taken a fair amount of beer, wine, therapy and song to get there, though. It's also been very complicated. I don't think it could ever have been simple.

'Give Me the Simple Life' is one of my favourite songs. It has become my daily mantra over the years, yet that simplicity eludes me. It seems that Squeeze are as popular as ever, Glenn and I are writing great songs again, my solo career is settling in, however chaotic it seems, and I'm loving the commitment to the future with Louise. All of this keeps me busy and the simple life is far away in the distance, which is just as well. I can't imagine myself shuffling about in the garden, or sitting and watching daytime TV like my dad ended up doing. Those twilight years need to be filled with ambition.

I've always wanted more in life, always looking over other people's shoulders to see if there is a greener field for me. The addict loves more, more of everything. My recovery meter often goes over into the red when I'm not on my game, when I'm seeking happiness in the out of reach. I will never be anybody other than myself and although I can dream of being more successful or more talented, I just have to accept that it's OK, there is no need to be wanting. I feel rewarded with love and happiness by just trying to stay in the moment.

When I was a young boy all I ever wanted was that red tractor in the toy-shop window, that ice cream with the 99 Flake. I wanted more pie, I wanted the best BMX bike, I wanted the latest Airfix model aeroplane. I just wanted. I have been trying to fill the hole in the doughnut for far too long, and that takes a lot of effort. I still want to have it all, but then who doesn't? I have everything I need really: a good wife and family, a great band and some wonderful friends. Songs and words for days, and a diary so full I can't even find the time to sit in the garden and listen to the birds sing.

There simply is nothing to complain about, but the fear that it all might go horribly wrong still follows me around like the old black dog.

Even now when I'm twenty-five years sober I have to stay alert, but also know when to celebrate with the still and sparkling. Celebrating my 25th sobriety birthday this 4th July, I looked out of the window at the panoramic view across Greenwich, a mile downstream. I was in a hotel, table for one, down by the O2 Arena built on the site of the old gasworks. Here many years ago I played in the mud while by father tended to the allotment and nodded to his mates as they passed on their way to work. Off in the distance I could see Greenwich Park and the Observatory on the hill, where I used to sit while hopping off school. I could see the church steeple of St Alfege's where I had been married in 1979. I could see the ever-changing skyline of London shimmering in the sunset which has risen up over the Isle of Dogs like masses of steel and glass Jenga pieces to obscure the evening sky. Over the horizon heading east of London I could see where my daughters Grace and Cissy now live, and by turning my head in the other direction I could see towards Charlton, where both my parents are buried. I was staying at the hotel to break the relentless journeys up to the studio each week. I was becoming my car and my car became me. Twenty-five years clean in the saddle was posing me some long questions, none of which I could answer. There I was, with this poetic view of my past life just beyond the glass window of the restaurant. I was thinking about friends and how many you can have in your life. How many real friends that would take that silver bullet for you are, of course, hard to number, but one thing was for sure that Louise would always stand by me if times got tough. My children also would do the same. They are all so wonderful and kind, sending me balloons, two golden ballons saying 25. I had so many calls and messages on the social media congratulating me I felt overwhelmed. It was a day of beauty and friendship. And a table for one. Home was not far away now, with the new house and the future being just one day at a time away. What else could I need in life? In some ways music has become the oil that keeps the wheels from squeaking, but it's never that simple. The squeaking wheel keeps on turning, and for the time being it's only me that confuses and complicates how that wheel turns.

When I was a child, to be told to speak when spoken to by my mother gave me the backstage pass to my imagination, and there I found the many songs and stories I have written and have yet to write. I still love being in a band, not the gang it might have been, but to hop around on stage is still a thrill for me. I still want to be that guy who sings 'Cool for Cats', and I still want to be a little bit famous. All the big cash is sadly gone but I have socks in my shoes, I have food on the table and a smiling face to wake up to. My dad always said if you join a band you will become an addict, a drunk and skint. Seems like his tender advice was right. However, I have amazing children who make me proud, and the escalators up to the next floor of adulthood seem to be running just fine. Over the years I have certainly idled and stood still where I could have taken in more of what went on around me, but that's what makes me who I am. I think I'm happy with that. I've never known from one day to the next what was going to happen, but something always did.

When the Beatles' van broke down in 1965 it was on the side of the road, having veered off it in some snow. Ringo said, 'What are we going to do now?' And John said, 'Something will happen,' and I'm very much like that, because something will happen – it always does.

Forty-five years ago in my little bedroom at Combe Avenue, on my single bed with my Bic pen and notepad by my side, I dreamt of being on *Top of the Pops* – tick. I dreamt of touring in America, which I used to visualise with my mother on the rocks at the Giant's Causeway – tick. I dreamt of having a family – tick. I was surrounded by posters of my favourite bands, vinyl records stacked up on the floor, my nylon-string guitar leant against the wardrobe. I was filled with dreams but lived mostly in fantasy, I was safe there. I think I was floating in a dream when I took a 50p piece from my mother's purse and placed an ad in a sweet-shop window for a guitarist to join a band. There was no band, there was also no record deal, there was nothing but me and my unmanageable grip on reality. I feel so blessed, and still I find it amazing that with that 50p, I found the rest of my life.

And now if you can excuse me, I'm going to have a little cry.

The Serenity Prayer

God grant me the serenity
to accept the things I cannot change;
courage to change the things I can;
and wisdom to know the difference.

Living one day at a time;
enjoying one moment at a time;
accepting hardships as the pathway to peace;
taking, as He did, this sinful world
as it is, not as I would have it;
trusting that He will make all things right
if I surrender to His Will;
that I may be reasonably happy in this life
and supremely happy with Him
forever in the next.

Reinhold Niebuhr

ACKNOWLEDGEMENTS

I would like to thank all the members of Squeeze who have given so much to the songs I have co-written, in performance and during various recordings. I would also like to remember Kevin Wilkinson and Matt Irving who have passed away gently along the way.

I take my hat off to all the crew who have pushed my amps around the many stages of the world and tuned my guitars, from Deptford to Detroit and back again.

Love and gratitude to managers David Enthoven, Matt Thomas, Julian Wright. Shep Gordon and John Lay, and to Suzanne Hunt.

The photography within these pages has kindly been provided by Jill Furmanovsky, Ron Reid, Lawrence Impey and Danny Clifford, among others. Thank you.

I would hold my umbrella open for the very generous Elvis Costello and Elton John, Christopher Guest, Cavan's own whippersnappers The Strypes, Niall Walsh, Marti Pellow and Bryan Ferry, and all of the inspirational people who have been the cornerstones of my musical career.

My ever-patient publisher Alan Samson, editors Rufus Purdy, Celia Hayley and Holly Harley, the Orion team Hannah Cox, Helen Ewing and Carey Brett, and my literary agent Clare Conville.

RONAN CASEY

Joe Dolan

The Official Biography

PENGUIN

IRELAND

PENGUIN IRELAND

Published by the Penguin Group
Penguin Ireland, 25 St Stephen's Green, Dublin 2, Ireland (a division of Penguin Books Ltd)
Penguin Books Ltd, 80 Strand, London WC2R ORL, England
Penguin Group (USA) Inc., 375 Hudson Street, New York, New York 10014, USA
Penguin Group (Australia), 250 Camberwell Road, Camberwell, Victoria 3124, Australia
(a division of Pearson Australia Group Pty Ltd)
Penguin Group (Canada), 90 Eglinton Avenue East, Suite 700, Toronto, Ontario, Canada M4P 2Y3
(a division of Pearson Penguin Canada Inc.)
Penguin Books India Pvt Ltd, 11 Community Centre, Panchsheel Park, New Delhi – 110 017, India
Penguin Group (NZ), 67 Apollo Drive, Rosedale, North Shore 0632, New Zealand
(a division of Pearson New Zealand Ltd)
Penguin Books (South Africa) (Pty) Ltd, 24 Sturdee Avenue,
Rosebank, Johannesburg 2196, South Africa

Penguin Books Ltd, Registered Offices: 80 Strand, London WC2R ORL, England

www.penguin.com

First published 2008
1

Copyright © Ronan Casey, 2008

The moral right of the author has been asserted

The Picture Credits on page 340 constitute an extension of this copyright page

Set in Sabon
Typeset by Palimpsest Book Production Limited, Grangemouth, Stirlingshire
Printed in Great Britain by Clays Ltd, St Ives plc

A CIP catalogue record for this book is available from the British Library

ISBN: 978-1-844-88196-3

Title page: the previous page shows Joe Dolan's distinctive signature autograph
– it didn't change a stroke in nearly fifty years

www.greenpenguin.co.uk

For
Mum and Dad,

and
Deirdre

I hope you'll say yes

Contents

Foreword

Not an hour goes by that I don't think about my beloved brother Joe and the magic he brought with him everywhere he went. Joe was my right hand. In the early years, when we lived together in a small cottage in Grange, Mullingar, we both dreamed that one day we might play in a band and entertain people. If you said to Joe back then that he would be having chart hits in every decade from the 1960s to the 2000s, he'd have laughed at you. We wouldn't have thought it possible. No way. But our dream came true. Joe became an international artist and, as they say in show business, he took me along for the ride! The last almost fifty years of my life with Joe have passed by in such a blur that it's hard to believe it all happened.

Joe was one of the best singers that ever came out of Ireland – if not *the* best. As a performer he was without equal. Joe always had a great style of singing; even when he was about ten years old he did not sing like anybody else. A huge chunk of my life was taken up with his success and travels all over the world, and now there's a void. I miss him so much. Joe was blessed with

good health and was rarely ill until the last year of his life; he seemed inde-
structible to me.

If Joe and I ever had a disagreement he would always win the argument,
but then he would say 'I'm sorry' and the next day when we met he'd say
'howaya!' and everything would be grand. He never held a grudge and always
saw the good in people. Even when suffering from a cold or flu, he would
smile and would be on good form. He was a real people person. Young or
old, no matter who they were or what age, Joe loved everyone the same. He
never acted the star, and he was never short with people. The only thing he
didn't like was rudeness.

Offstage, Joe wanted to be one of the lads and loved, as he used to say,
'having the craic'. He had a great sense of humour and simply adored telling
a joke. Joe was a great best man – the best man for the job! He could make a
speech about anything, even when he knew nothing about it.

He never spent any time thinking about money – not out of foolishness;
he just wasn't interested in making money for its own sake. So long as he had
some he was OK, but he would have been equally happy without any at all.

He had a great love for the game of golf and was very strict about the rules.
In fact he would carry a small rule book with him on a golf course and always
marked a card, no matter which way the round went.

But once he stepped on to the stage he was totally committed to his art,
and gave everything to the show. Even though I stood alongside him for
nearly fifty years, and played every show with him, I would have to say I was a
fan of Joe's first and foremost. Truly, there was no show like a Joe show. Success to Joe was the people, and I hope the people enjoy reading his story.

Ben Dolan
July 2008

Introduction

If you're in any way familiar with the late, great Irish singer Joe Dolan then he needs no introduction. But as he always got one throughout his fifty-year career, why break with tradition in this, the first fully authorized biography of his life?

Ever since his first official performance, on a creaky parish hall stage in the late 1950s, the young Mullingar man always seemed to merit some form of introduction. In those days he was the guitar player in a band, but his vocal prowess soon made him the star of the show and it was not long before he moved to the front of the stage. And as he stepped up to the microphone and dropped those first few words out into the night, he would introduce himself with a smile. All eyes on him would, in turn, twinkle in the glow of that broad, beaming smile of his, a smile that brought light into the corners of every venue he graced for five decades.

As Joe's stage entrance grew over the years and he began to arrive in his trademark white suit to a vast musical overture, he probably didn't need his smile in order to spread light to a room and into the lives of those inhabiting it, but it always did, and the smiles of the audience would fill whatever venue he happened to be playing. For the best part of fifty years there was no show for spreading collective happiness like a Joe Dolan show. And offstage the smiling continued.

Joe was the friendliest, happiest, most generous man going. He had a way about him that few others – and certainly very few in the entertainment industry – had. No matter where you met him he would be welcoming, enthusiastic and friendly. He spoke as if with an exclamation mark at the end of every sentence, much preferring to say 'we' rather than 'I' – for Joe, everyone was in it together. A man of great inclusive charm, Joe Dolan was the kind of person who made you feel good about yourself.

My own first official introduction to Joe and his smiling face of happiness was, I'm told, a couple of days after I was born. There can be no doubt that I smiled back, and there is a very good chance I had heard Joe long before I met him, carried around as I was in my mother's womb to his concerts and the places where Joe always seemed to hold court, no matter how many people were there. Joe could hold a conversation with forty or four hundred at the same time. He was at his happiest meeting people.

As I grew up, I met Joe quite a bit; he was, in everything but blood, part of the family, because my father, Seamus, was Joe's manager for over forty years. But they were more than just manager and charge. Together with Joe's brother Ben, they were friends, brothers-in-arms, colleagues and so much more. Everything and anything seemed to revolve and evolve around Joe, Ben and my father and the storm they kicked up around the world. They had their fair share of ups and downs, triumphs and tragedies, hits and misses and plenty more besides, but even when the going got tough for everyone, there smiling in the middle of it all was Joe Dolan, this great son of Éireann, a seemingly immortal man of music, magic and mischief. As a youngster with a rabid fascination for music, I found the regular exposure to Joe's world and the great characters that inhabited it an inspiration.

It seems that almost everybody I have ever met in Ireland and beyond has at least one Joe Dolan story to tell, and when they discover that I am from Mullingar, they not only insist on telling it to me, but ask if I knew him. When I confirm that, yes, I did know him, they want to talk about him until the steak-coated heels of the famous Mullingar heifers return home. It's something that everyone from Mullingar experiences, but the truth is *everybody* seems to have known Joe Dolan. In Mullingar (and, by extension, Ireland) he was just the same as anyone else. Sure, he was Ireland's first true pop star and a massive international star at that, but because he never lost sight of who he was, he was just Joe. The esteem in which he was held by others almost made him embarrassed.

But it seems that whilst lots of people knew Joe Dolan, or thought they knew him because he walked among them, they didn't really know the full story. A myth had built around him – nobody ever knew his age, for example – and few people in Ireland realized just how big a star he was in the rest of the world. At one stage, Joe was selling more records in France than there were people in Ireland, and he sold millions of discs to fans of all ages world-wide, but because he had this knack of reinventing himself every couple of years, very few of his Irish fans, fair-weather or loyal, knew just how far Joe's smile had spread.

I had interviewed Joe for different newspapers countless times, and for many years I had been quietly suggesting to him (and those around him) that he should write his autobiography, or at least allow someone to help him write it. However, Joe had always been extremely reluctant to do so. There were two Joes in real life, and he wasn't quite sure which one he should be on paper: the entertainer supreme who lit up the lives of thousands of people every week; or the ordinary Joe, who lived a relatively simple life. When he and I had talked about some of his key songs, it transpired that this initial reluctance or uncertainty was something of a character trait. Some of his biggest hits were songs that he didn't want to sing at first, and he claimed that he wasn't at all sure he liked his international breakthrough 'Make Me an Island' when he first heard a demo version of it. But Joe had been greatly impressed by *A Different Journey*, the autobiography of Fr Brian D'Arcy, and this may have swayed him to write his own story. A recurring illness throughout the year, which left him drained and tired though he hid it well, may have been another reason. Perhaps he wanted to put things in order, too. In 2007 I was finally given the green light to ghostwrite the book myself, and in the end he gave me glimpses of both lives as he prepared to put his life on paper for the first time.

We recorded some interviews, and it was just like the old days. Joe was a raconteur supreme, a joke-teller of the highest calibre and a man who loved to regale you with hilarious tales from on and off the road. When it came to his glittering, rollercoaster career, he was very matter of fact and remarkably modest; his achievements were just a small part of who he was. Whilst talking to Joe, I realized that his gift to entertain and to make people happy extended far beyond the personality you saw onstage in the white suit. Many stars are reputed to be unfriendly offstage, even to hate their own fame, but not Joe – he would shrug his shoulders at it all. He was happy with his lot even though he was not quite sure how he had got there.

When his health took a bad turn towards the end of 2007, we decided to park the book for a while and have another go in the New Year. I was looking forward to a year of further fun and insights and a chance to get behind some of his legendary evasiveness, but this was not to be. When Joe passed away on St Stephen's Day, instead I found myself writing a statement for the world's press detailing that the unthinkable had happened, that Joe Dolan was dead.

Although Joe wasn't well in what turned out to be the last year of his life, he still played some of the best gigs I have ever seen him perform. There was, as the famous saying about him went, 'No show like a Joe show', and he seemed unstoppable. Even when he was advised not to perform, he still carried on. There were no endings when it came to Joe Dolan, only introductions and beginnings. After he passed away it was decided that this book should also go on, and so, with the blessing of his family, here it is.

I

Remember when you were young

Joe Dolan was born at the then brand-new County Hospital in Mullingar on 16 October 1939. He claimed to remember it as a pleasant birth. His arrival came at a difficult time for his family, as they were adjusting to a new life away from the family business, which had recently closed, and away from the town itself; however, his older brother Paddy, who was thirteen when Joe first exercised his vocal chords, remembers a great sense of excitement taking over the house when news of Joe's birth reached home. Paddy, a raconteur with a razor-sharp memory and a playful sense of humour, vividly recalls going into Mullingar Hospital to welcome the new arrival: 'I remember going in and asking my mother how she was and I was delighted to see this little boy. Another brother, and just as lovely looking as the rest of us. When I was leaving, she asked me to ask my father to get her a new pair of shoes for when she got home. She had worn her last pair out carrying Joe, I suppose . . . I remember my father saying, "Does she think they grow on trees?"'

Although Joe was a relatively quiet baby, there were already a few signs that he could hit and hold a high note even before his distinctively high-pitched vocal chords began to form. 'He didn't cry that much,' Paddy remembers, 'but when he did, oh by God, you could hear him.'

Ben, who was four years old when Joe was born, recalls the great commotion in the house, particularly among his sisters, neighbours and visiting cousins. And when Joe was brought home to the bungalow from the hospital, Ben quivered in his tiny boots when his mother asked him to welcome Joe home with a kiss. 'My mother said to me, "Go on Ben, give your baby brother a kiss" and I said, shivering, "Brrrr . . . I will not!"'

Joe was born into a young family. Immediately above him were two brothers: Vincent, who was just two years old, and Ben. His sister Imelda was the next in line, aged seven; another sister, Ita, was ten. Then came Paddy, and then James, fifteen, and Dympna, who was eighteen. Joe's mother Ellen was forty-seven when she gave birth to Joe, and his father Patrick forty-nine. They had had another son, Michael, who had died from complications arising out of pneumonia in 1927, aged just four.

Although the Dolan family ancestry is in Scotland, Joe's Irish connection goes back three generations. Joe's great-grandfather moved to the gently lapping shores of Lough Owel in the 1700s. Joe's father, Patrick Dolan, belonged to a large, wealthy family whose home was on the Portloman shoreline of the large freshwater lake. Patrick's own father, Michael, was an only son who had lived there with his wife Alice Casey. Together they comfortably raised nine children there, and Joe remembered his father, Patrick, fondly recalling a youth spent by the water.

Patrick Dolan met and married Ellen 'Ellie' Brennan during the troubled years between 1916 and 1921 – a time when many people from the town of Mullingar took part in the struggle for Irish self-government. He first met his future wife on the farm at Portloman. Ellie Brennan was the third youngest child in a family of ten who lived nearby in Walshestown, in a thatched farmhouse adjacent to Walshestown church. Ellie had reason for visiting the Dolan home quite often, as her family, who were dairy farmers, supplied milk to families in the area and as a youngster Ellie helped on their milk rounds. This was a time when milk was sold by the jug rather than in bottles and cartons, and Ellie, who had a reputation for generosity, always ensured that the less well-off families got an extra cup or two.

After Patrick had completed his education, he moved into Mullingar town, where he opened a bicycle repair and retail business at Austin Friars Street, but he was still a frequent visitor to the home place and continued to date Ellen. They married on 26 April 1920, and she moved to join her new husband at Austin Friars Street. Their business and home was part of a splendid and long-since demolished building that stood at what is now the National Irish Bank premises at the gates of Mullingar Town Park. The jubilee nurse lived beside them, and, to the rear of their home, the county surgeon lived in Annebrook House, now part of a hotel complex adjacent to the town park. The gardens of Annebrook House were plush back then (they later became the town park), and the Dolans and dozens of other children had the run of them.

Patrick Dolan's bicycle business at Austin Friars Street appeared to be booming, but in reality it was floundering. An important market town not far from Dublin, Mullingar was dramatically expanding in all directions, and more and more cars were seen on its streets; yet Patrick was still not convinced of their staying power, believing two wheels to be king of the road. Patrick was also a generous man who gave his numerous customers credit, and some took advantage of him. Joe's eldest brother Paddy remembers that some people would rack up large accounts that were never settled, and his father found it hard to keep track of them: 'Their kids would come in to get their punctures fixed, but because they only paid monthly it would have to go down in the book. Sure half of them never paid him; they never turned up. He had a black book full of names. He was doing all the work, and not getting paid.'

Ellen always believed that Patrick was too soft. Ben recalls, 'She always reckoned that he was the worst man in the world to collect money. When people would come in to pay him, he'd say he might be busy, and for them to come back. Of course they never did. Other times, he'd say, "Come over and we'll have a drink," and they would go over and have a few drinks. Apart from that he was doing no work, so she used to feel that.'

Patrick began to drink and bills were often settled in a nearby pub. 'When people came in to pay him they would wind up in Hands' shop next door, which was also a pub, to try and settle their accounts,' Paddy remembers. 'And sure the money he was after getting, he would be treating the boys back to a drink and the next thing you know . . . gone.'

With the shop in deep trouble and haemorrhaging everything the family had in terms of resources, they were forced to accept an offer for the premises. Paddy remembers how the family ended up with 'nothing' and had to go to live with Ellen's family in Walshestown. However, Hands gave their former neighbour a recently renovated shed to keep his business afloat in their yard, and Patrick kept the business going there for as long as he could. He applied to the County Council for work and, a year before Joe was born, secured a job with the local authority, a new home for the family and a fresh start at Grange Cottages, a small council housing scheme of semi-detached cottages on the outskirts of the town.

Mullingar was also hoping for a fresh start in some ways. A factory in one's town was the gold standard of modernity for any Irish town, but despite its recent growth Mullingar only had a small pencil factory near the army barracks. The neighbouring towns of Athlone, Longford and Navan all had factories, whilst Tullamore and the tiny one-street town of Kilbeggan could both boast large-scale employment in their respective whiskey distilleries. Yet Mullingar's agricultural heritage and its markets had a good reputation – indeed, the phrase 'Beef to the heel like a Mullingar heifer' was well-known throughout Ireland – and although this might not be something that many bragged about when away from home, as it invariably conjured up an image (and an aroma) of the cattle and sheep fairs that were held on the streets of the town, Mullingar's attractive layout, the innate friendliness of its people and its strong sense of community all stood it in very good stead as it began to grow in size and stature.

The Dolans certainly had the best of both town and country growing up at Grange Cottages. 'We were only a mile and a half from the centre of town really, so it never really felt like we were too far away from the action, but we didn't go into town all that much; we didn't need to because everything we could want as kids was at our doorstep,' said Joe, as he reflected on a happy, carefree childhood playing in nature's playground. There was a mass of nearby green fields, a canal that flowed close to the Dolan back door, a railway line, farm buildings, old abandoned famine-era housing, a nearby racecourse and an abundance of lakes. With everything an adventurous child could wish for close to hand, it was very much an idyllic country upbringing for Joe, his brothers and sisters and their many friends, and the family certainly had no complaints. 'We were happy where we were, and happy with our lot,' asserted Joe. 'We didn't have much, but we didn't want for much, you know?'

Like his brothers before him, Joe was first educated at St Mary's Christian Brothers School in Mullingar. Situated next to the landmark Cathedral of Christ the King, the school complex housed a primary and a secondary school. Joe completed his education at the technical college on the other side of Mullingar, which was part of a complex of buildings that included the courthouse, the County Council buildings and the County Hall – Joe remembered looking in awe at the bands and musicians arriving at the County Hall for concerts. He was considered a good pupil who was keen to learn and contributed much to the classroom in both schools, but once the school day was over he couldn't wait to be as far away as possible from the place.

At one stage, the majority of the family walked to school together. As his sisters and elder brothers left school and one by one moved out of the family home, eventually only Joe, older brothers Vincent and Ben and sister Imelda made the daily walk, together with a wide and wild variety of neighbours, of which there was no shortage. 'In our area there were about fourteen houses full of kids. Every house had acres of children, so as far as having a good time went, we had! Looking at it in the context of growing up nowadays, the only thing we were short of, I suppose, was money, but we never noticed. Everything else was great,' Joe said, adding there was never any emphasis placed on money. Chestnuts and bragging rights were a much more important commodity. 'If someone said they had no money, you wouldn't say, "God, that's shocking." Things were poor enough everywhere, so as kids no one knew what it was like. When were you going to get out to play – that's all that counted.'

Joe has praised his mother and father for their fortitude, particularly as they had moved a few times, with children of greatly varying ages, which at a time of decreasing and almost non-existent wealth must have placed a great strain on them. Dympna, James, Paddy and Ita had enjoyed the larger part of their upbringing either in Austin Friars Street or in their mother's home place in Walshestown, whereas Imelda, Joe, Ben and Vincent only have clear and vivid memories of a Grange upbringing.

The children made their own entertainment, and Ellen and Paddy were relieved to learn that even the coldest weather out in the country could not put off their increasingly active bunch of kids. One of their favourite cold-weather pursuits also kept them within eyesight of the family home. 'As soon as the frost would come, everyone would be out with a bucket of water throwing it on the road so it would freeze up, and we would slide on it for hours,' Joe remembered fondly. 'We'd be down on our hunkers, sliding in groups, sliding on our ears, everything! There was no stopping us.' The only worry they had was the ever-decreasing soles of their shoes, as the unofficial Mullingar Winter Olympics took its toll on the family footwear collection – although not Joe's: 'Whatever pair of boots Joe would get, they'd be hobnails, almost lethal weapons,' said Ben. 'He'd be driving nails into them all the time just to give them better sliding power.'

Fortunately, in the 1940s and 1950s there were few cars trundling along the Mullingar to Ballymahon road on a frosty morning. 'ACC!' was the warning shout – short for 'A car coming!' – and Joe recalled that it was a warning that never lost its novelty, with competition cut-throat to be the first to spot a car.

When Joe got a little older, the long straight road was also used for some horse and cart theatrics, and he was admired in the area for his youthful agility in handling horses and ponies. The family had a pony called Kitty that Joe was fond of, and Paddy remembers his younger brother loved to ride this pony up and down the road. 'He was only a kid at the time, but he used to leap up on his back like a cowboy, even when the pony was running off without him. He could have been a good horseman if he wanted.' This interest in the equestrian world would evolve into a different type of preoccupation once Joe got to see his first-ever race meeting at the nearby Newbrook Race Course, of which more later on.

Paddy Dolan remembers Joe as a 'fierce' active child in his earliest years, and the gardens of the Grange bungalows were of particular interest to him. These were huge affairs, created in such a way that the families housed there could be self-sufficient. They often stretched to an acre and a half or more, and they offered endless opportunities for flora, fauna and food. Joe's father had started work on making their garden self-sufficient, but he struggled to bring his plans to fruition as recurring illnesses and fatigue laid him low. So

Joe made a good fist at ensuring that the yet-to-be-developed part of the 'Irish acre' was put to good use.

'Joe was like a fox,' Paddy laughs, as he remembers Joe and some of the younger boys digging huge holes, which were, in fact, elaborate tunnels with ridges and rooms hidden from view. Derek King, a friend who used to visit from afar, would be his co-digger and they used to enjoy the confusion caused when people would go looking for them. No one could ever find them, despite looking straight into the hole the boys had just dug. And if they weren't digging they would be playing with whatever horse or pony would be in the vicinity – something that was to leave an indelible mark on the life of Derek King, a lifelong friend of Joe's who would go on to become blacksmith to the First Lady of horse-racing, trainer Jenny Pitman. Needless to say, Joe availed himself of this friendship on a number of occasions when he just so happened to be close to a bookmaker's and Derek had rung him with a tip.

In fact, quite a few of the many children who played with Joe in the natural playground that was the western side of Mullingar over the years would become lifelong friends, with one even joining Joe and Ben on the road to stardom in later years. 'We used to knock around with everyone, and, you know, the people out of every house turned out well,' Joe recounted. 'A few doors down were the Horans, and Jimmy played with us for years. There was Tommy Rickard and his brother Jimmy, who are still great friends. There were the Tormeys, Corroons, Conlons, Owens, Dignams, Weldons, Morrisons and loads more. [They grew up to be] blacksmiths, boxers, post office workers, civil servants, gardeners, farmers, priests, engineers, nurses, doctors . . . and even gaming arcade men,' he added, referencing a glorious couple of decades that Tommy and Jimmy Rickard spent at the forefront of the amusement arcade industry in Ireland.

Joe's digging skills were utilized to the max later on in his childhood when rumbling bellies forced him and Ben into the seedy underground world of vegetable theft. Invariably, the target of the hungry pair was the substantial potato crop of neighbouring farmer Johnny Weldon. Their own potato yields had failed, and after their father died their 'Irish acre' could not sustain their appetite.

Weldon, whose own children were friendly with the Dolans, was a farmer with a fearsome reputation. It was not unheard of in the Grange area for him to deter green-fingered thieves with a blast of a shotgun over their heads.

Indeed, as a child in the 1980s, I myself was sent scarpering after an attempt to rob apples from his orchard ended when the boom of a shotgun blast filled the air. This was a good forty years after Joe and Ben's illicit moonlight raids, so poor Johnny Weldon must have been tormented with generations of garden raiders targeting his fertile lands.

Back in those days, Joe and Ben had what they thought was a foolproof method of stealing Weldon's potatoes. They would strike under the cover of darkness: Joe – being the smaller of the boys – was the soldier of misfortune sent into the vegetable patch, whilst Ben stood guard as a nearby watchman.

Joe would not dare unearth an entire potato plant as this would surely be noticed and would signal an end to their moonlight raids, so instead he targeted the furrows, digging his hands deep into them to steal a couple of tasty treasures from each individual plant. He often targeted a dozen plants at a time to get enough potatoes to fill the pot for a few days. The stolen spuds would then be brought to the Dolan home, often for immediate testing with midnight feasts of hot buttered new potatoes – a just and eagerly awaited reward for the youthful raiders. However, Weldon would soon note his declining potato yield, and his suspicions were confirmed one night when he confronted Joe with a jumper full of spuds. Somehow, Joe managed to talk his way out of trouble. 'I told him I was getting the lend of them,' Joe laughed.

It wasn't only vegetables that were targeted, though. For generations of children who grew up on the western side of Mullingar, no homeward-bound journey in the autumn would be complete without a raid on the Cleary family orchard at 'The Valley' (now a filling station), a large farmhouse on the edge of town that was ringed by a seemingly endless circle of juicy apple trees. On autumnal journeys home from school, Joe, with the aid of a boost, would scale the high walls to get his hands on some ripe apples – a precarious mission, as if you fell off the wall the only way out was via the farmhouse.

On hot summer days the boys from the Grange area could often be found swimming in the nearby Royal Canal. It was in these waters that Joe learned how to swim, and in later years swimming would become one of his favourite pastimes. If they were on for a spot of dive-bombing, the Grange gang generally launched themselves off Kilpatrick Bridge into the deep canal waters below. The handsome stone bridge features a natural ridge, so if Joe was feeling a little overwhelmed by the drop from the parapet, he would drop into the cool water from this ridge. The Dolan boys and their friends would also take refreshing dips in one of the many local lakes. It was, and still is, a rite of passage for anyone born in, around or near Mullingar to spend at least one full summer living the lakeside lifestyle. Whether launching oneself blindly into cool clear waters (and then pretending you weren't actually that cold, despite shivering), or desperately trying to appear cool as you stumbled around the shoreline in your bare feet, or being lucky enough to cadge a lift on a boat for a spot of fishing or island hopping, living near so many lakes afforded endless possibilities.

The nearest lake to Joe was Lough Ennell, where he often went. His sister Imelda remembers his first visit there very clearly. So excited was he at the expanse of water in front of him that he launched himself into it immediately, causing his elder sister to worry that he had disappeared for ever. His head bobbed up after a minute or two, though. She regularly brought him to Ennell, and the entire family visited several of its shores, particularly Ladestown and Lilliput.

The family still had relations living in Portloman, right on the shores of Lough Owel, so it too was an option, as was Lough Derravaragh – the home of the fabled 'Children of Lir' – which was close to the villages of Crookedwood and Multyfarnham. If Joe was feeling really adventurous and in the mood for a long bicycle journey, there was Lough Lene, near the village of Collinstown. In fact there are hundreds more lakes dotted around the north Westmeath countryside, and at one stage or another they have all been home to rampaging children in search of aquatic adventure.

One constant in the Dolan household in Grange was music, and the small cottage, with its warm, welcoming kitchen, was very much a musical haven for the family and for passing musicians. For as long as Joe could remember, songs, dancing and laughter echoed throughout the house. His mother Ellen ensured that an instrument of some sort was always close to hand, and if one couldn't be found then Joe and the boys were encouraged to improvise as best they could. 'We always had music in the house,' Joe recalled, 'and I suppose unbeknownst to ourselves we were becoming more and more interested in music. When visitors would come to the house our mother would put us up to sing a song. "Sing a song there, Joe. Sing a song there, Ben," she would say, and sure, off we went. God knows what we were like, but no one shut us up.'

Joe was initially mortified at the musical requests, as most children would be when asked to stand up and sing in front of their elders. However, Ben remembers that even when Joe was aged seven or eight, once he had stepped up to the fireplace to sing he did so oozing with confidence; and he always seemed to enjoy performing for any guests that might be in the house. 'He had to, because if you didn't sing you would wind up with the bucket over your head and you singing inside of it!' jokes Ben.

Many were songs that Joe would have been taught by the Christian Brothers at St Mary's. Others were Irish standards, sang *as Gaelige*. Some were by Delia Murphy – 'the Queen of Connemara' and one of Ireland's most popular singers and collectors of Irish ballads at the time. Delia's musical foundations were in the ballads of Travellers who were encouraged to camp on her family's estate, even when they were being ostracized elsewhere. Delia respected the Traveller tradition and was fascinated by their songs and culture, a respect that was passed on to Joe. Ballads such as 'The Blackbird' and 'The Spinning Wheel' were fireside staples not only for Joe, but for all the Dolan family. They were keeping the ballad and field-song flame burning at a time when there was almost a reluctance to sing these songs. With Ireland emerging from an era of great poverty, the Irish tradition they evoked was unfashionable, recalling as it did the maudlin, poverty-stricken bad old days, and any hint of a Traveller association was frowned upon in more settled quarters. But Patrick and Ellen Dolan encouraged their flock to embrace and learn the ballad and field-song heritage of Ireland. Thomas Connellan's seventeenth-century classic 'Dawning of the Day' was another particular favourite of Joe's.

As well as encouraging her children to sing, Ellen Dolan was herself a fine singer, and she frequently wrote to Waltons, the Dublin-based music institution, in search of sheet music and song lyrics. But as much as Joe's mother enjoyed singing, what delighted her most was that her love of music was being passed on to her children. Joe recalled his mother's unbridled joy when her daughters starting singing with the local choral society, and in choral lines at the many locally produced operas and Gilbert and Sullivan productions that were brought to life at Mullingar's County Hall. And when he was four, Joe himself finally got to see the inside of the hall when the family went along to hear their girls perform there.

When preparing themselves for the shows, Joe's sisters would practise their songs together at home – a routine that brought even more mysterious and magical music into the Dolan household – and Joe was delighted to join in with them. They were all accomplished singers and it is perhaps from them that he received his first vocal training. After the shows he buzzed with excitement and sang along to melodies he had heard onstage.

But the voice was not the only instrument heard in the household. 'There was always a fiddle in the house,' Joe remembered. 'My mother used to scrape the fiddle an odd time; she used to play a tremendous version of 'Father Flynn' and a few other songs and we'd dance away or sing along in the kitchen there. Ah, they were great times . . .'

However, these were also testing times, for their father Patrick had become seriously ill. Patrick was then working as part of the outdoor maintenance crew of Westmeath County Council, which was undertaking a vast infrastructure upgrade in and around Mullingar. He had suffered bouts of poor health throughout the 1940s, but these became more frequent in the latter part of the decade, and lean times were experienced in the Dolan household when, complaining of pains in his arms and back, he was unable to work for a period. Although he returned to work, he became sporadically unwell and he lost further days through feeling weak.

Paddy remembers well the time a 'ganger' of a council job his father had been on called in to the Dolan house to check on Patrick and to speak to Ellen. The conversation was very serious for a spell, and then the attention turned to him, with the 'ganger' suggesting to Mrs Dolan that 'the young lad' could fill in for his father. Ellen agreed that Paddy could work and, aged just fifteen, Paddy became the family breadwinner. Looking back on his sudden transition from schoolboy to a working man, Paddy equated the feeling to all his birthdays coming together. He was delighted to be given the chance to prove himself as a man at such a young age. 'I thought it was paradise, heading off to work in the morning,' he recalled. What he didn't love was the early morning search for the horse, that would often free itself to wander up the road in search of midnight nourishment. Paddy would frequently wake his brothers to help him in his search, and he remembers an early morning grumpiness beginning to manifest itself in Joe. 'Oh, he wasn't a morning person, no, and he never was!'

To bring in some extra income for the family, Paddy also worked – albeit for a short spell – at the County Hospital. He left after a row with a matron over a flower bed, and moved across the road to work at St Mary's Hospital, originally a workhouse in the famine years. The extra income also ensured his younger brothers received a good education. 'All this time Joe and Vincent were going to school, and sure the few shillings were keeping them there,' Paddy remembers. Not that the young Joe seemed to notice. 'All I'd see of him when I got home from work was this fella running around the place,' Paddy jokes. But Joe was eternally grateful for Paddy's efforts, and throughout life he spoke of the sacrifices Paddy had made. He reckoned that Paddy didn't see a penny of his own wages for a couple of years, such was his dedication to supporting the family through the lean period of their lives. Joe's other older siblings had already left home, taking advantage of the work on offer in war-torn England – Dympna and Ita to work in nursing, and James was in the air force – and they too regularly sent money home to support the family.

Joe's father returned to work for a short spell in the late 1940s, but young Paddy had impressed the council so much that he was made a full-time employee. Father and son worked together for a short while, but Patrick's health was up and down. Some weeks he was ready, willing and able for work; other weeks he would be complaining of exhaustion and fatigue. In the spring of 1950, he took a turn for the worst and became seriously ill. He had started to show signs of improvement when he suddenly succumbed to a stroke, and, on 30 June 1950, aged just sixty, Patrick passed away.

Joe was only eleven when his father died, 'a little gossoon in school', as he recalled. He could not remember much about that time, but said his one abiding memory was that there was no one to bring him out to Lilliput Sports on the shores of Lough Ennell any more. Because of his father's fluctuating health, Joe did not have as much time to bond with him as he did with his mother. In various interviews in later years he claimed to remember very little about him, and would tend to avoid questions on the subject. He did, however, fondly remember his father as a great fisherman, who spent nearly all of his weekends out on Westmeath's lakes.

By that time, Paddy had moved out of the family home. He was in a steady relationship with Caroline Fallon, a clerical officer at the hospital, and was beginning to settle down, still with two jobs to his credit, and high hopes for the future. In 1952, Paddy and Caroline married and took up residence on Mullingar's main thoroughfare, Dominick Street, which soon became a home from home for young Joe.

The Dolan household became even more musical in the aftermath of Patrick's untimely death. Music had always been a fabric of the house, but it became more important as the boys grew older and curbed their outdoor activities. Music sessions were encouraged and musicians always welcome. If passing musicians didn't want to call in to showcase their skills, then they were sometimes kidnapped with the promise of a hot meal. 'We had a cousin, Frank Gavigan, a great musician, who used to call into the house on occasion, but our mother would make us make *sure* he called in more than just the odd time,' Joe recalled.

Frank lived in Rathconrath, a tiny village between Mullingar and Ballymahon. It has always possessed an enviable pocket of fiercely talented traditional musicians, and Frank Gavigan was rated as one of the best. An accordion player by nature, he was also a dab hand at the violin and a fair man to sing when pushed far enough, although he always preferred to play.

In the 1950s, Frank's route home from his job at the post office passed the Dolan home. With eight or nine miles to go, he would be sidetracked, at Ellen's insistence, by Joe. Ben, who left school early to train as a carpenter, was also roped into the mission. 'She would put us sitting at the gate to wait for Frank to cycle past on his way home from work,' Joe laughs. 'So it might be half six when he would pass, and we'd be out at the gate from about six, and when he came one of us would say, "Frank, me mammy has your tea ready inside." And he nearly always came in. In those days you couldn't afford to refuse a feed. Now, the only thing we got him in for was to play the bit of music, you see. Frank would come in, and whatever would be going or whatever was on the pot he'd have it, we'd sit around, and the next thing me mother would hand him the fiddle and ask him to play, whatever, maybe "Peter Street", "Mason's Apron" and all these songs, and he'd play them one after another. We'd all be dancing and be yahoo-ing around the kitchen. We'd have a céilí in the kitchen, a half set. There'd be two of us on one side, and two on the other and we'd go up, down, back and step over across. That would last for as long as we could keep Frank in the place, maybe about two hours . . .'

Joe acknowledged that these informal céilís had a lasting impact. 'It probably gave us an opening into playing for others, you know, and for enjoying music not so much as something you did when you were a kid, but for what it was, that if you stuck with it you'd have it for life. It got us interested and these sessions influenced us, no doubt about it.'

In time the Dolan family preferred to have their own céilís for family, friends and neighbours. Other houses would also host informal sessions. Until the establishment of Comholtas Ceoltóirí Éireann in the 1950s, there was still a heavy church influence at 'formal' céilís. These would be overseen by a stern priest who scolded anyone who either danced out of place or – Heaven forbid! – touched another dancer in a manoeuvre that could not be classed as an official dance move. And, as Ben recalls, Joe's loose-limbed antics on the dance floor at these strictly controlled social outings invariably led to him getting in trouble. 'They used to shout, "*Gach duine ar an urlár*!*", and they'd hold everything up until they had the whole floor full. With Joe around, it was very easy to mess, especially when he swung someone around the place. He was like any young fella, I suppose, thinking "I'm as strong as anyone" as he stomped and swung around the place. But the next thing he'd be sent off the floor. So the formality kind of kept us from going to the céilís unless you made your mind up that you were going to do it the proper way, which wasn't Joe. He preferred to do it his way.'

At the informal sessions in their Grange bungalow, as well as taking lead vocals, Joe would often sing a lilt with the traditional music. He wasn't a great musician by any means as a young teenager, and he compensated for this by singing along as if he were an instrument. 'I was always a great man for a melody,' he once said in a very rare outburst of self-congratulation.

When Joe was twelve years old, Ellen realized it was time for him to harness his musical talent, and decided to buy something she had dreamed about for years: a piano. In a market town where cattle and sheep roamed the streets on market day, pianos were not as plentiful as one might imagine, so enquiries were wired to music shops in Dublin. In the meantime, Joe was to have piano lessons. Ellen found him a good teacher in Molly Carroll, who lived on nearby Patrick Street, a colourful residential street between Joe's house and the town. Ms Carroll came highly recommended, and it was also thought that the lessons would tame Joe's wilder inclinations to run loose with his friends. Even though he had passed the singing test at school, he had already refused to join the boys' choir as it entailed staying behind after school or, worse still, going to school on a Saturday morning for practice. He was slightly more amenable to the idea of playing the piano, and agreed to attend lessons on his way home from school once a week.

When Joe thought back at the effort his mother made for him at a time of disadvantage, he had nothing but admiration. As did Paddy – although he also admired the way she managed to tame Joe long enough to send him for piano lessons. 'Little could she afford them, but she stuck at it in any case,' he recalls. 'And for a while he did too.' 'I couldn't believe she was buying a piano for me,' Joe said. 'I thought, "What have I done to deserve this?"' Joe showed some signs of promise and, albeit begrudgingly at first as he felt he was missing out on valuable after-school playtime with his pals, just a little bit of passion for his first real instrument.

Ellen used her widow's pension to buy the piano, which cost £120, and the rest of the family all helped out too. 'My mother said to me once that she didn't mind about paying as long as she got it paid off before she died,' Paddy said. 'She thought Joe was going to be great,' he added. It was possibly the biggest purchase the family had ever made. The piano would be the making of Joe, or at least that's what his mother thought. In some ways, it was also a therapeutic purchase for the Dolan matriarch, even if meeting the weekly payments was sometimes tough. Having a piano in the house reminded Ellen of her own childhood and days at the big houses in Portloman where annual dances were the soundtrack to her teenage years. Indeed, she had first met Patrick Dolan at one such dance. She felt it fitting that the widow's pension she received be used for such a purchase.

At first the Dolan boys didn't believe it was happening at all, until one day some of the kids on the road roared, 'ACC!' When a futuristic-looking space-age Walton's wagon pulled up to the house carrying its tuneful cargo, the delivery man stepped out to a hero's welcome. Necks craned as local kids tried to get a look into the van. Vehicles such as this were certainly a rarity on the Ballymahon Road, so everyone came out to look. However, the delight that surrounded the new arrival was offset somewhat by the reluctance of the budding pianist to tinkle its shiny new ivories. 'When it was put up at home everyone thought Joe would leap in behind it and be able to play it, but he didn't at first,' Ben says with mild amusement. 'My mother was disgusted when he wouldn't go near it!'

Eventually Joe did take to the keys, and it was only then that the family realized that he had been skipping a few lessons. However, after a few days he improved, and Ben remembers hearing 'Over the Waves' and 'The Spinning Wheel' quite a lot as Joe got to grips with the new instrument and tried to showcase that he had, in fact, learned something from Ms Carroll. Ben also recalls that at this early stage Joe was beginning to show signs of the perfectionism that would later become a trademark of his career in music. 'He'd go so far, make a mistake and then he'd go at it again and again until he got it just so,' Ben remembers. 'Now, he wasn't great on the instrument at the time, let's be honest, but he was learning and trying hard to play and read music. He was getting there, so we forgave the occasional mistake.'

Ellen continued to send off for music, and Joe remembered that one of the last songs she wrote away for was 'Cottage by the Lee', a song by 'Isle of Innisfree' writer Dick Farrelly that was popularized in the late 1950s by the much-loved actor and singer Joe Lynch. In later years Joe Dolan became firm friends with Joe Lynch, and Joe always promised the actor, who is perhaps best remembered for his roles in long-running Irish soaps *Glenroe* and *Bracken*, that he would one day record 'Cottage by the Lee' in honour of both his mother and Lynch. 'Joe Lynch was a fine singer in his time, long before he started the acting. I used to call him a fiver. "If Pavarotti is a tenor, then you're a fiver!" I'd say to him. He didn't seem to mind,' laughed Joe. Joe Lynch died unexpectedly while on holidays in Alicante in August 2001, and six years later Joe made good his promise to the late actor when he began recording a selection of the Irish classics and traditional songs that had inspired him for an album he had wanted to make for some time. He was due to record 'Cottage by the Lee' in early 2008.

The musical sessions that would erupt in the Dolan house now had a new impetus, and a fresh new sound. As Joe joined in when the odd music session kicked off in the house, it seemed like the investment was beginning to pay off, even if it was costing Mrs Dolan an arm and a leg and leading to Joe and Ben's ongoing raids of the Weldon vegetable patch.

Not that Joe was a stickler for his lessons, especially during the summer months. 'I suppose, when you were asked to do anything at that age, you weren't quite so keen,' Ben recalls. 'He'd miss the odd lesson to play football or hurling or whatever. I remember once my mother met Mrs Carroll, who remarked that Joe hadn't been in lessons for four weeks. Well, there was war!' Enraged at his mitching, his mother gave Joe a stern reminder not to miss any more lessons. The rudiments of music and the sound of scales were more important than slotting a ball over a bar, so Joe was told he could play his football after his piano lessons, which in turn meant he was coming home later and later. Ellen would wait for him to return, and Ben remembers Joe 'swearing a hole through a pot' when he eventually came home that he had just been at practice that evening. 'Practice – it used to cover a multitude of sins, that word,' laughs Ben, remembering the many occasions when it was used to cover up Joe's non-practice endeavours, such as his growing fondness for games of cards with neighbours.

This same piano is still very much a part of the Dolan household, a permanent reminder of Joe's first big 'start' in the world of music, and it now has pride of place in Ben and his wife Helen's sitting room in their Mullingar home. Proudly sitting on top of it, among framed photos of all the Dolan family, is a photo of the man who reluctantly began his glittering career while playing its keys.

2

Teenage dreams, so hard to beat

Joe cut a distinctive dash as a teenager at both St Mary's and the Mullingar Technical College, and he was a well-known and well-regarded youngster who stood out from the crowd. He had a bright and breezy attitude to life, and his razor-sharp wit endeared him to his classmates and his teachers. He made many lifelong pals in the classroom. Even though his piano lessons were an open invitation to merciless teasing in the schoolyard, he had forged something of a reputation – unknown to those at home – of being somebody you didn't mess with, and he would always look out for the underdog.

Kevin Nugent, an old friend from Mullingar, remembers Joe and the Grange gang, a close-knit bunch, passing his house on their way into school. 'Sometimes I would slip in with them and bask in the ease of their well-practised banter, feeling grown-up and important,' he said. When he was six, Kevin was knocked down by a car and seriously injured. It was the stuff of nightmares for any youngster, not because of the injuries but because of the jibes that would surely be thrown around the schoolyard. After a spell in hospital, Kevin recuperated at home, but was reluctant to return to school. The lads from

Grange, of whom Joe became an instinctive ringleader, said they would keep an eye out for him. Kevin remembers that first day back. 'Joe took me protectively by the hand and led me right to the school door. "And if Sister Assumpta says a cross word to you," Joe said to me with a conspiratorial wink, "tell her to come and see me." I knew I was safe.'

Mullingar itself had come on a bit in the intervening years, but there was never much talk out in Grange of socializing in the town at night. Although Joe had plenty of pals in the town whom he hung around with before and after school, he still had everything he could possibly wish for on his doorstep, and if he went out at night it was usually to a neighbour's house. 'Going out on the town, or sneaking into a pub or places like that was not on the agenda at all,' said Joe years later. Looking back on his teenage years, he could barely remember going into town at all, save for the crafty visits to the Coliseum Cinema in Dominick Street, where Joe developed a foolproof way of sneaking into the best seats. 'The cheap seats were at the front and the dear seats were at the back, but to get to the cheap seats you had to walk through the dear seats, and you passed a ticket checker halfway up. What we would do was to wait outside until you heard the cheer when the lights were out. You'd pay for a cheap seat and sneak into the dear seats. You saw the picture from a good seat, and because you didn't pay full price you still had your shilling ticket for the next film.'

The only other times the Dolan boys and their pals can remember going to town for anything other than school was for a cheeky day at the Mullingar Races at Newbrook, literally a two-field hop from their doorsteps. On a rainy day, Joe and some of the boys would often run their own races past the finishing post and mill about in the grandstands. Growing up nearby gave the boys an insider's knowledge of how to gain access to the fortified track, and they became keen followers of the turf. The teenage Joe also began to forge a growing reputation as quite the card shark in the Grange area, and he honed his skills by playing anyone and everyone. These were skills he would demonstrate throughout his entertainment career, with card schools becoming a quintessential element of the Joe show before (and sometimes after) he and the band played.

The Dolan house still reverberated to music of all sorts, and the Dolan boys had begun to get a little more serious about it, much to their mother's delight, with plenty of teenage talk about forming a band starting to weave its

way across the dinner table. Music sessions were still very much the heartbeat
of the house, and they ranged from the traditional and the formal to the wild
and the improvised. Joe was a particular fan of a type of music that was beginning to take the world by storm: skiffle. The skiffle style meant that you didn't
necessarily need instruments to form a band, so it encouraged wannabe
musicians throughout the world to get started (indeed, bands such as The
Beatles and The Who owe their careers to their formative years as skiffle
groups). Pioneered and popularized by the young Scottish-born British musician Lonnie Donegan, initially as a way of killing time in the intervals of more
conventional jazz shows, skiffle music would see musicians belt out old blues
and folk standards on cheap guitars augmented by unconventional instruments such as washboards, tea chests, pots, pans and cans. As well as
delivering passionate versions of songs that traditionally would be played
steadily and studiously, one of the big factors in the emergence of skiffle
music was that anybody could do it.

By the time Joe was sixteen, his vocal skills, particularly in traditional, folk
and field songs, were indisputable. His emerging skills as a pianist were also
marking him out as one to watch and, thanks to skiffle, he could soon add
another instrument to his list – the washboard. A Grange-based skiffle group
of sorts formed in the Dolan kitchen, with Joe and Ben as the bandleaders.
There were no real members as such, as whoever happened to be around at
the time was welcome to join in. In some respects, what the boys were doing
could be viewed as a rebellion against traditional Irish music, although at the
time that was far from their minds, as they still heartily embraced the traditional music world. But then, as is the case today, this new music was met
with parental disapproval. 'We used to play in the kitchen at home in the
house; it used to drive our mother mad. It was always on a Sunday and whoever turned up could just play. There were a few rules, not many, and we'd all
play washboards, tea chests, old pans and bottles; anything that would make
a noise really. If it sounded in any way musical, then it was in. I reckon we
probably used instruments that nobody has ever heard of before or since.'

The next big thing to make an impact was – what else? – rock 'n' roll. Bill
Haley and his Comets, the pioneers of rock 'n' roll, were blazing a trail
across the globe at the time and the Dolan boys got caught up in its slip-
stream. The brothers were first bitten by the Bill Haley bug in a friend's
house on the way home from school, where they would listen to music on a

record player. 'Well, we'd listen to this Bill Haley's "Shake, Rattle and Roll" record over and over again. It was like nothing any of us had heard before. I thought it was the greatest thing I'd ever heard. I didn't understand anything about it, but I just thought it was the greatest. I couldn't wait to tell everyone back home about it!'

Back at Grange on a Sunday afternoon, Joe and Ben would then attempt to explain to the other members of their skiffle group how the song went, trying to play the song and other Haley numbers skiffle-style. The beauty of skiffle music was that you could get by with two or three chords and a bucket-ful of enthusiasm, so no matter how bad you were you weren't truly terrible. It wasn't quite rock 'n' roll, but it was near enough to it. Still, the seeds were sown, and soon enough the boys would be playing real instruments with some real musicians.

Joe's elder brother Paddy had landed a job at the County Hall in Mullingar. One of the perks of the job was that Paddy could see every musical act that came to town if he so wished. Knowing full well his music-mad brothers back home would appreciate this, he was able to sneak them in occasionally – although sadly Joe would have to wait a couple of years. Ben, being the right side of eighteen, was allowed to catch the odd show, and what he saw onstage inspired him to further his playing. Ben was also sometimes paid to man the cloakroom, and this gave him plenty of time to catch a band in full flight. 'Very few people put their coats in during a show. I must have heard every band that came to town. I'd be there every night, working you understand . . .' he recalled, with a nod and a wink.

There were dances (and hops) at the County Hall every Friday, Sunday and Tuesday night, so on average at least three bands would play a week. An unhappy Joe would wait up for his brother to return home from work in order to hear the latest happenings from the County Hall, and there would be plenty of them as 1955 progressed for it was the beginning of the show-band era. Although showbands would soon become ten-a-penny, only a few bands at that time were cutting loose from the staid and rigid mini-orchestra set-up of the 1940s and 1950s. Much to the envy of his younger brother, Ben got to see them all. Ben's experiences were enough to convince him that this band game was where it was at.

Ben had left school at the age of sixteen. He was a natural handy-man and had become an apprentice carpenter, eventually working for local builder

Frank Mulligan, who later would become a key man in building the Dolan business empire. Like Paddy, Ben also held down two jobs ('Two was better than none,' he says). His hours at the County Hall grew, and, if he wasn't working, he was there anyway as events onstage became his addiction. At home he had also been encouraged to take up an instrument, and whilst the piano was not his thing, he would be blown away by the brass instruments he was seeing at the County Hall. By 1956, the guitar had yet to make any significant impact and few bands came to the County Hall armed with six strings and the truth. The sexiest instrument of choice for any aspiring musician at the time was, without doubt, the saxophone. Having saved up enough money from his stints in the County Hall, Ben decided it was time he owned one. As he knew absolutely nothing about the instrument, he needed the advice of an expert.

Bands were few and far between in Mullingar at the time, but the best of them was a local band led by Denis 'Dinny' Hughes. 'He was my inspiration,' Ben admits. 'He was a very good sax player who always had a good band with him and, for me, he was the only real musician a young fella could look up to. There were loads of fellas in town at that time – luggers as we called them – who'd be able to play a couple of tunes, and play them badly. Dinny was a class apart though.' Having befriended Dinny and sought his advice on buying a sax, Ben then ponied up his savings to the musician so he could set Ben off on his own musical path. Joe was delighted with his brother's decision, and he waited at home by the piano, with the washboard at the ready just in case, for Ben's debut back in Grange.

When the sax arrived there was no initial reluctance to play it – much to the annoyance of those living either side of the Dolan house, as his tooting and parping shattered their relatively tranquil lives. Ben didn't confine himself to the saxophone either, and he began to develop a rabid fascination for all sorts of instruments. 'I used to fancy myself as a musician and I used to buy every instrument going. Dinny Hughes's wife played an accordion. I liked the idea of an accordion – as an instrument it was beautiful and I liked the way she played it, so I bought one. I fancied myself playing tangos, "barrr-ump-bum-bum!" and all that, but it didn't actually work out so I switched to the fiddle. I fixed up my mother's fiddle, did a right good job on it in fact, but then Joe started playing it.'

Joe reckoned that time was too precious to learn how to play the sax, but he got good at the fiddle. He also took a shine to Ben's neglected accordion. 'I loved it, but found it a bit too big to handle,' Joe would say of the bulky instrument. 'I'd come home from work and I'd find Joe with the accordion out,' an incredulous Ben remembered. 'He was playing it in secret at first because I'd be saying to him, "Don't damage that" and he'd jump up to say, "I didn't touch it!", but he would have been tricking away at it. I let him play it in the end.'

It was Frank Gavigan who really rumbled Joe's secret accordion practice, and Frank was impressed with Joe's playing, as Ben recalls. 'Frank liked it and said he had talent. Joe was picking out songs here and there, and when he'd hand the accordion over to Frank for him to play, he'd say, "That's not the same accordion" by way of a compliment. Sure Joe just lit up.'

Joe and Ben would play together often, with Joe on the piano and Ben on the sax. Ben had been learning saxophone by ear, but his keys were often wrong, so Joe started to teach him the rudiments of music, proving that he had learned something with Molly Carroll after all. They soon developed a good understanding of each other as players, and would experiment by incorporating their skiffle 'instruments' into their practice sessions.

Despite her obvious love for music and her constant encouragement, Ellen Dolan was often at her wits' end as her pair of budding bandsmen 'jammed' with saxophone, washboard, accordion and piano. One night they were playing so loudly she told them that if they continued with their skiffle orchestra racket, then they would have to do so in the horse's shed. Within minutes they had set up an unofficial band room there. The horse was sound asleep as the exiled musicians set up in his home, but not for long. The second Joe squeezed the accordion and Ben blew a loud note on his sax, the horse awoke from his reverie with an almighty fright, smashed the door down with one kick and ran away terrified. Determined to form a band, they continued to rehearse in the shed, even if it meant running after the horse for several miles after each performance.

Ben's playing improved with further tutelage from Denis Hughes, as did Joe's piano and accordion playing. Joe was also encouraged to sing at school, and was picked to sing in the choir, but once again he turned down the invitation, citing everything from playground politics to a sore throat. Although Joe could handle himself, Patrick Street could be a tough walk home – even tougher if you had choirboy jokes ringing in your ears. Again the after-hours commitment didn't suit. Piano lessons were enough after-school practice, thank you very much.

Joe's talents as a singer were also spotted by John McGrath, however, a Mullingar man with a keen interest in music and a leading authority on the late, great Irish tenor John McCormack. McGrath, from the Springfield area of the town, had seen something in Joe when he had heard him sing at school, and later he managed to get Joe to sing at Mass and other church functions. 'He saw a bit of a soprano in me,' Joe would say. His first singing engagement was in Gainstown, just outside Mullingar. Joe was part of a group who sang at the National School there as part of a special fundraising concert organized by the local parish priest, Fr Finian O'Connor. Delighted with Joe's performance, Fr O'Connor encouraged Joe even further, telling him that he would one day sing at the cathedral in Mullingar, which to a youngster like Joe was akin to being told you would play Carnegie Hall in New York. The sessions in the Dolan household had freed Joe from any fear of singing in front of his peers, and when encouraged to sing different styles of songs, even those of an operatic and religious sort, he did so with natural ease.

But Joe's real interest lay in rock 'n' roll and he loved emerging stars like Elvis. He also had an appreciation of jazz, and in particular the great Ella Fitzgerald, the 'First Lady of Song', who famously said, 'I sing like I feel', something Joe would take to heart. Joe liked the way Ella lived her songs, and he loved how Elvis performed. 'He wasn't living it, but he was living it up delivering it,' Joe said. But he admitted that as much as he liked both, they didn't influence the way he sang. 'As a teenager, I didn't set out to be what they were or to sing like they do, or do what they do. All I wanted to do was to listen to the rawness of their performances and the way they could put a song over.'

Joe was particularly aware of how the guitar brought an extra drama to Elvis's music. Determined to emulate the young American, but with no money and no idea where one would get a guitar, Joe managed to convince Ben to make him one. 'He did a great job on it, but he didn't put any frets on it,' Joe recalled. 'He was a long way ahead of his time ... it came out in the 1980s that fretless bass guitars were all the go. I suppose you could say it was a class of a bass guitar though, made from a box, with a big stick up through the middle of it and a couple of strings tied on ... Sure it was perfect!'

When Paddy saw the guitar he didn't know what to think. 'I couldn't say anything, but Joe was happy to be strumming away at it like a bass guitar so I left him at it.' But Paddy was happy to see the boys make the effort, and in a few years he would throw a couple of gauntlets down to his brothers that would set them off on the road to stardom.

Although Joe and Ben's two-man band was improving, Joe was frustrated that he was missing out on what Ben was getting to see three times a week: gigs. Every time Joe tried to convince his mother to let him go to the County Hall dances, he was told that he was too young. But with his two brothers working there he was sure he could get her to change her mind. Top of the tree and the one he really wanted to see was the great Clipper Carlton, the showband pioneers from Strabane in Northern Ireland. In the mid 1950s this colourful outfit in sharp suits was the hottest band in the land, an unstoppable and extraordinary musical force who have been credited with triggering the showband explosion.

The bands that emerged in the 1950s offered the youth of Ireland an escape route that didn't involve getting on a boat and moving to America or England. These bands came at a time when the absolute power of the Church was beginning to waver. For years, weekend entertainment in Irish towns had been closely monitored by the parish priest. Onstage, groups of older men would churn out old-time waltzes and variations of traditional songs, huddled over their instruments. Drink was certainly not allowed, and romance, as such, was limited to nervous shuffles around the dance floor. The orchestras that started to buck the trend were those led by Maurice Mulcahy, Mick Delahunty and Johnny Quigley. Their job was not to put on a show, but to make sure the band were providing a solid soundtrack to an evening's dancing in as steady a manner as possible. The crowd were only listening out for whether they were supposed to be dancing a waltz or a foxtrot. But by the late 1950s the social climate of Ireland was beginning to change. Motorcars and transistor radios offered freedoms that were unthinkable ten years earlier. Stations such as Radio Luxembourg gave youngsters something new and exotic to listen too, and the rise of popular music created a wave of new stars. In Northern Ireland in particular, bands were becoming more adventurous and would put more into the show, playing the hits that people were hearing on the radio, and they quickly did big business. Soon the parish halls were too small for them. The parish priest could only look on in horror as ballrooms sprang up in parishes around the country to meet a new, insatiable demand for dancing and showbands, and established venues like the County Hall in Mullingar started to book these new bands who were tearing up the rule book.

The Clipper Carlton had dispensed with the rules long before anyone else by incorporating a whole stage routine into their act that made the band members the centre of attention. They called the routine 'Jukebox Saturday Night', as it featured jukebox-perfect interpretations of the big rock and pop hit songs at the time, songs by bands and heart-throb pop stars that few (if any) Irish people would ever get to see in the flesh. It also featured a section of carefully rehearsed comedy routines, impressions, gags, and so on, as well as the usual big band songs to keep the old-school dancers in step.

Mullingar audiences had never seen anything like it when the band played a show there in early 1956. The Clippers' next County Hall appearance later that summer was highly anticipated, and Joe was desperate to go. It would have been cruel of Ben and Paddy not to try to get the young fella in, even though his mother had said no and Joe could not afford to buy a ticket. So Ben and Joe concocted an elaborate plan so that he could get in for free. The plan was put into effect the day before the dance, when Joe told his mother he would be practising that night and would be home a little later than normal.

The dance was due to start at 9 p.m., and Joe, having been warned by Ben to arrive early, was ready and waiting at the County Hall in the pouring rain from about six that evening. He attempted to keep a low profile in the grounds of the adjacent Mullingar Courthouse, but Joe was a distinctive-looking kid, his shock of black hair and big toothy grin his trademark. Inside the Hall, Ben was waiting for his chance. It eventually arose just before eight when some of the County Hall staff slipped over to a pub on the other side of the road for a swift half. Joe had to be ready to pounce at a moment's notice and even two hours in the rain hadn't damped his enthusiasm or his focus. Ben signalled from one of the County Hall doors that the coast was clear and it was now safe for Joe to sneak in. He bounded up the steps of the County Hall, his wet shoes squelching with every step. Finally, it was going to happen. He was going to see a big band in action, and not just any old band – the best, a band that played well, looked good, danced skilfully and put the show into show business. But before he could soak up the talents of the Strabane men, the wringing wet Joe Dolan would have to hide in the toilets until show time. Once the doors opened, Joe would be free to enter the hall as if he had just paid.

When the time came, Joe went up to the main door and pretended he had just been in but had realized he had forgotten something, and they gave him a pass out. Delighted with himself, he rushed home to Grange, giddy with excitement and safe in the knowledge that nothing was going to stop him from seeing the Clipper Carlton in action: he had his pass and all he needed now was his Sunday best and his dancing shoes. He raced home, pausing at the door to catch his breath so he could saunter in as if it were just a normal night. He told his mother he was tired after practice and that he was going to bed, but not for one minute did she believe him. Moments later she entered his room and caught him trying to sneak back out a window, having changed his clothes.

'And where do you think you're going?' she asked, as Joe groaned with the disappointment of being caught in the act.

Rumbled, Joe decided that honesty was the best policy. Surely his mother would appreciate that, he thought. 'I'm going to hear the Clipper Carlton in the County Hall,' he said meekly, adding that Ben and Paddy would both be there to look after him.

'You are in my hat going to the Clipper Carlton,' his mother retorted. 'Now get into that bed and let that be an end to it.'

A crestfallen Joe was forced to admit defeat. He went to bed, his heart still pounding with the anticipation of seeing the Clippers. But it wasn't to be. He lay awake on his bed until Ben arrived back home in the wee small hours, full of news about the extraordinary four-hour feast of entertainment he had just seen.

'Talk about an insult after he spent an hour in the toilet waiting to get his pass!' Ben laughed years afterwards. 'It was dreadful altogether for him and he was thick for days.'

Joe didn't speak to his mother for a few days after the Clipper Carlton dance that never was, and he didn't speak to Ben or Paddy either when they continued to rub it in by telling him what a fantastic dance it was.

Although she was firm about Joe not going to the show, for the most part Ellen Dolan was a very fair and generous woman. 'She wasn't strict,' Ben recalls. 'I don't remember Joe or any of us having any massive rows over not wanting to do things you were told.' If you did tell a lie, he said all that Ellen needed to do was to threaten you with the priest or the gardaí. 'To upset a priest wouldn't do, but the gardaí was a big one because they would be the last people you'd want to see coming around the house. If they were seen at the house, it would be around like wildfire – "The guards were down at Dolan's house!" – and you'd be tagged for life. So we always told the truth.'

A year later, Joe would finally get to see the Clipper Carlton in the Saint Francis Xavier Hall (demolished in 2006) in Dublin. Ellen had been convinced that Joe should go as it would be good for his piano playing and his singing to see such a professional outfit. The eye-opening gig was to be a musical epiphany for Joe, who was buzzing for weeks afterwards. There was no stopping him now, and he became a regular at County Hall shows, though always supervised by his brothers.

Music was the one constant throughout Joe's formative and teenage years. With the encouragement he was receiving from the likes of Fr O'Connor, John McGrath and another music man, Eamon Cloughessy, Joe was singing more and more, and Ben remembers Joe as a walking jukebox. 'He used to be always singing, always full of beans and full of songs. I wouldn't say that he knew that many songs, but he'd be singing the few he did know all the time.' As in later years, Joe always looked for a good melody.

The brothers used every available opportunity to practise, even when they were making their way into town by horse and cart. '[The horse's] clip-clop-ping trotting would give us a rhythm, and we'd be keeping time with him, singing along the whole way into town,' Joe recalled. 'We sang whatever was going, mainly Irish songs, but that was changing as we got into different stuff.'

Then Ben bought a spluttering beast of a motorbike, a noisy but eminently reliable machine that acted as a stopgap whilst he saved for something with four wheels. He had yet to form a band, but had set his sights on a band-wagon and had saved around £250, a massive amount of money at the time. Ben didn't want too many people to know about it, so he stashed it deep within the bowels of the family piano. He would take the money out on a Saturday , and he and Joe would go around the garages on the motorbike to see if they could find anything within budget. When he went home, he would carefully roll up the money and tuck it back into the piano. No one but Joe knew of the stash, and that was the way Ben wanted to keep it.

One Saturday morning, however, he opened the piano and when he took the money out, a good chunk of it fell to the ground in pieces. 'I thought to myself that if one half fell off out on the ground, then I must have the other half in the bundle. Maybe it had just torn with wear and tear. But I didn't have the other half in the bundle. Then I thought Joe was after cutting it and robbing the other half. I was livid.'

Suspecting that Joe was in town passing off the notes, Ben waited for his brother to return. As he opened the door Joe was met with a question: 'Did you cut up my money?'

'What money? What are you on about?' a shocked Joe replied.

Ben explained the situation and Joe laughed at him, even though he was taken aback by the accusation. Examining the notes that a suspicious Ben handed over to him, Joe laughed again as he protested his innocence. The pair then took the front off the piano and investigated its innards. They were greeted with a pile of rather expensive confetti. The thief was not a budding musician, but a hungry mouse with expensive tastes.

The next morning a hopeful Ben set off for the bank armed with the scraps of money and his tale of woe. Joe wished him well and asked for a cut; Ben didn't see the funny side. The bank manager said there was no way he could hand over money in return for half notes and the scraps that remained. As there was a chance that some of the missing money might have been stolen, he asked Ben to jot down the numbers of each note, promising that if nobody came into the bank with any notes (or bits of notes) that correlated with the numbers in the next twelve months, he would give the Dolan boys back their money.

Back home and seething with anger, Ben and Joe decided that the mouse was going to pay. They took the front off the piano, and set a trap. The lads then stocked up on bread, tea and whatever food they could find that would sustain them until the mouse was caught, and staked out the piano. After a few hours, the high-rolling vermin appeared. 'At this stage both our hearts were hopping,' Joe remembered as he recalled the stake-out. 'We could see the mouse, and for all the world it was like a cartoon. He ran down along the piano, turned around, and slipped back up, came back down and walked over to the mousetrap, sniffing the piece of cheese or whatever it was. My heart was pumping! I don't know why, but it was for the mouse. I nearly hated the thoughts of looking at him getting killed.' Finally the mouse went into the trap to get the cheese and – BANG! – he was caught. Ben decided to put the captured mouse in a jar, and as he tightened the lid he vowed to Joe that he would get his money back. He was going to show the criminal to the bank manager, along with the evidence, and demand his money back.

Joe told the story to a local newsagent who just happened to be a regular contributor to the local and national press. Thinking it a great story, she wrote it up and it appeared as a 'funny' in a letters page. Somehow the story took off and was wired around the world, without its protagonists knowing. Remarkably, Ben and Joe's brother Vincent, who had emigrated to Canada to work in the mines there, read the story in a newspaper and sent the clipping home. Joe couldn't believe it. 'Mouse in Piano Strikes Wrong Note' was the headline. Joe Dolan had made the newspapers for the first time, and he felt a little shocked about it. However, the shock was eased when the bank eventually came good and compensated the brothers for the money they had lost.

Joe's time in school was coming to an end, and he was unsure of what he wanted to do next. For all his musical talent, he didn't think he could make a career of it, and although hard, manual work didn't faze him and he loved the outdoors, he wasn't keen on working in a farm or learning a trade such as carpentry. It was hard for his teachers and his family to find out what he wanted to do. Emigration was an option, but not one he wanted to take. He was very close to his mother and brothers and too fond of Mullingar to leave. Several of his family had done so already, but Joe was keen to stay at home.

With Joe dithering, his mother took matters into her own hands, going into the offices of the *Westmeath Examiner* in the centre of Mullingar to sound out the possibility of their taking on her youngest. The *Examiner* was then, as it is today, the biggest-selling regional newspaper in the midlands. Its Mullingar offices on Dominick Street were also a busy printworks, which afforded a myriad of job opportunities once an apprenticeship was complete. However, the *Examiner* was also known as something of a closed shop. 'It was a hard place to get work in if there was no one belonging to you working there,' Joe recalled. 'It was impossible to get a job anywhere at the time, but it was probably harder to get a job in a newspaper at the time because it was tradition – the jobs were handed down from father to son.'

But Ellen Dolan had one string to pull: one of her cousins worked there.

Both she and Joe made a good impression, and Joe was taken on. Starting right at the bottom with a sweeping brush in one hand and a cloth in the other, Joe was to work his way up the ranks, but first he had to keep the *Examiner* offices and massive printworks tidy. Once a week, there was a break from cleaning when he went around the shops delivering the freshly printed weekly newspaper. 'I spent nearly twelve months at that,' Joe says, and eventually he hung up the brush and began training to become a compositor. The apprenticeship should have lasted seven years, but Joe was allowed to do it in five because he had finishing his schooling.

However, as his interest in music grew, his job satisfaction was beginning to wane. Even when he was meant to be studying printing, he was spending his free time playing music. Joe was even honing his performing skills at work. In fact, Joe often admitted that the shop floor of the *Examiner* printworks was where he developed as a performer. As he went about his work, he sang or whistled almost constantly. Popular music was infectious, and he could listen to it all day long on the assortment of radios that dotted the large *Examiner* premises. With his sweeping brush doubling up as a microphone, he often put on a show for the boys in the works . . . and would frequently be caught in the act by his boss, Kevin Cadogan, who would come up behind Joe as he was performing. Of course Joe's impromptu audience would see Cadogan approaching, but Joe wouldn't know until he got a tap on the shoulder. 'Mr Dolan,' he would declare sternly. 'If you want to join the circus then you had better leave!'

It was not long before Joe was handed his first 'proper' guitar. The acoustic guitar had belonged to a relative of Mullingar musician Ollie Kennedy (who would later play a key role in the international success of Foster and Allen as both a songwriter and a member of their band). On his way home from the UK to Mullingar for Christmas, the musician's trusty guitar broke into pieces. It was destined for the scrapheap until Ben offered to take it out of its misery, handing over a few shillings to its grieving owner. Ben was now a skilled carpenter, and his second attempt at creating a guitar was infinitely more successful than his first. He managed to restore the guitar to some semblance of its former glory, and although it now had a more rustic, patchwork charm, it was playable. When he gave it to Joe as a belated birthday present, his younger brother was thrilled, taking an immediate shine to it.

Joe began to play the guitar almost non-stop. Without telling anyone what he was doing, Joe had formulated a little stage routine for himself, which he was preparing to unleash on to an unsuspecting public when 'Beginners Please', a national talent contest that wanted to find the best hidden talent in the regions and bring it to Dublin to entertain the nation, came to Mullingar. It was the brainchild of radio personality and show-business impresario Roy Croft, whom Joe would later call 'the Louis Walsh of his day'. Roy hosted heats in each of the regions with the winner of each heat going forward to a pair of semi-finals. The lucky few who made it out of these would then compete in the grand final, broadcast on Radio Éireann to the whole country.

Croft and company rolled into town amid a flurry of excitement and anticipation. That excitement grew once they set up a marquee on the Fair Green, close to the Mullingar army barracks, as the temporary marquee could be seen for miles around and – crucially – from each of the town's main schools. A bumper crowd was guaranteed for the contest, which was going to be judged on the strength of the audience's applause – with that staple of light entertainment at the time, a clapometer, wheeled out at the end of every round.

Joe eventually let a select few know that he had entered, including his good friend Mick 'Jazzer' Mulligan, a larger-than-life character whom Joe knew from his early schooldays. Jazzer decided he would enter himself, and he told as many people as possible to come along, not to cheer for him, but to cheer on Joe.

The venue was packed as the show got underway, and Roy Croft introduced a succession of acts. At the back, 'Jazzer' marshalled his troops into place, warning them not to cheer for any acts other than Joe. The first act onstage was an unfortunate young accordionist who received a polite round of applause and even a few jeers. Then came a couple of Irish step dancers, a boy soprano who sang 'Marble Halls', a group called the Razzle Dazzles, a ventriloquist, a girl called Thelma Byrne with a voice like honey, and then Jazzer Mulligan himself, who mimicked birdsong. Finally, Mullingar was given its first ever glimpse of Joe Dolan, the singer.

Joe's old friend Kevin Nugent, whom Joe continued to look out for, was among those awestruck by what they saw onstage that night. 'A stranger in drainpipe trousers, frilled shirt, padded shoulders and swept-back black hair jumped out from behind the curtain, and with one bound landed in the middle of the stage, grabbing the microphone off the stand as if it was his and his alone,' Kevin remembered. 'We didn't recognize him at first. Could this be Joe Dolan? Our Joe Dolan?'

Joe launched into 'Ma, She's Making Eyes at Me', an old standard written in 1921 that Joe had updated as a tent-shaking rockabilly number. He delivered every line as if his life depended on it, whilst the shocked audience hung on every word.

'At first we were stunned into disbelief as he moved his body to the rhythmic beat, but it was his powerful voice that riveted us. This was as good as anything we had seen on television. Soon we were on our feet clapping and cheering. Here was Joe Dolan, our friend, the same Joe who worked in the *Examiner* office, singing and playing like a real pop singer,' Kevin remembered. 'Looking back, I think this may well have been the moment when our lives were changed for ever. It was as if Joe had catapulted us into another world, a world we had never imagined but one we had longed for, so that by the time the night was over Joe had dragged us into the twentieth century. Things would never be the same in Mullingar again. We were suddenly set down in modern times and there would be no turning back.'

At the end of the evening it came down to a tie between two acts: Joe and Thelma Byrne. So Roy Croft indicated that the audience would choose the winner. This was Jazzer's cue, and he went around and organized everyone in the venue, telling them to stay quiet for Thelma. When her name was read out, the applause was polite. When Joe's name was announced, the rallying call of 'Now, lads' coming from Jazzer was the cue for the crowd to go wild. But it was obvious to everyone that evening that they had just witnessed something very special indeed, and they didn't need the efforts of Jazzer Mulligan to get them clapping in appreciation of Joe's performance.

Joe was awarded a silver cup that he kept in his home all his life – although at the time he would have preferred the second prize, as Thelma received seven and sixpence for her efforts. 'I would have willingly given her the cup for the seven and sixpence,' joked Joe. 'I asked her in fact, and she told me to get lost!' He didn't make it to the final, but as far as first impressions went, he couldn't have asked for a better introduction to the stage.

After this, Joe became something of a celebrity among the youth of Mullingar. He was already a confident fellow, but Ben and everyone around him noticed that his confidence grew in the wake of his stage debut. A couple of weeks later, Joe appeared at the County Hall for another talent contest, reprising his 'Ma, She's Making Eyes at Me' routine to an equally stunned audience. He stood out even more, as Ben remembered. 'Everybody else was singing classy tunes, but he'd get up with "Ma" and blow them all away. It was a great routine for the yahoos he was palling around with, and anyway, it used to win for him.'

After working solidly for a couple of months, Joe got his first holidays from the *Westmeath Examiner*, and he and a gang of friends headed west for a week of fun in Galway City. As they wandered around the streets of Galway and the strand at Salthill looking for adventure and music, the gang had the time of their lives. It is said that Joe had his first kiss on this holiday. At home, there wasn't much in the way of teenage culture, and because everyone socialized in groups there was little time for intimacy.

Joe's knowledge of Irish song and dance made him a popular man to be around in a pub. Wild music sessions were the order of the holiday, and although innocence (allegedly) prevailed and most of the lads stuck to lemonade, it was in a pub late one night when Joe had another musical epiphany. A local musician was strumming along on an electric guitar, and the fiery-red instrument became the object of Joe's new-found six-stringed desire. Full of awe and admiration for the sounds being produced from the instrument and amazed by the 'feel' of it, Joe decided there and then that he was going to buy one.

When he returned home to Grange from the holiday, he informed Ben of his decision. Ben, who believed he had the sexiest instrument in the pack with the saxophone, thought Joe was insane. 'Guitars weren't in at the time. It was The Beatles really that brought in guitars in the 1960s, but in the late 1950s people used to be nearly laughing at lads playing guitars in bands. A lad would be strumming away, but no one would hear it with the sound of the band! And there was certainly no electric guitar in music, at least not in Ireland.'

But Joe was determined, and he told Ben that despite a financial handicap (he had blown all his savings on the Galway holiday) he was going to pick one up. Although he was the thriftiest of the pair, there was nothing Ben could do to help out his determined younger brother. He was saving for a van and had bills of his own, so he left Joe to his own devices. When Saturday came, Joe tucked his patchwork acoustic guitar under his arm and headed towards Dublin, thumbing lifts to get there and even treating one or two drivers to an impromptu song. He eventually arrived in the capital and made his way around the various musical instrument shops there. He was afforded a receptive ear in McCullough Piggott, one of the city's most reputable – and biggest.

Later that evening, Joe shocked his mother and brother when he arrived home armed with a top-of-the-range red and orange electric guitar, a guitar case and a brand-new amplifier. He was also covered from head-to-toe in coal dust. 'In the name of God, what have you done?' Joe's mother asked as he walked into the house.

Ben's first impression was also not a good one. 'I really thought he was after stealing it. The whole thing was like a fairytale.'

Asked how he had managed to convince a shop to hand over such grandiose goods valued close to £100, Joe replied, 'I used my charm' – his mischievous smirk hiding the string of lies he had fed the man in the shop.

'Where are we going to get the money to pay for that?' his mother wanted to know.

Joe told his mother and brother that he had set up a hire purchase agreement for the equipment – a statement that caused them both further worry because Joe had never displayed any signs of being a man who was unduly concerned about money. To Joe a bank account was a foreign country.

When it was firmly established that Joe had not stolen the musical gear, Ben noticed that something was missing. 'Good Jesus. Where's my guitar gone?' he asked.

It turned out that Joe had made the patchwork guitar a part of a unique trade-off deal in McCullough Piggott. He had traded it in for a pound, then convinced the shop assistant to let him sign up without a guarantor, and then cheekily borrowed the pound back so he could come home on the train and get a bite to eat. 'They basically gave me the guitar for nothing,' Joe revealed years later. 'I can't really remember signing anything and they never looked for a guarantor.' He had vowed to return with the next payment in a month.

Having nibbled into his train fare, Joe only had enough money left to bring him to Lucan. Standing at the edge of the village with his new equipment at his feet, he started to thumb a lift home. Luckily, a lorry from Whelan's Coal, a Mullingar fuel merchant, was passing through the village and the driver recognized Joe from 'Beginners Please'. Joe sat in the back among the coal bags for the hour-long drive home.

The new guitar was to have an immediate effect on his popularity. Word spread around Grange that Joe had one of these new-fangled electric guitars. 'Jesus Christ, but it attracted the crowds straight away!' Joe exclaimed. 'You didn't have to play a note on it. If you strummed it you'd nearly attract a crowd. Everyone was in awe of it.' Not quite everyone . . . as Joe recalled: 'We would be practising in the house and Ben would be blowing the sax and the dog would be howling away at it and me strumming the guitar,' Joe recalled. 'My mother would say, "Get up to your room, you're annoying the dog." So, we'd go up, but there would be no fire lit in the room and sure we'd be freezing. She'd then shout at us to come down. It got to the stage where we could play a few tunes perfectly. We thought we were the last word!'

Things were beginning to take shape for the brothers in 1957. Throughout the country the showband scene was also beginning to take shape, and from fairly quiet beginnings there was soon a plentiful supply of live music to enjoy, not just in the County Hall in Mullingar, but in parish halls and brand-new ballrooms throughout Westmeath. For the Dolan boys it was a case of 'right place, right time'. All they needed now was a band.

3
The Apprenticeship

As the showband scene began to take off, bands of all shapes and sizes were appearing out of the woodwork in every parish in the land. However, Mullingar was slow to catch up. Apart from the Mullingar Town Band, one of the most recognized and highly decorated marching bands in the country, there was no band 'scene' as such in the town. And despite the popular music bands that were now filling the County Hall on a regular basis, there was almost a sense of shame in saying that you belonged to one of the new breed. 'In some people's minds it was a slur!' Joe exclaimed. He often told a story about a musician he and Ben knew who used to play the trumpet in a dance band out of town. The musician's wife was dead set against the band, and was constantly giving out about his choice of instrument too. 'He said to us that if he was playing a tin whistle or an accordion or a fiddle, he wouldn't have been in as much trouble. It was as if playing the trumpet was bringing shame on the family.'

For the music-mad brothers this poor state of affairs was something they desperately wanted to change, and they often told elder brother Paddy that they were going to do just that by assembling their own band. 'Well, go and do it!' he would say, by way of stern encouragement.

Paddy remembers them as a quintessentially well-dressed pair of bachelor brothers who knew how to 'walk the walk' as musicians – the only thing they were missing was a band to play in. Paddy's home on Dominick Street and, later, on Ginnell Terrace, was always on their visiting list when they started to socialize in the town more regularly, and their arrival was always well flagged as he invariably heard them before he saw them.

Ben's motorbike was a noisy machine, but noisier still was its cargo, and in particular its all-singing pillion passenger, Joe. As the bike was a little more obstreperous than most other motorcycles, Joe had to sing that little bit louder to be heard above the din of the spluttering double-barrel exhaust. Ben would also be singing or humming along. 'I would hear them from inside the house,' Paddy recalled with an ever-so-visible trace of embarrassment. 'If you were at the door, you could hear Joe singing through the town – up Oliver Plunkett Street from the Market Square into Dominick Street. Honestly, you'd hear him as loud as anything. I suppose with the motorbike being the way it was, Joe didn't know he was singing that loud, but he'd a fine pair of lungs on him.'

When asked what Joe had been singing, Paddy reveals the two sides to Joe's music taste at the time: comhailes, representing the Irish tradition; and rock 'n' roll, pop and jazz, representing his new image as a slick rock 'n' roller. At work he was being exposed to different music courtesy of his co-workers' varied tastes, whilst in town and in the houses of friends with powerful radios he was able to tune into some of the long-wave continental channels coming through. At home his own radio would only pick up the rock and pop stations on a clear night, and he would often spend frustrating but ultimately rewarding hours trying to tune the dial. When he was successful, he would lie in bed utterly lost in the music.

Over dinner at Paddy's – where, coincidentally, a big radio awaited Ben and Joe's tuning fingers – they would again reiterate their desire to form a band, but it was down to Ben to make this a reality. With Mullingar a barren band desert, he looked at its outlying villages and discovered, much to his surprise, that the tiny hamlet of Ballynacargy, fifteen kilometres from Mullingar, was something of an unlikely oasis for new musical talent. It was here that Ben (and very shortly Joe) became a moonlighting member of not one but two bands at the same time.

The first band was led by the late Tommy Farrell. An accordion player, Tommy led the band from the front of the stage with traditional squeeze-box classics embellished with a big-band feel. The fluctuating line-up (more than one member was known to have been dragged home, often by the ear) had a rawness that pitched them somewhere between an orchestra and a show-band, so Ben was keen not only to join them as a player but to get to know Tommy. 'At that time Tommy and the band used to get an odd date,' he recalls, 'and I went with them a couple of times, just to see them play. But this one time they were in Ballinafid, County Westmeath, and Tommy asked me to sing a song with them. I think the song was "Blackbird of my Heart", so I got up on the stage, shaking, and sure I got through it all right . . .'

The next time he travelled with Tommy, instead of hanging around the hall he was hanging around onstage. Back at home, his younger brother was awestruck by Ben's assorted tales from the stage. Of course they were embellished with a few white lies, but nevertheless Joe wanted to join his musical partner in crime onstage as soon as possible. Ben told him to be patient; he himself was getting his bearings, and once there was an opening, Joe would be in.

Meanwhile, Ben became acquainted with another band in Ballynacargy, this one led by Henry J. Murtagh, or 'Henny' as most people called him. One night the band knew they would be down a man for a couple of nights, and Ben Dolan's name was recommended to them. They approached him asking if he would come to a dance they were playing at a venue in Tullamore, County Offaly. This gig went a little better for Ben, and he slotted into the line-up well. He knew a few of the boys who played with Henny, which helped him bed down. Sadly, Ben can remember little about the dance in question as 'It passed like a blur – one minute we were setting up, the next we were taking the gear down', but he remembers his heart pounding with excitement afterwards. 'I wanted to play again that night!' he exclaimed. For the most part, Ben played accordion, with some saxophone thrown in for good measure. 'I suppose I just made a few noises!' he laughs, unable to remember any of the songs they played that night.

Ben became a moonlighting member of this band as well as Farrell's outfit, and Joe went to see his brother in action. Although he was impressed with what he saw, it felt a little strange being on the dance floor while Ben played. 'I was desperate for a piece of the action, to get up there and play.'

As the weeks went by, Ben somehow managed to play and sing in both bands at the same time and not get caught out by either bandleader. As he skirted between the pair it was inevitable the bands would one day be booked to play on the same night, and should this ever arise a match-fit Joe Dolan was waiting on the sidelines. Bookings for both bands were beginning to stack up and, sure enough, in the run-up to Hallowe'en 1958, Ben was asked to play in both outfits on the same night.

He told each bandleader that he wasn't sure if he could make the gig, and, testing the water for Joe, suggested that his equally musically adept younger brother would do a fine job in his absence. Joe was about to get his first big band break, but with which band? Having gauged the reactions of both band-leaders, Ben eventually decided that Joe would be better served togging out with Henny Murtagh's more experienced band. The only trouble was that Joe was nowhere to be found when Ben went to tell him the good news. 'I was looking everywhere for him,' Ben recalls. 'I was fretting a bit and I went off to find him. I was beginning to think that the band would leave without him.'

Joe was eventually found playing cards in the Morrison family home. The Morrisons were faithful friends of the Dolans, and Joe was a regular visitor to their house, sauntering in without as much as a knock on the door. He had played cards with the Morrisons regularly from about the age of twelve or thirteen, and it was here that he really honed his card-playing skills. One of the Morrison boys, Jackie, eventually left Mullingar for Grey-stones, but Joe never lost contact with him. In later years he got to know Jackie's sons very well indeed, as fellow entertainers. Ciaran, the eldest of the trio, would see his childhood love of puppets bring him much success as one half of the TV puppet duo Zig and Zag, and later as Rodge in *The*

Podge and Rodge Show. Another brother, Johnny, would go on to become the man behind Dustin the Turkey, a creation that helped to revitalize Joe's career in the 1990s.

When Ben burst into the kitchen to tell his brother that he was about to make his first-ever concert appearance with a band, Joe bounced up from the table in delight. For quite possibly the only time in his life, Joe didn't get to finish a hand of cards. Excusing himself from the table, he flung the cards down and raced out the door, through the field which connected their homes, buck-leaping and clicking his heels in excitement.

At this time, if you were playing in a band then you had to have a dress suit, or at least a clean suit that with a few modifications could resemble a dress suit. Ben had already bought his own stage wear, but he wouldn't be handing it over to his younger brother just yet. For his first official stage appearance, Joe would wear an old suit that belonged to his late father, Patrick. His mother Ellen polished a pair of shoes for him, and although Joe recalled her muttering about all the fuss and panic just to play in a band, he detected some pride in her voice. 'Secretly she was quite happy, I think.' In a matter of minutes Joe looked the part, and he didn't seem remotely nervous about what lay ahead. Instead, he was oozing confidence and charisma.

'It was as if he was born for this moment. He was shaping around the house like a peacock – shifting around, checking himself out in the mirror, flicking up the collar of his shirt and making sure the hair was slick,' Ben remembers. His many weeks of preening himself for his 'Beginners Please' appearance had given him a good foundation in knowing how to look the part. On his own, he often practised a few moves in front of a mirror, as many a teenager has done.

Joe was almost too confident, and Ben had to remind him that although he thought he knew plenty of songs, this was Henny Murtagh's band – he directed the show and dictated the pace. Joe was not to let his keen edge and eagerness to impress become too obvious; he had to take it slow and steady. Like a boxer before a fight, Joe took it all in. He polished his guitar, even cleaning the dust out from underneath the strings to make sure he made a sparkling impression.

And so, on his first night as a working musician, Joe was waved away from his home by his mother as he left with Henny Murtagh and his band, whilst Ben went off to play with Tommy Farrell.

'It went by in an absolute flash, and what I do remember is that I loved it,' Joe laughed. 'I hadn't a clue what was going on, so I was watching the boys all night, playing catch up, but it was a blast.'

Joe didn't come home until six in the morning, and waiting up for him, with a mixture of pride and concern, was his worried mother. Joe was still ten feet high from the gig. 'Even though he only got to sing a handful of songs and didn't get to do much else onstage, he raved about it for as long as anyone would listen to him,' Ben revealed. But his late arrival also ensured the gig would be remembered for another reason – his mother grounded him for a few days, even though Joe had given her half his earnings from his first performance.

With his first gig under his belt, and Henny Murtagh suitably impressed, Joe found himself in demand and the Dolan brothers started to get more and more jobs with the two bands. Somehow the brothers had to keep both bands sweet and not pledge their full allegiance to either outfit. For some time they pulled this off, but they were beginning to attract serious attention as ones to watch. They became known throughout the county as talented musical guns for hire, and were highly rated by band members and audiences alike. Their days as moonlighters were surely numbered.

Even in these early appearances Joe was marking himself out as the showman of the pair, with a grasp of rhythm that saw him pushing other, more experienced band members to his preferred pace. Ben was the more serious musician, and kept an eye on learning the ropes so that he could form his own band. But from the outset it was clear that whatever band they formed, it would be centred on Joe.

With plenty of gigs under their belts and some extra money trickling into the Dolan household, there was a great sense of optimism and plenty of hope in the air when the family gathered for Christmas in 1958. Ellen was very much the proud matriarch, as all her brood were working and her love of music had been embraced wholeheartedly by almost all of them. The family were supporting her, and the generosity she had shown and the sacrifices she had made for their benefit in her younger days were coming back to roost. Life was very much on the up, and she was the life and soul of the neighbourhood, remembered as much for being a kind neighbour as a dear friend. She was also a proud and devoted grandmother, as Paddy, Dympna, Ita, Imelda and James had all married and some grandchildren were beginning to appear on the scene. With the war a distant memory, James was home more frequently than before, whilst the unmarried trio of brothers, Ben, Joe and Vincent, were all doing well for themselves.

But soon after the Christmas celebrations had wound down, Ellen took ill. After a brief illness fought with courage and conviction, she suffered a stroke on 16 January 1959 and died, just sixty-seven years old. She was buried at Walshestown church alongside her husband and their young son Michael. It was her local parish and her childhood home was only a short walk down the road.

Her passing hit all the family hard. Joe, then just nineteen, was inconsolable. He had been the apple of his mother's eye, and with no father figure save for his elder brothers, she was all he had. He would later admit to feeling her presence in venues, and in Moscow many, many years later when he was at the height of his international fame, he was to have a haunting encounter with a mysterious Russian psychic who claimed Joe's mother was proud of him. But the fact his parents never got to see him play was his biggest regret. 'I would dearly love if they had been alive to see me play – and to hear my records. But I suppose that was the will of God,' he said. 'What I missed most of all just after my mother dying was that when I came home after a dance, or after a show, or after anything, I couldn't tell her about everything that had happened, and after she went I felt alone.'

Her death brought silence to the Dolan home for the first time. 'There was nobody there – only Ben and I – and there was no music, no anything. We were numbed by it all,' Joe revealed.

Joe and Ben's band sharing lasted for a couple of months as they got over the death of their mother. They played with Henny's band the most, however, and, as his popularity grew, they left Tommy's group to become full-time members, travelling further afield to play gigs. (The picture on p. 37 is the first promotional photo of the young Joe.) The band would leave for these gigs quite early in the day. Often, Ben and Joe would ride for half an hour on the motorbike to meet the rest of them in Ballynacargy. They then all crammed into a car and, with most of their equipment bound to the roof, would set out on a marathon journey that always seemed to take longer than necessary. Sometimes the pick-up would be in Mullingar, but for Ben the journey was always a hassle. 'Even if you were going to

Roscommon, which was only forty miles away, you had to leave at two o'clock in the day,' Ben recalls with dismay. The other lads were a bit older than Joe and Ben, and there was still a very strong drinking culture at the time, so the journey would be punctuated by several pit stops for pints of porter – though the Dolan boys themselves had no interest in drink. 'We wouldn't be outside of whatever pub we'd stop in first but one of them lads would be dying to go to the loo; and you couldn't attempt to go on the side of the road even though everyone else did it. Fellas in a band had to go to the loo in a pub. So, three pints later, you'd come out and you wouldn't be able to get into the car, so more time would be lost. It was ridiculous. There'd be eight of us, including the driver, and we'd be crammed in, one on top of the other,' a shuddering Ben remembers. 'Of course you'd only be gone another five miles and the boys would be bursting again so we'd have to stop at another pub!'

Ben and Joe reckoned that investing in a bandwagon was the only solution. Ben bought a second-hand van in Dublin, and it was agreed that it would be delivered to the Dolan house in Grange the very next day. However, when Joe went to check out Ben's new arrival the next evening, he noticed that it had no lights. 'The seller had taken the spotlights off, and all there was at the front of the van were two holes and the front bumper,' laughed Joe. Ben was livid, but a discovery inside the van was to more than make up for the disappointment.

When Joe was cleaning out the van, he came across a mysterious case. Cracking it open, he found it full to the brim with sheet music for hundreds of songs from a wide variety of genres, from traditional to popular, rock to jazz, blues to folk. He also found the remains of a banjo, which he handed to Ben. He was in raptures with the sheet music and immediately scarpered inside to play 'Travelling Light' on his guitar. The Cliff Richard chart-topper was a favourite of Joe's, and for a couple of days he had been trying to master it by ear alone. He was also thrilled to find a load of Elvis Presley sheet music, and he set to work emulating the magic of his musical hero. 'Here we had Joe with a new guitar, a big pile of sheet music with all the chords and words and changes written on it, sure we had the makings of a full set there and then,' Ben recalls.

For days on end, Joe could barely bring himself to put down his guitar or even go to work, such was his determination to learn every song in the case.

'It was only a matter of him picking out the chords off the sheet and he had the song,' Ben recalls with admiration, even close to fifty years later. 'His progress was unreal, as it only seemed like a couple of days until he was able to play a good few tunes. He was astonishing, y'know? He had the chords perfect and he had the rhythm; he just had it. He picked it up so quickly, and what people forget was just how good a guitar player he was, and what a good rhythm man he was. He was a natural.'

The box of music and the new wagon gave them a sense of freedom and a taste for further musical adventure. Ben picked up a PSV licence and, with him behind the driving wheel and Joe acting as the 'ticket collector', the brothers started to use their wagon to ferry other bands and dancers to gigs. They were also using it to drive local drama groups to appearances at halls throughout the midlands. In these pre-coach hire days, they had the entertainment market sown up.

The gigs with Henny Murtagh kept rolling in, and Joe finally had the feeling he was part of something, part of a big band. But all the while Ben was working on other plans for the pair. 'I kind of wanted my own band and from his time out front, Joe really wanted his own band, so I started talking to fellas to get them to join up.'

There were still amusing times to be had with Henny's band. His instrument of choice was the piano, and his all-time favourite tune was an ancient folk song, 'The Shoemaker's Shop', which he would tap out a few times a night, telling Joe to sing each time even though Joe preferred to sing Elvis songs. Henny was so fond of the song that he would often launch into it without warning, or halfway through a completely different song. 'Unbeknownst to us, he'd start playing it, so we'd all stop what we were playing and we'd be coming in one after the other. There was neither head nor tail to it, we'd be on the hoof every night,' Joe recalled. If songs were short, Joe would be instructed to either repeat a couple of verses, or whistle a verse if he had run out of lyrics. 'I used to be a nervous wreck!' Joe remembers. 'Even though it would have nothing to do with me, because I was out front I'd get the blame!'

To add a percussive flavour to certain songs, Joe would rattle a set of homemade maracas (two tin cans full of sand crudely stuck on to sticks), which had a tendency to become much lighter as the show went on, courtesy of their unique air filtration systems – holes. Joe would often shake the maracas over Murtagh's back and, as the gig went on, sand would gently coat his suit jacket, much to the amusement of the other band members. 'He'd be covered in sand across the back. I used to think it was a shocking insulting altogether,' Ben says. 'I'd be trying to stop him onstage, which would lead to little scuffles as Henny played on, not noticing what was happening behind him at all.' 'It was all just accidental, I assure you,' was Joe's take on the situation.

Despite having much fun on the road with Henny Murtagh and the band, the lads' apprenticeship was over and their days as sidemen were fast coming to an end. Although they never got too serious, occasional rows and bicker-ing between band members were leading to poor performances. One such row concerned the growing use of Ben's bandwagon, as some of the band were jealous that he was getting an extra cut for being the driver, and this proved the final straw for the Dolan brothers.

Yet, like the box of music falling into their laps courtesy of the careless van owner, another piece of good fortune was about to befall the pair of budding bandsmen. 'It's shocking all the bits of luck that happened to us over the years,' Joe recalled, 'but out of the blue a musician called Eddie Deehy, who wasn't playing in any band we were in at the time, got a gig to play at a wedding in Killucan for a lassie he knew who was getting married.' With little or no time to practise, an ad-hoc band was formed with Joe on guitar, piano, violin and vocals, Eddie Deehy on drums, Tom Reilly, who had played in Henny's band, on accordion and vocals, and Ben on saxo-phone and vocals.

Killucan didn't know what hit it. As Westmeath villages go, Killucan was one of the quietest and not a place accustomed to four wild men belting out rock, pop and traditional music jams until the early hours. But despite having no band name and no time to practise, the lads went down a storm. Much of the impromptu set consisted of extended jams, and Joe took hold of the show as if it were his own. Although he was a little shy on the microphone between songs, once the music whipped up around him he let rip, and his vocal and musical theatrics set the dancers off into a maelstrom.

'Everyone, no more than at any wedding, I suppose, said it was the greatest wedding they were ever at. "The band was fantastic," they all said, so we believed them. But we kind of knew we were great anyway!' Joe laughs. 'We just played whatever we could play, and it went down very well, and we thought, "Ah, these are all friends, sure they'd say that any-way." But then we got serious about it, and we stayed together, a few of us, and we started to think we could play at a few other things if we went after them.'

Ben and Joe told Henny Murtagh the news and, naturally enough, he was reluctant to lose two handsome members who were causing quite a stir onstage and attracting plenty of women to his shows. He felt the lads were making the wrong decision, and he warned them in the nicest possible way that if they formed a band and based themselves in Mullingar, they would not stand a chance as the town had such a poor history when it came to jobbing bands.

With the deflating comments ringing in their ears, Joe and Ben sought solace at their brother Paddy's house, but having heard all their talk many times before about forming a band, he ran them. The boys were furious and even more determined to get their show on the road. 'He told us not to come back until we started a proper band,' remembered Ben. 'He kind of insulted us, saying we'd been wasting money on all these instruments if we weren't going to play any of them, so I says, "Right, I'll feckin' show you!" I really made my mind up we were going to start this band. Joe was full of it the whole time and was ready, so we just had to make it official.'

The lads agreed to do one last show with Henny, and the journey home from that show was filled with apprehension, anticipation and an air of sad-ness. 'We came home that night in a strange mood,' Joe recalls. 'As it happened, it turned out to have been a good night, the best gig in ages. The band had sounded well, there was a good turnout, everything had gone great and everyone was in good form.' Joe tried to stay solemn, to remain firm that they were leaving, but it proved difficult because onstage Joe transformed into a dynamic, all-pleasing being of warmth, charm and charisma, and after a good gig it took him an age to come down. He was laughing and joking away with the lads he was about to leave. It was left to Ben to bite his lip. 'I thought, I can't be too friendly now because I would have to go back on my word . . . It was the end of it as far as we were concerned, but because every-one was in such good humour it made it harder for Joe to say, "We won't be seeing yiz any more." So I had to stay thick, and stay in bad humour, but that wasn't Joe at all.'

With no gigs to play for the next few weeks, Ben was able to place his bandwagon on hire, and as showbands started to take Westmeath by storm he was in huge demand elsewhere as he transported bands, fans and anyone who would book him to dances. When Joe wasn't going to dances himself, or leading the Grange gang on their merry way to one, he would act as co-pilot, and if they were bringing a crowd to a dance then invariably the main topic of conversation was that Joe and Ben's band was going to be bigger and better than the one they were going to see.

4

Adventures on the rocky road to success

Not long after his successful first outing with the ad-hoc wedding band, Joe found that his vocal services were in demand and bookings for gigs began to mount up, even though the line-up of his band was by no means agreed. Although Joe and Ben had an innate understanding of each other, they weren't so sure about the rest of the players they had assembled, so practice – and plenty of it – was required. But with their mother's passing still fresh in their minds, they did not want rehearsals to be held at home. As they wondered where they could practise, a young local businessman with a big interest in music, Joe Healy, came to the rescue, and the Dolan brothers landed another lucky break.

The flamboyant Healy offered the lads the use of his Coliseum Cinema premises in the centre of Mullingar. The cinema was adjacent to his department store in Dominick Street, but a combination of factors had led to Healy closing down the old picture house. Its cavernous main auditorium, where Joe and Ben had watched so many films and newsreels in their childhood, offered the lads the chance to make as much of a racket as they wanted, which suited them, as their act was far from polished. However, there were a couple of snags: there was no power and no heat in the old cinema.

At first Joe and the outfit practised by candlelight in a little side room, but the lure of playing from a stage to a large theatre – albeit an empty one – was far too tempting and within a few days they had set up in front of the cinema's main screen. The lack of power was frustrating, especially for Joe as his electric guitar could not be heard above the racket the other members were making. And vocally he really had to strain himself to be heard. Something had to change, so he and Ben hatched an ambitious plan to bring the power back to the Coliseum.

Late one night Joe ever so delicately bored a hole in the wall into Healy's business premises next door. He then fed an electric cable through the hole, its exposed wires at the ready for connection on the other side. He had chosen the spot very carefully, knowing that on the other side was a former saddler's that was now a shoe-repair section. Such was the disarray of the shelving system, Joe was sure that the hole would not be noticed amid the clutter of shoes and old saddles. He was also sure it was close to a couple of power points.

The next day Joe took a break from work and met Ben in the cinema, where they went through the finer points of their plan. Because Ben had some relevant experience through his work as a carpenter and his knowledge of gadgets, Joe decided that it would be best if he handled the big switch and wired them into the power source next door. To avoid suspicion, Ben put on a big coat, and his electrician's equipment was then tucked into the pockets. They did a quick dry run, with Ben practising his wiring against the clock. Confident it could be done quickly and with little fuss, they marched out of the cinema, walked around the corner of Dominick Place and into Healy's store. Joe managed to distract Mr Healy by talking to him, and Ben sneaked swiftly down the back and got to work. He found the hole and the cable, and within a few seconds he had wired a plug on to it. But then, as he attempted to feed the cable inconspicuously around and under the shelves, disaster struck.

CRASH!

Some old saddlery chains had fallen off their hook and on to the floor. The clang of the metal hitting the wooden floorboards was heard all over the shop.

'What was that?' Mr Healy asked. 'Did you hear that, Joe?'

Knowing full well that Ben had been rumbled, Joe tried to buy some time. 'I didn't hear anything at all. Now, er, tell me about this thing again,' he said, reaching for a hat, the first available item he could grab. Smelling a rat, Healy turned to where the noise came from.

Having gone this far, there was no turning back for Ben. He had to feed the wire the whole way around the shelves and into the plug socket and then hide any evidence, or the plan would surely be found out. He needed to deflect attention from himself, and fast. 'Don't worry lads, it's only me!' he roared, trying to project his voice to another part of the store whilst working at the wire. 'I was looking at a yoke here, no need to panic. Be there in a minute.'

As Mr Healy rounded the corner he was confronted by a bolt-upright Ben, standing there sweating profusely. 'Howya, lads. Bad shelf here, Joe,' Ben quipped, as he tapped a shelf with the same screwdriver he had just used to wire up the cinema.

'Why don't you take that coat off you? You're covered in sweat, man,' Mr Healy remarked disdainfully.

'Sure it's cold outside,' Ben replied, directing an imaginary spit at the floor, a trademark of his.

Not wishing to arouse suspicions further, the Dolans made good their escape. They offered up prayers to the cheap seats as they plugged the cables in for the first time. Rather than wait to see if they had light or anything inconsequential like that, Joe strapped on his electric guitar, plugged the lead into his amplifier and tentatively switched it on. He heard a CLUNK, then a buzz of power surged through the amp. He was in business. The first thing Joe did was hit a celebratory power chord: TWANGGGGGGGGG!

However, his joy would be short lived. It had been such a job to finish the illicit wiring in Healy's store that the plug had not been fully tightened, and there were occasional power cuts and frequent surges. 'We patched it up again after that,' Joe recalled as he concluded the saga of the stolen power, but he remembered going back into Healy's to plug it back in after they had been inadvertently disconnected.

Eventually Joe Healy followed the lead and Joe was rumbled. 'He was nice about it, though,' Joe said. 'He didn't pass any remarks on it, and we often laughed about it over the years with him. We made it look like he gave us our start, and we promised him free tickets, which I don't think he accepted.'

Joe Healy's generosity was never forgotten by the Dolan family, and when things were not going too well for Healy's business, they offered him a partnership and invested in his Dominick Street property portfolio, including the former Coliseum Cinema, where Joe would eventually open a bar and a nightclub bearing his name.

Despite having all the electricity they wanted back in 1959, the cold of the former cinema still 'skinned them alive' according to Joe. But the set-up was working well and Ben recalls that Joe was really coming into his own, with the big stage bringing out the best in him as a front man and as a singer. Another thing that gave him a boost was a visit by an up-and-coming local photographer called Sean Magee, who took some of the first publicity photographs of the band. Posing for the camera excited them all, as it was a vindication of sorts that they were now truly in a band.

Their first major gig was in Castletown-Geoghegan, a gig that Ben had booked before the band was even fully formed. To augment the four-piece band, Joe had hired Sean Connolly, a tall, studious trumpet player with distinctive silver hair. A nurse in St Loman's Hospital in Mullingar, Sean had been playing music for years but not in a popular music group, so he was delighted to accept Joe's invitation. A piano player from Mullingar who was known only as Mrs FitzSimons also joined.

In October 1959, Joe found out that well-known showband man Donie Collins was performing at the Roseland Ballroom in Moate, a venue that for a short period in the late 1950s and '60s attracted the who's who of show business, from Roy Orbison to Johnny Cash. As a belated birthday present, Ben told Joe he had a couple of spare seats in his bandwagon if he wanted to bring some friends along for a night of dancing, fizzy pop and music galore with Collins and his eight-piece band.

They were waiting for the show to begin when a girl sitting on the ladies' side of the ballroom caught Ben's eye. He hadn't met her before, and instead of waiting for an opportunity to ask her to dance when the band came on, he went over to chat to her there and then before a note was struck. The girl,

Kathleen Maloney, told him that she was running a dance in Castletown-Geoghegan, a village just south of Mullingar, in a couple of months' time for the local Irish Countrywomen's Association (ICA), and Ben's eyes lit up when she said she had no band booked yet.

'Sure I have a band,' Ben said with confidence, and he pointed over the ballroom to Joe. 'That fella there, he's the singer and guitarist. We have a wagon and all, sure isn't it parked outside if you want a look.'

'Oh, really? That's great. What kind of stuff do you play?' Kathleen asked.

'All sorts,' Ben replied, as he listed a ream of songs that other bands were playing at the time.

'Oh Lord, it would be great if you could play, you sound perfect,' she said, before asking Ben if the band would be available to play at the dance.

'Oh yeah,' said Ben. 'No problem. I'll ... eh ... check the diary.' He produced a notebook that he had been using for carpentry measurements, opened a page at random and confirmed he was free for the date in question.

They agreed on a fee of £10 and enjoyed the rest of the evening, even sharing a dance to confirm the deal. Ben had a reputation as being one of the best dancers in Westmeath at the time, and he swept the ICA woman off her feet. He flicked a wink and a thumbs up at Joe, who decided not to interfere.

After the dance, Ben put Joe in the loop. 'We've got a date,' he whispered.

'Well done. Where are you bringing her? To the pictures?' Joe responded.

'No, you fool. A date for the band! We're playing a dance in Castletown-Geoghegan,' replied Ben.

'How in the name of Jaysus did you get that?' asked Joe, not really wanting to know, but curious all the same. However, he stopped questioning Ben when he realized that the dance was only two months away – less if you took Christmas into account.

The Dolan boys set about getting the band into shape at their new rehearsal space. They had lost their accordion player, so Ben's accordion was dusted off and, because he was free from piano commitments, Joe took it on.

On the night of 9 January 1960, as they went through their paces with a final rehearsal, Joe's first official band were finally a unit 'in a kind of a way, anyway', and ready to rock Castletown-Geoghegan. The only thing they were missing was a name, as no one would agree to the band being called The Dolans.

Ben's bandwagon was cleaned especially for the big night, with two new headlights glistening in the early evening darkness. Ben got a big crowd of what he now calls 'yahoos and young ones', whose ranks included several friends of Joe's, to come on board and show their country cousins how it was done. The ladies were resplendent in short skirts, whilst the men were dickied up in smart suits, and there was great excitement and anticipation in the crowded wagon.

When they arrived at Castletown-Geoghegan, Fr McGathey, the local parish priest, who was in charge of the hall, watched with abject worry and quite possibly a small degree of horror as Ben offloaded his boisterous cargo. Fr McGathey had to give the band the tour of the hall, and almost immediately the gig was in jeopardy as they discovered there was barely a note left to play on the in-house piano. All village halls at the time had an in-house piano, which was (allegedly) kept under lock and key, but more often than not its ivories were subject to much pounding by unmonitored children. Not only that, but the sound system they had hired for the night was causing them no end of problems. There was very little power in PA systems at that time, and they were never intended to be used by loud rock, pop and dance groups. They were usually the preserve of local drama groups, the organizers of raffles, eager announcers on sports days and the occasional singer. Once the volume increased, the levels of feedback could be unbearable.

'The PA we had for the first gig was just a big amplifier with no treble or bass or anything,' Joe remembered. 'When we said to the man who was setting it up for us, "That's a bit sharp there", he'd get a mike and go, "One, two, three; one, two, three" in a low voice. "That's not sharp at all, lads," he'd say. If we told him it was very bassy, he'd screech, "One, two, three; one, two, three" in a high voice – so we couldn't win!'

Bad PA aside, the gig went great for the band with no name. Joe, in particular, rose to the occasion as the band's lead vocalist and front man, and even though it was Ben who announced the songs, it was an enthusiastic Joe who led the floor in its merry dance. The only nervousness Joe displayed was when he was stuck for something to say between songs. When the band was in full flight he was a different person, taken over by the music and intent on lifting the crowd. 'He was always full of zip and that rubbed off on the audiences,' Ben says.

'We had a wonderful night altogether. Rock 'n' roll was the big thing at the time and we were playing quicksteps and jives galore – "Rock Around the Clock" and all that sort of stuff – and everyone seemed to be into it,' Joe recalled. 'Everyone said we were great, which was nice.'

Everyone, that is, except Fr McGathey, who feared that the 'yahoos and young ones' from Mullingar would corrupt his flock. 'He ran us out of the place!' Joe recalls. 'Fr McGathey was a stern enough PP out there, but he was enraged that night and put a barring order on us straight away, because of the crowd we brought with us. Some of the girls' skirts were so short you could see their underwear, so he went mad. Now, the other people out there, particularly the men of Castletown-Geoghegan, weren't complaining, but the priest thought otherwise.'

But Joe and the rest of the band were happy. 'We came home in great form. We were as happy as pigs in shite, to be honest. It was probably dreadful, but the fact was the crowd was with us the whole night [which] made it an incredible night for us. I don't know if we went back. The ban was lifted anyhow, but not for a good few years.'

Indeed, that ICA dance was to be a telling and fortuitous night, for one local man who attended the show was 26-year-old Seamus Casey, a schoolteacher in the neighbouring village of Dysart whose family were from Rathdrisogue in Castletown-Geoghegan. Seamus was a keen music man, and knew enough about music and show business to recognize talent when he saw it. He was impressed by the enthusiasm of the whole band, and in particular its livewire guitarist. Although Seamus and the band didn't know it at the time, the schoolteacher would soon play perhaps *the* most important role in the career of that young guitarist with the high voice, guiding him on an international journey that would last the next four decades.

In the days immediately after the band's Castletown-Geoghegan debut, all the talk was about the next date, but there was a slight problem. Because they had been so caught up in the rehearsals for the first gig, they had forgotten to organize a second one. 'I suppose we thought it would just take off,' Joe said, as he recalled those innocent early days. 'But there were no dates coming in.' He reckoned they wouldn't have been ready for them anyway as the band's line-up was far from complete.

However, impressed that they had actually got it together and played a gig, Paddy Dolan told them he had booked Mullingar parochial hall for a St

Patrick's night dance, and he wanted his younger brothers to play. The band spent each and every available hour practising under a single lightbulb in the old cinema, but Joe could only play a low-tuned guitar for so long. The band needed a bass player.

In 1960, a bass player was a stand-up guy with a big upright bass, but this didn't fit with the image Joe wanted for the band. He felt it was too stuffy and that a bass guitarist was the answer. The only trouble was that nobody knew any bass guitarists. Joe then suggested that Jimmy Horan, a neighbour from Grange who had played with them in their old skiffle group, would be the ideal candidate.

Jimmy was as musically minded as the Dolans and he had won a medal for singing at a *feis cheoil* as a youngster. His interest in the band business had been pricked by the informal skiffle sessions in the Dolan house, and he had joined a local group called The Skiffling Aces. Jimmy had been assigned the tea chest, so there was no doubt he had rhythm. But that band had disbanded, all emigrating to the UK except for Jimmy. With few bands in Mullingar to join, Jimmy was on the verge of emigrating too when Joe asked him to join his band. Jimmy accepted. But there was a slight problem. Not only did Jimmy not have a bass guitar, he had never even played one.

Joe told him not to worry about such a triviality and he left Ben to figure out where you could buy one at short notice. Meanwhile, Paddy Dolan told the band that he needed a band name so that he could advertise his St Patrick's night dance. After much debate, and a draw that was ever so slightly stacked in one direction (Ben having taken the other names out of the hat and replaced them with pre-prepared bits of paper), the band decided they were to be called The Drifters. 'I didn't know any Drifters at the time, but in my own stupid way and at the back of my mind I wanted something with a D in it,' Ben recalls. 'As much as I wanted to, we couldn't call ourselves The Dolans.'

Before the draw was made, trumpet player Sean Connolly had declared 'The Drifters' a terribly unbecoming name for the band, as Ben recalled. '"Drifters, eh? Do you know what a drifter is?" he said. I told him that it was a fella who moved and drifted around. Sean replied that a drifter was "a layabout, a waster, a no good, who does nothing. I wouldn't like to be called a drifter . . ." I thought, Jaysus, that's an awful thing, but that still mightn't be too bad because if everyone stopped to think about it, and could remember all that, then it mustn't be too bad a name. If someone could come up with lots of things wrong for it, then maybe it was a good name.'

But of course it was a name that had already been taken, not once but twice: it was the name of a chart-busting vocal harmony group that had had several big hits in the United States and were making inroads into Europe; and until 1959 (when they were forced to change their name to The Shadows after legal complications arose with the US Drifters) the name of Cliff Richard's backing band. Both Joe and Ben admit that they genuinely didn't realize there would be a problem in using the same name. 'Truth be told, we never thought we were going to be as big as we got,' Ben said, and in any case, The Drifters in America and those in Mullingar were 'that far apart it wasn't going to make that much of a difference'. Lawsuits were not going to complicate the life of a rural Irish band in 1960, or so he thought. Years later they would contact Joe, and he temporarily changed the band name to '*His* Drifters'.

Joe later confessed he was unaware of the name of Cliff's band, even though a couple of Cliff numbers had made it into his early sets. He didn't seem to mind what the band was called; he just wanted action. 'If we were called Paddymebollix he wouldn't have minded,' Ben laughs. 'With him it was "let's get going". He was very keen and practising like mad – really putting a lot of time into the guitar, and he was singing all the time.'

With just two days to spare before the dance, the bass guitar arrived and Joe dropped by Jimmy Horan's house to see if he was ready to play. Joe took it upon himself to familiarize young Jimmy with the chords, so Jimmy would be ready for the final full-band practice. 'I couldn't really play the bass guitar in the beginning,' Jimmy acknowledged in a Drifters fan-club newsletter a few years later. 'It took me three months to get to grips with it, but after that I never looked back.'

At the parochial hall the stage had been decked in green, white and gold for The Drifters' first gig in their hometown. By the time the band took to the stage, the hall was full. 'It was all movement, singing and playing and dancing. It was a huge night, and the place was stuffed,' Joe remembered. After a couple of numbers, with his confidence levels rising, the singer moved to the front of the stage to get closer to the crowd. As he did, the lead on his guitar came out with a bang. Jimmy offered Joe his lead and the band played on, without Jimmy, so he used the opportunity to familiarize himself with the material, miming away on his leadless bass with nobody in the hall any the wiser.

Even though Joe couldn't hear Jimmy, they bonded well onstage and everyone seemed happy with the performance. Indeed, after the show, when some of Jimmy's relations came up to tell Jimmy how fantastic he was, Joe didn't want to burst the bubble and joined in the praise. Even in this first gig, Joe noted approvingly that Jimmy had all the hallmarks of a 'nodder' – a bass player with plenty of movement and rhythm who leads with the head.

After paying for the ad in the paper and a few other bits and pieces, the band received the grand total of £30 (the equivalent of three weeks' wages for Joe at the time). They all knew they were on the right track. 'After it we played a couple of local things,' Joe recalled. 'We played at the Greville Arms, and in St Loman's Hospital. Then after that I realized we weren't sounding too bad at all.'

Ben went all out looking for gigs, and Paddy's wife Caroline became his secretary. Work on the Drifters' empire had officially begun.

The budding bandsmen refused to acknowledge that their name may have come from Cliff's now rebranded Shadows band, and they made things look official by having bill heads and cards printed, which Joe had arranged on the quiet at the printworks at the *Westmeath Examiner*. Ben still had some change from his famous mouse-money stash, and he bought some more equipment, including a couple of spare guitar leads for Joe.

Most of the gear was sourced via a long-since-departed general store in Mullingar's Mount Street, owned by the late Paddy Rourke. It was, by all accounts, the kind of shop where you could buy anything, from guitar strings to baling twine. It was also the place where Joe and Ben would get to know Seamus Casey. 'Around that time, you would go to town on a Saturday night but you really wouldn't be going anywhere – only up and down the town, into shops and meeting people,' Joe recalled. 'You might go to the pictures, and a big arrival was Woolworths, which was a great place to go in and look at stuff, y'know? But anyone who was into music nearly always hung out at Paddy's shop.' As well as stocking records and instruments, Paddy also sold single cigarettes at a keen price, which was a big draw for bands on a tight budget who wanted to look cool.

Ben, in particular, got to know Seamus very well at the shop, and their mutual love of music and just about everything in show business blossomed there. Ben was also drafted in as a driver for a drama group in Castletown-Geoghegan, of which Seamus was a member. As they drove in Ben's bandwagon, the two would often talk about what the band should be doing, little realizing that their plans would come to fruition in the near future.

In the autumn of 1960, Paddy got them their biggest Greville Arms dance yet: a fisherman's dance, one of the major events of the year. At the show, misfortune struck, but the boys were so hooked on their music that they couldn't stop playing. 'A rate collector in the town fainted in the middle of the dance floor during one of the dances,' Paddy relates, 'and Dan Mullally (whose son Jimmy would later play with the band) went up to the stage to tell the lads to stop the music. "I will not," roared Ben, and they kept blowing away. Sure they were mad to play. I got them £12 for the dance in any case, which wasn't bad money.' As well as securing them the occasional gig, Paddy used to travel with the band from time to time. He remembers a youthful Dickie Rock coming to one of The Drifters' early Ierne Ballroom shows in Dublin (where they played as a relief band) 'and desperately trying to get up on stage with them for a song'.

The dances always meant a late night for the band, and invariably Joe and Ben would arrive home at their bachelor pad in Grange around five or six o'clock, just a few hours before they were due in to work. Both of them were beginning to experience serious difficulties getting up in the morning, and with no one else in the house to make sure they got out of bed, they were starting to miss hours. Joe's long walk into work didn't help his timekeeping.

The boys now had quite a bit of extra money coming in, and, blessed with a gift that made him want to spend it straight away, Joe decided it would make sense for him to buy a car (so starting an addiction for cars that would take hold of him and never leave, causing him and countless others around him an abundance of worry and more than one broken heart). He justified the purchase in many ways, one of the reasons being that it would be advantageous for him to drive to work, though, as he later admitted, 'the truth was that it gave me an extra half hour in bed!' The car, a zippy VW Beetle, was bought on hire purchase. 'When he said he was buying a car, I thought we'd all end up in jail,' Ben revealed. 'At this stage I still didn't know how he had paid off the guitar, or even if he was paying it off.'

Ben invariably arrived home a little later in the evening, but not only because his boss allowed him to start work a little later: Joe was beginning to flourish as a cook, and, as well as being handy in the kitchen, he was quite the housekeeper and would light the fire almost immediately on his arrival home from work. So if Ben timed his arrival home late enough, Joe would already have made a start at the dinner and the fire would be lit. If Joe had not started the dinner, Ben would make his excuses and depart to the outside toilet until Joe got so hungry waiting for him that he would start cooking.

Nevertheless, despite the new car, Joe's timekeeping at the *Westmeath Examiner* was becoming a serious problem. Mrs Darby, a concerned neighbour and great friend of his late mother, would call over in the morning and knock on his window to wake him up, but often it was to no avail as he was a heavy sleeper with a ferocious snore. 'He loved to sleep,' Ben recalls. 'Often, he'd get up and fall asleep again in the kitchen.'

When he started to miss the occasional full day at work, warnings were issued. And eventually, just a year before he finished his apprenticeship, his boss, Kevin Cadogan, snapped after one too many late arrivals and fired him.

Ben went in to the office to plead Joe's case. Somehow Joe was accepted back and, as part of the agreement, Joe vowed to leave the bachelor pad in Grange. His brother Paddy came to the rescue and said Joe could move in with the family in Ginnell Terrace. Paddy was the epitome of hard work, as was his wife Caroline, and there was no slouching or lying in bed once you were in their house.

Joe recalled later that the *Examiner* was more than a little generous with him. 'Kevin Cadogan was very good to me at that time. We were beginning to play gigs in Donegal and places a long way away, and I was invariably late for work on a regular basis. He never once said a word to me except when he would catch us playing music.'

Joe would often be caught playing music or singing songs when he was supposed to be working, and finally an ultimatum was issued. 'I had two little sticks and I was playing drums one day and Kevin Cadogan said to me, "There's a lot going on, and I've been very lenient but you've got to make your mind up: it's either the printing or the music." I didn't tell him at that time, but I had already decided!'

As national gigs started to drift in on the strength of their Dublin debut at the Ierne Ballroom and their growing reputation, there was to be a bit of an upheaval in the ranks as drummer Eddie Deehy, who worked as a lorry driver with Westmeath County Council, did not want to play more than one or two nights a week. But Ben found a way around Eddie's reluctance to play. 'If we got a chance of two jobs in a week, I used to take them and I wouldn't tell Eddie about it until the day before the second job, which would lead to the odd row. I'd slip it in and sure, he couldn't say no.' They were also going through piano players at a rate of knots – three in their first year together.

Joe loved his time living at Paddy and Caroline's house, and he doted on their kids – three boys and four girls. He would go on to spend three or four years living there. 'He was more like a brother to them all than an uncle,' Ben recalled. All of Paddy and Caroline's children have fond memories of Joe. He struck up a particular bond with Kathleen from an early age, and they were great pals, but he had great fun with all the kids and was godfather to nearly all of them.

Joe shared a bedroom for a time with the toddlers, Vincent and PJ, which meant that the boys had to accommodate another bed in the room. 'Joe would arrive back from gigs every night between 3 and 5 a.m., depending on where they were playing,' Vincent remembers. 'Every night I would wake up when he came in and I would whisper, "Was there a big crowd at the dance, Joe?" and he would always answer, "The biggest yet, now go back to sleep and don't wake PJ." I never knew just how big the crowd got, but it was always the biggest yet.' Some nights if the lads were being noisy he would tell them about the dragon he saw on the way home, which led to immediate silence.

Joe would also scare Kathleen and the others with spooky tales of things that went bump in the night. 'He used to tell us stories about coming home late at night and seeing things on the stairs, like ghosts and monsters. He'd have the life frightened out of you,' Kathleen remembers. 'If he didn't say anything to us we'd be mad to wake him up to hear what he'd seen. He'd tell us he saw a ghost, a goat or a big dog. You'd be afraid to go to bed at night. You'd be standing looking up the stairs before you went to bed.'

But then, suddenly, the ghost tales stopped. It wasn't until years later that Kathleen found out why. Joe had come in from a show one night and as he went upstairs he heard the keys of the piano tinkling. When he looked into the sitting room he could see no one. As he went back up stairs he heard the keys tinkling again. He looked into the sitting room again and still couldn't see anything, so, terrified, he ran to wake Paddy and Caroline. Caroline accompanied him down stairs, and when she opened the sitting room door, she found a little black cat walking along the piano.

At Christmas, Joe was generous to a fault and would lavish gifts on the children, but one Christmas Eve Joe and Ben couldn't resist temptation themselves, and opened all the presents Santa had left. Paddy caught them in the act. 'I'd be running around after him, he'd be playing with all the toys, and then have to parcel them all up and put them under the tree again.'

Caroline used to work for the band, answering calls, letters and the fan mail that had started to trickle in. Ben would call up, ostensibly to find out if there were any bookings, but he always timed his arrival just as tea or dinner was about to be served.

With Caroline ensuring he got to work on time, Joe's timekeeping improved and he went on to qualify as a compositor eleven months after he had first been sacked. But on the first week of his full wage packet, in early 1962, he dropped a bombshell, telling his boss that he was leaving the *Westmeath Examiner* so he could take his music more seriously. He had no regrets about leaving, even if those around him were fearful. 'I could have gone to Dublin to work in some printing works, because at that time there was new technology coming in, but I decided I wanted to spend a bit more time at the music,' he said later.

Nevertheless, his qualification acted as a safety net, something he would tell anyone who was thinking of not finishing school, college or an apprenticeship. 'I was a qualified printer, and I had my card, so if in six months' time it didn't work out, then I could have applied to any place for a job and I would have had a job. I would always tell everyone thinking of stepping out into the unknown to make sure they had something to fall back on . . . I was [simply] going to give something else a shot. I just wanted to do something different. I had done my apprenticeship and I didn't want to be a printer, to be quite honest. I didn't want to be going into work every morning at nine o'clock and leaving at half five in the evening and trying to figure out what to do with the rest of the day. I took the bull by the horns and I said to Ben, "Look, I'm giving up working. I'm going at this full-time."'

Ben was initially unsure of Joe's decision, particularly as his job was relatively permanent and pensionable. 'It was a closed shop. Once you were in, you were in. It was a better job than my own, and he had real prospects. With the band it could have fallen apart the next day and he could have been left with nothing, but he said to me, "There are bands all over the country, so surely be to God I'll get a gig with one of them." I was delighted though that he went all the way with his apprenticeship.'

It did not take long, however, for Ben to realize that Joe was a big star in the making. His epiphany occurred midway through a dance in Kinnegad organized by Billy and Dermot Leavy for the local branch of the Irish Farmers' Association. At the time Ben and Joe used to share the songs fairly evenly, with Jimmy Horan chipping in with a couple of numbers. 'There were 150, maybe 200 people at the dance and I noticed that every time Joe sang a huge buzz came off everything and everyone. When I sang, everybody just danced and they didn't seem to notice, but when Joe stepped up it was something else. So I thought we'd better make sure Joe was singing more. When we'd go for practice, I'd say to him, "You'd better sing this one or that one." So he was singing more and the rest of the band was singing less. Joe was the man.'

Onstage Joe threw himself about the place even more, with an Elvis Presley routine now a big part of the show. All showbands had to have a gimmick to set them apart from the competition, and The Drifters' was Elvis. As part of the routine, Joe would leap on top of a piano and tap a tune out with his foot. He would swivel his hips and pump his pelvis like the King, sending the women in the audience into a frenzy. Joe's gyrating got the band noticed even more and crowds began to increase, as did the number of bookings. Halls began to lock their piano away if they heard Joe Dolan was coming to town.

Paddy roared with laughter when he recalled one such piano ban in Mullingar. 'If he was playing in the County Hall, the caretaker would lock the piano away. He'd say, "No black-haired fucker is going to leap on this piano to knock the shit out of it tonight!"'

With the band's popularity and workload on the rise, Joe seemingly timed his decision to leave the *Examiner* to perfection. However, Sean Connolly was not prepared to throw in his safe job at St Loman's Hospital in Mullingar, and drummer Eddie Deehy did not want to let go of his job with Westmeath County Council. Jimmy Horan, on the other hand, was only too happy to leave the shopkeeper's apron back in the shop once and for all.

When they had gone through almost as many piano players as there are keys on a piano, Longford man Frank Melia joined the band in 1962. Ben remembers him as 'a lovely player' who was always keen to play and to rehearse. Although he worked in the post office in Longford, over thirty miles away, Frank had no problem travelling to and from Mullingar for rehearsals and his early commitment endeared him to the Dolan boys.

Johnny Kelly, a trombone player originally from Mullingar, also joined the band – almost as soon as he had stepped off the boat he had taken home from the UK. A former Mullingar Town Band member, he slotted in nicely, even though there was a kind of unwritten rule that brass band members should not be in dance bands. Indeed, when Ben had tried to join Mullingar Town Band, he was not let in for that very reason. Johnny had a great ear for music – 'If you hummed anything he would play it,' Joe said of him – and sang in a low baritone like Fats Domino, which added another vocal dimension to the band. However, despite securing work with the ESB in Mullingar – 'you wanted a four-leaf shamrock to get in at the time,' Ben says – Johnny had moved to Kildare, and Joe would run Johnny home after gigs. Taking fellas home or picking them up was to prove 'an awful job' after long sets of up to four and five hours at a time.

Something had to change, and later in 1962 it did just that when the classic Drifters line-up began to fall into place.

5
The answer to everything

Following Joe's high-spirited performances, it was decided that the band should be rechristened 'Joe Dolan and The Drifters', only a few months after its core members had quit their jobs in favour of 'this showband thing'. Within a year everyone had started to talk about Joe Dolan, and the band had become one of Ireland's top ballroom attractions.

Joe was on the receiving end of his third significant bit of luck in as many years when in Easter 1962 supermarket supremo Pat Quinn booked them a dozen dates that summer for £25 a night as a relief/support band to The Rhythm Boys, a showband from Buncrana who were a big draw in much of the country. As he recalled the tour in 2008, Pat Quinn revealed that even though he knew most of the bands at the time, it was his wife Ann who suggested he take Joe Dolan and The Drifters on to the tour. 'Ann was working in the bank in Mullingar and she told me about this guy Joe Dolan. I went out to see Joe with Ann in a little village outside Mullingar called Delvin where he was performing, and I met Ben and Joe after the show and I asked them would they come and perform for me. And Ben, which was unusual for him, said that he was going to do a freebie for all the shows. And I said, "No freebies, Ben, I'll pay you." I was paying The Rhythm Boys £75 a night and I think the deal I did with Ben was for £25 a night. They had an old broken-down van I remember, so with the first £25 they went out and bought tyres for the back of the van, and the next night they bought tyres for the front!'

Noting the showband explosion taking hold of Ireland, the savvy Quinn – who would go on to promote a Beatles tour in Canada – decided it would be novel to tie showband dances in with a beauty contest his supermarket chain was promoting. As well as judging the girls on their looks, personality and fashion, Quinn replaced the usual 'party piece' routine with a dancing contest. Heats for the contest took place in ballrooms, county halls and festival marquees all over the country. And what better accompaniment than two of the hottest bands in the country – one an established act with proven box-office credentials, the other a hot up-and-coming outfit with star potential?

Securing the support slot was to prove the most significant break yet for the band, as they would perform to guaranteed capacity audiences around the country for the first time in their careers. 'You can rehearse all you like, but the only real rehearsal is up there onstage,' Joe said later.

Pat Quinn remembers that on the second night, in the Silver Slipper in Strandhill, County Sligo, the crowd would not let Joe leave the stage after he and the band had finished their set. The main act was pretty peeved. 'The Rhythm Boys said to me, "Pat, these guys have got to go," because they were stealing the show. So I said to The Rhythm Boys, "Guys, well, if that's the way you want it I'll pay you for the rest of the tour and I'll use Joe's band." To cut a long story short, they said, "Right, we'll go with it," and they played on.'

The tour also led to Joe's first encounter with the other pair of brothers who were making a big impression on the showband scene: Albert and Jim Reynolds. Jim had recently returned to Ireland from Australia, and he and his brother owned a chain of ballrooms across the country. If a band made it on to these Reynolds's books, they could expect countless bookings in the ever-expanding ballroom chain.

On the final night of the tour, in Rooskey, County Roscommon, the showbands literally took over the town and you had to pay to enter on the side of the road at both entrances to the town. 'I had the Maurice Mulcahy Orchestra, The Rhythm Boys and Joe Dolan,' Pat recalls with pride. 'Maurice and his Orchestra were playing in the Cloudland Ballroom, which was owned by Jim and Albert Reynolds. The Rhythm Boys were playing across in three marquees and Joe Dolan was playing in two marquees. Once you got over the bridge into Rooskey, Albert Reynolds was in a caravan on the Longford side with two or three fellas collecting tickets. I had a fellow on the other side. You could go into any of the ballrooms or the marquees. Admission was ten shillings, which was a fortune back then. The average price to get into a dance was about two and sixpence, or three shillings.'

After the tour, fan mail addressed to Joe started to arrive in droves to the Grange family home. (The picture on p. 65 is a promotional picture of Joe at home in Grange playing the piano his mother Ellen bought for him.) For Ben, this was the final vindication that he and his brother were doing the right thing. But managing the affairs of the band, driving them to and from dances, buying the equipment, announcing the songs as well as singing a good few of them, cleaning the matching suits that they had started to wear *and* taking the bookings was beginning to take its toll on Ben, who preferred being a more front-of-house kind of guy. Fortunately, he wouldn't have to worry about bookings for too much longer, as Seamus Casey was beginning to make a few inroads into the local music scene and his prowess at staging successful shows would impress the Dolan boys no end.

Seamus had made a handsome profit early in his fledgling music career when he booked the popular Northern Irish combo The Melody Aces for a gig in the Offaly town of Edenderry. However, the £75 profit was lost pretty quickly when another Melody Aces booking in Kilbeggan clashed with a Clipper Carlton booking in nearby Mullingar. The Clippers got most of the dancing crowd that night, but The Melody Aces were impressed with Seamus's humility in defeat, and even handed back some of their fee to him so he would live to fight another day.

One Saturday evening at Paddy Rourke's Mount Street shop, Seamus convinced Ben that The Drifters should play the town hall in Edenderry, as one successful night there would lead to several more. It would cost £12 to rent the hall, and Seamus felt that with the right promotion they could turn a decent profit, which could be ploughed back into doing more dates and building their reputation. To increase their profits, they decided they would also supply the suppers. Ben's girlfriend Moira was hired to make a host of sandwiches, and Paddy Dolan would run the mineral bar – Paddy still wonders how he managed to cart the soft drinks up the half-dozen flights of stairs.

It was two and sixpence on the door in Edenderry, and they managed to turn a tidy profit of £30. Paddy was happy as the bar sales were good, but Moira did not fare quite as well as she had overestimated the hunger of the audience and had made far too many sandwiches. Joe remembers that the band and everyone they knew 'spent the next three days eating nothing but sandwiches'.

The Drifters blew Seamus away. 'They were better than the Clipper Carlton that night,' Seamus recalls, and he was happy with another promise from Ben that they would do business again very soon.

Meanwhile, problems with the line-up were coming to a head, and by the Easter of 1962 Ben was searching for some new blood to fill a selection of suits he had purchased to give the band a 'look'. The Drifters piano chair was like a revolving door. In a little over two years they had gone through six piano players, all of them complaining about the ballroom pianos but unwilling or unable to do anything about it. And if it was not dissatisfaction with the pianos, it was commitment issues. Longford man Frank Melia left in the spring of 1962, and Joe was now looking for someone with stability, creativity and character. He got his hat trick (and a whole lot more) in Des Doherty.

Des wanted to give his all to The Drifters, and as he was a professional musician he did not have to worry about giving up a day job. Almost before Des had struck a note, Joe wanted him in the band. 'You just didn't find guys like this,' he would say of the talented keyboard man. Des had been a gifted musician from a very early age, and began playing the piano in a music-mad house in Athboy, County Meath, almost before he could walk. He was already well known around the country as something of a dab hand at traditional music, having played on Radio Éireann's *Céilí House* dozens of times, accompanying various artistes as well as performing on his own. He was also a familiar face on the nation's TV screens as he had appeared on Teilifís Éireann's *Club Céilí*. But it was his pedigree on numerous stages throughout the country that Joe really admired. Des had played, and could play, anything.

Des, or 'The Doc' as he was (and still is) affectionately known, was to

THE ANSWER TO EVERYTHING

prove the most valuable addition to The Drifters yet, and it was his original approach to music and his stylish, innovative playing that led to the band's trademark sound. A fan of just about every genre of music, Des brought a new musical edge to the band. He brought plenty of new technology too, and it was his pioneering use of the Hohner Pianet, an electric piano, in the early 1960s that pushed them into the super league of Irish bands. Tired of the tuneless pianos he encountered in venues throughout the country (and unable to wheel a grand piano around with him to dances), he was one of the first guys to import this groundbreaking new instrument from Germany.

The Hohner Pianet came with a built-in tremolo circuit or unit, and it was this that came to really define The Drifters' sound until the end of that decade. It can be heard dripping off all their early recordings.

The band was really starting to take shape when, a few weeks later, another line-up change was tabled. Drummer Eddie Deehy had taken ill and decided he could not carry on with The Drifters' punishing schedule. Joe went to meet Eddie and came back with the bad news that the man who had got them their first gig was leaving. His departure could not have come at a worse time, as Joe and the band had a show the very next night in nearby Athlone. It was suggested that at such short notice Joe himself should drum. 'Joe was a fantastic drummer, he was a really good swing man,' Ben disclosed. 'In the early days it used to create troubles when our drummer couldn't get the beat, or something would be missing, because Joe would get in behind the kit to show him and the drummer wouldn't like that at all.' However, unsurprisingly, Joe did not want to sit behind the drums for the full four-hour show in Athlone. (Later, during intervals in shows, Joe would sometimes show the world what it had missed.)

Word then reached Drifters' HQ that Donal 'Sid' Aughty was back in town. A noted sticksman from Monilea, just outside Mullingar, Sid had plenty of experience. He could play, he had the moves and he had the looks. Joe and Ben set out to find him, and eventually they were directed to a cornfield. Sid was cutting barley when the lads found him, and he was stunned to be flagged down in the middle of a Mullingar cornfield by a pair of lads in black suits. He pulled up to talk to these mystery men, but couldn't hear what they had to say over the din of the tractor.

'We're The Drifters, Joe and Ben Dolan, and we need you to play drums with us tonight in Athlone,' they roared.

'What?' replied Sid as he climbed down from the noisy piece of farm machinery.

When they repeated the offer, the drummer-turned-harvester didn't need too much convincing. He signalled to the boys that he would come with them there and then, not realizing he had left the tractor running. As he went off to find the farmer and tell him he was leaving, the tractor started to roll on through the field, zig-zagging through the golden crop.

Sid was well used to picking things up at short notice. At a dance in Dublin, the drummer belonging to British bandleader Sid Phillip's Big Band suddenly took ill and the gallant Monilea man offered to deputize. Despite the challenge of playing unfamiliar material with such a distinguished unit, he proved himself capable of the job, and when he informed pals of his percussive antics he suddenly found himself landed with his nickname.

He had also played drums with The Merry Minstrels, and in England with the Riverside Jazz Band, which brought an extra swing to his percussion skills, something that can be heard to dazzling effect on many Drifters recordings. And as for showband experience, he had stood in for Mike O'Hanlon of the famous Clipper Carlton on several occasions.

Ben and Seamus were delighted that a country and western music fan had been added to the ranks, whereas Joe was chuffed that Sid was a keen card player. Des also enjoyed a hand or two of cards, and he introduced a new sport to the band – golf.

The new boys made all the difference to The Drifters, with Joe readily admitting that 'they took us to another level'. There was more of a sense of unity about the group, as they all seemed focused on the prize, and publicity shots taken near the end of 1962 show a determined look in their young eyes. One of these featured prominently in the *Evening Press* on 20 October 1962, ahead of a show at the Ierne Ballroom in Dublin, showing a livewire bunch posing by their bandwagon (new wheels not pictured). Standing proudly in the back row was a confident-looking Joe Dolan, happy that he finally had the musicians to back up his vision.

Joe's Elvis routine (which he performed near the close of a Drifters show) was getting the band noticed, but they felt they needed something else to set them apart from the herd of showbands that was entertaining the masses in Ireland at the time. Not realizing they had that something else inside Joe's lungs, they purchased a set of retina-scorching red suits, a decision that probably seemed like a good idea at the time. However, in a town as unforgiving as Mullingar – where everybody seemed to know everybody else's business and have an opinion on it – it earned them some severe slagging. Having painted their bandwagon a matching red, they were quite a sight as they set off to gigs and dances, but Joe didn't mind. 'We were getting noticed, that was the main thing,' was his mantra.

Seamus decided that criticizing their latest clothing purchase was probably unwise, considering the amount of money that had just been handed over to the gleeful tailor, and instead christened the band 'the red devils of entertainment', a quip that they used almost immediately on their posters and which years later would land them in trouble. At the height of the showband craze, parish priests had had their fill of showband-related sins in their confession boxes, and started to warn dancers, particularly female dancers, that the devil was indeed on the dance floor preying on their innocence. Reports of cloven-hoofed dancers spread like wildfire, and could empty ballrooms overnight.

One such incident occurred at the Majestic Ballroom in Mallow one night. A girl had been dancing and getting on great with a man at a dance. They decided to slip outside, but when she looked down she saw he had cloven hooves. She screamed, ran back into the dancehall and announced that Satan was outside. There was widespread panic as the ballroom cleared. Even some of the band playing that night ran out the door. For several weeks afterwards the Majestic's crowds dipped from 2,000 a night to about 500.

A few days later, Joe Dolan and The Drifters rolled into Mallow with their posters proudly proclaiming that they were 'the red devils of entertainment'. Such was the fear of Satan, fewer than 500 people turned up to see them. It knocked the band for six as their earnings depended on the take at the door.

Pretty soon, canny ballroom owners all over Ireland made sure the devil began to appear at rival ballrooms on a regular basis. On one occasion he allegedly appeared at a ballroom in Tooreen, County Mayo, which was owned by no less a person than Monsignor James Horan, one of the most flamboyant and well-known holy men in the country.

Seamus Casey was beginning to play more of a role behind the scenes, and he started to get Joe and the band more bookings as he dabbled with various venues. Joe returned to Edenderry Town Hall a number of times for him, playing every Thursday night for six weeks, and there were further dates in midlands towns such as Tullamore, Athlone and Portlaoise. In hindsight, Seamus admits that he became a part of the band before he was officially offered the role. 'It was just a natural thing,' he said. 'He never really officially started with us,' Ben added. 'But we were glad he did!'

As well as easing the management burdens on Ben and his sister-in-law, Seamus came into his own when the band faced into a crisis following the departure of Sean Connolly on medical grounds. Although Sean had questioned just about every band decision – memorably asking, on one occasion, 'What will we do professionally that we don't already do as amateurs?'– he was still an enthusiastic member of the group who didn't let a heart condition get in the way of his great love of the band and their live performances. But his health was leading to some worries in the ranks, and Joe finally came to the conclusion that it would be best for Sean to step back from the stage as he was risking killing himself if he continued to play.

Ben was very friendly with Sean, so he broke the news to the trumpeter. 'It was an awful sad thing for me to let Sean Connolly go. When the break came, I pushed it off as far as I could before I could say to Sean I was going to have to take in a new fella on trumpet,' Ben recalls. 'It was the worst thing I had to do in my life. He had been there from the start and he had been great to Joe and me.' The decision to ask Sean to step down was made even harder as a few months earlier Ben himself had taken ill with a hernia problem, and being a bachelor boy who was shy in the kitchen, had convalesced in Sean's house where breakfast, dinner and tea was brought to his sickbed.

Seamus, still not the band's full-time manager at this stage, suggested a seventeen-year-old from Cavan as Sean's replacement. Tommy Swarbrigg was something of a musical prodigy on the showband scene, and in 1959, when only fourteen, he had joined The Jordanaires. Swarbrigg had come highly recommended by ballroom-owner John McCormack, who operated the Maple in Rockcorry and would later manage several bands. He had monitored Tommy's progress from his days with a skiffle band to his emergence as the youngest showband man in town. Seamus heard the youngster play and was impressed with him. Joe liked what Seamus told

THE ANSWER TO EVERYTHING

him and he was also impressed to learn Tommy had been writing his own songs from an early age and seemed to have an innate understanding of arrangements.

So, Seamus and Ben were dispatched to Tommy's house in Cootehill, County Cavan, to have a chat with the gifted player. It was to be an unusual meeting to say the least, one where just about every member of the Swarbrigg family would audition for a role in The Drifters. 'There was a rake of them in it,' Ben laughs. 'There were kids everywhere, and Tommy's parents and grandparents were all in the house to welcome us. Tommy took out the trumpet to play something with all the kids around. He sounded good. We asked if he sang, as it was important in a band that you had two jobs. So anyway, the kids started laughing when Tommy started singing. And then his grandfather decided *he* was going to sing for us. He sang some high-brow number like an opera singer, we were all in convulsions, and everyone else started singing then.'

When Joe heard Tommy sing in Mullingar a week later, the one-time electrician was hired. Cavan's loss was to be The Drifters' and eventually Ireland's gain, as Tommy would go on to become a household name in his own right after he left the band in 1968.

When he came to Mullingar he was put up in digs with local woman Josie Reid, where a piano furthered his musical education. He wrote several songs on it, which Joe would go on to record. His first week's wages was £14.50, three times what he had earned before.

Another casualty of the drive to go all-out professional was trombone player Johnny Kelly, who was just about to get married. With little or no security in the band business at the time, Johnny decided that he needed a more stable line of work. In his place came a friend of Seamus's from Castletown-Geoghegan, Noel Kirby, although Noel played saxophone rather than the trombone. 'The band now had two sax players, which wasn't the way forward as the classic combination was trumpet, trombone and sax, together with bass, guitar, drums, piano and as many vocalists as you could have,' Ben recalled. 'That line-up and its sound seemed to work, and it was a yardstick to go by.'

Noel Kirby filled in for a few weeks, but the search for a trombone player was ongoing, and about to turn towards Ulster. Joe had heard that a new band put together by Pat Campbell were receiving rave notices, with their trombonist Joey 'The Gill' Gilheaney coming in for particular praise. Having been told by Pat that they could talk to his man, Joe and Ben travelled to Swanlinbar in Joe's VW Beetle. Ben had some misgivings about driving blindly to an area that was so rural it was almost not on any map, but Joe wanted to call at his house, even if it meant spending several hours desperately searching for it. When they eventually found it, Joe whispered to his brother that if Joey could play the middle eight of 'Midnight in Moscow', then they could go.

It took a while for Joey to blow a note, and as he foostered around with his trombone, Joe and Ben became impatient. After close to two tea-filled hours, Joey's lips were eventually coaxed on to the trombone, and he not only played the middle eight of 'Midnight in Moscow', but owned the song. 'This is our man,' Joe said to Ben, who then offered him a place in the band. When Joey came down to Mullingar for a band rehearsal, he complemented Tommy and Ben perfectly in the brass section. What would become the classic Drifters line-up was now complete.

Seamus had been doing business with Joe and The Drifters for a couple of months when he heard on the grapevine that a manager of one of the top showbands in the country was taking an interest in them, so he and Ben met up and Seamus told him out straight, 'I want to be your manager full-time.' Ben agreed, but could only take him on part-time. At that time Seamus was still living on the family farm in Castletown-Geoghegan, working as a headmaster in Dysart whilst the band was based in Mullingar.

Seamus says he found Joe to be a little shy and vaguely aloof away from the stage in those early days of Drifterdom. 'At first I didn't really know Joe, he was the singer in the band all right, but it was just the same as Sid was the drummer, or Dessie was the keyboard player. At the start it was Ben and I that did most of the talking. I remembered Joe as a kind of a wild character. In my mind, he was half mad, you know? His VW Beetle was noisy and attracted a lot of attention, and he went around with a younger crowd than either Ben or I. He was quite young and restless, whereas Ben seemed quite sane and relaxed.'

Like Ben, when Seamus went to a dance, invariably all he wanted to do was talk to the band that was playing. It was through his enthusiasm for music that he had started to build up a number of contacts in the business. He knew

THE ANSWER TO EVERYTHING

most of the bandleaders and the big stars at the time, as well as their managers and crew, and they in turn knew of him. His favourite band in the early 1960s was Northern Irish showband The Melody Aces. When he was on a break from school while managing the band unofficially, he coincided a holiday in the North with a series of homecoming gigs The Melody Aces were about to undertake all over the province. He told Ben one night of his plans and suggested that he might do some sniffing about for Joe and the band to see if he could get them a few dates. On his way back from the holiday, Seamus took a detour to meet The Drifters at a ballroom in Leitrim, where they were playing.

'Well, how were the holidays?' asked Ben.

'The holidays were great,' replied Seamus, eager to spill the beans about what he had really been up to.

'So, erm, did you get us any work?'

'I got you sixty dates,' Seamus revealed.

Ben nearly dropped his saxophone.

Whilst Seamus was in the North, he had been pleasantly surprised to learn that people up North had heard of Joe Dolan and his 'red devils of entertainment', and that bands like the Melody Aces were also spreading the word. In places like Ballymena, Joe Dolan was better known than he was in parts of Westmeath.

Seamus started to make bookings, initially for fees between £30 and £40, and in venues where Joe Dolan wasn't known he hustled for deals far beyond the usual expectations of a fledgling group. A lucky break came when Bill Carvell, who looked after twenty halls and ballrooms, liked what he heard about Joe, and booked dates in each of his venues. At the time, for an outfit bedding in a new line-up, who were still scratching at the surface outside of the midlands, this was an enormous amount.

After Seamus had revealed the extent of his booking spree to the band, Joe himself declared that Seamus should be appointed full-time. 'I thought to myself, "Good fuck, I definitely needed a manager, if this is what a manager can do!"' Joe laughed. A meeting was called for Broders Hotel in Mullingar (now the Newbury Hotel), where they thrashed out terms. Ben wondered at first how they would strike a deal, as he had no idea what a manager should be paid. Some of the other bands he talked to didn't even know what their manager was actually doing. But with Seamus Casey it was different: he had nothing but the band's best interests at heart, and, although he was relatively new to the wheeling and dealing of the band business, he was getting good results.

There wasn't a whole deal of money in the kitty, so Ben couldn't offer Seamus a signing-on fee as such. 'We had all these dates, and it looked as if we had all this money, but we had to play the dates before we got the money,' Ben recalls.

A few weeks later another meeting was called, and it was here that Seamus said he was prepared to give up teaching to take on the manager's job. By this stage Ben had been paying Seamus £10 a week including expenses, but this would not sustain him if he gave up his plum position as principal of Dysart National School, where he was earning £65 a month. Joe agreed that Seamus should get a share in the band, and the brothers shook hands with him on a deal that lasted a lifetime. 'It was some commitment to give us,' Ben remarks. 'It had a good effect on the rest of the lads too, that here was a man putting his faith in us.'

Seamus had been the main breadwinner for his family since his teens. His own father had died in 1947, leaving Seamus, his sister Mary and mother Rose with a rambling farm between Castletown-Geoghegan and Dysart to manage. He had gone to college in Dublin and in Multyfarnham, County Westmeath, and returned home to teach when a vacancy arose in Dysart National School in 1951. He had taught for eleven years, but as soon as he had shook hands with the Dolans this (and the teacher's pension) was behind him.

'My mother thought I was stone mad!' he laughs. 'It was as if I was heading off to join the circus.' The local parish priest, who had the overall say in the affairs of the two-teacher school, also thought Seamus was mad, and he could not believe that Seamus was giving up his job to become a band manager. Even the Bishop of Meath intervened. However, although Seamus enjoyed teaching, the allure of show business was to prove infinitely more exciting. And the money wasn't bad either. In his first full week of employment as the manager of Joe Dolan and The Drifters, Seamus earned what it would have taken him a month to earn as a teacher – although he was in for a crash landing on the second week when he earned the equivalent of just three days' teaching.

Ben had also taken the plunge and had told Frank Mulligan that he was hanging up his chisel for ever, although he was a little scared. 'Here we were in the middle of this explosion of bands. Was it going to work, was it not going to work? Was it going to work for a month? Was it going to work for a year? Was it going to work for a couple of years?' Little did he realize what he was letting himself in for.

The first big job Joe wanted his new manager to do was to give them an edge that other showbands didn't have. Each band member had their individual strengths, and Seamus's job was to harness those as one complete package whilst also selling each member individually. Joe was a talismanic front man and a great guitar player – when he played the Shadows songs 'Apache', 'FBI' and 'The Savage' you would have sworn Hank Marvin was onstage – but in some ways the guitar was hampering his development as an out-and-out singer. The Drifters also had a secret weapon in Tommy Swarbrigg, who, unlike so many involved in the showband scene, was writing some original material himself. Des Doherty had a style all of his own, and his experience was crucial to the band. He did most of the arrangements and brought plenty of ideas to the plate. Jimmy Horan was a natural bass player with an unmistakable playing style and real stage presence. Ben Dolan ran the show from the side of the stage in a jovial and interactive way, which made the fans feel very much part of the extended family. Ben's whole life revolved around Joe and The Drifters, and it showed. 'The Gill' and 'Sid' both brought great talent and muscle to the band, with the former becoming one of the most recognized 'bone' players in the country, and the latter keeping it all steady. 'In the early days we were following on from a lot of the other showbands. We would still go to the bands and we'd listen to what they were doing. And whatever the latest hit was we would do it because the crowd wanted that. And we were doing material like "Danny Boy" and other songs in among the hits of the time,' Seamus recalls. 'But to truly set us apart we needed to record our own records and to have a set that no other band had.'

Joe certainly had a knack of identifying hit records before they became hits. He found a kindred spirit in his manager and they would have records marked as potential hits before they were officially released. By hook or crook, new records were obtained before their release. These were then rehearsed, and Joe's band would frequently be the first in the country to play whatever song would go on to become a hit. In the showband era, you were often judged on the strength of your covers, which gave bands bragging rights and near ownership of the song in question. It also ensured the fans knew that when they went to a dance with Joe Dolan and The Drifters, they were going to be dancing to the most up-to-date act in the country.

But what Seamus also did – and this was a pioneering move – was to identify and bring original and often obscure material to the plate. In the showband era original material was almost a dirty word. Bands might have been constantly trying to outfox each other with the hits of other bands, but most were more than happy to simply churn out the hits and watch the money roll in. Seamus knew Joe was not this kind of player.

Tommy Swarbrigg started to play a bigger role within the band and, alongside Joe, created new arrangements of different styles of songs. Tommy was encouraged to bring as many songs as he had written to the fore, which made the talented Mullingar outfit much more than just another jukebox band. 'We were very typical of the showbands, copying everything in the charts,' Joe said, looking back on the very early years of his Drifters. 'However, Tommy gave us an edge. And then, of course, he started to write his own songs, which in turn gave us something other bands didn't have.'

One of the band's biggest fans at the time was a youngster from the village of Castlepollard named Donal 'Donie' Cassidy. The man who would go on to become one of Ireland's best-known music impresarios and politicians, both in the Dáil and Seanad Éireann, noticed the transformation immediately. 'Joe Dolan was the star of the show as it was, but once you heard him sing this original material you really knew he was something special,' Donie recalls. 'There was not one song that he couldn't take on and make his own, but when he started to sing his own songs he moved into a different league altogether.' Donie claims that Joe inspired him to put down the hurling stick and take up a musical instrument when he first saw him play at an ICA dance in Collinstown, five miles away from Castlepollard.

About halfway through the gig, Donie was elated to be asked by Joe to come to the front of stage; he thought he was going to be invited up to sing. However, Joe whispered to him that he had just received a note to say Donie's father was outside. Donie had failed to secure permission to go to the show and his father was not happy. He then made the youngster run all the way home as he cycled behind him. The punishment was worth every yard, Donie claimed, and not long afterwards he started his own band and was going to see as many Joe shows as he could for inspiration. Joe and Seamus later made his acts their relief bands for years to come.

As Joe honed his performance, the outrageous coloured suits were slowly replaced with a more sober, elegant and altogether contemporary 1960s look. At one stage someone within the band had decided that canary yellow suits would be an ideal complement to the already garish red suits, and Joe wasn't afraid to point a finger at the guilty party. 'Ben had this ferocious idea to buy bright yellow suits, and you can imagine what we were called after that! The idea was to go onstage with the red suits and, over the course of the interval period when some of the lads would slip off the stage and those left behind would form a little three-piece, the others would have their tea and change into the yellow suits. When they came back on, the idea was to totally confuse the audience!' Sadly, it had the opposite effect, and there was little PR value in being called 'the canaries of entertainment'. However, the red suits were not confined completely to the bowels of fashion hell, as the 'red devils' tagline necessitated their retention for the time being.

Owing to their severe lack of dancing skills, The Drifters shied away from aping the many other acts who had their own trademark synchronized 'show-band step' dance moves. 'We never got into that, because we were all from the country, and sure, we could hardly walk, never mind dance on the stage,' Joe declared. 'We weren't sort of into that flash dancing stuff, whereas other bands were. Johnny Flynn was into it in a big way. The Clipper Carlton had great steps. The Miami, Freshmen and Capital too. Johnny Quigley was big into it.'

As they concentrated on their music Joe Dolan and The Drifters started to grab headlines in all the papers, with journalists only too happy to give them the occasional write-up alongside new photos. The band soon found that they could have great fun at the newspapers' expense, as quite often the write-ups were word-for-word what they had sent them.

Joe and The Drifters used to play what was then a standard set, four to five hours. 'All bands did it initially,' Joe recalled with a sense of awe at how they did it. After playing for two hours, around eleven o'clock some of the band would slip off for tea and a change of clothes. The others would stay onstage and play a different set. With Joe on drums for these breaks it would be like the old days in a way, with just him, Ben and Jimmy onstage – the Grange skiffle boys made good. When the other lads came back, Sid would perch himself back behind the kit whilst Joe went offstage for his tea. But, ever enthusiastic, he rarely put his feet up with a nice cuppa. 'Once he was on, he was on,' Ben recalls. 'He felt he had no need for a break.'

The breaks afforded the band the chance to play around with numbers, or to add a touch of comedy to the show: dressing up as folk singers for a folk segment was a favourite, or they would do three Shadows instrumentals in a row. Ben did most of the announcing between songs, and as elected band-leader he dictated the pace of the evening. Ben, Jimmy and Tommy also sang, and handled certain songs each, according to whether it was a hit, or in a particular range. About half the show would be well-known hits, the other half original material. 'Everyone had their own little niche,' Joe recalled. 'If someone sang like Roy Orbison, we might get him to sing a Roy Orbison song, but I tended to sing those. Ben did all the country songs in the band, Tommy could be Cliff and so on. It wasn't what we wanted to do at the time, we wanted to be different, but for a while everybody sang their songs as that was the whole point of showbands.'

For the purposes of the media, The Drifters suddenly got younger, with Joe losing three years to become a teenager again. No matter what kind of a relationship they were in at the time, each of them was marketed as young, free and single.

At gigs, most of the attention was inevitably focused on Joe, and the singer was subject to much attention and adulation from the female members of the crowd. As Ben had noticed a couple of years previously in Kinnegad, when Joe stood up to the microphone, there was an aura about him that created great excitement in the crowd. 'There was this magnetism about him,' Tommy Swarbrigg noted. 'The crowd seemed to take a breath when he sang.' Soon the other singers started to take a back seat; it was becoming the Joe show.

The clamour of Joe's fans would grow as 1963 became 1964. It was as if, finally, Ireland had a star that could match Cliff Richard, Adam Faith or even one of the Beatles. Ballroom owners, hurt by the big crowds the man from Mullingar was getting, started to make him more attractive offers, and Joe and the band secured themselves a prestigious string of dates in the growing ballroom chain operated by Albert and Jim Reynolds. At the peak of the showband business in 1966, the astute brothers would own fourteen ballrooms, and lease several others in areas where they couldn't build. They were the most influential men in the live music industry at the time, and to get on their books was a sign that you had made it into the big time. A full year of bookings could be made at the stroke of a pen, and that is exactly what the equally astute Seamus Casey did. Joe was thrilled, as he was beginning to tire of the same old dirty venues, and these were purpose-built rooms for bands.

One of the first dates in a Reynolds Ballroom was in the Roseland in Moate, as the relief band for The John Barry Seven. Barry, of course would go on to become one of the world's greatest modern-day composers, with his music for the James Bond series of movies among the greatest film music ever recorded. However, at that time he meant little to the people of Moate: all they wanted was for Joe Dolan to get back on that stage. 'One hour into Barry's act, the crowd started shouting, "We want The Drifters!"' Joe revealed. 'And we were only the relief band.'

With everything going according to plan, the stage was suddenly set for the beginning of what would become known as 'Driftermania'. The band had come through the early stages of the new line-up with a clear sense of purpose, foresight and identity, and in Joe they had a singer who, according to an article in Irish music bible *Spotlight*, 'began to incite uncontrolled spasms of enthusiasm and extreme delight'.

What would really set Joe Dolan and The Drifters apart from the competition was a hit record, and they soon had one. Of the few showbands that were releasing records, an even tinier number were making any sort of an impression as their cover versions lacked originality, spark and passion. Their choice of material was too obvious, and the cover versions were usually carbon copies of the originals. Invariably radio DJs would dismiss these efforts, and if it was a cover version of a well-known record they would often root out the original recording and play that instead. Studios in Ireland were few and far between, and the primitive recordings were also the subject of much scorn. 'The killer part of the business was that the DJs would run you down if the production wasn't good enough, whereas now they run you down when it's too good!' Joe later argued.

As Joe and The Drifters discussed what their first single should be, Seamus and a friend, music journalist Ken Stewart, talked it over. Ken had an incredible record collection, one of the biggest in the country, and he gave Burt Bacharach and Bob Hilliard's sentimental ballad 'The Answer to Everything' to Seamus, with a view to putting Joe's already unique vocal stamp on it.

'The Answer to Everything' was a B-side to Del Shannon's September 1961 US Top Thirty hit 'So Long Baby', and upon hearing it, Joe knew the track had potential. 'Joe's voice was unlike anything any of us had ever heard before, so we had to have something that showcased it in full,' Seamus noted. There were several other numbers that would have achieved this, but Joe didn't want to do an obvious hit; 'The Answer to Everything' ticked all the right boxes.

Ken was friendly with Pye Records Irish chief John Woods, who was releasing a lot of Irish artists at the time, and a deal was quickly negotiated for Joe. 'They agreed to release the record, but we had to deliver it to them, at our own expense, to *something* against a 4 per cent return on royalties. It was a good deal at the time,' Joe says.

Being newcomers to the recording game, they didn't know what to expect when they booked Pinewood Studios in Bray for a recording session. 'We set up as if we were on a stage, with Sid at the back, and the rest of us lined out as if we were in a ballroom. And we stood around, tuning, talking to each other as if we were pros. Sure we didn't know what was going on; we were just shuffling around the place, waiting for direction from above.' Above meant the control booth, which was located dozens of metres up a large flight of stairs almost attached to the roof. The engineer sat there waiting for the band to kick in. 'Yer man, the engineer, was up in his box, way up [*points up*] there somewhere in the sky. He says, "Are you guys ready down there?" We all said, "Yeah, OK," and looked at each other. "Right, give us a blast then," said the producer. "What, you want us to play? Now?"'

Up in the gantry, the engineer blessed himself. Down on the soundstage, Joe took a deep breath and rubbed his hands on his trousers. Ben shrugged his shoulders; Sid nervously lifted a drumstick high in the air to count them in; Dessie stretched his fingers and took a deep breath; Jimmy started to switch from foot to foot; Joey licked his lips; and Tommy Swarbrigg hoped they would remember the arrangement he had almost had to beat into one or two of them the night before.

Joe strummed the chord of C, then G, and they were away. Des, Sid and Jimmy led the charge with a gentle shuffle, with Doherty's keyboards leading the melody. Ben and Tommy were on backing vocals. The band did an assured take, and Joe ended the song with a guitar twang that reminded him of the day they got the power in the Coliseum Cinema.

'Cool. We've done it,' said the producer. 'That's great. That's just fantastic.'

'Excuse me?' asked Joe.

'That's it. It's good, we're finished,' said the engineer.

'What do you mean, we're finished?' Joe replied.

The band had pretty much nailed it on the first attempt, but they weren't so sure of the producer's confidence. Joe wasn't happy with the backing vocals – the phased 'shal-la-la-las' at the outro caused him some anguish – and a couple of takes were recorded to give them more colour. Ben would claim that they chose the take they did because the band grew tired of climbing the stairs to go into the control booth to listen to playbacks, but the final take is assured, and Joe's delight when the fast middle eight went smoothly is evident at the start of the final verse.

When Joe and I listened to the track years later, there was still a sparkle in his eyes as he picked out each part, and pretended to cringe at the backing vocals of his brother Ben, who he was secretly proud of 'even if he sounded like a bull'. It had been their first day in the recording studio, and the band were in full control, their first-day nerves offset by their confidence in each other's abilities.

'The Answer to Everything' became an overnight sensation, launching the band straight into the Top Ten.

Joe recalled how, close to forty years after he recorded 'The Answer to Everything', he met Burt Bacharach whilst playing golf in the K Club in County Kildare, and, as they spoke, Joe thanked him for the song. Excitement at meeting the man whose words set him on the road to stardom was to be offset by ironic disappointment. 'I told him about "The Answer to Everything" and he said, "Gee, I don't know, do I know this song?" I said, "You wrote the bloody thing, Burt!" So he asked, "Can you sing it for me?" I sang a bit of it for him. He said, "That's very nice, but I can't remember it."'

The single was backed up with a Tommy Swarbrigg-penned composition called 'When You Say I Love You', which was one of the first original songs to be recorded by any showband at the time. It was released on Pye Records in the first week of September, and Irish radio legend Larry Gogan was the first DJ to play it on air. A little birdie told Joe that the song would be spun on

Larry's Monday night show that week. Acting on the tip-off, Ben went off on his own in his car, armed with a transistor radio, whilst Joe and Seamus had gathered around a radio in Mullingar. The rest of the band also assembled in the town, full of excitement that they were going to be broadcast for the very first time.

Monday night was also when the official word came out about the charts. 'If you made the charts you were a totally different band,' Joe said. On 14 September, the second week of its release, the single came in at number eight, and from being an ordinary band they were suddenly in the big league. 'We played the town hall in Killarney on the Thursday night after the charts, and from averaging about 600 a night in the past, there were suddenly 1,600 there,' Joe recalled.

The following night they were playing at the Tullamore Harriers' Carnival in Offaly, and as it was their closest gig to home at the time, busloads of Mullingar fans were set to make the short journey to cheer on their man. Such was the demand the marquee had to be upgraded to three times its original size. It was Joe's biggest show yet and over 2,500 people turned up. They ran out of tickets and change long before they stopped trying to squeeze more people in. 'Everyone in the band was raging that the ticket price had been pegged so low,' Joe laughed.

Meanwhile some of the crowd were raging too, as the sound system was struggling to cope and the amps were cranked up to the last. The Drifters eventually got a bigger sound system for their subsequent shows, and they certainly needed it as the crowds just kept on getting bigger, all on the strength of one big hit. 'It was unreal. I thought then, what am I going to do, will we be able to manage this thing? It went huge almost overnight,' Ben says, excitement still coursing through him at the thoughts of their leap up the show-business pecking order.

Joe put the change in pace down to the arrival of the new manager. 'Seamus made the difference as his arrival got the whole thing moving. He was good at meeting fellas and not falling out with anybody, even if they gave him good reason to. From day one, Seamus steered us and we were very lucky that he was there. He was meeting fellas, and he knew what they were talking about, he had the same interests and he was able to talk to them. People higher up in the recording game liked him, and therefore liked us. If you didn't have a fella with a bit of foresight or vision you wouldn't have lasted.'

'The Answer to Everything' remained in the Top Ten for seven weeks, peaking at number four, a major achievement for any band. To have such a hit with a first single was astonishing, and Joe Dolan and The Drifters knew they would have to work hard to maintain this level of success.

6
Driftermania

With the success of 'The Answer to Everything,' the red devils of entertainment were causing such a frenzied reaction inside (and outside) ballrooms it seemed as if their fans were coming down with something. Cue the diagnosis of 'Driftermania'. Other bands could only look on in envy as The Drifters and their rugged, smiling front man became the objects of rampant female desire all over the country. Seamus readily admits that the idea of Driftermania was inspired by the kind of devotion The Beatles were enjoying, but there is no doubt that when the band returned to the road to promote their second single, 'I Love You More and More Every Day', Driftermania was a living, screaming reality. Joe's every move was monitored by adoring, shrieking fans.

They also returned to the road looking a little fancier, as Joe and the band had acquired new cars. Joe had spent nearly everything he had on a top-of-the-range Ford Zephyr, and even the band members who couldn't drive had bought cars. In fact, Tommy Swarbrigg had to get the garage owner to point his new car, a Mini Cooper, towards home, start the engine and then show him how to drive it *after* he had paid for it.

The second single was another smash hit and would spend eight weeks in Ireland's Top Ten. It came straight in at number four on 8 February 1965, and got as high as number three, Joe's highest chart position yet. Crucially, the single was billed as a Joe Dolan and The Drifters release, not just The Drifters. Recorded on the most basic equipment in just one assured take, the track still sounds fresh today.

With Driftermania taking off, the demand was there for Joe to capitalize and release a follow-up single almost immediately, but he decided to take his time picking a track, which proved to be a masterstroke, as anticipation for 'My Own Peculiar Way' had reached fever pitch by the time it was released.

The extent of Joe's fame finally hit home when he recorded that song in Eamonn Andrews Studios in Henry Street during the summer of 1965. As the day went on, a crowd of young women began to build up on the street below. Word had got out that Joe was in town, and soon there were hundreds on the street. The star gave them what they had come for when he leaned out the window to a chorus of screams. 'I was blowing kisses, pointing, waving and all that sort of stuff and, genuinely, I couldn't believe it. "Why me?" I was thinking. "Sure what have I got that others didn't have?" I really couldn't believe they were all there for me.'

A photographer who was there to capture the band at work managed to convince Joe to come down to the street to sign autographs, so that he could catch 'Driftermania' on camera. However, the young fans had other things in mind and started to tear at Joe's clothes, lunging at him for a kiss as he walked on to the street. Seamus had to rescue his young charge by bundling him into his car and driving away at speed. This soon became a daily occurrence.

A clever press advertisement in the second half of 1965 defined 'Driftermania' for those not yet in the know by way of a witty poem:

Dancers who as a rule are cool are
Reacting in ways that are most peculiar
In ballrooms where The Drifters appear
Frenzied thousands clap and cheer
Then of course you probably know
Everyone is wild about Joe
Requests for his records are made every day
Morning and night you can hear them being played
And the band's popularity just keeps on growing
Nobody knows how far this thing is going
It's spreading so fast that sometime soon
A Driftermaniac's Club will start on the moon

Competitions to spell as many words as possible with the letters DRIFTER-MANIA proved to be a big hit, and pretty soon the recently established fan club was snowed under with membership applications. Joe would spend every Monday, supposedly his only day off, answering fan mail and signing autographs before catching up with his pals in one of his local haunts.

With Driftermania stoked and flaring up all over the country, 'My Own Peculiar Way' sold like hot cakes for several months. Upon entering the charts on 26 July, it stayed in the Top Twenty for the entire summer, spending three months in the Top Ten alone. It got as high as number two, with only The Beatles selling more records.

By the end of September it had outsold 'Satisfaction' by The Rolling Stones, 'I Got You Babe' by Sonny and Cher, 'Like a Rolling Stone' by Bob Dylan and 'What's New, Pussycat?' by Tom Jones. It was the biggest record of the year for Pye Records.

Joe was a big Rolling Stones fan, so to outsell his heroes was a proud achievement for him. He even included 'Satisfaction' in The Drifters' set at that time as it gave him a chance to really let rip on the guitar, and to ape Mick Jagger, whom he became friendly with later on. The Driftermaniacs' reaction to this song was astounding, and it became commonplace for fans to rush the stage when he launched into it. 'The first time it happened I was taken aback. There was a sudden surge and the next thing I know there were seventeen Drifters onstage instead of seven! In the heat of the moment I came to the conclusion that whatever inspired these girls to join me couldn't be bad. We all had a marvellous time in fact – although I detected a trace of worry on Seamus's face. Of course, "Satisfaction" was a very exciting song, it gradually built up into an almighty roar which was hard on the voice, but I always enjoyed performing it.'

As Joe and The Drifters got bigger, they started to break box-office records in ballrooms all over the country. In one memorable week they broke attendance records in Moate, Athy, Drogheda, Cahir and the Olympic in Dublin, one of the biggest venues in the country at the time.

In an October 1965 edition of *Spotlight* magazine, its top columnists the Hand Twins, Michael and Jim, argued over just how long it had taken for The Drifters to become the number-one band in the country. Michael claimed it had only taken a few weeks, whereas Jim spoke of the truthful three-year slog. They ended up putting the band's success down to Joe being 'a sincere country boy with boundless energy, and that's what makes their fans happy'.

Joe was breaking the showband mould in concert as well as on record. Instead of dancing, Joe's fans began to congregate at the front of the stage, with the dancers finding themselves pushed to the back of the hall. With just three records to his credit, he was more of a pop star than a showband star. His popularity grew further in October 1965 when a TV appearance on *The Showband Show* garnered him thousands of new fans.

A brief Drifters tour of the UK during Lent (when all gigs were banned in Ireland) saw the band break three box-office attendance records, as thousands of homesick Irish emigrants packed into the clubs to get a taste of Driftermania. This first overseas tour would not be the luxurious five-star trip Joe had imagined, however. They were met off the ferry by Bill Foley, who worked for well-known ballroom owner Bill Fuller. Foley had a 1,000-weight van with just two good seats – one for the driver and one for the passenger. Joe grabbed the front seat and the rest of the band had to sit on two tiny benches, military style, for the arduous seven-hour journey to London. They stayed four or five to a room in a tiny apartment over the Buffalo Ballroom in Camden Town, where they spent most of their time arguing over whose turn it was to switch off the light, an argument often settled by someone throwing a shoe at the light bulb.

The gigs were great, though, and not for the first time Joe had his suit torn off after being pulled into the crowd. He was rated as the biggest emerging Irish star in the UK press.

The band was a real 'last gang in town' and they went everywhere together, as Joe fondly recalled. 'We had great fun in these places when we all used to stay in the same hotel. The first time we went to London, I'll always remember all eight of us walking around together in awe of the place. We went for breakfast together, lunch together, dinner together, we did everything together.'

Joe never dreamed that they would be able to release records in the UK, although Seamus was trying to convince Pye otherwise. 'Pye Records in London and Pye Records in Dublin were poles apart,' Seamus says. 'Even though the Irish singles sales were huge, they were separate identities and it took a lot of effort to get them interested in us.' When it finally happened in 1969, it would prove to be well worth the wait.

The continued success of 'My Own Peculiar Way' in Ireland delayed the release of their next single by two months. The new single, 'Aching Breaking Heart', marked a radical departure for Joe and the band, and his country-and-western-music-mad brother and manager were delighted to see him wrap his vocals around a country song by a true American great, George Jones.

Although 'Aching Breaking Heart' got to number two in the Irish charts, Joe was not hugely satisfied with the recording. He didn't want to copy the distinctive velvet singing style of George Jones, and the song was transformed with an up-tempo bossa nova beat, which recalled The Royal's 'Hucklebuck'. Joe's performance was a bit distant, and his fans did not become as involved with the record as they had done its predecessor, 'My Own Peculiar Way'. Joe would joke for years afterwards that he was 'never doing a song by that Jones fella again', even though he secretly liked him.

Joe felt the opening lines of the song reflected his own state of mind at the time, as it described a man who was suddenly alone. He had been seeing a local Mullingar girl, Carmel Barrett, for a number of years and they had become very close. They went everywhere together in Mullingar, often looking after Paddy's kids when he and Caroline were away, and at one stage it looked like they would get engaged. But Joe had broken up with her because of work pressures, and offstage he was not in the best of form. The relationship had been kept quiet for fear of upsetting his fans.

In an interview with *Spotlight* a year later, he said, 'I don't agree with all this falseness about images and the like. I'll tell you out straight that I was in love. I was even to get engaged last August. Anyhow, things didn't work out. It wasn't my fault though, and that was that. I'm not in love now. It's all over a long time ago.' He added he was back in the market, but not for a serious relationship. 'I'd like also to go out on dates with girls, who wouldn't expect to have a serious line after one or two dates.'

It was sometimes tough on Joe to be the centre of attention in 1965 while the band's musical arrangements were developing, with both his vocals and his guitar playing becoming more complex. He had also taken on a role in an all-star Christmas panto of *Cinderella* for Teilifís Éireann, had fronted a TV campaign for *Club Orange*, and for four Saturday mornings late in the year he hosted a radio show for Radio Éireann. The pressure to keep the hits coming was also immense, and recording on the band's next release began almost as soon as they were happy with the last one. 'You had to keep records coming out all the time, we had to play every night, and take whatever promotional steps were necessary. You had to continue that momentum,' Seamus said. But despite one or two members of the band falling ill (Peter Barden of The Greenbeats joined the band temporarily), Joe was showing few signs that the hectic schedule was getting to him: 'I never complained of having to work too hard, I enjoyed every second of it.'

The year 1965 came to a fitting and prestigious close when the late Jim Aiken invited Joe to headline the Ulster Hall in Belfast on Christmas Night. 'It didn't get much better than that,' recalled Joe, who still remembered that the attendance that night was 3,514, their biggest crowd to date. When Joe was told the booking was confirmed, his answer was, 'Does that mean I'll have to have my Christmas dinner for breakfast?' Away from the public eye many of the band had started families, but they all agreed to play the gig and Aiken was delighted.

They played there every Christmas for many years until the Troubles made it difficult for a short spell. Joe loved the Christmas show, and was always thrilled that both communities in the North came out in force and enjoyed the show together. It made for a special atmosphere, and Joe always rose to that, rating it as one of his favourite gigs of the year. The band loved it too as there were plenty of show-stopping moments. One in particular stood out for Tommy Swarbrigg. 'That first time we played there was the first time I really realized Joe's power. During the show he stepped forward, and a hush descended on the hall. He sang "Silent Night" unaccompanied and you could have heard a pin drop. At the end of the song there was total silence, and then one person started clapping and the whole place erupted, the people on the balconies rising to their feet.'

On St Stephen's Night Joe played to 4,000 at Limerick's Jetland Ballroom with the doors closed hours before he went onstage. Such was his increasing profile, his only day off throughout December 1965 and January 1966 was Christmas Eve.

Joe ended the year on a further high when he was voted Showband Personality of the Year in the *Spotlight* Show Business Poll 1965. The Drifters, meanwhile, were voted the second-best Showband of the Year, just behind The Royal. 'My Own Peculiar Way' was voted the second-best Record of the Year, and the band was voted the second-favourite Recording Band. Joe was voted second-best Male Vocalist and Des Doherty was in the top ten of the Favourite Showband Instrumentalist category.

But 1965 could have been so different had Joe accepted a tempting offer early in the year for a potentially lucrative residency in Las Vegas. He did fly over to the United States for a whistle-stop tour though. (The picture on p. 86 shows Joe and Seamus about to take off for the States.) Surprisingly, a song that Joe was quick to ditch from his repertoire, 'The Jolly Tinker', was one of the best-received songs of his maiden American voyage, where he played to big Irish-American crowds in Boston, New York and Chicago. It was also on this tour that avid record-buyer and country-music aficionado Seamus Casey picked up several songs for Joe to record in the years ahead, including what would eventually be his first number-one smash, 'Pretty Brown Eyes'. Joe remembered that they were travelling between shows from Boston to Chicago by bus when he was first alerted to the future number one. Seamus – 'always on the lookout for new sounds', according to Joe – had bought a portable radio for the journey, and he and Joe were permanently tuned into it. Back home, radio was stiff and risk-free, and the music of this new radio frontier enthralled and inspired them. Even before he got near to recording it, Joe confided in the band that 'Pretty Brown Eyes' was a sure-fire hit. 'Jaysus, lads, it's a great song,' he told them. When they got to Chicago, Seamus immediately set off in search of a record store to find a copy.

On the first night in New York, they opened with 'Concrete and Clay', a catchy number one at home and a Top Thirty smash in the States at the time for a band called Unit 4+2. Joe thought the song was a good opener as it was full of vocal harmonies that would keep all the singers in the band happy. It was also felt that the song's idealistic and romantic lyrics of love in the big city would be perfect for a New York crowd. But it left the largely Irish-American crowd cold. On the second night the band set a different tone, and learned a lesson that would stay with Joe wherever he and his band went after that: surroundings didn't matter, they should just play as themselves.

Going to America was 'like going to the moon', according to Joe. 'We used to imagine being there. To be in New York, you know, was just incredible. It was beyond our wildest dreams.' The trip was memorable for any number of reasons – from the band bringing nothing but warm winter clothing and big coats with them and then to be confronted by a heatwave the moment they disembarked, to their first ever attempts at bowling. Joe loved to tell the tale of Des Doherty's first run with a bowling ball. Des reckoned because he was the keyboard player he would have the best fingers for a bowling ball. He grabbed a ball and, kitted out in the best bowling attire, 'looking every inch the pro', he made a run for the bowling lane. However, as he moved to launch his bowling ball, his fingers would not give and he followed the ball down the line for a couple of feet.

In the Woodward Hotel in New York, half the band got stuck in the lift, making it to a gig with only seconds to spare. Some of them also got lost.

The tour ended with a return visit to New York for a trio of dates. It was on this return trip that Joe first began to enjoy a drink, although Ben, who did not encourage drinking, was kept in the dark about it. But only just. 'Lads, you'll have to try this drink,' the Kerry-born Bill Fuller told the band one night as they prepared to go on stage. 'Have a little shot of this and a dart of 7-Up,' he said, as he handed several glasses of sweet-smelling amber liquid to the band. The Drifters suddenly discovered Seven and Seven, and Joe Dolan suddenly discovered alcohol.

'Instead of taking one, we took about six or seven each,' Joe laughs, as he recalls them downing the drinks and rubbing their mouths like cowboys after each sup. 'Sure it went straight to the head and we were all in convulsions when we went on stage.'

Seamus was at the side of the stage watching the band play through their moment of weakness. 'The whole lot of them were all over the place. Ben didn't know what they were at. They were all laughing and pointing down to me and then Joe started saying he couldn't feel his arms.' He rubs his head as he remembers the shambolic scenes. 'At one stage during the opening few numbers, Ben went over to Jimmy, disgusted that the band were half-cut. "I think some of these boys have been drinking," he said. "You're damn right about that, Ben!" Jimmy roared. He was absolutely raging over it.' The band were then barred from having pre-show drinks.

The next few times Joe had a drink on the road, he kept a soft drink or a glass of water close to hand, pushing the alcoholic drink out of the way if Ben came into the room. Tommy Swarbrigg and Des Doherty were marked out as big drinkers by Ben because invariably when he entered a bar after a show one of them would have two drinks lined up. Joe admitted to being fearful of alcohol, and his brother's attitude to it was understandable. Their father's drinking had contributed in some way to the closure of the family business before their move to Grange, and there can be no doubt that this made them wary of drink, particularly in those early days.

The dates all went remarkably well, and Fuller was delighted that he was putting up the 'house full' notices each night. Perhaps not surprisingly, he wanted the band to return as soon as they could. 'The band was really cooking,' Tommy Swarbrigg remembers of that first American tour, and the trip gave the band a new zest in more ways than one. As well as picking up new material, their friendships and trust in each other grew, and onstage their playing improved even more as they were removed from the comfort zone of an Irish audience. They were elated with the response and loved the royal treatment laid on for them. When they got back home, Ireland was still in the grip of Driftermania and the princes who had left the island a few weeks previously returned as high kings.

At the start of 1966, over 3,000 Driftermania car stickers were distributed to the fans, as were a few thousand calendars. The fan-club postbox in Ginnell Terrace was besieged as fans tried to get in touch with their heroes, answer competitions and attempt to join one of the most generous (and one of the first) showband fan clubs.

The calendars would be a lasting and enduring gift to the fans, given away free to them every Christmas for the next forty-one years, and the signed photos and postcards each member received became collectors' items. Fan-club secretary Mary Curtain (née O'Dowd) remembers those heady days well. 'I remember when Seamus decided that we should run a fan club. That was really original back then; in fact, it was unheard of in Ireland. He bought me a portable typewriter and I would have typed a couple of hundred newsletters every month.' Members joined in their droves, and newsletters with free gifts were sent out to fans all over Ireland and, increasingly, to England. Her younger sisters, who helped seal the envelopes, can still remember the taste of the glue.

Mary was only seventeen when she became fan-club secretary, and remembers how the rise of Joe Dolan seemed to signal a changing Ireland. 'The 1960s was the start of everything, and it was a very exciting time for young people. We were just beginning to enjoy a little bit of freedom, getting to go out, and there at the head of it all was Joe Dolan. He represented so much for people – the dancehalls, the showbands and rock 'n' roll – and yet people felt they knew him. They looked to him, a local star, and they thought, "If he can do it, I can do it."'

Even with his increasing fame and the rising hysteria surrounding him, Mary says that Joe never changed, remaining the same, down-to-earth person that she first met when she took the job. 'The Drifters were bigger than Elvis or The Beatles for the people of Ireland. Today, you hear about a sold-out gig or a popular night out and people are talking about hundreds of people. Joe brought in thousands of people to his gigs. And yet, you were just as likely to pass Joe on the street or see him in the cinema. He was always about, ordinary and friendly; the fame never went to his head, not then, in fact never,' Mary said.

Things were so busy that Sean Connolly, the trumpet player whose heart condition had made it impossible for him to continue playing with the band a few years earlier, was drafted back in for a little admin work, and he became Seamus's cover when the manager was out of the office – which was quite often as he and Joe set about getting a number-one hit. In Dublin, Seamus would be hustling for radio plays on Radio Éireann, whose studios were then in Henry Street. This invariably meant more than a few trips into Madigans' Pub on Moore Street, which was the hangout for disc jockeys and anyone associated with the national broadcaster at the time. Eamonn Andrews Studios was also in the vicinity, so the pub became a favourite haunt of most of the band business. It was not for a carvery lunch or a quiet coffee either: drink culture was in, and even on lunch breaks the pints flowed freely. Most deals were toasted with a few drinks.

The first big Drifters release of 1966 was to be a curious one, the five-track 'Two of a Kind' EP. Its release date was carefully timed, as every one of The Drifters' singles the previous year had clashed with releases by The Beatles and they wanted to avoid that this time. The EP was then something of an unknown quantity. 'Change was important in the showband business,' said Joe, justifying its release. The band didn't want to hoard material, and with four-track EPs now eligible for the singles charts they thought it would be a nice gift to the fans, whilst they readied material for the first album.

Joe, Ben and Tommy Swarbrigg all shared vocals on the EP. Two of Tommy's compositions were included, with most of the PR at the time focusing on these. However, despite Seamus's best efforts to show the band as equally multi-talented, there was no escaping the fact that Joe was the one the people wanted, and the EP confirmed him as the band's main vocalist.

The EP didn't do so well, and it took a few weeks to break the Top Ten. One of the reasons was a ban on one of its tracks, the ill-advised 'The Jolly Tinker', which, on reflection, should have stayed as a live 'favourite'. Its dated and rude lyrics meant it wasn't favoured by Radio Éireann, who immediately blacklisted it. Other tracks on the EP included 'I've Got Five Dollars and It's Saturday Night' (a country number that featured Ben Dolan's first recorded vocal) and 'Minutes to Midnight' (which found Tommy taking the vocal credit). The latter was a staple of their shows, and would have been a worthy single in its own right. There was even talk that Cliff Richard was thinking of covering it, and other bands started asking Tommy to write for them. The title track on the EP was an obscure Roy Orbison ballad first heard in America, and whilst Joe's sincere vocal on it was impressive, it lacked the spark of the previous singles.

Live, Joe and the band were developing a set that was anything but showband-style. Swarbrigg compositions such as 'The Wrong Impression', 'I'll Sit on your Doorstep' and 'When I Say I Love You' were now concert staples, as were songs from some of the other band members, Irish writers and emerging international writers such as Willie Nelson. But even though the material was setting them apart, back in those halcyon days the majority of Joe Dolan's success was down to putting the fans first. In a 1966 interview, he said, 'Hand on my heart I always put the fans first. If you don't please the fans you won't succeed. It's really as simple as that. No amount of records or publicity will do anything if you don't satisfy the basic requirements of fans.'

His manager agreed. 'I liked to go around and listen to as many bands as I'd time to hear, and I can honestly say that I've never heard an outfit that can communicate with audiences as well as The Drifters. And it is this communication – you can call it rapport or family atmosphere or any number of things – [that] binds The Drifters so close to their audiences.'

This close rapport with the fans would last for the whole of Joe's career. The very same girls who were screaming for Joe when they were sixteen or seventeen were still screaming for him over forty years later. He got to know them by name, to love them and to cherish their support. He made the fans his bosses and he always looked out for them. It is this star quality that ensured that only Joe Dolan would ride out the decline of the showbands which, in 1966, was just around the corner.

The first UK tour of 1966 was to be another revelation for Joe. The England World Cup win brought a new-found sense of optimism and pride. London was swinging, and the world swung with it in arts and culture, fashion and music. It was the year The Beatles controversially proclaimed that they were 'more popular than Jesus' before they turned rock and pop on its head with the release of the seminal *Revolver* album. There was a sense of world-beating bravado that would not be felt again until the high times of the first Tony Blair government and Brit Pop some thirty years later. The world looked to London, and 1966 became a sort of cultural 'year zero'. And into the middle of that maelstrom dropped Joe.

The tour eclipsed their previous UK jaunts, and no one could believe the reception Joe was getting. Driftermania was being diagnosed in towns and cities from John O'Groats to Land's End, and there was a feeling that if Pye Ireland could convince its UK counterparts to write a prescription in the form of a big UK release, then Ireland could have its first international music star. 'Everywhere we went on that tour it was the same story – packed halls, record-breaking crowds and scenes that really underlined the meaning of the word "mobbed"!' Joe recalled. 'They had heard our records just the same way as an Irish person might hear discs by an American group. They thought they might never see us in person, so they were surprised to find us touring England.'

In Glasgow, The Drifters played encore after encore for a rabid crowd of over 3,000. At the close of one show in the famous Irish club the Galtymore in Cricklewood, London, Joe was pulled off the stage and it took him two hours to get back to the sanctuary of the dressing room. But he never complained about the adulation. In fact, he used to say he would only start to worry when it didn't happen.

Pye in London were considering taking a gamble on 'I'll Sit on your Doorstep', a Tommy Swarbrigg original that featured a powerful and energetic vocal performance from Joe. 'It had both quality and commercial impact, and we thought it could break through,' Seamus said. But it wasn't to be, and Pye stalled on releasing it at the last minute. Pye had released a limited number of the band's records on Irish import, but these were difficult to buy. Fortunately, the BBC took notice of this hot Irish act, and they filmed the band for a thirty-minute programme called *The Showband Sound*, which charted the rise of the movement in Ireland and featured Joe and the band performing eleven numbers. It had a peak-time viewing audience of several million when it was broadcast in 1966 at 6.30 p.m. While recording it, Joe met and befriended The Who, and they offered each other advice on the UK and Irish music scenes and found they were playing some of the same covers.

But the big revelation for Joe on the tour was that all of the crowds watched the band from start to finish without distraction. Dancing was not at the forefront of their minds, and this really opened Joe's eyes to the art of performance. He returned from the tour more determined than ever to make it outside of the thirty-two counties.

On his return, the Driftermaniacs nearly drowned out the boys with screaming when Joe attempted to record a *17 Club* show for Larry Gogan on Radio Éireann. Larry couldn't believe the reception, whilst Joe thought they weren't loud enough.

Joe also undertook his first significant charity work, playing what became an annual free concert for a boys' club in Mullingar, and taking part in the Jimmy Magee charity football matches. These were curious and often bruising encounters that raised hundreds of thousands for charity by pitching show-business stars against former footballing stars. 'They were the height of madness!' laughed Joe as he lifted his trouser leg to reveal minute scars that at one time may have resembled the aftermath of a studs-first challenge. 'We would be playing, say, the 1949 All-Ireland winning Meath team, or the 1952 Cavan team, and the lads on the other teams would be huge, big hulks of players, and we only slight fellas.' Joe recalled that even a shoulder given in jest had consequences. 'If a footballer hit you, you knew all about it. I remember one night this fella came over and gave me a shoulder and nearly knocked me off the pitch. A fella who was on the sideline watching it went over and gave yer man an earful, telling him this was for charity and to leave me alone. The minute you went near a ball, a lad would give you a belt. I suppose they were trying to prove they were the best, but we hadn't played football since we were kids, and these lads played all the time so we were crippled by the time we came off the pitch.' Joe didn't have the heart to tell Jimmy he was stopping. 'I just didn't turn up to a good few of them!' he joked. On one of his last outings, against an All-Ireland winning team from Kerry, Joe suffered off-the-pitch indignation when his football boots were stolen by a fan. 'Sure I couldn't play after that. They were me lucky boots!' he said with a wink.

Ben took part in just two matches, and having being shouldered off a pitch into a ditch he reckoned making a donation was wiser. 'Everyone was going around not able to stand up. Des Doherty left a game on crutches, Doc Carroll nearly got killed in a game I played in, so that was it for me.'

Meanwhile, Sid and Des had joined a local GAA club and their last junior hurling match saw Des marked by a 6' 5" man-mountain. He complained to Sid, who said, 'Stay close to him and he can't hit you when he's swinging.' Shortly after this, all members of the band resigned from the GAA and their dreams of gracing the hallowed turf at Croke Park were over.

An appeal from the fan-club newsletter for members to fill the mailbags of music magazines, radio shows and newspapers was beginning to build up the hype ahead of the release of 'Pretty Brown Eyes'. In August 1966, a letter from Athlone man Aidan Clark in *Spotlight* spoke for many Driftermaniacs:

> *Dear Editor,*
> *Please stop printing articles on The Beatles, Beach Boys and Monkees, and give us more of the fabulous Joe Dolan.*
> *I think Joe and the boys are great and I have all their records. Joe's latest is his best yet and it is far better than the records being made by the English and American groups!*

Another letter in the same issue asked for Joe's life story to be printed 'in the name of thousands of Drifters fans', and Seamus managed to secure a column entitled 'A Drifter a Month' in the same magazine, in which the band members were subject to a short profile. These profiles, invariably written by Seamus himself, continued the myth that all of them were single and unattached, as well as their being aged between seventeen and twenty. Joe was said to be nineteen, although he was really twenty-six.

'Pretty Brown Eyes', their sixth release (and fifth single), marked a return to a gentler, almost ballad-esque pace, and it made Joe Ireland's biggest star. He updated the straightforward Willie Nelson country and western number to a beautifully pitched love song, perfect for the dancing era, Des Doherty's keyboards lifting the song and carrying the steel guitar riff Nelson had written. It became the ultimate Joe Dolan number for dance-floor seduction, and it is estimated that hundreds of thousands of relationships and marriages started with a slow dance in Irish ballrooms as Joe sang the song. The lyrics, about a broken man who had realized that his new girlfriend held a torch for her ex, would see hundreds of female fans rush to comfort Joe, feeling his heartbreak (even though it was imaginary) and thinking the unappreciative brown-eyed girl should be dumped and replaced by them.

Seamus had done his homework, as there were no Beatles releases to compete with it – well, almost. Although 'Paperback Writer' had been released in the summer, the follow-up single 'Yellow Submarine' was not due until autumn. Thinking they had a couple of weeks' grace to promote the single, the band proposed to take their annual holidays. Meanwhile, their manager had a proposal of his own, as some months earlier he had proposed to his girlfriend, Doreen (who he had met at a Joe Dolan show), and the wedding was set for 5 September – a week after the release of 'Pretty Brown Eyes'. Joe was his best man, and Seamus and Doreen were due to fly off on their honeymoon the night of the wedding.

Radio Éireann had fallen head over heels in love with the song, and they were playing it non-stop. As Driftermania mobilized the fans, it was looking like Joe would finally get his first number one. Sure enough, after just one week, it hit the top spot – on Seamus and Doreen's wedding day.

The couple had been blessed with a beautiful day of blinding sunshine for what was the showbiz wedding of the year. As much as the happiness of the day was evident earlier on, there was also keen anticipation of the chart rundown due that night. as they assembled for the Wedding Mass and the reception at the Crofton Hotel in Dublin. Early in the evening, as the time of the chart countdown approached, a wedding guest was quietly dispatched to a corner of the hotel function room with a transistor radio. As everyone toasted the bride and groom, Joe was frequently observed glancing over to the man with the radio. It was only after the happy couple had left for the airport that word finally filtered through that Joe had knocked The Beatles, whose 'Yellow Submarine' had been brought forward, off the top spot.

Inside the hotel there was bedlam, as champagne corks bounced off the ceiling and people danced on tables, but Joe felt it unfair that the man who had set them off on the road to their first number one was not there to share the celebrations. So, he did what any best man would do – he decided to take them to the newlyweds. He gathered together the jubilant band and a huge crowd of wedding guests and they piled into cars, racing to the airport to catch the bride and groom before they jetted off.

Seamus and Doreen had just arrived hand in hand in the Departures lounge when a herd of mad Mullingar men in their best suits came crashing through the terminal's doors, followed by a bunch of elated and emotional wedding guests. The airport came to a standstill, as the screams of the rampaging group filled the building. Customs and police tried to stop them, but it was no use. They bounded over the security gates and into the Departures area, where they found their startled manager.

A beaming Joe asked Doreen if he could have a quiet word with her husband, and roaring, 'We're number one!' he picked up Seamus and carried him shoulder high through the airport as everyone sang, danced and buck-leaped around. As it was evidently so good-humoured, the security guards who had been called in to deal with the invasion decided not to interfere and left the revellers to it. 'Joe was carrying me around the airport, people were taking photos of us, and everyone was just elated. Sure it was madness,' Seamus recalled.

Joe and the band then went on their own holidays, and Seamus's honeymoon was peppered with phone calls as he hastily tried to rearrange dates to take advantage of the chart success. The band were scattered all over the Mediterranean coast, and when they reassembled after their holidays they were inundated with work and tempting offers. As they filled every venue as chart-conquering heroes, Joe Dolan and The Drifters were officially Ireland's biggest-drawing and biggest-selling band.

The twelve months of Driftermania in 1966 'flared like an Australian bush-fire all over the country' according to the *Spotlight* Christmas annual of that year. 'Bandstand consistency' and Joe's 'heart-throb' status were cited as the main reasons behind their success, but the magazine also said no one was recording or writing songs quite like The Drifters.

As 1966 came to a close, with 'Pretty Brown Eyes' still selling well and the gig revenue pouring in, Joe's car addiction saw him add to his growing fleet and he swapped his affections from Ford to Mercedes. It was a romance that would last a lifetime, with a couple of interruptions in between. As they had done after their first hit, every other member went out and bought new cars, as well as new homes. Seamus and Doreen built a house across the road from the racetrack in Grange, just yards from Joe's childhood home. Ben and his wife Moira moved from Grange to Ballinderry; Joe was best man at their wedding. And one by one, several band members, who for a number of years had lived next door to each other in Ginnell Terrace, all moved, some keeping their weddings and relationships a secret from the Driftermaniacs. Joe still lived with his brother Paddy, but he would soon take up residence in a Mullingar town-centre apartment, christened 'The Haven', which would become something of a party destination.

Ben bought a very expensive custom-built bandwagon replete with airplane seats, tables and all the luxuries a fast-rising band of The Drifters' stature required. But, with Joe and the band keen to show off their flash new motors, they invariably only used the bandwagon when there was a long journey ahead.

One night, they were nearly all wiped out when they had a serious crash after a dance in Kanturk, County Cork. 'We were driving back in the new bus on a really frosty night and it was kind of nice as we were rarely all in the bus,' explained Joe. 'Ben was tired and none of the rest of us wanted to drive, but Seamus offered and he took the wheel at Abbeyleix. We were on the far side of Mountmellick when we met black ice on the road and, after slipping all over the place, those of us who were still awake felt the wheels rising and then the wagon went over on its side. We thought we were goners! Lads woke up on top of other lads and there was pandemonium.'

Still recoiling in horror and embarrassment, Seamus remembers the crash for different reasons, as band members, sensing an inferno, literally walked all over him to get out of the bus. Joe still found it funny. 'Dessie started to panic and screamed we should get out as he could smell petrol. We had to get out through the side window on to the roof, which was now the side, and Dessie walked on Seamus in the panic to get out. Poor Seamus was in shock after, and the rest of the lads were claiming he had fallen asleep, which he hadn't. Ben was even worse.'

They took all the gear out, and a highly emotional Ben ordered the laughing band to push the stricken bandwagon up on to its wheels, but warned them to hang on when the bus righted so it wouldn't roll over the other way. 'Sure we were all in bits laughing, and when we got it over we all let go, leaving Ben hanging on to the side of the bus!' They managed to get the engine going, and drove the 200 miles home in the freezing cold as there were no windows left. Much to his delight, Seamus was then given a lifetime ban from driving any bandwagons or tour buses.

Because no one would get on the bus after that, Ben decided he'd get rid of it without telling anyone. 'He traded it in for a small transit van with no windows, and it just so happened that we were going to Cork on the night we found out,' Joe remembers. 'None of the lads fancied driving so they decided to take the wagon, only there wasn't a wagon any more. There was a big hullabaloo, so Ben put two armchairs in the back of this little van and told the lads to get in!'

The idea of driving separately to gigs dismayed Ben, because if anything happened to one member en route the gig might not happen, and if it went ahead without key men, punters would not feel they were getting value for money. Despite the growing attention on Joe, each member was a star in his own right and that member's fans would be disappointed if he wasn't there. 'Ben preferred the security of the unit,' Joe says, recalling a story of a Clipper Carlton visit to the UK when the lads had become so used to going to gigs separately that no one noticed they had left their bandwagon and their equipment on the dock back home in Ireland. Bands also had a tendency to leave fellas behind, Joe recollected. In the days before mobile phones, the sight of stray band members waiting at their gates for a bandwagon to roll up was a familiar site on Irish country roads. 'So Ben wanted us all together. He was right, I suppose, but in other ways we were beginning to drift apart. Things were changing.'

7

Split happens

As their name suggests, The Drifters were not a band one would ever find standing still. For almost all of 1967, Joe and the band consolidated their gains at home and covered an awful lot of terrain, with their year-round ballroom blitz only interrupted by further touring in the USA and the UK. In addition, Joe's eagerly awaited debut album was recorded at various intervals during the year, and when he wasn't on the road or in the studio, he appeared on numerous television shows. Determined to remain on top in Ireland, he turned down another lucrative Las Vegas invitation. 'Practically all of that year was spent on the road,' Joe recalled, as he struggled to recall any particular moments that stood out. 'I don't know how we did it. We were almost too busy.'

Their next single, 'House with the Whitewashed Gable', which hit the top spot on 20 February, unseating 'I'm a Believer' by The Monkees, was a curious one. Initially a hit record for American pop singer, and future Barry Manilow producer, Ronnie 'Ron' Dante in 1966, the Neil Levenson-penned ditty was originally called '221 East Maple' and concerned a girl who lived not in a brightly painted Irish cottage in Mullingar, but a pretty little house in American suburbia. It was a happy, spring-in-your-step pop number, as far removed from 'Pretty Brown Eyes' as you could get, and its success surprised even Joe himself. 'It was quite an insane single to be honest,' he admitted. 'But people loved it.' The single went on to stay in the upper reaches of the Irish charts for well over three months, and it became a fixture in Joe's live sets for over thirty years.

Behind the happy-go-lucky 'dum-de-dums' of the song lies a complex and intricate arrangement. Jimmy Horan's bass is the lead instrument, whilst Des Doherty has fun with chiming bells, vibraphone and vibraharp, which augment his playful piano. About a minute in, the brass section flexes its muscle and the song is raised to even jauntier heights. Joe's guitar work, too, consists of more than just a few simple chords. The complex layers of the song and its decent production were highly unusual for recordings by an Irish band at the time, as state-of-the-art equipment was often lacking in Irish studios. If you wanted fancy sound effects and studio trickery, then you had to follow the lead of The Beatles and Pink Floyd and make Abbey Road in London your home for months on end. The band did go to the UK to record 'House with the Whitewashed Gable', and it shows.

Following its release, Joe and the band were playing almost every night, and the dances were not without their controversial moments, not least a St Patrick's night dance in Castlebar that nearly ended in a riot when over 3,000 angry locals found out that tickets for a raffle with a top prize of £10,000 had been sold as far afield as America and Britain.

During Lent in 1967, Joe and the band went on their second US tour. This time, the tour hit both coasts, and was even more memorable than their stateside sojourn two years earlier, with an eye-popping trip to San Francisco a highlight.

Previously they had played ballrooms and venues in Irish enclaves, but by 1967 their American promoter was thinking big, and they performed in theatres and rock music hangouts. The tour was heavily promoted, with radio ads and billboards proudly boasting Joe was 'direct from Ireland' and ready to rock. Although crowds at some of the shows were again predominantly Irish-American and prone to crying when Joe launched into nostalgic Irish numbers like 'Danny Boy', as the tour progressed he won over plenty of new fans.

For the country and western lovers in the band, the tour was a living dream. Seamus, Ben and Sid were like children in a sweetshop when they got to Nashville, Tennessee, for a two-day orgy of country and western gigs, record buying and an obligatory worship at the Grand Ole Opry. Joe, however, was much more enamoured by the thoughts of wearing a flower in his hair in San Francisco, and he rolled into the city at the height of flower power, with the Summer of Love in full swing. The outdoor 'Human Be-In' at Golden Gate Park in January that year had popularized hippie culture across the US, and hundreds of thousands were flocking to the city to 'turn on, tune in and drop out'. The Haight-Ashbury neighbourhood was where it all happened. On to this fulcrum of peace and love arrived nine innocent midlands' ambassadors whose clean-cut image, sober suits and neat haircuts were completely out of place amid the sea of long hair, tie-dye shirts and bell-bottomed pants. Joe ordered everyone to lose their ties and unbutton their shirts as they walked slowly around this alien world. Everything they had read in the papers proved to be true, and quite a bit of it was even more outlandish than they'd expected.

That night they played their show dressed more casually than usual, but they still stuck out like sore thumbs. Not only that, but only twelve people turned up to see them play, and six of these were Christian Brothers, although Joe would joke that they weren't. 'There were six nuns there,' he said. 'They told me they weren't in the habit of coming to this place!'

Years later, when Joe was playing Las Vegas he met a woman who claimed to have been among the audience that night. 'Joe, do you remember playing in San Francisco and there was nobody at the dance?' she asked him.

'Yes, of course I do,' he replied. 'Sure wasn't I there myself!'

Being a rocker, Joe brought the band to check out Bay Area legends Grateful Dead and Canned Heat, some of the antics of the free-lovin' crowd shocking the more conservative members of the band.

After they had completed more dates on the West Coast, where numbers picked up, the band made a diversion to Las Vegas, where Rocky Senas, who had brought the Royal Showband out and had tried to bring The Drifters out in 1965, had arranged an audition. The band only had two nights in town to impress the casino bosses, who were beginning to fall for the numerous charms an Irish band could bring. With a three-month contract on offer but with Driftermania showing no signs of abating back home, Joe questioned the need for an audition. In the end, they were offered the contract on the basis of their soundcheck. 'We went for the audition far earlier than we had to, and were deciding which numbers we would do,' Joe recalled. 'We were chopping and changing things and half-playing songs. So anyway, we decided we might do a run-through of "Danny Boy" to check the equipment. When we finished the song we heard this clapping from the back of the venue. We didn't know, but there was a lad sitting down the back. Turned out he was the fella we were supposed to be auditioning for.'

But the band decided to decline the attractive offer, as they would have had to cancel months of dates that had already been booked back home. 'At that time if you were cancelling dates you'd nearly be shot for it, especially if you were doing well, or if you were tied into particular dates with particular ball-room chains. You'd end up in court over it, which we did for other cancellations but we won't go into that!' Joe explained with a wink. The band would also have missed out on valuable recording time, and Joe reckoned that it might endanger the sanity of the band, as doing two shows a night every night for months on end in each other's company 'would definitely lead to a punch up!' The band were also worried they would not have been allowed to do their own thing. The promoter had suggested more of an Irish flavour in the show and wanted them to exploit their Irishness to the full. 'There would be no Aran sweaters, folk songs and "top o' the mornin' to ya" coming from us,' Joe says.

Moreover, playing Vegas at this time was not as glamorous as some thought. To most of those back home in the 1960s, Vegas conjured up images of gold-plated venues and glittering stage wear topped off with fillet steaks for breakfast followed by cocktails with Sinatra and the Rat Pack. However, although it all seemed very alluring when bands such as The Royal returned to Ireland in the winter with perma-tans and bulging wallets, these Irish bands were not the big stars over there that they appeared to be as they posed for photographs at Shannon Airport prior to their departure. Whilst the rooms they played were huge, the band would habitually be tucked into the corner of a lounge playing to a handful of drinkers on one side and huge embank-ments of slot machines on the other. As a further indignity, the speakers would be turned in towards the walls to minimize the impact on the concen-tration of gamblers. Even the dirtiest rural Irish ballroom, with a filthy dressing room, no running water and stale ham sandwiches, had more to offer a jobbing musician than playing to thousands of slot machines. And although Joe and the band were offered bigger 'real-life' venues and theatres, they decided to keep their focus on Ireland for the time being. They knew that Vegas would come calling again one day.

The short Vegas trip was not without its usual quota of high jinks, however. As country boys faced with slot machines, card tables and so much more, there was only one thing they could do. And so, over two days and one (long) night, they proceeded to lose every dime they had . . . with the exception of one man: Des Doherty. He managed to win an absolute fortune on the first night, taking to the casino like a true pro, and as the sun rose over Vegas, long after Joe and everyone else had gone to bed, Des smashed into Joe's bedroom, bright with success. He announced his good fortune by throwing hundreds of dollar bills into the air and, in true Las Vegas style, rolling around in the winnings on his bed. Over breakfast, the band were heartened to hear Des's announcement that he was not going to blow all the money back at the tables, but would instead hand it over to his wife, Audrey. However, as soon as backs were turned he was down in the casino again. Somehow, the winning streak continued, with the money piling up all around on their last day on the Strip, and finally, with a plane to catch, Des had to be literally dragged out and back to the airport.

Despite his growing fame, back home in Mullingar Joe still thought of himself as 'just an ordinary Joe' who liked a drink with his pals. His best friends at the time 'were people who knew nothing about the band business' and that was where he seemed to be most content. 'When I'm with the band it's OK, but on my nights off I like to be able to go out with the boys and have a good time.' Joe partied a bit, and his apartment in Mullingar was the scene of many a late night. Journalist and broadcaster Sam Smyth, at the time a young entrepreneur with an interest in the band game, remembers some wild nights there. In the summer of 1967, Sam travelled from Belfast to visit him, thinking he was about to enter a rock star's paradise, a gated mansion by the lakeside, but instead he found an ordinary man in an ordinary apartment with an eclectic group of pals. The two became great friends, raising hell together for years to come.

Most of the rest of the time when Joe was at home, he doted on his extended family. Both Ben and Paddy's families had grown and his sisters also had children, so he was never lonely or without the comfort of a family around him. It was also around this time that Joe got into golf in a big way. In fact most of the band took up the sport, and dates in towns where there was a golf club began to look very appealing.

But 1967 was not all fun and games, and that summer Joe had a big record coming out, 'Tar and Cement', a beautiful song that was brought to Joe's attention by members of Ireland's growing Italian community. In the 1950s and 1960s the gaps in Irish bellies were increasingly being filled by canny Italian restaurateurs, who had started to set up family restaurants nationwide. They were surprised that, aside from Wimpy Bars, few Irish had grasped the concept of fast food restaurants. The Irish market for high-speed, tasty and affordable food was ripe for exploitation, and it was Italian families who brought the basic American-style concept to the Irish market. They were blessed that there was one food item the Irish would never tire of: the potato. This had been the main staple of the Irish diet for generations, and the chance to eat a couple of spuds without washing, boiling, roasting or peeling them was seized by the Irish, who fell in love with the humble chip. The Italians fell for Joe's semi-classical continental voice in an equally big way. It lent itself to the European and Italian taste for big operatic vocalists, and, homesick for some of the great singers, the Italians found a kindred voice in Joe. Joe and the band were pleasantly surprised to find themselves invited to play a lot of Irish-Italian dances.

The Copolla family, who had set up restaurant businesses in Mullingar, were one of the first Italian families to actively support Joe. They became firm friends of Joe and the band, encouraging him to learn Italian and helping him to adopt a unique Mullingar version of the language. Joe learned Italian songs, and often blindsided pals with Italian sayings.

It was at an Italian dance where Joe met Mario Fusco, a budding Italian restaurateur who suggested that Joe should sing the beautiful Italian song 'Il Ragazzo Della Via Gluck'. The song had been a smash hit back home in Italy for Adriano Celentano, who wrote it after he had revisited his birthplace to find it utterly changed. Joe loved its resonance with Mullingar and the sentiments it evoked.

Joe sang the song in Italian first, before learning an English version translated for him by his Italian pals. When he got to the studio to cut it, he recorded both Italian and English versions. With its beautiful ballroom-silencing intro, the track was given an organic, earthy feel by the band, in keeping with its lyrics. The trademarks of The Drifters are all over the recording: the trademark piano stabs bring urgency to the pace, whilst the brass section's arrival in the last verse is uplifting, even though the lyrics are full of regret for the disappearing lilacs, meadows and children. The spirit of Adriano Celentano's original is fully intact, despite a few subtle changes to the lyrics.

The song would spend four months in the Irish charts, rising as high as number three in late July 1967. Joe felt it was an injustice that it didn't become his third number one in a row, but The Beatles put paid to his dreams with 'All You Need Is Love'. 'Tar and Cement' was a major departure for Joe, and further proof that, for him, the showband era was coming to an end. The soaring vocals and high production values were a sure sign that Joe had surpassed that era, and the Italian connection saw him develop a full-blown case of itchy feet. He was keen to make a break elsewhere, but so too were his band.

Joe Dolan opened 1968 with his most ambitious plan yet. Many celebrities in the elevated financial position Joe found himself in would consider making relatively safe investments – houses, cars, bars, businesses, or maybe even a share in a horse if they fancied a short-term flutter. But not Joe Dolan. Instead of investing in a horse, he would try to buy an entire racecourse.

Newbrook Racecourse on the outskirts of Mullingar had run into financial difficulties, and in 1961, after 109 years, it stopped hosting meetings. In the latter half of 1967, word got out that the entire racecourse – including a showground, rugby field and its very own private mini-station on the old Galway–Dublin railway line – was coming up for sale via private treaty with auctioneers optimistic that a hammer would fall when £20,000 was secured. Joe somehow convinced the rest of the band to open their wallets and pool together some of their available resources, as he had ambitious plans to turn the 128 acres into an entertainment playground – with horses – and was proposing to host outdoor music festivals (or jamborees as they were then known) on the site.

Joe was ahead of his time. From his trip to the West Coast of America he had seen first-hand the excitement music festivals brought to an area, and he wanted to bring some of that musical magic to Mullingar. Of course, it wasn't just about the music. Racing was also at the forefront of his mind. The racecourse had started to canter into decline when it had been left with only six race meetings a year a few years earlier. Joe wanted to double this to twelve, with plenty of side attractions to justify the increase. The railway station would be reopened, and new bars, restaurants and seating would attract a different sort of punter, one there for the craic and the social aspect of a day at the races as much as the actual racing itself. He also proposed building a multi-purpose ballroom-style building, which could be used for anything from concerts to conferences. Other sports organizations would be encouraged to set up camp inside the track, and any spare ground could be used for commercial developments. The band had planned to write songs about the track and use their fame to spread the word about Mullingar racing, which they feared might be lost for ever.

Although Joe would later admit that the plans had started out as a publicity stunt to plug his debut album, there was nothing fanciful about his notions for the track's redevelopment. The Drifters had done their sums and were pleasantly surprised by their calculations. Although the bank managers were not necessarily impressed, others were inspired to back Joe's ambitious bet.

The daring bid made the national newspapers and created a massive stir locally, with much of the Mullingar population getting behind it. Joe, Ben and Seamus met with the Irish Racing Board in Dublin to present their proposal. 'We thought they would fall over themselves,' Joe said. Sadly, the stakes were too high and the Racing Board was not convinced. There were not enough race meetings to go around. The company that owned the course were similarly unconvinced.

Joe and the band were prepared to invest £28,000 in the course, and the saga carried on for most of the year, but then the band started to experience a few internal problems, which cast a shadow over their plans. Although they never withdrew their interest, and promised to return with another proposal, other businessmen came in and bought the course. Regrettably for racing in Mullingar, they sold it on six months later to the Industrial Development Authority for a substantial profit. To add insult to injury, the site was not developed for many years, although it would eventually host a music festival when local music promoter Tommy McManus brought several big-name bands there. The unsuccessful bid would haunt Joe for some years, as he felt his proposal would have brought in millions to the local economy and could have helped put Mullingar on the map (although he did a good job of doing just that himself).

*

Joe's debut album, *The Answer to Everything*, was released in the summer of 1968. Few showbands dared to release albums like this at the time. It was the norm for showbands to contribute to compilation albums, and something like *The Answer to Everything* was practically unheard of, but Joe Dolan and The Drifters were not another Irish showband. They had broken the mould a long time before that. 'We were one of the only ones brave enough to do originals, to put them on EPs and on albums. At the time everyone was releasing singles to get radio plays, publicity, and almost to get one up on rival bands. It was a competitive thing. There were so many venues, so with singles you were just trying to put yourself that little bit higher in the public's minds. We always wanted to aim a little higher!' Joe said with a laugh.

When you listen to the debut now, it almost sounds like a modern boy-band album – a mix of covers, some well known and others obscure, and plenty of originals. Four of the album's twelve tracks were written by Tommy Swarbrigg, another two were written especially for Joe, whilst the remainder were specially sourced covers. Producer Gay McKeon had managed to entice the RTÉ Light Orchestra to record strings for a re-recorded version of the debut single and a soaring poetic take on 'Unchained Melody' among others. Ben was captured on disc, lending his dulcet tones to the George Jones song 'World of Forgotten People'; Jimmy Horan also sang a number, 'Some Kinda Fun'; and Tommy Swarbrigg sang a few.

The iconic cover image was taken at Belvedere House on the shores of Lough Ennell, then owned by Joe's friend and great Westmeath bon viveur Rex Beaumont. Joe loved Beaumont's flamboyance and his larger-than-life character, and the two became great friends from the second they met. Indeed, when Joe hosted a RTÉ chat show in the 1980s he almost enticed Rex to appear on it. Rex was a great personal friend of Mick Jagger and Marianne Faithfull, and the showbiz couple visited him and Joe in his home by the lake on several occasions.

The strains of keeping the band together manifested themselves as they promoted the album, but whispers of dissatisfaction in the ranks became a chorus of discontent just after the band released their ninth Top Ten hit in a row, 'Love of the Common People'. Within a few weeks of the track breaking into the charts, the band broke up.

They went out with a great track. The band's growing musical maturity had blossomed into full-blown adulthood, and this top-class recording stood out from the common herd; the song was as far removed from the traditional showband style as you could get. It had been first recorded by country and western outlaw Waylon Jennings for an album of the same name in 1967, and Joe broke his country music 'ban' to really make this song of dreams, love and family pride his own. He immediately identified with the song's lyrics and sentiment, and went all out to put his stamp on the track. His vocal is a magnificent example of his range, rising from a gentle start to a climactic crescendo. Remembering the session, Joe said he 'knew it was a risky song to do', but it was a great vehicle for his voice, as it just kept going up, and up and up. Yet when asked how he staggered his vocals, he would shrug his shoulders: 'I just sang it as I normally sang.'

It was thanks to Seamus's ear for a classic song that Joe became the first of many artists to cover it. Over the years, acts as diverse as Elton John, Pat Boone, John Denver, Paul Young, Stiff Little Fingers, Indigo Girls, The Everly Brothers and several reggae artists have recorded it, whilst Bruce Springsteen performed it on his *Seeger Sessions* World Tour of 2006. Each has done it differently, with few emulating Joe's soaring take.

The Drifters were at the peak of their powers, with Jimmy Horan really shining, but soon after the record's release they informed Joe that they did not want to continue with him any more. A number of reasons have been given for the split of the country's biggest band, ranging from musical differences to medical reasons to money. The cooperative structure of the band had been causing unease for some time – some members seeing it as anything but cooperative – and it was difficult to agree on certain things. 'As a co-op it was difficult to make a decision,' Joe said. 'Even when it came to recording new records, what someone thought was a great idea, someone else saw as a terrible idea. Others wanted to do other things but it was hard to adapt. It limited a lot of bands and with us, it all blew up one day.'

The Drifters' cooperative structure was based on a shareholder model, initially agreed in 1964, with each band member entitled to a share. However, Joe and Ben had the controlling shares, owning two each, whilst each of the Drifters and the manager held a share each. This agreement held firm until two years of almost constant successes led to calls for a change. 'Little jibes and some asides had begun to appear again throughout 1968,' Ben says. Joe did not necessarily notice them, he reckons, because he was just too happy with how things were going. 'It was one big happy family, so I guess he didn't see it coming, or maybe he was blindsided by it all. If there was a bad night, some of the lads would be going on about it saying they could have done it differently. A bad night might have affected Joe inside, but he never ran down a venue, a hall or a crowd. I suppose that's what made him a great artist, he was built in a way that things like that didn't affect him, you know? He put all his effort into the work instead of worrying about the business. But some of the rest of the lads wanted to be more involved in the business, whilst a few others wanted out altogether.'

Some of the band wanted a change in the structure, and they were also beginning to tire of the treadmill of gigs they were on, as Joe was. They felt other musical avenues were there to be explored. They made their feelings known to Joe, Ben and Seamus at a dramatic showdown at the Dun Mhuire Hall in Wexford in July 1968.

In the late 1960s, bands were splitting up all over the place, whilst other bands were replacing more experienced members with more youthful stock in a bid to prolong their shelf life. 'Lads were being sacked and poached with equal measure all the time,' Ben says. 'The first thing I thought when the lads came in was that they wanted to get rid of me, as I was older than the rest of them. I thought I was [going] back to carpentry.' The lads said they wanted a chat. 'Now, I was told as a young fella that when a lad wanted "a chat" you had to keep your hand tight in your pocket as that's what they were going for,' Ben recalls.

At the time, it was impossible to say what the band was earning in an average week, as there was no such thing as an *average* week. Some weeks, earnings could be as much as £500 a week, but they could be as low as £80 – not that that was low, as the average industrial wage was about £30 a week. With Joe and The Drifters at the very top of the show-business pile, they all wanted an equal footing. Ben reckoned there was only one available share – and that was one of his. Joe was the figurehead of the band, the lead vocalist and the one attracting all the attention, so there was no question of him relinquishing a share. 'The only thing they could fight over was one share. They couldn't fight over two shares for Joe because at the very least he was worth two shares. The only thing was my one share. So I said, "Well, lads, you're fighting over one share and when it's divided between you all it doesn't amount to much." They all had a bit to say and each man stood up and said

Joe's parents, Ellen and Patrick.

Joe and a friend stand outside his home at Grange Cottages, just outside Mullingar.

Ben astride his first big purchase, a noisy motorbike upon which he and Joe travelled the length and breadth of the county in searc of music. In the background is their cousin Frank Gavigan, about to be 'kidnapped' for another impromptu music session.

Paddy Dolan's late wife Caroline (pictured here with Joe and baby Maeve). When Joe was beginning to miss work due to his late nights on the road with his early groups, she and Paddy took him under their wing. She also handled some of The Drifters' early bookings.

Joe loved his extended family, and he was godfather to several children. He is pictured here with god-daughter and niece Kathleen, March 1961.

n early photograph of Joe and Ben Dolan in action on a tiny parish hall stage.

The perfect clean-cut young singer, in the early 1960s.

e on one of his first photo shoots, on a boat on his beloved Lough Owel in 1962.

ven early in his career Joe was adored by his fans, and would sign autographs for hours ter shows.

To promote the debut single 'The Answer to Everything' Ben carved a large wooden 'record' th[a]
he and Joe hauled around the country. The wooden disc (Ben's last carpentry job) would soon [b]
swapped for golden discs when it became the first of many hits for Joe. In a career that saw hi[m]
rack up hits in five decades, Joe spent a combined total of five years in the Irish singles charts.

Bandwagons like this early Driftersmobile were all the rage during the showband era. The band
is pictured somewhere in rural Westmeath.

An image from a Christmas card for the first incarnation of The Drifters – one of the printing jobs the young Joe Dolan created 'on the sly' at the offices of the *Westmeath Examiner.*

he second incarnation of The Drifters. From left: Jimmy Horan, Noel Kirby, Joe Dolan, Sean onnolly, Eddie Deehy, Ben Dolan and Des Doherty.

he Drifters, mark 3, the classic line-up. From left: Jimmy Horan, Joe, Ben Dolan, Sid Aughey, mmy Swarbrigg, Des Doherty and Joey Gilheaney.

WHAT IS

DRIFTERMANIA?

DANCERS WHO AS A RULE ARE COOL ARE
REACTING IN WAYS THAT ARE MOST PECULIAR
IN BALLROOMS WHERE THE DRIFTERS APPEAR
FRENZIED THOUSANDS CLAP AND CHEER
THEN OF COURSE YOU PROBABLY KNOW
EVERYONE IS WILD ABOUT JOE
REQUESTS FOR HIS RECORDS ARE MADE EVERY DAY
MORNING AND NIGHT YOU CAN HEAR THEM BEING PLAYED
AND THE BAND'S POPULARITY JUST KEEPS ON GROWING
NOBODY KNOWS HOW FAR THIS THING IS GOING
IT'S SPREADING SO FAST THAT SOMETIME QUITE SOON
A DRIFTERMANIACS' CLUB WILL START ON THE MOON.

The country was gripped by 'Driftermania' for much of the 1960s, with nearly all of the fans'
attention focused on Joe.

Joe was the best man at the wedding of his manager, Seamus Casey, to Doreen McCormack in September 1966. Later that day the Irish charts would reveal that he had bagged his first number one.

Joe dated Mullingar woman Carmel Barrett (*far right*) for much of the 1960s. They are pictured here with Seamus and Doreen Casey.

The 'tug-of-war' publicity shot of The Drifters in 1963 would prove sadly apt when band members decided to go their separate ways.

FAMOUS SHOWBAND BREAKS UP

Evening Press reporter

THE showband scene was surprised today at the news of the breaking-up of the Drifters Showband, from Mullingar, which, with singer Joe Dolan, has been one of Ireland's top three bands for the past five years.

Five members of the band have decided to quit, leaving just lead singer Dolan (25), his brother Ben, the leader, and manager Seamus Casey. The bombshell came after the band had played at a dance in Mallow last night, when Seamus Casey announced that because of a difference of ... "band policy"...they had decided to go their separate ways.

The split was completely un- expected, as the Drifters had been going from strength to strength, and were due to release their first L.P. record in a month's time.

Mr. Ben Casey, however, said today that the row had been brewing for "quite a while, for the past few months." He said: "There was a difference of opinion between the five who are leaving and the three of us on band policy, such as what type of numbers to play."

Amicable

"We came to a decision last night that it was no use carry- ing on and so we decided to split up. The break-up was very amicable, and both ourselves and the other five are going to start their own bands."

The five are Tommy Swar- brigg, Jim Horan, Des Doherty, Joey Gilheany and Sid Aughey.

Mr. Casey said it was hoped that a new Drifters band would be on the road again in a month's time, and it would start looking for new members on Monday. The band plays its last date in the Casino in Castle- ... tonight, and one last Dublin date in the Arcadia in Bray tonight, he said.

Already £600 has been spent on recording their first L.P. to be called "The Answer to Everything," and Mr. Casey said that it would be definitely released.

Holiday

The band, which has just come back from a two-weeks Majorca holiday, has undertaken a 13-weeks radio series, and the first programme is being transmitted on Monday night. Mr. Casey said they would have a meeting of the whole band on Monday to see what they would do with the other 12 weeks.

The Drifters have been to- gether for six years, and their meteoric rise to stardom began five years ago with the record "The Answer to Everything." This was followed by a string of hits, which included "My Own Peculiar Way," "Pretty Brown Eyes," "Tar and Cement," and their most recent one, "Love of the Common People."

"It has been a really great run since we made our first record," said Mr. C...

The split shocked the nation and was front-page news on all the national papers.

New Drifters, new suits. The post-split Drifters line-up.

'Driftermania is back,' pronounced the ads for the new band's early gigs. The ads proved prophetic as Joe was hauled into the audience on his very first night back onstage.

Joe relaxes by the pool just prior to the release of 'Make Me an Island' in April 1969. This would be the last holiday he would enjoy in years, as the single made him a star around the world.

in Britain

britain's top ten

1 (1) HONKY TONK WOMEN—Rolling Stones
2 (3) SAVED BY THE BELL—Robin Gibb
3 (7) MAKE ME AN ISLAND—Joe Dolan
4 (2) GIVE PEACE A CHANCE—
       Plastic Ono Band
5 (6) MY CHERIE 'AMOUR—Stevie Wonder
6 (4) GOODNIGHT MIDNIGHT—
       Clodagh Rodgers
7 (8) CONVERSATIONS—Cilla Black
8 (—) EARLY IN THE MORNING—Vanity Fair
9 (—) BRINGING ON BACK THE GOOD TIMES
       —Love Affair
10 (—) WET DREAM—Max Romeo
By arrangement with the Record Retailer to be played
on the B.B.C. this Sunday.

Tony Prince (Luxembourg Disc Jockey)
presenting "Singer of The Year Award".

Top Radio Luxembourg DJ Tony Prince presents Joe with its Singer of the Year award in 1969. 'Make Me an Island' had some illustrious company at the top of the UK charts.

immy Saville, one of the biggest television personalities of the time, tries to rescue Joe from the
lutches of a rabid audience.

he band in the mid 1970s looking very happy and relaxed.

Adoring fans reach
out to their hero.

Joe signs an autograph
after a concert appearance.

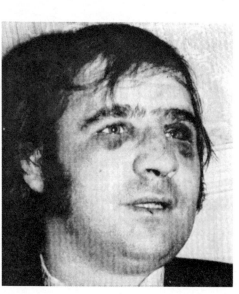

Joe pictured after his savage
beating in Liverpool in 1970.

relaxed Joe takes a break from the rigours of his hectic 1970s schedule.

...e was not one to align himself to any political cause; he was happy to leave that kind of work
...Bono and Bob Geldof. However, he did break a vow not to get political when he marched
...support of an anti-paid parking in his native Mullingar. Leading the march is one of Joe's
...hoolfriends, Des Walsh.

A whole new audience discovers Joe in the 1990s, when he cements his place in the annals of Irish music with a series of hugely successful albums for EMI and on his own label.

their bit,' Ben says. 'I said, "I don't know, lads, I can't do it." There was no sense in it, but they went on with it, and I sensed there was more to it.'

He reckoned there was a touch of jealousy and disappointment in the ranks with the amount of attention focused on Joe. Tracks such as 'Tar and Cement', 'Love of the Common People' and 'Unchained Melody' had shown that the band could operate on a different musical plane from other showbands. But they were still playing to showband crowds in showband-style venues and they wanted to start on a clean slate. Ben admits to getting 'horse thick' as he realized it was nearly all over. 'I nearly got a heart attack I was that thick, but I decided not to say anything bad. But I was really churning inside . . .'

He privately shed a tear at the time, and forty years on, another tear was shed as he remembered how it all ended. There are a few regrets there too. 'I took it to heart that they weren't happy as every fella was well looked after. We always had everything that was needed; we made sure we had it.'

Joe also tried to keep calm in the midst of the 'showdown', but he remembers it being very uncomfortable. He said, 'The whole thing just blew up. It was bad.' He was equally hurt and shocked that it came to a make-or-break decision. 'I was very pally with them all. We were always the best of friends, we played golf together, we partied together, we did everything together, and then this happened.'

Having said their piece and made their demands, The Drifters left, and Joe and Ben were left sitting facing each other, their band teetering on the brink of its very existence.

'What do you think?' Ben asked his younger brother.

'Whatever you want to do is OK with me,' Joe replied.

Joe's calmness confused Ben even more. 'I began to think to myself, will Joe stay with me, or will he go with the lads? So I asked him.'

'I'm staying with you, what the fuck is wrong with you?' Joe is said to have told his elder brother. 'Isn't that the way it's always been?'

Attempts were then made to reason with the five unhappy members. Seamus realized something special was around the corner if the band continued to focus on progressive material, but he couldn't argue with their desire for a fresh start.

Even though they had originally planned to stay over in Wexford that night, Ben and Seamus decided they would head home to Mullingar. Ben asked Joe if he wanted to go home too, and he remembers being surprised at his answer. 'At first I couldn't believe it. "No, I don't want to go home. Why should I go home?" Joe said to me. "I've no problem with the lads." Joe didn't take it to heart, which, looking back, was him all over. He would keep his cool, and stay friendly with you no matter what.'

Ever-dependable stage manager and roadie John Delamere, who had recently joined them, drove the shocked pair home. En route Ben asked Seamus what he thought about the situation, and Seamus told him the words he wanted to hear: 'I'm staying with you anyway.'

'So I thought, we have management, we have a lead singer, and we have almost the best sax player in the world. We're not too bad ... Then, out of the blue, John Delamere said, "I'm staying with you too," so I thought, well, we're going to carry on now. It was awful, but that was how it had to be,' Ben said.

Ben and Seamus talked all the way home to Mullingar, and all the way from Mullingar to Mallow in Cork the next night. As they arrived in the Rebel County, any thoughts of a rebellion were dismissed. Their minds were united. 'If we had agreed a settlement, it would only have been a matter of time until it all started again. Seamus and I decided, if it's over it's over.'

Unknown to the management, Joe Healy and a caucus of good friends and cohorts, including the legendary Mullingar figure Tommy Roche (aka Roche T) and Frank 'Twiggy' Daly, had travelled ahead of them to Mallow in a last-ditch attempt to prevent the band from splitting. The unofficial delegation met separately with The Drifters and with Joe, but reconciliation could not be achieved.

Everyone assembled at the bandwagon, and Ben remembers holding the door and asking the band, 'Well, lads. Did you make your mind up what you're going to do?'

The band members said they had come to a conclusion, that if they did not get what they were looking for, then they were leaving.

Ben replied, 'Well, you can take it that you're leaving ...'

Amicably, they agreed it would be for the best to split the band. Seamus rang the national newspapers and told them the band was splitting after three more shows: Mallow, Bray and Castlerea.

The story appeared in every newspaper on Saturday 3 July and almost all of Sunday's, with Saturday's *Evening Press* and *Evening Herald* both running it as their lead story. It was also front-page news on the *Irish Independent* and the *Cork Examiner*, and was all over television and the radio. 'Even though a lot of bands were breaking up or shedding members at the time – The Miami and The Royal both had their differences – word that this famous band were breaking up was a huge news story, bigger than even we expected,' Seamus remembers. Looking back, he recalls only the decision of Take That to split in the 1990s garnering as much front-page coverage. The story also dominated the entertainment and social columns of the midweek regional papers.

Tears flowed into cornflakes bowls all over the country on Saturday morning as Joe Dolan fans learned that their favourite band was breaking up. In the best show-business tradition, the reasons behind the break-up were kept carefully concealed from the fans behind the euphemistic music-industry term 'musical differences'. 'When you were too long together,' Seamus says, 'we used to always say the thing that happened was "musical differences". It's not, it never is. It's just that people get fed up with each other and it gets to a point where they just can't work together. It's as simple as that.'

The final shows were absolutely crammed. Over 4,000 fans turned up each night to bid an emotional farewell to a much-loved band, who, after an unhappy gig in Mallow, tried to rise to the occasion for the last two shows. The Arcadia in Bray, scene of some of the most memorable gigs in Ireland in the 1960s, had never seen a night like it. Thousands were turned away at the doors as people flooded in from all over the country to bid a tearful farewell. 'There was consternation in the place and it was jammed to the doors,' Joe revealed. 'There were women crying, fellas crying, everyone on the floor was crying and it was stuffed to the doors.'

Before the final dance in Castlerea, there had not been much in the way of chat between the band beforehand, and one thing that still hurts many of those involved was that there was no big emotional farewell, either onstage or off. 'It was totally us and them,' remembers Ben with sadness. 'Even onstage that night the thrill had gone, but we got through it.'

'The atmosphere in the band was terrible that night,' Joe observed. 'We worked, fair play, the lads played what they had to play. I couldn't . . . I like to refer to the band all the time when I'm working. I'll have a bit of banter with the drummer or whoever. I'll send him up, and he'll send me up and all that sort of stuff; but not that night. There was none of that. You'd look over at one of the lads and he would look somewhere else.' Joe said later that he just got on with the job. 'I was feeling rotten really but I had a job to do and I went out and did it, like I always did. Big crowd, small crowd, it never mattered to me.'

They played well enough, Seamus recalls. Joe sang the first couple of songs of the evening, with Ben calling the next set, as he had done for the last eight years. And he called the next one, and the next one, and the next one after that. Anger was to rear its head momentarily when one of the lads walked across the stage to say to Ben, in earshot of the microphone, that other lads in the band sang as well. Joe had been singing the lion's share of songs that night. 'They'll have loads of time next week to sing!' Ben is alleged to have joked back.

Ben felt he was doing the right thing in pushing Joe throughout the show. 'We nearly had Joe hoarse with the amount of songs we had him sing that night,' he recalled. 'We told the crowd that we were breaking up and that we were starting our own band, that we would be back, then some of the other boys took the microphone to reveal their plans.' Ben paid everyone their 'shares' of the spoils from the money on the door, and a couple of halcyon years at the top came to a sad and abrupt end.

Looking back on the split and assessing Joe's feelings at the time, Seamus reveals that Joe would have accepted the boys back, if a deal could have been struck.

'Strangely enough, he would have kept working with them. But Joe passed no remarks. He just went on ahead as if it had never happened,' he says. 'They were thinking and saying we weren't as popular as we were, but that was a natural progression as bands did not have the pulling power they once had. All bands like us were beginning to suffer at the box office, but we had to keep doing these gigs as the gigs were paying for the records and there were few other places where you could make money to keep progressing the recordings.'

Seamus still has some regrets, but he remembers that there *were* genuine musical differences. 'We were progressing nicely, but what we have to remember is that we were called Joe Dolan and The Drifters, and as much as we wanted and encouraged everyone to write and sing, to the people at the concerts it was all about Joe. And I guess when you were as talented as some of the lads were, it was hard to take in that you were just a Drifter.'

Tommy Swarbrigg had proved to be the most musically savvy, and Joe says he had always known Tommy would one day leave to lead his own band. 'Tommy was a great arranger, a really good addition to a band in getting people playing to their strengths,' he said. 'He knew what would sound well, and he could hear pieces and runs that others couldn't hear. We were devastated to see him go, but that was show business.'

Speaking about the split for the first time, Tommy denies that money ever came into it on his part. He says the seeds of the split were sown not in a darkened corner of a dressing room, but rather in a hospital. For several months leading up to the split, Tommy's trumpet playing had been suffering, and he was finding it increasingly difficult and painful to play because of a callus on his upper lip. A specialist had told him that sadly his trumpet playing days were coming to an end, and Tommy and his brother Jimmy, who had been in the UK, had been talking for some time about forming a harmony-led vocal outfit, akin to Simon and Garfunkel. The other members of The Drifters had also decided they wanted to pursue new musical challenges, and that the five would eventually leave as one.

'My brother and I decided we would form a band, and that I would leave The Drifters. I honestly wasn't really that interested in money at that age [he was twenty-two]. There were frictions in the band about money, among some of the older guys, but all I wanted at the time was money for me car, for birds and for a good time. I was young and having fun. I was finished as a trumpet player so I was leaving anyway. My only escape was to become a singer/songwriter, and the only way to do that was to get out of The Drifters. I knew I wasn't going to be the lead singer. No one could compete with Joe. I was about to give my notice when the boys said they would leave with me.'

Tommy does not remember the final gigs as being particularly acrimonious. 'To me it just felt as if we'd all moved on. Joe was the star. If anything, we were taking a much bigger chance in leaving as we had no idea how it was going to go for us.'

The lads decided to reassemble as The Times. It was not long, however, before some started to have second thoughts. 'We were only back in Mullingar when I got a phone call from two of the lads,' Ben revealed. They wanted back in. Ben was faced with a dilemma, and admits today that if he had handled it differently, things could have taken a different path.

'I went down to see them, and we talked for a while, but we couldn't reach an agreement,' Ben said. The crux of the matter was whether they would come back on a wage, or a share. There was a pang of regret as Ben remembered the talks, but the show was officially over. There was never going to be a show like an original Drifters show again, but there would be plenty of Joe shows.

Years later, Joe said that in many ways the split was 'for the best' for both bands. 'When you were working six nights a week and constantly in each other's faces, friction does appear and it would probably have gotten worse for us.' And despite the suddenness of the break-up, the fall-out was not as bad as many thought it would be. There was a friendly rivalry at first between the two outfits, and a couple of clandestine efforts to lure one or two members back into the fold, but Joe always treated all the lads as his friends – and played golf with quite a few of them – and within a few days of the split everyone was back on speaking terms. They would reunite frequently and spend many a late night reminiscing on those golden olden days when Driftermania swept the land.

In fact, the split could not have come at a better time for Joe Dolan. Just after he was seemingly cast adrift on his own island, he received a phone call concerning a certain island that was being made in a London recording studio. As it turned out, it was an island that would only accommodate one man . . .

8
The new Drifters

For fans of Joe and the band, the split was a cruel and sad blow. The postmen sighed with the weight of correspondence arriving in Mullingar and sent to newspapers and magazines, and fans vented their sorrow in public. 'The break-up of The Drifters seems to me the saddest thing in Irish show business,' wrote a fan, Kay Jordan from Rathfarnham, in an August edition of *Spotlight*. 'Seven of the nicest personalities on the scene combined to make The Drifters the most popular band on the road. Individually they had tremendous talent and versatility – these assets moulded into a unit producing a show always

JOE DOLAN

worth travelling to see and hear. I could not begin to count how many times I have seen them in action and never once was I disappointed.'

Joe, his brother and his manager needed to put together a new band, and quickly. One of the first things Joe told them was that he was not going to play the guitar any more. 'It was holding me back. I felt chained down to the knee with the guitar,' he recalled in an interview with a Sunday newspaper. 'This was bad news for Ben as it meant another mouth to feed!'

Seamus was overjoyed with Joe's decision; however, he remembers Ben's initial dismay. 'But with Joe, a four-word sentence or remark was an order. There would be no discussion; Joe just said it and that was it.'

The only trouble was that they had just four weeks to find the other band members. A number of shows were cancelled, but other bookings that had been made long in advance were held by promoters and venue owners who were confident the Mullingar men would bounce back.

It was almost a given that Mullingar man Pat Hoey, a friend of Joe's, would join on bass. He came into the fold almost immediately, handing in his notice with The Swingtime Aces in Galway. A giant of a man in more ways than one, Pat's unique bass-playing style (he played it almost vertically) had marked him out as one to watch, and he didn't disappoint. Joe knew of a drummer who had caught his ear in the past, and he went over to Longford to hear the sticks man play with the band he was in at the time. Ironically, guitarist Sean Kenny, from Boyle, County Roscommon, was in the same band. Sean didn't make it into the Drifters' line-up that time, but he would in the future. In fact, he would have to wait until 2005 for Joe to tell him to tog out, but he claims the wait was worth it. The breakaway Drifters also had their eye on the talented six-stringer, and they managed to entice him into their new Times band, despite being warned by his manager – who owned several ballrooms – that if they did they would never play for him again.

Joe realized that shuffling around the country in search of members was not the best way of doing business, especially as he was so recognizable. He also did not want to poach members directly from other bands, and decided instead to hold open auditions. He expected a few dozen at most to turn up for the auditions in Dublin's Ierne Ballroom, as the band name wasn't mentioned in the ad, but word got out and they were besieged by wannabe Drifters – close to 300 turned up. There were musicians, wannabe musicians, singers pretending to be musicians, painters covered in paint, a fella in a chef's jacket and mechanics in their work clothes, their dirty oil-coated hands clutching a pair of sticks in the hope of bagging the drummer's stool (and quite possibly a kit). 'They were all kinds of everything, some of them were all over the place!' Joe recalled.

Armed with notebooks, pens and their selection criteria, Seamus and Sean Connolly started the laborious process of taking down the details of each hopeful. Joe, who was meant to be in charge of finding a rhythm section, instead signed a few autographs and chatted to the hopefuls, whilst Ben tried to remain cool in his dual role as musical director and brass-section selector. Eventually, each musician auditioned onstage.

Among the first men to perform was rising beat-group star Maurice Walsh. A real true-blue Dub, he oozed confidence, and his personality impressed the boys. Joe got on with Maurice straight away, and he asked the long-haired Dubliner to keep drumming for the remainder of the auditions that morning. Maurice also made an impression on Ben, but in an altogether different way, as the nineteen-year-old insisted on calling Ben 'Paddy' from the off, despite Ben's constant corrections. (To the inner-city man, everyone from the country was called Paddy.) Maurice was an unusual man to find behind a kit, as although he had originally been the drummer with Dublin beat group The Bye-Laws, he was now their lead singer, and they had built up a good following in the capital. However, with Joe's band needing new direction, the energetic and creatively minded musician was the perfect choice to have in the engine room alongside the equally flamboyant and skilful Pat Hoey.

The day dragged on and on, and few others made a significant impact. 'The auditions were a bit of a nightmare to be honest,' Joe would reveal. 'A lot of the musicians who turned up simply didn't make the grade.' As a succession of poor musicians took to the stage, it became obvious that stricter criteria should have been put in place.

However, a shining light smashed through the gloom when 21-year-old Cork man Gordon Coleman strapped on a guitar. Gordon had been playing and singing across the Channel and at home for many years, and his stage experience, coupled with his dexterous playing and knowledge of the material, made him a perfect and almost immediate fit. He was soon christened 'Corky'.

One man who didn't make the audition but who desperately wanted to join was Red Hurley, who was playing drums in a showband at the time. Red requested a late audition, but was told that Joe and Ben had already settled on Maurice Walsh.

At the end of an arduous day, there were still some key positions to be filled, but Joe was happy with his two finds. Both Gordon and Maurice were taken aside and told to come down to Mullingar the following weekend so Joe and Ben could have a closer look at them.

A few days later, Maurice Walsh nervously entered the band's rehearsal room, at that time set up at the Horizon Ballroom on the outskirts of Mullingar. He found only Ben in the venue, and after they had exchanged formalities and pleasantries, Maurice uttered the immortal line, 'Paddy [meaning Ben], Seamus said you wanted to have a look at me. Do I have to take off all me clothes?' Ben was aghast. 'I didn't know where to fucking look. The man was mad!'

Meanwhile, in the days leading up to that first official rehearsal, some good fortune was to fall Joe's way. Little had he realized, when he packed the car for the Ierne Ballroom a few days earlier, that right under his nose were two of the most talented brass players around.

Nineteen-year-old Seamus Shannon, from neighbouring Roscommon, arrived, quite literally, on Ben Dolan's doorstep. Shannon was a talented traditional musician and a champion accordion player with the Gallowglass Céilí Band. He had won three Connaught Fleadh Cheoil titles in a row, as well as an All-Ireland award. The youngster had also been a regular (again on the accordion) in cabaret, entertaining tourists at the Old Shieling Hotel in Raheny, County Dublin. However, this night he arrived armed with a trombone and told Ben, rather off-handedly, that he did some trombone work and that it was his second instrument. At first Ben didn't know what to think, and he brought young Seamus into the house. Ben had a long-player from The Capitol close to hand, and he asked Seamus to blow along to it. Ben went to get one of his own saxophones to see if they could play together, but Shannon literally blew him away instantly. 'I'm after landing on me feet here!' Ben thought as he rang Joe to tell him the good news. Joe was thrilled, and said he would love to hear Shannon.

As they waited for Joe to appear, Shannon asked if Ben wanted to hear him play the accordion. Many bands thought the accordion was old hat, but the Dolans had always had a soft spot for it and Ben couldn't resist the temptation to hear an award-winner perform. Shannon brought his five-row button-key accordion out of the car and started to play, his notes evoking fond memories of Grange for Ben, where the traditional music of Frank Gavigan and other assorted players used to fill the house. If Shannon hadn't done enough to convince Ben he was the right man for the job, then he was surely in after this. 'The hairs stood on the back of my neck. It was magnificent,' Ben recalls. 'So I rang Joe again, and roared at him to come quick! "He plays the accordion?" Joe said. "Get him in!"'

Another nineteen-year-old, organist Ciaran McDonnell, was next to join. Ciaran came from Strabane, the spiritual home of Irish showbands, and so the young man's formative years as a musician had been soundtracked by the great Clipper Carlton – although, like Joe, Ciaran was now keen to move away from the showband era. A highly talented organist and pianist from a young age, the quiet Northern Irish man had been recommended to Joe by friends involved in bands up north. Ciaran came down to Mullingar for an audition, and surprised all concerned with his knowledge of Joe's material and his talent.

The arrival of Frankie McDonald – the last man to join the new-look band – was a pivotal moment in Joe Dolan's career. At twenty-two, Frankie was one of the most gifted musicians and finest trumpet players in the country, and had been a fan of the band for quite some time when he saw the headline 'DRIFTERS SPLIT' splashed across the front page of a newspaper in June. He made a few phone calls to see if there was an opening for him – although he needn't have worried, as a few calls had been made in the opposite direction too, and despite Joe's initial plea not to poach members from other bands, a movement was underway to entice the Clones-born Athlone man to Mullingar. There was a slight problem, however. Even though he was playing trumpet with Athlone band Syd and The Saints, and with Kieran Kelly (who was also his father-in-law), Frankie was still a member of the Western Command Army No. 4 band, and he would have to be bought out of the armed forces if he wanted a career as a professional Drifter.

Frankie and his pal Liam Meade had been with the Army School of Music and then the Western Command Band, the best marching band in the army, since they were kids. They were stationed as part of a UN force in Cyprus for most of 1965, but as non-combatant members of the army, their non-band duties were menial. Bored, they formed a splinter group called The Irish Rovers, to entertain themselves and keep up morale among their fellow troops. It was not long before forces from other countries started to book them for gigs. One such booking was for the Klondike Day celebrations at the Canadian forces army base (the Irish Army was given a lorry load of soup in exchange). The boys played the popular Dixieland stuff and, notably, some songs that were hot back home for a young singer by the name of Joe Dolan.

Frankie had been a fan of Joe's for quite a while. 'I was a big Joe Dolan fan. In 1962 and 1963 I played with a band on the same circuit as them; I saw them play in the Royal Hoey Hotel before they had any hit records, and I always remember the room gasping when, about halfway through, Joe took off his guitar and did an Elvis set. Now I'm a big Elvis fan, I always was, and I just couldn't believe how good he was. All of a sudden I picked him out as the guy in the band, the star in the making. He just blew me away. The band had this magic about them, they were always enthusiastic about what they were doing and they were full of beans onstage. They were definitely going for it. There was no holding back, and I knew then that they were going to be *the* band.'

The fast-rising popularity of The Drifters was brought home to Frankie when he played with Eamon Robinson and The Central Seven in Kilcormack, County Offaly, in Christmas 1963: 'It was a big gig for us as it was more upmarket, and the venue could hold around about a thousand. We were used to playing to 200 or so, maybe 300 if it was a big social. We had the same type of gear as Joe and The Drifters, and were doing that little circuit for around the same money. It was a great night and we went down very well, so much so that the owner of the hall came up onstage afterwards and grabbed the microphone. He talked to the crowd just as we finished our last number, and said, "Ladies and gentlemen, do you want more?" There was a big roar, and we were made up. We thought we were The Rolling Stones or someone. It was the pinnacle of our career. "In three weeks' time I have a free Sunday night," the owner continued. "I'd love to bring this band back." There was another big cheer. "I know there are a few bands that go down very well here, and there's a band called The Drifters. So it's your decision. I can bring back The Central Seven, or The Drifters. Who do you want?" And the crowd roared, "The Drifters!" We just put our heads down, turned off the equipment and went off home with our tails between our legs.'

Seamus and John Delamere had heard Frankie play before and were sure he would be a good addition, but Joe and Ben wanted to see him in action, so they launched what was to be a botched attempt to covertly see him play with Kieran Kelly's band (which also featured Brendan Shine) at a festival marquee in Rhode, County Offaly. Frankie was on fire that night – 'Man, it was beautiful,' Joe remarked. 'I'd never heard anything like it' – and outside the tent (where the sound was invariably better) they decided there and then that he was in. It looked like they had got away with their poaching mission when Ben bumped into Kieran Kelly and they were rumbled.

However, they rang Frankie the next day and arranged to meet him incognito in Ballymore, a tiny country village between Mullingar and Athlone. Frankie said he was interested, and after they had arranged the transfer fee of £300 to buy Frankie out of the army, Frankie was in.

Joe and Frankie clicked immediately. The Clones man had a twinkle in his eye that matched Joe's, and they had a lot in common musically too. 'I was brought up in poor times, as Joe and everybody else were,' Frankie recalled as he looked back on his Monaghan upbringing. 'That was the way it was. My father sold insurance, but he rode a bicycle, for a fiver a week. Your lifestyle was accepted at the time, you know? What you did was what you did. Ireland was a poor country.' Frankie's father, Peter, played violin with a couple of acts, and on Saturday nights, musicians from all around the area, including Bernard and Dympna McCabe (whose son Pat became one of Ireland's most celebrated writers) descended on the McDonald family home for sessions. Kathleen, Frankie's mother, was a great singer and welcomed them in. Frankie's brother was a sax and clarinet player, and it didn't take Frankie long to follow behind. 'Before I could count to ten I was able to sing "In the Mood". Whatever was popular at the time I was able to sing it,' he says in his warm, friendly, half-Ulster, half-midlands drawl. 'If a child is listening to music when they are very young, their brain is active. The brain is very active when you're a young child so I had music on the mind from day one – way before I went to school.' He was an All-Ireland Feis Cheoil Champion at the age of twelve, and joined the Cathal Brugha Barracks Army School of Music aged just fourteen. It was there that he met future band colleague Liam Meade, and in 1962 both men joined the Band of the Western Command in Athlone.

Frankie would prove a natural successor to Tommy Swarbrigg, bringing not only musical skills but singing and arranging skills too. Each night, for as long as he or any Joe fan can remember, Frankie signalled Joe's departure from stage with a memorable solo at the end of 'Goodbye Venice Goodbye', an album track from the early 1970s that closed a Joe show, and he became the longest-serving member of Joe's band, playing by Joe's side for thirty-nine years.

Everything was looking up when the new Drifters line-up met for the first time at Ben's house. However, it all came crashing down again when the new band tried to play together. 'The first few rehearsals were disastrous,' Joe recalled. 'Songs that were good one day would fall apart the next. Sometimes it gelled with more familiar numbers, and other times it didn't. But within a few days we had it, and that's when the magic really started.'

Frankie recalls Joe driving them that extra mile. 'He always said he had the best band in the world. He gave it everything, so we responded in kind.'

For their return to the coalface, Seamus reignited the flames of Drifter-mania – but he need not have bothered as there was a full house for every show. The first date was the Las Vegas Ballroom in Templemore on 15 August. The show was not without a few mistakes and first-night nerves, but Joe was a different man. Now free of guitar duties, he blossomed as both a front man and controller of the show, and was able to dictate the pace, interact more with the band, change the show or set-list at will and respond even more to the fans. This, of course, was fraught with dangers as Joe used to be pulled from the stage into the crowd if he got too close. While still sad that some of their former heart-throbs were not onstage with Joe, the fans took to the new band almost immediately.

Letterkenny's Fiesta Ballroom was the destination for the second show, and this was followed by the Commercial Ballroom in the Tyrone town of Dungannon. A show at the Granada in Kingscourt completed the first round of toe-in-the-water dates. After a short break to assess how things were going, Joe and his new band played ten straight nights to ten full houses, including the first Dublin date of the new era, a riotous Monday night at the TV Club in Harcourt Street on 26 August.

Although Joe thrived as a front man, the shows were still marathon affairs and he would occasionally find himself behind the drum kit when the band took their breaks, with Maurice Walsh taking the mic. Maurice really gave it his all, and was only too happy to be pulled from the stage by the fans. The tailoring bills were going through the roof, thanks to Maurice having his suits ripped from his back by over-excited fans, a trademark of a Joe show back in the day. 'I knew how to deal with them, even though they'd be grabbing me and everything else, but when Maurice went near them, he'd be delighted to be pulled asunder. Ben decided that a microphone set up behind the drum kit would be cheaper because every time Maurice went out we had to get him a new suit.'

One of the last songs Joe had recorded with the old Drifters was earmarked to be the first release for the new line-up: 'Westmeath Bachelor', a traditional arrangement written by Castletown-Geoghegan 'singing postman' Billy Whelan. Joe had picked the song up having heard Billy play it many years earlier, and as Joe had been billed in newspapers and magazines as one of Ireland's most eligible bachelors, he decided it would be a good fun song to put into his set. It was given its first airing during his Lenten shows at cinemas when he decided the band should throw in a traditional music set. As a bit of a laugh, Joe bought a selection of big chunky white Aran sweaters and fisherman's hats for the lads to sport. To have a traditional song set in their hometown, with lyrics that alluded to Joe's status as the most eligible bachelor in the county, was something Joe's audiences adored, particularly his home county audiences. When he recorded it, he made sure he did so in the right spirit, and coaxed a few friends into the studio to recreate a carefree hooley. 'It was like someone had turned back time to those days in the kitchen,' Joe remembered. Only instead of his family dancing around the range, he had a herd of musicians and friends stomping around a studio like 'pure bogmen'.

The song was a real oul' fellas' lament about the advantages of the single life and the get-up of the modern Mullingar woman, who paraded around the market town covered head to toe in make-up. It was always a fun song to play live, and Joe played it at almost every show he performed, from Mullingar to Moscow. When the song broke into a wild jig, Joe would attempt some Irish dancing, which, even with a new hip in 2005, never failed to please his audiences.

However, at the last minute Joe decided to pull the release of the single, feeling that he should not go down the Irish *comhaille* road, especially as the first release with a new-look backing band. 'I love the song, and always enjoyed playing it live, but at the time I just didn't feel it reflected the new journey we were about to take,' Joe said.

JOE DOLAN

Also undertaking a new journey were his ex-bandmates, as The Times. Tommy Swarbrigg had put his trumpet aside for ever, and set up a two-brother axis with his brother Jimmy at the front of the stage. Joining the ex-Drifters were guitarist Sean Kenny and saxophonist Gene Bannon. Their first release came in November 1968, and it was followed by over a dozen massive Top Twenty hits. 'They did very well and we did great business,' Joe said. 'There was a kind of rivalry between the two of us, but we didn't care that much. You'd like to say that we always had the edge, although they were saying that they had the edge!'

But they too would split as the Swarbrigg brothers' popularity grew. While still playing with The Times, the Swarbriggs also enjoyed several hits as a duo, as well as flying the flag at the Eurovision Song Contest in 1975, finishing sixth with 'That's What Friends are For', and again in 1977, taking third place with 'It's Nice to be in Love Again'. Perhaps in a small tribute to Tommy's formative years onstage with The Drifters, they performed on one such occasion in bright canary yellow suits. They left the band after this, but The Times carried on until 1982 with a new line-up. Tommy and Jimmy Swarbrigg retired from performance in the 1980s and are now successful businessmen and music promoters. They still write songs and reunite for occasional charity shows, and Joe had expressed an interest in recording one of their songs, 'The Music of My Life', in 2007.

As Joe got used to life without his old band and got to know what made the new members tick, Seamus Casey was working hard at finding new songs for Joe. Visits to the UK to talk to Pye Records were beginning to have an impact, so much so that the very same month as Joe Dolan's new band returned to the stage, Joe was finally made an offer that he simply couldn't refuse.

9
Just the *one* Island, sir?

It was an almost impossible task for Irish musicians and acts to find success outside of Ireland in the 1960s and only Van Morrison, who had played with The Monarchs and The Manhattan showbands in the North, had done it before, firstly with the band Them and then as a solo artist. One of the main obstacles was record company parochialism. Although Pye Records was *the* major record label as far as Irish acts were concerned, the links between its Irish operation and its international parent company were, at best, cordial, the latter believing that Irish acts were for Irish audiences. But the radar at Pye's London HQ had been picking up signals from Mullingar for some time, and in 1969, together with Europe's biggest music publisher, Shaftesbury Music, they would make Joe the biggest Irish star in the world.

Joe had come to the attention of Shaftesbury long before The Drifters had split. Shaftesbury wanted their songs to be recorded by singers with conviction, longevity and great voices, and Joe Dolan was just that sort of artist. Their MD Geoffrey Everett felt that Joe was so far ahead of the showband pack that to call him a showband singer would be to do him a disservice. Joe's vocals on progressive tracks such as 'Tar and Cement', 'Love of the Common People' and 'Unchained Melody' had showcased an operatic, emotional and unique voice and, given the right material, they felt he could do massive international business.

Everett had asked the hot in-house songwriting partners Albert Hammond and Mike Hazelwood to come up with some material that would suit Joe's voice. They came back with a number of tracks, and Shaftesbury's Joy Nicholls was dispatched to Dublin to make contact with Joe and his record label.

When Joy Nicholls confidently told Joe that the demo she was about to play would make him an international star, Joe was sceptical. She then played an early, stripped-down version of a song called 'Make Me an Island'. As the tape rolled, Joe and his manager shuffled in their seats, not really knowing what to make of it at first. 'It was just a rough demo that had been done by Albert Hammond. There was no big arrangement as such,' Joe remembered of that first awkward listen. The demo was played again in Mullingar, and even though Joe could see some potential in the composition, he was still not convinced of its merits. However, he liked its romance, as it was about a cad suddenly prepared to change his bed-hopping ways for the love of a beautiful woman, and he noted a cheeky synergy in the lyrics with what was happening in his life at the time. Strip away the boy-meets-girl nature of the song, and it is about a man undergoing big changes. That each verse concludes with an emphatically sung 'and I'm different now' said something to him. He had been tired and uninspired with the whole showband scene, and he now wanted to wipe his slate clean.

'Make Me an Island' was also a clever variation of the basic verse-chorus-verse-chorus pop song, a euphoric, arms-in-the-air singalong. Its chorus was tailor-made for a good front man, and Joe's decision to emphasize certain words − such as 'take', 'break', 'close', 'shut', 'cut' and 'make' − gave it further urgency and even more singalong appeal. (Although some audience members chose to sing their own, more sinister version, leaving Joe to wonder if he was harbouring serial killers. 'Some of them would be roaring, "Hang me and break me and smash all your windows . . . Shoot me and kill me" and all that sort of stuff,' he laughed.)

When Joe agreed to record the song, Joy revealed that another singer had

been snapping at her heels for it: Tom Jones. Shaftesbury's London neighbours, a management company called MAM, had heard the demo and were
impressed. Jones was their star man at the time, but after a few misses he was
in need of a big UK hit. If Joe didn't want the song, then they would gladly
take it for Jones. In fact, the MAM Agency would go on to sign Joe and promote him around the world after 'Make Me an Island' broke.

It was decided that his new band would not contribute to the track, as
both Shaftesbury and Pye wanted this to be as big an introduction to Joe
Dolan as possible, and so they hired an orchestra instead. The London
recording sessions were therefore a complete step into the unknown for Joe,
and he was astonished to be greeted by over fifty enthusiastic musicians when
he entered the studio. 'The atmosphere in the studio was fantastic,' he
recalled. 'I suppose everyone could sense this was going to be a great song.'
Geoffrey Everett was in the executive producer's chair, but the majority of the
work was done by arranger and co-producer Johnny Arthey, alongside former
Eamonn Andrews Studios engineer Bill Somerville-Large, who had worked
with Joe several times before. His reassuring presence would be an essential
ingredient as the sessions progressed.

Arthey had carved out a huge reputation in the 1960s for big-sounding
records. He had worked with everyone, from singing starlets and Eurovision
hopefuls to big bands and orchestras, and had scores of hits to his credit.
Arthey and Joe initially set about getting a feel for the song, and immediately
Joe showed his worth in a studio.

'We rehearsed it on the first day, to bring this demo to life really, and find
the key, the tempo, and everything else. We did it a few times with just Johnny
Arthey and me at the piano in different keys.' When they found what they
thought was the right tempo, the song bore little resemblance to the original
demo. It had sped up, and Joe was singing it in a higher key. As they were doing
this, Arthey was singing and humming little arrangements with a view to bringing in even more musicians. 'When Johnny arranged something everybody got
a job!' laughed Joe. 'He used the full orchestra and there would be no pulling
punches or introductions with a piano. Everyone got a job, even the little fella
playing the triangle – ping! – he's in there somewhere.'

As this was his song and not band songs like his initial run of hits, Joe was
not scared of getting his hands dirty in the studio. Seamus recalls that if things
were dragging a bit, Joe had no fear in going down into the orchestra pit to

change things. 'He was a bit scatter-brained and wild at the best of times, but he took his recording very seriously indeed.'

At one stage, he felt the drummer was playing too quietly, too stiffly and too steadily, so he encouraged more percussive flair to give the song a lift and the kind of rolling flavour that was in keeping with its continental-sounding chorus. The drums are one of the most prominently featured instruments on the track – something that was practically unheard of in mainstream pop music at the time. 'Joe was a good musician first and foremost, and because he appreciated rhythm and tempo so much, there was always a great relationship between him and his drummers. He wanted the power behind him to drive the song and the show,' his nephew and future producer Adrian recalled.

Seamus remembers Joe being a perfectionist about his own vocal on the track. 'After listening to playbacks of his own vocals in the control booth he would usually say he would sing that better. From day one this is what he always said, and engineers would plead with him, and say, "No, Joe, it's OK," but he would insist on another take. And do you know what? He would do better each time.'

'We were blessed with the team we had,' Joe recalls. 'We couldn't have done it in Eamonn Andrews Studios or anywhere else in Ireland for that matter. We literally could have whatever we wanted on the track, and Johnny put everything on to it.'

One thing that endeared Joe to the musicians even more than his insight and interest was his generosity. The musicians were all union guys, so no matter how a recording session was going, union rules were observed, which meant that every three hours there was a tea or meal break, and Joe would lead everyone to the pub and buy them all their lunches. 'None of Johnny Arthey's people could believe it,' Seamus says. 'They told us that of all the acts they worked with through the years, Joe was the only one to have bought them a drink or a bite to eat.'

Joe and Arthey got on well, and the producer found Joe's Irishness amusing, in particular the Irish Friendly Matches that Joe (who had taken up smoking) would use to light his cigarettes. Arthey couldn't believe that there was such a thing as a 'friendly' match, and he and some of the orchestra were in hysterics at what they thought was a real-life example of a Paddy Irishman joke. When Joe returned to the same studio a few weeks later, he came armed with a huge package from which he presented each person in the studio with their very own box of Irish Friendly Matches.

However, above all, he treated the musicians with respect and courtesy. They were used to singers who would stomp in, do their bit, bark a few orders and walk out without so much as a thank you. Joe's innate friendliness made for a great atmosphere in the studio, and it can be heard all over the finished product. 'Joe just treated them as if he had always known them, and there were no airs and graces about him. He just put them at their ease and that's what stood him in good stead throughout his life. Joe was able to mix with anyone,' Seamus recalled. 'Even the few people he didn't like!' The warm atmosphere remained as Joe returned to the same team over the next few years, and with the session musicians giving their all, the recordings never once sounded like an ensemble going through the motions.

The B-side of 'Make Me an Island' wasn't bad either. A jaunty 1960s pop track about actions speaking louder than words, 'If You Care a Little Bit About Me' was a quick, two-minute Motown-influenced number that would have made a good single in its own right. Joe's ideas are all over it, including a dramatic pause before the final chorus. When both tracks were finished, further recording was discussed, and Joe felt good about doing an album with Arthey and his rather large ensemble. Additional dates were pencilled into the diary, and writing team Hammond and Hazelwood got to work on some new ideas.

When Joe's band first heard the tapes from the 'Make Me an Island' sessions, they had mixed feelings. 'The first thing I thought was it was too fast,' Ben says. 'It nearly sounds as if it was a waltz, but it wasn't in waltz time, y'know? It was hard for me to make my mind up at first. But there was something different about it – it was a new song, a new style, a new arrangement . . . And then it came to me, it was a new singer! Up until that, we had recorded everything with the band, and you could hear the band. With this, it was all about Joe. It was incredible, after hearing it a couple of times we all loved it; and we loved that there were bits in it for us all to play!'

Surprisingly, Joe's hopes for the new single were not as high as those around him. 'To be honest we expected, at most, to get a hit in Ireland with it. Geoffrey and Joy loved it, and because we had been burned before with proposed UK releases we kind of didn't share that belief.' The Shaftesbury pair were so confident it was going to be a big international hit that they convinced Radio Luxembourg to feature it prominently before Pye had even agreed to give it a release outside Ireland. By a happy coincidence, Shaftesbury also had a stake in the world-famous radio station, which meant they had a say in the playlists. Indeed, Geoffrey Everett had even deejayed for the station before returning to a management position. In 1969 Radio Luxembourg reigned supreme; it was a colossus in the world of long-wave radio, and the youth of Europe lived their lives through it. In the mid 1960s it had seen off formidable offshore challenges by swashbuckling pirate radio stations such as Radio Caroline, and even the all-new BBC Radio One couldn't topple it. Big-name DJs such as Tony Prince and David 'Kid' Jensen gave the station a hip attitude and a confident cockiness. Armed with the knowledge the single would feature on the popular radio station, a humbled Pye executive informed Joe that they would finally be giving his record a full UK release. Joe was ecstatic. If it made an impression in London, he knew it would make a similar impression elsewhere. 'England, and London in particular, was the centre of the music industry at that time. If something went into the charts there, it automatically did the same all around Europe. America was the place, but when The Beatles came along they changed all that. They were a world power, so naturally all eyes were focused on England as leader of the pop world.'

The 7-inch was released in the UK in mid April, and in Ireland two weeks later. Larry Gogan, one of Joe's biggest supporters on Irish radio and in print, gave the single a scathing review in *Spotlight* magazine. He later revealed he had been told to be 'harder' on Irish artists, and Joe just happened to be the first one he picked on. 'It did OK at first, but it didn't exactly set the world on fire,' Joe remarked. But as it picked up radio plays, it slowly crept into the Top 100.

Joe and the band decided to reward themselves after six months of hard work with a two-week sun holiday – just as they had done before the release of 'Pretty Brown Eyes', Joe's first number one in 1966 – and went to the south of Spain. Unfortunately they had forgotten to inform anyone in either Pye or Shaftesbury, and with no such thing as mobile phones, emails or fax machines, they were not contactable. They certainly weren't to know that the new single was beginning to take off. When a relaxed and freshly tanned Joe checked into his Mullingar office to see how things had been going in his absence, hundreds of messages awaited him from people in Pye Records

offices around the world, from newspapers, radio stations and, most importantly, from the team that had brought him his new, original material:
Shaftesbury. They had a big hit on their hands.

Joe barely had time to unpack his duty free at his apartment before being
whisked back to the airport to go to London. 'It was quite foolish of us
always to take holidays when we released big singles,' he later said with a
laugh. 'I suppose we should have learned from what had happened a few
years earlier. Actually, we should have booked holidays every time we
released a record!'

Within a few weeks, requests for it were so numerous on Radio Luxembourg that it had become a coveted 'Power Play' record, with a guaranteed
twenty-four plays a day, ensuring that millions of listeners throughout Europe
would hear the Mullingar maestro at some stage of the day or night. Whilst
there can be no doubt Shaftesbury's Geoffrey Everett played a role in this, the
sheer class of the single and its singalong chorus ensured Luxembourg DJs
simply could not ignore it. 'Make Me an Island' started to climb the UK
charts.

'Within a couple of weeks, all hell suddenly broke loose,' Joe recalls. 'We
were invited on to *Top of the Pops*, we were all over Europe, we were doing
interviews, everybody wanted me to do this, do that, and do the other; and I
did it. It was madness, but brilliant madness, you know?'

When Joe broke into the Top Forty in June 1969, The Beatles were at the
top of the charts with 'The Ballad of John and Yoko'. Joe's was the second
highest new entry that week, only Amen Corner's 'Hello Suzie' landing in
above him. Also competing for the attentions of record buyers in the UK Top
Forty that week was Elvis Presley, who was undergoing a renaissance of sorts
with his new single 'In the Ghetto'; Frank Sinatra, who was on his way up the
charts with his signature track 'My Way'; and Steppenwolf with 'Born to be
Wild'; together with Glen Campbell's 'Galveston', Smokey Robinson's 'The
Tracks of my Tears', Bob Dylan's 'I Threw it All Away', Jethro Tull's 'Living
in the Past' and Scott Walker's 'Lights in Cincinnati'. In his third week in the
chart, Joe had leapfrogged Sinatra, Tom Jones, Glen Campbell, Simon and
Garfunkel, Jim Reeves, Andy Williams and Marvin Gaye and landed in the
Top Thirty.

With Radio Luxembourg's 'Power Play' status beginning to kick in, Joe made
significant gains in his fourth week in the UK charts, and in mid July he rose to

number nineteen, with even more big names in his rear-view mirror, including Cilla Black, The Four Tops, Cliff Richard, The Bee Gees and Stevie Wonder. Back in Ireland, he was an instant Top Ten success, but all eyes were focused on the UK chart. Describing the feeling of climbing up the charts, Joe would say it was like 'walking on the moon', a nod to what had happened that same week, as astronaut Neil Armstrong took his famous steps on the moon's surface. (Joe, a big science-fiction buff, had tuned into the live coverage in awe.)

Joe continued to outsell some of the biggest names in show business the following week, reaching number sixteen. Above him, The Rolling Stones, riding on a crest of sympathy surrounding the death of guitarist Brian Jones and their emotional Hyde Park concert, grabbed the number-one spot with 'Honky Tonk Woman'.

Pye's record-makers couldn't press enough copies of Joe's single as it was released all over Europe to cope with the demand following its high showing in the UK and its 'Power Play' status. From thinking it would only be an Irish success, Joe was knocked for six to learn it was about to be released across Europe and elsewhere, including Australia and New Zealand. In one amazing night, Joe recorded versions of 'Make Me an Island' in Italian, Spanish and German. All were mixed and sent to the record manufacturers for immediate pressing. In Spain, the song was released as 'Haz de mi una Isla', and in Italy it became 'Apri la Porta'. Meanwhile, plans were unveiled for the song to be released in America in both English and Spanish. In Israel it rose to the top of the charts, packaged as a special EP with 'I Love You More and More Every Day', 'Time of My Life' and 'But I Do'.

As Radio Luxembourg pumped it up across their schedule, 'Make Me an Island' rose up the charts all over the continent. July gave way to August, and the British public really fell for Joe when he entered the UK Top Ten. His sales went through the roof that week and he was the biggest climber, rising an impressive nine places from sixteen to his lucky number seven, leaping over The Beatles.

A carefully choreographed campaign then saw a wave of releases in Czechoslovakia, the former Yugoslavia, Greece, Poland, Bulgaria, Hungary and Romania. He landed into the Top Ten of nearly every one of them.

So, how did it feel to be emerging as one of Europe's biggest stars?

'It felt good,' Joe remembered. 'But we were too busy to notice, there was little time for it to sink in.' He often joked that he thought the release schedule was decided by his management throwing darts at a map of Europe; the promotional schedule, even by today's jet-setting standards, was almost Herculean. A typical day for Joe could start with him waking up as a plane touched down on the runway at Schiphol airport in Holland. From here he would be whisked to a radio station in Amsterdam. By lunchtime that same day he would be in Belgium for a television appearance. By dinner time he would be in London for a BBC radio interview. He would then be back in Ireland for a show, and the next day he would wake up in Germany, the following day in Portugal, and so on.

Germany had been particularly quick to pick up on Joe's epic singles. Almost a year earlier 'Tar and Cement' had made a big impression on German radio, and they had played other Dolan songs too, with 'Love of the Common People' another favourite, but neither Joe nor the record company realized this until they promoted 'Make Me an Island' there. Joe was angry that his label had not cottoned on to this, but there was little time to remain bitter as things were becoming increasingly manic for him.

He became one of the biggest-selling artists in Germany that year, helped by an appearance on *Vergißmeinnicht*, the biggest entertainment show in the country at the time, where he was backed by no less an outfit than James Last's Orchestra. 'We were three days doing that one,' Joe recalled. 'It was an immense show in Germany. Helen Shapiro was on it too, and for some strange reason they imported a black London taxi for me, which I had to drive on to the stage, stop, and get out of it and start to sing! Why they had me in a taxi I'll never know.'

Joe thought he would never get home from the show. After a four-hour car journey, he and Seamus arrived at Hamburg airport, a little worse for wear only to be confronted by thousands of anxious and angry American troops trying to return home from the Vietnam conflict. All flights were delayed due to fog, and they ended up being the only two men not in military uniform in a packed Departures lounge, taking it in turns to sleep on the one seat over the course of the night.

Chat shows and music shows from all over Europe wanted Joe on their stage, but because of his hectic schedule he could not bring his new band with him to all engagements, so it was Joe and Seamus who buzzed from country to country. Meanwhile, back home, there was a band to pay and gigs to be played. Before the single had taken off they had booked a huge number of dates into the diary (some bookings taken years in advance) that they simply had to play. Out of loyalty to his Irish fans, Joe didn't want to cancel any of them, and he somehow combined the rigours of a European career with that of the Irish ballroom circuit, commuting between Europe and Ireland at a rate of knots. Sometimes they were lucky in that TV bookings would be early in the week when the band wasn't working. More often than not, Joe would have to fly home directly from a showpiece European engagement to a gig in 'the back of beyond' in Ireland – even if that meant honouring both commitments in the space of twenty-four hours.

'To this day, I still do not know how Joe did it,' Seamus recalls in disbelief and admiration. 'When the single took off in Europe, we were coming into the busy season for us at home – from June to August – and we had dates all over the country. Joe felt we couldn't let the fans down at home either. He never complained about the schedule he was undertaking, which made it all the more impressive.'

At one stage, as 'Make Me an Island' was beginning its incredible climb up the charts, Joe had to be in London every Monday morning for five weeks in a row. Sunday night was still a big night in the ballrooms, so Joe would perform until after 2 a.m., and then stick around signing autographs. A few hours later, he and Seamus would catch the 6.15 a.m. flight out of Dublin to compress a week's worth of work into two days. Often, Joe would come home for a gig on the Tuesday and fly out again on the Wednesday, criss-crossing the continent as and when his availability allowed. He cut a video for the song at one point in a rowing boat on a Belgian lake, which was sent out to TV stations around Europe to cope with the demands placed on him.

'I don't know how he did it without having a breakdown,' Frankie McDonald remembers with his typically dry humour. 'We'd finish in Cork; he'd drive back to Mullingar and fly out to London or Lisbon the next morning. On Tuesday night he'd be back for a show in Limerick and still be full of beans, and able to put in a full four-hour show knowing that he was probably flying off the following day to some place else!'

Ben still scratches his head as he wonders how his brother did it. 'It must have taken incredible stamina, but Joe never seemed to tire of doing it. I remember one time he flew back to Belfast from Germany or someplace, and drove to Muff in Donegal for a gig, then drove back to Mullingar, and flew out to London the next morning for a recording session.'

They really winged it on the historic night when Joe was booked to appear on the biggest music programme in the world, the BBC's *Top of the Pops*. It was every musician's dream to appear on *Top of the Pops*. 'This was real fairytale, dream-come-true stuff,' Joe said, and he wanted to savour every minute of it. The trouble was that on the same night he was to appear on the programme, he had also been booked to play a massive Dublin show. The Ags Dance was the Trinity Ball of its day for Dublin students, and Joe had been booked to headline it almost a year before the release of 'Make Me an Island'. Despite the prestige and the big audience, Joe and the band were being paid buttons to play it. Four days before the ball, the BBC rang to inform him he was wanted for *Top of the Pops* – an offer they simply couldn't refuse, as the show had an estimated audience of 14 million.

Frantic efforts were made to reschedule the Dublin show, and Joe and his team tried to reach a middle ground. Somehow the BBC were persuaded to charter a private jet to fly Joe back to Dublin after his spot was filmed. If all went according to plan, he would be back in time for the gig, which was being held in the Olympic Ballroom in the south of the city. Just in case, an extra relief band was added to the bill, with Joe and his band due to go onstage a little later than previously billed.

Joe and Seamus flew over to London and into the BBC that Wednesday morning, rehearsed 'Make Me an Island' and then enjoyed a day in the television centre, chatting with other musicians and stars of the day. The Rolling Stones were also appearing on that week's broadcast, but Joe was not in the least bit star-struck about meeting a band he idolized. 'He was just as happy chatting to the tea lady,' Seamus says, without any trace of exaggeration. However, he became friendly with Mick Jagger, and in later years they shared many a drink together.

Using his charm (and cheekiness), Joe convinced the director to film his performance first. It went perfectly, and Seamus realized that Joe was a natural in front of the cameras, instinctively knowing which camera was on him and which way to turn. 'He'd eyeball one, then on cue turn to the other. He was amazing. His gestures and his posture were magnificent, and it was complete in just one take.' Although the footage from the show is now sadly lost, Seamus said Joe was more akin to a professional actor than a singer that night, and the crowd were delighted. 'He was quite animated, and the studio audience loved him,' he remembered.

Joe and Seamus had little time to hang around and catch the performances of the other acts recording that night, and as soon as the director gave
Joe the thumbs up they literally ran out the door to a waiting taxi. They were
met at Heathrow by members of the airport police and a customs man, who
had cleared a route for them to follow, avoiding the normal checks and
searches, right on to the runway, where they were bundled into a small four-
seat Cessna plane. Joe remembered the customs man banging the side of the
airplane as if they were heading off in a car. They barely had time to catch
their breath before the jet was airborne.

The plane was tiny and Joe began to feel a little edgy. 'It was like sitting in
a Morris Minor,' he said later, laughing, but at the time he remembers feeling
as if he were trapped in a box. The familiar sights of Dublin, alongside some
of its newer sights such as the seven fifteen-storey towers of Ballymun which
had recently been opened to tenants, were shrouded in dusky darkness as
they approached the capital. Ben's wife Moira was waiting at the other end
with the engine running. However, not everything went according to plan.

'The pilot was being told to come in on a different runway – off the main
runway – but he misjudged it completely and came in on the wrong runway,' he remembers. Luckily, it was not in service at that time. Unluckily, it
was blocked off from the rest of the airport site by wooden barriers. With
the pilot and air-traffic control blaming each other over the radio and the
plane stopped some distance from the airport building, Joe leaped from his
seat and out of the door, on to the plane's wing, and slid down on to
the runway, where he single-handedly moved, pushed and then threw the
wooden barriers out of the plane's way. Some 'colourful' language was
exchanged between Joe and the pilot, and the tiny aircraft eventually taxied
into the airport, where once again customs waved Joe through. Joe jumped
into the waiting car, and Moira raced towards Dublin city centre, where
Joe's band had already taken to the stage.

For his *Top of the Pops* appearance, Joe had bought an expensively
tailored crushed velvet suit, which was now stuck to him with sweat – and
boy, could Joe sweat! Everything had happened so fast that evening that he
did not have time to change. The band had been onstage for about forty-five
minutes when Joe pulled up outside the Olympic just before midnight. He
was lucky that most of the new line-up had some semblance of singing talent,
so there were plenty of varied numbers to go around, with Maurice Walsh

particularly enjoying an extended spell back in the spotlight. Having relin-
quished his master of ceremonies duties to Joe, Ben was loving every minute
of building up the big arrival of Ireland's new continental star.

When Joe stepped out from the car, frenzied scenes greeted him. Such
was his popularity, hundreds had been turned away, and the venue was
ringed by fans eager to welcome their all-conquering chart hero back to
Ireland. They probably didn't expect him to turn up on the street. Driftermania was back! Eventually Joe managed to get into the Olympic, where he
went straight up onstage to a wild and rapturous welcome. He started
singing 'Make Me an Island' and the venue nearly fell apart. Everyone's
attention was focused on Joe, and hands from the first few rows were thrust
out to touch this big, burly star who had brought the island of Ireland to
charts all over the world and made everyone feel good to be Irish again. By
the time he got to the end of the first chorus, a whole new generation of
Driftermaniacs pulled him off the stage. Ben went into the crowd after him,
but when he got a hold of his younger brother he found an entire arm had
been ripped off Joe's new suit. As Ben tried to haul Joe back up onstage, the
fans got hold of him again and ripped the rest of the jacket off his back. Joe
escaped their clutches and threw the remnants of his suit into the baying
crowd. Even without most of his costly clothing, he went on to play one of
the best gigs he'd done in a long, long time. There were no regrets on leaving
the glamour of *Top of the Pops* behind – even at the height of his fame Joe
was happier among his own people.

In the aftermath of his memorable *Top of the Pops* appearance, Joe
became the first ever Irish artist to crack the Top Five in the UK. Mullingar
(and Ireland) rejoiced as its favourite son took the number-three spot, comfortably outselling the likes of John Lennon (with 'Give Peace a Chance') and
Stevie Wonder (with 'My Cherie Amour'). Any fingernails that were left
among his Irish fans were nibbled to the quick, as they wondered whether
one of their own would go all the way to number one the following week.
Only The Rolling Stones and Robin Gibb (with 'Saved by the Bell') stood
between Joe and the top, and they'd been there for a couple of weeks. In
Europe, sales were going through the roof, and Joe now occupied the top
spots in several countries. At one point, Joe was number one at the same time
in seven European countries. And when he fell off the top spot in one country, he would grab it in another. In all, he topped the charts in an

unprecedented fourteen countries that summer. The only country where 'Make Me an Island' failed to make a significant impact was the US.

Sadly, hopes of a number-one spot in the UK were dashed, and both Stevie Wonder and Zager and Evans (with the apocalyptic 'In the Year 2525') outsold Joe in the last week of August and he slipped two places to number five. However, there was barely any disappointment about not reaching the top spot in the British charts. It was a major achievement for an Irish artist to be in such exalted company, and only The Beatles and The Rolling Stones could match his European form.

And there was more to come. 'Make Me an Island' was a massive hit in Australia, and by the end of 1969 it was the ninth biggest-selling single of the year. It was also released in South Africa (where it spent ten weeks at the top), India, the Philippines and the Lebanon, and Joe's Spanish version of the song was released in various South American countries, although to this day nobody knows how many copies it sold. 'We certainly never saw any money from South America!' Joe quipped when asked about his track record there. It would, however, get an official release in Brazil. Argentina followed a year later, and Joe, or 'José Dolano' as he was nicknamed in the Irish press, would go on to become a massive Latin American star, releasing specially recorded singles, EPs and albums throughout the 1970s.

There was little time to absorb the highlights of these halcyon days, but the year-long promotional campaign paid off. Joe held on to the number-five spot in the UK charts for two weeks, a full three months after the song had first charted. All in all he would spend five months in the UK Top Forty. The song also took up extended residencies elsewhere, staying in the Top Twenty in the Netherlands for ten weeks, and in Belgium and Germany for four months apiece. It also spent at least a month in the upper reaches of the Israeli, Portuguese, Norwegian, Turkish and French charts. Joe's Spanish and Italian versions also did remarkably well, with both of them reaching the Top Twenty in their target markets.

The walls of his Mullingar office started to groan under the weight of the gold and platinum discs and the awards Joe had started to accumulate. In the UK he went from silver to gold disc status in just three months, with sales in excess of a million. Radio Luxembourg awarded Joe their highest possible honour as 1969 came to a close, with the prestigious 'Radio Luxembourg Award'. The single was also voted 'Record of the Year' by the music industry in Germany, Sweden and, most importantly, in Ireland, where ironically the single had not made number one.

It had first entered the Irish charts on 17 May and although it reached the number two in a week, four men from Liverpool blocked the number-one spot (again), firstly with 'Get Back' and then with 'The Ballad of John and Yoko'. On 19 July 1969, Elvis's 'In the Ghetto' made it to the top for a month, and then The Rolling Stones nabbed number one. Nevertheless, Joe held on in the Top Ten for close to four months, and spent six months in the Top Twenty.

With such an enormous hit, Joe was on great form, yet he never allowed his success to go to his head. 'I can't describe how I was feeling. You couldn't help but be happy, but there was still work to do so we never allowed ourselves to get too carried away with it.' Those around him remember Joe being enthusiastic about the promotional process, and he did everything that was asked of him – although getting him up in the morning was proving increasingly difficult. Seamus was the only other person to have a key to Joe's apartment, and he often had to drag Joe out of bed to catch early morning flights to England, which became their base of operations as the 1970s dawned. 'I would hear Joe's snoring nearly from Dominick Street itself,' said Seamus. 'I'd get there, having warned him to be up for, say, six, and he'd be fast asleep. Often he had only just gone to bed because he would have been back from a show or something. I'd an awful job waking him up. I'd throw bottles of water on him, and he'd tell me to fuck off out of it, but once he got into the car he was great, not a bother on him.' Joe knew that every appearance counted.

Joe's professional outlook, which was at odds with his devil-may-care personality when he wasn't working, was even more startling given that he was still managing four or five gigs a week with his band. He never once thought of chucking that in to base himself permanently in the UK or Europe, despite his huge success on his maiden voyage. 'He always said he wanted to stay at home no matter what,' Seamus reflected. 'He was just a down-to-earth kind of guy, and being at home kept him that way.'

'He never thought of himself as being an international star,' Ben reveals. 'Even though he had achieved this huge success, he was still the same fella who had been upsetting the horse and the neighbours by playing the guitar too loud.' And he would still spend hours signing autographs after shows, always stopping to talk to his fans. He started to get to know his most loyal fans, and he had an incredible memory for names and faces. 'If you had been to a Joe show twice he would have been familiar with your face,' Ben recalls. 'And if you had been there three times then he knew your name!'

There was now an urgent and pressing need for an album, but so far Joe had only laid down a couple of new tracks with Johnny Arthey. Fearing the ship of stardom could sail away as soon as it had docked, Joe's record company pressurized him into releasing a compilation that featured some earlier Drifters material plus his big hit single. Joe would have preferred to have waited and released a true representation of 'Joe Dolan' (which he managed to do that Christmas, with the *Make Me an Island* album), but the record company were insistent. The compilation album served as a good introduction to his talents, though, and as well as featuring 'Pretty Brown Eyes', 'Aching Breaking Heart', 'Unchained Melody', 'Tar and Cement', 'Love of the Common People', 'House with the Whitewashed Gable' and 'The Answer to Everything', it also included a powerful take on the Don Gibson song 'I'd Be a Legend in My Time' and a rousing take on '(I Don't Know Why) But I Do', an R&B hit for Clarence 'Frogman' Henry in 1961. The album was a huge hit, and the pressure on Joe's young shoulders to follow up the success of his international breakthrough with a new single was immense.

It would be with regret that Joe looked back on the follow-up single to 'Make Me an Island'. His gut reaction was to release 'You're Such a Good Looking Woman', but instead the record company talked him into releasing 'Teresa', another Hammond and Hazelwood composition, which Joe had recorded at the same time. Joe felt that 'Teresa' was just too similar to 'Make Me an Island'. And, having grown to appreciate rock music over the past couple of years, and in particular hard rock music, Joe wanted to hit his new audience with a punch; he felt 'You're Such a Good Looking Woman' delivered that knock-out blow. Band members and management agreed.

But the powers that be thought otherwise. Even though 'Teresa' had been recorded in 1968 by Leapy Lee, who had a big international hit with 'Little Arrows' (also written by Hammond and Hazelwood), Shaftesbury and Pye felt the record-buying public would not be familiar with it. They were wrong.

'They insisted that we bring out "Teresa" for the second single, and I thought, "These guys made a hit out of me and 'Make Me an Island' with what they did, so who am I to say they are wrong?" So I went with it, and I think to this day if I had gone with "Good Looking Woman" it would have been a totally different ballgame,' Joe said. In quiet moments he told Fr Brian D'Arcy, who became the unofficial parish priest of the music industry, of his regrets, and not pushing for 'Good Looking Woman' was one of his biggest. 'Ultimately, it wasn't his decision and I told him that,' Fr D'Arcy recalls.

Seamus Casey was a little blunter on the subject. 'The reality was that if we had followed "Make Me an Island" with "Good Looking Woman" we would probably have had a UK number one with it. "Teresa" was huge in Europe as it had a big European sound, but it just didn't work in the UK. It was a great song, but it was a very plaintive song which seemed to hang around for a bit and disappear.'

However, frustration and regret cannot diminish the quality of the recording, or indeed the song itself, and its B-side, 'My First Love', would go on to become one of Joe's favourite and most commonly requested songs. Commentators in America felt 'My First Love' would have made a good American single, and many years later, in 1981, a reviewer of one of Joe's Las Vegas shows in the *Las Vegas Mirror* said, 'It could probably top the charts in this country,' not realizing it had been released twelve years earlier.

'Teresa' was released on 31 October 1969, and in its second week in the UK charts, it jumped nineteen places to number thirty. 'Make Me an Island' was still selling at this time, and in the first week of November, Joe had two singles in the Top Fifty. In its third week, 'Teresa' rose to number twenty-eight. Things were looking good despite Joe's worries about the song, and a second big *Top of the Pops* appearance and a further promotional blitz saw it rise to number twenty on its fourth week of release. However, when the charts for the last week in November came out, 'Teresa' had slipped back to number twenty-eight, and in mid December it fell to number thirty-eight, just as Christmas shoppers began to fill the record stores. As Rolf Harris took the coveted Christmas number-one spot with 'Two Little Boys', 'Teresa' slipped quietly out the back door of the charts after a seven-week relationship.

Nevertheless, its stay allowed Joe to write himself into the history books as one of Ireland's only acts to remain in the Top Fifty of the biggest and busiest music chart in the world for over half a year without a break. And

'Teresa' did very brisk business elsewhere, becoming a Top Ten hit in Belgium, where it reached number six, as well as being a big hit in Sweden, Portugal, France, Holland and Germany. It was Joe's second Top Ten smash in South Africa.

Back home in Ireland, 'Teresa' shot straight to the top of the charts after two weeks, replacing Bobbie Gentry's 'I'll Never Fall in Love Again' at the top spot on 7 November 1969 and becoming Joe's third number one in Ireland. 'Teresa' would stay in the Top Twenty there for a very respectable fifteen weeks, and at one stage in November Joe had two singles in the Top Ten, so there was plenty to smile about when Joe spent (most of) Christmas 1969 at home with family and friends.

Plenty of Europeans enjoyed the gift of Joe Dolan that Christmas as the *Make Me an Island* album was released just in time for the festive season. It was decided to keep some numbers in the tank: 'You're Such a Good Looking Woman' was not included, even though the track had been finished. But there were a selection of new songs and covers, with Joe lending his ample vocal charm to songs such as 'Games People Play', 'Lover Come Back to Me' (one of Ben Dolan's favourite Joe tracks), Frank Sinatra's 'My Way', 'Here Am I' and, of course, the multi-million-selling, award-winning title track that reinvented him.

10

Oh me oh my

Joe consolidated his international success in 1970 with a song that became his theme tune almost from the moment he first heard it: 'You're Such a Good Looking Woman'. His instincts about it being a better choice of single than 'Teresa' proved to be correct when it became an even bigger international hit upon its release in January that year.

He had included the song in his live sets long before its release, and the audience response had been very positive. 'Almost from the moment we first played it,' he said, 'fans were always asking us to play it.' It was the quintessential Joe Dolan song: a groovy, swinging, rocky anthem, with great singalong potential, and it soon became one of his most popular and most requested songs. Joe would open concerts with it, right up to his last ever show in Abbeyleix on 27 September 2007, as it made an immediate impact and the intro gave the entire band the opportunity to flex their muscles and build up anticipation for Joe's arrival onstage. When asked by RTÉ's Gerry Ryan in 2003 to reveal his biggest fear, he told viewers it would not be dying or losing his voice. 'The day I'm going to die is the day when I walk out on the stage and I sing "Good Looking Woman" and I stop in the chorus to let the audience sing . . . and nothing happens. Would I run off the stage? I'd be gone. I'd say that would be a killer.' Joe only had to sing half of the song anyhow; after that, the audience invariably took over. 'I think it's a great accolade for people to know enough about your music to sing them for you,' he said. 'It feels absolutely tremendous. I always try to bring the band down a little bit so they [the audience] can hear themselves singing, and that makes people sing. When that starts it really buzzes me up.'

It wasn't long before some of the song's lyrics became something of a catchphrase for Joe. When playing golf at a charity pro-am in the UK just after it had been released, British comedian Jimmy Tarbuck came running over to him. Instead of saying hello, he started pointing his fingers and singing, 'Oh me oh my!' Joe reckoned that from that moment onwards not one day passed without someone saying 'Oh me oh my' to him. He even sent himself up by singing it with Dustin the Turkey for a charity single in 1997, and for a television advert for a mobile phone company in 2007.

'The crowds at gigs loved [the song] and latched on to it. Quite early at cabaret shows, the crowd used to sing along to it,' Joe remembered. 'It wasn't me that got them singing; it was, I think, because they all wanted to sing "Oh me oh my!" It was simple stuff, but they loved it.' Other bands loved it too, and Joe found himself in an unusual position when Irish showbands began covering his material, chiefly 'Good Looking Woman' and 'Make Me an Island'. He was no longer a showband singer covering other people's material, he was an artist and a hit-maker worthy of being covered himself.

He told RTÉ's *Musical Vistas* programme in 2005 that showbands were thankful there was such a big production value to the songs. 'Lads [in bands] said to me afterwards, "Everybody in the country got a job on that song" because there was everything in it, you name any instrument and it was in there on "Make Me an Island". On "Good Looking Woman" Johnny Arthey put everything including the kitchen sink in. They were beautiful arrangements, absolutely gorgeous arrangements. He wrote for a big band and they were exciting songs for bands to play.'

Recording it had been exciting and good-spirited too, and very much 'on the hop' as he had laid down his vocal while busy jetting around Europe in support of 'Make Me an Island'. The musicians gave it their all for him. The piano player, who features prominently, did just that but then forgot what he had done. 'There was this amazing riff on the piano that went right up into the air. When we listened to the take we liked it, and I thought, "This is working." But when we went through it again, the piano break wasn't in there. I discovered it hadn't been written, that it just came out of his head, but after about four more takes he found it again. I was singing to the end of it, and I'd hoped Bill [Somerville-Large] had put it down. After, I signalled, "That's the one!"'

Joe delivered the delirious lyrics with real passion, creativity and flair. There was a chord change at the start and finish of each line, and Joe shifted up or down a key on each line accordingly, holding notes and then letting them go in a flash before launching into the next line. The intonation of the held words – complete with a quiver – at the end of each line was his suggestion, and the famous groan came from pure excitement at the quality of the playing. Joe just remembered 'giving it socks' in the recording booth, and it shows.

The song's playful lyrics are among the best Joe ever recorded, and Joe would praise Hammond and Hazelwood's clever wordplay at every available opportunity; he was particularly fond of the song's final line, in which the woman of the song is described as an angel without wings. The B-side, the under-rated 'Something Happens', is an equally clever love song. Even though Joe is a little subdued vocally in its verses, he still rises above the ranges of most pop singers, singing with real passion in the joyous chorus. It was *almost* the perfect Joe Dolan love song but surprisingly he rarely performed it live.

Joe once again criss-crossed the globe in support of 'You're Such a Good Looking Woman', never allowing the fame to go to his head. 'There were a lot of big stars around at the time, and Joe was one of them, but he never thought of himself as a big star,' Seamus recalled. 'After a show or whatever, he just switched off and was the same Joe.' He was extremely sociable, and would treat everyone the same. But the boredom factor was beginning to creep in. The novelty of sightseeing and the attractions of the big European cities had worn off by the time they travelled Europe for the third time in a little under a year, and in Bruges in Belgium, where Joe and Seamus were snowbound for a couple of days, they were bored out of their brains. Some parts of the European promotional world were being exposed as a waste of time, and Joe wasn't too happy about some of the TV shows he had to do. He was far happier on big stations like RTL than on localized ones. In addition, Joe still had gigs in Ireland every Thursday, Friday, Saturday and Sunday night, so he barely had time to take it all in – a gruelling schedule he kept up for much of the 1970s.

'It was extraordinary on Joe. A real killer. But he never outwardly showed it,' Seamus remembers. 'He might be grumpy on a flight over, but once we touched down he just picked up and put on the charm.' What made it more difficult for Joe was that he was invariably singing in a foreign language. He had already recorded versions of 'Make Me an Island' and 'Teresa' in different languages, and 'Good Looking Woman' joined them, with versions in Spanish, Italian, French, Portuguese and German.

It was a hit in Spain and in South America (as 'Eras una Mujer tan Singular'), in France (as 'Tu es une si Belle Femme'), and in Holland, Norway, Portugal, Sweden, West Germany, Spain, Italy, Turkey and Brazil. In Australia it was packaged as a special four-track EP with 'Bridge over Troubled Waters', 'Games People Play' and an alternative mix of 'Make Me an Island'. Joe's Israeli fans were also treated to an EP, which featured 'Love Grows', 'Teresa' and 'You and the Looking Glass'. The single had a limited release in America, with promo copies dispatched to hundreds of radio stations.

In Ireland, 'Good Looking Woman' first appeared as a new entry in the charts on 30 January, and within a week it had broken into the Top Five, rising as high as number four. However, once again, it was the UK charts that everyone had their eyes on, as it was still the centre of the music universe. It entered the UK charts at number thirty-eight, the second highest new entry that week after Elvis Presley's 'Don't Cry Daddy'. Following some energetic television appearances and coupled with support from Radio Luxembourg, the BBC and other radio stations, it climbed to number twenty-eight. A warning bell was sounded by The Beatles, though, who entered the charts that week with 'Let It Be'.

After a round of club dates in the UK, the single broke the Top Twenty on its fifth week of release, rising to number eighteen in its sixteenth week in the charts. But Joe was to be gazumped by another Irish native, Eurovision winner Dana, whose 'All Kinds of Everything' started selling like crazy in the wake of her Eurovision triumph that week. Joe reached number seventeen in mid April, but the following week, Dana tiptoed over Simon and Garfunkel's 'Bridge Over Troubled Water' and grabbed the top spot.

Joe held on in the UK Top Forty for over three months, but that was to be as good as it got for 'Good Looking Woman' in the UK, and by the end of April, after nine weeks, it slipped to number twenty-one. He still outsold The Who, The Beatles, Elvis and countless others, and he was in the Top Twenty all over Europe and the Top Five back home, so there was to be little disappointment in the Dolan camp, but he would have to wait until November 1997 for the track finally to top the charts, when a re-recorded version with Dustin went all the way to the top, initiating a rebirth of his career.

In 1970, as Joe had now logged a couple of European tours, plans were being solidified for full-scale assaults elsewhere. South Africa and Australia were mentioned, but he needed a few more hits in the latter country to justify the expense.

Having experienced some of the exquisite venues and big theatres Europe had to offer, Joe was sometimes finding it tough coming back home to play spartan Irish ballrooms, which had been hastily built to cash in on the ballroom boom of the 1960s. 'Some of the venues were appalling: there was no dressing room in some of them, no running water, and nowhere to hang up your clothes – no chairs even. You had to go outside if you wanted to go to the toilet,' he remembered. 'Or go in the hall. Now, I always liked to mix with the fans, but not like that.' Some of the band used to pee in bottles and leave them behind them as a message to mean ballroom owners to get their act together. Unfortunately one night, a certain band member – who shall remain nameless as it is feared he still doesn't know about it – drank one by accident when he entered a dressing room thirsty after a show.

Joe had signed with the MAM Agency, who had booked him residencies in some of the leading UK venues and plenty of dates in the rest of Europe, and Joe and the band would soon be regulars in some of Europe's top venues, the first Irish act to really break out. This led to a couple of eye-opening and often chaotic years on the road, years that would hone Joe as a supreme entertainer, but would also test his commitment to his career to the absolute limit.

Even as he was touring on the strength of 'Good Looking Woman', Joe kept dipping into studios to lay down further tracks, including a handful of Hammond and Hazelwood compositions, three of which were earmarked as future singles. Joe was thrilled to be recording more of their tracks as they 'fitted like a glove' and were the perfect showcase for his tenor voice. He also teamed up with Roger Cook and Roger Greenaway, two of the hottest songwriters on the block, for 'It Makes No Difference'. Several sentimental love songs, such as 'Audrey', 'Falling in Love' and 'Sometimes a Man Just Has to Cry', were recorded too, along with harder-sounding material such as 'Friend in a Bottle'. He would also record several cinematic versions of well-known songs for his European fans, and his takes on 'Bridge Over Troubled Water', 'Can't Help Falling in Love' and 'Something's Burning' rivalled the originals.

As a showband singer who had covered the big hits of the early 1960s, Joe was rated as one of the best interpreters of other people's songs in the business. In the early days of his career, hundreds of thousands had danced, sang and maybe even shared their first kiss to the sounds of the big international stars they might never get to see. To his ballroom audiences Joe *was* Elvis, Frank Sinatra, Roy Orbison, Tony Bennett and even Mick Jagger. These new-era covers were a nice reminder of that golden era. To his European audience, who had never experienced the showband phenomenon, they were a good showcase of a great voice singing great songs.

In May 1970, a little over six months since his last album, Joe released his second big-league long-player, *You're Such a Good Looking Woman*. Even though he had had little time to record cohesively, Joe had given his all to the recording sessions and very much dictated the 'all killer-no filler' flow of the album. Because he sang mainly in minor keys, the sessions had been lengthy as musicians kept pace with his unusual voice, but his enthusiasm had never dipped, despite the gruelling hours. Joe often emerged from the studio shielding his eyes from the morning sun, as he headed straight to Heathrow to catch a flight back to Ireland to perform a concert later that same day.

But there was an anger gnawing away at him owing to the way his last two singles had been handled. If his second single had been a bigger hit, it would have made it easier to establish himself with his third. Joe felt that 'Good Looking Woman' should have done better and been given a bigger push. He would also be disappointed with his next single, 'It Makes No Difference'.

It was touted as a big summer single, but failed to make a significant impact on the UK charts, hovering about outside the Top Fifty for several weeks. In Europe, it was a different story and it did very well in several countries. Back home the single was his thirteenth consecutive smash hit, peaking at eleven and going on to spend close to two months in the Top Twenty.

The failure of 'It Makes No Difference' to break into the Top Ten came as a surprise, but not to Joe, who didn't rate it that much. It was not a thoroughbred love song, and record buyers and radio programmers didn't warm to its stop-start nature, which seemed to limit Joe's vocal style. When he did let rip it sounded forced, his tenor more aggressive than agreeable. The song's bittersweet lyrics didn't seem to match its production style, and Joe said he never felt comfortable with it; in fact, he would rarely perform it live, claiming it was almost two songs in one.

However, its writers, Roger Cook and Roger Greenaway, were sizzling in 1970, and with rumours circulating that Hammond and Hazelwood were about to leave for America, Shaftesbury felt Cook and Greenaway were a tailor-made replacement. They had enjoyed multiple chart successes with artists such as Gene Pitney (who topped the charts with their composition 'Something's Gotten Hold of My Heart' in 1967), Cliff Richard, Andy Williams, Gino Washington, Cilla Black, The Hollies and a young Elton John. The same year they worked with Joe, they would write the foundations of 'I'd Like to Teach the World to Sing', which became one of the all-time greatest selling singles after Coca-Cola adapted it for a worldwide advertisement campaign. But 'It Makes No Difference' was not one of their finest moments. Neither was the single's flip-side, a funky country ballad called 'I'll Be Home in About a Day or So', the first (and only) song Joe would record with a drifter as its central character.

Joe was also frustrated that there had been such a long gap between releases – there had been a couple of months between 'It Makes No Difference' and 'Good Looking Woman', when the norm in the UK and Ireland was to follow up hits one after another. And not only that, but as the material on the *You're Such a Good Looking Woman* album was so rich and varied, his record label had decided to release a number of different singles in different countries at the same time. In the summer of 1970 Joe found himself promoting 'It Makes No Difference' in the UK, Ireland and parts of mainland Europe, 'Something's Burning' in Spain and Portugal and 'Love of the Common People' in Germany (over two years after it had been a hit elsewhere); meanwhile, 'My First Love' was released in South Africa. Nevertheless, the album was still a huge hit across the globe.

Joe's creeping unhappiness had been compounded by Hammond and Hazelwood's official announcement that they were packing their bags for a songwriting career in the States. It would take Joe a full two years to find writers who could comfortably fill their shoes. 'It was a big downer for me when they left,' Joe later revealed. 'Theirs was a songwriting partnership that was made for me. They understood me, and I could really "become" their songs, so I was very sad to see them go.' As Joe struggled with a succession of Irish, English and American writers, he began to question himself as an artist, and he openly admitted in later years that he was beginning to lose interest in the music business. Without Hammond and Hazelwood, it seemed that the hits were harder to come by. 'When Hammond and Hazelwood stopped writing for me, I sort of lost a lot of interest in the game. I was getting songs by different people, from everywhere, mainly from London and different parts of the world. But I discovered on looking at them and hearing them they were just a remake of 'Good Looking Woman' or a remake of 'Make Me an Island' or a hash-up of something we had already done. I wasn't thinking of giving it up, but I was a bit depressed if you like, a bit despondent about the whole future of the Joe show.'

Joe's next single in Western Europe was the swinging 'Sometimes a Man Just Has to Cry', which came with the spirited B-side 'Friend in a Bottle', about one man's battle with the booze. The single again led to numerous TV appearances and a European promotional tour, but Joe began to turn down certain offers, a tell-tale sign of his lack of interest in playing the game. At the same time he was promoting this release, the slushy ballad 'Falling in Love' was being primed as a single elsewhere. He showed no outward signs of despair, though, and the Joe show carried on, even in Northern Ireland, where the Troubles had begun to take hold. Many acts turned their backs on the Province and refused to play there, but Joe never did.

Joe's band had developed into a well-honed and watertight unit while touring the UK and the rest of Europe, capable of reproducing Johnny Arthey's big-time arrangements with ease, while still maintaining a rugged charm. At this stage the billing was invariably for Joe only – in Europe there was no such thing as Joe Dolan and The Drifters, it was just Joe Dolan – so, free of expectations, they cut loose. The time that Joe spent away from the band while performing solo across Europe saw him develop into a confident and powerful front man, which in turn rubbed off on the band.

When Joe was away they still assembled, not for gigs but for rehearsals, where Joe's new material was deconstructed, remastered and augmented. 'It's hard to believe it now, but we were one of the few bands playing original music at the time, so we rehearsed almost non-stop,' Ben remembered. Ben said the band were particularly fond of the album *You're Such a Good Looking Woman*, as it 'was a dream for the brass section', and its free-flowing drums, perky piano runs and scintillating guitar licks gave every member of the band something to sink their teeth into. Where there wasn't brass they would add it in, subject to Joe's approval of course. Ben says that the songs, particularly the lead singles, had such a freshness about them and such passion, that they never went stale. 'When you'd play them, it was like you were in a new band. Every time we did them there was a lift. We never grew tired of playing them.'

But Ben was torn between two worlds when Joe and the band prepared for a bout of touring at the end of 1970 (a run of dates that would continue almost non-stop for a couple of years). With a vast army of Irish fans to please on one hand, and a battalion of new fans on the other, Ben wondered how they would get the mix right. Irish gigs were still lengthy, drawn-out affairs (often four hours long), but in the UK and on the continent gigs rarely went over the two-hour mark. The right balance had to be struck, and eventually a showband armistice was reached – they would leave the past behind.

'At first I thought we did too much of the new stuff, which was ridiculous really, because it was *our* stuff, but I had this fear. It worked out a dream, of course, but to get over that initial problem was unnerving, y'know? Joe, on the other hand, had complete confidence in the material,' Ben recalls.

Joe's long-term fans rated the live shows at this time as some of the most electrifying they had seen, and Joe pulled out all the stops to ensure a memorable evening of entertainment. However, he would never allow too much of the past to be forgotten, and songs such as 'The Answer to Everything', 'My Own Peculiar Way', 'Pretty Brown Eyes', 'I Love You More and More Every Day' and 'Tar and Cement' always found a place in the live set.

Joe started working the big cabaret clubs and theatres in the UK for the first half of the 1970s, and its cities became second homes for Joe and the band for much of the decade that followed. Joe's decision to sign with the MAM Agency had been crucial as they opened dozens of doors for him. With their guidance he would do a week in some venues, longer runs in others, and he would also slot in occasional one-night performances in key venues dotted around the country.

A big eye-opener for Joe and the band was their maiden residency in a cabaret venue, Tito's in Cardiff, in April 1970. This was the first time that Joe would front and take complete charge of a show. Previous English tours had largely been confined to Irish halls and ballrooms, where the crowd was 90 per cent Irish ex-pat. These new gigs were light years away from all that and were in front of a predominantly British audience. He was also following a week of shows by legendary jazz man Acker Bilk at the club, so expectations were high.

For the maiden voyage they had brought their own PA system, even though the club had offered them one. The one-man army that was John Delamere looked after it, and the driving. Joe recalled that as they set up on the first night, bright-eyed and bushy-tailed, a worker in the club came in and asked for a lighting spec. His request was met with silence. 'None of us knew what he was on about,' Joe laughs. In Irish venues at the time there was no such thing as a lighting rig: the hall was either bathed in all its house lights' glory or the lights were dimmed a bit. 'So I said, "Oh yes, put the lights up for fast songs and down for slow songs." Well, yer man thought I had two heads!'

Joe was also unsure about what he should say on his opening night. 'What will I say? When should I say it?' he asked the band.

'Maybe you should wait until after you sing the first three numbers to talk?' Ben suggested. 'Warm them up a bit.' He winked at the band to let Joe sort this one out on his own.

As Joe struggled, he asked his manager to come up with an intro. 'Here, you write out something,' Joe said, thrusting a marker and paper into Seamus's hands.

OH ME OH MY

Seamus thought for a minute then wrote out, in capital letters, 'LADIES AND GENTLEMEN'. Then he got stuck.

'Have you anything written? Here, give us that!' an impatient Joe said as he swiped the paper from his manager, thinking Seamus had written out an intro for him.

As he got ready to take to the stage he unfolded the piece of paper to learn his lines. 'Ladies and gentlemen.' He turned to Ben. 'Is that it? Am I not going to say it's great to be here or anything?'

It became an in-joke for years after that, and when Joe knew Seamus was watching he would say to the crowd, 'Ladies and gentlemen . . .' and then pause. The band would kick in without Joe saying another word.

For his entire career Joe would suffer from nerves before a show, but these would vanish when he took to the stage, and it was no different that first night in Tito's. 'He came up with things himself; he never needed a prompt or anything like that. He might show a few nerves, but they say all the great performers get nervous before a show. If you're not nervous about facing an audience then there must be something wrong with you,' the author of 'Ladies and gentlemen' remarked.

From the moment he came offstage at Tito's, Joe said these were the kind of shows he wanted to do. 'I didn't want to be singing in a dance band any longer,' he remarked.

The week-long run would also open Joe's eyes to a whole new way of getting paid – or rather, of not getting paid, as after they took their hotel charges and expenses out of the equation, each member of the eleven-man touring party was left with barely a fiver. As Seamus recalls, they had to 'cut their cloth according to their measure', but things improved as the months progressed and Joe's name got even bigger.

Joe then played all over the UK in cities such as Birmingham, Sheffield, Leeds, Manchester, Bolton, Liverpool and Glasgow as often as he could. In venues such as Fagan's, Talk of the North and the Batley Variety Club, he would play for over 1,500 people a night, seven nights a week. 'The North of England was great at that time, and it was a brilliant place for these venues. They all seemed to do well and we made a lot of friends.'

As he had done in the Irish showband era, Joe became good friends with a massive array of acts on the same circuit: Tom Jones, Gene Pitney, Shirley Bassey, Roy Orbison, Kenny Ball, Frankie Laine, Engelbert Humperdinck and others. 'Every week we'd see these people, and we got a right shock when we met Gene Pitney in the Dolce Vita in Leeds after we had finished a run. We got about £1,000 for the week, and Gene Pitney came in after us and he was getting £11,000!' Comedians such as Morecambe and Wise, Tommy Cooper, Larry Grayson, Freddie Starr, Ted Rogers, Stan Boardman, Tom O'Connor and Jim Bowen were all playing the same venues, and Joe often shared the bill with them. Memorably for Joe, Frank Carson, who was then a big name in the UK, supported Joe on a couple of early tours.

'Frank had been there on those tours a long time before us, and I had great respect for him,' Joe said. 'He was Mr Show Business in England as far as I was concerned. We were only upstarts coming in on his territory. To me, he was a far bigger star, and here he was coming on *before* us!'

To maximize his profile and income, Joe and the band sometimes played in two different venues in two different cities on the same night, particularly in the northern cities, where Joe was a big draw. 'There was something about the north of England character, and love of a good singer, that seemed to bond them to Joe,' Seamus would remark.

Sometimes this plan backfired. On one occasion they were booked to play an early evening date in a club in Sheffield with a late night date booked for a club on the outskirts of Leeds. Stage manager John Delamere had the schedule worked out to military precision, and had drilled the band on what they were to do between shows. They would finish in one club at 10.30 p.m., and be ready to start in the other one just before midnight. After the first gig ended, the band would take the gear down and load everything into Delamere's van. He would then race off ahead of the band to make a head start on setting the gear up for the later show. Once Joe had been convinced there was no need to talk to everyone in the venue, he would be bundled into another bandwagon. Somehow this night they took the wrong turn and it was only after ten minutes of straight motorway driving that they realized they were en route to London – the opposite end of the country. It took them a good while before they figured out how they could get off the motorway and turn their bandwagon in the opposite direction.

'John made it and had the gear up, but we didn't; we were about an hour late and were politely told to eff off,' Joe laughed. They made it the next night though, but only after a crash course in the rules of the road, which made road maps mandatory bedtime reading. Two shows a night became a norm in later years, and they had it down to a fine art by the time they reached Las Vegas at the end of the decade.

Some of these initial gigs were held in tough working-men's clubs, which could be daunting places to play. The band stayed where all show-business people stayed at the time – B&Bs and residential hotels offering an evening meal in lieu of a breakfast. Remembering in horror the dodgy platefuls of mystery meat and cramped rooms, all the band members wonder how they coped with it. In particular they were surprised and humbled that Joe never acted the star of the show, but stayed with them.

'I often think about it and wonder why Joe didn't stay in a hotel on his own. But he refused to stay anywhere else; he insisted the band stayed with him,' Seamus remembers. 'Although these big tours sounded glamorous, they were poor days for us, as we had to work our way up over a few years to get to the point where we were making any sort of money. And we were paying for most of the promotion of our own records too, so any money we did make went directly into that. We struggled for three or four years until we started to make it big. Everyone thought it must have been fantastic to be these fellas on the road all over the place, but it was hard work.'

On the way home from the club dates, Joe always made a point of playing at least one big show to the Irish community, with two main motives: firstly to ensure the Irish in England had a taste of home; and secondly to get extra money for his band members. It was usually the Galtymore in Cricklewood, London, and Joe and the band would earn more on that night than they got on the other six.

Joe and the band also continued to perform across Europe, where the singles, although often different from the ones released back home, did very well for Joe. The orchestral 'Falling in Love', for example, was tailor-made for a Mediterranean market, and it was a hit in France, Spain, Greece and Turkey. Even songs such as 'Sometimes a Man Just Has to Cry' were better received in Europe than at home.

The UK became the hub of Joe Dolan operations in 1970, and he was making a big impression there. Having proved his worth and commitment with the often-gruelling club dates, it was perhaps inevitable that Joe would be made a series of tempting offers for longer and more lucrative residencies. The MAM Agency were keen to strike when the iron was hot, but Joe was less so.

One such offer, for a long-term residency in Blackpool, the British Las Vegas, could have made him a permanent and well-paid fixture on the UK circuit, but the terms of the offer – though financially very attractive – dictated that it was for Joe only. The season would be from June to October – two shows a night for twenty-two weeks, with every Sunday night off – in a 'beautiful, 2,000-seat venue'. The offer stipulated that Joe must go with a tried and tested musical director as well as some seasoned session musicians, and he would be part of a packaged variety show – a big-name comedian would join him on the bill, with an up-and-coming pop act and an MC. He would be given guaranteed TV exposure and a Royal Command Performance would be a certainty. The likes of Val Doonican, Cilla Black and Ken Dodd were all doing these shows at the time and were becoming household names in the UK in the process.

Joe turned it down, fearing it would spell the end of his musical relationship with his brother as well as the loss of his band, and although he was made the offer two years in a row, with the money significantly increased each time, he turned those down too. Years later, similar offers would be made in different countries, but Joe rejected them all. 'As was apparent afterwards, he never wanted to be more than four weeks away. Whatever was in his head, he used to get bored. In hindsight he was right, but he could have become a huge star. It wasn't what he wanted and we respected that. It was seen as being a big thing to have a summer season in a place like Blackpool. As it turned out the summer seasons tapered off just as the club scene in England did. People had different ideas of entertainment and holidays. There was a big social change at the time,' Seamus reflected.

There were big social changes in Ireland too in the early 1970s. The showbands had been dying for some years, and for many of the big names it was a slow and agonizing death. From the highs of 3,000 and 4,000 people on a Friday and Sunday night, bands were now getting 2,000 or 1,500 people if they were lucky. For the smaller names and also-rans it was a merciless cull: a quick death and a return to a job on a farm or wherever. Although he bucked the trend, Joe was not immune to the falling numbers. Television, discos and visiting performers had changed people's perception of a night out. Women were being welcomed into more pubs, and men followed in hot pursuit. This situation was making Joe more and more determined to bring his band with him to as many places as possible, but to keep the show on the road they still had to log in Irish dates.

Newspaper coverage of the latest acts had also declined, and *Spotlight* magazine, once the voice of Ireland's youth, was floundering as the voice of yesteryear. In some ways Joe was tarred with the same brush. 'Joe had a history and a status at home, and he was something that people thought was from the past,' Seamus says. 'The Irish people honestly didn't know how big he was abroad, which was perhaps the greatest shame of that whole period.' His triumph at an international song contest in Romania in March 1970, for example, was barely reported back home, despite attracting a live TV audience of several million throughout Eastern Europe. Some of the biggest names in world music competed in the event, and Joe became a household name in Eastern Europe, although few of his records would be officially released there. In fact, it is reckoned he became one of the most bootlegged acts of the 1970s in Eastern Europe.

But it was hard to change a mindset when the ballrooms were closing down and there were few venues to do it in. In Dublin, the Olympia and the Gaiety Theatres had yet to embrace popular music, and the Adelphi and Carlton cinemas alongside the National Stadium in the South Circular Road were seen as venues for international acts, who were now leaving Ireland off their itineraries. The Beatles, The Rolling Stones and Bob Dylan had all visited in the 1960s, and Belfast had become a favoured destination for acts like Led Zeppelin and Pink Floyd, but the Troubles soon left the whole country with few visiting acts.

Joe also believed that the Irish record-buying public were slaves to the tastes of the British record-buying public. What became a hit in the UK also became a hit in Ireland, and *Top of the Pops* was still the main shop window. Joe told *Evening Herald* reporter Tony Wilson at the time: 'It's a proven thing to me now that if I don't get a hit in England, then I won't get a hit in Ireland. If "Sometimes a Man Has to Cry" went into the charts in England, it would have gone into the charts here . . . the Irish are beautiful, dedicated followers of fashion.' He reckoned that artists such as Van Morrison, Rory Gallagher and even Val Doonican had to 'give it away before they got it back' by having to leave Ireland before they were 'accepted' by an Irish audience, but despite further offers to base himself abroad, where he was considered a big act, he continued to stay in Ireland.

Joe began another major UK tour in September 1970 in better form. He was performing in classier, bigger venues than he had earlier in the year, and mentally, he was in better shape too. Doubts that had arisen early in 1970 after 'Good Looking Woman' did not do as well as he had hoped were not as prevalent as they had been, and the highs of touring outside Ireland started to eclipse the lows he experienced in the wake of the break-up of his songwriting team.

However, just when things seemed to be on the up, the rough and ready nature of the UK club circuit reared its head on the second night of a week-long tour that September, at the Wookie Hollow in Liverpool. The venue was more of a theatre than a club, and Joe had just wowed a full house with a high-octane two-hour show. He had refined and restructured his set, and hammy songs that he had been reluctantly performing in Ireland for a couple of years were no longer part of his show. It was an all-out assault from Dolan, with his eight-piece band in peak form. Any time Joe played Liverpool he was always afforded a reception as passionate as his performance, and he had given it his all that night.

After the show, Joe and some of his band had a few drinks in the venue. A smattering of fans remained, keeping a respectful distance, as they always did over the years. A few bought their hero a drink and thanked him for another great show. If a Joe show had gone particularly well, Joe would be on a high for hours afterwards, and the only way he could come down was to attempt to switch off and have a few quiet drinks, talking about anything from golf and fishing to food and cars. As the band and crew drifted off to their hotel for the night, Joe and another member of his road crew, Hubert 'Shotgun' Crowley, stayed behind for a few more.

A girl who had been at the show began to pester Joe at the bar, and eventually he told her to leave him alone – albeit in a trademark Joe Dolan way, politely with a smile. The girl had been sitting with three men at another table and all had been drinking heavily that night. One of the men became boisterous and began to take his ire out on a young assistant manager at the venue. The man claimed he was owed a bottle of champagne, as he had ordered one earlier from a member of the bar staff who had gone home. He persisted with this for some time, but the assistant manager explained there was no way he could get champagne as it had been locked up for the night. Joe was always a machine gun when it came to firing off a quip, and he casually remarked to the man that he would have to come back in the morning and have himself a champagne breakfast. The man didn't see the funny side and he started to call Joe a 'Paddy', telling him the drinks were none of his business. Joe tried to laugh it off and said nothing as he carried on with his drink, although he did signal to Shotgun that perhaps it might be in their best interests to join his brother Ben and the band in the nearby hotel.

The girl then returned to the men's table, and the man's taunts grew more persistent. As Joe attempted to brush them off and leave the club, he was grabbed by the man, who asked Joe where he thought he was going. Joe replied he was going home, but was told he was not leaving until he apologized to the woman. The man then headbutted Joe, shattering his nose. Joe fell to the ground as blood flowed from his smashed nose, and although what happened next is something of a mystery, Joe claimed the assistant manager backed away and other people left the club in a hurry, as the men were known to them. Shotgun leaped to Joe's rescue but was grabbed by one of the attacker's pals. The attacker was joined by his other pal and the two started to kick and punch Joe as the girl egged them on. Shotgun was also punched and kicked as he tried to free himself and he was chased into a corner.

Meanwhile Joe managed to get up from the floor and attempted to shield himself from his attackers, but was kicked and punched to the ground a second time. He bravely fought off the blows and managed to get to his feet again and escape through the nearest door. His eyes were swollen and blackened with blood, and he fell through into a toilet as he was pursued by his attackers. He managed to lock himself into a cubicle, but his assailants kept taunting him, calling him 'an Irish bastard' and a 'fucking Paddy'.

They started to kick the door of the cubicle and Joe managed to hold them off for a couple of minutes. However, the force of the kicking broke the door free from its hinges, and the two stormed into the cubicle. They then proceeded to attack Joe even more viciously. One of the men grabbed Joe by the neck and shoved his head into the toilet bowl. As he held it there, the other man stamped on his head. Joe managed to fight back and somehow avoided getting his neck broken as he pushed one of the men back out through the cubicle doorframe. But his bravery only delayed the onslaught, and pushing him to the floor again they landed further blows on to his bloodied frame. One of the men literally pulled lumps of hair out of his head, and Joe's flamboyant fringe was torn out completely. Another slammed Joe's head into the wall, on top of one of his own concert posters. 'You won't look like this again, you Irish c——!' the ringleader is alleged to have said as he ordered the other man to search for a piece of rope. 'We're going to fucking throw what's left of you in the Mersey,' he sneered. Terrified, Joe tried to fight back, but blows and kicks continued to rain down on him.

Shotgun eventually managed to free himself from the third attacker and outran him, raising the alarm. The police were summoned and he then ran to alert Joe's brother and the rest of the band. Shotgun's attacker raced back into the club to tell his two pals to finish the job and get out. As the sound of distant police sirens filled the Merseyside air, the main attacker told Joe that tonight was his lucky night. He punched Joe back on to the floor, and Joe slumped to the tiled surface. The three men and the drunken girl raced out of the club just as the band and crew rushed to Joe's aid. By the time the police arrived, the attackers were probably a couple of streets away.

An ambulance was immediately summoned, and Ben sat by his brother's side as he was rushed to hospital. Joe had received multiple injuries, lacerations, cuts and severe bruising to the face, head and body. He was also suffering from internal bleeding, and on doctors' orders he was not allowed to travel home. He and Ben then tried to help the Merseyside police identify the attackers. Meanwhile, the rest of the band returned home, the remainder of the tour cancelled. News of the attack spread rapidly, and Joe was front-page news in all the Irish papers and the international music press, photographs of Joe's bloated and battered face shocking his fans. Joe wanted to return home, but the police insisted he stay and help with their enquiries. However, the search would prove to be a frustrating and traumatic episode for him, especially as some of the policemen on the case had an idea who the attackers were but could not pin the assault on them as alibis appeared out of nowhere.

After six days, Joe returned home. He had to cancel a full six weeks of European engagements. The release of a new single in Europe – 'One Way Woman' – went almost unnoticed, and plans for the release of 'You and the Looking Glass' at home and in South Africa, Australia, Japan, Brazil, Israel and other countries were stalled as Joe recovered from his savage assault. As he looked in the looking glass all he could see was a face left disfigured, his nose flat and smashed into his head. He became deeply depressed. Joe's agency commenced proceedings to sue the club for assault and for loss of earnings, but they were in for a severe shock when the club suddenly closed and went into liquidation, leaving little hope of recompense.

Joe and Shotgun returned to Liverpool when the police told him they had made a breakthrough, and he was faced with the unenviable task of inspecting a police line-up face to face. He couldn't identify any of his attackers, and attempts at jogging his memory with the aid of sketches and police photos of previously convicted thugs proved futile.

The beating led to a sense of despondency that would not leave Joe for a while. It was a blow to his confidence, which had just been regained with the initial success of his UK tours, and, despite continued success all over the world – he would soon rack up hit singles in Brazil, South Africa, Australia, New Zealand, Japan, the Philippines, India, Israel, Romania, Yugoslavia, Scandinavia, Italy, Spain, Portugal, Holland, Belgium and at home in Ireland and England – that night in the Wookie Hollow would have a long-term effect on Joe's international popularity, as he became even more attached to Ireland and more determined to break the country out of its showband cycle.

Joe hadn't taken a proper holiday since 'Make Me an Island', and he started to cancel some promotional appearances as he tried to get a break. 'To break into, say, Czechoslovakia, we would be told that we needed to do this TV show and that TV show,' Seamus reveals. 'But nobody ever told us what shows – and sometimes we were flying off for two days to do an afternoon show there with a couple of thousand viewers when we should have been doing a late-night show in France or someplace else with millions of viewers. Joe needed a bit of time to savour what had happened to him, but we were being pulled and pushed all over the place, so he started saying no to certain invitations.'

'I got lazy as far as looking after my own side of the business was concerned. I was making excuses all the time, saying I couldn't do this, when I could really have done it. I used to phone up and say I missed the plane or something,' Joe said. The post-traumatic stress of the beating would prove hard to shift.

A rethink was required to reignite Joe's passion. Luckily, Hammond and Hazelwood's parting gift, 'You and the Looking Glass', came to the rescue: a classy, amorous song that extolled the virtues of natural beauty. If there were any doubts about Joe Dolan's aphrodisiac qualities as he emerged from the slow-dancing showband era, then they were answered with this track. Its B-side was 'Make Me Act the Fool', a high-energy Hammond and Hazelwood album track that Joe loved. Its 'let me entertain you' theme was perfect for the live arena and he played it for years, making it a big part of his Las Vegas shows in the 1980s.

Released internationally in 1971, 'You and the Looking Glass' went to the top end of the charts in South Africa and stayed in its upper echelons for several weeks. The timing of its success there was the perfect tonic for Joe, as he had just confirmed details of his first South African tour, so even though it failed to make an impact at home or in previous Dolan strongholds, there was to be a glimmer of happiness reflected in Joe's bruised and battered face as the year ended.

11

Wait a minute, this isn't Rio

The effects of Joe's savage beating would linger for much of 1971 and 1972, but he had little time to mope about. He and the band toured England and the rest of Europe, performing in over a dozen countries in just a few exhausting weeks. He also undertook his first mammoth tour of South Africa in early 1972, spending six weeks on the road as the headliner of a major package tour (of which more later). This was immediately followed by a six-day tour of Israel, which reached a fitting climax when they topped the bill in an open-air festival attended by over 70,000. Joe was subsequently voted Israel's most popular international star, and his fame began to spread throughout the Middle East. In the space of just five months between 1971 and 1972, the Irish ambassador of song performed in five continents as single releases mushroomed around the world. He also managed to record several further singles, working in different languages with some of Europe's top writers and producers.

Big international song contests were all the rage in the 1960s and early 1970s, and Joe competed at quite a few of them, as did all the big league artists of the time. The biggest competition of them all was the International Song Contest of Rio de Janeiro, which was first staged in 1965. Its 1971 staging would be Joe's first official engagement after his savage Liverpool beating, and he would be flying the green, white and gold for Ireland with 'One Way Woman'. With a powerful song behind him, expectations were high.

The contest received huge international coverage and, having been won by a few Americans over the years, it was beamed live into millions of American and South American homes, where Joe had already started to rack up some hits recorded in Spanish and Portuguese. It was also filmed for distribution to the major TV networks around the world, which meant even more exposure. However, it was very nearly a one-way trip, and were it not for the bravery of one pilot, Joe might never have got there.

'Seamus and I had to fly to London to get the plane to Rio de Janeiro, so we were a little stressed when we got to the airport, even though we were masters of the art of catching planes at the last minute. When we got on the plane we knew a load of the guys on it; there was some of Tom Jones's people on it, and loads of really good guys from the English newspapers and magazines and record industry people, so we relaxed a bit.' At midnight on 16 October, the captain wished Joe a happy birthday and the initial dozen or so who had been enjoying a drink swelled as extra well-wishers joined the party. 'We were having a right old laugh, and we were singing a few songs, clapping and telling yarns and what have you, but it got a bit too loud for the other passengers so the captain ordered that we be moved down to the back of the plane.'

Free from disapproving eyes, the group partied on even more loudly. At one stage Joe was spotted dancing up the aisle in just a pair of shorts and his stockinged feet. 'We ended up drinking everything on the plane. When we ran out of wine, gin, vodka, whiskey, brandy and beer we moved on to Dubonnet, Campari and Martini and all this stuff that no one drank, and we drank it all. It was probably one of the best sing-songs I've ever had,' Joe recalled, amid fits of guilty laughter. With no more drink left on the plane, one by one the revellers began to fall asleep. However, as they slept, the pilot, crew and everyone else not involved in the celebrations were subject to a terrifying experience.

'I woke up with all these people shaking me. I just thought, "We're land-ing, thanks be to God." But I looked out the window and saw all these army men, and the jungle behind them. I thought, "Wait a minute, this isn't Rio." All these people were barking orders at us. I honestly thought we'd flown into a military coup. We were put on a bus, everyone in our group hungover and not knowing what was going on.'

From the mystery military base they were brought to Recife International Airport. Joe fell asleep and eventually woke up in Rio. The official explana-tion was that they had landed in the military base to refuel, and Joe thought nothing of it.

'Two years later Peter O'Sullivan, a guy who was on the plane, rang me and said, "Do you remember the time we landed in Brazil?" As it turned out, when we were all asleep the plane flew into an electrical storm and lightning had hit it. All the electronics were wiped out and they couldn't contact the ground and the ground couldn't contact them. The plane flew off-course over the sea, but the pilot changed course back over land and started to fly low to find somewhere to land. He couldn't be found on radar at the time, and he had no radio, so the plane was officially listed as missing, presumed crashed, and search parties were sent out to try and locate the plane. I believe they were getting ready to contact priests and embassies.'

The pilot flew by eye without the aid of any directional tools towards the city of Recife, and decided to take a chance at landing the plane either at Recife Air Force Base or at Recife's own airport, whichever came into view first. The air force base won out. He was not able to warn the base of his plans to land a civilian jet on military property, but somehow, as soldiers were scrambled, he managed to do so without being shot down. It turned out that the plane was just about to run out of fuel and it was only when it touched down that some of the electrics started working again. The pilot contacted Rio, who called off the search. 'Well, it was a miracle, apparently, but they forgot to mention it to us!' Joe remarked. 'It was only years later that I got a flashback of waking up to the sound of this bang, and I felt the plane dipping. But I fell back to sleep! I thought I was dreaming!'

Seamus remembers that when they landed at the air force base, the pas-sengers were ordered off the plane and everyone except Joe complied. He was fast asleep. Air-base personnel and some of the beleaguered crew went back in to wake Joe, and Seamus recalls standing on the concrete of the military base trying to take it all in. 'We were all standing around confused on this runway and all you could hear was Joe's snoring from the plane, then him shouting when he was woken up!'

However, despite its shaky start, the trip ended up being, for Joe, 'The best ten days I have ever had. Just fun and laughter and craic every day from the moment we got up. We used to love waking up – even me – because we knew we had a great day ahead.' Joe got through the first two rounds of the contest (ringed by dancers and a full orchestra) in front of 20,000, but didn't mind finishing 'nowhere' in the final because he was having so much fun. Every night Joe and Seamus were invited out to parties, receptions and outrageous ten-course dinners. One night in the British embassy Joe was serenaded by the British ambassador and his staff with a cappella versions of 'Make Me an Island' and 'Good Looking Woman'. 'It was quite strange,' Joe remembers of the black-tie singalong. He was pleased to discover how big he was in South America, and he made several promotional appearances and played a couple of solo gigs while there. One incident that stuck in his mind was a late-night walk down a Rio street when he heard 'Make Me an Island' booming out of a jukebox in an arcade.

However, because they had such fun on the trip, when they went to pay the hotel bill, neither Joe nor Seamus had any money left to pay for the 'extras'. There was only one thing they could do – leave without paying. 'The barman loved us, and sure we were buying drink for everyone. The tab we ran up was unmercifully large, so all we could do was run. Seamus had about £50 left and I had less.' So, international singing star Joe Dolan, with sales of over 2 million records to his credit, threw some of his luggage out the window and calmly walked out through the hotel reception carrying some light baggage, waving at the receptionist and hotel manager as he strolled past the desk. 'It was as if we were going sightseeing for the day. We walked out and, calm as you like, picked up our bags and got into a taxi. I'll always remember it because it had no front seats. Anyway, we got to the airport and that was it.'

However, with their flights delayed and a couple of penniless hours to kill in the Departures area, panic and guilt about what they had just done began to set in. A few nights earlier on the trip, one of the journalists travelling with them had attempted to leave a restaurant without paying, having 'treated' a large party to an extravagant meal. He was stopped by a cleaver-wielding chef and threatened with more than an order to wash dishes and peel spuds for the night. Seamus expected the police to come in at any minute, so he attempted to hide under a hat. Joe tied a handkerchief necktie around his neck and sat there reading a comic. Realizing there may be financial trouble ahead when they landed in London, they spent the last of their money calling Pye Records begging them to organize someone to meet them in London with a loaded wallet.

Onstage, Joe was on fire and never more so than on his first full tour of South Africa in 1972, which was organized by the Quibells, the legendary South African music-industry family. Joe's South African record company, Teal Records, who had guided tracks such as 'Make Me an Island' and 'You and the Looking Glass' right to the top of the charts, promoted and released new records to coincide with the tour. Joe's music was known everywhere, from townships to isolated rural communities to rich enclaves deep within the cities.

South African tours at the dawn of the 1970s tended to be package shows, and Joe and Chris Andrews were the big names on the bill. Well-known Irish funnyman Hal Roach was the comic glue, and prototype boyband groups The Dallas Boys and The Paper Dolls were the cubs. A momentary lapse of reason saw Joe placed second on the bill to Andrews, who had topped the charts in the 1960s with 'Yesterday Man' and 'To Whom it Concerns' (which most people will recognize as the theme tune to *The Late Late Show*) and who was number one in the charts with 'Carole OK' just before the tour began.

However, a failure to read the small print led to some acute embarrassment (and anger) as Joe's band had unwittingly agreed to back *all* the acts on the bill. They only found out when they arrived sweating to the rehearsal venue, the Three Arts Theatre in Cape Town, after an arduous two-day journey. There, they were met by the producer of the show, who started handing out sheet music to the dumbstruck band. Some guffawed as they looked at the alien music. All eyes soon focused on Frankie McDonald and new boy Liam Meade, the only fully trained musicians in the band. 'This isn't our music, boys,' Frankie said as he flicked through the books. A row immediately broke out, The Drifters saying there was no way they would have agreed to back all the acts on the bill.

'This stuff would have taken them ten years to rehearse,' Frankie said, laughing, as he recalled the complex arrangements for the other acts. 'The row was pure comedy as there were only two days to go before the show,' said Joe. With the band exhausted, rough around the edges and irritable, Joe casually slipped away to leave it to his brother and manager to sort out.

After a couple of tense hours the producer managed to get a session band together, and Frankie agreed to act as musical director to guide them through the six-hour show. Gordon 'Corky' Coleman joined on guitar. Well used to playing mammoth sets back home, they didn't seem to mind, although they did negotiate extra payments for themselves. However, the air was still rife with tension, and the producer was disgusted with The Drifters. They were also disgusted with him, as he had not let them slip off for something to eat, and after several hours of slouching around the venue, they were in even worse form than when they had arrived.

'The other acts were dressed to the nines, the kinds of lads with a suit for every occasion. We, on the other hand, looked like complete tramps,' Ben recalls.

The producer snapped. 'What do you actually do?' he asked them. 'Can I hear it? Do you actually play?'

Joe was summoned, and he arrived seemingly oblivious to the tension still in the air. 'He bounded in shaking hands with them all as if he had known them this hundred years,' Ben said, laughing. 'It was like they were all long-lost friends. He was slapping lads on the back, finding out where they were from – "Oh, you're from there? A relation of mine was there last year." He had hugs for all the crew and workers in the theatre until he finally got to the producer, whom he grabbed by the hand and slapped on the back. "Pleased to meet you, I just love producers!" he roared.'

Any patience that the producer had left was fading fast. Through gritted teeth he asked the lads if they were ready to do something.

'All right, lads,' says Joe. 'We'll do "Good Looking Woman", yeah?'

Maurice Walsh counted them in and – bang – the producer's jaw dropped to the floor. 'Jesus. It's fantastic!' he said. 'If you played with the rest of them, you'd ruin the show!'

Any lingering animosity was quickly forgotten about and Joe became the centre of attention on the tour, holding court and making everyone feel part of a team.

'After a few nights we were all Paddies together,' he said. 'A few jars and the whole thing mellowed greatly. The groups got on great, and we all helped each other out, even though my lads couldn't help in the way the contract stipulated. But it was great fun, and it was wonderful to have Hal Roach on the road with us.'

The tour, which played in big theatres, halls and arenas, was a big boost for Joe's own confidence. After just a handful of nights, he was promoted to the top of the bill. Joe remembered that Chris was 'very gracious' about his demotion. 'In fact, when the decision was made, he came running out to me one night pleading to have my band when the tour was over!'

Although there were whispers of discontent from certain quarters of the Irish media regarding Joe's decision to perform in South Africa, Joe was dismissive of these and he recalls no signs of segregation or apartheid at his shows. 'We sold records to whoever wanted to buy them or listen to them; there was never any disparity as to who we would perform to. We played to mixed audiences all the time, and certainly on that first big tour the South African situation wasn't as bad as it would become in later years, but even in those tours there was never any segregation and we had guys on the shows working hand in hand with other races. There was no problem. The only problem would be in Ireland with people who never actually went to any of my shows there to see for themselves who was at them.'

Favourable early reactions from the country's music writers ensured Joe got huge crowds wherever he went. A big hit on the tour was Joe's passionate rendition of 'My Way'. As he held the final high note, the stage curtain dropped, making it a killer pay-off.

Joe's female following was reminiscent of the Driftermaniacs back home. 'Joe's thrusting movements drew screams of ecstasy from female members of the audience,' wrote the *Rand Daily Mail*. The *Johannesburg Express* reported that Joe's act was 'an educative example of how to make the most of the talent you've got . . . On one side he has a considerably better-than-average voice; on the reverse he is a visually non-romantic Romeo.' *The Sunday Times* said all he had to do to prove his star quality was 'step up on stage'. The band were 'strident' young men who 'looked good in their neat, elegant suits and they set about their performance with the assured authority of people who know their business'. *The Johannesburg Star* went all out with the Irish stereotypes: 'It's almost as if the South

African heat had combined with the kissing of the Blarney Stone to form a frenzied chemistry that hurtles Mr Dolan through pop, rock 'n' roll and rollicking Irish jiggery.'

After his maiden tour Joe returned to Ireland clutching a selection of gold and platinum discs. Almost every second year Joe would return to South Africa to tour until the pressure of the anti-apartheid movement and a series of stinging newspaper articles forced him to cease touring there in the 1980s. 'I loved working there. Every tour was great and Ronnie Quibell was an absolute gentleman to work for. He treated all the band like they were stars and they all responded onstage. It was really as if they were family. Every night after a show he would tell us he had a beautiful restaurant opened especially for us and in the venues and in the hotels everything was laid out for us. He was a really special guy.'

Joe was extremely happy with his record label there, Teal, who put everything into promoting him. 'If you had some of the top guys in a record company interested in you, then you were home and dry. Teal really made a big effort to break us there, which we appreciated.'

He played the promotional game perfectly, and the band didn't seem to mind that he was the one garnering all the attention. Personal appearances and record signings became the norm for Joe, and despite the previous year's beating everything seemed to be on the up.

As he continued his search for a writing team to match Hammond and Hazelwood, Joe worked with a variety of up-and-coming names, many of whom would go on to become huge stars in their own right. These included a young Giorgio Moroder, a groundbreaking Italian producer, songwriter and musician who was cutting his teeth with his partner Pete Bellotte. They hooked up with Joe on tracks such as 'Girl For All Seasons', 'Roots and Rafters' and the German-only releases 'Tina (Mama Did You Really Think)' and 'Wenn du Einen Bruder Hast'. Joe allowed the duo free reign in the studio to experiment as they pleased, and was impressed with their commitment to innovative recording techniques and their desire to try out new sounds.

It was when they were working on further tracks for Joe (and others) at Munich's Musicland Studios in 1973 that Moroder and Bellotte met a young German-based American session singer and actress called Donna Summer.

She was starring in musicals such as *Hair* and *Godspell* but also began to work as a backing singer for Moroder on an assortment of sessions, including Joe's. She would become Moroder's passport to international fame and glory in 1975 when she cut 'Love to Love You Baby', the highly charged erotic opus widely credited with signalling the birth of disco, as well as the 12-inch single format.

Their work with Joe featured plenty of the trademark flair and studio trickery that would bring them into disco-supernova with Summer, and they paid meticulous attention to detail. Behind the main Fender Rhodes piano, brass line and sustained, electronically treated guitar of 'Girl For All Seasons', a Moog synthesizer (which was frowned upon until Moroder, and later Stevie Wonder popularized its use) lends some sensual string effects to the track without ever sounding artificial. Despite the novel production and the inventive musical polish, Joe's vocals were largely left untreated and they sound a little out of place on 'Girl For All Seasons', where the emphasis is on the song rather than the singer. However, the tracks demonstrated that Joe was not afraid to experiment or to reinvent himself.

They were due to do more work together, but then in 1975 Summer broke into the big time. Joe was sad to lose another talented writing team, but he was thrilled when they made it big. Moroder would go on to work with many of the most famous names in music, including Barbra Streisand, Elton John, Freddie Mercury, Cher, David Bowie and Blondie.

Joe then hooked up with Mitch Murray and Peter Callander, who had written hits for a variety of acts including Cliff Richard, Tom Jones, Shirley Bassey, Cilla Black, Nana Mouskouri, The Tremeloes and Georgie Fame. They would become two of the most internationally respected songwriters in the business.

'Home Isn't Home Anymore' was one song of theirs that did well for Joe. An epic track dripping with strings and brass, it showcases all that is powerful about Joe's soaring voice, which rises to a glass-breaking crescendo at the end. It was a song that musical purists would love, even if it eventually became a notable album track rather than a memorable single. It did, however, get an Italian release and it became Joe's third consecutive hit record there.

Joe had another crack at the UK market in early 1972 with the Marty Wilde production 'Take the Money and Run'. Wilde was among the first generation of young English singers who were turned into rock 'n' roll stars by 1950s music impresario Larry Parnes, and in the late 1960s and early 1970s Wilde turned his attentions away from his band, The Wildcats, to songwriting and production, working with the likes of Status Quo (before they discovered three chords and denims), Lulu and later his daughter Kim.

The single was a powerful number, and Joe was hoping it would be a hit in the UK. Seamus Casey masterminded a brazen PR campaign for it when he printed up thousands of fake £100 notes which had Joe's big smiling Irish face in place of the Queen's. The notes were distributed throughout England, with the bearer entitled to a special gift at a Joe Dolan concert. However, this particular PR campaign saw Joe enjoy his first big brush with authority when the Bank of England signalled their intentions to take High Court action against him. They ordered the notes to be destroyed, and after much grovelling, apologies and claims of Irish innocence, the case was dropped. Tragically, the single also dropped – out of the Top 100.

The song fared better in Ireland, where it became Joe's fourteenth Top Twenty hit in August. There would be no qualms from the Bank of Ireland about Joe's head appearing on £100 notes at home when the same stunt was pulled.

He tried a country direction after this, with a version of 'Here We Go Again', a steel guitar ballad from the Steagall and Lanier writing team that would also be recorded by Ray Charles and Dean Martin. He also dipped his toe into glam rock waters with the thumping 'Ginny, Come to Me', written by Guy Fletcher and Doug Flett, an award-winning partnership who were the first British writers to have a song recorded by Elvis and had hits with Cliff Richard, Ray Charles, Tom Jones, Joe Cocker, The Hollies, Frankie Valli and the Bay City Rollers.

Joe would take an extended break from the rigours of touring and recording for much of 1972 and 1973, spending time back in his beloved Mullingar. Although he didn't admit it back then, he was suffering from exhaustion and there was also a lingering touch of post-traumatic stress from his beating. He wanted to be back among his people, where he could 'rest a little, work a little and play a little'. 'I thought it was time to get out for a bit,' he said later. 'It was becoming a ferocious drag.'

Having acquired a taste for outlandish clothes early in his career, he started a clothing business. He also played a lot of golf, crashed a couple of cars (including Ben's beloved Jaguar XJ6, which he smashed into a cow), lent his own cars out for others to crash (he lost two in 1972 alone – 'Every time I've lent a car out it's been crashed, and if I borrow a car, it crashes. I don't know what it is.') Finally, he got a chance to reflect on what had been a couple of whirlwind years, not knowing that more were just around the corner.

Joe was proud of Mullingar, and in every interview he did, no matter if it was in Preston, Paris or Pretoria, and in his promotional material, he would mention the county town of Westmeath, and the place of his birth. Mullingar was equally proud of him, but in the town the singer was every inch 'an ordinary Joe'. He had a wide circle of friends, ranging in age from eight to eighty. For Joe, everybody was equal, and in the hotels, bars and restaurants and out at Mullingar Golf Club he would be as friendly with flamboyant businessmen as he would be with the man on the street, old friends from Grange and his former bandmates from The Drifters. He was also very close to his family, doting on Paddy, Vincent and Ben's children, who all grew up to be good pals with their uncle.

Monday evening was the big night out for working musicians, and Joe would usually knock around with a motley crew of musicians, roadies and wannabe musicians. He was in 'Rank' O'Reilly's – a spit-and-sawdust hotel bar – one famous night when gardaí raided it, looking for illegal late-night drinkers. He managed to slip away but his great pal Tommy Roche was found in a darkened dining room. When gardaí asked what he was doing there he replied he was waiting for his breakfast. Other band members were found in upstairs bedrooms with their boots on. Drink culture was in, and Joe and his brother Ben would soon invest in their own bar, located at the front of the old Coliseum Cinema site where they had first rehearsed under one light bulb. Joe was perhaps at his most comfortable when he was having a drink with the ordinary man or woman, finding in them friends whose lifestyles he identified with more than the lifestyles of the rich and famous.

As a big star and rated as Ireland's most eligible bachelor, Joe had women falling all over him, but he was only interested in them on his terms. Many of the women were only keen because he was famous, which annoyed the singer. 'If a girl chases me then I don't want to know. When I have to do a bit of work, then I'm interested,' he said – although regular visitors to his apartment at the time attest that Joe was only too happy to entertain women who had been chasing him. His apartment was the focus of some serious partying, and if there wasn't a party going on there, then there would be at Joe Healy's, his neighbour. In a newspaper interview in 1972, Healy revealed he had lost count of the women Joe was seeing at one stage. Inevitably, it was left to Healy to source gifts for Joe, and thankfully Healy had his own network of shops to do just that. 'You can tell if he's interested in a girl because he'll come into the shop and buy her something. If he isn't interested, you couldn't sell him a thing!' Joe Healy had been a close friend of Joe ever since those early days when Joe rehearsed in Healy's cinema. He knew that Joe had been hurt before, and admitted it had an effect on him. 'I think it's true to say that Joe doesn't chase that many girls. There was only one girl that he was seriously interested in as far as I know.'

Joe rarely discussed his private life. He was the epitome of the man who lived for the moment, and he gave little away in interviews throughout the years. But in a 1972 interview with *Evening Herald* reporter Tony Wilson, he revealed something of himself, saying, 'I've got no plans. Lots of girls, but no plans . . . I don't like girls who chase. That's something I do! If there's a bird chasing you then fair enough, you feel great, who doesn't? But it gets you down after a while . . . I'm not the romantic type. I'll take a bird out, but I won't sit and croon over her all night and say, "Are you all right, sweetheart?" or "Are you enjoying your meal, darling?" or any of this old muck. I have no time for that. In fact, in a way I really agree with Women's Lib, I really do. I'll open a door for a woman, yes, stand up when she walks in a room or let her sit down before I do, this type of thing. I won't allow a woman to buy a drink. But I think if you're out for a meal or whatever, you don't have to give her all your attention. You mess about, talk to other people, be with everybody at the same time and she can do the same. She can be independent.'

He also revealed that marriage didn't hold much appeal for him. 'If I never got married, it wouldn't worry me too much,' he said. 'Not a terrible lot anyway. A lot of people have said to me I should marry and settle down. It would be nice to come home to the wife and kids, but that's something you just can't turn around and do. It has to be right or it's no good. I see too many people settling down and getting married and six months later walking out of the pub every night at closing time. They would be better off if they didn't bother their heads. If they got the right woman, she might be with them for starters, or they'd have had a couple of pints and gone home early, or better still spent the night with the wife.'

Joe was painted by Wilson as something of a wild man, but Joe was keen to stress to him that offstage he was different. 'When I'm offstage I figure I don't have any image. Fair enough, when I'm working I have. People are bound to have an image of you anyhow, but when you're not working there is no image. I figure I can do what I like, when I like, within reason. I can go out when I like, meet who I like. So I don't think there's any sort of image to uphold.'

As far as money went, it really held no meaning for him, and he was seen as extravagant because he literally threw it about the place. 'I'm a bad handler of money!' he would admit. From the off, his brother Ben looked after that side of things, and Joe never had any real interest in how much he was earning. 'After a gig, Joe would never ask me or Seamus how much we got,' Ben said. 'If he asked about anything, it was about how many were in. And if it was a bad crowd he never seemed to mind, and he never complained either.' Ben reckoned it was this detachment from the business side that made Joe such a good showman. 'It allowed him to concentrate and put his efforts fully into what he was doing onstage and in the studio.'

Ben became more of a father figure than a brother as Joe's fame spread, and despite Ben's pleas for Joe to use his self-imposed break from the road to settle down and perhaps get married, Joe continued to live the single life. But Joe's loyalty to his friends and to the people of Mullingar filled Ben with admiration. 'He was pretty much the same guy as he always was when he was home in Mullingar, and that break really helped him to focus on where he was going next, though this wouldn't be apparent to anyone as he was having the craic,' Ben said.

Joe's break gave him time to get over his disappointment that some of his singles had failed to sparkle at home and in the UK, but there were numerous triumphs to look back on, and things to look forward to: a further South African jaunt was one, another trip to Brazil was on the cards and an Australian tour was being lined up in the wake of a promotional appearance there in 1972. And the discovery of Italian songwriter, producer and musician Roberto Danova in 1973 would be the greatest blessing of them all.

Arguably, Roberto Danova had a greater impact on the career of Joe Dolan than any other songwriter or producer. His arrival was a breath of fresh air, and he was the catalyst of Joe's most successful years as an international artist.

Danova was an avid record buyer and a committed Driftermaniac since he had first heard one of Joe's earliest recordings with the 'classic' Drifters. He had been writing material with Joe in mind since 1970 and had been trying to make contact with him for some time. Unable to get to him, he hooked up with another big admirer of Joe, Peter Yellowstone, and they gelled as a writing team, crafting songs with Joe in mind. With the music industry whispering that Joe was damaging his career by taking a year off, Roberto was not prepared to let him disappear without a struggle.

Things were not getting desperate for Joe, but his manager felt Joe needed a leaner, meaner hit. The balladry and big orchestral numbers he had been releasing were not in vogue. Music lovers were rocking to a chunkier beat, and Joe needed to adapt to that. Seamus was in London for a make-or-break meeting with Shaftesbury/MAM when an emotional Roberto Danova sang his way into the life of Joe Dolan.

'I was waiting to meet Joy Nicholls and Geoffrey Everett, when this fella walked into the foyer and came straight over to me, and in this big Italian-English accent said, "Hello, who are you?"' Seamus recalls. 'I remember thinking to myself, this fella must be mad. He kept asking me what I did, where I was from, and why I was here so I told him that I looked after a singer from Ireland.'

'Who is theees singer?' Roberto asked.

'It's a guy called Joe Dolan,' Seamus told him.

'Oh my God!' screamed the Italian as he leapt to his feet and started to sing 'Good Looking Woman'. '"Oh me oh my, *you* make me sigh!" This is unbelievable! I came here to find out how to get this man! I write to him, but he no answer, I meet him but he no want to listen! Argh! This is a dream. This is meant to be!' He then fell to his knees in front of Seamus, arms extended and sobbing. 'I beg of you. I have songs for Joe Dolan. They are magnificent songs. I write them for Joe. These are Joe's songs!' And he started to sing some of them for an increasingly embarrassed and blushing Seamus. The girl in reception had to come over to quieten Roberto down and to tell him the music company didn't normally appreciate sales pitches in its foyer, but Roberto grabbed Seamus and continued singing lines from his songs. '"Oh lady in blue! With this love we can last for ever!"' he roared. 'I have more. Listen! Listen!'

As Roberto continued to sing songs, a gobsmacked Seamus was then whisked away by the receptionist to meet Joy and Geoffrey. 'There's a mad man on the loose out there,' Seamus told Everett as he entered the board-room.

'Oh, you've met Roberto, have you?' Mr Everett replied.

Joy then admitted he had been in with songs for Joe but as yet she had not given them much attention. At the time they were looking elsewhere, to writers like Guy Fletcher and Doug Flett. They proceeded to play Seamus some new demos they had received, but he was unimpressed.

When Seamus came out after his meeting, Roberto started singing again and followed him out of the office. They exchanged phone numbers and agreed to meet the following day. Roberto handed the cautious manager some demo tapes and that was that, or so Seamus thought. Armed with the phone number, Roberto bombarded Joe's office with letters, telephone calls and tapes of his songs until Joe finally agreed to meet him.

'I thought I'd better visit this Danova fella,' Joe recalls. 'I was a bit scared at first but, do you know what? He was great. We hit it off straight away, and he played me some songs, and he even sounded like me, and before I even left London I had agreed to work with him.' Joe laughed when he remembered a press cutting that Roberto proudly displayed in his London base which described Roberto as 'Italy's Joe Dolan', a further indication as to how popular the Irishman was on the continent.

After that historic meeting, Joe felt confident that for the first time in a couple of years he had a writer and producer who really understood him. 'My records were mainly ballads and I just seemed to get stuck in that bag. People were writing me these styles of tunes, or country tunes or big roman-tic songs. But I was brought up on really expressing myself, with skiffle and rock 'n' roll and even traditional, and I've always been a rocker at heart, so when I heard Roberto's "Sweet Little Rock 'n' Roller" demo it completely blew me away.'

Roberto and Peter Yellowstone became a familiar sight wherever Joe and the band travelled, and they began to turn up at concerts armed with guitars and new songs. 'We didn't know who he was at the time,' one band member remembers of Roberto's backstage invasions. 'We just thought he was a mad fan. When he played us these songs we couldn't believe it, you would almost swear it was Joe. He was doing all the moves, he sounded similar to him. A nice fella, a wild fella, but he was quiet underneath it all.'

Released worldwide in March and April 1974, 'Sweet Little Rock 'n' Roller' proved to be just the song that Joe needed, propelling him back into the spotlight at home and in the UK but, most pertinently, Europe as a whole. A powerful, pounding, yet complex rocker, it is a timeless song, and Joe never dropped it from his sets as it 'sort of sets out my stall that I'm a rocker'. 'It turned out brilliant. It was a stunning take, and I loved the drive of it,' Joe remembers. 'If I had released it two years earlier it probably would have gone top after "Good Looking Woman", but I was glad to get it when I did.' When he recorded with Roberto and Peter he was more enthusiastic in the studio than he had been in years. 'I was on the same wavelength as the boys, and we had some great times,' he recalled. As well as being highly productive in the studio, they all became firm friends, and had a fearsome reputation in the musical hangouts of London where they socialized.

As they readied 'Sweet Little Rock 'n' Roller' for release, Joe received a makeover, with his Irish and Italian tailors cast aside for some of Carnaby Street's finest. The new image saw Joe sport diamond-studded Las Vegas-style black suits and leathers. The lapels of his specially tailored suits came with a diamond-studded 'J' on one side and a 'D' on the other, costing over £1,000 each. In the UK a major press day was called in Hyde Park to unveil his new image, and a big promotional push to get him back in the British charts ensued. The single was picked up by BBC Radio 1 and there was a strong possibility it would be made a 'Power Play' on Radio Luxembourg. Every known disco in the country received free copies, and Joe was booked for a number of high-profile TV and concert appearances.

Irish and British releases were followed by releases across the rest of Europe, except in France where a French-language single called 'Maria' was released. Although it would not get an official release in the USA, promo copies were distributed to thousands of record stations and discos there. There was a good buzz in the Dolan camp. 'We got a lot of write-ups and a good deal of praise, and when it charted we were glad, but it charted in the lower regions and just didn't get up,' Joe recalls. In Ireland it got to number 14, a poor showing. 'I was beginning to wonder if I was old hat in my own country.'

All around him things had moved on. Joe had become more adventurous in where he played, with gigs booked in more intimate venues – hotel function rooms and purpose-built cabaret venues where fans could have a drink and a meal. He became an Irish cabaret attraction with no equal as very few acts were doing it. Comedians and other acts started looking to Joe as a man who could give them a break, and in Ireland Joe effectively invented the cabaret show, with up-and-coming and established comedians like Frank Carson and Bal Moane playing a key part.

Even in the remaining ballrooms, Joe was the act doing the most business. As *Spotlight* magazine noted in 1974, 'The popularity of Joe remains undiminished. Driftermania dies hard and the Mullingar band has the most loyal, and at times the most fanatical fans of any band in the country.'

While a nice compliment, it did Joe a disservice. 'We weren't The Drifters any more, yet we were constantly referred to as The Drifters. It kinda made it hard to progress in Ireland because all they [the media] could think about was your past,' he noted.

'Sweet Little Rock 'n' Roller' did much better in Europe, however. The track won the European Pop Jury single of that year, and saw Joe once again promote it around the world, where his new direction was lapped up. He was disappointed that after so much effort it didn't make a huge impact in the UK. 'I was a bit upset, but we had left Shaftesbury, and by leaving them we lost a bit of clout. But what it did do was make us more determined,' Joe recalls. 'Sweet Little Rock 'n' Roller' would eventually become a big hit in the UK in 1979 when it was covered by Showadawaddy, who also invented a dance move for it. And Rod Stewart would play it in the years to come.

'16 Brothers' would be Joe's next single. The titular brothers allegedly existed (along with a sister), belonging to a large Italian family that Roberto knew. Joe, however, was not too aware of the over-protective nature of their family, and when one night he started to chat up the blonde sister in a London bar, one of the brothers approached him and politely threatened that if he didn't move away from the girl, all sixteen brothers would be set on him. Not surprisingly Joe backed off, but light bulbs went off for Roberto and Peter, who used the concept for the song.

Again, a big promotional push was instigated, and the single was unleashed in half a dozen European countries, South Africa and several South American countries. A version recorded in Spanish did particularly well there and in Spain. It didn't do quite as well as expected in Ireland, but Joe was away from the country for practically six months on end, so he never got a chance to give it a proper push.

On one such 1974 excursion, Joe flew to Tokyo to represent Ireland at the famous World Popular Song Festival at the historic octagonal Budokan Hall. He sang 'Lady Laura', a lush continental love song about falling for the kind of woman your mother warned you about. The song would be notable for Joe's incredible display of vocal agility at its conclusion, where he sings an operatic melody of his own devising to counterbalance the fade-out. It was an improvised trick he would repeat to even further devastating effect on 'Sister Mary' a couple of years later, and it became a vocal trademark of his. He didn't win the 1974 competition, but he did make the final and he was in good company: other acts who would do well at the same competition (and not win it) until its final staging in 1989 included Roy Budd, Tony Christie, John Farnham, Demis Roussos, ABBA, Christopher Cross, Bryan Adams, Bonnie Tyler, Erasure, Kylie Minogue and Celine Dion.

A new dawn for Joe Dolan came when he moved to the Red Bus Music Group – publishers, bookers and a record label combined (although Joe kept Pye Records as his record label for the time being as they were still one of the biggest labels in Europe). Dates had been decreasing in the UK with the closure of clubs in the south of England, but Red Bus started putting Joe back into theatres there. And as ever, Joe and the band still finished their UK tours with a round of dates in Irish ballrooms such as the Leeds Irish Centre, and the Galtymore in Cricklewood.

As Joe jetted around the world, he did so in the company of some new band members: the increasingly nameless Drifters (the billing was always Joe Dolan) had been subject to a number of line-up changes. Keyboardist Ciaran McDonnell had been the first to leave. A deeply spiritual man, McDonnell had decided to become a priest. 'We couldn't believe it at first, but Ciaran was firm in his faith, and there was no arguing with a decision like that, was there?' Joe said. 'Who could we appeal it to? The Pope? I don't think you'd have much luck getting a legal team to take that one on!' As a mark of Joe's respect for McDonnell's decision, he himself drove the Strabane man to the seminary at St Patrick's College in Thurles, County Tipperary, and as McDonnell got out of the car, Joe handed him a sum of money and a guitar. Joe was always a regular Mass attendee, and he kept in touch with McDonnell long after he was ordained.

McDonnell was replaced by genial Derry keyboardist Kevin Cowley, who slotted into the line-up relatively quickly and comfortably. But Kevin's fear of flying and Joe's ever-expanding international touring commitments would mean a new man had to be found a couple of years later. There would be several replacements as Joe's keyboard curse continued, until Mullingar man Jimmy Mullally, aka 'The Mull', joined in the mid 1970s. Jimmy was from the same lakeshore, a short paddle up the shore from the original Dolan family farm, and had been a fine piano player from his youth. He brought a virtuoso touch to the ivories and he loved touring; his enthusiasm, coupled with his great playing skills, made him a popular member of the group for many years.

Trombonist Seamus Shannon was tempted away to join a 'supergroup' Brendan Shine was putting together in 1972. It is understood that Shine also approached Frankie McDonald and Joe strongly advised both him and Seamus against leaving. Frankie was enjoying himself too much to leave, but Seamus wanted a fresh musical challenge and after four years in the brass section he went back to his beloved accordion. He went on to become one of Ireland's most noted and highly regarded players of that instrument.

Frankie knew just the man to replace him: Liam Meade. Frankie and Liam had known each other and played music together in the army band since they were kids. When Liam was asked to join a band that had been put together by Michael O'Callaghan, he was told he would have to buy himself out of the army. With the buy-out fee out of his reach, the plucky trombonist trooped off to see the then Minister for Justice, Brian Lenihan, to negotiate his way out. His plan worked. He went on to play with a few other acts and was rated as one of the best trombonists in the country, so there was much surprise when, frustrated with the lack of big breaks, he hung up his trombone. He married and went to work with Youghal Carpets in Cork. The lads in the factory couldn't believe that there was a well-known musician in their midst who had given up music when all around showbands were still cleaning up. Whenever he was asked whether he would go back to it, he would reply, 'There's only one man that I would go back to play with, and that's Joe Dolan.'

Liam was a huge Joe Dolan fan and, like so many in Ireland, Joe's tenor had been the soundtrack of his 1960s. His first Joe Dolan gig of many was in Ballinasloe in 1962. 'I saw Joe and The Drifters in the Emerald Ballroom one night, and it was so exciting. I had heard plenty of buzz surrounding them, and the excitement in the music just blew me away. There was no one like them. I got a feeling when I saw him. It was something that got to me, his presence; I knew he was something special. He had a brilliant voice, and his aura onstage was incredible. I was a fan straight away.'

Despite not having blown a trombone in over twelve months, Liam passed the audition – although his move to Westmeath 'didn't go down too well with my wife and my four-week-old baby!' Liam soon settled into the Dolan groove and would go on to become the second-longest serving man in the band after Frankie, with over twenty-two years of service. 'Joe was brilliant to play behind,' he said. 'He was *the* star, and he was a star. Onstage you would still be in awe of him, every night for over twenty years. He was so confident in himself and competent and he was never, ever going to let the show down . . . You could feel the build-up of the crowd; it was an amazing ride.'

After six steady years in the Drifters' engine room, bassist Pat Hoey took a break, and in his place came Mick Bagnell, who would play for two years until Pat rejoined. Bagnell went on to become a publican, and achieved local notoriety as being one of the few venue owners in the world to kick U2 off his stage when Bono and the boys went down badly with a small crowd. Like most young bands they were finding their feet, but they also found the boot of an unimpressed owner, who kicked them out of his venue, refusing to pay them for their set.

When Pat Hoey returned, Joe had a band that, in his own words, 'was the envy of every other band in Ireland', and what many would regard as the 'classic' new Drifters.

It was a Roberto Danova and Peter Yellowstone composition called 'Lady in Blue' that would mark the beginning of another big new era in Joe's career. 'From the moment I heard it I said to myself, "That song is going to be a big hit,"' Joe said. 'It had this melody and swing, this continental flavour to it that I just knew. It was made for me.'

But before he could unleash it, Pye released 'The Most Wanted Man in the USA', a rocker in the same mould as 'Sweet Little Rock 'n' Roller'. It had been written with America in mind, as 'Sweet Little Rock 'n' Roller' had caused a bit of a stir there. 'They felt that going too soft too soon might have record buyers thinking that this was the same old Joe Dolan, the big romantic singer,' Joe said. 'I agreed in some ways, but I was keen to get "Lady in Blue" out there.'

Starting with the sound effects of a car crash followed by the pounding footsteps of a man on the run, 'The Most Wanted Man in the USA' is a fun knockabout track which paints Joe as a bad guy, a man who has stolen a con- siderable sum of money and is prepared to go to any lengths to avoid capture, using his gun if necessary. Conmen and bad guys were in vogue at the time, as Hollywood ushered in a golden era of cinema with classic crime films such as *Mean Streets, The Sting, The Godfather: Part II, Thunderbolt and Lightfoot* and *Chinatown*. All featured bad guys or flawed heroes whom the audience could in some strange way sympathize with, and this rubbed off on Joe and Roberto, who were both avid movie-goers.

The single did brisk business in the charts. Together with 'Lady Laura', the 7-inch package got a full European release in the spring and summer of 1975, with Australian, South African and South American releases sched- uled to follow later in the year. In Ireland it rose to number twelve and stayed there for four weeks. In the UK record buyers failed to catch up with the wanted man and it hovered outside the Top Fifty for a couple of weeks. The fugitive was duly captured in South Africa, where it reached number one. It also made an impression in the Soviet Union, despite the fact that the record could not be released there as the country was under the firm grip of communism. 'I think people from Eastern Europe and from Scandinavia started to bring my records into the Soviet Union, and when we started making cassettes they started to arrive there too. We never knew it until much later, but the songs were beginning to be heard in the East.'

Joe didn't mind that the single wasn't a huge success, as he had 'Lady in Blue' primed. 'I knew that we were coming out with something much better afterwards, so it didn't concern me.' Nevertheless, he gave it his all, and in promotional appearances on an assortment of TV shows and shoots he would play the character of a wanted man, sometimes brandishing a gun – an image that would be shattered with the great romantic lead character of what would be one of his greatest-selling singles.

12

I need you, lady in blue

'Lady in Blue', Joe's big 1975 release, would set dance floors alight like no other Joe Dolan song before or since. It would become one of his best-selling records, re-establishing him as one of Europe's biggest stars after a couple of up-and-down years. It would also lead to some of the most intensive international touring that any Irish performer had ever undertaken, a non-stop eight-year jaunt that would culminate with Joe making history behind the Iron Curtain and then turning his back on millions in Las Vegas.

The song that ushered in this golden era was a tinkling romantic tango written by Roberto Danova and Peter Yellowstone. It opens with a confident, almost cocky Joe walking into a venue where he sees the eponymous lady alone and dressed in blue, a painted smile on her face. He asks her for a dance and they go on to enjoy an intimate night together. But beneath his smooth dance moves and his charm, he reveals in the melodic but slightly melancholic chorus that he too is hiding behind a painted smile.

'There's an everyman feel to "Lady in Blue",' Joe said. 'It was written in such a way that even those with the most basic grasp of English would understand the sentiment.' This was one of Danova and Yellowstone's greatest strengths – their ability to write vast and complex arrangements with simple lyrics, designed to accentuate and flaunt Joe's voice. His operatic vocals here are astounding, and astonishingly it was all done in one take. Over the course of a couple of single lines in the first verse, he moves effortlessly from the highest to the lowest notes without even pausing for breath, and as the song progresses he accentuates and holds certain words, letting the lines flow into one another before launching into that memorable chorus.

When he holds a word, he highlights his vibrato technique by varying the speed of his pitch in order to convey different emotions; so, for example, the way that he holds the word 'blue' when it refers to the woman's clothes is quite different from the way he holds the same word when it refers to loneliness. This technique of changing the note or pitch of a single syllable of text, known as melisma, was seldom used in popular music at the time. In fact, outside of soul and gospel music, it was rarely heard. Among its greatest and most popular practitioners are Aretha Franklin, Stevie Wonder and, in more recent times, Whitney Houston and Mariah Carey, but in their wake, many a talent-show contestant has strangled the art form to death. Joe was one of the few male European singers to master it, even though he admitted he never set out to sing like that. Interestingly, when asked who he would like to record a duet with, Joe said either Houston or Carey.

Joe would play down his passionate display of vocal agility in the song. 'Roberto encouraged me to give it my all, and he just brought the best out of me, I suppose. I never thought to myself that it was operatic. I just sang it melodically.' Bar his youthful piano training and a few informal vocal lessons in Mullingar, Joe never received any formal training. 'I have an extraordinary range. I don't know how though, it was just *there*. I didn't develop it from anything, it was just what was there when I opened my mouth and that came out,' he said. 'At school, my friends used to joke about it, asking where did I get this old man's voice!'

When asked if he liked it, he replied, 'I don't think there's anything wrong with it. In fact, I can listen to it. Not that I listen to a lot of my own stuff or anything, but I can listen to it. I can find fault, naturally. I don't think you'd call my voice smooth. It's high, and that's about it. I can sing low as well! But I tend to sing high notes. I try to get songs that will suit that range.' In Danova and Yellowstone, working together or apart, Joe would get plenty of these.

He seemed happy to have a distinctive voice. 'It's not a contrived voice, it's nothing else; it's just the way the voice comes out, and if it sounds good, you do it. It's my voice and that's it – good, bad or indifferent, like it or don't like it. You'll get the same sound tomorrow as you did today, and next year and last year.'

With plenty of radio play and pre-release buzz, 'Lady in Blue' received as big a release as that other great romantic Joe Dolan single, 'Make Me an Island'. Joe was more of a known quantity this time around, however, and it shot to the top of the charts in several countries, becoming one of Europe's biggest records in 1975. It quickly became a staple at European discos and the big chance for Latin lovers to show off their dance moves. Once the DJ dropped it, a scream would erupt and within seconds of the intro, the dance floor would be awash with couples. Dance moves were invented for it and it became a dance-floor phenomenon. After two weeks it rose to the top spot in France, selling 2 million copies in the process and earning Joe seven gold discs. It was also a South African number one for Christmas 1975 and was still there two months later, outselling big hits such as 'Dancing Queen' and 'Fernando' by ABBA, and 'Don't Go Breaking My Heart' by Elton John and Kiki Dee, to become the biggest-selling record of 1976.

'Lady in Blue' also danced her way to the Top Ten in Belgium (spending four months there), Holland, Spain, Portugal, Germany, Israel, Australia, Turkey, Greece, Argentina and Brazil. It was also released in Canada, India, across Scandinavia and copies even turned up in Eastern Europe. It sold well in countries such as Bolivia and Peru where few, if any, European artists were even known. Indeed, a few years later, one member of Joe's band was on a trail to the ancient city of Machu Picchu when he heard 'Lady in Blue' blaring out of a radio and nearly fell off the mountainside.

The hit record led to another huge round of globetrotting for Joe, and he and his manager were once again Aer Lingus's most frequent flyers. Up until now Joe had shared a room with his manager when abroad, but after several years of Joe's notoriously smelly feet, and his propensity to stay up late and invite the occasional fan back for a coffee, Seamus had had enough and, armed with a more flexible credit card, they booked into separate rooms.

The exact sales figures are not known, but it is estimated that 'Lady in Blue' sold over 5 million copies in Europe alone. Astonishingly, the single failed to make a significant impact on Irish and UK charts.

Unsurprisingly, Joe's next album, released not long afterwards, was called *Lady in Blue*, and its sleeve was a comical hand-painted 'remix' of the 7-inch single sleeve, with the lonely dancing lady in blue now joined by an all-smiling, all-dancing Joe Dolan. The album would be dominated by Danova and Yellowstone, who wrote the four lead singles ('Lady in Blue', 'Sweet Little Rock 'n' Roller', 'Most Wanted Man in the USA' and '16 Brothers'). The album also included 'My Darling Michelle', 'What Have You Done', 'Lady Laura' and 'Hush Hush Maria' (which went on to become a big European hit single), as well as the quasi-religious 'Send an Angel of the Lord' and 'Anuschka Balalaika', a daft but lavishly produced song about a rural Russian ballet dancer who dreams of escaping to join the Bolshoi Ballet, hooking up with a Leningrad cowboy who promises her the world but betrays her. It features a huge chorus line and a balalaika, and even if the images the song evoked were tantamount to a send-up, Joe's Russian profile began to rise.

As an extra treat for Joe fans, Johnny Arthey would return with three songs, which was good news for Joe's brass section. The highlight of these was the married-life-is-bliss idyll of 'Real Good Woman', a live favourite for many years to come. Other Arthey tracks included the stirring soul of 'Day Time, Night Time' and the country-tinged 'The Feeling I Feel'.

The *Lady in Blue* album also did huge business in Europe, selling well over 2 million copies, with strong sales in France, Holland and Belgium. It also sold well in South Africa, Israel and Australia (a country Joe would finally tour that year). Ireland belatedly caught up with the single when the album came out, and the latter went Top Ten upon its release, but Joe was not in Ireland for much of 1975 as the album's success kept him abroad.

'I was very happy with that album,' Joe said. 'It had everything – from rockers, to big ballads, to soul and pop numbers – and it was probably the best-sounding album I've ever done.' In the studio Joe pushed the musicians to the limit, and he brought out the best in some seasoned players. Joe too was pushed to the limit, and he could not have had better men in the control booth than Danova, Yellowstone and Arthey. They let Joe improvise at will, and many of his most memorable vocal stylings on the album were made up on the spot.

In the wake of his latest wave of international success, Joe needed a big follow-up single, and Danova delivered it in 1976 with the disco-influenced 'Crazy Woman'. Joe hated the song, and demanded it be remixed. 'The key to recording Joe was to get his high pitch right and very few producers could capture that,' Seamus Casey says. 'Roberto knew how to record him, and he pushed Joe to the limits to get this high voice, but it was just a little too high with "Crazy Woman" and Joe never liked it.'

However, it had already been picked up by radio stations in France, Holland, Belgium, Germany and England, and pretty soon it had topped several European charts. In France, sales of over 200,000 in its first week heralded the start of another downpour of gold discs. The RTL Radio Group, the biggest in France at the time and fast becoming part of Europe's biggest media group, made it their Record of the Year. It went on to make an impression in Australia, as well as New Zealand, Brazil and Argentina, and disco and 1970s compilations for decades after featured the manic song.

At the start of the decade, Joe had kept the Irish show on the road along with his international commitments. But successive big-selling singles abroad had given him the box-office clout to sustain longer periods of touring away from home with his band, and they made the most of it. His European and Middle Eastern tours became more frequent, as did his African adventures. Countries such as Turkey, Lebanon and some of the more far-flung European states were visited for the first time. Joe also undertook a daunting and lengthy tour of Japan and Australia in October 1976.

This particular tour was to be another big eye-opener for Joe. Because of the prohibitive cost factor, it was decided he would go solo. Although they were disappointed, the band didn't mind too much as they would still be getting paid a full wage. It was a testament to Joe that he always wanted to retain his band. 'In a strange way, Joe's family was the band and the road crew. He lived with them in a way, and he never tired of their company,' Seamus maintains. 'For some of us, you were often glad to get back to your family after a show or a tour. But when Joe got back, it was with the lads, and everything revolved around the lads. Countless times he'd ring me to tell me something that had happened at one of the shows, and he'd be roaring laughing. He was always so loyal to his bands over the years. But it wasn't because they were all that he had; it was because they were all he wanted. When I think of Joe I think of him right there in the centre of things with the lads.'

A musical director had been hired before the tour, and when Joe arrived in Sydney a rehearsed band was ready and waiting for him, although after just one rehearsal Joe had whipped them into a very different shape. Stiff session men were allowed to express themselves, and Joe made a beeline for the drummer, telling him to play a bit louder and therefore drive the show.

As well as arena and concert hall performances in Australia – his biggest crowd of the tour was a 2,500 attendance at a Sydney show and 5,000 in Japan – Joe had a hectic promotional schedule to undertake, as a deadpan letter home to his manager revealed.

Down Under

9 – 10 – '76

Dear Seamus,

I thought I'd drop a line and tell you a bit about the trip, but I'll probably be home before the letter. I've just sent a card but there's not much room on them.

Well, Japan was very good, I think we did a very good promotion there. It was very organised for a change; all the top magazines and TV, the latter being very good.

Here in Australia it's been all go, have done all the radio stations, there are six in all, each one has done about 20 minutes' interview plus us playing four songs, mainly 'Good Looking Woman', 'Make Me an Island', 'Lady Blue'[, and] after that they pick one from an album, so, we've had a lot of coverage. Up to the time of writing I've done one TV and have three more lined up. When I say there are six stations, I mean here in Sydney. I've also done several telephone interviews on stations all around the country.

The show at St George was a bit slow to pick up, but they told me the first three nights are always bad. According to reports we had the best opening for a long time. The band is pretty good, nice people, took them a few days to get it together, but it's fine now.

That car sounds expensive but never mind I think we'll have it, make sure it's got electric windows and all that jazz, for that sort of money it should have a shithouse.

I heard about the record in France, it's very good, I hope what you say about England is right, if it happens there it will make my life much easier. 'Crazy Woman' is released here now, and getting a great reception on the show. The record company is very good, at least they have a great interest and seem to be working very hard, they've organised all the promotion and they ring all the time to make sure everything is all right, so it's pretty nice.

I don't know when I can get out of here, they say the Sunday flight goes all over the place, stopping in a lot of countries and takes about 36 hours, whereas on Monday there's a direct flight which gets to London about 7 a.m. Tuesday, but I'm going to check it out myself – when I know for sure I'll send a telegram.

I think that is about all so, until I get home,

God bless,

Joe.

P.S. If I've forgotten anything, fuck it.

While Joe was performing in Australia, an unlikely song was creeping up the charts back home in the form of the conceptual medical melodrama 'Sister Mary'. Joe had been working on material in the studio with Danova and Yellowstone on and off throughout 1975 and 1976, and the sessions were yielding great results. But when they got to 'Sister Mary' they hit a brick wall. The song, co-written with Steve Voice, details the anguish of a man whose lover is in a coma after an undisclosed tragedy. By her hospital bedside Joe begs medical staff for news about his beloved, but it's not looking good. Recording it, Joe thought it needed a female vocalist to offset the feeling of grief and despair, and perhaps give the track further depth, but he was at a loss as to who he should ask.

Meanwhile, in an adjacent studio, young Scottish singer Kelly Marie was recording her debut single. Joe was so smitten with Kelly's voice that he invited her in to sing with him. They acted out a hospital bedside scene of 'Sister Mary' and it clicked. Both were good improvisers and they cut loose at the end of the track, with Joe's breathtaking and anguished howls as the track fades out as evocative as any opera singer's.

JOE DOLAN

The Scottish singer would follow Joe to the top of many a European chart in later years. She appeared at the same World Popular Song Festival in Tokyo where Joe performed, before being bitten by the disco bug that would eventually lead to her signature song, the infectious 'Feels Like I'm in Love' – a song originally intended for Elvis that was turned into disco gold by Kelly and Peter Yellowstone.

'Sister Mary' struck a chord with Joe's Irish audience, and it would enjoy not one but two lengthy sojourns in the Irish Top Three, registering as high as number two, before it dropped out after seven weeks. It was resuscitated two months later and enjoyed a further seven-week run in the charts, climbing to number three.

The single also did very well in Europe, where it sold over a million copies. A lengthy promotional jaunt saw Kelly Marie come along for the ride, and the pair appeared on several European television shows together, adding fuel to the fire that they were more than just singing partners. The rumours were denied by both of them, but their chemistry was undeniable.

As the recording sessions continued throughout 1976, something originally written as an album track began to evolve into something quite different. 'Goodbye Venice Goodbye' was conceived by Roberto Danova as both a love song and a romantic love letter to his favourite Italian city, and as they recorded the song Joe gave it such depth and conveyed such emotion in his delivery that it became more epic and musically ambitious. The dramatic 'Goodbye Venice Goodbye' that would go on to close Joe's shows for nearly thirty years and, ultimately, provide the soundtrack for his last journey down the aisle of the Cathedral of Christ the King in Mullingar, was born.

The song was in the plaintive key of D minor, and to maximize its emotional impact Roberto added a heavily struck electric guitar and the clang of a real Venice church bell. Backing singers and a melancholy piano and bass line added to the drama, carrying the song through its first funereal verse into its bombastic, unforgettable chorus. Still, it would take a couple of years for it to find its place as the concluding song of a Joe show.

'"Venice" was an album track we just did – in the middle of the show on occasion, or sometimes even closer to the start of the show,' Joe remembered. 'Believe it or not, we didn't do it all the time. But we had been doing it for a while in the show and we just started tricking around with the arrangement a bit. Ben, Liam and Frankie were playing the violin runs very quietly,

198

but I felt the end of the tune had to mean something; it had to deviate from the actual melody I was singing. The lads worked around it and I think it was after Vegas when it became our anthem to shape the end of the show after "Sweet Little Rock 'n' Roller" and "More and More". You couldn't go out with a better bang than that!' What was a heart-rending song with a sad ending about leaving both a relationship and a city behind became an anthem of hope and happiness.

Frankie McDonald remembers that he relished writing the new brass movement for the song's finale. Although to the untrained ear it may have sounded improvised each night, the soul-stirring conclusion of the song was meticulously planned, as Frankie reveals. 'I started playing riffs at the end of it and it became part of the show, so much so that when Joe was shaking hands with the fans at the front there was 16 or 32 bars, or measures, where he would shake hands and we would carry on according to how many people he was greeting. When he would be coming to the end of meeting the people, he'd put up his hand and we'd lead him out of the room. When he was gone, the band and the arrangement would carry on and we'd do little brass riffs and end with a run I did on the trumpet. It was quite an honour to finish the show with a solo like that every night. I was on a high, the crowd were on a high and if it was a good night Joe and all the band would be on a high.'

A tearful Ben Dolan says that when it comes to summing up the all-time greatest Joe Dolan songs, 'Venice' is high on the list. 'If you ask a dozen people to name a Joe Dolan song, chances are that most of them will say "Goodbye Venice Goodbye". Nearly everyone remembers it, which is great because at the time [when it was being recorded] it was just another LP track, but it was a very apt closing number, as the lines summed up how Joe felt at the end of a show. He was bidding goodbye to his lovely friends. He knew that it would all end, and didn't want to leave, but he had to. They're lovely lyrics, as the crowd was his friend. Every night they were there for him, and he was there for them.'

The album 'Venice' belonged to is a long-player chock-full of hits and songs that would remain in Joe's repertoire for years to come. Released at home and in some parts of Europe as *Sister Mary* (complete with a crazy picture of a beaming, sun-tanned Joe) and in the rest of the world as *Crazy Woman* (with a more modest cover of Joe in a white shirt and red suit), it would top the charts in 1976 and sell well for years to come.

As well as the stand-out 'Goodbye Venice Goodbye', the album featured another epic that would have a similar resonance – the thoughtful 'If I Could Put My Life on Paper'. A captivating and moving album track about looking back and taking stock, it highlighted Joe's growing maturity. Whenever he was asked for a song that reflected how he felt about his life and career, Joe would name this song of regret and hope. He had an uncredited input into the lyrics, which were autobiographical in some respects. Joe's single life sometimes got to him and he often opened up to friends about his romantic regrets, which ranged from being unable to have a lasting relationship because of his commitment to being Joe Dolan, to his feelings for some of his earlier, first loves.

He would laugh when fans referred to it as 'the war song' on account of the military-style brass and marching drums at its conclusion. It seemed that even when he got serious, his fans still saw the lighter side.

The album *Crazy Woman* is one of Joe's best, but it's an album of mixed messages and musical moods. 'Caterina Ballerina' opened the album on a rocky note, and after that it was a case of 'spot the genre' as glam rock ('Boogie Mama') and hard rock ('Be My Fire') rubbed shoulders with all-out disco ('Crazy Woman'), gently strummed continental pop ('Lady of the Night'), smart show-stopping pop ('You Belong to Me'), streamlined disco-pop ('Fly Me Atlantic') as well as some Mediterranean balladry ('Morena') and the more plaintive epic material of 'If I Could Put My Life on Paper' and 'Goodbye Venice Goodbye'. It also featured a single that had only been previously released in South America, 'My Blue Tango', a sequel of sorts to 'Lady in Blue'.

The album certainly reached for the dance floor, and as he promoted it Joe donned the full white suit for the first time. Originally intended to be a 'king of the dance floor' look, the white suit struck a chord with Joe and he intended making it his stage wear from then on. 'It just made me feel more of a showman, it just turned me into a different Joe and I felt I could express myself more with it and get away with wilder dancing and stuff,' he claimed.

In a world of big solo singers in fancy shirts and diamanté suits, the white suit gave Joe a clearly identifiable and marketable image, but surprisingly his record company was not keen on it, as the white suit (albeit studded with millions of dollars' worth of precious stones) was Elvis's Las Vegas image, so in publicity shots Joe still sported the latest gear, much of it his own offstage clothes. As Ben recalls, he was a snappy dresser: 'Aside from cars, his only other vice was clothes. He always had to have the latest fashions, even back in the sixties when he couldn't afford a haircut. And if he saw something that was good, he'd make sure others got it too, like these sheepskin jackets. Sure you could buy them anywhere but Joe spotted a good one in Cork, and a few days later drove down and bought a load of them to give to the fellas in the band.'

It was around this time that Joe made perhaps his most lavish four-wheeled purchase: a top-of-the-range, hand-built, limited-edition Jensen Interceptor, a British sports car of immense power. Joe bought it from a friend in the UK, Tony Clarke, after a show in Birmingham. Tony had just bought the luxurious, gleaming golden-brown car ostensibly for his wife, and was showing it to Joe when Joe made him an offer he simply couldn't refuse.

So smitten was Joe with the Jensen that he decided he would drive it straight back to Ireland from the UK tour. He drove on to the ferry, apparently 'forgetting' to declare the car to Customs. 'Sure he was bound to get caught but he didn't listen,' Ben recalled, still shaking his head in disapproval over thirty years later. From Dublin, Joe drove straight to Mullingar, where it became the talk of the town. In the 1970s, the car's trimmings – electric curved windows, reclining real leather seats, air-conditioning, wood-trimmed steering wheel and dashboard, power steering, a state-of-the-art stereo system – were the stuff of dreams for car lovers. Not to mention its 300-horsepower engine.

Joe used to take great pleasure in taking people out for drives. 'He was never a show-off, but once he had the Jensen he became one,' chortled his manager. 'He was kind of proud to be bringing people off for drives, and when they wouldn't be expecting it, he'd take off at top speed. He was like a child with it.' However, Joe's Jensen dreams would come crashing down around him when early one morning, Customs pounced.

'I was in the office when Joe came running in crying,' Seamus remembers. 'It was the first time I had ever seen him cry in fact. "They're taking my effing car!" he roared. "Why would they do such a thing?!" "Well, Joe, we told you..." So we went around to the street and there they were, seizing the car.'

As the officials took it, Joe scrambled to rescue his golf clubs, clothes and a crystal Entertainer of the Year award that he had just won in Galway. Amid the scramble, the award – which was in the shape of a crystal sword – got chipped. Joe cried again.

The sassy sports car was impounded in Dublin for a couple of weeks as Joe tried to come up with a plan. He negotiated a settlement and ended up paying the then substantial fine of £500 before driving it straight back to England, where he sold it on.

While Joe's next batch of cars exuded a certain class, and were invariably Mercedes, the Jensen would be the last of Joe's OTT car purchases, as Ben explains. 'He didn't go in for big flashy sports cars after that.' Luxury for a long drive was all he wanted. 'If he was driving from Mullingar to Killarney, he wanted luxury in the car he was driving. It wasn't this icon idea, of showing that "I can drive a top-of-the-range Merc" – that meant nothing to him. He liked to drive to shows and he also liked to listen to music in the car, and he liked that comfort of listening to songs alone and living with them for a while.'

However, Joe was to suffer something a bit more humiliating than an impounded sports car in October 1976 when an alleged air-rage incident saw him receive a lifetime flying ban from the airline Aer Lingus, and nearly led to him being shot at a Greek airport.

Joe and a big group of friends, including his brother, manager and several other entertainers, were on their way to Corfu having just finished a sell-out run of shows, and were in good form. 'A group of us were flying to Greece for a golfing trip – it was my first holiday in years,' Joe recalled. 'But the flight was delayed by a couple of hours. Anyway, when we were about to take off I followed all the instructions. The seat-belt and no-smoking signs came on, so I tightened my seat belt and put out my cigarette – you could smoke on planes in those days. Then we were in the air and everything was grand. I was chatting to a few people and to a friend of mine, a priest, in a row of seats further up the plane from where I was sitting when this air hostess started asking me to move because she said I was causing an obstruction. I was sitting on the arm rest, not in anybody's way at all, having a drink and I might have been smoking a cigarette, but this air hostess kept at me that I was in the way. She was crabby and in bad form. Anyway, there might have been a few words spoken so she made a complaint to the pilot and he and the chief hostess came down and asked me to sit in my seat – or else. There was a bit of an argument, but I sat down in the end.'

Joe's recall of events was rather more diplomatic and a little less detailed than others remember. When he and the group arrived at Dublin Airport to find the flight delayed, they had a meal and a few drinks. When they boarded the plane they were, as one of the party remembered, 'quite merry' and when the plane finally took off some of the travelling party cracked open their bottles of duty-free and spirits were high. Joe was wandering about the plane chatting to people when the hostess told him to sit down – rather curtly, as one witness remembered. Joe brushed off the warning and later sat on an arm rest talking to Fr Dick Kelly and a couple of friends in the same row, almost sitting on the lap of the girl at the edge. The air hostess asked him to move, but Joe claimed he wasn't causing an obstruction. The captain then told Joe that if he didn't sit in his seat he would have to be restrained. Joe could not see the logic as he felt he was doing nothing wrong, and he was reluctantly brought back to his seat, where he remained for the rest of the flight.

When they landed in Corfu Joe stormed off the plane, angry at his treat-ment. To add insult to injury, his luggage did not appear in the baggage hall and he began to lose his temper. Rather than publicly make a scene, he chose to leave the airport and, without his baggage and his passport, went to walk through the Customs checkpoint, which was manned by armed guards. His friends tried to haul him back, but to no avail. 'He wouldn't take no for an answer and he tried to barge his way through Customs,' Seamus remem-bered. 'It got pretty serious when one of the armed guards drew his gun.'

Joe was held at gunpoint for a few minutes until he calmed down. His bags were eventually located and his passport produced. Everything was put down to experience and nothing further would happen – or so Joe thought.

A week later the organizer of the tour, Sean Skehan, was sent a telex by Aer Lingus informing him that they were refusing to fly Joe back. Skehan telexed back offering guarantees of Joe's good behaviour, and even offered a cash deposit, but Aer Lingus stood firm. Joe was unable to book a flight to Dublin or London with another airline, so he had to be left behind. Even the Corfu airport manager intervened and vouched for Joe, but Aer Lingus still refused.

When the rest of the group landed back in Dublin they immediately went to the papers. It was front-page news and the pressure was on. 'AER LINGUS BANS JOE DOLAN' reported the front page of the *Evening Herald*. A more sober line was taken by the *Irish Independent*: 'AER LINGUS REFUSES TO FLY POP SINGER HOME'. Several other newspapers made Joe's story and the shock resignation of Irish President Cearbhall Ó Dálaigh – ironically after an incident in Joe's hometown when the then defence minister called the President a 'thundering disgrace' – the main stories of the week.

Pushed for a statement, Aer Lingus issued the following: 'We carried Mr Dolan on an inclusive tour holiday from Dublin to Corfu, and on the basis of reports received from our staff, including the crew on the aircraft, we decided it was inadvisable to carry him again. At the moment we are happy to be without Mr Dolan's business.'

The official line from the band, reported in the press, was that 'a mountain was made out of a molehill. The whole incident could have been averted if Joe had not been treated in a grumpy manner. Joe was in a holiday mood. It was his first holiday in four years. If airline staff are not able to deal with people in high spirits then they should give up. The incident could have been averted were Joe dealt with more diplomatically.'

Meanwhile, as all this was happening at home, Joe was stuck in Corfu and the first dates of a big UK tour were edging closer. Eventually, after several days, Skehan managed to island-hop Joe to London just in time for the tour.

The ban lasted for close to two years, and, looking back, Joe found it all amusing: 'It was a complete overreaction and I'm sure in the end they were very sorry for doing it because it landed in their faces afterwards. I was glad of all the publicity! I got over £100,000 worth of free publicity over the whole thing. I was on the front pages of all the papers for days on end. We issued one comment and we allowed them to comment, and then they kept on commenting and the story refused to leave the papers. The album started to do well then and all the shows were packed! I didn't mind being in the papers for things like that. So long as they spelt my name correctly, I didn't give a damn.'

Joe appeared on *The Late Late Show* and on numerous radio broadcasts to discuss the incident. He then started to play it up in his live shows. As it turned out, Ben had bought the band new green suits before the ban, but Joe would say to the audience, 'I want you all to give a big hand of thanks to Aer Lingus; as you can see, they have compensated me by buying new suits for the band.'

'It's the way it happens when you're a public figure,' reflected Seamus. 'Joe kind of did wrong, but the people sided with him and Aer Lingus were the enemy.'

Eventually, Aer Lingus pleaded with Joe to stop poking fun at them. He met them and a resolution was thrashed out, and the ban was quietly lifted. 'I never held a grudge against them, honest,' Joe said. 'It was just one of those things. I flew with them everywhere after that and they treated me beautifully!'

Joe started selling out shows at the National Stadium on the South Circular Road in Dublin, and RTÉ would film one of them for national broadcast as *On Stage at the Stadium* in the summer of 1976. The broadcast proved so popular it was repeated in the autumn and then again at Christmas. It would be the first of many Joe shows that the national broadcaster would record all over the country.

With further hit singles including 'You Belong To Me', the French-only single 'Bonjour Mademoiselle' and a Portuguese version of 'Lady Laura', there was little time for Joe to rest on his laurels. Having become something of a disco king, he set about pushing this genre further with his next album release, which this time would be guided by Peter Yellowstone, with the assistance of Steve Voice and Mike Tinsley. Roberto Danova had been expanding his horizons somewhat, and in 1977 he established his first production company and record label. He was also beginning to write and work with other artists, including Georgie, a gruff British rock band whose vocalist, Brian Johnson, would replace the late Bon Scott as singer in AC/DC in 1980.

Joe's international releases became somewhat scattered ahead of his new album. 'Hush Hush Maria', a song that had previously been released in 1974, climbed to the top of the South African charts and stayed there for most of the summer of 1977. It would go on to become one of the biggest-selling singles of the year, outselling such classics as ELO's 'Living Thing', Chicago's 'If You Leave Me Now' and Boney M's 'Daddy Cool'. Meanwhile, in Portugal, a belated release of 'Sister Mary' saw the song do well a year after it had charted elsewhere, and a French-only release, 'Rock and Roll Fever', did brisk business.

However, with more and more material being released at different times, Joe often didn't know which single he was promoting. He wanted one big push with a cohesive, united release. Big questions were asked whether to go all-out disco (with 'Midnight Lover' or 'Disco Crazy') or whether to stick with the same winning formula that had made 'Lady in Blue' such a worldwide hit. In the end they went for the gentler, slower side of the dance floor, and once the decks were cleared of stray singles, the smooth and silky 'I Need You' was given a worldwide release in July 1977.

The track is probably one of the most romantic songs Joe would ever record. Like the Joe of 'Good Looking Woman' and 'Real Good Woman', there is just one thing on his mind, and that is praise of his woman. In the song's description of finding a heaven on earth, it knowingly tipped its head in the direction of the angel who featured in 'Good Looking Woman', a religious theme he would carry in many of his songs. The lyrics are lush and romantic and unusually there is no chorus as such, just the high-pitched purr of certain lines and the lilt of the song's title.

Confidence in the single was extremely high, and Pye gave it their biggest simultaneous release across a continent since 'Lady in Blue'. The single slow-danced its way up the charts all across Europe and climbed to the outer reaches of the UK Top Fifty. Indications that it would rise higher in the weeks ahead led to the tantalizing prospect of a further *Top of the Pops* appearance. It was still the biggest televised music show in the world, and although Joe had appeared on just about every other music programme ever filmed, he hadn't appeared on this one since the start of the decade. As sales started to take off in the wake of an onslaught of daytime radio plays on the BBC and other stations, excitement began to mount. Then, on 12 August, Joe received the news he had been waiting for: he was on standby to appear on *Top of the Pops* the following week – and if that didn't happen, he would definitely appear the week after. The song was taking off: radio plays were on the up, daily sales were rising and everything was falling into place . . . when on 16 August, Elvis Presley died. Within a week his record company re-released a slew of his hits, and mourning music fans honoured the King by putting him back in the charts. In one week alone, eight Elvis singles entered the Top Forty, pushing Joe out of it. Then, a week later, another six singles joined them.

'We really went through the mill that time. At first, we couldn't believe it, because suddenly we were back in the big time, and sales were good. Had the Elvis reissues not made the impact they did, we were certs to go Top Thirty,' Joe said, stressing that there were no sour grapes against the King. 'Sure wasn't I in mourning myself? Elvis was always the King as far as I was concerned.'

When the Elvis singles disappeared from the charts two weeks later, Joe's sales were still strong enough to place him at number forty-three, but it was over a month since 'I Need You' had been all over the radio and the momentum was lost.

Elsewhere it was a different story. There was great joy in Mullingar when Joe landed the top spot in the Irish charts at the start of August. The record would enjoy a long run at the top end of the charts, spending three months there. In South Africa, it took the number-one spot on 11 November after Elvis had been sufficiently mourned, and it stayed in the Top Ten for seventeen weeks. In Spain, Germany, Belgium, Holland, France, Italy and Brazil, Joe repeated the trick. Again, Brazilian and Argentinian record buyers were in for a treat as the single was released as an EP with songs in Portuguese and Spanish on the flipside. Australia also fell for the balmy, mellow song, giving Joe another big Aussie hit.

Once again, Joe undertook a worldwide promotional campaign in support of the single, but continued to play a large number of gigs in Ireland. Diaries at the time show hundreds of bookings. Like Bob Dylan, Joe seemed to be on a never-ending tour. 'Joe did a serious amount of work. Looking back on it I don't know how he did it as he seemed to do it for all the big singles, but it wasn't a bother to him,' Ben recalls. 'Joe would get a call to go to Spain on a Monday and he would just pack a bag and go.'

Joe had the dual life down to a fine art by the end of the 1970s, but he often still cut it very close. One day, he had a French TV appearance in the afternoon and a date at the Gleneagle in County Kerry that night. There was a lot of anxious 'will he/won't he?' whispering, as Ben recalls: 'Everyone was anxious about what time Joe would arrive at and we couldn't cancel the gig because we were fierce friendly with the Gleneagle people. There were no mobiles or anything at the time, so all we had to go on was this call from Joe in the afternoon when he said they were running a little late but they would make it. "Be out there and watch the sky," he said to us.' Little did Ben and the band realize just how serious Joe was.

En route to the airstrip at Farranfore, which was not yet open to major commercial travel, the pilot had got lost and had landed the small private airplane at Shannon Airport. Joe takes up the story: 'He didn't know the way to Farranfore airport and with time ticking away, we encouraged him to maybe bend the rules a bit and fly down along the railway line to get to Kerry. Sure he couldn't miss!'

At Farranfore, Ben and a few of the band were indeed out watching the skies. The ETA had been between 6 p.m. and 8 p.m., but there was still no sign of Joe. Ben was getting anxious when suddenly, from out of nowhere, 'this plane came over the hedge in front of us.' It was Joe. 'So, the plane lands for a second on the airstrip, lets Joe out and immediately takes off again. Joe bounded across the tarmac to us, roared, "Howyiz lads" as if he was getting out of a bus, hopped over a fence and into the car.'

Coming back from jet-setting around the globe to rural Irish gigs was often rather odd for Joe, but he still loved it, and he and the band enjoyed some great (and often hair-raising) nights on the road together. On one particular frosty November night, Joe and the band were coming back to Mullingar from a gig in Castlebar, driving 'as the crow flies' on a network of country lanes. At about 5 a.m. in the middle of nowhere they hit a bull and the bandwagon crashed into a ditch. With no way of raising the alarm, there was nothing to do but start walking. Some of the lads brought their instruments with them, but few had coats. There was great banter for the first mile or so, but this soon turned to silence as the icy cold began to take hold. After three-quarters of an hour the shivering group came to a little country cottage. When there was no answer at the door, Joe did what he used to do in Grange and decided to make himself at home, opening the latch and walking on into the house. A concerned female voice from upstairs asked, 'Who's that?' and after Joe explained who they were, the old lady told them to make themselves at home and to make some tea. However, with no phone in the house the band wanted to move on.

Eventually, around 8 a.m., freezing and in foul humour, Joe and the band came upon a village, Williamstown. Upon spotting a phone box they made an immediate charge to get into it to stay warm. As they tried to cram into it, they heard a church bell ring: salvation was close at hand. Ben rang for help, while Joe and the boys raced over the road to the village church. Once inside, they found a small portable gas heater on the altar. They all huddled in the front pew, shivering and exhausted.

A voice then echoed around the church. 'Now lads, I don't think you're here for morning Mass.' Spotting Joe and telling him he was a fan, the priest brought the band to the nearby parochial house. Inside there was a friendly housekeeper, a big fire, lashings of tea and round after round of hot toast. The priest came back in after Mass and, like so many parish priests did over the years, asked Joe to do a gig in aid of a new church roof. A few hours later, a rescue team from Mullingar arrived and Joe said his goodbyes, promising to return for a fundraising gig.

Nearly twenty years later, Joe was playing nearby and Frankie McDonald found himself passing through Williamstown. He decided to stop and say a prayer in the church. He found it full of workmen and, among them, a new parish priest, who asked if he could help Frankie. Frankie explained he had come in to reminisce more than anything, but before he could even finish his sentence the priest said, 'Let me guess. You were here with Joe Dolan. Well, it's about time . . .' They were in the process of putting a new roof on the church, and once again Joe was asked to lend a hand. When he heard the price tag for the roof, he replied it was 'a very expensive breakfast'.

Just in time for Christmas 1978, Pye cashed in with the imaginatively titled album *I Need You and Other Great Hits*. Because many of the songs had not been big hits at home or in the UK, the album enabled fans to catch up on the many records that had kept Joe high in the charts throughout the world. Large quantities of the album soon found their way into the Soviet Union, where Joe had been building up quite a following without even trying. With the cassette tape market prone to mass bootlegging, Joe became even more well known as the year progressed, so much so that the Soviets would soon come knocking on his door.

Joe's band went through a couple of key personnel changes as the decade came to a close. After the energetic Maurice Walsh left the band to pursue other musical interests, he was replaced by Jimmy Walsh (no relation), another great character who stayed with the band for three years. (Jimmy would go on to write 'In Your Eyes', which won the Eurovision Song Contest in 1993.) When he left, he was replaced by Mullingar man Tony Newman, a larger-than-life individual with a remarkable gift for one-liners. 'He was the kind of fella who caused people to walk on the far side of the street if they met him out walking,' Joe grinned. 'He was like a lion!' But he became one of the most fondly remembered players in Joe's band.

Tony had been playing drums for Irish country star Roly Daniels, and he was so confident that he had got the Joe Dolan job that he handed in his notice before he even auditioned. At the audition itself, he made an instant impression, initially saying nothing as he surveyed the scene before him.

When they performed a country song, Ben told him he preferred slower drumming. When they ran through 'Good Looking Woman', Joe told him he preferred faster drumming. Tony snapped. 'Now, lads, I just want you to remember one thing,' he stated. 'I am the fucking drummer here!' 'He wasn't even in the band and he was tearing us apart!' Joe said. Tony was hired.

A consummate pro whose bark was worse than his bite, Tony had played in many bands before he joined Joe's, and on hit records all over the world. He was a voracious reader and a lucid thinker who had an opinion on anything. 'Tony exploded the musical myth about drummers being stupid,' Joe recalled. 'He could talk about anything at length. Himself and Joe Healy used to fight as to who knew most about World War II! He was passionate about what he believed in, and he had great command of the English language, which he'd use to slay you.'

Tony was the bandwagon's navigator for some time, and one of his many memorable lines was directed at a new member of the road crew who, on his first trip to England, turned the bandwagon left after Tony had directed him to turn right. Tony turned to him and said, 'You know, if intelligence was fatal, you'd live for ever.' Dozens of Joe's favourite stories on the road involved Tony, from the time Tony was 'adopted' by a family in Moscow, to the time he awoke on a wall in New York City, to filling his father's pipe with marijuana to keep him quiet. Yet behind the razor-sharp repartee and his wild streak was a remarkably mellow man, a classical music and opera buff who could dance the steps to *Swan Lake*, no mean feat for a sixteen-stone drummer. And Joe and Tony's chemistry was even more evident at show time.

'There was a healthy friction of sorts between Tony and Joe, and Tony used to drive the whole show,' Adrian Dolan recalls. 'There is a way for drummers, you can play with the singer, or you can push the singer. Tony was able to get the balance perfect and he was able to push Joe that little bit further, to take him off. Joe loved that, he really did. It was that chemistry between Tony and Joe that made the live shows. The converse of that relationship was when Joe was in the studio, and he would be pushing exactly the same way as Tony would have pushed him on the stage.'

Livewire guitarist Gerry Kelly was another new recruit, and he filled the shoes of Mullingar guitarist Jimmy Murray, who had replaced Gordon Coleman a few years earlier. Jimmy was another great character, and a put-down aimed at Ben one night would become an eternal part of Joe's bandwagon banter, as Joe recalled: 'He asked Ben for some wages up front one night. So Ben got his sax out – he used to keep the money in the bell of the sax after a show – and took out a few pound for Jimmy who quipped, "That's the best note to come out of that sax in a long time!"'

Gerry was another dedicated pro, and played with the band for several years before being replaced by Mullingar man and guitar virtuoso Joe Meehan. Joe loved the camaraderie that came from having lots of band members from his hometown, and Meehan fitted the bill perfectly. He would go on to become one of the longest-serving members of the band.

13
From Mullingar to Moscow

Keeping track of Joe's gold discs at the end of the decade required a map of the world and plenty of pins: he had turned vinyl into gold in over two dozen countries, with massive sales on practically every continent. Two countries still remained elusive: America and the Soviet Union; however, by the end of the decade, Joe would play to hundreds of thousands in both nations as they succumbed to Mullingar's singing ambassador.

But before all this, in 1978, Joe had his biggest South African tour to date: a non-stop two-month trip that saw him play to over 160,000 delirious fans. Indeed, he had a tough job to meet the voracious appetite of his many fans, and soon found himself playing two shows a night to meet demand.

Joe's arrival at Cape Town International Airport on 6 January 1978 was televised live, and the following morning he awoke to find himself splashed all over the front pages of South Africa's national newspapers. Pop music magazines featured poster spreads and colourful interviews geared for Joe's younger audience. He would garner more newspaper and magazine column inches in two months than he had done in an entire year back home. At first, Joe tried to paint an accurate picture of himself as being 'one of the guys', but the South African media were having none of it. From then on, Joe had fun with them, spinning them several yarns. He described his home to one journalist as a Georgian structure overlooking a golf course 'which had collapsed'. He made Mullingar twice the size it was. In another interview he claimed that only Gaelic was spoken at home as he grew up. 'I think I've learned English pretty well,' he quipped. For the rest of the tour he would be asked if it was difficult adjusting to English when he had been reared on the native Irish tongue.

The coverage was largely full of praise for Joe, as – just like in Northern Ireland – he was not afraid to play where other artists had refused to tread. 'People have said to me, "You're mad – what about the bombs and the fighting?" But I tell you something, if I believed half of what I read about Ireland I'd be afraid to go home!' he told one interviewer. He did, however, refuse to play certain shows, including a potentially lucrative residency in Sun City, the controversial whites-only Vegas-style entertainment enclave. Joe also insisted that his shows and his crew be multi-racial, which at the time of apartheid rule was a brave move. In fact, when audience members and Joe's crew were refused entry to one venue on account of the colour of their skin, Joe pulled the show.

The tour hit the biggest venues South Africa could offer at the time. Positive first-night reviews added to the clamour for tickets, and even with two shows a night in cities such as Johannesburg, Durban, Cape Town, Pretoria, Port Elizabeth, East London and Bloemfontein, extra dates were added in February. Critics were united in their praise of Joe's show. The leading music critic in the *Cape Times*, Ted Partridge, felt 'Danny Boy' and 'Goodbye Venice Goodbye' were the standouts of Joe's week-long Cape

Town run. 'Both songs require exceptional talent, class and application. Dolan has all that and it is tied up with a sparkling professionalism that makes him really special for me. You can't help liking this little dynamo of a man because he gets straight into his music and keeps belting it out. The audience participation is largely spontaneous and the atmosphere is electric. He never misses a trick, and when he is called back for more he looks genuinely surprised . . . He is class – and onstage it comes beaming through like a beacon on a misty night.' 'Joe brings the sunshine,' said *The Star*, urging its readers not to miss him.

In Durban's Playhouse Theatre, towards the end of the tour, Pat Boone made a surprise appearance onstage to present him with . . . a glass of milk! As the perspiring Dolan took a sip, Boone grabbed the microphone to say, 'I have never seen anyone work so hard in my life.' Boone was genuinely blown away by Joe's 'hip-swinging, air-punching routine', but more so by Joe's voice, which was 'high and strong and clear'. The entertainers went on to become firm friends.

Nevertheless, although Joe was delighted to play to so many full houses and to receive an endorsement from a singer he admired, the tour was hard on him. 'It was a tough, tough tour. I think we covered 8,000 miles by road, and had five or six flights to contend with as well, with a pick up at eight in the morning, and the only day we had off was a Sunday when *everything* in South Africa shut down.' Even on these supposed days of rest, everyone wanted a piece of Joe. He was the biggest solo star to play the country in a long time, and there were queues around the block for any personal appearances at record stores. He found himself doing promotional work for others, including South African Airlines, who co-sponsored the tour, and he even opened a supermarket. But when he wasn't playing, all he wanted to do was to relax beside the pool with the band, who took full advantage of the sun, knowing that Ireland was enveloped in deep, heavy snow. When they eventually got home they were like strawberries in cream.

Following Joe into many of the venues was top comedian Spike Milligan. They met on a number of occasions, but had little time to swap jokes as Joe was in such demand. His concerts varied in length according to the demands of the particular venue. If it was a two-show-per-night gig, each set would last an hour and a quarter; if it was one show, two hours. The reception each night was loud, boisterous and highly appreciative. In a divided country, Joe managed to unite both communities – black and white – under one roof, at least for the duration of his show.

Coming back home was a bit of an anti-climax for Joe and the band, but Joe never seemed to show any despondency, and he gave it just the same as he had done in the palatial venues he had just left. He played an increasing number of cabaret shows, together with a series of Northern Irish dates – something bands from the South were reluctant to do in the wake of the Miami Showband massacre of 1974.

A new album, *Midnight Lover*, released in Ireland in December 1977 and around the world the following month, heralded the first truly regular appearance of the white suit, and the album did big business for Joe at home and abroad, particularly in mainland Europe and Australia. It was largely made up of Peter Yellowstone productions, such as the heavily disco-influenced title track, the latter winning further gold discs in France. This song was also a big hit in Germany and all over mainland Europe, its upbeat tempo the perfect tonic for late-night groovers. Also on the album was a disco update of 'Unchained Melody', which would set dance floors alight in Spain, Italy, Greece and all around the Mediterranean. It was the subject of much derision at the time, but Joe would have the last laugh decades later when dance-floor updates of classics like this became a staple of commercial clubland. 'Disco Crazy' was another big dance-floor hit, and it was also Joe's first 12-inch single. Its extended mix made it a firm favourite of Joe's brother Ben because of the *huge* sax solo at its conclusion. The album also featured the European hit single 'Gypsy Lady' and the similarly successful punchy power pop of 'Don't Ever Change Your Mind'.

The undisputed highlight of the album, however, was another massive romantic love song, the moving 'My Love', an epic in the same mould as 'I Need You' but with an even greater vocal performance from Joe, who hits and holds remarkable Everest-high notes. It is one of the saddest songs Joe would ever record, and bucked the trend set by his previous romantic epics as here there are no two-way declarations of love and no happy ending. Instead, the song is about a man alone, spending his long dark nights dreaming of his departed love, the backing vocals and Joe's wails at the song's meditative, dreamlike conclusion making for some of the most spine-tingling yet uplifting few minutes he has ever recorded.

It was probably too sad a song for Joe's Irish fans, particularly those still shocked by the way he had embraced Euro pop and reinvented himself as a white-suit-sporting disco king. Despite a gruelling thirteen-week Irish tour around its release, it reached a disappointing number twenty-seven in the charts. In the UK, it performed equally poorly. At the time, Joe was also beginning negotiations with Pye and Red Bus to free himself from his contract. Elsewhere the single did considerably better, and it took the top spot in the South African charts for a fortnight, spending three months in the Top Twenty. It also did well in Latin America, Portugal and in Northern and Eastern Europe. And although Joe did not know at the time, 'My Love' became a very well-known song in the Soviet Union. (In some respects, 'My Love' was rooted in the Soviet musical tradition, as it turned into a more reflective, almost classical piece after the bridge, with no need for lyrics to convey its emotion. Joe would often slag off Peter Yellowstone about the song's conclusion, saying that he had forgotten to finish it.)

The *Midnight Lover* LP also broke Joe into the big time behind the Iron Curtain, although, as with his last couple of albums, not via conventional distribution channels. Joe would discover just how big he was when the Soviet Ambassador to Ireland, Vladimir Khorev, made a surprising phone call to his office, inviting him to become the first-ever Western artist to undertake a major tour of the then communist Soviet Union.

'I didn't believe it at first, I really thought someone was pulling my leg,' he remarked of that phone call. 'I was thinking, "How did they hear about me?"'

As it turned out, the Soviets were well aware of Joe Dolan, so much so that over the course of his groundbreaking 1978 tour there, close to 200,000 of them would serenade him from the stalls – 100,000 of them in Leningrad alone. 'It was the most moving experience I think I have ever had in show business,' he would remark about hearing his own songs being sung back to him by an audience who, by rights, should not have known about him or his material.

As he recalled how the historic tour to the USSR came about, Joe still sounded astonished by it all. 'Seamus received a call from the Soviet Embassy, which he thought was a big joke at first. When he told me about it, I was sure it was a joke as well. Anyway, the call was for us to visit the Russian Embassy, where there was only one item on the agenda, what they called a "cultural relations trip".'

If Joe was unsure about how popular he was in the Soviet Union, the rouble dropped when they got to the Embassy. 'We were met by the Ambassador and the Cultural Officer. They were really into us, and they knew everything about my career. They told us that they wanted to bring us to the Soviet Union for a big tour. They had even gone to see me in concert at the Chariot Inn in Ranelagh and said they were big fans!'

As they talked about Joe's career, Cultural Officer Andrei Romanov revealed that the man from Mullingar was one of the biggest and best-known Western artists there, even though, technically, he wasn't supposed to be. For many decades music had been closely monitored to keep it within certain boundaries. Censorship and seizures were commonplace, and even folk songs were suppressed. But the rise of the cassette tape, which was easy to bootleg, as well as the drift of longwave radio waves from Europe, had led to a seismic shift and people had greater access to music that the State had no control over. Rather than try to control this growing taste for music from the 'free West', the authorities reluctantly accepted it and, subject to presidential approval, some Western entertainers were being invited to perform one-off shows. Although this was not something that the authorities encouraged, particularly as pop was not deemed 'pure' music, the forward-thinking Soviet consulate in Ireland felt that because of his popularity in the East, Joe was just the man to lead a popular music revolution. They had proposed to their Red Square bosses that he could bring a live popular music presentation to the Soviet people. When they told an awestruck Joe this, he agreed to 'look into' doing a tour there in the not-too-distant future.

The provisional agreement was toasted with a glass of neat vodka and a traditional Russian lunch. 'We left with the idea that we'd look to go out there in November. We couldn't refuse something like that. I had to pinch myself in the car on the way home,' Joe said.

Within a few days, the entire tour was arranged for November that year, giving Joe just a couple of months' notice. At the government's behest Joe would play venues built especially for the Olympics, which were due to be held there in 1980, as well as some of the state's top theatres. In all, he would play twenty-three shows. A press photo call was arranged at the embassy to announce the tour, the first-ever major tour to be undertaken by a Western artist in any musical genre. Irish and Russian television news and newspapers all featured the historic news.

To celebrate the deal, every member of the Soviet Embassy staff, and other dignitaries and government officials flown in from Moscow, attended a Joe show at the National Stadium. Joe brought an entourage of his Mullingar pals to meet the VIPs, among them the late Tommy Roche, aka Roche T, possessor of one of the most famous stutters in Ireland. Backstage after the show, Joe introduced him to the Ambassador, pretending to him that Tommy was part of his team for the upcoming tour.

'Pleased to meet you; and vot do you do?' the Ambassador enquired.

'I'm th-th-th-th-th-th-the int-t-t-t-t-t-t-t-t-t-t-t-terp-p-p-p-p-p-pret-t-t-t-t-t-ter,' Tommy replied in his trademark stammer.

In November 1978 Joe flew from London to Moscow. Because he was still banned by Aer Lingus, he had to make his own way to London, where he hooked up with the rest of the group. When they touched down in Moscow after a fun-filled five-hour flight, they realized that they should have learned a little bit more about the place in advance, particularly when it came to the climate. 'It was a bit of a stupid time to go out really; it was freezing! There we were, nine Paddies chilled to the bone in clothes that would barely keep us warm at home! Poor old Tony Newman only brought a cardigan with him!' Joe said, laughing.

They didn't bring any equipment, road crew or a translator with them, only their cherished instruments. The band arrived at their Moscow hotel looking, as Joe recalled, 'like men who had just touched down from the moon. I don't think they'd ever seen a band like us before. It was all classical musicians and maybe some folk and traditional musicians at that time. The night we arrived at the hotel, a classical quartet was playing in the dining room. They stopped when we walked in armed with instruments and wearing denim.'

The first night in Moscow was a hoot, according to Joe. 'We were treated like royalty that first night, and this extraordinary meal was laid on for us. We all had fillet steaks, and I think they had imported Irish beef especially for us. We were on two tables, and Seamus, Tony Newman, Pat Hoey and I were on one and we all tried some caviar, as you do. After the meal, Ben came over to see what we had thought of the meal. As he was talking he picked up a piece of bread, buttered it and spread a load of caviar on it. He tasted it, and spat it out saying, "Jesus Christ, lads, there's an awful taste of fish off this jam!" After dinner we walked around Moscow in awe of the whole place, we walked to Red Square and our jaws just dropped. The square was about the size of Mullingar.'

On that first night they were introduced to their cultural attaché for the trip, Marina, and an interpreter, Bella. 'The first thing Marina said to us was that we were not to call the country Russia, it was the USSR, so I called it Russia from then on to drive her mad! She would get extremely annoyed, as Russia was a country, but not the whole country,' Joe said, grinning. Although they did not know it at the time, they were also being shadowed by KGB men, acting as bodyguards.

The next morning he and the band were back to the airport for a flight to their first tour destination, Kishinev, a city of over half a million by the Black Sea in the state (now the Republic) of Moldova. Flying into the city, they were a little apprehensive as all they could see in the snow-covered city were tower blocks and factories. However, their jaws were back on the floor when they were brought to the theatre where Joe would officially begin his history-making tour: 'The theatre was a beautiful palace of a place,' he said. 'It seated 3,500 people and the stage was as big as any Irish ballroom we'd played in; it was massive. It was fully kitted out with balconies, royal boxes, and huge foyers for eating. I sat in one of the ordinary seats and even they were beautiful. Everything was magnificent about the place, the in-house sound was top notch and the auditorium had great acoustics. There were TVs and CCTV cameras for the lads doing the lights, who were all keen, and the dressing rooms were beautiful . . . You know, we'd been all over Europe and played in every sort of venue imaginable, but never had we seen anything like this place.'

Seven shows had been lined up over five days in Kishinev, all of them sold out. The format of the shows was unlike anything Joe had experienced before. 'There was no warm-up band. My band went out and played an intro, then I was introduced on to the stage by a beautiful woman called Tatiana and off I went, until this interval, which we knew nothing about. We only found out when we were about to go onstage that the interval was mandatory. They had to split the show in two so the crowd could go out for a drink and a bite to eat halfway through. We had to change the show a bit to take account of it; we didn't want them to be too relaxed after their feed.'

They would build up the show to a high before the fifteen-minute break, and then finish with an hour-and-a-quarter set, raising the tempo and temperature as they went.

Although Joe had done a little homework before he headed out, and he understood that the crowds would probably be very reserved and discouraged from letting go, he found the audience to be completely the opposite. 'The crowd clapped immediately after he went onstage,' recalled Seamus, who watched the first show from the back of the theatre. 'And he kept them going all the way through. They loved big slow numbers like "Danny Boy", "I Need You" and "My Love" and they were incredibly impressed with his voice.' The crowd would stand up and applaud him during songs when he hit the high notes.

'Jesus, it was beautiful to behold; to have that effect on people,' Joe recalled. 'It frightened some of the lads [in the band] though, but to me it was the ultimate compliment.'

They would continue to pay him compliments by demanding encore after encore at every show, but Joe didn't appreciate their manner at first, as Seamus recalls. 'They confused us because they would slow handclap you if they wanted more, which was extraordinary compared to what we were used to. Joe thought it was an insult on the first night, and we had to tell him it wasn't. Once he got over it, he was on an incredible high after the shows. He was really buzzing.'

'I was surprised that they knew so many of the songs,' Joe said. 'We did a good, big set which we thought would have across-the-board appeal, with a little bit of everything in it. But of the twenty-four numbers we did that night they knew about eight of the hits really well, so we put more of those numbers in. We balanced the programme with the big songs spread here and there.'

After the first show in Kishinev the band went back to the hotel, where the plan was to pore over the show and have something to eat. 'We then discovered that the entire seventeenth floor was a bar, so we spent a good part of the first night there!' Joe said, laughing. 'Even the lads who didn't drink in the band let their hair down that night.'

The next morning, free from any lingering first-night nerves, Joe was quite shocked by what he saw in the city as he walked around it. Although Kishinev was known as a great resort area in the summer, in the winter it was a bleak place, and away from the concert hall there was little joy to be had. 'It was probably this amazing city back in the 1930s or 1940s – but even as we flew in we could sense this depression about the place. On the first day I went into this huge shop, and all that was in it was carbolic soap and potatoes. I couldn't believe it. The people seemed to have nothing. We saw the real flipside of life in the Soviet era there. It was a very strange place, and we weren't allowed really to go anywhere in it. Men would crop up out of nowhere and go, "No, you can't go there, Mr Dolan."'

The divide between the haves and the have-nots was obvious all over the country. The hotels were for tourists only; locals could only work there. 'There was nothing for the Russians themselves. They couldn't go to the touristy shops, where you could use your credit card or spend dollars. I just thought it wasn't right.' Although Joe had all the luxuries he could possibly desire and was treated like royalty, he preferred to be out among the people. In Kishinev he found a small local restaurant that became a sort of home from home for him and some of the band. But an increasingly edgy Joe was looking forward to returning to Moscow. Unfortunately, because of heavy snow, they had to stay another night. Joe would curse Kishinev for years to come as it was when he was holed up there for that extra night that he started smoking again – having stopped for almost two years. 'I was sitting in this hotel lobby staring out the window at a wall of snow that surrounded the hotel. Nothing or nobody was moving that day and I reached for a packet of cigarettes,' he said, regretfully.

When Joe was brought to the airport, the royal treatment continued and he was left with little option but to accept it. 'We were brought on to the plane in front of everybody – skipped every queue going. Then loads of soldiers got on board; one after another they all filed on. I started to get a bit worried that the plane wouldn't take off with the weight on it. I kept thinking, "This plane is going to crash, this thing will never take off." Seamus started to get worried then, and we thought about Brazil. But it took off OK. I think everybody was scared too, as there was no craic on the plane. Everybody stayed quiet, which was a first for the boys. Although, looking back, that could have been because we were the only civilians on it.'

After they had touched down in Moscow, they were taken to their next accommodation. 'We stayed in a beautiful old hotel, the Metropol, right beside Red Square. All the boys were jealous because I had this massive suite with a grand piano, a magnificent marble bathroom and a bed as big as a house, while the rest of the lads had normal rooms. The opulence was just something else. I felt guilty though. Down below us there were old ladies sweeping the streets, and here I was in the presidential suite with a corridor outside so long you could play golf down it.'

In Moscow, Joe was to play a week of sold-out concerts in another impressive theatre, this time a 3,900-seater. Gosconcert, the Soviet state agency who were promoting the tour, had created plenty of hype for the Moscow dates, and Joe was the centre of attention for the Russian media, and for fans on the street. 'We did loads of press, and a photo shoot on Red Square, which was a bit of a disaster. I arrived for the photo session wearing only a light pair of Spanish leather boots, which genuinely stuck to the ground with the cold. It was 15 degrees below freezing. There was a massive buzz surrounding the shows, this sense of anticipation, you know? When we finally got onstage, Moscow was just in a different league to anything we had done before. It was unreal.'

Marina had a few snags to iron out, and her diplomatic management skills were needed on a number of occasions, not least when it came to equipment. Drummer Tony Newman, a percussion perfectionist, was responsible for one big fright, as Joe recalled: 'When we walked into this beautiful theatre in Moscow, we were gasping looking at this huge stage and this incredible layout, but all we could see up on the stage was this tiny little drum kit – like one you'd buy a child for Christmas. Tony walked around it a few times, announced, "I'm not playing these *effing* drums," and walked out.' A drum kit was effectively seized from a Moscow musician in exchange for free tickets. 'They just took a kit from a poor ould divil's house,' Joe said. 'It was decent kit but still way down the line to what Tony was used to back home, but it was probably the best there was in Russia. This poor divil used to come along, and he'd be at the side of the stage looking in horror at Tony beating the drums on him.'

As the band rehearsed, an audience of classical musicians, orchestra conductors and dancers from the nearby Bolshoi came along to check out this Western phenomenon. Noting the VIP presence, Seamus and an interpreter casually listened in to what they were saying.

'They were discussing among themselves how Joe could sing so high without going into falsetto. They were amazed with the sound of the voice, and they couldn't understand how he went up to high notes and didn't break, how he kept pushing out and holding this big note,' he said. Needless to say, they were all invited to the show that night.

'All the bigwigs came to see us, including the top conductor with the Russian Symphony Orchestra,' Joe remembered. 'We invited them back for a drink at the hotel. We got incredibly friendly with the conductor, he was a lovely guy. He kept saying to me, "Stay in Russia, don't go back to that troubled country of yours." At the time there was a lot going on in the North, but I was thinking to myself, "If only you knew what I was going back to. I have so much freedom it is ridiculous!" He ended up conducting the band in a mass singalong of the *1812 Overture*, much to the disapproval of Joe's 'shadows'. They arranged to meet him the following day for lunch, but he never turned up. 'We all suspected that he had been sent to the Gulags!' Joe recalls. 'Tony used to accuse the girls of being KGB agents, which they weren't, but in Tony's mind they were. "You are KGB!" he'd roar at them.'

There was ample opportunity to see the sights. Gosconcert had laid on a luxury coach and a limousine, so Joe and the band were driven anywhere they wanted. Quite ludicrously, the engines of both manned vehicles were left on around the clock outside the hotel in case the band decided that some 4 a.m. sightseeing was in order. They were suitably astonished by Lenin's tomb and everything else Moscow had to offer, and were also amazed at the lack of cars and other vehicles on the streets and the queues. Some of the band were a little cheeky out and about in Moscow, as Joe remembered. 'People would be queuing everywhere, so some of the lads would stop and form a queue outside of a different doorway, and loads of locals would start to queue up behind them thinking a door was going to open! People queued for everything. You would walk down past the queue and find they were queuing for a mat, or a carpet or something; it was incredible. We went shopping in the GUM, a big department store right beside us, and there was nothing in it. Russia really was on its knees at that stage.'

Joe found that he was being mobbed by fans on the street, so he spent a lot of his time in his suite playing the piano and entertaining dignitaries. 'A couple of the lads would get up early and go for a walk or go looking for Western newspapers, but I couldn't do that. I'd watch the news on the TV, but it was all in Russian so it was no use to me.' One of Joe's concerts was filmed for state television and Joe was also interviewed.

Even though he was suffering from some cold-weather blues – 'It was too cold really to do anything' – the shows were sensational and probably among the best the band had ever played together at that stage. 'Joe knew from Kishinev how to work the thing and it went better in Moscow,' his manager recalls. 'I would be either on the side of the stage, or walking around. It was great to be at them, they were exciting shows, and Joe really sang his heart out and gave it his all onstage. Every night he received an ovation, and they always wanted an encore. It was incredible for him to be getting this reaction from a crowd who had never seen him before, and whom he thought wouldn't get him.'

Joe danced like a man possessed in Moscow, and sensing a slightly conservative edge to the crowd he had plenty of fun getting them involved in the show, changing the arrangement of some of the songs to ensure there were opportunities for them to clap along. The big hit in Moscow was, surprisingly, 'Westmeath Bachelor', which sent the audience wild with its traditional Irish flavour and Joe's Irish dancing routine. Rockers like 'Sweet Little Rock 'n' Roller', 'Make Me Act the Fool' and 'Good Looking Woman' also got a great reaction. Sadly, 'Midnight in Moscow', a jazz hit for Kenny Ball, played Dixieland-style, went down like a lead balloon, so it was dropped after one night. The shows were high-octane performances and Joe's white suit started to become his permanent stage wear, albeit with a black shirt at this stage. As well as almost making him feel like a new man, the suit also looked very good under all the lights. 'The suit looked very flash under the slick lighting; it was really knocking off the white suits!' The rest of the band, meanwhile, cut a dash in dark suits offset by crisp white shirts, complete with the obligatory massive collars almost touching their elbows.

It was during the Moscow run that 'Goodbye Venice Goodbye' first became the closing number of the show. 'We introduced a couple of numbers, and if a number wasn't going well we'd throw in another one,' Joe recalled. '"Venice" just seemed to click on that tour.' Joe learned several Russian phrases to use onstage (including the 'ladies and gentlemen' running joke) and this endeared him further to the crowd. 'Moscow was an absolutely fantastic audience, and they reacted to the *cúpla focal* immediately,' he said, revealing that as the tour went on he became a little more adventurous in what he was saying to them. The crowd also had an understanding of English. 'English was the second language in most of the universities over there, so we used a bit as well and I probably left some of them talking English with Mullingar accents!'

After the shows, such was the clamour of the fans that Joe had to be whisked out of the auditorium back to the hotel almost immediately. But each night there was a haunting encounter with an old woman who would wait for Joe at the gate beneath the theatre. 'Joe was really spooked by this old lady,' Seamus reveals. 'I don't know how this old woman knew Joe, but she waited there for him, humped over, and every night, she used to stop the car and say, "Joe, Joe, Joe" and we'd stop – we had to. Joe would roll down the window. She'd come over, saying, "Joe, Joe, Joe," and then she'd speak in Russian and hand him little trinkets and relics. The first night it was a cross. The next night a little pressed flower, rosary beads and little religious orthodox items. He kept them all when we got back. The driver, who could speak a little English, said, "Joe, she says your mother is looking after you." As we drove up to this gate, he would say each night, "Joe, your mother is here," and Joe would shout, "Stop, stop!" and he'd talk to this woman. She'd give him a little something, a hug, and a blessing and then she'd walk off. It troubled Joe for a bit. We often talked about it. "How did she know?" he'd ask. She wasn't even at the show, this poor little woman. Joe looked for her from the stage but could never see her, but yet she had this love and this message for Joe. We didn't know where she came out of. For seven nights in a row she was there waiting each night. We tried to find out where she came from or who she was but we couldn't find out anything about her. The security guards at the theatre had never seen her before. It was strange, but nice in a way.'

There were no journalists on the trip, but the stories were sent home every day and the Irish papers snapped up any titbit. A photographer was hired from a Moscow press agency, but the pictures were poor and few remain today of that tour. The only other cameras were the band's own, which weren't working very well in the freezing cold, but the few sightseeing pictures that exist reveal a very happy, if rather cold, group.

The band then departed for the next leg of the tour: Leningrad (now St Petersburg). For eleven straight nights Joe played to a sell-out crowd of 9,000 a night in Leningrad's Olympic Winter Sports Palace. Even though he had played to crowds of up to 5,000 at the height of Ireland's ballroom boom, and had entertained tens of thousands at big outdoor shows in

Israel and across Europe, this was far more special. 'Without question, Leningrad was one of the highlights of my career,' he enthused. 'When I walked on to the stage it was the most moving and spine-chilling experience I have ever had in show business. I felt like a bullfighter walking into the arena.' Behind him onstage was a massive sixty-foot hand-painted effigy of himself; the stage itself was as big as a venue back home, and the band were spread over raised platforms. Joe was positioned about thirty feet out on the arena floor on another raised platform, a black circular disc cut into the shape of a record with the words 'Joe Dolan' spelled out in strip lighting. It was even more Las Vegas than Las Vegas itself. Surrounding Joe's personal stage were three main stands full of screaming fans. Joe was in heaven. 'Everything about Leningrad had this sort of magic about it. I could have lived there. The city was breathtakingly beautiful, the people very friendly, and then this big production in the arena. When I went into my act and spoke my first big word of Russian while sipping water – "*Nasdarovia*", meaning 'cheers' – a voice shouted back from the darkened auditorium, "*Sláinte!*" I could have cried.'

Cliff Richard had played some shows in Leningrad in 1976, and had told Joe the crowd would be warm and appreciative, but quite cool and reserved at the same time. However, Joe found the Leningrad crowd to be the wildest of the tour. 'They knocked me out,' he said. Because of their proximity to Europe they knew practically every song Joe performed, from the 1960s classics of his early Drifters days to 'My Love'. They sang along and roared their approval afterwards, stomping their feet as well as clapping. 'I was still innocent enough in this business to get the tingle in my spine when I got applause, but I became quite emotional with my reception in Leningrad,' Joe observed. 'There aren't enough words to describe how magic those shows were; it was amazing, packed every night. They were more like happenings than gigs.'

He opened the show on the first night with his own unique take on 'River Deep Mountain High', the Ike and Tina Turner classic, which was received well. But the applause and response from the crowd was even greater when Joe launched into his second song, 'Good Looking Woman', and it would soon become his opening number. Ben remembers Joe changing the set-list during the first Leningrad show to reflect the enthusiastic response of the Leningrad audience. 'Joe had a great sense of a crowd, he could feel how it

ne of the earliest known photographs of the young guitar slinger onstage, taken by his
other Paddy.

ne Drifters in the mid 1960s. Relax, girls, they were nearly all married.

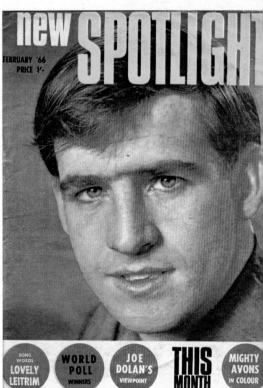

FEBRUARY '66
PRICE 1'-

SONG WORDS
LOVELY LEITRIM

WORLD POLL
WINNERS

JOE DOLAN'S
VIEWPOINT

THIS MONTH

MIGHTY AVONS
IN COLOUR

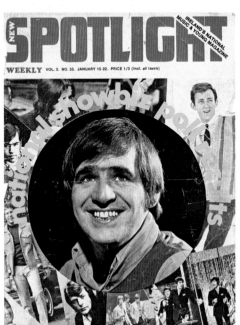

IRELAND'S NATIONAL
MUSIC & YOUNG MAGAZINE

WEEKLY   VOL. 3. NO. 33. JANUARY 15-22. PRICE 1/3 (Incl. all taxes)

VOL 7. No. 39 MARCH 28th 1974

Spotlight

IRELANDS NATIONAL MUSIC/ENTERTAINMENT MAG.

10P

CAN JOE ROCK BACK?

IN GIANT FULL COLOUR
NAZARETH

2 GREAT SONGS

EXCLUSIVE

TINA'S "Cross your Heart"

PAPERLACE'S "Billy don't be a hero"

We talk to GLEN CAMPBELL in Nashville

A selection of Joe's numerous appearances on the cover of *Spotlight* magazine, from the early 1960s to the mid 1970s.

Sleeves from Joe's
hundreds of recordings
through five decades.

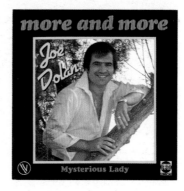

Black suit, big smile: an energetic Joe performs on European television as his career goes into overdrive with the release of 'Lady in Blue' in 1975.

Onstage in Leningrad in 1978, Joe performs in front of over 9,000 fans every night and is dwarfed by the sixty-foot backdrop of himself.

Joe, live in Las Vegas in 1980. The show would be marked by lasers and the green flowers he said he had had flown in from his very own garden.

The quintessential '90s Joe, resplendent in white suit.

...e in Belgium, back on the road after his savage beating in 1970 as he starts to rack up hit after ...t. He never got his nose fixed.

...e and his band, ready to take on the world in 1974 ahead of the release of 'Lady in Blue'. ...om left: Ben Dolan, Kevin Cowley, Liam Meade, Maurice Walsh, Joe Dolan, Gordon Coleman ...d Frankie McDonald.

Joe and the gang on holiday in the 1960s.

Joe dons a tracksuit for a very brief time in the 1980s. A restless soul, he hated for things to get too quiet and laid-back. If someone was not paying him full attention, he would try to get their attention – perhaps by setting fire to their newspaper, as he has done here to long-time band member Liam Meade.

Golf was Joe's great love and he's pictured here on one of his many favourite courses, in Mullingar.

integral part of any Joe Show from the 1980s onwards was the ceremonial handing out of his
nature ties.

oodbye Venice Goodbye': Joe always took the time to thank his front row at the end of a
g show.

Joe and his brother Paddy ride a Honda 50 through Paddy's Mullingar home, a photograph Joe cherished and kept on his mantelpiece at his home in Foxrock.

Joe with his niece and god-daughter Kathleen, one of his closest friends and confidantes.

r once Joe was happy to let someone else do the singing as Ben leads his brothers and sisters in
ng. From left: Dympna, Paddy, Ben, Vincent, Joe and Imelda.

e, Ben, Paddy and Vincent at a family function. Joe doted on all his family, especially
s brothers.

Joe backstage in Vicar Street in February 2006, just after his first show – billed as a 'comeback' show – with his new hip. It would be the last incarnation of The Drifters. From left: Ray Dolan (drums and percussion), Johnny McCafferty (keyboards), Adrian Dolan (bass), Joe, Ben Dolan (saxophone), Seamus Casey (manager), Sean Kenny (guitars) and Frankie McDonald (trumpet).

Forty-seven years of friendship – Joe and h
manager, Seamus Case

Welcome to Mullingar – Joe put the Westmeath [to]wn on the map …

… And now Westmeath is honouring its distinguished son by erecting a statue in the town centre.

[...]n, Paddy and Vincent, with a model of their brother's statue.

Joe clowning around during filming of a *Nationwide* special in 2004 in his hometown

Joe was a patron of many charitable and voluntary organizations, and he always held St Brigid School in Mullingar close to his heart. He is pictured here during a visit to the school in 2004.

e playing his last ever hometown show on 14 August 2007. He looked the picture of health
fore, during and after the show, and as ever he gave it his all. However, within a month he
ould leave the stage for the last time.

The crowd outside the Cathedral of Christ the King in Mullingar.

's coffin is carried from the church. His nephew Adrian Dolan can be seen gripping the handle the upper left-hand corner.

Fans in mourning ...

... Including then Finance Minister and fellow Midlander Brian Cowen.

was going and he was able to switch a programme mid-stream. You had to be on your toes, and I thought I knew him pretty well!'

Looking around the arena, and looking at his boys on the massive stage dwarfed by a sixty-foot painting of Joe, Seamus said he felt like 'the proudest man in the world'. Everything from the sound to the lights was perfect, and the technicians gave it their all. But the audience made it. 'It was incredible to take in. I will always remember the sight of 9,000 people as one standing up to applaud Joe hitting a certain note. They were in awe at this voice and the heights it scaled.'

Joe was delighted. 'I never forced the notes, they were just the way I sang, I've always been known as a sort of high-voiced singer, but you'd hit that high note and they'd all stand up and cheer and then they'd settle back again until you came to something like that again and – bang! – they're all up on their feet again. They liked that effort you put in to get that note; it was a super feeling.'

To build the massive stage, over 1,000 seats had been removed. Thousands stood outside each night in the hope of snatching even a whisper from inside the venue. 'We probably could have fitted another few thousand in on the floor as well,' Joe said, laughing, although at the time there had been a few worries in the camp about audience numbers. 'When the lads saw the arena they were a bit worried that there'd be no people in and I was a bit worried about the ticket price. Seamus was asking Marina if there would be people in. She would be getting thick almost and would say, "Of course, of course. Why do you keep asking this question? I tell you, it will be filled, every night will be filled."'

As they set up on the first night, Joe and Seamus checked out Joe's route from dressing room to stage. 'I had to come out in the middle and run up through this huge space in front of the stage to my platform, so we practised it,' Joe recalled, stifling chuckles at what happened next. 'When I came out on to the arena there was this step and Seamus was worried I'd trip over it en route to the stage, so we decided he was going to lead me on.'

'It was about two yards out,' Seamus remembers. 'I was going to walk Joe out to the step and let him off. But what I didn't know was that when the show began, and the announcer roared, "Joe Dolan!", four huge spotlights would be directed into the corner. I came out first and they hit me, blinded me and I fell over the step. Joe had to walk across me to get over the step and keep going! Sure the laughs that night were unbelievable and Joe told that story for years.'

When not playing, Joe and the band would go and see something new every day, including all the historic sites associated with the 900-day Siege of Leningrad, one of the most epic, destructive and savage sieges of the Second World War, together with palaces, museums and local restaurants. 'We were treated like tsars and were brought everywhere – they brought us to the Hermitage, once the main residence of the tsars, for a private tour one day. They opened the Gold Room especially for us,' Joe recalled. 'They brought us to all their armouries, museums, St Isaac's Cathedral, the palace where all these famous paintings were. We came from simple, humble backgrounds, you know? It was like Venice on ice, all these dark colours and canals, just a beautiful place.'

Overall, Joe had a better time in Leningrad than anywhere else in the Soviet Union. 'It seemed a bit more cosmopolitan, and it seemed to me that the people had more freedom, you know? You also felt there was more prosperity and happiness there, and even though it had been bombed to bits in the war it had this remarkable character about it; this resolve. They were a very cultured people. We went to see some local musicians and they were great players. There wasn't a stiffness that the musicians elsewhere had. We could also use roubles there, which was a bonus, as we weren't allowed to use them in Moscow or Kishinev, and we were all loaded with them!'

A recurring theme on any Joe Dolan jaunt was 'the feed', and Leningrad didn't disappoint. 'We were always hungry on the road,' Joe said, 'but we were adventurous too. We'd eat anything. We used to have a big sit-down meal together after the show. We would be back in the hotel by eleven and it was a nice thing to do.' Meanwhile, some of the band became addicted to caviar. The rhythm section, Pat Hoey and Tony Newman, got friendly with some chefs and decided they were going to smuggle some enormous cans of black caviar back to Ireland. In Leningrad, as he had done in Moscow despite the 'shadows', Tony lived 'underground' as Joe remembered. 'He got friendly with a couple who worked in the hotel and who bought and sold all kinds of stuff on the street – money, denims, smoke, everything. He looked after them, and babysat their children for them a couple of times. Years later, Seamus Whelan, whose father wrote "Westmeath Bachelor", was in Leningrad and he was asked by this taxi-man where he was from. So he said Ireland. "And where do you come from in Ireland?" the Russian asked. "Oh, a little place in the centre of the country, you wouldn't know it, a town called Mull—" and before he could even finish the taxi-man roared, "Oh, do you know Tony Newman, 6 Harbour Street, Mullingar?" He couldn't believe it. They gave him a clock to bring home to Tony! God knows what was in it.'

Russian culture was geared towards food and drink, and it was tempting to drink as much as one possibly could. Despite his reputation as something of a hellraiser, Joe took it easy on the tour, and although he was still the first man to get a round in, he was careful not to drink too much and instead enjoy the company and camaraderie. During one such session, the hard-core element of the band managed to outdrink a delegation of Russian dignitaries. 'We did it, lads, we knocked them out,' declared Tony Newman at the end of the lunch. 'Now let's go back to the hotel and have a real drink!' Marina, in particular, made sure there was little funny business. She kept Joe and the band on track, and as they were ambassadors for their country, big drinking sessions were few and far between.

She had difficulty keeping them on track on the way to Leningrad from Moscow, though, and had she known that Joe was hiding a dark secret in his suitcase she may not have been so protective of him. 'We decided we wanted to go from Moscow to Leningrad by train,' Joe explains. 'It was an overnight sleeper and we thought it would give us a better chance to experience the country, plus it was something exciting to do.' Some of the touring party were interested in seeing the sights on the approach into Leningrad, particularly Lake Ladoga and 'Doroga Zhizni' (the 'Road of Life'), the only route to connect the besieged city to the mainland during the war. Meanwhile, some of the others had their sights set on attacking the card table.

Everyone shared two to a cabin, apart from Joe, who, owing to his notoriously funky feet and his room-shaking snoring, had a cabin to himself. Leaving the others to play cards, Ben and Seamus settled down early for the night and ordered tea. 'We were amazed by the presentation of the tea, and these silver holders that the "cup" sat in. They drank tea by the gallon there, which suited us, and this little friendly old lady really looked after us,' Ben remembered. In the cabins down below, however, something stronger than tea was being consumed.

Ben and Seamus wanted to get up early to take in the dramatic approach into the city. 'I had this great historic moment planned as we came into Leningrad and I went out on to the corridor at five in the morning to get my bearings,' Seamus remembered. 'Ben got up and the old lady came down and offered us tea, but she was a little edgy and not as friendly as the night before. There was something wrong, and we sensed there was a problem. We had our tea in less refined cups and we looked over the battlefield. I was thinking of the army surrounding Leningrad, thinking about how terrible it was to be in the city cut off from everything and to be one of the soldiers dug in. It was all dead flat with snow and nothing but an odd tree going sideways. Eventually we got in towards Leningrad, but before it pulled into the station the train was stopped and Marina told us that we were all being held, and that the police were coming on board.'

Marina gathered as many of the band together as she could. Joe was left in his cabin, his snores piercing the sudden unease in the air. 'There is a problem,' she said, revealing that all twelve of the little silver tea holders from the carriage were missing. The old woman had called the police in Leningrad, claiming the Westerners had robbed her. The band stood in amazement.

'Some of the boys had stayed up most of the night so I was worried about Joe, because it transpired he had only been asleep for a while and he could be ratty when you got him up in a hurry,' Seamus said. 'Plus he had a busy day ahead, so I said to Marina, "I have to get Joe out; get me a car ASAP and I'll get him to the hotel." She knew his form in the morning, knew he needed sleep, so she let us off.'

As the police boarded the train, a bleary-eyed Joe and his manager were given a police escort to their hotel. 'I got away with Joe and when we got to the hotel he went to bed and I went downstairs and waited for Ben and the lads. When they eventually got there they were all a bit shocked. They had been interrogated and searched, but the police couldn't find anything. So, there was nothing else said about it, that was the end of it and we laughed it off.'

Six months later, Ben was in Joe's Mullingar apartment when he noticed some familiar-looking silver holders on a shelf.

'Joe, where did you get them yokes?' Ben asked his brother.

'Ah, I got them that time we went to Leningrad from Moscow on the train. Why?'

Joe had taken them as a souvenir of the journey. He later divulged that after he had had a few jars he saw them and thought, 'Jayz, they're nice,' so he started gathering them up.

Joe's final show in Leningrad would be an emotional one, and he cried for much of it. Afterwards, the atmosphere was somewhat muted. The tour had been so successful, however, that Gosconcert officials immediately began to plan a return leg. Joe was sure the Iron Curtain would be opened again for him. 'We desperately wanted to go back for the Olympics, and everything was in place for us to go back in 1980, but then that fell apart. I was crushed. I would certainly have gone back.' Joe always held the Soviet Union dear to his heart, and was dismayed when certain countries refused to attend the 1980 Olympics. Further attempts to return were also un-successful: in 1990, Joe was going to return to take part in a documentary. The contracts were signed and he was set to 'go walkabout' in Moscow and Leningrad, miming his songs for Russian TV, but at the last minute it fell through. He was also planning a return in September 2007, and some dates in Moscow and Leningrad had been booked, but as he started to encounter health problems, the dates were postponed.

Despite the 1978 tour's great success, however, it was nowhere near as lucrative as the numbers on seats suggested. Although well over 160,000 Russians saw him, Joe ensured that the ticket price was kept as low as possible. He had learned from South Africa that charging too much excluded the ordinary fan. 'Although some of the band no doubt had thoughts that the tour would see them drive home in a Rolls Royce, money could not buy the experience we had on the tour. It really opened everyone's eyes,' Joe said. 'The Russians seemed to be more interested in culture than we were, but we were cultural to them even though at home we never felt as if we were. Everything was about the now in Ireland, but coming back we felt a bit special all right.' When Joe arrived home newspapers were full of his triumph, and the extra publicity ensured that he would have the 'house full' signs erected wherever he went for the foreseeable future.

This was just as well, as Joe did not make a single rouble from the huge Russian and Eastern European bootlegged cassette sales. 'We tried to do a deal but we kind of knew everything was bootlegged over there at the time, and there wasn't much point. That was the system behind the old Iron Curtain and we couldn't do anything about it.' Despite efforts to import official material, he was not allowed to sell merchandise at the concerts either. And neither were they allowed to bring any roubles they had out of the country.

However, Joe made a lasting impression in the East with the tour, and his music is still heard on Russian radio; some of his 1970s records are regarded as classics there in the same way the Irish appreciate old Bob Dylan, Neil Young and Neil Diamond tracks. And everyone, from Latvia to Lithuania, Estonia to Belarus, the Ukraine to Georgia, Kazakhstan to Armenia, knew Joe's name. 'When a lot of people from the East started to move over to Ireland in the late 1990s they were seeing this big star in their midst and he'd be buying petrol off them or having a coffee with them in the bar. They couldn't believe it!' Seamus says. 'He was played and bootlegged all over the East, and even today we're still only finding out how big he was there.'

Ben recalled the story of a Lithuanian woman who arrived in Ireland and chose to come to Mullingar because it was the town where Joe Dolan was from. She couldn't believe it when she ended up almost working for Joe in Dolan's Bar and Mojo's night club in the town. She often asked Adrian Dolan for old tapes to send back home. 'Tapes are still the musical currency in Eastern Europe, and there is still demand from Eastern Europe, from Lithuania and places like that, for them,' said Adrian, who controls Joe's online shop and studio. 'Every day I answer emails from the East enquiring about Joe.'

An Internet search using the Russian Google engine today reveals over 360,000 pages devoted to him and his music. He frequently crops up on radio station playlists, and thousands of Irish tourists have returned home from Russia and its former states with stories of how they heard Joe Dolan songs being played in taxis, bars and restaurants. After Joe's death, several Russian newspapers carried pieces about him, one obituary saying that he paved the way for other acts to tour the Soviet Union. Another remembered him as being 'a true star' in that he put his music first. Joe was never one for a carefully cultivated image, and this was something the Russians appreciated. 'In terms of his appearance Joe Dolan was strikingly different from the polished stereotypical dandies on the Anglo-American commercial stage,' one of the obituaries noted, adding that although Joe's face was 'thickset and angular', once he sang 'his constraints suddenly disappeared'.

Looking back over that astonishing tour, Ben remembers Joe as being the 'ultimate showman' onstage and the same old Joe offstage. 'Onstage he was brilliant; he gave it his all for every date on that tour. Offstage he was just an ordinary Joe. The band and Joe always stayed together. They were all Joe's friends so it was one big happy family out there. We didn't feel like we were making history or anything like that, we just did our thing.'

14
Viva Las Vegas!

Joe Dolan had it all at the outset of the 1980s and he was about to have even more when he pulled off one of the biggest gambles of his career to play a couple of successful seasons at the entertainment playground of the world: Las Vegas. The dice started rolling for Joe's first big Vegas tour, like the Russian trip in some ways, after a show in Dublin when Joe belatedly found out that he was well known out there. The late Dublin businessman and concert promoter Joe O'Neill ('a man who really could sell sand to Arabs and snow to Eskimos', according to Joe) had returned from Vegas claiming that Joe's name was on the lips of several casino bosses. After Russia, Joe had started to attract a good bit of American attention, and unbeknownst to Joe, Ben and Seamus, O'Neill had been in talks with the people who owned the famous Silverbird Casino and Resort about bringing Joe to Vegas. 'Now at first I thought he was talking about a holiday,' Joe laughed. 'Go over for a little flutter, like. "Jaysus aye, I'd love to go," I said, and I thought nothing else of it.'

O'Neill then brought four of the top men from the Silverbird, including its president, Fred Crossley, general manager Lee Fisher and two other directors to hear Joe play at the Clare Manor Hotel in Dublin. At first, Joe's brother Ben thought it was a set-up. 'I didn't believe it when these lads came in with real "how-ya-doin" American accents. They weren't young men, and I was thinking to myself, "These are after coming off a plane from Vegas at their age, to hear Joe Dolan?" Give me a break . . .' Having established it wasn't a wind-up, Joe went on to perform the show as he always did, giving it everything. Joe never allowed the presence of a VIP to affect a concert; the fans were more important than a handful of VIPs as far as he was concerned, and from the moment he went onstage he had forgotten they were even in the room. Ben, however, kept a close eye on them. 'The Vegas boys were blown away,' he said.

After the show everyone went out for a meal. Joe made an immediate impression. 'Five minutes in their company and it was as if he'd known them for a lifetime. It was all yarns about this, that and stories about Vegas. Sure the boys were over the moon with him,' Ben remembers. The Vegas guys told Joe he had what it took to be a big Vegas star. The heroes of Vegas were safe old pros like Sinatra, Dean Martin, Sammy Davis Jr and Tony Bennett, and what the Silverbird was trying to do was to bring a bit of youthful action back on to the Strip. They felt Joe had the voice, the moves, the material and the band to do just that. His voice was rich, strong and unique, and his performance was akin to that of a young Elvis, they said. They made him an offer.

Joe accepted the offer almost immediately, rising from his feet to shake the hands of the Vegas veterans. 'I'd love to go out there,' he said. After all, over a dozen years earlier he had been booked to play Vegas but never played, so an appearance there was long overdue, especially if he was known as well as they were making him out to be. But Ben thought differently.

'Everything was great, but what worried me was that there was no mention of money or anything like that,' he recalled. 'We were all on tour, and Joe was going to be doing this and that and the other, but I'm thinking to myself, "We're going halfway around the world, and how exactly are we going to do that?"'

The Americans offered the band $10,000 a week, and agreed to fly them out and put them up in the finest Silverbird rooms available. 'Right, that's settled then,' Joe said as he rose from the table to shake hands on the deal for the second time.

'Wait a minute, lads, what about the food?' Ben asked to loud groans from his younger brother, who flopped back in his seat.

'Aw Jaysus, lads, do you know you can get a breakfast out there for fifty cents?' he roared, insisting they tie up the deal.

But, as most bands will attest, if there's one thing that will cause consternation on the road morning, noon and night, it's food, and for Joe Dolan's band 'the feed' was all-important. Ben realized that the novelty of a fifty-cent breakfast would soon wear off, and he made a passionate case for all food to be included free of charge. Joe O'Neill couldn't believe what he was hearing. But the Americans eventually agreed to put all food and drink on the tab. Everyone seemed satisfied and it was third time lucky as Joe rose to his feet finally to accept their offer.

Joe was booked to play six weeks of shows at the Continental Theatre of the Silverbird throughout September and a chunk of October 1980. Vegas newspaper columnists such as Joe Delaney, a famous Irish-American writer with the *Las Vegas Sun*, started to drop Joe's name into their columns. Ads were booked, interviews were conducted and hundreds of thousands of bill posters, flyers and postcards were printed. Months before he even set foot on American soil, Joe's name went up in neon lights outside the Silverbird: 'Ireland's Number One Singing Star' proclaimed the massive roadside billboard.

At home, newspapers speculated on how much it was worth to Joe. An *Irish Independent* headline declared, '£50,000 CALL TO "THE STRIP" FOR SINGER JOE' and continued, 'The Mullingar-based star hopes his breakthrough on the American scene will result in a major boost to his show-business career, earning him repeat visits and international appearances ... The opportunity could also result in a flood of bookings from all over the world if Joe is the success the Americans believe he will be.'

'It was kind of typical of the Irish media at the time,' Seamus says. 'Nobody seemed to accept that Joe was *already* a huge star abroad. It was painted like it was his first tour out of the country.'

Joe's relationship with airplanes was never the steadiest at the best of times, but for once it would not be him who would put the latest trip in jeopardy. Everyone had arrived at Dublin airport in plenty of time for the connecting flight to London. Joe was taken directly to the gate by his manager in order to keep him out of potential danger. His flight ban and subsequent slating of Aer Lingus were still a little too raw in the memories of some to take a chance. Some of the band went with him, while Ben and a few others milled about the airport. They took their time strolling down to the departure gate, where a security guard stood looking at his watch.

'You're too late, lads,' he said.

'No, we're not going to *late*,' Ben replied, chuckling. 'We're going to Las Vegas.'

The guard didn't see the funny side. 'No. You're *too* late lads,' he repeated. 'You were called ages ago; there's your flight.'

They looked out the terminal window to see the heartbreaking sight of their plane edging out on to the runway without them. For perhaps the only time in his life, Ben used the line that people in show business try to avoid using: 'Do you know who we are? We're meant to be on that plane. How are we going to get there now? Can we get on another flight?' Ben asked.

'I dunno, can you?' the attendant said, winking to the others.

There was another flight going to Heathrow in half an hour, but it would leave the stragglers with only a slim chance of making the solitary London to Vegas flight that afternoon. Luckily, the guard turned out to be a big Joe Dolan fan, and he pulled a few strings to make sure they didn't miss the main Vegas flight. Once they reached Heathrow, a luggage wagon brought them across the runway to the Vegas flight.

'Talk about panic, the sweat was pouring out of us. We thought we would die if we missed it because we'd have to wait a good few days for the next flight out,' Ben says, remembering that direct flights to Vegas were few and far between in 1980. They made the flight with only seconds to spare. As they were literally pushed through the doors of the plane, the first person they saw in first class was Joe, reclining shoeless in his chair, a large vodka and soda in his hand.

'Well lads. What kept yez?' he asked, before bursting into laughter. Sitting pretty in the seat beside him was a very content Joe O'Neill. 'You nearly missed the fifty-cent breakfast, boys,' he quipped.

The band were in for a further shock when they touched down in Las Vegas. The captain had been asked to keep the other passengers on-board and to make sure Joe led the band off the plane first. As Joe stumbled on to the walkway he was greeted by a full-scale Vegas reception. As he got his bearings amid flashing lights (see picture on page 234), Joe couldn't help but notice a string of glamorous models – all blonde, pencil-thin, six-foot tall and dressed as ... leprechauns. They roared, '*Céad Míle Fáilte*' and threw shamrocks at him. And then a band piped up. If that wasn't enough to take in, there were TV cameras, reporters, over a dozen policemen on motorbikes and, finally, a fleet of open-topped limousines waiting at the end of the walkway. Sitting on the bonnet of each car was another pair of blonde, six-foot leprechauns.

Tony Newman and a few of the other lads were tired and emotional after the long flight, and the last thing they expected was a clatter of models, the prying eyes of the press and, worse still, the police. When Tony was asked by a TV reporter if he was glad to be in Vegas, he replied, 'What the fuck is this?', looking around him. Joe was a little more eloquent, and even though he was stunned at the circus that greeted him, he soon clicked into life and soaked up the adulation and attention, giving an interview to a local TV crew. With police outriders driving alongside them, a waving Joe then led a cavalcade from the airport through Las Vegas, where further police outriders had closed all the junctions along the Strip and stopped traffic to allow him a clear path. The cavalcade ran through red lights as it edged its way towards the Silverbird complex at the end of the Strip.

'The whole arrival was such a buzz,' Joe said. 'I suppose coming into Vegas at any time is a buzz and to come into Vegas at night is an even bigger buzz with the lights and everything. If you came in during the day it could have been any town. To be the centre of so much attention was a little weird. You wouldn't realize that you were a star back home, but yet they felt we were all stars, every one of us.'

After arriving at the hotel, Joe disappeared with the blondes to a nearby room for a press conference while the rest of the band made a beeline for the nearest restaurant. It didn't take them too long to discover that drink was on a slate too, and they soon made the most of it in a Silverbird cocktail lounge.

At the press conference, Silverbird president Fred Crossley told the dozens of reporters that Joe was 'the biggest new continental star since Tom Jones' and he detailed how the resort was going to make him an even bigger star. Vegas reporters were particularly keen to find out how Joe had been treated by the 'enemy' in the Soviet Union.

The Silverbird had earned a reputation for booking many 'firsts' and for establishing the star-making rep of acts such as Judy Garland, Rosemary

Clooney, Ray Charles, Rodney Dangerfield, Nat King Cole, Frankie Laine, Duke Ellington, Buddy Rich and Jack Benny. In the 1950s and 1960s it was a hip hangout for Sinatra and the Rat Pack, who ate in its seafood restaurant, 'Big Joe's Oyster Bar', rated as the pearl in the crown of Vegas restaurants. Affectionately known as 'the Fourth Lady of the Strip', as it was the fourth hotel and casino complex to open in Vegas (it started doing business in 1948, when it was called the Thunderbird), the Silverbird was also one of the biggest: a colossal 24-hour-a-day entertainment playground, with 400 state-of-the-art guestrooms and suites, an 80,000-square-foot casino, three major venues, scores of lounges, bars and restaurants, an Olympic-sized swimming pool and a concourse of shops the size of a small Westmeath town. When Joe asked the owner, Major Auterburn Riddle, if the Silverbird ever slept, he replied, 'Hell no, after we built it we threw away the goddamn keys.'

Joe's jaw dropped when he first saw the Continental Theatre, his venue for the next six weeks. 'It was magnificent,' Joe remembers. 'I'd been delighted that venues were improving back home, but this was so far beyond the next level it was off the scale! It was near enough a triangular building with the stage deep down in the corner and every seat and booth angled towards it. Every seat was a good seat, and it was lovely to play because everyone was right in front of you at their little tables. In Ireland there was always a tendency for people to be watching you from the side of the stage, or from behind a pillar, but this was just a class place. The acoustics were great in it too; it was perfect.'

Joe had just two days to get the band in shape for their big Vegas debut in front of a VIP audience of Vegas movers, shakers and fellow artists. Tom Jones and a myriad of big names were on the guest list. But surrounded by a multitude of Vegas temptations, and with cards a big feature of nightly life on the road for Joe and the boys, it was only natural that they were a little distracted. Surprisingly, however, the lure of the casino tables wore off quickly. Joe was thrown off a blackjack table for being too slow to make his mind up. 'Hey, buddy, the beginner's table is that way,' the dealer told him as he took his cards away. And Joe was amazed at the amount of money being gambled. 'If you came in with money, then the people in the casinos couldn't care less how you spent it, so long as you didn't leave with it.' So Joe retreated back to his own trusted card pools. 'We were surrounded by casinos, card dealers and high-stakes poker games and do you know what we did? We played cards amongst ourselves sitting by the pool!' he said, laughing.

Meanwhile, a new laser system for the show was being prepared, devised by a Dolan fan who was trying to make a name for himself in show business. Some of the band members weren't completely convinced.

'What if it hits us?' one member asked. 'Will it hurt?'

'Is it like the James Bond lasers?' another asked.

'They'll kill you stone dead,' Joe joked.

It would be the first time lasers were used in a Vegas show to such dazzling effect.

'He built this cone of lasers which I stepped into at the end of the night and disappeared under. The crowd used to be astonished,' Joe said. It appeared to the audience that Joe had been swallowed up whole by the lasers.

Joe was proving to his new employers at the Silverbird that he was not just another refined old pro on the Strip. His positive attitude was exactly what they wanted, but because he was untested and still relatively unknown in Vegas, Joe's first fortnight of shows took place during the 'graveyard shift', at 2 a.m. This was no demotion though, as the late-night shows were invariably attended by taxi-drivers, bartenders, casino workers and waitresses: service-industry people who could spread the word. If Joe could prove to the owners that what they saw in Ireland was no fluke, he was promised an earlier slot.

His first show, on 12 September, was packed, complimentary tickets and a guest list as long as your arm ensuring there wasn't a spare seat in the house. Joe went down a storm and the band was hotter than ever. Opening night reviews in the press were highly positive, and Joe was beaming, but the next few shows were a reality check as Joe tried to build up his rep in front of a sparse crowd. 'It was very depressing at first, especially as the first night had gone so well. After that night, there might be a dozen in the venue after we opened the doors, and by the time I came onstage there might be a couple of hundred,' Joe remembered.

'Even if there was one man and a dog there Joe still would have given it his all. Outwardly, a small crowd never got to him,' Seamus added.

But many people arrived expecting the American Drifters to be up onstage with 'Ireland's Number One Singing Star', and Seamus remembers a few shocked punters looking for their money back when they realized the white guys onstage in green suits were not the American R&B doo-wop group responsible for such hits as 'Under the Boardwalk', 'Save the Last Dance For Me' or 'Saturday Night at the Movies' (a song Joe played). 'Groups of people would arrive excited that such a legendary vocal group were playing with an Irish singer,' Seamus said, laughing. Any confusion was soon cleared up with new publicity material announcing that 'Joe Dolan and *his* Drifters' were playing the Silverbird.

Crowds were picking up though, and within a week it became notoriously difficult to secure a seat in the 900-seater theatre even though there were big, big acts on elsewhere. Cher was at Caesar's Palace, Joan Rivers and Bobby Vinton were at the Frontier, Donny and Marie Osmond were at the MGM Grand, and Bobbie Gentry, Frankie Avalon and Buddy Rich were at the Sahara.

And by the start of October, even heavier-hitters were being lined up in every other venue, as the city was due to be packed with fight fans ahead of Muhammad Ali's big comeback fight against the World Heavyweight Champion Larry Holmes at Caesar's Palace. Joe met Ali at his training camp, his second time meeting the boxer.

As Vegas began to buzz in anticipation of the big fight, the management at the Silverbird took advantage of the increase in daytime traffic by putting Joe on at the unusual time of 2 p.m., and a whirlwind of publicity was geared up around him. The price was kept keen, with a free drink or cocktail thrown in for good measure. He was also on at 2 a.m.

In his 'On and Off the Record' column in the *Las Vegas Sun*, Joe Delaney gave the switch a big boost, writing that Joe was 'a delightful touch of present-day Ireland' who 'has a great way with an audience, quick wit and a clear, pleasing tenor sound'. However, Joe found the 2 p.m. show 'very strange', and he made alterations to the set for each show, nearly overhauling it completely. He found, much to his surprise and delight, that Americans in the audience started calling for his own songs that he had dropped from the set rather than covers.

'We thought they had never heard them before, but we were getting calls from the audience. "Hey, Joe, what about this song?" "Jesus, why are we changing the programme?" I thought. This is what they wanted to hear!'

'From Ireland with Love' flyers had been distributed throughout the city and, as an extra touch of Irishness, Joe hatched a cunning plan. When he was singing the Irish chestnut 'Forty Shades of Green', he handed out carnations that he had had hand-dyed green. 'I gave this big spiel telling the audience about Mullingar and how its meadows were full of green carnations that only grow in Westmeath, and then I told them I had a special delivery flown in from Ireland for them, cut from my very own garden, and I'd hand out these beautiful Irish carnations. They used to take them and mind them like they had been given a million dollars. They really believed they were from Ireland!'

Positive word of mouth, glowing reviews and even compliments from acts such as Tom Jones all contributed to the Joe Dolan show becoming one of the hottest tickets in town, and the 2 p.m. and 2 a.m. gamble paid off.

On 1 October, the day before the Holmes–Ali fight, Joe was informed he would be upgraded to a prime-time Vegas slot. He celebrated the next night by joining 25,000 fight fans at the open-air arena at Caesar's Palace in 100-degree heat to witness one of the most tragic nights in boxing history as the once-great champion Ali fell apart in the ring against the undefeated Holmes. 'Once the fight began it was obvious something wasn't right with Ali,' Joe remembered. 'He looked tired and he barely threw a punch.'

Downhearted fight fans needed a pick-me-up, and new Vegas sensation Joe Dolan was just the tonic. Within a few weeks of his arrival, he had become a prime-time Vegas attraction, playing two full houses a night at 9 p.m. and at midnight – the most coveted slots on the Strip – six nights a week. Joe was in direct competition with some of the heaviest hitters in Vegas, including Tom Jones at Caesar's Palace, Tony Bennett at the Sands, Glen Campbell at the Frontier, Liberace at the Hilton, Dean Martin and Engelbert Humperdinck at the MGM Grand, Bob Newhart, Neil Sedaka and Joan Rivers at the Riviera, Siegfried and Roy at the Stardust and Rosemary Clooney at the Sahara. Against these odds, thousands of punters took a gamble on him, and by the end of Joe's Vegas run, you had to tip the doormen even more than the ticket price (which itself had trebled) to get a good seat.

Away from the stage, Joe led a relatively simple life by Las Vegas standards. After the last show, Seamus would accompany Joe to his dressing room and then bring him back to his suite and back down to the hotel. 'When we went down to the bar there was always between forty and a hundred people there, all friends. A big Italian fella called Frank who was looking after the bar used to announce, "Oh, everything is all right, Joe is here! Joe, what are you having?" and there would be a big cheer and everything was on the house for everyone after that. We'd stay there from two or three until five or six in the morning. Joe was a night owl, but he didn't drink much. He liked to give the impression that maybe he did, but he'd only have a few. I'd get up at ten or so, but Joe would stay in bed and get up at one. He'd loll around the pool all day, maybe go for a walk up the town, have another swim and that was it. At 7.30 p.m. he'd get ready for the first show of the night. He wouldn't leave the dressing room until long after 2 a.m.'

After the first show had finished, around 10.30 p.m., Joe would sit on his own in the dressing room and drink water to replenish the liquid lost during his energetic performance, preferring the solitude. 'Some of the rest of the lads would be out chatting to women or fans, or would go for a quick feed, but Joe never left the dressing room. On the odd occasion there'd be a few people in,' Seamus says. 'It was a ritual for him, this solitude.'

Even though the Silverbird was blessed with an assortment of restaurants, the band used to assemble at the same table at the Silverbird Buffet, a large coffee shop, where they chowed down on what the brochure describes as 'southern fried chicken, succulent ham and "just right" roast baron of beef' alongside 'twenty-four assorted salads, meats and cheeses, ten hot entrées, and fabulous desserts.' The lads ate the lot.

'To the boys a coffee shop at home was a place you got a cup of tea and a bun if you were lucky,' Frankie McDonald remembered. 'In Vegas a coffee shop offered you everything, and we took full advantage. We would have all sorts. We used to look at the desserts for hours, then eat them all.'

Joe also developed an addiction for huge crates of spare ribs, and when the munchies got to him he and Tony Newman would go out in search of what Joe affectionately termed 'a bullock in a bucket'. There was a restaurant nearby that offered such a delicacy and, after they had finished, 'the restaurant would be like an elephant's graveyard – bones everywhere!'

Away from the hustle and bustle of life on the Strip, Joe was in constant demand, meeting prominent members of the Irish community one minute and posing for a variety of photo shoots the next. He even lent his name to a home video games system, as he had done in South Africa, and filmed a few scenes for a long-since lost movie. 'We really didn't know what was happening,' he said. 'There were all sorts of deals in place that we only found out about when we got there.'

He didn't even get to play golf, despite 'huge, incredible plans' to wake up every morning and play a round before the Vegas sun got too hot. Instead, Joe and his manager found a golf shop and got friendly with the owner. They used to have putting competitions and would tee off a drive into a net there. It was as close to the real thing as they got.

Joe finished his maiden Vegas residency in triumph, having played sixty-four shows and managing to sell out far more of them than even the Silverbird's Vegas veterans could have predicted. The Silverbird immediately booked him for a return visit starting on 9 January 1981. End-of-year polls in the Vegas newspapers rated him as one of the 'sleeper hits of the year', with the *Las Vegas Mirror* describing him as one to watch. However, Joe was slightly disappointed he never got the chance to see some of the other Vegas stars in action because they were going up against each other at the prime-time 9 p.m. and midnight slots. He did, however, get to meet Glen Campbell and the pair clicked. Any chance of seeing any of the big Vegas names playing when Joe finished his run was scalped as he had to fly straight back to Ireland after he had finished his run of shows.

Joe returned home in good form, but there was little time to rest and barely any time to celebrate Christmas as he was gigging non-stop in Ireland and the UK. When he wasn't onstage that Christmas, Joe was playing a demo of a new song – 'More and More' from the returning pen of Roberto Danova – to anyone who would listen, a song Joe was convinced was a major hit. Initial reactions to the song were not good. 'The lads laughed when they heard it first,' Joe remembered, visibly upset at the memory. 'Tony Newman, Gerry Kelly and Jimmy Mullally – the three of them were at a party in my apartment when I played it and they all started laughing, so I got thick and I threw them all out. I think I might have fired the three of them as well, but sure they were back the next day.'

After his first big sprinkling of hits, Roberto's pen had gone a bit dry, but Joe knew they were on to a winner when 'More and More' came together perfectly at a Christmas show at the Gleneagle Hotel, where they had experimented with it during the soundcheck. 'Funnily enough, whatever we came up with on the day turned out to be what was on the finished record,' Joe said. That night they played a version of the song 'and the crowd went wild for it', so much so that Joe played it three times 'and they kept shouting for more (and more)'.

*

Vegas aside, Joe had enjoyed a successful year on and off the stage in 1980. On the back of publicity surrounding the Soviet Union trip, the epic 'My Love' had been re-released and entered the charts back home, and the slick *Turn Out the Lights* album (with its risqué sleeve) signalled another musical reinvention for Joe as it embraced adult-orientated rock that saw Joe wrap himself around sophisticated, lyrically rich songs. Joe retained the services of Peter Yellowstone and Steve Voice for the album, but he also worked on it with Tony Swain and Steve Jolley, a pair of writer-producers who would go on to become one of the most successful musical partnerships of the 1980s.

Swain and Jolley, who had worked on *The Muppet Show* together, were hungry for a break when they presented songs to Joe. He spotted their potential almost from the first bar and agreed to record with them. Among the songs he did with them were 'Moving In and Out of Love', the clever 'Maybe Someday My Love' and the epic 'False Promises', which features a high C note that even Pavarotti himself couldn't hit, or so Joe claimed, laughing. These tracks were among the many standouts on the new album. Joe's knack for talent-spotting was confirmed within a few months when the duo brought one of the first ever manufactured boy-bands, Imagination, to the top of the charts with their debut single 'Body Talk', and followed it with several other hits. They broke into the real big time when they co-wrote and produced several massive hits for groups such as Bananarama and Spandau Ballet, including 'Cruel Summer', 'True' and 'Gold'.

The album proved to be Joe's last major release with Pye and Red Bus, however. He had grown impatient that his records were not getting the necessary promotional push, and although he had complete creative control over what he recorded, he was tired of record company promises that didn't amount to much. The song 'False Promises' expressed how he felt at this time. He struck a deal with Release Records and his first single for them was the show-stopper from his annual Christmas shows in Belfast, 'Silent Night'. It was his first (and only) Christmas single, and a beautiful take on the seasonal favourite. With it, Joe captured Irish hearts all over again and it reached number two in the Christmas charts, only kept off the top spot by Pink Floyd's 'Another Brick in the Wall (Part 2)'.

*

In January 1981 Joe set off for his second Vegas residency. As ever, the band had problems making the connecting flights. With minutes to spare in Dublin, Joe looked around to find only himself, his manager, trombonist and guitarist waiting to board the plane. Ben was coming in the van with the rest of the band, but they had been held up. Joe and the others got to London, where they were to catch a flight to JFK in New York before flying on to Vegas. They made the New York flight by the skin of their teeth, but were delayed in New York as they waited for clearance on some cases of vinyl records and tapes. Seamus and Liam Meade stayed, as it was vital for Joe to arrive on time – once again, a grand reception awaited him at the airport. Having missed their flights, Seamus and Liam decided to re-route with the discs, eventually catching a flight to Los Angeles. Armed with over a thousand LPs, they decided to drive to Vegas to see a bit of 'the real America', and rented a station wagon, arriving at the Silverbird two days later to a big emotional greeting from Joe. When they cracked open the boot to take out the precious cargo, they were horrified to discover that many of the vinyl albums had warped in the searing heat while in transit. Luckily, Joe saw the funny side.

The car gave the rest of the band ideas, and they soon rented a fleet of cars to explore more of Vegas and Nevada. 'There was great freedom,' Seamus recalls. 'We'd drive up a mountain and we'd run back down, having a race – innocent stuff, but a great laugh.'

It took just a handful of shows to build up the buzz the second time around, although a stumbling block was put in Joe's way by his support act, the acrobatic, all-singing, all-dancing family group known as The Muglestons. 'Even though they were a great act, they nearly ruined the show for us as they had this kind of a cult following who'd come in early, get the best seats and then leave after they had finished,' Joe commented. 'Before I'd go on, I'd look out to see a packed theatre. By the time I went onstage, the front rows would be empty, which I hated; it kind of took the pleasure out of the show as the buzz was too far away from me.' Joe had become good friends with the Silverbird maître d', however, a tough little Italian called Gino Pardini, who soon made sure there were only Joe Dolan fans in the front rows.

The second residency was a little harder on Joe, mentally and physically. Once they were offstage the rest of the band usually went off to enjoy the delights of the Las Vegas pleasure dome, but Joe invariably stayed in his suite, by the pool or in his dressing room. Onstage, though, any trace of lethargy disappeared and the smiling musical ambassador returned. He would play over thirty songs between his two nightly sets, changing the set-list for the second (midnight) show to keep things fresh. The set was peppered with the now-mandatory Irish staples 'Westmeath Bachelor', 'Forty Shades of Green', 'When Irish Eyes Are Smiling' and the show-stopping 'Danny Boy', which closed the show before Joe came back for one or two encores; the rest of the show consisted of his own material.

His prime-time slot was to run for a full six weeks, and Joe was up against even bigger guns the second time around: Frank Sinatra, Cher and Tom Jones were playing up the Strip at Caesar's Palace; Bill Cosby, Natalie Cole and Andy Williams were performing at the Hilton; while Kenny Rogers and Dolly Parton were at the Riviera. But Joe was 'better 'n ever' according to the *Las Vegas Mirror* editor, Joe Cross: 'If someone could figure out a way of tapping the energy that flows in the Silverbird's Continental Room every night these days they could come close to matching the output of the Hoover Dam. Joe Dolan's back in town, you see, and if there is an entertainer anywhere in the world who expends more energy than the Irish superstar, then it's probably dangerous to even sit in the audience.' Glowing reviews and endorsements in the press and, most importantly, on the Strip itself from service-industry workers ensured that Joe's second run was even more successful than the first.

There were more Irish visitors for the second trip, including a handful of the band's friends from Mullingar. 'When the boys arrived they hadn't a bob,' Joe remembered of their impromptu arrival. 'They figured in Vegas they gave you money to play. The people in the casinos would expect you to have money, so some of the boys would get tokens. Once you were gambling you would be getting free drink and after a few hours you might get a voucher to go for a meal. The boys were living in the lap of luxury. We put them up for a couple of the nights, but we made them work for it – they handed out flyers for us!'

Frankie had a brother who lived in Edmonton, Canada, and he also came down. When Frankie got a cab to the airport to pick him up, the driver had heard about Joe, so Frankie invited him down to the show – 'just the way you would do in Ireland', he said. The cab driver, Myles Mavaar, and his family were given VIP treatment, meeting Joe and enjoying the best seats in the house, and Frankie and a few of the boys got friendly with him. Myles then returned the compliment by driving them around, buying them presents, lending them cars and more. At the end of the tour Frankie asked, 'How come you did all this for me?'

'Frankie,' Myles said. 'You're the only star who ever invited me backstage, and I'm in Vegas a long, long time.'

'It brought it home to me,' said Frankie. 'He reckoned we were all stars, yet none of us thought we were and Joe never thought he was. It was an incredible eye-opener. We thought we were just a band, but in Vegas we were a whole lot more.'

With the success of the second residency it was perhaps inevitable that Joe would be offered a longer stay. An approach was made to extend his stay to six months, and a lot of money was put on the table – more than Joe would earn in two years of Irish gigs – but surprisingly, Joe declined. Some of the band couldn't believe it. Although morale in the camp was good, Ben remembers that Joe was beginning to count down the shows. 'He'd say before a show, "Only twenty-seven shows left, lads" and so on. He just wanted to be back home.'

'I just couldn't handle it any more,' Joe said. 'I remember feeling depressed three weeks into the second Vegas residency, saying, "Jaysus, I wanna be somewhere else." Everyone was having a ball, but I wasn't. I was in the one place. My room is over there, there's a swimming pool over there, and the venue is over there. When I had a show I had to be focused, so I couldn't head off for the day, I had to stay around. Now, it's grand for three weeks, but I bet you couldn't do it any longer. Maybe you would, it depends on the person themselves of course, but not me. I could never live in one place for six months and play the same place night after night. I couldn't do that. I have to be on the road. Maybe there's a Traveller in me or something, I dunno. I just like to keep moving. I like to go to another venue. It's fresh. It keeps your mind fresh. I don't like the idea of being trapped anywhere, to be honest. I'd prefer to be in Dublin today, Donegal tomorrow and London or Paris the next.

'We were used to doing a show, chatting to people, then leaving, going to bed, getting up in the morning and driving someplace else for a different show and so on. I didn't want to be like some car in a showroom. I don't know how any act does years in a theatre, I really don't. You would be all right if you had your house there, and your family and friends were there and you just ran down to do your show and it was your day's work, but we only had ourselves, and in any band it gets a bit crabby after a while.'

Word that Joe turned down a substantial offer spread throughout Las Vegas. They thought he was playing a hand. Within a few days he was approached by the people who looked after Stevie Wonder and Tony Bennett, who made an offer for a different resort. Again, Joe declined. Further offers were made, and again, Joe rejected them.

'To build up a really good Vegas rep meant long stays on the Strip. Only acts like Sinatra and Elvis could do a quick turn and then leave. I just didn't want to devote my life to one place. Vegas had a big effect on me in terms of my act, but it just wasn't for me.'

Over the years there were several attempts to lure Joe back to play Las Vegas, but they all failed. Nevertheless, he looked back on his time in Vegas with some degree of affection, and he did return on holidays. On a trip to Los Angeles for a friend's wedding in the late 1980s, Joe decided to pay the Strip a visit for old time's sake. He was disappointed to learn his venue had been renamed El Rancho, but he decided to stay there nonetheless to retrace his steps. 'It was great to go somewhere and not have to work! I'd great fun back there, but it didn't make me change my mind about the place. I wouldn't have been able [to do] it.'

Despite Joe's obvious discomfort in staying in one place for too long, his Vegas residencies had signalled a crucial rebirth in Joe's performances. Vegas audiences wanted a spectacular show (even Elvis bombed on his first run there in 1956, with *Newsweek* likening his appearance to 'a jug of corn liquor at a champagne party'), and Joe had strained every sinew in his body to give them something to remember. Joe had spent decades driving home his feel-good message – and making his younger fans scream and cry with delight in the process (it was not for nothing that he was known as 'the national aphrodisiac' in the 1960s) – but he was now playing to audiences aged forty and above, and he really had to push himself to impress and seduce them. It was here that he honed his performance to the older crowd, and he oozed confident, maturing sexuality.

Joe always appreciated the value of a held pose as he brought a song to a big show-business climax, but in Vegas they became even more dramatic, particularly as he clad himself in sharp, tight-fitting suits. Instead of being launched or pulled into the audience as he was in the heyday of the 1960s and 1970s, he showed the older crowd due respect, kneeling down to kiss the entire front row and reaching out to them in a gentle, tactile manner. At opportune moments during the show, he would use special 'JD' handkerchiefs to mop the sweat from his brow and then hand them to the audience. And his show was still peppered with jokes and thrusting, dancing songs that brought him to his knees. Joe was sending a new, more mature breed of fan home sweating – and often without their underwear as the Silverbird stage would be strewn with panties thrown up by some of the more excitable members of the audience. It was a phenomenon that Joe would encounter at almost every Irish venue right up until the end of his career. As a fan said on an RTÉ documentary, Joe got to her in places that her own husband couldn't reach.

Vegas set Joe Dolan off on a completely new path, and was in many ways the last throw of the dice for him internationally. The gruelling nature of the shows was nothing new to him: he had been doing two shows a night, six nights a week for a full decade before the curtain rose at the Silverbird's Continental Theatre. But his growing feelings of confinement, and his sense that the international stage was almost becoming a treadmill, would soon reach its nadir.

15
Bringing it all back home

While Joe Dolan began the 1980s calling for 'More and More', the truth of the matter was that he was actually seeking less and less. The pounding song became the soundtrack to the summer from Cahirciveen to Cape Town in 1981, keeping big international hit singles such as Phil Collins's 'In the Air Tonight' and Ultravox's 'Vienna' off the top of several hit parades around the world. It perched itself at the top of the South African chart for most of June and July, spending a further two months in the Top Ten, and was a number one and a big radio smash in an assortment of European strongholds, as well as performing well in Australia and Canada. It was also extremely popular on bootleg compilations in the Soviet Union. However, although it did well in America, it didn't blow them away – something that surprised Joe, as the big-hearted song, with its country-and-western, Johnny Cash-style, 'boom-chicka-boom' guitar line and thundering chorus, is probably *the* most all-American track Joe has ever recorded.

At home, 'More and More' spent several weeks at number one and over four months in the singles charts, the majority of those in the Top Ten, making it Joe's biggest Irish hit in some time. Tours were being lined up all over Europe to promote the track, but in Ireland Joe became an overnight sensation all over again, and this was enough to convince Joe once and for all that his home audience was the one he really wanted.

In August, RTÉ screened a full concert live from Tralee in Kerry. Sadly, Joe's white suits were all at the dry cleaner's that day (or so he claimed) and so instead he sported a tailor-made grey suit, not realizing the effect the amount of sweat he produced over the course of a show would have on it. Front-row fans at any Joe show would tell you that from the opening number they were (quite gratefully) subjected to an occasional few drips of Dolan sweat, but in grey his perspiration was all too obvious, and in none-too-flattering places either. It led to a memorable review in the *Sunday World* when the TV critic at the time said he tried to watch the concert, 'but it got too wet so I turned over to *Mutiny on the Bounty*'.

Joe seemed to have the run of the island. Concerts and cabaret shows that would normally take a couple of weeks to sell out were doing so within days, and a juggling act was required to try to fit more dates into a schedule that was tighter than Tony Newman's drumming.

A sold-out National Stadium concert in Dublin almost turned into a riot when a massive crowd outside did their utmost to get in, waving money around and propositioning the ticket collectors. When Joe heard that the touts were charging over four times the ticket price, he didn't know whether to laugh or cry. Pumped and primed, the crowd were then blown away with the same show Joe had been using to devastating effect abroad. His wit, charm and sheer hard work onstage turned the adoring audience on from the first number that night. A *Sunday World* review by Micheline McCormack wondered how he did it. 'It's difficult to pin-point what Dolan's appeal is – apart from his magnificent voice. He's not good looking. Even his beautifully tailored suit with its satin lined jacket and his white satin shirt couldn't hide his obvious paunch. And his hair is thinning out. It doesn't matter, though. He's got what it takes, for me, and for everyone in the audience the other night.'

The gig was the vote of appreciation that Joe needed, and he cited it as a turning point in his career. He had played the venue several times before, but never like this. For several years afterwards his Dublin shows took the form of extended residencies either back at the Stadium, or in the Gaiety or Olympia Theatres or the National Concert Hall. He would play a week at a time, the tickets selling out just as soon as concerts were announced. He would do the same in big Dublin hotels, and in venues all over the country. In the Belgard in Tallaght alone he would play up to nine nights at a time to over a thousand people a night. In fact, Joe estimated that for most of the 1980s he was playing to, on average, over 5,000 fans a week – month-after-month, year-after-year, with two months off for a holiday. Contemporaries of his from the 1960s were lucky to play to a couple of hundred a year. Ireland in the 1980s was a gloomy place of mass unemployment, but Joe shone like a beacon, bringing some light into the lives of ordinary people for a low ticket price.

Joe followed 'More and More' with an almost identikit single in the form of 'It's You, It's You, It's You', again penned and produced by Roberto Danova. Released in September, the sister song was another massive Irish and international hit, and also charted in the UK, Joe's first big hit there since 'I Need You' in 1977. He toured the UK extensively for most of October – almost reluctantly, although the radio patronage of top DJs Terry Wogan and Jimmy Young was too good a vote of confidence to ignore.

This song had that same cowboy charm as 'More and More', and its relatively simple lyrics made it a firm favourite among Joe's younger fans. Kids would point at Joe and say, 'It's you, it's you, it's you', as would plenty of his show-business associates. When Joe met fellow entertainers at shows or award ceremonies, he had a habit of singing a line of their most famous song to them by way of a hello. One night backstage at the Galtymore, Big Tom turned the tables on Joe, becoming the first to use the 'It's you, it's you, it's you' line back at him. It became a daily occurrence after that.

This track was Joe's first official release on Ritz Records, a new London-based Irish record label that Joe had invested in and that was run by Mick

Clerkin, a well-known Irish music-industry figure and the Svengali behind Release Records, one of the most successful Irish record labels of all-time. Ritz would specialize in releases by established and up-and-coming artists with a big emphasis on Irish talent, and Joe and his good friend Daniel O'Donnell were its two biggest names.

Just as things really took off back home at the end of 1981, Joe kicked off another extensive tour of South Africa, but attitudes to his success there in certain quarters were not as positive as they once were. With the rise of anti-apartheid movements throughout the world, countries had begun to boycott South Africa, while others considered banning the import of its products, and major companies were being pressurized to pull out of the country altogether. Joe began to feel the heat at home just as the Irish national rugby team had done when they played the South African Spring-boks during the summer of 1981. He always held firm that he was anti-apartheid and that he played to a mixed crowd – unlike some inter-national megastars, he was not playing to whites-only crowds in entertainment enclaves like Sun City – however, he could not always count on the support of the venues themselves.

As the biggest cross-community pop star in South Africa, Joe's arrival in 1981 was front-page news, and the tour had been going well for over a month when he found himself on the front pages of the papers once more – but for the wrong reasons: a venue in the mining city of Newcastle in the northern province of Natal had refused to allow blacks entry to a Joe show at the Iscor Club. They had tried to keep the ban from Joe, and when he found out he refused to take the stage unless a compromise was reached. But it was too late for the newspapers, who led with the story from the angle of Joe's dis-gruntled black fans. 'Does this mean we are only allowed to listen to him on the radio and not hear him sing live? I think it's sick,' one fan told the *Natal Post*. Joe agreed, and the ban angered him deeply. As reports of internal vio-lence between blacks and whites began to become part of the daily routine of South African life in 1981, Joe began to feel uncomfortable and homesick, but he was still one of the biggest stars in the country and he felt he could not let his fans down.

Things reached a head with his 1983 tour. Prior to his departure Joe had been subject to much public scorn, and anti-apartheid activists had person-ally targeted him. The campaign against him grew more vocal, and for several weeks a Sunday newspaper repeatedly asked him to comment on the South Africa situation. Joe refused, and each time he refused they printed a blank space. Eventually, he made his anti-apartheid views clear when a week-long run of shows at the Gaiety Theatre in Dublin were picketed. The picket was organized by the Irish Anti-Apartheid Movement, led by Kader Asmal, who went on to become an ANC government minister under Nelson Mandela. Asmal was totally opposed to Joe's 1983 tour and said it went against sanctions that the United Nations had called for. He accused Joe of ignorance, but Joe was well aware of the political situation and he made a public statement saying he would not tour South Africa again unless political changes were made. His forthcoming tour would, officially, be his last.

The criticism hurt and saddened Joe in many ways. The country had been very good to him, and his promoter there, Ronnie Quibell, was keen to promote freedom for all with multi-racial shows, crews and staff. But in the politically charged climate at the time, Ronnie's multi-racial dreams were often a non-runner. Even so, at Joe's first three sold-out shows of the 1983 tour, at the 2,100-capacity Rand Afrikaans University, a ban on blacks was temporarily lifted after the outcry from the previous tour.

The country was in turmoil, with the ANC's political resistance to apartheid becoming increasingly violent (bombs were a routine part of daily life), but Joe's arrival was once again still big news, with hundreds of female fans waving bunches of flowers at Johannesburg airport. A huge press conference was organized at his hotel, and although he was asked some tricky questions about the political situation, he endeared himself to all sides with his diplomatic grasp of the situation.

This tour would become the most exhaustive the band had ever undertaken with Joe – eight full weeks from 23 October to 21 December, with just seven Sundays off. In all, Joe sang his heart out for seventy-two shows – usually performing two shows a night, one at 6 p.m. and another at 9 p.m. It was also their most extensive tour to date, taking in thirty-eight different towns and cities.

It was the first tour for Joe's nephew Ray, who joined the band on percussion straight from school. 'It was some baptism,' he said. As it was Joe's final jaunt, several friends from home accompanied him on the tour, including Chris Ferwick, a promoter and friend from Kiltimagh in Mayo, whose town was unwittingly used as a motivational tool to keep Joe going when he was down in the dumps after a show about four weeks in. Denis Mee, the stage manager and PA for the tour, asked Joe which he preferred: the dusty, concrete dressing room in Kiltimagh, or the opulent one he was in.

Still, there were few opportunities for Joe to relax during the tour. He was on a curfew, so aftershow parties were a thing of the past, and he had a serious promotional timetable to keep as he had just released a new album there. Called *Yours Faithfully*, and billed as 'his most powerful and exciting album to date', it was his sixth album release in South Africa in as many years. Joe spent most mornings in either radio or television studios. After that he would face any number of print interviews, photoshoots and in-store appearances, and then it was show time. He was on this treadmill for eight straight weeks, six days a week. And he wanted off.

Despite the challenge of so many shows in so little time (and in sweltering heat), Joe's voice remained sweet, its quality never diminishing. One night a well-known South African soprano singer in the audience challenged Joe to a vocal duel during 'Danny Boy' and she joined him onstage in song, but failed to match the Mullingar man on the high notes.

Joe covered plenty of new ground on tour, including the Orange Free State, although in Bloemfontein he and the band walked out of a hotel because staff there refused to serve one of the black members of their crew. They were more insulted than he was at the refusal, and a nasty confrontation was avoided only at the last second. The band also broke new ground in Namibia, where shows were booked in Windhoek and Walvis Bay on the Skeleton Coast – all white-knuckle journeys in a variety of ancient aircraft. Leaving Walvis Bay (which, according to Joe, was 'like coming across Clifton in a cowboy movie'), there weren't enough seats on the plane to Cape Town for all the touring party, so they drew lots. Joe secured a seat but when he saw that the plane was a Second World War-era twin propeller Dakota, panic set in and he refused to board it. Eventually he was coaxed on. However, as everyone settled themselves into the wooden seats, Joe started muttering about infamous plane crashes involving Jim Reeves, the Manchester United team and Buddy Holly. He had a panic attack, terrifying the band, and had to be taken off and put into a jeep for the long drive down the coast. Meanwhile the rest of the band started to get a little edgy.

'We took off, and after about ten miles we touched down again on an airstrip in a desert,' trumpeter Frankie McDonald remembered. 'Then this fella with a fishing rod came on and just stood there. We took off and he was standing up as if he was on a bus! Some chickens broke loose and people were beginning to panic. When we were up high the pilot would cut the engines and glide for a bit, then start them up again ... It was the craziest thing of all time. Joe was lucky not to travel on it.'

In Vryburg, they all stayed in mud huts in a wildlife reserve as Joe wanted the band to see Africa as it should be. Over three nights they bonded by the barbecue, and every morning Frankie woke the whole reserve up by playing a military-style reveille. 'You could hear the animals telling him to be quiet!' Joe chuckled. The Zen-like Frankie had a habit of taking his trumpet out when they were least expecting it. When Pope John Paul II flew into Clonmacnoise in 1979, Frankie calmly walked through the 30,000-strong crowd, past the security barrier to the helicopter pad, explaining he was part of the official welcoming party. He then welcomed the pontiff to the Midlands with a toot of his trumpet.

Joe and the band eventually came home the day before Christmas Eve.

Several offers were made for Joe to return to South Africa, and stadium gigs were even proposed, but he quietly turned them all down. As the years progressed and apartheid was abolished, he was tempted to return but never did. With the currency destabilized, he would have been forced to charge a high ticket price, which would have excluded the ordinary music fan whom he had entertained for all those years. Joe always kept his ticket prices within the range of the working man.

But even without touring, his records continued to sell there. Indeed, Joe is in the all-time South African Top Ten for the most weeks spent in the charts, his 123-week stay putting him ahead of Elvis, Madonna, Queen, Rod Stewart, Diana Ross, Billy Joel, David Bowie, Paul McCartney and Dolly Parton. Only Abba and The Bee Gees racked up more Top Three hits than him.

His popularity was underlined to Fr Brian D'Arcy when he went out there to work in the townships in 1988: 'On one of my first days there I got the fright of my life when I turned a corner and saw Joe Dolan standing in front of me! It was a life-size cardboard cutout and he was in the white suit with the finger pointed out. It was weird, so I went into the shop and saw rows and rows of his records. I couldn't believe it. You heard him on the radio regular.

Even in 1994 when I was back there you still heard him on the radio. He could have gone back out there at any stage, because he was still a very, very big name out there with both blacks and whites. He had that sort of music that appealed to all and I felt a lot of the stick he got for going over there was very unjustified.'

Joe was annoyed by the level of bad feeling his tours in South Africa generated in the media, as he felt he was only going out to help the underdog, to bring a bit of life, happiness and music to the people. 'There was no agenda to any of my tours there at all. None of any sort,' he said. 'And I shouldn't have been judged by that. Apartheid was a horrible rule. It wasn't right. I thought that by going out to work there I was bringing a little light into their lives, but others saw it differently.' And the threats to his life that he received from certain sections of the anti-apartheid crowd would take him several years to get over. Joe found out the hard way that music and politics don't mix. It was a valuable lesson, and he would never publicly display his politics again (aside from taking sides in an anti-paid parking march in Mullingar in 1985, that is). His trust in the Irish media also took a tumble.

A number of other international tours undertaken in the early 1980s ended on a slightly disappointing note for Joe, increasing his desire to focus on his home market. He completed another major tour in Israel in 1983, but the promoter had forgotten to inform him that the tour coincided with the tenth anniversary of the Yom Kippur War, the 1973 Arab–Israeli conflict. A curfew of sorts was in place throughout the country, and while the shows did well, they were nothing like the last shows Joe had played there. In Tel Aviv in 1979, he headlined what was Europe's biggest open-air festival at the time in front of over 80,000 people; but with tensions running high throughout the Middle East in 1983, the tour came to a quiet close and Joe had to almost island-hop his way home. It would also be the last time he would play Israel, despite the many lucrative offers he received.

Like other divided regions, the Middle East had taken to Joe, but in 1981 a tour to Iran, Lebanon, Saudi Arabia and Egypt was postponed due to the escalating conflicts in the region. Like the Russians, the Lebanese had got into Joe via bootleg tapes, and Irish peacekeeping troops sent to Lebanon in the 1980s were shocked to find that wherever they went all they could hear was Joe Dolan. The United Nations made an effort to bring Joe to Lebanon in the late 1980s, but the trip was postponed for a variety of reasons. (When the Special Olympics World Games were held in Ireland in 2003, however, the Lebanese team chose to stay in Mullingar and Joe was there to greet them on their arrival. Many of the athletes and their touring party were fans and Joe happily entertained them throughout their stay.)

A poorly promoted Canadian tour in 1984 was also hit and miss – Joe rated it as one of his worst ever – and while the following European tour went well, Joe's desire to keep things closer to home grew even stronger.

Joe never officially indicated that these would be his last major international tours. His decision to concentrate on his home audience had been made gradually. From the 1960s onwards, he had been made dozens of tempting offers to base himself abroad. The riches, he was told, would be unimaginable. He could throw those curtains wide each morning to a view of the Mediterranean or the Eiffel Tower, whichever he preferred. 'I can't explain it, I'm just happier to be at home, I'm a homebird at heart,' he would say. Had he gone to France when a major attempt was made to lure him there in 1975, he would have become an overnight millionaire. Had he gone back in 1978 at the request of the country's top record label, the purse would have been even greater. Offers from further afield were sent to tempt him, but Joe was happy to entertain thousands at home rather than millions in the bank. Rather than try to spread the Joe Dolan gospel further, he preferred to be a prophet among his people. A great socializer, Joe could be himself in Ireland and no one bothered him unduly. He loved the Irish pace of life and he loved that the Irish people knew when to draw the line between Joe Dolan the performer and Joe Dolan the man.

Joe was secure with his family and fans, and that was all he wanted. Although many newspapers made an issue out of his bachelor status, it didn't bother him unduly and he never once admitted to feeling lonely. He had started seeing long-term girlfriend Isabella Fogarty in the early 1980s, having met her in 1977, and although they holidayed together, lived together and Joe's friends all knew and loved her, Joe was careful to keep her from the public eye. He had moved to Foxrock in Dublin around the same time (although he kept a Mullingar home too), and he became even more settled, entertaining and putting up plenty of friends there over the years, but he was still a deeply private man. Joe always maintained that his private life was just that – his private life. When Joe was onstage he was public property, but offstage he was just Joe, and that was the way he liked it. He had lived out of a suitcase in party-friendly apartments in Mullingar for close to twenty years, but now Joe finally had what he wanted: a stable home, which he cherished.

At Foxrock, Joe loved nothing better than to have people over for dinner. Dinner parties were his speciality, although his signature dishes varied. He was also a delightful host at post-night-out parties, and parties after other people's parties. Joe's neighbours were all good friends, and no one thought twice about Joe's being an international entertainer: on the street, Joe was just Joe.

However, as much as he enjoyed having people in his home, Joe was reluctant to have it mentioned in any dispatches. Only on one occasion did his fans get a peek 'through the keyhole', when in April 1995 the *Sunday World* devoted a lavish spread to the house. The piece, written by the newspaper's chief show-business reporter Eddie Rowley, described the house in detail, from the stairway to the dining room and kitchen (which 'were like a little restaurant'). But despite the crystal (Joe had a passion for crystal and often asked friends to bring him back pieces from around the world), the numerous awards, the piano in the sitting room, the upstairs jacuzzi, the sauna room, the conservatory and the impressive sound system (Joe ensured there were stereo speakers in every room), Eddie couldn't help but be more impressed by Joe's relatively 'simple life of luxury': 'It lived up to the image of a star's home, but in contrast Joe's lifestyle was relatively simple. Outside of music, golf was his other passion. He enjoyed the simple things in life, like cooking, reading, watching sport and soaps on telly, or entertaining family and friends,' he said.

Joe's day would start with a peek out through the curtains. No matter what time he went to bed, even if he had only had a few hours' sleep after driving home from a show, if the weather was looking good then golf was on the menu – after a nice cooked breakfast of course. 'You were only out on the golf course a while and you'd be as fresh as a daisy and ready to go again you know?' he'd say.

After a pot of tea he would then return home for dinner. If he wasn't onstage that night he would take his time over dinner, and then he loved to watch television. Joe was a soap addict and *Coronation Street* and *Fair City* were his favourites. He was a big fan of sitcoms too, and loved the timeless comedy of *Fawlty Towers* and *Father Ted*. One of his guilty pleasures in recent years was reality TV music shows such as *X Factor* and *You're a Star*, though he would be at pains to tell you he hated them.

When guests were visiting, he would never allow the television to take over – unless, that is, he was watching a good film. Joe loved a good film – in any genre from horror to comedy – and when he got into one he would become transfixed. Arms criss-crossed high upon his chest, he would sit there totally closed off from what was going on around him. You could try talking to him, but you'd get no reply. He wouldn't even hear you. Films got right into his system and he was known to shed a tear or two at a few. The classic Western *Shane* was a particular favourite. 'I'm a romantic person and very emotional. I can't watch sad movies for too long because if something is going bad for somebody, I tend to fill up a bit,' he said. He couldn't go to the cinema for this very reason, as when he tried to mask the tears by pretending to blow his nose, people would ask him to be quiet.

Joe's partying days were almost behind in the 1980s, and relaxation and smaller social gatherings at home were what it was all about. 'We were all getting that little bit older, the days of going out at night were long gone,' Isabella says. 'We just didn't. He preferred to be at home.' He still went out for dinner dances, weddings (of which there were quite a few with so many nieces and nephews) and the odd cinema or theatre premiere, and at a dinner dance or a wedding he loved to just get up and dance. 'He was a lovely dancer. He really enjoyed it,' Isabella remembers. A family wedding was something he always cherished.

A regular caller to Joe's house was Fr Brian D'Arcy. He thinks that when Joe created a home he could share with friends, it was the making of him. 'Any man who's gone around singing, entertaining and being happy has to be another person behind that. You can't just be a man up on the stage. It wasn't until the 1980s that Joe came to terms with the fact that he was a man off the stage as well as on the stage. Up until then he was working six nights a week and had no other life. He began to take more time to himself and changed from dances in halls to concerts and cabaret. Joe had a dignity about himself when he went to cabaret and he became more show business and then he began to be really confident in himself as a person. Las Vegas gave him a bit of that, to be honest. He could see the difference and that you didn't have to kill yourself working, that you could relax, and that's when he began to reach out and stretch out and do different things. He was surrounded by his friends at home and he was happy. He got respect from others and he began to see he was different himself. He got a certain confidence, a certain self-respect, and changed dramatically as a person for the better at that stage. He suddenly realized he wasn't running around with the self-destruction button on any more.'

At home, Joe's favourite time of the year, even though it also tended to be his busiest onstage, was Christmas. Joe was like a bold child on Christmas morning, and he loved opening his presents – and other people's given half the chance – and the earlier the better. Isabella remembers that when he came home from Mass on Christmas morning, the first thing he would say was, 'Can I open my presents?'

Joe really began to embrace the festive season when he lived with Paddy and Caroline and their children in Ginnell Terrace in Mullingar. Joe was often the biggest child of them all, even though he was supposed to be the responsible uncle. 'He was more excited about Christmas than the kids and even up to recently he was just like one of them, tearing little bits of wrapping paper to get a sneak preview of the presents, and he was a great one for annuals. He'd take the annuals, read them, and he'd put them back after,' Paddy's daughter Kathleen remembers.

When Kathleen married Gerry Oakes and set up a home, Joe was still the same and he would visit a few days before Christmas, to see the kids and give them their presents. 'He would always come back a few days after Christmas and ask, "What did Santa bring you?" and he'd be mad to test out the new toys and if it made noise all the better. He used to fly around the house and he'd have all the kids hyper, and they loved him. He was the same with us and with everyone else, with generations of kids. Joe was Christmas.'

When he wasn't in Mullingar spending Christmas night with his family, it was always a huge night in Joe's Dublin home. That other great rural bachelor, Fr D'Arcy, was nearly always there. 'It was a lovely time to visit Joe. The house would always be full of friends, people from the business and people from all walks of life,' he reveals. 'Joe had an affinity for Travellers, and sometimes they were there in the evening and he would be giving them Christmas presents. They would be asking Joe to sing a song, they loved his voice, but Joe wanted to hear them sing, to hear true Traveller songs and Irish ballads, but more often than not one of them would start to sing, "It's you, it's you, it's you ..." and sure we'd all fall around the place laughing. There would be other friends who might have had a broken marriage that year, or guys who lost someone belonging to them; they were the people he wanted to make happy. It wasn't as if he was doing them a big favour or anything, he was just a noble sort of fella who looked out for everyone.'

Throughout his life Joe gave to many charities. Joe had a kinship and a feeling for the underdog and for the poor, and in the earliest days of The Drifters he would play free dances for the Mullingar Boys' Club. Indeed, the proceeds of most of his Mullingar shows went to local charities and schools. As his career took off he became a generous philanthropist who gave away a large proportion of his earnings to a variety of charities and to the poor. Few, if any, know the full extent of Joe's generosity, but it is estimated that he gave away millions.

Fr D'Arcy knew first hand of Joe's charitable nature. 'Every time I met him, without fail, he would always give me a roll of notes and quietly ask me to give it to the poor.' These donations were never formal, and could occur anywhere and everywhere. 'Backstage at shows, even just before he went onstage he would shake my hand and press notes into it saying he'd wish I took it for myself, but he knew I wouldn't and he knew that someone would benefit.'

Other priests also felt the full force of Joe's generosity in the 1980s. Indeed, the roofs of many churches and cathedrals on the island were put there by the proceeds of a Joe Dolan concert, Mullingar included. The door takings from dozens of other concerts every year went straight to charities or voluntary groups in the area. Joe also became a patron to the disabled and those with special needs, and raised funds for a number of organizations and schools, including St Bridget's in Mullingar; he also used his love of golf to raise millions for a wide variety of charities.

Asked what career he would have chosen had he not become a singer, Joe declared he would have liked to have been a professional golfer – but a pro-golfer who could sing. 'If there had been some way of doing it, I would have loved to have been a pro-golfer and still do what I'm doing. I could compete at the US Masters, the British Open and all these big tournaments, play a few rounds, and then do a concert at night in the clubhouse or in a big marquee by the eighteenth. Now that would be my dream job!'

Joe lived for his golf and he played almost every day. His perfect day was to play a round of golf first thing, enjoy dinner at home or with friends or family, catch up on a soap opera, and then walk out onstage and play a two-and-a-half-hour concert to a venue of adoring fans. By the summer of 2007 he reckoned that he had played every single golf course in Ireland. Despite his best efforts, course managers repeatedly refused to let him pay green fees, preferring instead to have the honour of being able to say that Ireland's best-known non-pro golfer had teed off on their course.

Joe took up golf quite early in his show-business career, at a time when it was still considered an elitist sport. He became a lifelong member of Mullingar Golf Club, and he rated his hometown course, designed by golfing legend James Braid, as the best inland course in the country. The clubhouse became a home from home for him and his many friends from the town, and whenever television crews wanted to make a documentary or a feature on Joe, he would invite them out there to film some scenes.

Although he never sought special treatment on a golf course, Joe always seemed to receive it. His nephew Vincent remembers one such occasion on a busy Sunday afternoon at the club when he and a friend were trying to get out for a round. 'We were only starting out on the golf scene around 1975 and the place was packed, with little hope of getting out to play. We waited around for two hours when Joe happened to arrive out. There was a backlog on the first tee and the captain at the time along with the club president were awaiting their turn. Joe runs up and says, "Hiya, lads, listen, I have a gig to go to later, any chance of me getting a few holes in?" A chorus of people said, "Go ahead, Joe, no problem" and they parted. With that, Joe turned around to us two teenagers and said, "Come on, boys, we're on." We played the full eighteen holes and when I asked Joe where the gig was that night, he whispered to me, "A film on RTÉ tonight at 8 p.m.!"'

Joe had many caddies during the years and because he was known as a big tipper, youngsters would literally queue up to carry his bag. His main bagman was Frank Daly, a lifelong friend from Mullingar. But in the 1970s, one caddy who nearly always hauled Joe's clubs around the rolling Mullingar course was future Ryanair boss Michael O'Leary, a son of one of Joe's pals, Edward 'Ted' O'Leary. The youngster gave an early indication of his business acumen by guarding Joe as a prized 'client'. Some golf-club veterans said it was because O'Leary knew he would get paid. Indeed, one day, Joe asked the youngster why he never caddied for his father, Ted, who often played in the same four-ball as Joe, and O'Leary told him that his father wouldn't pay him as well as Joe did.

From the 1980s onwards, Joe held his own annual golf 'classic' (a mini-tournament that would usually involve a golf competition, an auction and some entertainment), which raised more than a million euro for his favour-ite charities over the years. His friends Thomas Murphy and Cecil Whelan helped him to organize it, and dozens of show-business and sporting personalities as well as friends took to the course, usually at his Dublin 'local', Powerscourt Golf Club. Joe would play in as many 'classics' organ-ized by fellow entertainers or friends as he could, often providing the entertainment at them for free. He played with many pros around the world, from Des Smyth to Seve Ballesteros, and Seve even joined him onstage one night in Portlaoise to say hello. The Spanish golfing legend was in the Laois town to oversee the development of a golf course, and he and Joe enjoyed a meal together. That night Joe introduced Seve to the audience, but when some people in the crowd rushed the stage looking for Seve's autograph, Joe was left with only one option: he ran him!

Joe's game improved remarkably in the 1970s thanks to his friends on the professional circuit, especially Christy O'Connor Jr, Des Smyth and Joey Purcell, the latter a tenacious young pro from Mullingar whom Joe and Seamus managed at one point. Joey was with Joe when he played his best ever round of golf (in Headford) and also when he picked up his fabled putter, one that allegedly came with a built-in bottle opener. Despite losing patience with the putter and purposely leaving it behind on many an occasion (includ-ing one memorable time, when he launched it into a tree), he always got it back, and kept the club for the rest of his life. It eventually accompanied him on his final journey. Joe was not interested in material things, so changing his clubs, as many golfers in his elevated position would do each year, was not for him. An electric golf buggy was his only golfing luxury, especially after he and four-ball partner Damien Ryan had their hips replaced. Joe would invariably use the buggy as a bumper car.

Christy O'Connor Jr remembered Joe as an incredible player who never gave up on a round, with one notable exception – a pro-am in Bundoran. Joe didn't compete in the first two rounds because it was too wet, leaving O'Connor's team (of which Joe was a member) languishing down the scoreboard. After O'Connor warned Joe he would never speak to him again, Joe then appeared for the third round and played a magical eighteen holes which left the team one shot off the top prize. O'Connor also spoke of the many thousands Joe donated to charities over the years.

Des Smyth, a big fan who has been known to take the microphone to sing a few Joe Dolan numbers on occasion, recalled Joe's charity in another way. Pro-golf was not always the lucrative game it is now, and when Des and Joey were feeling a little strapped for cash, Joe used to let them win. 'I think he was generous to lose to us – we needed it!' Smyth also spoke of Joe's role with the Links Golfing Society, a group that has raised millions for charities.

In later years, when Joe decided he wanted to play some of the world's most famous courses, he and his friends became golfing globe-trotters. Accompanying him on many of these trips were brother Ben, tailor Chas Fagan and friends Sean Skehan, Damien Ryan and Paul Claffey. The latter remembered one particular round of golf in America which Joe had won. As the vanquished arrived back at the caddyshack after Joe had taken their money, an old caddy asked them how they had played. 'Terrible. We lost,' Claffey said. Just then, Joe arrived around the corner singing 'We are the Champions'. The caddy turned to Joe and said, 'You might be the champion, but you can't sing for shit!'

Golf was Joe's great love, but it was also his primary source of exercise (aside from the miles he covered onstage every night). 'I play golf most days, so on average I walk three and a half miles a round, which can't be too bad for you,' he said. Although he maintained a healthy diet and always ate very well, his other keep-fit regimes were always doomed to failure. In London sometime in the 1980s, stage manager and PA Denis Mee remembers Joe waking up one morning declaring that the route to supreme fitness was jogging. He then went out and bought two tracksuits, runners, sweatbands and the whole works, and Joe and Denis togged out for their maiden run. They ran at a variety of paces (most of them slow) from the hotel into Hyde Park. 'This is great,' Joe enthused as they jogged along, but from a distance he could hear people singing 'It's You, It's You, It's You'. He thought nothing of it until he noticed a group of Irish builders running towards him, saluting him in song. 'Right, that'll do, Denis. We'll go back to the hotel,' Joe pronounced as they did an about turn, and that was the end of that.

16

There's no show like a Joe show

Joe Dolan's biggest challenge in bringing it all back home was changing people's ideas of what a Joe Dolan performance should be. Having had his eyes opened abroad to what an audience could and should get, he made Ireland his 'project' in the 1980s. Outside of the major city-based concert venues and theatres, big venues for sit-down shows were still something of a rarity at the time. There were still a few ballrooms standing, and although they had put Joe on the road and kept a lot of his fans coming back, Joe wanted to move on from this type of show and the ballroom mentality. In certain parts of the country, Joe was still playing over the audience's heads. 'A lot of them were only there because they knew there was going to be a big crowd there,' Joe said, adding that 'the fellas are here because they know there's going to be lots of women, and the women are here because there's going to be loads of fellas. OK, you did have a scattering of fans, but the main thing was that people weren't there to hear you.' His international adventures had given Joe a taste for shows where the audience appreciated every song and hung on his every word. But even before his first run of international hits, he had been getting frustrated: 'I remember saying one time,

"God, I wish they'd listen for a while", because we weren't bad, you know? I just wanted the people to listen to what we were doing, rather than the shows being some sort of a cattle market.'

It killed Joe to come back from the continent where he was a big star and then play to an apathetic crowd. Something had to change, and the tipping point was the first night back on the road in Ireland after the final tour to South Africa in 1983. From heaving arenas, packed theatres and scrums in record shops, Joe walked out onstage to play to a few hundred people on a freezing cold January night in Glenamaddy, County Galway. His reaction backstage was one of boiling frustration, one of the few times his band saw him lose it. 'I remember thinking, "What the fuck am I doing here?" They don't care!'

By two o'clock in the morning there was 1,500 there, all shouting for more, and this annihilated Joe mentally. 'I wasn't in control at a show like that and I didn't like that,' he said. He issued an ultimatum to his manager and brother.

'One day, soon after this, we decided we weren't doing dances; that was it, finished, goodbye and good luck,' Seamus recalled.

From then on, Joe insisted on only playing concerts and sit-down shows – although he didn't necessarily want his audience to sit down the whole way through. 'I never insisted on them sitting down all night,' he scoffed. 'But I do believe in having a place for them to sit.' Joe didn't like an audience to be 'running about the place'. No matter if they were dancing on tables or chucking their underwear at him: Joe was happy because he knew they were actually listening to his music in order to have that good a time.

There were few acts exclusively playing those types of sit-down gigs and so he had to re-educate the audience, especially his older fans, who were used to dancing around a venue. He did so by crafting a show that made each Joe Dolan concert an event. The Joe show was born.

For much of the 1980s, the late Bal Moane, an old-school marksman of the one-liner and Joe's favourite stand-up comedian, was the first man the audience saw. A comedian was the perfect warm-up act, and Bal (and later Shaun Connors and Sil Fox) left the audience in good spirits for what lay ahead. Joe's band, almost without being noticed, would then sneak on to the stage amid the hum of pre-gig conversation and break into a short instrumental overture featuring riffs from some of his hits. As the temperature rose, all eyes would be on the stage as Bal intoned, 'Ladies and gentlemen, let me introduce Ireland's greatest singer, the great –', the rest of the sentence drowned out by the screams greeting Joe's arrival. The spotlight would shine on Joe, dressed in his dazzling white suit, and the audience would jump to their feet, 'Good Looking Woman' generating even more euphoria, and bounce in time to the hot-wired opening. Picking out familiar faces and welcoming others, Joe seemed to enjoy the opening number even more than the audience. Even when he had driven half a day to reach the venue, or when suffering from a cold or flu, Joe would forget it all as soon as he hit the stage and launched into that opening line, the audience's reaction, the surge of the room and the energy within making it all worthwhile. The audience would become even more delirious after the hip-shaking routine that brought 'Good Looking Woman' to a close, Joe pointing to the heavens in a sensual frozen pose as the song ended. He probably performed the song at least ten thousand times, but he never tired of it.

Barely giving the audience time to catch its breath, he would launch into a selection of show-stoppers from different eras of his career, bringing the evening to an early crescendo before he and the band had even warmed up. Unhooking the buttons of his white suit and loosening his famous white tie from his neck, the temperature in the venue would rise a couple of notches and squeals of anticipation pierce the ears. Before the end of the night, someone would be bringing that tie home.

He would then peel off a few powerful ballads to bed the audience down for a bit, but not for long as he would then whip out anthem after anthem. By now, the audience's inhibitions had vanished completely, and when they had reached fever pitch again, Joe would carefully wrap them up in their favourite blanket – usually 'Make Me an Island', 'I Need You' or 'Unchained Melody' – before whipping it off and sending them home sweating with the likes of 'Deeper and Deeper', 'More and More' and the penultimate 'Sweet Little Rock 'n' Roller'. After close to two and a half hours, the show would reach its powerful denouement with the rousingly theatrical 'Goodbye Venice Goodbye', and Joe would shake, grab and high-five as many hands as possible, reaching out to the same arms that had swayed to the music all night long. Joe's greatest pleasure was his audiences' pleasure, and he was never shy in letting them know how much he appreciated them. Before they knew it, he left the building.

There was more to the show than just a selection of greatest hits, though. When Joe slowed the show down, he delighted in involving his audience: notes passed up to the stage would be read out; and requests would be acted upon immediately by the tightly drilled band. 'Some of the boys weren't keen on the requests as they felt it was killing the momentum of the show, especially in a concert situation in theatres around the country like the Olympia, but it was an element of the show I loved for a number of reasons, not least because I could catch me breath!' Joe said, laughing.

The requests also enabled Joe to connect with his audience. He loved to chat to them and get to know them, and he enjoyed the stories they would tell about events in their lives. He could alter the whole mood of the room without even playing a song by offering a simple hello or by highlighting the story of a particular fan. And night after night they returned. The front rows would usually be full of the hard-core fans who attended as many Joe shows as they could. When familiar faces in certain towns and cities didn't show, Joe would be concerned. He would often ring his friends to tell them his fans' latest news. Few entertainers, Irish or otherwise, cared this much about their audience, and his genuine interest in them made them feel special.

Ceremony was a big part of a Joe show. When Joe peeled off his jacket and loosened his tie with its famous signature, a forest of arms would reach out almost immediately in a desperate bid to get their hands on the most sought-after piece of tailoring in show business. After teasing the crowd for a bit, Joe would give the tie away, either picking an audience member out at random or giving it to someone he had heard about in advance. A tie was all many needed to feel their burdens had been lifted. Thousands of fans have their own stories to tell about getting one of Joe's white ties – from those who had been ill, to children with special needs, to ordinary fans finally able to bring a piece of Joe home with them. For many, it was a ray of light in their lives. Joe cherished the ties almost as much as his fans, and kept them locked up at a secret location, only taking one out at a time. The tie was part of a Joe show, and Joe would never give them away unless it was at a show, despite the many thousands of requests he received.

The gesture itself almost came about by complete accident. One night at a Dublin show, Joe arrived at a venue having forgotten his tie and asked a friend if he could borrow his. The man explained that the expensive silk tie had been given to him as a birthday present by his wife. 'Oh, that's nice,' Joe said, half-listening as he looped the silk around his neck. About three songs into the show, sweat beginning to moisten his collar, Joe loosened the tie and a fan roared up, in her loudest Dublin accent, 'Hai, Jow, give us yer toi!' Without thinking, Joe unfurled it and went to hand it out to the woman, but a melee ensued as other fans tried desperately to get their hands on that same little piece of Joe. Meanwhile, the man who had given Joe the tie looked on in abject horror. Standing next to him, his wife remarked that the tie was just like the one she had given him for his birthday.

The day after the show, Joe went to his tailor, Chas Fagan, who had been making stage clothes for Joe since the 1960s, with the idea of making ties with his signature on them. Chas went on to hand-make tens of thousands of them over the years, skilfully stitching Joe's signature on to them himself.

Fans also gave Joe little gifts, and Joe cherished them, especially those given to him by his numerous young fans with special needs. He knew all their names and years later would remember who had given him which gift. Joe always had incredible time for his special needs fans, and would phone some of them quite often to see how they were doing, even stopping rounds of golf or interrupting films to do so.

No matter what sized venue he played in, Joe felt like the audience were his friends. 'You can get a sort of a rapport going with people, and the show became more of a party,' he said. 'I feed off the audience in a huge way. When I get a buzz off the audience straight away you're not working any more, you're at a party. This is my party. It's the biggest karaoke in town on the night because everyone is singing with my band.' Joe would often let audience members sing a line or two into his microphone and it didn't matter if they could sing or not. It was all in aid of a good time, and that's exactly what the fans got with a Joe show.

From the first song to the last, Joe ensured the set-list was always full of hits. 'Not doing a hit record or a song the audience likes or expects is letting down an audience in a way,' he said. Joe hated going to shows where artists would either leave out their big hits or save them for the encore. 'What was the point? Making people happy is what music is all about,' he argued. His favourite live acts were The Rolling Stones and Neil Diamond, acts who knew that a live show should be hit-heavy and full of fun.

He had little time for artists who complained about being famous. 'This isn't rocket science, it's meant to be fun. I have never liked performers who go onstage and then moan about what a bloody miserable life they're having. I have always been a bit of a road hog – I do a couple of hundred gigs a year and I love them. Obviously there are times when you'd love to be at home or out and about with your friends, but that is not an option. Travelling is the only thing that kills me, but when I get there the journey is all forgotten about. And when I go onstage, man, all hell breaks loose and it's great. It's a great high when people start to react. They lift you up and you want to stay there for ever.'

As entertainment was his chosen profession, Joe felt it was his responsibility to entertain and give it 100 per cent: 'If you go to work in a factory or a job that you hate, then you have a reason to moan. But if you are doing my job, which is the best in the world, I think you are treating your audience with contempt if you just put in half a show. When I see people going to gigs, not just mine, but any good show, and I see the smiles on their faces, and the fact that they might have arrived in a bad mood but, for an hour or whatever, the music and the singer can make them forget why they were in a bad mood, I feel proud. It's a huge responsibility and one that should not be taken lightly.' For Joe, the audience was the absolute king, and in charge of his destiny. 'You might think you're the ringmaster, but at the end of the day, they are the bosses. If they don't come with you, I mean, what can you do? If you don't give them what they want then you're in trouble. Without the audience you're sunk. The atmosphere at our shows – I can't speak about many shows, but I'll talk about our own – lifts you. I'm lifted off the stage when the crowd start buzzing and it makes the whole night. I have seen people looking at their watches because we're finishing, and they're looking, "Jaysus, he can't be finished yet?" That means that it's been a good show because time has just flown away. When you see that happening, when they look at their watches and look at each other, "Oh no, it's not the end, is it? Two hours have gone by already" – that to me is a good indication of a show that swung along.'

When asked if he could live without his audience, Joe said, 'I wouldn't be happy, I seriously wouldn't be happy if I didn't have the audience. You can play golf once a day; or you can watch television in the evening, but I think at the end of the day when you finish up your day by walking on in front of a full hall of people and they are joining in with what you are doing, that is a real high, a big buzz, and I don't think I could live without that.'

Joe would allow nothing to get in the way of giving his all for a show. 'Even if I'm tired and have had a hard day, that's got nothing to do with the audience. You just have to perk yourself up and go for it. If I sense people aren't enjoying themselves, I don't blame them, I blame me ... I feel that if the people are not singing for me, then I'm doing something wrong.' The only time he would consider getting out of the business was 'when the people out there don't want me. As long as they are there and they want to hear what I do then I don't see any reason to retire from the business and play golf full-time. I can't visualize myself being off the road. I'd be bored for starters. There are a lot of people out there and I want to be there with them.'

The package-deal concert, a notable Irish show-business first, with accommodation, transport and a couple of concerts as part of an all-in deal, was something that Joe pioneered. Effectively, he brought the fans on holiday with him. He would play five nights a week for almost a month in places such as the Gleneagle Hotel in Killarney, which became the focal point of many a Joe Dolan-soundtracked break in the 1980s. The shows were attended by anyone and everyone; a young Ronan Keating was a regular. The biggest name in World Championship Snooker at the time, Denis Taylor, was there one summer and caused quite a stir. Indeed, Denis had met his wife at a Joe Dolan concert, and had spread the word about Joe among his fellow pros. Every big name in snooker had seen Joe in concert at one stage thanks to the patronage of the genial Ulsterman, and in 1985 Joe reunited the original Drifters for a one-off performance to mark Taylor's appearance on *This Is Your Life* with Eamonn Andrews. It was the first time they had played together since 1968.

Together with his friend and promoter James Cafferty, who had been a fan of Joe's from the early days, Joe went on to devise the concept of the 'Showtime Express', which brought fans from all over the country to a series of Joe Dolan-themed bank holiday weekend festivals in cities such as Cork and Galway. The first such weekend, in 1987, was in Cork, for which James hired a train carriage from CIÉ to bring fans down from Dublin. After one ad in the *Evening Herald*, the eighty-seat carriage had sold out. He ended up booking a series of carriages and then CIÉ had to charter a special train for the weekend. It was the same story in Galway.

These shows led indirectly to the Isle of Man Festival in 1990 – the first in a series of weekend-long festivals on the island that would see Joe headline a concert a night with a massive selection of support acts. Because the weather was anything but predictable and had led to cancelled ferries, James moved the weekend festival to Bundoran in 1996, and for many years Joe returned as its headlining attraction. Joe was initially reluctant to play, as the northern coastal town had lost some of its lustre in the 1980s and it was thought that only 600 people would come, but Joe's pulling power saw over 2,600 beds booked for that first festival. So successful were the subsequent Bundoran festivals that in 1999 the effervescent Cafferty was presented with the Freedom of Bundoran in recognition of his outstanding contribution to tourism and business in the town and the North-West. Cafferty's Showtours company would go on to repeat the magic formula in Mayo, Sligo and Killarney.

As he moved into the 1990s, Joe was content that he had accomplished what he had set out to do. People who didn't do disco, who didn't do night clubs and who certainly didn't want to travel to cities for big concerts, could now go out again in comfort. Even people who didn't 'do' Joe Dolan would end up enjoying a Joe show, as you just couldn't ignore his physical, musical and vocal energy for long.

Some of his own band had thought he was mad turning his back on the dances, the echoing halls and the fusty ballrooms. They were lucrative and you could get as many people to come through the door as you wanted, they argued. But the pay packet didn't matter to Joe; all he cared about was how he performed and whether the people enjoyed it. 'I don't ever remember going onstage thinking, "I'm going to make money tonight," because that's not me. The only thing I'm interested in is the people.'

The Joe show made it personal for Joe again, and he thrived. His manager had known all along that 'there was no show like a Joe show', and almost by accident his casual remark became the slogan that would define Joe's marketing right up until his last shows in 2007.

Joe almost created a new Irish circuit by playing places that wouldn't ordinarily host gigs. His favourite gigs were those in the class venues: the big theatres and opera houses. However, he loved the hotel circuit and although he could easily have survived by performing a couple of dozen big theatre shows a year, he continued to play all over the country a couple of hundred times a year. By playing venues such as hotels, arts centres and theatres, which were readily accessible to all, fans of all ages came to worship.

Joe allowed his band plenty of freedom to express themselves as he never wanted any concert to sound the same, but he would always rein players in with a quiet word backstage if they were becoming a little *too* expressive. It was, after all, the Joe show.

From his centre-stage position, Joe directed the show. The minute Joe signalled, he had to have what he wanted. Despite the band's name, they could never just drift along when they were playing with Joe. 'I like to have a good band around me, and I like to try and keep the same band together,' Joe said. 'It's important because the lads need to know exactly what I do onstage. It's not as if I do the same thing all the time or that I do certain things at certain times during the night – I don't. I'm a total freak like that. I change everything every night to keep it interesting for myself as well as everybody else because I don't like singing the same note in the same place.'

The Joe show also allowed Joe to keep a steady road crew in full-time employment. The pre-show card schools (poker or twenty-five) that the crew and the band played in were legendary, uninterruptible affairs that sometimes became so heated they had to be continued after the show. One venue Joe loved playing because of the card schools was the Headford Arms in Kells, the owner of which was a card player whose game was as impressive as Joe's. One night, as she held Joe, Ben and promoters Joe O'Neill and James Cafferty to ransom, they were interrupted by a former squeeze of Cafferty's. Such was Joe's determination to continue playing that he kindly asked, 'Would you politely close the door, preferably from the outside.' He could be cutting in the nicest possible way, but nothing got in the way of his card playing. One of the few times he really lost his temper was playing poker with Ben and James. The pair of them spent a night 'bluffing' Joe with false hands and he stormed out, sacking them both. They were reinstated the next morning.

Another thing keeping Joe on home ground was his recording career. Because he was out of the country for so long in the early 1980s, Joe felt he had dented some of the momentum that 'More and More' and 'It's You, It's You, It's You' had built up. In fact, the release of the *More and More* album had been delayed because he wasn't in the country to promote it.

One of Joe's most successful discs, it features many Joe-show favourites, from the two high-flying singles to Joe's third big hit single of the 1980s, 'It's

Only Make Believe', an electrifying rocker that rose to number thirteen in the Irish charts in April 1982 and spent close to three months in the Top Thirty. Other standouts on the album included a long-awaited recording of 'Ave Maria', in which Joe reaches for the heavens with one of his most celestial vocals.

Striving to keep his sound as fresh as he could, for his next release he hooked up with one of Ireland's greatest songwriters and producers, Phil Coulter. The Derry man – who had written such seminal classics as 'Congratulations', 'All Kinds of Everything' and 'Scorn Not His Simplicity', and who had worked with everyone from Planxty to Van Morrison – had been working on tracks with Joe's voice in mind for some time. They teamed up at London's Mayfair Studios at the end of 1982, and over a few months assembled the *Here and Now* album, one of Joe's most cohesive long-players. Coulter's musical direction ensured it was more than just a schizophrenic collection of big singles of varying genres. The first single, 'Deeper and Deeper', was the ultimate Joe Dolan track. Another in a long line of powerful, big-hearted love songs, it was a Top Ten hit in November 1983, spending eleven weeks on the Irish charts. Other big hits (and concert favourites) on the album included 'Sometimes When We Touch' and a sprightly cover of the ELO song 'The Way Life's Meant to Be'.

The album title came about almost by accident. For months nobody could agree on one, and Joe had about ten in mind. Eventually a meeting was called and initially it proved equally fruitless. With time running out, a frazzled and frustrated Harmac Records chief Brendan Harvey banged his fists on the table and declared, 'Look, lads, will you make up your minds. I need a title, and I need it here and now!' Joe looked at him: 'That's it! *Here and Now*. That's the title.' The album cover was a cheeky shot of Joe smoking a cigarette, an unfeasible thing to do these days, and it was a theme that was used on promotional posters at the time.

Despite giving up smoking for some years in the 1970s, Joe was now smoking heavily, which was extraordinary given the nightly strain his voice was under. 'I hate the stuff and don't know why I do it,' he would say of his on-off tobacco addiction. 'I don't need them physically; it's just a habit I can't break.' He eventually broke the habit in the late 1990s, but was still known to sneak the occasional quick smoke when he thought nobody was looking, before giving it up for good in the early 2000s.

For a while, nearly everyone in the band and crew smoked, and with so much smoke in the wagon, Joe announced a smoking ban long before it was a twinkle in a government ashtray. Banning smoking while in transit wasn't a popular decision, but it was followed right up until the last tour. It was even less popular as Joe was the sort of smoker that fellow smokers hate: he would decide one day that he was giving them up and that would be it, he wouldn't smoke for three months. It was the same with drink: if he decided he wasn't going to drink for a while, he would stick to his guns, despite the many after-show temptations.

In 1984, the one-off 'Come Back Home' was released. Although ostensibly a song about a marriage break-up that leaves a little boy, Danny, without his mum, the song can also be read as a triumphant declaration of Joe's decision to bring it all back home. The following year saw the release of the *Always On My Mind* album, which marked another change of direction, Joe adding a contemporary 1980s touch to some of his favourite love songs by artists such as Elvis, Kris Kristofferson, Bonnie Tyler, Del Shannon, The Platters, and even little Leo Sayer, whom Joe had become friendly with over the years.

A concept album of sorts, *Always On My Mind* has a track-listing that reads like a carefully sequenced jukebox, detailing the trials and tribulations of a recently reunited couple. The cover art gave listeners an indication of the album's theme: the front image was of Joe and an attractive model, together but separate; while on the back cover, Joe and the girl were nowhere to be seen, an empty bottle of champagne and the girl's negligee the only trace of their earlier reconciliation. The album, which was produced by Terry Bradford, can be viewed as a predecessor to the covers collections that would reinvent Joe for a whole new generation of fans at the end of the century.

In 1987, he followed this with *This Is My Life*, a collection of originals that are also loosely linked to tell a life story. This album marked the return of Peter Yellowstone both as songwriter and producer, and it is a smooth work. It features plenty of Joe-show mainstays, such as the title track and 'Take Me I'm Yours', together with the particularly apt 'Home Is Where the Heart Is'. The cover was designed by U2 designer Steve Averill, with pictures by renowned photographer Amelia Stein. The first single, 'Take Me I'm Yours' was a Top Ten hit, its summery flavour and smooth tempo taking it to number nine for a couple of weeks in July and August 1986. The next single, 'Don't

Set Me Free', also charted. However, despite its success the album did not mark much of a progression, and in a bid to spice things up, in 1988 he went to Georgia, in the States, to record with Bagatelle man Liam Reilly.

The recording of this album, *Always Loved You*, nearly broke the bank, but it was worth every dime as it marked a significant shift in sound for Joe. For fans of great Irish rockers doing what they do best – in Reilly's case writing powerful anthems, and in Joe's case bringing them to life – it is an album worthy of investigation. The album's softest moment, 'Wait 'Til the Clouds Roll By (Jenny)', was the first single, but the punchy follow-up singles 'She Doesn't Live Here Anymore' and 'When You Walk in the Room' were more indicative of the disc as a whole. The singles all fared well in the Irish charts and the album received good reviews. Trademark Liam Reilly songs such as 'Over You' and 'Is it Raining in Paris Tonight' fitted Joe's voice like a glove, and recording it in America had given Joe a leaner, meaner FM-radio edge. But Joe found that he had become a sort of heritage act, with his music now played on RTÉ Radio 1 as opposed to the hipper 2FM.

The arrival of Adrian Dolan, Ben's eldest son, in the band would change all that. Adrian joined the band on bass guitar for a round of US dates, Joe's first American concerts in eight years, just before Joe recorded *Always Loved You*. He took over from long-serving bassist Pat Hoey who, ironically, had just moved to America. 'I'd been on the road with the band for a good bit as a youngster, but never thought I'd actually play in the band,' admits Adrian. He had just cut a single with Beyond Words, one of Ireland's best-known live acts in the 1980s, when Joe asked Adrian if he would be interested in joining his band, and the decision was not easy for him.

Even though Joe had intended to take things easier, by the time Adrian joined he had increased his Irish gig count considerably to over 250 shows a year – almost resembling his workload at the height of the showband boom. And when Joe wasn't on the road at home, he was in a recording studio – usually abroad, as there were few top-notch studios in Ireland at the time. Although Joe liked to take his time on albums, he found he was unable to do this as he was so busy on the road. So, with a thriving band scene back home in Mullingar and a derelict building at his disposal to the rear of Dolan's Bar, Joe and Adrian conspired to build Joe's very own studio complex.

Joe hired Ben's old boss, Frank Mulligan, to oversee the construction of the studio, while London studio designer Andy Monroe, who had designed the Windmill Lane Studios in Dublin, was in charge of the interiors. Joe's studio was completed in 1992 and christened the Bandroom Studios, and in 1993 they recorded the first song there, an Adrian Dolan composition called 'Ciara'.

Joe had first heard a raw take of the song on Christmas night 1992 in Mullingar. He and Adrian had sat up long into the night discussing music, and when Adrian played the song to Joe, he was impressed and they played around with a few ideas for it. A few weeks later, when Joe heard a demo, he was even more impressed, and he told Adrian he wanted to record it. The two got to work in the freshly built studio. Things were going well, but Adrian was still unsure about the final verse. He was kicking around the line 'There were times when I needed somebody . . .' but had hit a blank. Joe read it, and without thinking immediately added, '. . . but then you came along and turned the world the right way up for me', and then launched straight into the chorus again. It was the perfect fit, the new verse making for a rousing conclusion.

'Ciara' broke the Top Twenty in August 1993, giving Joe his first big hit in three years. When Adrian first heard the song on the radio, he was blown away: 'To hear it on our local radio station, Midlands 103, was something else, but to hear it on 2FM was just incredible,' he said.

It was full steam ahead for a new album, *Can't Give Enough*. The majority of it was recorded in Mullingar, and Joe worked with a variety of writers. The album was released in spring 1994 and did well, but it was the first major release for a relatively new record company, Ainm Records, who were still finding their feet. Joe decided that the next album from the Bandroom would be far better, and as well as being paid for by JBS Music, the new company he had set up with Ben and Seamus to oversee his affairs, it would be released on his own record label, the recently established Gable Records. He got to work almost immediately.

Meanwhile, the critics began to claim Joe was in cruise control, and to a certain degree they were right as he had found a comfort zone. In concert, he was giving the fans exactly what they wanted. The winning Joe-show formula had been going for a while, and although Joe would always try to include new material in the set, he was sticking to a winner. He told the *RTÉ Guide* that the show was like a round of golf. 'If you're hitting the ball fairly well, why change your swing? It's the same with my stage performances. Why change what I'm doing when it's successful and making people happy?'

But the merry-go-round was not without its tragedies, and Joe suffered a hammer blow in Tullamore one night in 1994 when trombonist Liam Meade suffered an onstage heart attack. The second-longest-serving member of Joe's band can remember only fragments of the night. He recalls feeling a little unwell and warm when he got onstage, and that he found it hard to hit the notes, as his puff was going. His fellow brassmen noticed and Liam whispered to Ben that he wasn't feeling well. Concerned, Ben said Liam should have a rest, but just as Liam turned to leave the stage he began to fall. He remembered the confusion and panic of trying to locate the stage door before everything stopped. Denis Mee managed to carry Liam off the stage and into the dressing room, where he immediately began CPR on the stricken trombonist. Joe stopped the show and uttered something he never thought he'd have to say from the stage: 'Is there a doctor in the house?' There wasn't, but a nurse came in and helped Liam until the ambulance arrived. Amid the panic he never found out who she was. As he fell in and out of consciousness, he remembers worrying about being the cause of a stopped show. 'I remember this ferocious feeling of sickness, and then I thought, "Poor Joe" and was out for the count again.' He woke up a few days later in hospital. As it turned out, he had been only inches from death and had been saved just in time by an injection which kick-started him back to life.

Sadly the long-serving trombonist was unable to rejoin the band because of the seriousness of his heart attack. He was only fifty-one, and would never be replaced in the band.

Joe took a very hands-on approach with his next album, particularly as it was on his own record label. Joe could never be accused of not giving his fans value for money, and *Endless Magic*, released in 1997, features a whopping fifteen tracks, including live favourites 'I'll Give All My Love to You', 'Angel Lover', 'When I Dream' and the title track. It is a defiantly romantic and thought-provoking album, and it was apt that Joe revisited his old 1970s hits 'Lady in Blue' and 'If I Could Put My Life on Paper'. Never one to forget his continental market, Joe also included 'Latino Lover' and the playful 'Tropical Girl'.

There was more of an autobiographical feel to the album than some of its more recent predecessors: 'I'm Coming Home' was an anthem about leaving the bright lights of the city for the flames of the hometown he'd been away

JOE DOLAN

from for too long; and 'The Right Side of Love' also showcased Joe's happiness at forging a new path.

Produced by Adrian, the album features the talents of all the Drifters, who recorded it as a band – Ben, Adrian and Ray Dolan, Tony Newman, Jimmy Mullally, Frankie McDonald and new guitarist Conor Kenny – as well as those of several special guests, including guitarist Des Moore, former Christy Moore and Different World keyboardist Declan O'Farrell, and several local musicians. Ollie Hennessy, who would play a key role on several future Dolan releases, was the musical glue. 'It was a great record to put together, because everybody was doing their own little bit,' Joe said of the long-player. 'We had good fun recording it and there was a real buzz about it.'

Adrian and Joe struck up a good working relationship during the recording process, and Adrian was unafraid to point Joe in different directions and towards new things. He'd suggest different moods, rhythms and lyrics, and Joe would bring his own ideas to bear too. However, the same old Joe would emerge in the studio: 'As with most albums he did over the years, there were songs he didn't like doing which ended up being the songs he loved the most,' Adrian said, chuckling.

The album was launched by Larry Gogan in the 2FM Roadcaster amid massive fanfare on Dublin's Henry Street on a fresh February morning in 1997, and on its first week of release it entered the Irish album charts at number nine – a placing that made Joe the first Irish star to have a Top Ten hit in every decade from the 1960s to the 1990s.

'I was absolutely delirious. If anyone would have told me I'd be having hits in four decades when Ben and I were on the motorbike hustling for gigs, I would have asked them to get their heads examined,' he said. 'The record was really well done and I knew it had a chance of doing well, but to get to number nine in the first week was just extraordinary, and very satisfying.'

Praise rolled in for Joe, and Irish chat-show king Gay Byrne suggested that it might be time to honour him with a coveted *Late Late Show* special. Only a handful of these rare tribute shows were ever made in the forty-year-plus history of the show. It was flattering to say the least. 'It looks like I've been rediscovered, but I've never been away, you know. I've been here all the time,' a delighted Joe told Richie Taylor in the *Irish Mirror* in one of the dozens of big spreads the newspapers devoted to him at the time. 'But I must say it's a lovely feeling to be rubbing shoulders with U2 and The Spice Girls in the charts! I can't believe I'm actually hip again.'

Joe's big gamble to bring it all back home had paid off.

'Everything was on the up,' he would say later. 'There was a sort of industry at the time, all centred around the Bandroom Studios and Seamus and Helen's office in Dominick Place, Mullingar. I was around the town more so than in previous years, there was talk of documentaries and the *Late Late*, the concerts were selling out, and it felt good. I began to enjoy it more than I ever did really. I'd a real get up and go about me. I enjoyed tricking around in the studio and it felt good to be in complete control of everything.'

The *Endless Magic* album was soon joined in the charts by the second major release on the Gable Label, *This Is Joe Dolan*, a concert video filmed at the old Mullingar County Hall. Fittingly, as the hall had given both Joe and Ben their first taste of popular music and show business, Joe became the last major act to perform there before it was rebuilt as the Mullingar Arts Centre. 'It was a nice send-off to have the cameras in there one last time,' he recalled of the final curtain at the old hall. Filled with new material, the video also served as a reminder that Joe was not one to trade on past glories. But when he did decide to re-record two of his old hits, the results led to the biggest reinvention of his career.

17
Let's all meet up in the year 2000

A glove puppet operated by the son of a childhood friend was the unlikely catalyst for the most triumphant and surprising of all Joe Dolan's 're-inventions'. For over a dozen years Joe had been doing his own thing at his own pace, and the Joe show was a tried and tested trademark that he wasn't about to change in a hurry. However, he had drifted away from the main-stream, and in certain quarters of the media and the music industry he was cast as a dogged survivor, a yesterday man going through the motions and pleasing those hankering for the sound of yesteryear. But Joe was to prove the naysayers wrong . . .

The renaissance started on daytime television. Irish children's television was an anarchic place in the early 1990s, with Zig and Zag leading a charge of irresponsible glove-puppet behaviour. Their complete disregard for conven-tional presenting norms, and their wicked sense of humour (which habitually flew over the heads of its intended audience), on the afternoon kids' TV slot *Dempsey's Den*, with straight man Ian Dempsey, made them cult figures for a much older audience. They were loved and loathed equally by students, parents and pensioners. Joe, who was a fan, found himself frequently name-checked by the pair of puppets, who were created, voiced and operated by design students Ciaran Morrison and Mick O'Hara. At Christmas 1990 they were looking for a seasonal element, so Ciaran's younger brother Johnny joined the team as Dustin, a wise-cracking Dublin turkey. Saved from the oven, Dustin became a regular on the show and developed into a ribald central character: a cowboy builder right at the cusp of the Celtic Tiger building boom with a cult following all of his own.

Joe knew the Morrison boys well. Their father, Jackie, had been a good friend of Joe's, and Joe stayed in touch with the family after Jackie had passed away.

When Zig and Zag left to pursue a career on UK television in 1993, Dustin gobbled up the chance to become RTÉ's top children's television presenter, with another Morrison brother coming in as Socky the sock monster. A big part of Dustin's character was his atrocious attempts at singing and his love for 'culchie' Irish stars such as Joe Dolan. It was met with much derision from his *Den* co-stars, but record company executives looking on saw Dustin's desperately out-of-tune singing as a golden egg. In 1994, with the guidance of EMI A&R man Darren Smith and label boss Willie Kavanagh, Dustin started to plan his first album. It was important that the album had big names on it to reflect Dustin's tastes on and off the construction site, and the names that immediately sprang up were Joe Dolan and Ronnie Drew – two singers who represented the culchie and townie characters more than any others.

Initial contact was made with Joe in early 1994 to record a duet of one of his iconic tracks. Joe was nervous about the idea, but those around him thought it was too good an opportunity to pass up, and so he tentatively agreed to record 'Make Me an Island'. A new backing track was cut in Mullingar, and Joe and Dustin laid down the vocals with producers Dave McCune and Ronan Johnson. Joe particularly enjoyed working with Johnny Morrison, who he had last seen when he was just a kid. 'It was a real treat to work with John . . . sorry, Dustin and to meet all the [Morrison] lads again. They were a fantastic bunch of lads, real good guys and a lot of fun,' Joe said.

'Make Me an Island' appeared alongside duets with Ronnie Drew, The Saw Doctors and Zig and Zag, as well as several other Dustin originals and 'interpretations' on the *Not Just a Pretty Face* album, which topped the Christmas charts. EMI were unsure whether to release the Joe/Dustin duet as a single and in the end decided against it. However, radio stations started to pick up on it and its popularity grew.

Joe was flattered and more than a little surprised by its reception. 'To be honest I didn't know what to expect after we had laid the track down, I really didn't, and we certainly weren't building on anything major coming from it.' However, that's just what happened. People began talking about Joe again. At his shows he noticed an increase in the number of younger faces in the crowd, and although 'Make Me an Island' had always been a stand-out moment, a chance for his audience to come together in a unifying singalong, Joe's old hit began to sparkle even more.

Having gone through a few fallow years, with his television appearances limited to sporadic chat-show appearances, award ceremonies or the occasional sarcastic name check, Joe started to become a familiar and welcome face on Ireland's TV screens again. He was comfortable and casual, firing jokes and not taking himself too seriously, which appealed to programmers and presenters alike. When he wasn't on *The Den* in person, they would often play his music. Children loved him, and his cultish image also started to appeal to an older generation of kids and students.

Newspaper and magazine editors dispatched reporters to Joe shows, and on the radio, top DJs such as Tony Fenton, Larry Gogan and Gerry Ryan played Joe's hits – old and new – and some of his greatest hits collections and recent albums reappeared in the charts as people started to rediscover him. As he said himself, he was 'hip again'.

Nevertheless, Joe remained unfazed by it all, focusing all of his energies on the *Endless Magic* album – a focus that paid off when it became one of the biggest-selling independent releases of 1997. And just as Joe was becoming used to being a totally independent artist, he was snapped up by EMI himself.

The success of Joe's duet with Dustin had ruffled plenty of feathers in EMI, and for the third Dustin album they wanted the 'hip-again' Joe back, with 'Good Looking Woman' the next song in their sights. Again Joe wasn't so sure of the merits of re-recording old gold, but he eventually agreed to record it on his terms – with all proceeds going to Barnardo's, Ireland's leading children's charity. Joe and his band recorded a new backing track, and once again he had great fun ad-libbing with Dustin. They changed plenty of the song's original lyrics, the final chorus descending from 'good looking woman' to 'good looking turkey' to 'dog ugly turkey'.

The label loved it, and persuaded Joe to film a lavish video. He was delighted to be sent up and to allow one of his greatest songs to be sent up too. Model and TV personality Amanda Byram was enlisted, and many an eyebrow was raised as she danced provocatively among Joe's hot-under-the-collar band. When the single was released in November 1997, it flew straight to the number-one spot.

An avid chart watcher, Joe couldn't believe it. In the space of a year he had seen the *Endless Magic* album go Top Ten and now he was top of the singles charts. It was a cause for celebration, and Joe's sold-out run of gigs at the end of 1997 were some of the wildest in years.

'Working with Dustin was probably one of the biggest risks we ever took,' Joe reflected. 'It was worth it as there really is no finer feeling in the world than when you find out you're the number-one hit record, it was something we hadn't felt in sixteen years, but boy was it worth the wait.'

Darren Smith, EMI's main A&R man, had become friendly with Joe over the course of the Dustin singles, and when Joe and his manager told him that if the label were interested in furthering their relationship, they would be receptive, Darren went to work on a few ideas with label bosses Willie Kavanagh and David Gogan. They were particularly excited at the thought of cementing Joe's iconic status by complementing what he already could offer – his incredible voice – with something that people would not be expecting from him. They thought he could show the younger guns how it should be done, if given the right material, and so proposed that Joe cover the music that was huge at the time – British indie music, contemporary songs that no one would have associated with Joe. 'We knew he still had a great voice, but did everybody else know that? If he had the right songs then there was no reason why it couldn't regenerate his career,' Willie Kavanagh says.

Joe gave the pitch his blessing and record collections were raided and listened to afresh with Joe's voice in mind. Short-lists of potential songs were drawn up and Joe listened to dozens of compilation tapes. There were some outrageous tracks and plenty of names that Joe himself liked and knew already, but before he would consider recording any, some ground rules had to be established.

'The one thing he was always conscious of with any of the albums he did for us was that they would never sound like a karaoke album,' David Gogan explained. 'Joe had to put his own mark on it. We were also conscious that if you went to a Joe gig, would these new songs fit into his set? That was the brief – the songs had to suit him and they had to work at his gigs.'

Willie Kavanagh agreed: 'If Joe wasn't comfortable with a song then it was off the table. We never wanted to put him in a situation where he might be embarrassed or people would think, "What's yer man doing? That's sad." There had to be some element of credibility to it all.'

Several meetings were held as Joe weighed up certain songs and brought suggestions of his own to the table. Everyone had their own favourites, with Blur's 1995 hit 'The Universal' an immediate standout for many. But the song orbited outside of Joe's musical solar system, and his reaction came as a surprise.

'It really stood out and I told Joe to listen to it carefully,' his manager said. 'He rang me about two days later and said, "What the hell were you saying about that 'Universal' song? It's a load of shit." He was more into the rockier numbers, and there were a few other Blur songs he preferred.'

He eventually grew to like it. 'I genuinely didn't know at first,' Joe admitted. 'I mean, I liked Blur a lot, but when I heard it I just listened to Damon Albarn's voice, which was quite alien to mine, almost spoken word, so it became a difficult song for me to sing until I just forgot about it for a while and came back to it one day and it clicked. I'm glad it did, because if I had sung something like "Country House" it would have sounded daft! I liked the song they did with Françoise Hardy ('To the End') and their albums all had incredible moments that would stop you in your tracks. Albarn was ahead of the game really, a very talented guy.'

Joe changed the song completely. Where the Blur man finished a word quickly, Joe instead held on to it, and his phrasing and expressive voice turned what was originally a slow, meditative song about the loss of free will and individuality into a celebration of life.

One of Joe's provisos was that no expense was to be spared on the production. If he was doing a cover of an already lavishly produced song then he wanted his to sound equally, if not more, lavish. Production team Dave McCune and Ronan Johnston did just that, adding a raw, rockier crunch to proceedings. Their enthusiasm rubbed off on Joe and the recording sessions were going so well that the born-again rocker didn't want them to end. 'The boys used to have to lock up the studio to try and keep me out,' he said, laughing. 'I was mad to get this done, and that done and the other done. I was really enjoying it. They were two of the nicest fellas you could work with.'

Although he was working with a new production team, Joe ensured that Adrian Dolan was not forgotten about, and a couple of songs they had been working on with another Mullingar musician, Peter Carroll, were also recorded.

'Joe was enjoying life again,' Ben recalls. 'There was a real buzz about him, and he was probably as happy as I'd seen him in years.' The shows were better than ever, and with guitarist Joe Meehan's return after a short break, the band was hotter than they had been in a long time. Meehan's guitar work always added an extra dimension to the Joe show, and with the musical challenges ahead, his return could not have been better timed.

The album complete, 'The Universal' was, as predicted, getting the most feedback. 'When we listened to that album,' Willie Kavanagh remembers, 'the second we heard that song we thought, "Jesus, this is definitely the right thing to do. He definitely still has it!"' When it was released as a single, it launched Joe into a different stratosphere. Even Joe's own family couldn't believe it when they heard Gerry Ryan play the single on the radio for the first time on a September morning.

'Now, just listen to this,' Ryan said as the track faded in. 'You won't believe how good this is . . . and you won't believe who's singing it . . .'

'I thought it was the Blur track, and then I was astonished to hear Joe's vocals come in,' Adrian recalled, admitting he almost dropped his coffee cup to the floor, as, undoubtedly, did thousands of fans across the country.

Within days it took off for Joe in a big way. Ronan Collins, who had been playing Joe for years on RTÉ Radio 1, must have felt that his artist had been stolen as RTÉ 2FM were all over it. Tony Fenton and Larry Gogan played it all the time, and over at the newly launched Today FM, Ian Dempsey was also loving the song.

The moving video won Joe even more fans, even though it didn't actually feature Joe. It instead starred a hand-made puppet that bore a striking resemblance to the singer, embarking on a journey of rediscovery in an old attic. He yearns to be the real Joe Dolan, and eventually gets his wish. Two puppets, worth £25,000 apiece, were specially made for the shoot, which was directed by Caboom. The puppet concept was also an affectionate tribute to *Joe 90*, a

1960s string-puppet secret-agent series, and a reference to the album's title, *Joe's 90s*.

'I didn't get the notion of not being in the video, but when I saw this puppet they had made, well, I knew it was the right decision – he was better looking than me for a start!' Joe said, laughing. He loved the video and admitted that the first time he saw it, he shed a tear.

As Joe didn't appear directly in the video, people were able to judge the song entirely on the strength of his voice. 'Joe's voice was fantastic – it's a better version than Blur's own; substantially better in fact,' says Willie Kavanagh. 'The voice won through. He always looked great anyway, and the white suit was the best image going in Irish show business, so when people eventually saw him, he looked even better than they had imagined or remembered him looking.'

'Because he had been off the radar we were worried that if we stuck him in front of a camera in the white suit, people wouldn't take him seriously or they would think we were taking the piss out of him,' David Gogan added.

Within a week of its release the single went into the Top Ten and Joe Dolan was everywhere (again). Even the English media reported on the song's high chart placing, with music bible *NME* featuring Joe for the first time in over thirty years. Blur's manager wasn't happy at first and asked Tony Wadsworth, the worldwide boss of EMI, to find out what was going on, but once he heard Joe's version he gave it the band's blessing. 'I hoped Damon approved of it,' Joe said. 'I wanted to meet him to thank him for the song, but it never happened.'

The song became an integral part of Joe's live shows, a scarf-waving singalong comparable to 'Make Me an Island'. Joe would say that it was 'up there with the best of them' in terms of his own material.

The album *Joe's 90s* was launched at Ireland's biggest music store of the time, the Virgin Megastore on Dublin's Aston Quay, and all the staff were decked out in white suits and Joe Dolan ties for the day as Joe and the band performed live. 'Everyone there was into it, shaping all round the place. I thought to myself, "This is very rock and roll." It was like the old days again; it felt great.'

Flushed with success and an ever-increasing audience, the singles kept coming, with a version of Reef's 'Place Your Hands' (which featured another

LET'S ALL MEET UP IN THE YEAR 2000

hip video, this time with Joe in a variety of outfits), followed by his highly spirited take of Pulp's coming-of-age saga 'Disco 2000', a song that became an immediate (and lasting) hit at Joe's live shows. Joe was an enormous fan of Jarvis Cocker and always had a lot of fun performing the song live.

The album was the perfect encapsulation of what Joe did best. His reading of Elvis Costello's 'Alison' was affectionate, as was his take on Radiohead's 'High and Dry'. He was honoured to sing Neil Young's 'Only Love Can Break Your Heart', and his vocal was full of rocktastic fire and brimstone on a dance version of Rainbow's 'I Surrender'. He also added his own pathos and experience to Suede's 'Beautiful Ones'.

Although a few critics scoffed at the notion of Joe covering indie bands like Radiohead, Blur and Pulp, Joe had this to say to them: 'You know, it doesn't matter where the material comes from or who has recorded it before – a good song is a good song; it's as simple as that. When I listen to a song the first thing I look out for is the vocals and if you listen to the songs I did they are all singer's songs.'

He noticed the effect of the new material at the shows straight away. 'Any single gigs we had booked, suddenly we had to do an extra night. We sold out all the November and December gigs, and then all the gigs we had for the following February, March and April sold out. It was just amazing the way the whole thing just went boom from there,' he recalled. The album held on to the number-one spot for a couple of weeks as Joe appeared on just about every television and radio show in the country.

The crowning achievement of this incredibly hectic period was a series of sold-out shows at the Olympia Theatre. Joe had been worried that he might have alienated some of his audience by recording the new material, but it all fell into place during those hot, steamy nights in the Grand Old Lady of Dublin's Dame Street.

'It was two stand-up concerts, the first time I had done shows like that in the Olympia for a good while. I was a bit scared, to be honest. I paced around backstage for a bit and I sort of didn't want to know if there was anybody in, I didn't want to know how many tickets we had sold or hadn't sold because I didn't want to be disappointed. I reckoned if I left it until I went out onstage I'd be able to be disappointed quicker. When I walked out the place was just stuffed with people and they were two of the greatest sing-songs I've ever played. The reception was unreal; just fantastic and it gave me such a high. Everything turned itself upside down again over those nights. The older crowd were singing all the new ones and the younger crowd were singing the older songs such as "The Answer to Everything", "I Love You More and More Every Day" and "Make Me an Island". It was unbelievable to be able to cross that bridge and I knew then that we had made the right decision.

'Before *Joe's 90s* and the Dustin thing, the kids weren't really coming to the shows, but these records brought them and involved them in the show, and when they heard me singing "The Answer to Everything" they probably remembered hearing that record at home in the house. At the show you'd see them say, "Jaysus, that's the song" and they already knew it. It's a strange feeling. It made me feel like a king.'

Joe finally received his crown when Gay Byrne devoted a full two-and-a-half-hour edition of *The Late Late Show* to him. The atmosphere in RTÉ Studio 1 that day was electrifying, and with a large crowd of Joe's family, friends and fans, as well as dozens of his fellow stars present, it felt every inch like a coronation. After Joe opened the show to a rapturous welcome with 'More and More', Gay told Joe he looked well. 'When you get a reception like that, how can you get tired,' Joe said of wild cheers. 'It's just beautiful. I put all my success down to people like that, it makes you feel good; but for them I wouldn't be anywhere.'

Gay interviewed Joe on all aspects of his career, and Joe's replies were full of warm, self-deprecating wit, which was lapped up by the enthusiastic crowd. The celebration was also full of glowing tributes and dozens of humorous anecdotes – most of them at Joe's expense. Ronan Keating, Christy O'Connor Jr, Des Smyth, Larry Gogan, Louis Walsh, Jean Costello from *Fair City* (who was Joe's favourite actress), Dustin and writer Liam Fay all spoke about the impact that Joe had had on their lives – but perhaps the greatest tributes came from Joe's family and from his fans.

One young woman, Teresa Heavy, spoke of how Joe helped her through a heartbreaking period after she was diagnosed with breast cancer. Because she was ill, she couldn't go to a Joe show at the Spa Hotel and, noticing her absence, Joe instead came to her, arriving on her doorstep the next morning to wish her well. 'It was the miracle I needed,' she told Gay. Other fans shared memories of great shows, and Joe's friends also spoke of his lasting friendship and generosity.

The show ended when Gay presented Joe with an enormous one-off piece of Waterford Crystal that had been painstakingly hand-cut for Joe and featured a 3D representation of his face. Joe was a big crystal collector, and his eyes lit up when he saw the piece.

RTÉ's cameras followed Joe around several times after his *Late Late Show* appearance. In 1999, a documentary named *The Mullingar Mojo* centred on the magic of a Joe show and featured plenty of behind-the-scenes footage and interviews with Joe and those who made it happen. It also featured interviews with his fans – from Lottery winners to taxi drivers to the legions of women who have loved Joe since childhood – including Dubliner Tommy Murphy, undoubtedly one of Joe's biggest fans and a man who saw Joe perform close to a thousand times over the years. Tommy always sat front and centre at a concert and was one of the few people in the country to own a black Joe Dolan tie.

The documentary also speculated on how long Joe would continue performing. Joe said he would never give up. 'You can't put a time limit on it. I have no intention of going anywhere.'

'He can go on as long as he wants,' said his manager. 'I think he's getting better with age. As long as he feels he wants to do it, he'll go on. I doubt if he will ever give up, he'll keep going for ever. And I hope Ben does too. I'll be right there behind them.'

Dozens of other programmes would capture Joe at work, rest and play in the following years. In 2004, with the help of broadcaster Alasdair Jackson, Joe hosted a travelogue of sorts about Mullingar. This *Nationwide* special saw him bring the cameras on a guided tour of his hometown and its environs, and featured Joe chatting to traffic warden Joe Cronin, friends and neighbours, and at work in his studio. He was even re-interviewed for his old job at the *Westmeath Examiner* and filmed getting a haircut in the barber shop of County Councillor Frank McIntyre, who played a key role in making Joe a Freeman of Mullingar in 1987, and it finished with footage of Joe live onstage at his annual homecoming show at the Greville Arms Hotel.

One of Joe's own particular favourites was a *Ryan Confidential* special with Gerry Ryan, which was filmed in a Dublin restaurant in May 2003. It was one of the most revealing interviews Joe ever gave on television. Joe enjoyed Gerry's company and the two bonded as they discussed subjects such as the Drifters' split, his international triumphs and his relationship with his fans.

Other, more controversial, TV appearances were not so enjoyable, however.

The first of these had come in October 1982 when he was banned from driving for a year and fined £360 following an incident on St Patrick's Day when Joe had hit a parked car while well over the legal limit. But it was his series of court appearances in 2003 that would become something of a media circus. Joe had been charged with drink driving at Cullohill, County Laois, on 10 December 2001. He had been out for a long lunch in Dublin ahead of a Cork show the next evening, and had drunk some wine with it. He went home and started making plans to drive to Cork a day early. When told he couldn't drive because of the wine, he got thick and drove anyway. By the time he got to Abbeyleix he was exhausted so he stopped for a coffee, but the taste of the grass makes a rogue of the ass, so he had a nip of brandy on top of it. As he drove away from the town, a garda noticed that he was driving quite slowly and, suspecting that Joe was over the limit, pulled him over. His breath was tested and charges were brought against him.

Joe reckoned he could fight the charges, so he hired an equally confident barrister to defend him. When the case was first heard in Rathdowney District Court Joe couldn't appear, so his manager went on his behalf. At the court, the barrister stood up and, according to Seamus, 'threw in a few hand grenades'; a legal argument ensued. The judge adjourned the case to another court (which Joe was also unable to attend), and, following another legal argument, the case was re-submitted to Castlecomer District Court for a June 2003 sitting. The absent Joe was warned to appear.

The press were out in force for the June hearing, and they got more than they bargained for when the keys to Castlecomer Courthouse mysteriously vanished, leaving everyone locked out of the court. The judge ordered the court to be brought twenty miles down the road to Portlaoise for an afternoon sitting.

Joe was caught by television cameras signing autographs for gardaí, solicitors and other defendants in the court foyer prior to the sitting. When the case was heard, a legal argument ensued for nearly two hours over the issuing of summonses: Joe had given his address as Dominick Street, Mullingar, when he was stopped, but gardaí could not find him at the address and although legally it could have been served on any member of his family, the garda did not think it fit to serve it on a family member in the bar below the apartment. Gardaí established Joe had another address in Dublin, but they couldn't catch him there either. Eventually, after some months, a garda managed to serve the summons on Joe just before he was due onstage – ironically in Port-laoise. No inference was made in court that Joe had been trying to evade the summonses, but the argument of its validity held up the case, which was eventually adjourned to September – the judge warning that there would be a full and final hearing on that day.

On the day of the hearing, 11 September 2003, the original judge was on holiday, as was the garda who took the breath test. Inspector Liam Delaney from Portlaoise Garda Station appealed to the judge to adjourn the case; however, the judge told Inspector Delaney that the case was marked to go ahead, that despite Inspector Delaney's concerns he was familiar with it, and that the garda witness should have been there. The judge then dismissed the entire case against Joe.

With a major media presence inside and outside the courthouse, Joe pre-pared a statement. On the steps, he began by thanking everyone for their support, adding that the case had caused him great stress as it had been going on for almost two years. 'Please God, this is the end of it,' he said. However, before he could get to the end of his statement he was almost drowned out by a large crowd of local schoolchildren who began singing 'Good Looking Woman', and asked him for autographs. Eventually, somewhat embarrassed, Joe was able to make his escape.

When Joe had time to come down after the success of the *Joe's 90s* album, he immediately got to work on a follow-up. As it was 1999 and millennium fever had gripped the world, Joe decided to look back at a whole century of music, and *21st Century Joe* saw him tackle such certified classics as Mark Bolan's '20th Century Boy', REM's 'Everybody Hurts' and David Bowie's 'Starman', as well as edgier affairs such as Talking Heads' 'Psycho Killer', Alanis Morri-sette's 'One Hand in My Pocket', The Clash classic 'Should I Stay Or Should I Go' and the Oasis anthem 'Live Forever'. Joe was delighted to cover U2, and he chose 'Who's Gonna Ride Your Wild Horses' from their *Achtung Baby* album, itself a long-player of brave reinvention.

The first single was a smooth take on REM's 'Everybody Hurts', one of Joe's all-time favourite songs. Its video was another memorable one, a tongue-in-cheek fictional day in Joe's life depicting anything and everything going wrong. The shoot itself, which took place around Maynooth and Leixlip, was full of good humour. When the crew started holding up traffic in order to get a better shot of Joe walking across the street, a garda initially ordered them to stop as they had no permission to do so. 'Who are you stopping the traffic for anyway, lads?' he asked.

'Joe Dolan,' the director responded.

'Ahh Jaysus, sure why didn't you say?! I'll stop the traffic for yiz . . .'

EMI's Willie Kavanagh remembered local shopkeepers and others also helping out, offering their services as extras. 'Nothing was too much trouble for anyone. It was amazing. It just goes to show the huge goodwill that was out there for Joe.'

The next single, a spirited take on Bruce Springsteen's 'Brilliant Disguise', would see dozens of big names – from members of Boyzone to well-known Irish personalities such as Lorraine Keane, Neil Toibin, Dustin, Gerry Ryan, Dave Fanning, Ian Dempsey, Larry Gogan and Seán Moncrieff – don a white suit in tribute to Joe as they jokingly auditioned as 'the new Joe Dolan', a pun at the reinvention tags that accompanied this period of Joe's career. Joe himself made an appearance as 'evil Joe', sporting a black suit and tie. The singles worked, and when *21st Century Joe* was released it put Joe back on top of the charts.

The shows, enjoyed by a mix of old and new fans, went even better than before. 'It was so fresh because nobody at the shows ever thought of any of the music we were playing as old,' he attested with a smile as broad as the one on the album cover.

It was while touring *21st Century Joe* that Joe fell head over heels in love with a venue for the first time since walking into those majestic theatres on his Russian tours: Dublin's Vicar Street. The 1,500-capacity theatre, built in the late 1990s and world-renowned for its customized acoustics and spacious layout, was tailor-made for the Joe show. 'I felt like saying, "After all these years where have you been?" when I played there. It's such a magic place to perform. The Aikens [the late Jim and son Peter who ran the venue] were always great people to work for, and I think the fans always liked it there too. The layout and the tables all made for a great show.'

Joe was always keen to play there, and once he entered the venue's name into his diary he would almost dance a little jig of joy. He endeared himself to the staff by buying them all a drink and they got to like him too. Indeed, some of the security guards there became friends and also looked after Joe outside of the venue. One such occasion was when he travelled to Pollerton, Carlow, to play a gig in the home of Angela Nolan, who had won a competition searching for Joe's biggest fan, on Gerry Ryan's 2FM show. When they arrived at the house, hundreds of women had turned up, and it was only the stable presence of the security guards that prevented his suit from being ripped from his back.

Cork was his favourite city to play, but sadly it was while playing a trio of sold-out dates there that Joe was dealt another hammer blow when Tony Newman, one of his greatest friends, became ill. After the penultimate show, Tony rang Joe from his hotel room late at night to tell him he would be unable to play the following night as he was in a great deal of pain. A doctor was called, and later told Joe and Ben that the drummer was 'a very sick man'. They were surprised – they had known that Tony had not been feeling well, but were not aware of just how seriously ill he was. 'He would talk off the pain as a side effect from a car crash decades previously. Or he'd say his troubles were related to a hernia. It was always something else until that night in Cork when we found out how sick he was,' Joe remembered. Tony had cancer.

They immediately considered cancelling the following night's show, but Tony wouldn't allow them. Even though he was advised not to play, he took painkillers so that he could get through it. 'He was wrecked; but he played that night as good as ever he played. He never missed a beat,' Joe recalled. After the show Joe wanted to bring Tony home in his car, but Tony refused. Perhaps knowing this had been his last show, he wanted to travel with the lads in the bandwagon. Back in Mullingar, Tony's doctor broke the news that Tony would not be drumming again. His cancer was terminal. Within a few months, Tony passed away.

Jason Fallon, a powerful and flamboyant drummer, joined the band, and he was a hit with the fans and with Joe, who admired his enthusiasm and his backing vocals. But Tony's loss, coupled with Liam Meade's departure, was a blow for Joe: for close to twenty years he had had 'the perfect backing band' and, for many fans, this was the definitive Drifters line-up. Joe managed to pick up the pieces in time for New Year's Eve 1999, however, when his millennium concert was beamed into over a million Irish homes from the Gleneagle in Killarney. It was a fitting tribute to Joe, and he was honoured to lead his country into the new century.

*

After the success of *21st Century Joe*, Joe released more albums and settled into a six-months-on/six-months-off routine that limited him to 'just' 200 shows a year. This gave him time to play around in his Mullingar studio, as well as play lots of golf and take some much-needed holidays.

The live shows were better than ever before and the Vicar Street shows were 'event' concerts. Such was the clamour for tickets that even the likes of Shane MacGowan would be forced to buy tickets from the touts outside the venue. MacGowan had an in-depth knowledge of Joe's songs and lyrics, and indicated to Joe on several occasions that he wanted to work with him, claiming to have written songs with Joe's voice in mind. Celebrities from all walks of show business would turn up to see Joe perform. Actor Colin Farrell, fast becoming Hollywood's hottest bright young thing, had been a Joe Dolan fan from his youth, and his parents Rita and Eamon had been big Joe fans for years. Farrell would regularly block-book rows of seats for himself and his family at Joe's concerts, and he and Joe got on like a house on fire backstage. Ronan Keating became even more of a regular at Joe shows, as did dozens of other entertainment and sporting stars.

Celebrity manager Louis Walsh paid Joe the ultimate compliment when he included two of his songs on his *History of Pop* compilation album, and film-maker Neil Jordan used Joe's 'Good Looking Woman' at a pivotal moment in his vibrant adaptation of Patrick McCabe's *Breakfast on Pluto*. Joe himself made an appearance in a *D'Unbelievables* film, and his songs featured in a number of other big Irish films and dramas.

Not only that, but Joe could even hold up sporting messiahs. On the day Páidí O'Sé arrived (by helicopter) at Bloomfield House Hotel in Mullingar on his first official day as Westmeath Football Manager in October 2003, he noticed Joe in the foyer and promptly disappeared with the singer for a few hours, leaving several top Westmeath GAA officials and Supporters Club officials waiting as Páidí and Joe had an impromptu lunch. They were great friends, and the larger-than-life GAA legend would often jest that Joe was the real reason he came to manage Westmeath.

Joe was always glad to meet and greet the big star, but he was just as happy – if not more – meeting the ordinary fan. To him, everybody was equal – no matter if you were Hollywood's brightest thing or just in off the ferry from Holyhead.

*

They say imitation is the sincerest form of flattery, and that was certainly how Joe Dolan felt when his concept began to be copied by artists all over the world. EMI MD Willie Kavanagh felt that the original *Joe's 90s* album started a genre all of its own. Many of Joe's former contemporaries on the Irish music scene of the 1960s, such as Dickie Rock and Brendan Bowyer, tried to emulate the concept with albums of their own for other labels, but none would come close to Joe's either commercially or musically. Even Pat Boone, Joe's old friend, tried his hand at more edgy material with an album of hard-rock covers.

One artist for whom it worked well was Tom Jones. A year after *Joe's 90s*, Jones released *Reload*, a collection of contemporary songs, and there was no doubt in EMI's eyes that the success of Joe's albums had been acutely observed by Jones's people. 'Was it coincidental? Did someone look and say, "You know that Joe Dolan album worked? Let's get Tom to do something similar"?' asked Willie Kavanagh. 'I think so . . .'

Joe's immaculate reinvention was not without its downsides though, as the renewed interest in him led to the release of dozens of opportunist compilation albums, the majority of which were haphazard, badly designed and poorly sequenced cash-ins that Joe had little or no control over. After Pye had ceased to exist, its back catalogue had been absorbed into a variety of other companies and the rights of many of Joe's hits up to the 1980s were scattered and difficult to control.

Compilations that got Joe's seal of approval included those from a Dutch record label, BR Music: *Singles +* and *The Story of Joe Dolan*. They were real labours of love for label boss Bert Van Breda, who was a massive Joe fan. Like so many in Europe, Bert first heard Joe in 1969 on Radio Luxembourg when 'Make Me an Island' broke. He bought the single and managed to pick up just about every other record Joe released. 'I was such a fan and I still am,' he said. 'To me Joe was the best singer in Europe. No one could sing like him and no one had songs like his.'

Like promoter James Cafferty, Bert was inspired by Joe's music to follow a certain career path. When he set up his own record label, he made sure the first release was a Joe Dolan one and, unlike the makers of other compilations, he always sought Joe's permission. Indeed, Joe's favourite compilation of his own music was *Singles +* as he appreciated that Bert had literally gone to the ends of the earth to source the material.

For his next studio album with EMI, Joe was keen to pay tribute to some of his favourite Irish songwriters and performers, and so *Home Grown* was born, released in spring 2003. Deeply impressed by the music and attitude of fellow midlands musician Mundy, who had overcome many obstacles to become one of Ireland's biggest stars on his own label, Joe wanted to record one of his songs for the album, but choosing just one proved difficult as Joe liked them all. In the end he went for the rocky 'Mexico', which he performed with Mundy on the first episode of Eamon Dunphy's short-lived TV3 chat show. Joe also thought highly of Aslan and their mercurial singer Christy Dignam, so he was happy to pay tribute to them with a spirited take of 'Crazy World'. And he couldn't pass up the opportunity to record something by Phil Lynott, who he had been friendly with – delivering a nice, continental take of 'Sarah'. Van Morrison's 'Have I Told You Lately That I Love You' was another in a long line of songs that Joe had performed live but never previously recorded. Christy Moore's reference to Joe on 'Lisdoonvarna' always pleased him and he had tried to repay the compliment in some shape or form over the years. Unfortunately, his souped-up version of 'Ride On' was not quite it. Much better was his version of The Frank and Walters hit 'After All', The Stunning's 'Brewing Up a Storm', David Gray's 'This Year's Love' and A House's 'Here Come the Good Times'. There was lyrical significance to the lyrics of U2's 'Stuck in a Moment', which Joe liked, and Joe's fellow *Father Ted* fans could rejoice with his take on the Divine Comedy's 'Songs of Love'. The best song on the album, though, would be 'Dreaming of You', a song seemingly hand-engineered for Joe by Liverpool band The Coral. The ragged, deeply romantic song is one of the best contemporary songs Joe ever recorded for EMI, and was one of his favourites too.

The follow-up to *Home Grown* would be *Double 0-Joe*, released in late 2004. With it, Joe brought a winning formula home. Recording in Mullingar, he created an album where several all-time classics rubbed shoulders with a handful of original tracks by Adrian Dolan, Peter Carroll and Ollie Hennessy. The title and cover image had a James Bond theme, and while fans expecting an album of James Bond classic themes would be disappointed, 'Have You Ever Been in Love' could have featured in any Bond film. 'The Air That I Breathe' saw Joe return to cover the first big American hit of Albert Hammond and Mike Hazelwood, his one-time writing team. Other tracks included Joe's favourite Paul Brady song, 'Crazy Dreams' (which they performed on television together), a lively take of Roy Orbison's 'I Drove All Night' and some classics that Joe had sung for years but never properly recorded: 'I Can See Clearly Now', 'Under the Boardwalk' and 'You've Lost That Loving Feeling'. He also recorded a song that many people thought was originally by him, George Baker's 'Little Green Bag', together with Freddie Mercury's moving final song with Queen, 'These Are the Days of Our Lives'. On the night Mercury died, the BBC showed the poignant and brave video that accompanied the song, and Joe remembers being moved to tears by it.

The originals on the album were all excellent too: 'Sometime Love Must Say Goodbye' is a classic Joe Dolan love song, while 'The Way I Feel About You' reaches for the dance floor, and the ballad 'The Only One' went on to become a highlight of the live show. 'Girl of My Dreams' rounded off the album on a high note.

Because the album contained fewer contemporary hits, it lacked the novelty value factor, but there was more of an original, organic feel to what he was doing and *Double 0-Joe* was something of a natural progression to a steadier pace for Joe.

18
Let there be love

There are few people in this world who can claim to have thrown Robbie Williams out of a bed, but Joe Dolan was one of them! Joe made plenty of fans and firm friends around the UK during his tours, and among his earliest fans was a youngster from Stoke-on-Trent in Staffordshire called Robert Williams. Joe regularly performed in and around the northern England town, and he became good friends with Peter and Janet 'Teresa' Williams, their children Robert and Sally and grandmother Betty. The Williams were a family of Irish ancestry who also ran one of Joe's favourite pubs in the city, the

Red Lion, and Joe had got to know the family as Peter Williams (under the stage name 'Pete Conway') had supported Joe on many of his UK engagements as a stand-up comedian and cabaret artist. Joe's music was played regularly in the Williams house, especially 'Teresa', which was Janet's first name.

Joe used to call into their house after shows in the region, and he would often stay for a couple of drinks and a chat. He always remembered their warm hospitality and spoke fondly about them over the years, laughing at what used to happen late at night. Instead of him going back to his hotel, Janet would offer to put Joe up for the night, which meant disturbing the sleeping arrangements in the Williams household. Inevitably it was young Robert who would have to sacrifice his resting place to allow Joe to put his head down for the night. EMI MD Willie Kavanagh said that Robbie often spoke highly about Joe, and even paid tribute to Joe on a documentary the label made: 'He said to me, "My first memories of Joe Dolan are that I had to give him me bed!" but he knew Joe from the time he was a kid.'

Years later, after Robert became Robbie and achieved international superstardom firstly with Take That and then as a solo star, Williams and Dolan found themselves sharing the same record label. Joe was delighted to be on the same label as the young star, and was even more delighted when word started to buzz around the Dublin office of EMI that a duet was on the cards.

'We talked about Joe doing a duet with Robbie,' Willie Kavanagh revealed. 'It was well talked about, believe you me.' Plans were first mooted when EMI in Ireland were trying to get Joe to do a swing album and there was a suggestion that he and Robbie could record an old Rat Pack standard. But Williams also had plans for a swing album, and the duet idea was put on ice as the timing was wrong. EMI promised to look at it again and right up until Joe's death, plans were still afoot.

Joe was a big fan of Robbie's work, and he kept a close eye on his career. His favourite Williams song was 'Better Man'. He loved the lyrics, the melody and Robbie's delivery, and he also appreciated the fact that Robbie had recorded it in Spanish, as it reminded Joe of his own Spanish-language discs from the 1970s. Joe had been keen to record a Williams song for some time, and when he was putting together a new album in 2001 he recorded 'Better Man'. He loved the song so much he kept it from the album and instead used it on a Greatest Hits collection he was putting together, even referring to the song in the collection's title, *No Better Man*.

In 1999 there was a real possibility that Joe would perform on the supporting bill for Williams's massive outdoor Slane Castle show, as EMI's David Gogan remembered: 'We were talking to Robbie's people about it, but the problem was that it was the biggest gig that Robbie had ever done in his career at that stage and he was shitting himself and he didn't want to be worrying about another element that they didn't really have any control over. They just wanted supports that he had nothing to do with essentially. It was before he had done Knebworth or anything. It was such a big gig, being filmed to go out live for Sky and the pressure was on. We were talking to them about it for a good while, but it didn't happen.' In the end, the support slots were filled by other acts, but Joe wasn't disappointed. He was glad of the chance to watch a young heir to the Dolan throne, and even joked that Robbie stole some of his moves that night.

But in 2004, as he celebrated his fortieth year on top of the Irish show-business pile, it was Joe's moves that would cause him to slow down a bit. All those years of hip shaking and pelvic thrusting had finally caught up with him. For most of the year Joe found himself leaving the stage in a small degree of pain, his legs and back the main source of his discomfort. Joe was usually quite loose-limbed and sprightly after a show, but for the first time in his career he was beginning to feel stiff and less agile. He even developed a slight limp. A hearty breakfast and a nimble round of golf the next morning would have sorted him before, but even this seemed to only exacerbate the pain and discomfort he was experiencing. He was also feeling a little tired, but he put this down to his hectic schedule. Proud and defiantly old school in that he tended to keep his complaints to himself, Joe didn't tell too many people of his struggles, but eventually it became obvious that something wasn't right. Band mates and friends noted he was not able to put the same levels of boundless energy into his shows, and medical counsel was sought. Specialists confirmed he needed a new hip bone.

On learning that he would have to be off the road for at least six months, Joe postponed the operation to allow him to complete a round of concert dates. Ever loyal to his fans, band and crew, he didn't want to just up sticks and cancel dates, even though he was playing through a lot of pain. He arranged redundancy for his players and riggers and he underwent the operation in Kilkenny, his presence in the hospital ward enough to send many of the nurses doolally.

As he recuperated, the six months soon became eleven months. Joe admitted that it 'killed him' to be off the road for so long, for both the fans' and band's sake alike. But the break gave him some time to reflect on his life, and realizing that he was not as invincible as he once thought, he decided to scale things back a bit. He would reduce the gig count and begin to take things a little easier.

While he was in hospital for his hip, the cause of his low energy levels and fatigue was discovered to be Type 2 Diabetes, a form of diabetes that usually develops slowly in adulthood.

Ever restless, even though he was off the road and not able to play music or golf, he still put his all into charity work, and dozens of charities benefited from his generosity during this time. He also started to work on new ideas and a few projects with his nephew Adrian.

The second he was able to swing a golf club again, rather than go straight back into the competitive throws of his regular four-ball, he played at several big charity events where he could take things a little easier. It was at one of these that he managed to see the funny side of his hip operation. (All the jokes were trotted out on the first tee: 'So, how does it feel to be hip again, Joe?' being one of many groan-inducing puns.) Following a conversation with Keith Duffy about his work with Irish Autism Action, Joe decided he would sell the old hip bone for the autism charity. He announced his intentions on the *Podge and Rodge* TV chat show, and the autographed hip bone was auctioned on eBay for close to €1,000.

Joe eventually returned to live action with a sold-out Vicar Street performance on 25 February 2006. He was back to his usual energetic self, striding across the famous stage as if he had never been away and even (against doctor's advice) attempting an Irish jig during 'Westmeath Bachelor'. It was hard to equate the graceful, grateful and confident Joe onstage that night with the nervous wreck backstage. He hadn't been as nervous about a show in years, and couldn't even meet anyone before he went on.

His nerves were compounded because in the year off the road he had lost long-term guitarist Joe Meehan, keyboardist Jimmy Mullally and drummer Jason Fallon, and this was his first live performance with his new band. Fallon, who had gone solo after appearing on RTÉ's *You're a Star*, was replaced by Ray Dolan, who had been Joe's percussionist for just under twenty years. Ray seized the opportunity to be behind the kit, and that first night he literally channelled the spirit of the late Tony Newman through his playing by listening to a tape of Tony's drumming in his headphones. Ray didn't need the tracks after a while and did a fine job as the drummer, striking up a good relationship with his godfather out front and with his brother Adrian in the engine room. Ray's new role was also a big hit with the fans, many of whom had taken Ray to their hearts.

As well as adding an extra dimension to Joe's live and studio sound via his percussion, easy-going Ray also ventured out to the front of the stage as a solo act, and he started to play as a support act to Joe, who had encouraged him to take up the guitar, telling him he could go anywhere in the world once he could sing a few songs. 'Everyone wants music,' Joe says. 'Everywhere in the world there is an audience for music. It's as good as having a trade just to be able to sing and play a few songs.'

Joe Meehan had played and recorded with a number of acts when Joe was off the road, and by the time Joe was able to return, Meehan had committed himself to tours with Keith McDonald and The Showband Show. Sean Kenny, whose son Conor played with Joe in the early 1990s, was brought in on guitar. Ironically, back in 1969 when Joe's original Drifters split, Joe had considered Sean but was too slow to snap him up, and he had joined the breakaway Drifters in The Times. Sean added great charm to the Joe show in its last few years. Enthusiastic and genuinely excited to be up onstage every night, his eagerness and striking guitar style rubbed off on those around him, and he and Joe enjoyed the banter onstage.

The search for a new keyboard man was not as easy, or as successful. A few auditioned but none seemed right. Just as it looked like the curse of the revolving piano stool was about to strike Joe again, events took a strange twist. Joe remembered seeing a keyboard player 'who had plenty of go in him' in Alicante; he and Ben had joined the piano man onstage one night to sing a couple of songs. That man was Johnny McCafferty, once a member of The Mighty Avons, who, like Liam Meade many years before, had said his big ambition in life was to play with Joe Dolan. A call went back out to Alicante and plane tickets were booked almost as soon as McCafferty could recover his jaw from the floor.

McCafferty was an enthusiastic addition to the band. 'He was mad into show business, and into the keyboards, although Adrian had to stop him waving and winking a few times,' Joe recalled. 'He had him a nervous wreck after a few days!' He then became a commuting member of the Joe Dolan band, jetting between Irish tours and his own gigs in the sweltering Alicante sunshine.

Because he surrounded himself with skilled musicians (and as many from Mullingar as possible), it didn't take long for Joe to feel confident in his new band, and although they took it deadly seriously they had fun onstage every single night. When the new-look band became totally comfortable with each other, they really hit their stride, particularly on what turned out to be Joe's last year onstage in 2007. 'As a matter of fact they were as good a band as ever we had,' Ben recalled. 'The banter was brilliant and Joe came with us in the bandwagon a good bit. There was a nice vibe to it.'

For the year he had been off the stage, life without Joe had been difficult for his fans, and it showed in the turnout, the adulation and the wild abandon displayed throughout the spring tour that followed the comeback show. Every subsequent show was a sell-out, and after taking a few months off in the summer to rest his new hip and come to terms with his diabetes, Joe bounced back with a season of shows in his beloved Killarney, where he had played almost 350 times. His bank holiday appearances there were always special, with many building their holidays around them, and Joe gave it his all.

In the early hours of a bank holiday Monday morning, as he drove back from Killarney to Mullingar, he stopped at the side of the road to take in the dawn chorus. He had a habit of ringing people at all hours, and this time he decided to ring his manager, Seamus Casey, for no other reason but to tell him how much he loved his job. 'Haven't I a great job? There's no job in Ireland like it,' he said, going on to detail how much he loved it, his fans, his family, his friends and his golf, and how his job allowed him the freedom to combine those loves. It was an unusually reflective call from a man who lived for today and only thought about tomorrow when he had to. But throughout the year Joe was becoming more reflective. It was as if he knew what lay ahead, and he wanted to get his thanks in early.

The tour continued sporadically into Christmas 2006, with plenty of breaks for the star man, who was grateful for the opportunity to add several rubber stamps to his passport. Golf was always the deciding factor in where Joe went on holidays, and he made the most of it as in earlier years his holiday destinations were decided upon by the band. For many years in the 1960s, '70s and '80s Joe and the band had holidayed together, even heading off on honeymoon with one band member.

Joe was usually the centre of attention, the first man to get a round in and to crack a joke, and everyone who went on these holidays has fond memories of him. One of Joe's great strengths was making instant friends with every staff member in a hotel, bar or restaurant. On one occasion in Spain in the early 1970s, Joe stood up to an unruly guest who was pestering some of the staff, and the following day, as Joe and the band departed for the airport, nearly all the staff stood in a line waving him and the band off.

A trip to play a show in Turkey in the mid 1970s acted as a cue for one particular holiday in the Balkans and the Black Sea. The region was trying to put itself on the tourism map when Joe and a gang of legendary Mullingar characters arrived. They stayed in Romania, Bulgaria and Turkey, and because the economies of the countries were so poor at the time, the gang were akin to billionaires. Joe won big in a casino and sat with a sack of notes at his feet. As he went to leave, he gave all of his winnings away to hard-pressed locals.

His generosity on holiday was legendary. 'Most show-business people are slow to buy a round, shall we say, but Joe was generous to a fault; he was the decentest man you could ever go out with. We'd all be out for a meal and he'd insist, "I'm getting this," and there would be no stopping him. He enjoyed the enjoyment of others,' his manager remembered.

Joe tipped well if the staff were as friendly to him as he was to them, recalled his brother Ben. 'He'd be great friends with the waitresses. He respected them and always left a few bob when he was going. Joe was also good at remembering people's names. If he made friends with anyone, he would remember them. Even the fans, the majority of them he knew well as friends. It didn't matter where he was in the world, he'd strike up a friendship the minute he'd arrive. If it was in a hotel, or a restaurant, the first thing he'd do would be to ask their name. He would then address them by name all night: "Ok, Mary, I think I'm going to have a nice steak tonight, Mary." You could go back to the same hotel three or four years later and he'd be looking for Mary first and foremost.'

Joe hated to relax too much on holidays and preferred to be doing things. To Joe's mind you could relax all you want between shows so why relax on holidays? If others didn't share that view, he would try to change their minds. A speciality of his was to burn newspapers as people read them.

As he scaled back his international ambitions, Joe enjoyed returning to countries where he had played before but never had time to truly experience. He was always a fan of Mediterranean countries, and returned to the Med many times, either with a group or with a few close friends, always spearheaded by his brother Ben and wife Helen, together with close friends Isabella Fogarty, Gene Harnett, Damien Ryan, James Cafferty and others.

With golf on the top of the agenda, certain countries emerged as favourites, with Spain, America and Thailand among Joe's top destinations. But he and his golfing buddies would literally play anywhere that had a good golf course, and they liked to visit any that hosted big tournaments. However, there was little chance of really getting away from it all.

Denis Mee, who went to Thailand with Joe several times, remembers that even in far-flung places people would make a beeline for him. 'He'd attract people from all over the world, and they'd all sit down with him and everyone would be waiting for every word to drop out of his mouth. I don't know whether they liked him because of who he was, or because he could tell a yarn, but when we'd be away he'd attract people like a magnet.' Sometimes people would pester him to sing. If he was on a big golfing trip with fellow musicians and pro-golfers, he would gladly sing, but when he was on his own holidays it often rattled him.

'It was the one thing that got to him on holidays,' Ben recalls, 'but he was always good humoured about it. If someone came up and said, "Are you going to sing a song, Joe?" it didn't sound so bad, but when people almost demanded him to sing, then that got to him. If anyone got a bit stroppy, he'd say, "Now I'm on my holidays," and it usually worked.'

In Thailand he would often succumb to request fatigue, and if people pestered him for songs too much he would signal to Denis to get a motorbike. 'I'd put him on the back of an oul' motorbike and we'd go off about ten miles up the beach, and we'd sit in a restaurant with no one in it who was either in the business or who knew who we were and we'd watch the sun go down over the Gulf of Siam. Those are my happiest memories of Joe.'

Joe, Ben, Denis and a variety of pals including Peter Boyle, Damien Ryan, Paul Claffey, Sean Skehan and others used to love eating at a little beach restaurant in Thailand run by an elderly couple. 'The shack would be Joe's place.

He'd lie on the beach for a while to top off the tan, but you'd always find him sitting at the counter of that little shack drinking tea,' Denis said, laughing. The same restaurant now has a little shrine to its favourite customer, 'Mister Joe'.

Joe certainly loved to indulge in his food while on holiday, and if he could get it, a bottle of Chef sauce would be on every table. Joe's love of brown sauce was legendary. And not any old brown sauce, it had to be Chef sauce, a staple of any Irish table. He would be just as happy eating fish cooked fresh off a boat or a kebab at the side of the street as he was in a fancy restaurant.

Joe's golfing adventures ensured he also had plenty of holidays on his native sod, but there were other times when he preferred a break much, much closer to home, on one of Westmeath's many lakes. 'I used to love going out for a day's fishing on Lough Owel,' he revealed with a smile. As well as being one of Ireland's largest freshwater lakes and one of the main sources of drinking water for Westmeath, Lough Owel is also a popular trout-fishing lake. The best time for a summer angler to catch any of the lake's treasures is in the evening, after dark, which suited Joe to a tee as it meant he could be away from it all for a day and night.

He would usually only give a few hours' notice to his regular boatmen, Denis Mee and sound technician Jim Fox. 'He'd ring me some nights – at two or three or four in the morning, his usual time to call people – and say, "We'll go out on the lake tomorrow." That was Denis's cue to make the necessary arrangements and to prepare some food.

'We never fished, but we ate well and we drank like fish. It was great craic,' Joe joked. 'Ahh no, we did fish but we were useless.'

Owel's water quality is remarkable, and on a bright, sunny day you can see down to a depth of over twenty feet. Often Joe would not be able to resist and he'd dive in. As they waited for sun down, the boat would usually head for Srudarra Island – or 'Sooder Island' as Joe called it – a secluded suntrap, where they usually set up camp. If someone else had got there first, they would head instead for the smaller Lady's Island or Carrickphilbin Island, where Denis would set up a barbecue, the moment Joe had been waiting for. 'He would bring this big bag of food – chopped vegetables, spices, meat, sauce, the works – and he always brought a wok with him. We'd light an open fire and cook the best of stuff on it,' Joe enthused. Even though Joe was no slouch in the kitchen himself, he thought the world of

Denis's cooking, often bragging about Denis's culinary skills when they holidayed abroad. 'Jaysus, I used to think that they'd be thinking I was his personal chef, I'd be cringing,' Denis laughs.

Then it was time to fish. Once back on the boat and surrounded by night, Joe would let go on the ebb and flow and cast his rod into the water. A blue earthly heaven lit by a sparkling midnight moon, his evening in paradise always ended too soon. Joe was never too starry-eyed about his angling skills, however, and he rarely troubled a trout out of its watery habitat. Instead, he was happy that his father's talent had been passed on to his elder brother Paddy, who was noted as one of the top anglers in the country.

Paddy would often be at Joe to learn how to fish properly and to see more of the lakes and get more fresh air, as Joe remembered. 'I'd say to him, "Sure aren't I going out with Denis and Jim and they with a field kitchen?" I loved it out there; we'd laugh, talk and crack jokes, swim and eat and drink. Simple pleasures really, but lovely.' Joe would sometimes land the boat up on the shore and call in to his cousin, also named Joe Dolan, who lived by the lake.

However, even when at his most relaxed, Joe was beginning to show signs that all was not well. While on holiday in Cadiz in September 2005 with a group of friends, Joe collapsed in the foyer one night after complaining of feeling weak. Both Ben and James remember him coming to as if nothing had happened, and the blackout was put down to his diabetes. Ben was concerned that he wasn't taking his diabetes seriously enough, and James felt that his dearest friend was showing signs that his health was more delicate than he was letting on.

In late 2006 and early 2007, Joe really got to work on some projects that relied more on his voice than on showmanship, something that suited him down to the ground as he knew he couldn't continue at the same pace. The plan was for a gradual slow-down, but instead of consolidating his fanbase as he moved into the twilight of his career, he extended it even further by working harder and harder.

At the start of 2007, the Irish mobile-phone operator Meteor pitched an idea for an advertisement that Joe felt would help him connect to another generation of young fans. The advert played on Joe's legendary status by placing him in an opulent bathroom as a friend rang him up to ask for the correct lyrics to 'Good Looking Woman'. Though the Meteor advert was a hard shoot to do because he was immersed in a bath full of water for several hours, Joe enjoyed it. 'Is it "Oh me oh my" or "Oh my oh me"?' the friend asks as she calls Joe. From his gold-plated bath tub, a champagne-quaffing Joe says, "Just follow me" and then clicks his fingers to reveal an in-house band who start playing the song for Joe to sing along to. A send-up of both the song and Joe himself, the ad was scheduled to run on Irish TV in the summer of 2007, and Joe hoped to release an album at the same time to coincide with it.

The first of his ongoing projects was a jazzy collection of swing classics for EMI. Smoke signals had also been sent out for a duets album, and other plans were afoot as he set about redefining his voice for another century. When he was off the road, he delighted his country-and-western-loving brother Ben and manager Seamus by finally agreeing to lay down vocal guides for an album of country-flavoured songs. He also began working on an album of traditional Irish, folk and field songs, something he had promised himself for years. In an interview on Midlands 103FM with Noel O'Farrell in 2004, he had signalled his trad intentions by singing an unaccompanied version of 'The Rising of the Moon', the 1798 Irish Rebellion song written by John Keegan Casey. Casey, known as 'the poet of the Fenians', was born in Milltown, near Rathconrath, just outside Mullingar, close to where Joe's inspirational uncle Frank Gavigan lived, and the song was one of the most famous of all the 1798 songs that Joe had sung since childhood.

But the sessions were put off for a while as Joe was complaining of feeling drained and tired. He began to feel low, and didn't know what was wrong with him. Everything seemed to be pointing to his diabetes, but Joe wasn't convinced. He was also complaining of a pain in his leg. His blues were compounded by the passing of legendary concert promoter Jim Aiken in February 2007. Aiken had promoted hundreds if not thousands of Joe Dolan shows since the early 1960s, and Joe always spoke highly of him, remembering his generosity and warmth.

He was given a big lift in March 2007 when the *Irish World* in London awarded him their ultimate accolade, an Outstanding Contribution to Music award. He travelled to London for the gala ceremony and wowed the crowds with a couple of impromptu songs. He then played a series of rapturously received UK dates, returning to the Galtymore in Cricklewood for his first show there in years. Even he was astounded by the welcome he received at the famous London venue, which closed its doors for ever in May 2008. He also played a dazzling show at Cheltenham Town Hall on 15 March. The crowd went wild, and Joe said he would be back for a full UK tour. Both he and the band were on top form, and as a tribute to James Brown (who died in Christmas 2006), the original 'hardest working man in show business', and to show he was back on the way to good health, Joe included Brown's 'I Feel Good' into his sets.

Joe then returned to the stage in Ireland for a series of spring concerts. An Easter show at the Pavillion Theatre in Dun Laoghaire was attended by dozens of his closest friends, and was the first show Isabella had been to in about a year. She couldn't believe how good he was that night. 'It was one of the best shows I ever saw him play. I remember saying to him after, "Fair play, pet, you haven't lost it." He laughed and said, "Oh God, babe, we must have been great then!"'

Everything was on the up for Joe, and he was even talking about a return to Russia, to mark the thirtieth anniversary of his historic trip there, to the point where a few dates were booked. But it was around this time that those close to him noticed his recurring nosebleeds, which were leaving him quite pale. He had also started to lose weight. As it transpired, he had been suffering from the nosebleeds for some time, but he had not made an issue of them. At first doctors thought it was related to a pancreatic problem associated with his diabetes, but it was discovered that he had a low blood platelet count. Doctors could not identify the cause, but gave him a blood transfusion, which seemed to help. Ben remembers he was 'as right as rain, jumping out of his skin' for a couple of months. Then he would be down again, and another transfusion would give him a boost.

Joe had taken a break after his Easter 2007 dates and he would not be back on the road until July, so he refocused his energies on the collection of swing-era big band and jazz classics. Joe wanted to call the album *Let There Be Love*, after the classic 1940 song popularized by Nat King Cole in the 1960s, and it was one of the first songs Joe recorded for the album. The laid-back collection was something he had been born to make, and Joe's tuneful phrasing is almost perfect throughout, even when he is singing in Italian.

Although he was ill when he started to record the album in the summer of 2007, he didn't let on to anyone, saying it was just a cold or low energy levels due to his diabetes. 'You honestly couldn't talk to him about his health, you wouldn't get a straight answer, or he might turn the question back on you,'

Ben recalled. 'He didn't want you to pass remarks on his appearance. He never passed his troubles on to anyone else, which he probably should have. You always felt that you were sort of working against the grain if you tried to help him, or were asking him how he was.' Ben reckoned this reluctance was almost hereditary. 'In general our family are like that. They didn't want to annoy you,' he said.

Ben also said that Joe sometimes forgot his diabetes medication, which used to infuriate the elder brother. 'He'd turn up at places and say he'd forgotten his tablets and we'd send someone out and get his doctor to OK the prescription. The fact of him needing them and going without them used to drive me mad. He never forgot about a gig or was late for one, never forgot about golf or was late for a round, but it seemed that he didn't put his health on the same scale . . .'

Following a blood transfusion, Joe was always in good form for a couple of weeks, and his studio work was excellent. 'Even though, as it turned out, he wasn't in great shape, his voice was in great shape,' says Ben, reflecting on his brother's singing. 'Some of it was sung in a lower key to what he would normally sing, but he really embraced it and he was still singing in a higher key than he probably should have been. I wouldn't say Sinatra or Pavarotti recorded anything as high at that age.'

Recording was then put on hold as rehearsals got underway in Mullingar for his summer and autumn tours. Joe was looking forward to the tours, as earlier in the year he had bought a new Mercedes and this would be an opportune time to test it out as he drove between shows. He sold his old one on to his brother Ben, but when a few things started to go wrong with it, Joe scolded Ben for 'abusing' his old car. 'That was the sort of love/hate relationship we had. Everything that went wrong was my fault!' Ben joked.

Anyone who met Joe during that summer remembers he was on good, if reflective, form. In Mullingar and elsewhere he caught up with a lot of old friends, including some he hadn't seen in several years. The Meteor television advertisement started to run in June and July, and pretty soon everyone was talking about Joe Dolan again. Backed up by a billboard campaign, the ads meant that ticket sales for Joe's autumn shows were going through the roof, and even before he had started the tour every date was sold out. Dates announced for Christmas were also snapped up, and a few shows announced for February followed suit. More were added to meet demand, and soon the man who had promised to take things a little easier had an extraordinarily busy schedule ahead.

Joe's health was beginning to fluctuate as the summer tour progressed. Joe put a brave face on it and continued to put his heart and soul into the gigs, but after the initial dates in Killarney, his energy levels were beginning to suffer. Preferring to save everything for the shows, he decided he would not take part in every afternoon soundcheck. The tour was a biggie: Joe was calling into Nenagh on 29 July, followed by Monastrevin and Bantry, then back to Killarney on 4 August. The second leg would begin on 10 August in Cork, with Joe playing further dates in Mullingar, Dublin, Limerick and Killarney.

The first series of dates were rated by long-time fans as some of the best he ever did. With Joe and the band in scintillating form, the set-list became braver, reflecting the direction Joe was hoping to take the following year, with some of his epics from yesteryear polished up and given a fresh coat of paint. To the audience, all was fine onstage. But what very few people outside of the band and Joe's inner circle knew was that Joe was struggling after the shows.

At the Greville Arms Hotel in Mullingar on Tuesday 14 August, Joe played what would turn out to be his last ever hometown show. Even though no one knew that at the time, there was something in the air that night that made it the most electrifying Joe Dolan show in Mullingar in over a decade. For the first time in many years, though, Joe didn't stick around for drinks after the gig, and he was soon in his car and bound for Dublin, where he would be taking to the stage at the Red Cow the next night.

James Cafferty was again proud to be promoting his friend at Moran's Red Cow. He remembers in particular the anticipation and expectation before the gig. 'Joe was the only artist who gave me a buzz. I always looked forward to the show, getting it organized and everything. What I enjoyed the most was to see the reaction of the audience, how happy he made them. They adored him that night, they absolutely adored him,' he said. Tellingly, for the second night in a row, Joe was too tired to see any fans after the show.

Joe was in Limerick on 17 August, and a night later he was back for a final full house at the Gleneagle in Killarney. A few days off the road followed, and Joe was then in Navan on 22 August. The following night Joe officially opened the Carlton Slearwater Hotel in Ballinasloe with a sold-out show, his thirteenth straight sell-out in a row. A major fuss was made about him, and photo shoots had been organized. From the moment he arrived in the town, Joe was the centre of attention, and although he was tired, feeling a big 'chesty', and his bandmates thought he looked pale, he was happy to give freely of his time, as he always had done. A big crew from Mullingar were among the 700-plus crowd, and they agreed that it was another outstanding, committed performance from Joe. He really put on the ritz for the new hotel and it was rated by dozens of seasoned Joe-watchers as one of the best shows he had played in County Galway in a number of years, certainly the best in Ballinasloe.

But Joe could remember little of that night, and such was his fatigue he could barely walk coming offstage that night. Denis Mee, who always led him from the stage to the sanctuary of his dressing room, remembers Joe was 'very, very tired' that night and delicate on his feet. Joe told others he was 'wrecked', and he admitted that he could not remember the last twenty minutes of the concert. He said the crowd were driving him along but it had been a blur. Some fans and old friends came into his room that night and although he was friendly and forthcoming, he just wanted to be left alone. He wanted to go home.

The morning after Ballinasloe, Joe sought medical counsel. His blood platelet count was low again, and over the past few weeks he had contracted pleurisy. Although he had been taking his diabetes medication, his diabetes may have contributed to the Ballinasloe blackout. He was advised to move the remaining August dates to the second leg of the autumn tour, which was scheduled to start on 27 September in Abbeyleix, County Laois.

Over thirteen hot August nights, Joe had worked his magic almost non-stop. Each show was equally exhilarating and exhausting for him, but he had given them his absolute all for the full two and a half hours, pumping out a tail-spinning set of old classics and new favourites. Joe and the band had never sounded so good.

Astonishingly, Joe completed the recording sessions for the *Let There Be Love* album between 2 September and 23 September. He had been told to take things easier after Ballinasloe, but Joe didn't know the meaning of the word. He seemed to be in good form as he recorded the album, even if he was a little up and down with his energy levels and his weight. 'We had no idea he was ill,' EMI's Willie Kavanagh says. 'He was in the office and he looked like he had lost weight. I remember saying to him that he had lost weight and he said, "Oh yeah, I had a bit of a cold." . . . But some of the vocals are wonderful. I think he put his heart and soul into it, I really do. When you listen to it now I think you realize maybe he knew a lot more then than he was pretending to us or anybody else.'

Joe had been adamant that he did not want to go down the clichéd, zipp-ity-doo-dah Rat Pack route with this album. He wanted to distance himself from standards that were too obvious, as definitive versions of these had already been done by Sinatra & Co, and both Robbie Williams and Westlife had already released crooner-style albums. Joe was keen to broaden the spec-trum, and with songs like Dusty Springfield's 'Spooky', he did just that. Another stand-out track is the Italian 'Volare (Nel Blu, Di Pinto Di Blu)', and more thoughtful material, such as the title track and 'It Had to Be You', dem-onstrate that age and his recent bout of ill-health had done little to affect Joe's big voice on a slow song. Joe's voice was so unique that some of the more familiar material was given a new twist, and 'Ain't That a Kick in the Head' certainly has Joe's own stamp on it. He even sneaks in a bit of his Mullingar brogue on 'The More I See You', one of the few times he did so. Joe was particularly keen to put down a class cut of 'Just a Gigolo/I Ain't Got Nobody', and this was intended to be released as a Christmas single.

Dave McCune assembled a crack squad of seasoned rhythm, blues and jazz players for the album, including the Phil Ware Trio, one of Ireland's finest jazz trios, and Michael Buckley, the saxophone star of the Irish jazz scene. Joe knew the album was going to sound great live, and a gala presenta-tion of the album was on the cards. Willie Kavanagh made it clear that the label had plenty of faith in Joe's future. 'Someone asked us, "What's next for Joe Dolan?" When you do the standards, the contemporary and the Irish stuff, there are only so many songs that you can do. You can't go and do the same thing again, so we had a number of plans for him.' Among these ideas were a light opera album, a collection of contemporary international songs and a duets album.

There were also plans for some huge one-off shows with a full big band and orchestra at select venues around the country, including the National Concert Hall, the INEC in Killarney, the Royal Theatre in Castlebar and Cork Opera House. These concerts would have given him a chance to perform some of the swing classics and possibly some of his more operatic tracks, as well as orchestral reworkings of his greatest hits and some lesser-known classics. If there were still people out there who doubted that Joe was Irish musical royalty, then these stately shows would have proved them wrong; they would have been crowning moments in a glittering career.

19
Goodbye my lovely friend . . .

The fans started to arrive at the Abbeyleix Manor Hotel on that warm and balmy 27 September evening from about 6 p.m., but the anticipation and excitement had built up much earlier in the day. A Joe Dolan show was always a big event, and Abbeyleix was buzzing, especially as this was Joe's first concert there since he had played the Happyland Ballroom in the 1960s. Hairdressers and beauticians had been booked out, restaurants were seating more covers than usual and pubs were bustling with the hum of expectant concert-goers. Tickets had sold out long in advance and the hotel itself was booked up months ago. There wasn't a room to be had in the town. Joe himself couldn't even get a room for the night, although if many in the audience had known that there would have been plenty of salacious offers of bed and breakfast.

From about 6.30 p.m. onwards, a steady queue started to wind its way through the hotel complex as concert-goers wanted to make sure they got the best seats, the band of loyal fans who went to nearly every Joe show, as ever, at the top of the queue. The band had finished their soundcheck earlier that afternoon, and they chilled out and lounged around in their dressing room backstage, some playing cards while others were just happy to relax and chat. All the boys were in relatively good spirits considering most of them harboured some worries from the previous day's tour rehearsal. Joe had not been on good form and he sat down with his head bowed for most of it, singing with his arm resting on his knee holding the microphone. Although his voice was impeccable, he was pale and withdrawn and after rehearsing a handful of songs he stopped singing. He just wasn't himself and seemed troubled.

Joe hadn't made the soundcheck either. Earlier that day, Joe and his manager met for lunch in Mullingar. Before they sat down to eat, Joe told Seamus that he wasn't feeling too well, that he was a bit tired. Seamus remarked that he was pale and suggested that Joe should see a doctor. Joe said he would, but in true Joe style he added that he was hungry and they ordered lunch. His manager remembers that Joe ate well, cleared his plate in fact, and they shared a final pot of tea. When Seamus suggested he should cancel that night's show, Joe wouldn't hear of it. They went to the doctor and afterwards Joe went for a lie-down in his Mullingar apartment. Again Seamus suggested Joe should cancel Abbeyleix, and Joe refused once more, saying he would be 'all right in a while'.

Later that afternoon, Ben picked up Joe and they set out for Abbeyleix in Joe's recently purchased car. As they pulled up outside the hotel a little after six o'clock, some lucky fans managed to grab Joe for a photograph and an autograph. Joe always had time for his fans, in sickness or in health. There must be more photos of Joe with his fans than any other entertainer. That evening, one remarked that Joe was looking a bit pale. He explained he had a cold.

Although on relatively good form when he arrived at the dressing room, it was noticeable that he was not his normal jovial self. He was still experiencing some mild chest pains, and Joe confided in his older brother that he was feeling a bit weak and one of his hands was ablaze with pins and needles. Ben, thinking that this could have been related to his diabetes, told him that if he wasn't feeling up to it then there would be no problem in cancelling the show, but Joe refused to entertain such a notion.

After taking his medication and drinking some tea, Joe perked up considerably and, with an hour to go until show time, he, Ben, Denis Mee and Johnny McCafferty played cards in the dressing room as the venue filled up. Adrian and Ray Dolan, Frankie McDonald and Sean Kenny were also there. They talked about the shows coming up, joking that their manager must have been playing darts on a map of Ireland again, as the following night they were due to play in County Meath, and then on Saturday they were due at the Burnavon Theatre in Cookstown, County Tyrone, followed by Vicar Street in Dublin on Monday night. There was no let-up after this either, as the tour was due to call in to Carrickfergus, Omagh, Letterkenny, Tullamore, Wexford, Kells, Dún Laoghaire, Lisburn and Killarney before finishing with three sold-out October bank holiday dates in Sligo. A *Late Late Show* appearance on 9 November would be the last date before a Christmas tour.

The band all signed a sixtieth birthday card for a friend of Joe's, music promoter Patsy Rogers, who was expected to attend the show that night. Joe signed it twice, which caused some in the band to worry, but other than that he appeared to be well.

When the band got ready to take their positions onstage, Joe wished everyone the best of luck. It was highly unusual for Joe to be with the band at the last minute, as he almost always changed in a hotel suite or a bedroom before being brought to the stage. Indeed, for well over twenty years, a room or suite in which to change was the only item on Joe's hospitality rider. But on this September night he was happy to be with the band and they were glad of his company.

'We had good oul' craic at the cards, and he seemed to be in good form,' Denis Mee, his PA for over twenty years, remembers. 'But when Ben and the boys went off for the stage he said to me, "Jaysus I really don't feel like this tonight." I told him, "Sure don't go on." He said, "Ah no, I'll go out and see how I get on."'

As they walked from the dressing room to the stage, Denis noticed that

Joe seemed unsteady on his feet. He asked him if he was okay, but Joe motioned for Denis to keep walking. They then heard the band launch into their usual sixteen-bar overture. Inside the room, the sound of rolling drums and bass guitar, a golden blast of brass and the timeless melodies of the guitar and piano, overpowered the clinking of glasses and the hum of pre-gig conversation. The crowd started to clap and cheer, knowing their man would be with them in little under a minute. Close to 500 necks craned forward, all eyes fixed on the set of double doors at the side of the stage.

Outside, Joe stood alone in his thoughts for a few seconds as Denis made one final check to ensure that the path to the doors was clear. Joe blessed himself and whispered a prayer to St Blaise, the patron saint of throats, as he did every night before he went onstage. Every year, on the Feast of St Blaise on 3 February, Joe's throat was blessed, and he always carried some of St Blaise's oil with him, spreading a drop on his throat every night. When he finished his prayer, Joe and Denis rolled a few playful punches to each other's chests, as they typically did to get Joe fired up, although the strength didn't seem to be there that night.

Denis asked Joe if he was ready, and Joe nodded that he was. As the band's overture switched into the time-honoured intro of 'Good Looking Woman', Joe took a deep breath and blessed himself again. Inside, the spotlight was fired up and an arc of brilliant white light opened out at the doors. Five hundred fans took a deep breath.

Denis pushed open the door and Joe Dolan entered the room. As the spotlight picked him out, it reflected off his white suit and filled the room with (de)light. The crowd roared, their screams of approval enough to knock out any last-minute doubts or nerves. His smile wide, his arms outstretched, Joe greeted his people. He arrived centre-stage right on cue for the first breakdown of the song he had played every night since 1970 and never once grown tired of performing. He took his position, saluted the front row, grabbed the microphone and sang, "When God created a woman for me . . .' The venue erupted. A forest of arms rose into the air to wave, point and sway, and everyone sang along. The swell of goodwill filling the room soon raised everyone to their feet, their collective smile enough to make the spotlight seem almost redundant. The crowd barely had time to show their appreciation before Joe and the band followed it with the Jeff Lynne song 'The Way Life's Meant To Be', with Joe ablaze as he accentuated certain lines. Joe thanked the crowd and then launched into his big hit from 1964, 'The Answer to Everything', the starting point for a medley of his first hits. To the casual observer, all appeared to be well onstage. Joe's voice was strong and he was putting everything he had into the performance, just as he had always done. But some of his regular fans could tell that Joe was not looking well. Some remarked afterwards that they had never seen him as pale.

As soon as Joe launched into 'Ciara', his first big hit of the 1990s and his fourth song of the night, he began to struggle for breath, and his fire started to go out. Although he gamely tried to sing the up-tempo number, for the first time in his life the power simply wasn't there. He glanced at his nephew Adrian. The band knew he was struggling and they tried to carry him to the end of the song so he could take a breather. The brass section, who sang backing vocals on this song, found themselves handling the lead vocals, and they brought the song home a few bars early, just on the verse that Joe and Adrian co-wrote almost fifteen years before. Joe turned around to Adrian and told him that he couldn't continue the concert.

'He always gave it 100 per cent, but that last night onstage was the very first time I saw Joe and I thought, "You know, he's not well,"' Adrian recalls. 'He looked around to me and said, "I can't go on . . ." and it was tearing me apart to see him like that. He was nearly the same colour as the suit. And I just thought, "This is not fair, we're whipping him." But he went up and he sang the songs one after another, and sang them as best he could, but he just turned around after 'Ciara' and looked at me like this [nods head from side to side] and he kind of smiled at me as he said, "I can't go on . . ." It was the saddest smile I've ever seen. It must have ripped him apart.'

Joe then turned to the audience and apologized. 'I'm very, very sorry, and I have never had to do this in the last forty years, but I just can't go on,' he said. 'I don't know what's wrong with me . . . I'm sorry for the disappointment I've caused . . .' Before he could finish the sentence he began to well up, and one by one the audience rose in spontaneous applause. As he moved off the stage, it was to a standing ovation.

Waiting for him at the side of the stage was Denis Mee. 'He walked over to the side of the stage and I put my arm up for him to hold. You could see the tears in his eyes. I gently brought him off the stage and down on to the ground where I put my leather jacket around him to keep him warm, and we moved out gently. The crowd were still applauding him as he left the room, and when we got outside he just broke down crying. He kept saying, "I've let everybody down, I've let everybody down." I said, "No, you let nobody down, don't be like that. If you can't do it you can't do it." But he was in tears still. I brought him back into the dressing room and he broke down again.'

After a while there was a knock on the door and the secretary of Joe's GP, who happened to be at the show that night, came in. They talked for a bit and Joe phoned his doctor. The rest of the band and a few others arrived, but Joe just wanted to be left on his own. He wanted to go home. Numerous offers to drive him home to either Dublin or Mullingar were made, but Joe refused them all. 'No, I'll be all right, I'll be all right,' he insisted. A garda friend at the show offered to make sure Joe got home safely, but Joe didn't want any fuss, insisting that it was just a dizzy spell. After a short rest he went to his car and, despite numerous pleas for him not to, he drove back to his Dublin home. He was monitored with phone calls as he made his way back, and an hour and a half after leaving the hotel he arrived at Foxrock safe, sound and emotional. It was the first time in his entire career that he had to abandon a show like that, and it hurt.

He told Seamus the next morning that by the time he got to Dublin he felt better, and could have turned the car back and finished the show. As a precaution, however, Joe checked into the Mater Private Hospital, and on medical advice the rest of the tour was postponed. Joe optimistically rescheduled all the dates for November and December, with others pushed into February.

Joe received another blood platelet boost, but doctors could still not get to the root of his blood disorder and his lethargy. He was released from hospital early the next week and, despite being tired, was in relatively cheerful form. Nevertheless, friends, family and colleagues were all worried. For the first time in their lives they saw a vulnerable Joe Dolan. The only health complaint Joe had had previously was a sore throat, and most people thought that Joe's voice would go before Joe. When hoarse after a run of gigs, Joe had been told by a doctor as early as 1963 that unless he gave up singing for at least six months he was likely to lose his singing voice for ever, the doctor warning him that if his advice went unheeded, Joe would only be able to sing for a couple more months. But Joe decided to take the gamble. In the early 1980s, another doctor had told Joe that he would have to stop singing because his throat had been so badly damaged by his vocal histrionics, but yet again Joe had stood firm, telling his brother Ben, when he had asked what Joe was going to do next, 'Well, I'm not giving up singing.' In more recent years, another doctor had said the same thing, but, well-acquainted with Joe's determination, he knew there was no point in recommending a time when Joe should stop: 'Joe will tell you when he doesn't want to work any more, because he won't be able to,' he would say.

However, this time, having been told to rest, Joe did just that, despite being keen to get back on the road (and to the golf course). To keep busy, he made plans to do up his house in Dublin and he visited friends and family in Mullingar. He was in and out of hospital over a couple of weeks. During this time, he never lost his sense of loyalty to the band and his road crew, and Adrian remembers visiting Joe in hospital when the only thing on his mind was the lads and how they were getting on.

'I asked Joe how he was feeling and all he wanted to talk about was the lads. I told him that Gerry Oakes was doing a bit of work with Alan and Paddy Nolan and that Dave Hughes was at something else; Frankie had a couple of gigs coming up and Ray had a couple of gigs, and he said, "I'm glad. I'm glad they have something. It's just that I feel guilty because I'm not able to be out there." None of us minded about the shows, because Joe was ill and needed time to get back on his feet, but here he was feeling guilty, thinking that he had let the lads down, which he hadn't. He had that feeling whenever he wasn't working. "When I'm out there I'm working and I demand a lot but, you know, I'm glad I have ye," he would say.'

Joe had plenty of visitors when he was in the Mater and he kept in touch with everyone by phone and by text. He was a dab hand at text messaging, even though he felt they were destroying the art of joke telling, something he was a grand master in.

Several people have kept the text messages they received from Joe when he was in hospital, and they are cherished items. When James Cafferty thought he had misplaced his mobile, all he cared about was a text message on it that Joe had sent in November. James had sent Joe a get-well-soon card and Joe had replied with a text: 'Thanks James, you're the man. Hope I didn't upset everything. Back rocking soon. Love to all.'

When Seamus visited Joe in hospital, they would reminisce about their adventures together on the road, from the red suits to the Red Square, promising each other that those days would never end. They would enthusiastically discuss how they would change the whole show around, with Joe scaling things back completely to just a few dozen shows a year. Joe was looking forward to the following year, and Seamus was heartened by his positivity. Joe had been told that by Christmas everything would be OK, and he was excited about getting back on the road to recovery.

Others remember Joe's sadness about being unable to promote his *Let There Be Love* album, which had been released in November. He loved the songs and even in his hospital bed he was still singing them, and signing copies of the album for nurses and other staff.

After each blood transfusion he would feel much better, and after one particular 'top up' in November, Joe even felt good enough to play golf, joining Ben, his nephew Ray and his regular four-ball partner Damien Ryan on a bright, but cool and crisp morning at Rathcore Golf Club. At the first tee they separated into pairs and Joe teamed up with Ray for the round. The match was all-square as the players came down the eighteenth hole. Both Ben and Damien then hit into the water while Joe and Ray saw their shots sail over the lake and on to the green. They converted their putts and won the round by a margin of one hole. Joe was delighted. Ben remembers the round as being 'great craic', with plenty of laughs and jokes as the four players sampled all the challenges the relatively new course had to offer, although Joe had been a little anxious on the first hole as he had forgotten to pack any confectionary to give his blood sugar levels a boost. Damien came to the rescue, and Joe perked up as he nibbled on a Mars Bar. 'Joe was in great form afterwards, and we talked about some of the shots we had made – good and bad – and arranged to play again as soon as we could,' Ben remembers.

Joe was also proud as punch to officially open a hair and beauty salon over his studio, called Joli. The business was the brainchild of his sister-in-law Helen, who had been at the centre of operations in his office for many years, and Joe was delighted for her that day, posing for photographs and even granting a short interview to the *Sunday World*.

But within a couple of days Joe would be back in hospital for more tests, and for the rest of November and early December he would be in and out of hospital quite regularly. Joe's platelets were wearing down a little quicker than they had been previously, and they were breaking little veins, which caused Joe some problems. His nosebleeds, which had stopped for a while, also came back. He told friends that the slightest thing brought on the bleeding, and in mid conversation he would often tilt his head back when he felt one coming on. Doctors eventually cauterized the veins in his nose, and Joe was delighted as it stopped the bleeding. But he was getting noticeably weaker.

Fr Brian D'Arcy was among those who visited him, and he remembers that mentally Joe was great, but physically he looked frail. As ever they discussed faith, and Joe asked Fr Brian to say a prayer for him. He remembers Joe being frustrated because he genuinely didn't seem to know what was wrong. 'I was worried about him, I could see him going down, but I never thought he was going to die at that point,' the priest says. 'He said to me, "Look, after Christmas I should be better. They tell me I should be out on the road again by April. When I'm better, call down to the house and we'll have something." And I did think I would be down for St Blaise's on 3 February.'

The next time Fr Brian saw Joe it was on a cold, troubled December night. 'I left the hospital very worried about him. I was very fearful that it might not work out for him. What he was telling me was not matching what I was seeing. I just thought he wasn't as well as he thought, and maybe as others thought he was. He wasn't getting better.' They chatted as normal, and Joe was delighted to learn Fr Brian was reappearing on the *Podge and Rodge Show*. In April 2006, Joe and Fr Brian had appeared together during its first series, and they had a great laugh as they remembered it and the subsequent publicity surrounding Joe's decision to auction his hip bone. Joe told Fr Brian to tell the boys he was asking after them.

But Fr Brian saw sadness in Joe's eyes, and Joe seemed in a reflective mood. He asked Fr Brian to say a prayer. 'I read from the Book of Ecclesiastes for him. Ecclesiastes Three: "To every thing there is a season . . . A time to be born, and a time to die . . . A time to weep, and a time to laugh; a time to mourn, and a time to dance" and all the rest of it. Joe said to me, "Where did I hear that before?" and we talked about how funny it was that most people think of it as "Turn, Turn, Turn (To Everything There Is a Season)" by The Byrds instead of it being 4,000 years old. And he said it was a lovely piece, and that there was a lot of sense to it. I gave him a blessing and I wished him all the best. He even apologized to me, saying, "I wish I was in better form, Fr Brian, but it was good of you to call." And that was the last conversation we had. The room was kind of darkened because he wasn't well. He had been brought in the night before and I think he knew that it was nearing the time for him to say goodbye. There was a little tear in his eye when we prayed.'

Joe was in and out of hospital a couple more times in December, but he always remained positive and enjoyed the attention of the nurses, still able to crack a toothy grin upon hearing the latest joke from one of his regular visitors. His niece Kathleen was at home with her father Paddy one Thursday evening when she got a feeling she should stay with Joe. She got the train up on the Friday morning and surprised Joe by popping her head around his door. Since the day she was born, Joe and Kathleen had been the best of friends, and he was delighted and a little surprised to see her. She stayed with him all that Friday and brought him home to his own house on the Saturday. 'I would have been up and down a good few times before that but we would have driven up and down. I don't know what made me go that weekend. When he saw me he said, "What in the name of God are you doing here?!" He was delighted. We sat down and chatted. He was worried about where I'd parked, but I told him I'd got the train, and that I had to stand the whole way up from Mullingar to Dublin and he went mad at CIÉ. He couldn't believe that I had to stand on the train. When I was going on the Sunday he rang me to make sure I had got a seat.' Joe was happy to be at home, and was in good form despite having to use a walking stick as support.

He was back in hospital a week later. He was experiencing some difficulty with his blood vessels, and his blood was thinning more quickly than before. He went home again, this time with the aid of crutches. Again, Joe put a brave face on things, and he was still talking about being back on the road after Christmas.

He was unable to drive, so a friend brought him to Mullingar in the middle of December to visit his family. He called in to several family members and stayed for a few hours in each home. He visited Paddy in Ginnell Terrace and they sat in his sitting room in front of a big turf fire as grandchildren poured in and out of the house. 'God, isn't this great. You don't know how lucky you are with all the kids coming in to you,' Joe told Paddy. The brothers enjoyed a long chat, and other family members who called over were delighted to see Joe out and about, albeit with limited mobility.

But the prognosis for Joe was not good. Although he had no terminal illness, he was not showing any significant signs of improvement. He returned to hospital a week before Christmas unable to walk. His blood did not seem to be getting around, and his legs were weak. It was as if his body was beginning to break down. All the while, Joe desperately wanted to be at home for Christmas. 'He used to want to get out of hospital for a day or two,' Ben remembers. 'He was at them about Christmas, and they gave him his wish. Nobody knew; maybe they knew he didn't have long.'

On the evening of 23 December, Joe left the Mater for his home in Foxrock. His legs were too weak to carry him to the car, and he left the hospital building in a wheelchair. On Christmas Eve he was good humoured and just a little mischievous as he always was at this time of the year about presents and the all-important Christmas dinner the following day. He rang around his large circle of friends, and friends who had heard he was home for Christmas rang him. But he was tired, and his trademark long chats were somewhat abridged. On Christmas morning he was bright and breezy, enjoying a joke or two, but still in some pain and discomfort.

He spent Christmas Day, as he had nearly always spent it while living in Dublin, in the company of his best friends. Several callers came to the house early in the day and wished him well, and he spoke to a variety of family members, colleagues and friends on the phone, as was his Christmas tradition. He spoke to Ben and Seamus in the late afternoon, and both men remember having almost the exact same conversation with him. They only spoke for a short time, and Joe told them he was probably going to go to sleep a little earlier than he normally would on Christmas night, that although enjoying himself he wasn't feeling too well. Ben and Seamus both rang each other after that and spoke about Joe.

Kathleen also spoke to him and he said the same thing. 'He said to me, "Kathleen, I'm not great." I said to him that he mustn't be great if he was calling me Kathleen on Christmas Day. He always called me Goggeen.' It was his pet name for his niece, coined when her brothers and sisters were young and couldn't pronounce 'Kathleen'. Joe was the only one ever to call her that after she had grown up. 'I told him to hang on in there until tomorrow, because he was due to go back to hospital on St Stephen's morning, that everything would be okay,' Kathleen said.

A few hours later, however, Joe's discomfort grew. He rang his doctor, who agreed he should go back to hospital earlier than planned. An ambulance was summoned, and Joe immediately rang Ben to inform him of his plans; Ben rang around the family and friends. Emotions were running high, and Joe's nearest and dearest began to fear the worst, even if the man himself was putting a brave face on it.

'Joe was his jolly happy self up to about ten minutes before the ambulance came,' Isabella remembers. 'He was in a bit of pain, but he enjoyed his day. We had giggles and laughs up until ten minutes beforehand. He was still Joe, and in great form. He was still joking and making funny faces . . . That sort of stuff. He was smiling and seemed happy.' But Joe then paused for breath, closed his eyes and seemed to doze off. The ambulance arrived and its crew managed to communicate to Joe who, although dozy, was receptive to what was going on around him. He was carefully put on to an ambulance stretcher and brought out of his house.

As the ambulance raced towards Dublin city centre, Isabella held Joe's hand. She then felt him squeeze her hand, and it was at that moment that doctors believe Joe suffered a brain haemorrhage. 'He certainly knew nothing about it. He just got a bit dozy and then slipped off. He just drifted off . . . He just squeezed my hand and kind of let go . . .'

Joe was put on a life-support machine as soon as he arrived at the hospital. At first it was thought that he had suffered a stroke. His brothers Ben, Paddy and Vincent and sisters Imelda and Dympna were contacted, and they and their families rushed to his bedside. Over an hour later, as he clung on for life, Joe was surrounded by his nearest and dearest.

'None of us ever thought he was *that* ill, even his doctors. I don't think they ever thought it was going to come to that. You know what I mean? It was far removed from that . . .' Ben said. When Ben saw him hooked up to the life-support machine, it was 'the worst thing imaginable'. 'I kind of knew then that he was going to die.'

Early on St Stephen's morning a scan revealed that Joe had suffered a brain haemorrhage, more than likely en route to the hospital. His family had stayed with him from the night before. All were still in a state of shock. A doctor explained that there was little hope, that the machine was keeping Joe alive and that although it could do so indefinitely, he would not be Joe. He explained to them that it was their decision.

A few hours later, at approximately 2.30 p.m. on St Stephen's afternoon, surrounded by his extended family and friends and with his family's consent, Joe Dolan's life-support machine was switched off.

He breathed unaided as his body closed down, and a little over twenty minutes later, as he drifted off, something remarkable happened: Joe's arms gradually rose and crossed over themselves on his chest. When Joe was at rest, he always sat with his arms gently crossed in this way. At 3.04 p.m. Joe Dolan was officially pronounced dead.

In the immediate aftermath of Joe Dolan's death, Ireland seemed to pause in shock as it reappraised Joe, his success and his impact on the country. For days Irish newspapers were dominated by that familiar, friendly face and that winning smile; radio stations pumped out Joe's hits and he was all over television news broadcasts. Past and present Taoiseachs paid tribute, as did President McAleese, who privately expressed her sorrow to the Dolan family. Joe's passing was noted and mourned throughout the globe, with reports in newspapers in every continent and in magazines such as *Time* in America and *Mojo* in the UK. As tributes flooded in and mourners began to arrive in Westmeath, it is fair to say that not even Joe himself realized the esteem and regard in which he was held.

Like any sudden passing, shock was the abiding emotion as tens of thousands of mourners assembled in Mullingar to bid farewell to its favourite son. Mullingar had never seen – nor ever will see – anything like it. Indeed, it's quite possible that Ireland will never again witness anything quite like the scenes that greeted Joe's final journey.

At his Removal on Friday 28 December, over 10,000 people queued up in gale-driven rain to pay their respects and to sympathize with Joe's family, friends and colleagues and to say a final goodbye to the man himself. Inside Con Gilsenan's Funeral Home, Joe effectively lay in state, making his last public appearance in his trademark white suit, a white tie gently tied around his collar, his hair ever so slightly ruffled, just as it always had been. The only thing missing was the bright light of his beaming smile.

As mourners filed past Joe, there were few dry eyes. For those waiting in the lengthy queue, which stretched down adjacent streets, the sound of sobbing and the sight of inconsolable fans and friends exiting the funeral home must have been heart-rending. After several hours, the thousands dispersed, and as the doors of the small funeral home were closed only Joe's heartbroken family, relatives and friends remained inside.

The Revd Fr Sean Neylon, a great friend of Joe's for many years, prepared them for what lay ahead, and his warm kindly nature gave all present great comfort. As he blessed Joe one final time, he led everyone in a moving fare-well prayer:

Joe, go from this world upon your final journey. Go from this world and rest in peace in the presence of God the Father who created you, in the love of Jesus who called you his friend and in the warmth of the Holy Spirit who gifted you and blessed you with so many talents and gifts.

Joe, you gave so much joy, happiness and love to thousands of people over the past forty-seven years. You were blessed with a wonderful personal-ity and a unique voice. Now that your voice is silent it will live in the hearts of people for ever. Your amazing repertoire of music and song will for ever remind us of the genius and talent you were blessed with.

In death we believe that life has changed and not ended, and we give back to our faithful God our faithful and loving brother, Joe. You truly left a great footprint on the lives and hearts of those who really appreciated your great talent.

Joe, on our journey in life, our paths will change direction this weekend. We have accompanied you as far as we can go together. Our ways will part now but beyond the coldness and stillness of your cemetery space you will be met by Jesus, who is the Way, the Truth and the Life.

Joe, may the angels lead you into Paradise and may the saints take you by the hand and walk with you into the presence of God the Father and reward you for a life well lived and a singing voice that gave light in times of darkness, and hope in times of despair.

Joe, you were a wonderful entertainer, a most loving and caring human being and a man that really made a difference. May your loving God reward you for a life well and truly lived and for the years of joy and happiness you gave to so many people.

Joe, your talent, personality and voice touched so many people and will be remembered for ever more. You leave the world a better and happier place than it had been before. As one door closes, so another opens, as one bird ends his song, another sings. Thank you for your song.

Joe's casket was then carried shoulder high by his family from the funeral home across the street to the Cathedral of Christ the King, the journey accompanied the whole way by warm, appreciative applause. Joe's remains were received at the door of the cathedral by the visibly shaken Bishop of

Meath, Dr Michael Smith. As had happened so many times in his glittering five-decade career, Joe's arrival was marked by the crowd inside rising as one to give him a prolonged standing ovation.

The cathedral had been busy all day as thousands of mourners chose not to go to the funeral home, preferring instead to remember Joe as they had last seen him. Others quietly signed some of the many books of condolence that had been established all over the town and, as it turned out, all over the country.

Speaking to a packed, darkened cathedral and addressing Joe's grieving family, Fr Mark English CC said that the thoughts and the prayers of the world were with them. He said it was 'right and proper' that Joe's passing had been acknowledged as it had been, adding that one's task in life is to make the most of the gifts of life and to share them as Joe did, but that Joe's gifts were greater than others and deserved recognition. 'Most of us will live and die, quietly making our impression upon the earthly patch we inhabit, but a few will be more widely known and contribute greatly to the society around them.' He said it was fitting that Joe had been brought back to the cathedral in the shadow of which he grew up and where he was treated 'purely as a local lad'. Fr English also gave comfort when he noted that even though Joe's distinctive voice was now fading from its earthly stage, it would forever echo in the memory of those who loved him, as family, friend or fan.

Joe's passing ensured that Christmas had been all but forgotten, but a haunting 'Silent Night', sung by his niece Maeve Dolan-Corroon, and other hymns sung by nieces Sandra Dolan and Ester Behan, brought it back to vivid life on that poignant night.

The following morning, over 3,000 people packed into the pews and aisles at the cathedral for Joe's Funeral Mass. Indeed, crowds packed the cathedral hours before the Mass began. Another thousand braced themselves against the chill wind outside on what was a dull, wet and cloudy winter's morning, and hundreds more began to line the streets below the cathedral.

There can be no doubt that Ireland's first major show-business star would have approved of the rousing and moving send-off he received. Like a Joe show, the funeral lasted over two hours, but appeared to pass by in a matter of minutes. In death, as he did in life, Joe managed to gather together all strands of society, regardless of age or status. Many people travelled long distances (and even across continents) to attend, all those present united in

their admiration and grief. Famous names and faces mixed freely with everyone, and in the end it was the fans who took centre-stage, just as Joe would
have wanted it.

Fr Mark English presided over the Funeral Mass, and he was assisted by
an array of other clergy including Fr Brian D'Arcy, who delivered a moving
and compelling eulogy remembering the man behind the voice. As he remi-
nisced about sad and happy times in Joe's company, Fr Brian peppered his
tribute with humorous asides, genuine heartfelt emotion and more than a
little mischief, which Joe himself would have enjoyed. On the verge of tears
throughout, Fr Brian revealed that he and Joe had made a pact – that if Fr
Brian went first Joe would sing at his funeral, and if Joe went first Fr Brian
would have to tell a few stories. He also revealed the extent of some of Joe's
charity work, perhaps not realizing that this would be the first that many
people had heard of it, as Joe had kept it under wraps all his life. Fr Brian
ultimately broke down when he recalled a quote Joe had asked him to write
down as he lay in his hospital bed: 'Death can leave a heartache that no one
can heal, but love leaves a memory that no one can steal.' Fr Brian left the
pulpit to rounds of warm, spontaneous applause.

The readings were given by Joe's sister Dympna, who read from the Book
of Ecclesiastes, the same prayer that Joe had wanted to hear in hospital, and
by his nephew Adrian. They were joined on the altar by Joe's sister Imelda
and a stream of Joe's nieces and nephews and his manager Seamus who all
delivered the Prayers of the Faithful with grace and fortitude. The Eucharist
and gifts that reflected Joe's life – his final album, a framed photo of the
'ordinary' Joe and his famous golf putter – were brought to the altar by his
brothers Paddy, Ben and Vincent and sisters Imelda and Dympna.

As one would have expected, the final celebration contained beautifully
stirring musical tributes, including songs from his nieces Sandra Dolan,
Maeve Dolan-Corroon and Ester Behan as well as the cathedral choir, aided
by some of Joe's former bandmates. As they reached for the heavens in song,
the clouds and rain disappeared and beams of bright sunlight pierced the
stained-glass windows of the cathedral.

As he had done onstage for close to forty years, Frankie McDonald
sounded the last musical note as he accompanied Sandra and the entire congregation on a stirring version of 'Goodbye Venice Goodbye'. Joe's casket
was raised on to the shoulders of his nephews, whom he counted as his best

friends, and he began his final journey. Again, rapturous applause filled the cathedral. Mourners reached out to touch his coffin as it made its way down through the packed cathedral and on to the packed plinth outside, where thousands of mourners welcomed him in song and applause.

Joe never tired of talking about his hometown, and it was little wonder that the town came to a halt to pay tribute to its greatest son as he was borne from the cathedral grounds. Few people will ever forget the silence that descended on the town that afternoon. As Joe's funeral cortège paused outside his Dominick Street public house, the former cinema site where it all began for Joe Dolan and The Drifters under one light bulb, it seemed as if the world itself was in mourning. The hum of daily life in town disappeared; the birds stopped singing; footfall and vehicles became soundless. You couldn't even hear the breeze.

Townspeople lined the six-mile journey to Walshestown Cemetery as the funeral cortège slowly wound its way around the country roads. Many stood there with tear-stained faces, some applauded, others bowed their heads in dignified silence. Some even erected homemade signs outside their homes as a final farewell.

At Walshestown church, Joe passed by his parents' grave for the very last time. His own coffin would soon join theirs in the hallowed ground of his family's parish. The air was filled with sorrow and the ground was wet with tears as he was carried to his own final resting place. Taoiseach Brian Cowen was among the hundreds of mourners who wept openly. As Joe received a final blessing, the sun once again shone down to welcome Joseph Francis Robert Dolan to a new way of living.

Since Joe's funeral, many thousands of tearful fans, heartbroken friends and family members have visited his grave, its black marble and stone the reminder of the remarkable man beneath. Joe's timeless appeal is demonstrated by the absence of a birth date on his grave, with only the date of his passing noted. He is as ageless in death as he was in life.

Dozens of posthumous awards and reappraisals have followed his passing, each one greatly appreciated by his family and fans. Indeed, over 10,000 fans reunited for a special celebratory weekend in Killarney in the summer of 2008. A life-size statue to be erected in 2008 in the centre of Mullingar will add to the sense of permanence surrounding Joe's contribution. With a musical career that spanned close to fifty years and entertained at least three generations across every continent before ultimately focusing on the place he loved best, Joe Dolan will never be forgotten, and will live on in the memories of generations to come.

Joe would never have wanted anyone to grieve. A few weeks before he died, he quoted a poem by Brendan Kenneally that makes the point that as long as someone is remembered, that person will never die. His Mass card featured the following poem, which sums up exactly how Joe felt about death:

You can shed tears that I have gone
Or you can smile that I have lived.
You can close your eyes and pray that I'll come back
Or you can open your eyes and see all that I have left.
Your heart can be empty because you can't see me
Or can be full of the love we shared.
You can turn your back on tomorrow and live yesterday
Or you can be happy for tomorrow because of yesterday.
You can remember me and only that I've gone
Or you can cherish my memory and let it live on.
You can try to close your mind,
Be empty and turn your back,
Or you can do what I'd want:
Laugh, open your eyes, love and go on.

Anon.

Going on has been tough for those closest to Joe, but they are managing it. Life has to go on. There will never be another show like the Joe show and there will never be another entertainer like Joe Dolan, but as his brother Ben points out, Joe is always there.

'You can press a button and hear him at any stage,' Ben says. 'It's not always the easiest thing to do. But sometimes it's very soothing. Sometimes it helps. Sometimes it hurts. But Joe is never too far away. He's with us every single day.'

Acknowledgements

Everything in this book is down to the efforts of three men: Joe Dolan, Ben Dolan and Seamus Casey. With Joe gone, it fell on the shoulders of Ben and Seamus to fill in the blanks, and I honestly don't know how to express my gratitude to you both. The interviews and chats were often tough and tearful, but Joe's story is as much your story and what a privilege it has been to share your memories. For giving so freely of your time at what has been a very difficult period in your lives, I am eternally grateful.

My father Seamus has been the greatest inspiration in my life, a man who always seems to know how to do the right thing and who has always been there for me and all the family. His love of life, music and the people who make it is an incredible gift, and I am forever in awe of his positive outlook, spirit and peace of mind. The opportunity to get even closer as this book was being prepared is something I will always treasure. Thank you, Dad, for everything.

My deepest thanks to my wonderful mother Doreen, sister Celina and brother Justin: your individual and collective support has been immeasurable and has kept me going even without you realizing it. Thanks also to Chris Ferwick, Mamta Chudasama and to everyone else in the family who has been there for me over the years.

Thanks to everyone in the Dolan family, far and wide: to Paddy and all his family, especially Kathleen; to Vincent, Dympna and Imelda and their families; and to Ben's family and his wife Helen.

Deirdre Duncan is an amazing girl whose love, support (and patience!) are the stuff of dreams. She has kept the faith, even though it must seem like years since that dawn-coloured vase was filled. Thank you for everything, my dear, for continuing to set my heart aflutter and for making me smile every day; I am blessed to have an angel as lovely as you.

This book wouldn't have been possible without the valued guidance and support of Patricia Deevy and Michael McLoughlin at Penguin Ireland. My wholehearted thanks to my editor, Deirdre O'Neill, whose perceptive mind and tireless slicing and dicing ensured that nobody would be asleep by the second page. An extra special thanks to Caroline Pretty for her expertise and sympathetic copy-editing during the final push. Thanks also to Cliona Lewis, Patricia McVeigh, Keith Taylor and Ellie Smith. Your collective interest, belief and encouragement has been a tonic, and made the creation of this book an utter pleasure.

My sincerest thanks must go to everyone who helped with the preparation of this book and who asked for nothing in return. So many agreed to be interviewed and gave freely of their time, with many opening up their personal archives. Particular thanks must go to Adrian Dolan, Liam Meade, Frankie McDonald, Ray Dolan and Denis Mee. A big thanks also to Des Doherty, Tommy Swarbrigg, Sid Aughey, Joe Meehan, Jimmy Horan, Pat Hoey, Jimmy Mullally, Joey Gilheaney, Sandra Dolan, Sean Kenny, Johnny McCafferty, Gordon Coleman, Maurice Walsh, Kieran McDonnell, Seamus Shannon, Kevin Cowley, Mick Bagnell, Jimmy Walsh, Gerry Kelly, Jason Fallon, Conor Kenny, Gerry Oakes, Tommy Begley, John Delamere, Joe Bustin, Joe McAuley, Paddy Nolan and all his staff, and all those who ensured Joe was always on the right note. May the rock be with you.

Extended thanks to broadcaster Gerry Ryan and David Blake Knox and all at Blueprint Pictures; James Cafferty and all at Showtours; Willie Kavanagh, David Gogan and all at EMI Ireland; Bert van Breda at BR Music Two in Holland; Roberto Danova; Peter Yellowstone; Paula Murray in RTÉ Athlone; Jimmy Magee; and Larry Gogan. Gracious thanks to Isabella Fogarty, and to Fr Brian D'Arcy and all at the Graan, and to Fr Sean Neylon and Fr Mark English.

Thanks to my esteemed former colleague in the *Westmeath Examiner*, John FitzSimons, and to RTÉ's Ciaran Mullooly, for their unerring professionalism and big hearts when it mattered most on 26 December 2007.

For their photographic expertise, my heartfelt thanks to Sean Magee, John McAuley, John Mulvihill, Colin Watters, Matt Nolan and everyone else who contributed images.

Author and journalist Eddie Rowley came to the rescue on several occasions, and his valuable advice and help throughout this project has been much appreciated.

My thanks also to Lindsey Holmes, Susan O'Grady and Deirdre Crookes at LHP, Paddy Dunning, John Reynolds and all at POD Concerts, Aiken Promotions, Hugo Straney at CHIN Radio, Donie Cassidy, Pat Quinn, Sharon Newman, Leagues O'Toole, Jim Carroll, Liam Horan, Finian Coughlan, Tommy McManus & Co., Gerry Buckley, Darren Smith and Louis Walsh.

A very special word of appreciation to everyone at the *Westmeath Examiner* (past and present), Celtic Media Group and to all those I have worked with in RTÉ, Tyrone Productions, Newstalk and Midlands 103.

My warmest thanks must go to the countless Joe Dolan fans who got in touch by email, phone or good old-fashioned post. There are far too many of you to thank individually here, but your memories, photographs and words of encouragement have been greatly appreciated. You have proved that a good thing never dies and there can be no doubt Joe and his music will live on thanks to your devotion. Thanks to Helen at *http://joe-dolan.it-all-starts-here.com*, *www.irish-showbands.com*, and *www.joedolan.com*.

Thanks to Con Houlihan for convincing me to throw in the teacloth on a career in catering. Thanks also to Mullingar's master wordsmiths, Leo Daly, J. P. Donleavy and Padraic O'Farrell (RIP). A big thank you to Patrick Whitelaw and John O'Hara; a warm handshake and a carriage clock to Ronan O'Donoghue, and a poetic thanks to Marty Mulligan.

Thanks to all my dear friends for their support, encouragement and friendship. You all know who you are.

A number of magazine and newspaper articles and TV and radio features proved invaluable in the preparation and research of this book, including several from the archives of RTÉ; *Spotlight* magazine (thanks to John Coughlan); *Irish Independent* (thanks to Joe Jackson); *The Irish Times*; *Evening Herald* (thanks to Tony Wilson); *Sunday World*; *Sunday Independent*; *Evening Press*; *Las Vegas Mirror* and *Westmeath Examiner*.

Finally, in writing this book, the words and music of David Gilmour, Roger Waters, Nick Mason, Richard Wright and Syd Barrett helped a great deal, as did that of Robin Proper-Sheppard, Mogwai, The Jimmy Cake, Elbow, Karl Hyde, Rick Smith, Alex Paterson and, of course, Joe Dolan.

Grá agus síocháin.

Ronan Casey
September 2008

ACKNOWLEDGEMENTS

Picture credits

The author and publisher would like to thank the following for permission to use pictures: the Dolan family, for pictures opening the Foreword and chapters 1 and 13, pages 1, 2, 6 (bottom) and 7 (top two images) of the black-and-white inset and pages 1, 8 and 9 of the colour inset; James Cafferty, for pictures opening chapter 16 and pages 4 (bottom right) and 7 (top) of the colour inset; Seamus Casey, for pictures opening chapters 3, 6 and 10, pages 3, 5 (bottom), 9 (top), 11 (top), 12 (top) and 15 (top) of the black-and-white inset and page 10 (bottom) of the colour inset; EMI Ireland, for pictures opening chapters 17, 18 and 19 and page 16 of the colour inset; JBS Music, for pages 11 (bottom) and 16 of the black-and-white inset and pages 4 (top right and bottom left) and 6 (bottom right) of the colour inset; Las Vegas News Bureau, for picture opening chapter 14; John McAuley, for pages 7 (bottom), 11 (top right and bottom) and 13 of the colour inset; Sean Magee, for pictures opening chapters 2, 5 and 7 and pages 4, 5 (top), 6 (top), 7 (bottom), 10 (top) and 13 (bottom) of the black-and-white inset; Liam Meade, for pages 5 (bottom) and 6 (bottom left) of the colour inset; John Mulvihill, for page 15 (bottom) of the black-and-white inset and pages 12 (bottom) and 15 of the colour inset; Bert Van Breda, for pictures opening chapters 11 and 12, pages 3 (covers to the albums *Lady in Blue* and *Crazy Woman*), 4 (top left) and 5 (top) of the colour inset; Colin Watters, for pages 11 (top left), 12 (top) and 14 of the colour inset. Every effort has been made to identify and credit copyright owners of all images. We will rectify any omissions in future editions.

Index

Kelly, Gerry 210–11, 244
Kelly, Johnny 64, 73
Kelly, Kieran 127
Kenneally, Brendan 336
Kennedy, Ollie 31
Kenny, Sean 122, 130, 306
Khorev, Vladimir 216
Kilpatrick Bridge 8
King, Derek 7
Kirby, Noel 73
Kishinev (USSR) 219–21
Klondike Day celebrations 126

Las Vegas 92, 106–8, 234–44, 246–50
Last, James 139
Late Late Show 282, 292–3
Lebanon 258–9
Leningrad 225–30
Links Golfing Society 266
Lough Ennell 9
Lough Owel 310
Lynch, Joe 16

McCabe, Bernard and Dympna 127
McCabe, Pat 127
McCafferty, Johnny 306–7
McCormack, John 72
McCormack, Micheline 252–3
McCullough Piggott 34–5
McCune, Dave 288
McDonald, Frankie
    joins the band 125–8
    remembers Joe 140
    on South African tours 173–4, 257
    and Liam Meade 187
    and 'Goodbye Venice Goodbye'
        199
    and Williamstown incident 209
    at Joe's funeral 334

McDonald, Kathleen 127
McDonnell, Ciaran 125, 186–7
McGathey, Fr 54–5
MacGowan, Shane 298
McGrath, John 24
McIntyre, Frank 293
McKeon, Gay 112
Madigans' Pub 95
Magee, Sean 52
Majestic Ballroom, Mallow 71
Maloney, Kathleen 52–3
MAM Agency 133, 153, 161
Marie, Kelly 197-8
Meade, Liam 173, 187–8, 246, 281, 297
Mee, Denis 256, 266, 281, 309–10,
        316, 323
Meehan, Joe 211, 289, 305–6
Melia, Frank 63–4, 68
Melody Aces, The 67, 75
Meteor mobile phone network 311
Milligan, Spike 214
Moane, Bal 269–70
Monroe, Andy 279–80
Moroder, Giorgio 176–7
Morrison, Ciaran 40–41, 285
Morrison, Jackie 40
Morrison, Johnny 41
Morrison, Van 131
Moscow 222–5
Muglestons, The 246
Mullally, Jimmy 'The Mull' 187, 244,
        305
Mulligan, Frank 21–2, 76, 279
Mulligan, Mick 'Jazzer' 32–3
Mullingar
    County Hospital 1
    Dolan family home in 2–4
    Joe's childhood in 6–8
    locally produced operas in 10